Fodor's

ESSENTIAL SWITZERLAND

WELCOME TO SWITZERLAND

Whether on snowcapped mountains or in glitzy resort towns, you can experience the high life in Switzerland. Visitors are elated by its soaring outdoor recreation, riding cable cars up peaks near the Matterhorn, sipping Swiss wine while cruising on a crystalline Alpine lake, and skiing the immaculate slopes of St. Moritz. At the end of the day, lavish spas beckon, along with lively après-ski scenes and pots of fondue. Sophisticated cities like Zürich and Geneva take luxury to new heights, with posh boutiques and upscale restaurants lining their cobblestone streets.

TOP REASONS TO GO

★ **The Alps:** Majestic views from commanding peaks and storybook Alpine hamlets.

★ **Urban Pleasures:** Cosmopolitan Geneva, flashy Zürich, artsy Basel, and historic Bern.

★ **Food and Drink:** Haute cuisine, local wine, and, of course, Swiss cheese and chocolate.

★ **Winter Fun:** You can whoosh down premier ski slopes and then relax in opulent spas.

★ **Scenic Journeys:** Trains provide panoramic views of spectacular mountainous landscapes.

★ **Shopping:** Chic designer boutiques, extravagant luxury shops, festive holiday markets.

25 ULTIMATE EXPERIENCES

Switzerland offers terrific experiences that should be on every traveler's list. Here are Fodor's top picks for a memorable trip.

1 Go for a Hike

You'll find nearly 40,000 miles of hiking trails throughout Switzerland, including the Swiss National Park, a UNESCO biosphere reserve with nearly 50 miles of trails along winding rivers and through dense Alpine forest. *(Ch. 4)*

2 Visit Switzerland's Oldest Town

Chur, Switzerland's oldest town, has been inhabited for more than 5,000 years; its picturesque, narrow streets and cobblestone alleys are lined with shops and cafés. *(Ch. 4)*

3 Listen to Music

The Swiss hills are alive with the sound of roughly 300 music festivals, including the world-famous Montreaux Jazz Festival, which features jazz and pop stars every July. *(Ch. 12)*

4 Visit Appenzell

Car-free Appenzell village, with its brightly colored and intricately decorated chalets, is a center for traditional Swiss arts like cheese making and embroidery. *(Ch. 3)*

5 Eat like James Bond

Not far from Interlaken, atop the Schilthorn's 9,700-foot summit, sits the revolving Piz Gloria restaurant, famous from the 1969 film *On Her Majesty's Secret Service.* *(Ch. 10)*

6 Go Medieval

Switzerland is littered with castles, but the most famous is the well-preserved 12th-century Château de Chillon, perched on a rock in Lake Geneva just outside of Montreaux. *(Ch. 12)*

7 Go to the Top of Europe

At 11,333 feet, the Jungfraujoch is easily accessed by train; at the very top is the Aletsch Glacier, the longest in the Swiss Alps and a UNESCO World Heritage Site. *(Ch. 10)*

8 See the Waterfalls

The unforgettable Lauterbrunnen Valley, with more than 70 waterfalls plummeting from its cliffs, is considered one of the most beautiful places in Switzerland. *(Ch. 10)*

9 Ride the Steepest Cog Railway

Mt. Pilatus can be reached on a ride on the world's steepest cog railway, which drops you off a quick stroll from magnificent views of Luzern and the lake. *(Ch. 6)*

10 Raft through the Swiss Grand Canyon

The stretch of the Rhine that runs through the Vorderrhein Gorge offers white-water rafting, with popular tours departing from May through October. *(Ch. 4)*

11 Eat Chocolate

Whether you do a tasting at Maison Cailler in Broc or at Confiserie Bachman in Luzern, you'll quickly realize that it's hard to resist chocolate in Switzerland. *(Ch. 8)*

12 Stroll through Luzern

Luzern offers a quintessential experience: a medieval town and waterfront promenades crisscrossed by picturesque wooden bridges. *(Ch. 6)*

13 Discover the Origins of the Universe

CERN offers guided tours of the world's largest particle accelerator, which allowed scientists to identify the so-called "God particle" in 2012. *(Ch. 13)*

14 Attend Switzerland's Hottest Party

Basel Fasnacht is celebrated with four days of revelry starting the Monday after Ash Wednesday, when parades fill the streets and the city is lit by lanterns. *(Ch. 7)*

15 Enjoy Some Cheese

Celebrate the many types of cheese that are produced in Switzerland by partaking in either fondue or raclette, two wintertime favorites, often served with white wine. *(Ch. 8)*

16 See Chagall

Five stained-glass windows designed by Marc Chagall for the choir of Zürich's Fraumünster have drawn art lovers and tourists since they were installed in 1970. *(Ch. 2)*

17 Ski in the Shadow of the Matterhorn

In Zermatt, swoosh down first-class slopes past the country's most recognizable peak, the snaggletooth-shaped Matterhorn, which reigns over the car-free town. *(Ch. 11)*

18 Paddle the Lakes

Almost every town on Lago Maggiore and Lago di Lugano has paddleboats, kayaks, or canoes for rent so you can take to the water for an hour or the whole day. *(Ch. 5)*

19 Take the Waters

For centuries, the Swiss soaked in the thermal waters and the natural springs that bubble up in such famous spa towns as Brig and Leukerbad, in the Valais region. *(Ch. 11)*

20 Visit Grindelwald

Before the Eiger's treacherous north face, bucolic Grindelwald is a charming Alpine village and an excellent base for summer and winter adventures. *(Ch. 10)*

21 Visit the Olympic Museum

On a gentle slope in Lausanne above Lake Geneva this interactive, modern-day shrine to the competitors, creators, and engineers behind the games, is a must-see. *(Ch. 12)*

22 Float down the Aare River

A relaxing float on the Aare, which winds through charming Bern, is a popular summer activity on any warm, sunny day, with or without a boat. *(Ch. 9)*

23 Grapple with Swiss Tradition

The Swiss are known to love skiing and hiking, but in summer they also cheer for *schwingen* (*lutte Suisse* in French areas), traditional Swiss-style wrestling. *(Ch. 11)*

24 Ride the Rails

Swiss trains are both an efficient and scenic way to get around. The route of the Glacier Express between Zermatt and St. Moritz is among the most spectacular. *(Ch. 4)*

25 Celebrate the Cows

In fall, farmers adorn their beloved cows with crowns of flowers and huge bells to join the parade down the slopes for the Alpabfahrt (La Désalpe in French regions). *(Ch. 10)*

Fodor's ESSENTIAL SWITZERLAND

Editorial: Douglas Stallings, *Editorial Director*; Margaret Kelly, Jacinta O'Halloran, *Senior Editors*; Kayla Becker, Alexis Kelly, Amanda Sadlowski, *Editors*; Teddy Minford, *Content Editor*; Rachael Roth, *Content Manager*

Design: Tina Malaney, *Design and Production Director;* Jessica Gonzalez, *Production Designer*

Photography: Jennifer Arnow, *Senior Photo Editor*

Maps: Rebecca Baer, *Senior Map Editor*; David Lindroth and Mark Stroud (Moon Street Cartography), *Cartographers*

Production: Jennifer DePrima, *Editorial Production Manager*; Carrie Parker, *Senior Production Editor*; Elyse Rozelle, *Production Editor*

Business & Operations: Chuck Hoover, *Chief Marketing Officer*; Joy Lai, *Vice President and General Manager*; Stephen Horowitz, *Director of Business Development and Revenue Operations;* Tara McCrillis, *Director of Publishing Operations;* Eliza D. Aceves, *Content Operations Manager and Strategist*

Public Relations and Marketing: Joe Ewaskiw, *Manager;* Esther Su, *Marketing Manager*

Writers: Kelly DiNardo, Liz Humphreys, Susan Misicka, Alexis Munier, Chantal Panozzo

Editor: Douglas Stallings

Production Editor: Jennifer DePrima

1st Edition

ISBN 978-1-64097-032-8

ISSN 2576–0386

PRINTED IN THE UNITED STATES OF AMERICA

10 9 8 7 6 5 4 3 2 1

CONTENTS

1 EXPERIENCE SWITZERLAND .. 19
What's Where ... 20
Need to Know ... 24
If You Like ... 26
Flavors of Switzerland ... 28
Switzerland Today ... 30
Best Hikes ... 32
Money-Saving Tips ... 33
Great Itineraries ... 34

2 ZÜRICH ... 45
Welcome to Zürich ... 46
Zürich Planner ... 49
Exploring ... 52
Where to Eat ... 64
Where to Stay ... 71
Nightlife and Performing Arts ... 79
Shopping ... 83
Spas ... 85

3 EASTERN SWITZERLAND AND LIECHTENSTEIN ... 87
Welcome to Eastern Switzerland and Liechtenstein ... 88
Eating Well in Eastern Switzerland ... 90
Eastern Switzerland and Liechtenstein Planner ... 93
Schaffhausen and the Rhine ... 96
Bodensee to Walensee ... 105
Liechtenstein ... 120

4 GRAUBÜNDEN ... 125
Welcome to Graubünden ... 126
Graubünden Planner ... 129
Heidiland ... 132
Prättigau and Davos ... 145
The Lower Engadine ... 155
The Upper Engadine ... 164

5 TICINO ... 179
Welcome to Ticino ... 180
Ticino Lakes ... 182

Fodor's Features

Scenic Train Rides and Drives ... 38
The Bernese Alps ... 370
The Vineyards of Lavaux ... 474

Ticino Planner ... 185
Sopraceneri ... 188
Sottoceneri ... 202

6 LUZERN AND CENTRAL SWITZERLAND ... 215
Welcome to Luzern and Central Switzerland ... 216
Lake Luzern ... 218
Luzern Planner ... 221
Luzern ... 223
Around Luzern ... 238
Urnersee ... 246

7 BASEL ... 253
Welcome to Basel ... 254
Basel Planner ... 257
Exploring ... 259
Where to Eat ... 272
Where to Stay ... 276
Nightlife and Performing Arts ... 278
Shopping ... 280
Greater Basel ... 283

8 FRIBOURG AND NEUCHÂTEL . 285
Welcome to Fribourg and Neuchâtel ... 286

Cheese: Fribourg's Calling Card... 288
Fribourg and Neuchâtel Planner.. 291
Fribourg ... 293
Murten... 307
Lac de Neuchâtel and Nearby.... 310

9 BERN ... 319
Welcome to Bern... 320
Bern Planner ... 323
Exploring ... 325
Where to Eat ... 335
Where to Stay ... 339
Nightlife and Performing Arts 341
Sports and the Outdoors ... 345
Shopping ... 345
Spas ... 348

10 BERNER OBERLAND ... 349
Welcome to Berner Oberland 350
Berner Oberland Planner... 353
The Jungfrau Region... 355
Brienzersee... 384
Thunersee ... 389
Simmental and Gstaad ... 394

11 VALAIS ... 399
Welcome to Valais... 400
Valais Planner ... 403
Bas Valais and Sion... 406
Conversion de la Vallée ... 417
Zermatt and Saas-Fee ... 426
Brig and the Alpine Passes... 439

12 VAUD ... 443
Welcome to Vaud... 444
Eating Well in Vaud... 446
Vaud Planner ... 449
La Côte ... 452
Lausanne ... 458
Lavaux Vignobles and Riviera..... 470

13 GENEVA... 489
Welcome to Geneva ... 490
Geneva Planner ... 493
Exploring ... 496
Where to Eat ... 510
Where to Stay ... 517
Nightlife ... 521
Performing Arts... 522
Shopping and Spas... 523

TRAVEL SMART SWITZERLAND ... 527

VOCABULARY... 543

INDEX ... 550

ABOUT OUR WRITERS... 560

MAPS

Cantons of Switzerland ... 37
Zürich... 58–59
Where to Eat and Stay in Zürich... 72–73
Schaffhausen and the Rhine... 97
Schaffhausen ... 100
Bodensee to Liechtenstein ... 107
Chur to Davos ... 133
Upper and Lower Engadine... 156
Sopraceneri... 189
Sottoceneri ... 202
Lugano ... 207
Luzern (Lucerne)... 226
Central Switzerland... 236
Basel ... 262–263
Fribourg and Neuchâtel ... 295
Bern ... 327
The Jungfrau Region... 356
Brienzersee... 385
Thunersee, Simmental, and Gstaad ... 392
Bas Valais and Sion... 406
Conversion de la Vallèe ... 418
Zermatt to Aletsch... 427
La Côte ... 453
Lausanne ... 460
Lavaux Vignobles and Riviera..... 471
Geneva (Genëve) ... 502–503
Where to Eat and Stay in Geneva ... 514–515
Language Regions of Switzerland ... 536

ABOUT THIS GUIDE

Fodor's Recommendations

Everything in this guide is worth doing—we don't cover what isn't—but exceptional sights, hotels, and restaurants are recognized with additional accolades. Fodor'sChoice★ indicates our top recommendation. Care to nominate a new place? Visit Fodors.com/contact-us.

Trip Costs

We list prices wherever possible to help you budget well. Hotel and restaurant price categories from **$** to **$$$$** are noted alongside each recommendation. For hotels, we include the lowest cost of a standard double room in high season. For restaurants, we cite the average price of a main course at dinner or, if dinner isn't served, at lunch. For attractions, we always list adult admission fees; discounts are usually available for children, students, and senior citizens.

Hotels

Our local writers vet every hotel to recommend the best overnights in each price category, from budget to expensive. Unless otherwise specified, you can expect private bath, phone, and TV in your room. For expanded hotel reviews, facilities, and deals visit Fodors.com.

Top Picks

★ Fodor'sChoice

Listings

- ✉ Address
- Branch address
- ☎ Telephone
- Fax
- Website
- E-mail
- Admission fee
- Open/closed times
- Ⓜ Subway
- Directions or Map coordinates

Hotels & Restaurants

- Hotel
- Number of rooms
- Meal plans
- ✕ Restaurant
- Reservations
- Dress code
- No credit cards
- $ Price

Other

- ⇨ See also
- ☞ Take note
- Golf facilities

Restaurants

Unless we state otherwise, restaurants are open for lunch and dinner daily. We mention dress code only when there's a specific requirement and reservations only when they're essential or not accepted.

Credit Cards

The hotels and restaurants in this guide typically accept credit cards. If not, we'll say so.

EUGENE FODOR

Hungarian-born Eugene Fodor (1905–91) began his travel career as an interpreter on a French cruise ship. The experience inspired him to write *On the Continent* (1936), the first guidebook to receive annual updates and discuss a country's way of life as well as its sights. Fodor later joined the U.S. Army and worked for the OSS in World War II. After the war, he kept up his intelligence work while expanding his guidebook series. During the Cold War, many guides were written by fellow agents who understood the value of insider information. Today's guides continue Fodor's legacy by providing travelers with timely coverage, insider tips, and cultural context.

EXPERIENCE SWITZERLAND

WHAT'S WHERE

1 Zürich. Zürich is surprisingly small, but its wealth of cultural riches more than makes up for its size. Tour the luxuriously gentrified **Altstadt** (Old Town), then take in the hulking **Grossmünster** cathedral, great modern art at the **Bührle** museum, and top old masters at Winterthur's **Oskar Reinhart Collection.**

2 Eastern Switzerland. East of Zürich the Rhine snakes through some of the most untouched regions of Switzerland. Amid wood-shingle farmhouses and grand baroque churches, discover the old Rhine city of **Schaffhausen,** known for its medieval frescoes; **St. Gallen,** a busy textile center with an active Old Town; and princely **Liechtenstein.**

3 Graubünden. The mountains of what used to be called Rhaetia once made the region of Graubünden difficult to rule. Today, emperors and kings have been replaced by new conquerors: tourists, who take the gorgeous train ride to **Arosa,** visit "Heidi country" in **Maienfeld,** hang out with writers in **Klosters** and billionaires in **Davos,** and ski in glitzy **St. Moritz.**

4 Ticino. With its intoxicating *italianità* (Italian flair), Ticino is an irresistible combination of Mediterranean pleasures and

Swiss efficiency. The region's sinuous lakes, perhaps its greatest attraction, beckon with strolls along fashionable waterfront promenades. Concentrate on beauteous **Lugano**, serene **Locarno**, and elegant **Ascona**, set on the shore of Lago Maggiore.

5 Luzern and Central Switzerland. Central Switzerland is the most visited region in the country. No wonder: you can take a paddleboat steamer on the **Vierwaldstättersee** (Lake Luzern) past some of the most beautiful lakeside vistas to the **Rütli Meadow**—"birthplace" of Switzerland—and the fabled Wilhelm Tell chapel. **Luzern** itself has an Old Town so cleanly refurbished, it could be mistaken for a museum exhibit.

6 Basel. Set where Switzerland meets Germany and France, Basel's lovely Old Town, Rhine River walk, and great modern art—including **Museum Tinguely** and **Fondation Beyeler**—make it a best bet. In the 15th century, the city won the right to hold an unlimited number of fairs, which today range from the famous Fasnacht carnival to the chic ArtBasel.

WHAT'S WHERE

7 Fribourg and Neuchâtel. Largely undiscovered, these two cantons (states) are favorite western Switzerland getaways. Fribourg, part German and part French, is divided into a checkerboard of fields—the highlight is the stunningly picturesque castle at **Gruyères.** Other treasures: lakeside **Neuchâtel** and Gothic-era **Fribourg.**

8 Bern. A city of broad medieval streets, Switzerland's federal capital sits in the country's largest canton, whose size and influence mirror the pride of its citizens. The famed sandstone arcades, painted fountains, performing mechanical clock of the **Zytglogge,** Gothic **Münster,** and art-filled **Zentrum Paul Klee** are as ardently protected as the country's neutrality.

9 Berner Oberland. Kiss the sky in this hypermagical province—a "summit of summits" that includes the peaks of the **Eiger, Mönch, and Jungfrau.** From the hub of **Interlaken,** journey up to gorgeous eagle's-nest towns like **Mürren** and **Wengen** and down to the "Shangri-la" valley that is **Lauterbrunnen.** A taste of the high life awaits in glam **Gstaad.**

10 Valais. This is the Switzerland of raclette eaters, wine makers, yodelers—and, oh,

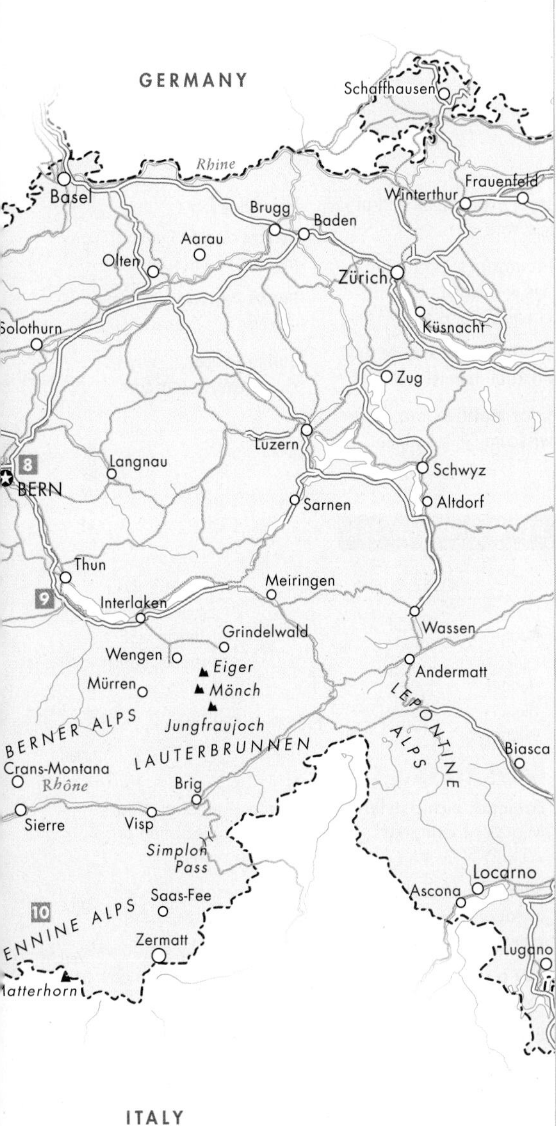

yes, the **Matterhorn.** From the Rhône Valley explore the citadel of **Sion** and take resort luxury to new heights in **Saas-Fee, Verbier,** and **Crans-Montana.** Of course, you'll feel unsated if you miss Switzerland's most photographed icon, the Matterhorn, so stop by its lovely home, **Zermatt.**

11 **Vaud.** Centered on **Lac Léman** (Lake Geneva), this French-speaking canton harbors Alpine villages, glamorous lake resorts, and verdant vineyards. But be sure to visit the Old Town and waterfront of **Lausanne,** harbor-front **Vevey,** Riviera-like **Montreux,** and lakeside **Château de Chillon**—Switzerland's most fabled castle.

12 **Geneva.** As the birthplace of Calvinism and the International Red Cross, home to the European headquarters of the United Nations, and a stronghold of private banks and exclusive boutiques, Geneva is, in many ways, a paradox. To get into its international vibe, begin by exploring the **Palais des Nations,** then after the **Vieille Ville** (Old City), head to the downtown waterfront and the feathery **Jet d'Eau.**

NEED TO KNOW

AT A GLANCE

Capital: Bern

Population: 8,236,600

Currency: Swiss franc (SF)

Money: ATMs are common; credit cards widely accepted

Language: German, French, Italian, Romansh

Country Code: 41

Emergencies: 117

Driving: On the right

Electricity: 200v/50 cycles; electrical plugs have two or three round prongs

Time: Six hours ahead of New York

Documents: Up to 90 days with valid passport; Schengen rules apply

Mobile Phones: GSM (900 and 1800 bands)

Major Mobile Companies: Swisscom, Salt, Sunrise

WEBSITES

Switzerland: *www.myswitzerland.com*

Swiss Railways: *www.sbb.ch*

Swiss Travel: *www.swisstravelsystem.com*

GETTING AROUND

Air Travel: The major airports are Geneva Cointrin and Zürich Airport.

Bus Travel: Bus travel is good for traveling between smaller regional towns to and from isolated villages.

Car Travel: Rent a car to explore at your own pace, and buy a vignette for the autobahn if your rental doesn't already have one (40 SF at the border or in gas stations).

Train Travel: The Swiss train network is exemplary; Swiss Rail passes also include buses, boats, city trams, and discounts on cable cars and funicular trains up to most Alpine peaks.

PLAN YOUR BUDGET

	HOTEL ROOM	MEAL	ATTRACTIONS
Low Budget	118 SF	20 SF	Grossmünster Tower, Zürich, 4 SF
Mid-Budget	340 SF	40 SF	Kunsthaus Zürich, 25 SF
High Budget	1,250 SF	150 SF	Opera ticket, 250 SF

WAYS TO SAVE

Eat lunch picnic-style. Take advantage of Coop and Migros supermarkets. Prices for perishables often drop 25% to 50% after 5 pm. Then have a picnic.

Ski in the afternoon. Most mountain resorts offer a cheaper half-day ski pass, with runs usually closing between 4 or 5 pm.

Buy a rail pass. Transit passes let you explore the country by rail, boat, bus, and city tram.

Experience markets and festivals. Every town has a festival (*Dorffest*) between June and September; markets are held weekly.

PLAN YOUR TIME

Hassle Factor	Low. Flights to Zürich are frequent, and Switzerland has a great transport network.
3 days	You can see some of the magic of Zürich and perhaps take a half-day trip out to Winterthur or Luzern.
1 week	Combine a short trip to Zürich with at least one day trip to Luzern or Interlaken as well as an additional day or two in a place within easy reach like Geneva or Lugano.
2 weeks	You have time to move around and for the highlights, including a stop in Zürich, excursions to Lake Luzern, and a trip to take in the highlights of atmospheric Graubünden and ritzy Montreux.

WHEN TO GO

High Season: July, August, and December are the most expensive and popular times to visit Switzerland. In December, the Berner Oberland is crowded with skiers; the season runs from December to March. July/August is busy in Luzern. Zürich is busiest from May through October.

Low Season: November is quiet, which also means many family-run hotels are closed. The lowlands (Zürich, Luzern) go gray and foggy in November, but above that are blue skies and fabulous mountain views. November to March is pretty much gray and wet anywhere under 3,000 feet.

Value Season: September and October still have great weather, though temperatures start to drop by late October. Late April and May is a good time to visit, before the masses arrive but when the fields are green and dotted with flowers.

BIG EVENTS

February: The White Turf horse race in St. Moritz attracts international high society. 🌐 *www.whiteturf.ch*

May: Cows are led to pasture with great pomp and circumstance for the traditional Alpine ascent. 🌐 *www.appenzell.info*

July: The legendary Montreux Jazz Festival offers three weeks of exemplary music. 🌐 *www.montreuxjazz.com*

September/October: The Zürich Film Festival is an intimate place to rub shoulders with filmmakers. 🌐 *www.zff.com*

READ THIS

- ***In the Cradle of Liberty,*** Mark Twain. A witty report on Twain's mid-19th-century trip to Switzerland.
- ***Jakob von Gunten,*** Robert Walser. A classic novel from a writer deemed a genius by J. M. Coetzee.
- ***Dunant's Dream: War, Switzerland and the History of the Red Cross,*** Caroline Moorehead. The title says it all.

WATCH THIS

- ***On Her Majesty's Secret Service.*** Bond and Blofeld match wits in the Berner Oberland.
- ***The Swissmakers.*** A satirical comedy about xenophobia in Switzerland.
- ***Vitus.*** A pianist wunderkind rebels against his parents' plan for his future.

EAT THIS

- ***Fondue***: cheese mixtures vary according to region
- ***Zürcher Geschnetzeltes***: veal strips in cream sauce
- ***Pike perch***: fresh from local lakes
- ***Cheese***: every region has its own variety
- ***Birchermüesli***: authentic with wheat germ, fresh berries, and cream
- ***Chocolate***: Zürich especially has a wealth of specialty shops

IF YOU LIKE

"Peak" Experiences

"Mountains are the beginning and end of all scenery," the great 19th-century writer John Ruskin once observed. And if mountains have a "home," it is truly Switzerland—a summit of summits. View collectors flock to that big schlock candy mountain, the Matterhorn. Adventurers are seduced by the "sheer" excitement of the Jungfrau. "Social climbers" head to the chic villages of Wengen and Mürren, which seem to levitate at either end of the Lauterbrunnen Valley, and daredevils worship at the foot of the Eiger's notorious north face. No matter where you head, you'll find that hillside footpaths can be almost as crowded as supermarket checkout lines (remember: the higher the trail, the less "conversation"—you need to concentrate!). Here are some places that will leave you with that top-of-the-world feeling.

Matterhorn, Valais. From the summit station of Gornergrat, this jagged mountain steals the thunder from all surrounding peaks.

Jungfraujoch, the Berner Oberland. From the top of the 11,333-foot-high Jungfraujoch, the Aletsch Glacier looks like a vast sea of ice.

Neuhausen am Rheinfall, Eastern Switzerland. With its mists, roaring water, jutting rocks, and bushy crags, the Rheinfall, from the Neuhausen side, appears truly Wagnerian.

Lauterbrunnen Valley, the Berner Oberland. Looking more like a painting than real life, the jaw-dropping vista of this valley is spectacularly threaded by 72 waterfalls that plummet from sky-high cliffs.

Christmas Markets

Nothing evokes Switzerland in winter like a *Weinachtsmarkt* or *marché de Noël.* These seasonal markets are held from the end of November to Christmas Eve, or even longer in some areas. You'll typically find stands brimming with handmade Swiss goods, including leather items, silver jewelry, and wooden toys. Alongside these treasures are imported market wares like South American sweaters, Indian fabrics, and soaps from Provence. With festive live music and plenty of drinking and dining options, you'll have your choice of savory local cheeses and dried meat specialties, all washed down with a hot *Glühwein* (mulled wine).

Montreux. At the largest market in Switzerland, more than 150 illuminated chalets line the lakeside promenade and main street. This is one of the best places to find handcrafted jewelry from local artists that won't break the bank. Got little ones in tow? Take the winding train up to nearby Rochers-de Naye to see Chez Santa Claus, or to the authentic Christmas village in Caux for breathtaking views over Lac Léman.

Basel. Two distinct markets circle Basel's Barfüsserplatz and Münsterplatz, next to the landmark cathedral. In the city's Old Town, you'll bask in the glow of twinkling lights while browsing through traditional handicrafts. Don't forget to sample the famous Basler Läckerli spiced cookies, the perfect accompaniment to a hot cider with schnapps or rum-infused *Punsch.*

Bern. Set among historic 15th-century buildings on Münsterplatz, Bern's Christmas market is one of the loveliest in Switzerland. A magical mix of roasted chestnuts, smoky incense, cinnamon, and pine wafts freely here. Shop for arts and crafts in the main square, and then head just down the road to Waisenhausplatz for more traditional wares.

Zürich. The best Christmas market in Zürich is held in the train station. This market charms with its handmade wooden toys and vast selection of cheeses and dried meats. Stands are centered on a stunning showpiece: a 40-foot Christmas tree laden with Swarovski crystals.

Traveling Through Time

Wander the slopes of Klewenalp above the Vierwaldstättersee on a still spring day, gaze across the placid waters beneath, and it is easy to identify Switzerland as a land of peace. Continue on a mile or so and you are reminded that for much of its time, Switzerland has been nothing of the kind. Here is the Rütli, the meadow where legend avers that the men of the three forest cantons, Uri, Schwyz, and Unterwalden, met in 1291 to plot the overthrow of their Habsburg landlords (thereby creating the world's first democracy). But move beyond this spot—hallowed by Wilhelm Tell—and you'll find Switzerland is practically crawling with history from border to border.

Old Town, Basel. When the sound of fife-and-drum music drifts from the upstairs windows of guild houses in Basel's Old Town, you'll think the Middle Ages have dawned again.

Tellfreilichtspiele, Interlaken, Berner Oberland. For a festive evening, rent a lap blanket and settle in to watch a grand retelling of the life of Wilhelm Tell, performed under the stars.

Monument de la Réformation, Geneva. The complex history of the Protestant Reformation as it unfolded across Europe is boldly rendered in granite.

Stiftsbibliothek and Kathedrale, St. Gallen. For rococo splendor and opulence, nothing beats this complex of Abbey Library and Cathedral, adorned with spectacular excesses of 18th-century wedding-cake trim.

The Most Beautiful Villages

Whatever town or valley you pick, you'll be pulled into discussions about what *the* top place in Switzerland is. The *whole* of Switzerland is undeniably beautiful. But there are certain places where the needle would fly right off the scale if they were rated on a beauty-measuring gauge. With scores of half-timber houses and chapels, these storybook places have a sense of tranquility not even tour buses can ruin.

Guarda, Graubünden. This federally protected hamlet in the Lower Engadine is full of architectural photo ops, with cobblestone streets and flower boxes filled with red geraniums.

Stein-am-Rhein, Eastern Switzerland. A nearly perfectly preserved medieval village, Stein is replete with shingled, half-timber town houses boasting ornate oriels and flamboyant frescoes.

Gandria, Ticino. Clinging vertiginously to a hillside, its flower-filled balconies overlooking Lake Lugano, the tiny town of Gandria retains the ambience of an ancient fishing village.

Mürren, Berner Oberland. Closer to the sky than the earth, this jewel presides over the majestic Lauterbrunnen Valley and offers a so-close-you-can-touch-it vista of the Eiger.

Gruyères, Fribourg. Right out of a fairy tale, this village is crowned with one of the most picture-perfect castles in Switzerland.

FLAVORS OF SWITZERLAND

Although fast food has made inroads in Switzerland, it's still a country deeply rooted in seasonality and fresh produce—it's been locavore all along. Wherever that has wavered, it's coming back as farmers and environmentalists encourage a move away from mass-food production. Other trends? Revived interest in Swiss recipes and regional cuisines: Swiss-German, Swiss-French, and Swiss-Italian, as well as the cuisine specific to Graubünden. In addition, Swiss wines are coming into their own as never before.

Natural Bounty

The countryside is a patchwork of farms, vineyards, and fields of cereals and plants used for cooking oil, like sunflower and rapeseed. Various "belts" include Vully (Vaud, Fribourg), known for its rhubarb; Bern's Guerbetal for cabbage (and sauerkraut); and Geneva, which grows its own specific type of cardoon. Apples and pears are also common, as are natural or cultivated walnuts, chestnuts, and berries. Wild mushrooming is a national pastime during summer and fall, and honeybee keeping is popular: those houselike boxes, often painted in primary colors, that you see along forest edges are hives. Saffron crocuses grown in Mund (Valais) produce the highly prized spice. Alpine herbs flavor teas and bitters.

The country's lakes and rivers provide a bounty—some 50 delicacies, including crayfish. And the Swiss like their (fall) hunting season fare: hare, deer, wild boar, and game birds.

Cheese

More than 450 types of cheese are produced in Switzerland; some 11, including the quintessential "Swiss cheese," Emmental, are labeled AOC, which means production is controlled and protected. The term "Alp cheese" designates cheese produced from summer milk when cows graze in high-altitude meadows. But there aren't only semihard cow's milk wheels—there are hard cheeses, too, like Sbrinz AOC (made in central Switzerland), and soft patties like Tomme (made in Vaud). An October-through-March must-try is spoonable Vacherin Mont d'Or AOC. Unusual regional items include Schabziger from Glarus: small, green, cone shaped, and redolent with the smell of blue fenugreek.

Fondue and Raclette

Whether a mix of Gruyère and Vacherin (known as *moitié-moitié*) or a less pungent mix of hard cheeses, fondue is a countrywide staple. Although locals prefer it in winter, rest assured that in the summer high up in the Alps, fondue is not only for tourists. When temperatures fall in the evenings and a cool breeze sets in, a caquelon of melted goodness will leave you warm and satisfied.

If fondue seems too rich, try *raclette*. Originally a dish from the Haute-Savoie region in France, this heated half wheel of full-bodied cheese is scraped piping hot onto boiled potatoes and consumed alongside pickled cucumbers, onions, and a selection of dried meats. It's a full, delicious meal in itself.

Meats

There's a reason meat is pricey in Switzerland—farmers here receive the second-highest subsidies in the world. These taxpayer funds allow farmers to continue dairy farming and ranching in a traditional manner, much as their families did several generations ago. Tens of thousands of small-to-medium family farms coexist alongside larger facilities, many with "Bio" (organic) distinction.

Each canton has its dried-meat specialties, but the most well known comes from Graubünden. *Bündnerfleisch* is made from beef shoulder marinated in white wine and herbs before the lengthy five-month drying process begins. Pressed periodically to rid the meat of excess moisture, the final product is rectangular shaped, deep red in color, and eaten in very thin slices.

Switzerland might not be as sausage-crazy as Germany, but there are several distinct types that merit tasting. *Cervelat,* the national sausage, is made from a mixture of beef and pork. It can be found at every barbecue, grilled with the ends sliced in quarters to resemble a flower. St. Gallen is the country's top spot for sausage making; its famous smoky Schüblig and milky-white St. Galler bratwurst are tasty options available in most cities.

Desserts

A national treasure, Swiss chocolate ranges from the ubiquitous Lindt to handcrafted pieces from boutique chocolatiers. But there's more to Swiss desserts than simply chocolate. Specialties featuring local ingredients abound, from the Vaudois *carac,* a bright-green tart filled with sweet chocolate ganache, to the popular chocolate mousse. In a country teeming with fresh, creamy milk, it's no surprise that this rich, whipped blend of chocolate, cream, and eggs can be found on nearly every menu.

For a lighter way to end a meal, sample some of the sorbets and gelati in Ticino. Traditional favorites like salted caramel and pistachio can be found alongside experimental flavors such as basil lemongrass and lemon ricotta.

Wine

October is harvest season in Switzerland's six main wine regions: Valais, Vaud, Geneva, Ticino, the Swiss-German area including Graubünden, and the Three-Lakes area around Neuchâtel. Following a trend to diversify grape varieties, there are now hundreds, but top players include red Pinot Noir and Gamay, Merlot in Ticino, and Chasselas white.

Fall wine festivals abound—participants revel in freshly pressed grape juice called *Most* or *moût*. Slightly fermented, lightly effervescent wine called *Sauser* is a favorite with hunt-season meals in German-speaking parts. In May, some areas feature "Open House Days" when wineries open for tastings to launch wines made from the previous year's harvest. You can get more information from the Swiss Wine Exporters' Association (🌐 *www.swiss-wine.ch*).

SWITZERLAND TODAY

People

After centuries of poverty, with fathers sending sons abroad as mercenaries (resulting in Swiss Guards at the Vatican, for example) and citizens emigrating in hopes of a better life, today's prosperity has led to a decrease in population growth and a marked increase in immigration.

These days, a large international population (about a quarter of the populace) lives alongside the Meiers, the Favres, and the Bernasconis. They came to Switzerland because of unrest around the world, the need for workers, and that old familiar search for a better life. The resulting cultural mix has unnerved some, but it also works world-flattening magic—in the traditional town of Brütten there is a "Stars and Stripes" American-style restaurant in an old Swiss farmhouse run by a family from Sri Lanka.

Politics

Quick: can you name the president of Switzerland? Don't feel bad if you can't—the position is refilled once a year.

Every December the Swiss parliament elects or reconfirms seven of its members to make up the executive Federal Council. These seven are each the heads of an administrative department (Foreign Affairs, Home Affairs, Justice, and so on). They rotate annually to act as a "first among equals" president who has no individual power of his or her own.

Simply said, the president gets to represent the country in international and domestic matters, but still has to keep a day job.

Switzerland is also one of the most democratic countries in the world as far as citizen participation is concerned. Within this "direct democracy" any citizen can try to change a law—or propose a new one—by collecting at least 50,000 signatures within 100 days and presenting them to the local, regional, or federal government (depending on which level presides over the issue). The result is referendums and initiatives voted on by the population as many as six times a year.

Economics

With an economy that is stable, thanks mainly to its banking and taxation system (even in these volatile times), Switzerland enjoys a rare prosperity.

It is home to multinational corporations (often drawn here by low and flat-rate taxes) and local companies active in pharmaceuticals, chemicals, precision instruments, insurance, real estate, and, of course, banking.

With a decidedly business-friendly government, one area stands out in this capitalist utopia: agriculture. Farmers receive approximately 60% of their income from hefty government aid, making Switzerland's agricultural industry one of the most highly subsidized in the world.

Given that there is only so much space in roughly 16,000 square miles of country—much of which is made up of steep mountains that are hard to develop—and that green Alps are an essential draw for the tourism industry, great efforts are made to ensure that what Mark Twain once called "a large, humpy, solid rock, with a thin skin of grass stretched over it" doesn't all get paved over.

Culture

The rural traditions you'd expect—alphorns, yodeling, cows festooned with flowers—are alive and well, and not just a show put on for the tourists (although that's not unheard of either).

Almost every town has some kind of festival at least once a season, where you can sample the local food and do the local dance, with an added Italian, German, or French flavor. Thanks to full government coffers and charitable businesses, you'll also find a wide variety of art, dance, and musical offerings ranging from the cutting edge to the traditional highbrow.

And you'll find unexpected cultural offerings not just in the expected urban settings, as evidenced by the gallery of surrealist artist H. R. Giger (the designer of the monster in Ridley Scott's 1979 movie *Alien*) in the tiny and quintessentially Swiss town of Gruyères.

Gender Parity

Switzerland tends to lag behind in terms of equality of the sexes. Granted, in most cities and large towns the issue is disappearing, but a surprising number of companies still have a corporate culture that feels like an episode of *Mad Men*. In more rural cantons, there still is a certain stigma attached to mothers who send their children to (hard-to-find) day care.

In Appenzell in eastern Switzerland, women were prohibited from voting in cantonal elections until the federal court intervened on their behalf in 1991. Federal law overall didn't grant women the national vote until 1971. Nonetheless, much progress has been made recently. For example, several women sit on the executive Federal Council, and women outnumber men at universities.

Although Switzerland may still have some catching up to do with regard to the sexes, there is a flip side to this equation: women are typically able to secure part-time employment, with many working at 60% or 80% while their children are young. And although Swiss maternity leave is not the most generous in Europe, mothers still receive a minimum of 14 weeks, which can often be extended to include another two months for breastfeeding.

Sports

Switzerland is an extremely active country. Hiking, biking, windsurfing, kayaking, hang gliding, and golf are just some of the amusements practiced by young and old. Traditional Swiss sports are played by only a small fraction of the population but are beloved nonetheless as an important part of the culture. Schwingen or Hosenlupf wrestling competitions feature scantily clad opponents who grip, trip, and throw their opponents to the ground. These odd competitions are held throughout Switzerland.

There is also an interesting pastime called *Hornussen*: a puck is placed on a ramp and shot into the air with a whiplike staff. As it comes down, the opposing team members try to swat it with boards on posts that look like giant picket signs. Although not technically a sport, Trotti bikes—scooters with large, fat tires—are a popular family-friendly way to descend the Alpine heights on a sunny summer day. Rentals and dedicated trails can be found in many resort areas.

And then there's skiing. It's a sport enjoyed by Swiss of all ages, from preschoolers to hardy mountain folk in their nineties. Slopes are rated by level of difficulty, and there are areas reserved for everyone from newbies to experts. Snowboarding has made inroads as well, and is especially popular with the younger crowd. If you'd rather watch, catch a ski-jumping competition where the participants reach death-defying heights.

As far as spectator sports go, in summer it's soccer; in winter, hockey.

BEST HIKES

Hiking is practically a religion for the Swiss, and it's easy to see why: more than 37,000 miles of marked and maintained trails are braided across a landscape bursting with Alpine farms, flower-filled meadows, and towering peaks—not bad for a country slightly smaller than Massachusetts and New Hampshire combined. Here are a few of the best routes that can be done in a day or less.

Vaud

The Lavaux Vineyard Terraces (Lutry–St. Saphorin). This 11-km (6¾-mile) stretch perched above Lac Léman offers the beauty trifecta: massive mountains, a deep blue lake, and lush green vineyards. One look and you'll see why it's a UNESCO World Heritage Site. You can always pop down to Lac Léman below to catch a boat (or train), rather than walk the entire way. *Easy to Moderate.*

Berner Oberland

Eiger Trail (Alpiglen–Eigergletscher). If you think the brooding north face of the Eiger is impressive from afar, try walking right below it. The entire 6-km (3¾-mile) trail (built in 1997 in just 39 days with hand tools) bathes in breathtaking views of Grindelwald and the surrounding peaks. Hike it in reverse if your knees can handle the pounding descent on an uneven trail. *Strenuous.*

Graubünden

Muottas Muragl to Alp Languard. The ruggedness of Switzerland's most uninhabited canton is on full display on this 9-km (5½-mile) trail. The craggy mountain views of the entire Engadine valley make the effort worth it, as does a plate of yummy smoked meats at the rustic Unterer Scharberg hut at the halfway point. *Moderate.*

HIKING TIPS

■ Remember to wear practical shoes with good soles and ankle support and to always bring water, a few snacks, and extra clothing.

■ Always check your transport connections before setting out—you don't want to miss the last bus.

■ Bring cash, because huts rarely take credit cards, and you never know when you'll run across a farm selling cheese or locally made wine.

■ Have an iPhone? Switzerland Tourism (🌐 *www.myswitzerland.com*) has a superb (and free) app offering descriptions, maps, and practical information on dozens of the country's top hikes.

Valais

Zermatt Lake Trail. With the iconic Matterhorn as a backdrop, just about any hike over Zermatt will be worth the toil. Particularly special is a 9-km (5½-mile) route from Blauherd to Riffelalp; the path is relatively easy (no major ups or downs), but you'll still climb 800 vertical feet and lose almost 2,000. Numerous huts dot the route, offering plenty of chances to soak up refreshments with some of the region's most spectacular views. *Easy to Moderate.*

Ticino

Valle Verzasca (Sonogno–Lavertezzo). It's not hard to imagine life here centuries ago as you stroll over Roman bridges and past stone houses in this narrow valley, nestled in Switzerland's Italian-speaking canton. *Easy.*

MONEY-SAVING TIPS

Switzerland ranks as one of the most expensive countries in the world, but that doesn't mean you have to mortgage your home or sell a kidney to visit. Deals may not be plentiful, but occasional discounts do exist, especially during low season. Don't be afraid to ask for one—the answer might surprise you.

Transportation

Prices for rental cars in Switzerland can be nearly double the rate you'd find at home. If you decide on a car after you've arrived, it is worth the time to book one online. You'll save roughly the equivalent of a night at a four-star hotel by avoiding the rental counter.

One secret to staying solvent while riding Swiss trains is the Swiss Half-Fare Card. Available monthly, it allows you to pay only 50% of the regular ticket price on nearly every train, boat, bus, and tram in the country. This deal is not available in Switzerland, so buy this pass online or at a travel agency before you arrive.

Willing to travel on a specific train at a specific time? Surf the Swiss Federal Railways website (🌐 *www.sbb.ch*), which is loaded with money-saving goodies like the SuperSaver ticket. Simply click on your starting location to view destination and schedule options. There are even first-class tickets to choose from. Note: you must print the tickets yourself or have them sent directly to your mobile phones with the free app.

Sightseeing and Activities

Culture buffs on a budget can plan their visits around the free nights offered by local museums. These nights differ by museum and frequently by region, but most often occur on the first Saturday, Sunday, or Monday of each month.

In exchange for your passport and a small deposit, many Swiss cities offer free bikes from May to October. Whether you cruise up the Rhône River, stopping into vineyards and quaint chalet-strewn villages, or carefully navigate traffic in the trendy Zürich West district, you'll work off that heavy fondue without lightening your wallet.

Summer brings free festivals, concerts, and events to much of Switzerland. Dance into the wee hours of the morning at Zürich's famous Street Parade or bask in the glow of the biggest fireworks display in Switzerland at the Fêtes de Genève, both in August and absolutely free.

Food and Drink

For less than 20 SF, you can dine like a king at lunchtime by ordering a *Tagesmenu,* plat du jour, or *piatto del giorno.* These specials are cooked up fresh each day for less than half the price of a similar main dish in the evening.

Shop for snacks after 5 pm, when most grocery stores knock 25% to 50% off certain perishable items. If you're determined not to raid your hotel's extravagantly priced minibar, you can find chips, soda, pastries, and even prepared to-go dishes like fruit salad, sliced veggies, and pasta salad at bargain rates.

Every city, town, and village has a fountain where you can fill up a bottle with clean, fresh drinking water. Don't mind the pigeons—even Zürich's more than 1,000 fountains are frequently tested to meet strict quality standards.

GREAT ITINERARIES

SWITZERLAND SAMPLER: A FIRST-TIMER'S TOUR

10 Days. This route offers a taste of this tiny country's various cultures and landscapes. From cosmopolitan Zürich and Geneva to the quaint charms of Luzern and Zermatt to sleepy Lauterbrunnen, this tour gives you a good sense of what's to be seen here.

Zürich

2 nights. Switzerland's commercial heart and largest city offers something for everyone. Visit the Grossmünster church, updated in a Gothic style in the 1700s. Then make your way through the maze of tiny cobblestone streets toward Bahnhofstrasse, where designer boutiques cater to the city's elite. ⇨ *Chapter 2.*

Luzern

2 nights. Cross this lovely city's Wooden Bridge, the oldest in Europe, before ascending the heights of nearby Mt. Pilatus for a view over classic "Wilhelm Tell country." Hungry? Don't forget to try a *Lözarner Chögelipastete*, a meat-filled pastry that you can't find anywhere else. ⇨ *Chapter 6*

Lauterbrunnen

2 nights. Lauterbrunnen is a gorgeous base from which to explore the Berner Oberland. Trek from Interlaken to St. Beatus-Höhlen's natural caverns and hillside pavilion. When your feet can't take you any farther, take the funicular from Grindelwald up to picturesque Mürren, a tiny, delightful town perched on a rocky cliff 5,361 feet up. ⇨ *Chapter 10*

Zermatt

1 night. This picturesque, car-free village sits in the shadow of the iconic Matterhorn ... need we say more? ⇨ *Chapter 11*

BY PUBLIC TRANSPORTATION

All points on this tour are easily, and comfortably, reached by train. Note that the villages of Zermatt and Mürren are off-limits to private cars—you'll have to park outside town and take a shuttle, train, or funicular into town.

Geneva

2 nights. After learning all about the Protestant Reformation that began here, stand in the spray of Geneva's Jet d'Eau, the tallest fountain in Europe. Take a cruise on Lac Léman for breathtaking views of Mont Blanc while enjoying a glass of Chasselas, grown next door in the celebrated vineyards of Canton Vaud. ⇨ *Chapter 13*

SWISS GASTRONOMY

9 Days. This food-intensive itinerary offers aficionados an opportunity to travel from one great dining experience to another, sampling the finest *haute gastronomie* at one stop, the most authentic regional classics—even the earthiest peasant cuisines—at another. Incidental pleasures—wandering in the Alps, for example, or strolling through medieval town centers in Switzerland's greatest cities—can be squeezed in between meals. Remember that reservations must be made well in advance.

Geneva

2 nights. Your first night, indulge in a hearty Lyonnaise meal at the Bistrot du Bœuf Rouge. For lunch the next day, head out to the vineyards for exquisite seasonal cuisine at the Domaine de Châteauvieux. Back in Geneva, have a relatively light Ticinese supper at La Favola. Fill the time between meals with a brisk stroll along

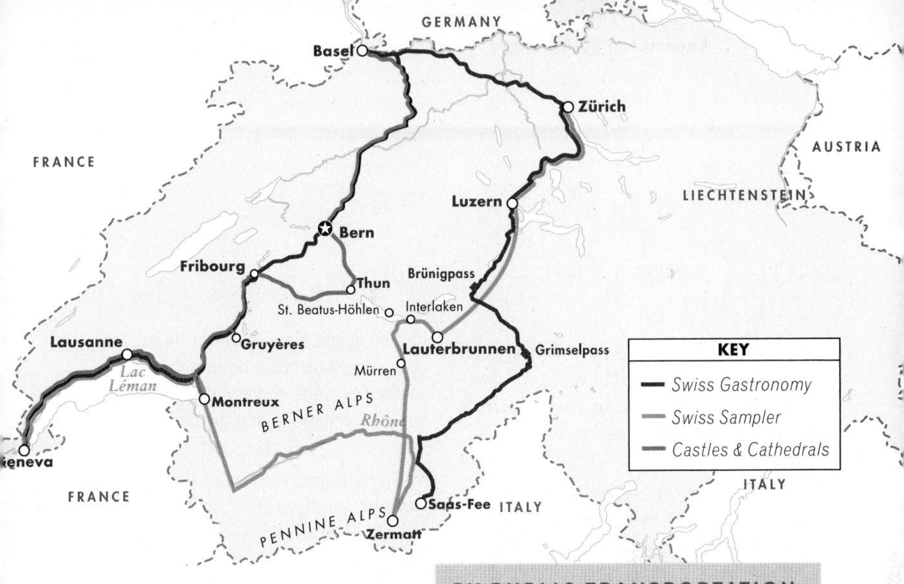

the quais or a visit to one of the city's many museums. ⇨ *Chapter 13*

Lausanne

1 night. Despite the tragic death of star chef Benoit Violier, the Restaurant de l'Hôtel de Ville has remained one of the world's top dining experiences. His widow, Brigitte, has kept the culinary passion alive, winning hearts—and stomachs—with current chef Franck Giovannani's fresh twist on haute cuisine. This may be the triumph of the trip, but reserve judgment for after Basel and Zürich. At night, head down to the waterfront at Ouchy and have a chic, light supper at the Café Beau-Rivage. ⇨ *Chapter 12*

Basel

1 night. Two hours north, lunch at Bruderholz, which gives Restaurant de l'Hôtel de Ville a run for its money. Then, after visiting, say, the Münster and the history museum, relax in the downstairs bistro at the Teufelhof: the light specialties are prepared by Michael Baader, who is chef for the top-notch restaurant upstairs as well. ⇨ *Chapter 7*

Zürich

2 nights. Step back in time for a meal at Zunfthaus zur Zimmerleuten, a medieval guildhall dating back to 1708. Then, after a thorough walking tour of Zürich's Old Town, you can settle in for an atmospheric, old-world evening at the Picasso- and Matisse-lined Kronenhalle. ⇨ *Chapter 2*

Luzern

1 night. For a total contrast and perhaps the most authentically *Swiss* meal of your tour, head for Galliker and a lunch of real farm food. Having absorbed the Lion Monument, crossed the Kapellbrücke, and toured the history museum, you can think about the evening meal: a light, sophisticated river-fish entrée at Rotes Gatter, in the Hotel Des Balances, affords waterfront views. ⇨ *Chapter 6*

Saas-Fee

1 night. From Luzern allow for a full day's scenic mountain drive south over the Brünigpass, then on over the Grimselpass and down the Rhône Valley to Brig and the spectacular little resort of Saas-Fee. Once there, retreat to the isolated Waldhotel Fletschhorn for a sophisticated dinner and a bare minimum of one night to take in the mountain air. ⇨ *Chapter 11*

BY PUBLIC TRANSPORTATION

Each of the stopovers is accessible by train, though some of the restaurants may require cabs or tram rides; a rental car will give you more flexibility for reaching country inns.

CASTLES AND CATHEDRALS

8 Days. Romantics, history buffs, and architecture fans can circle western Switzerland to take in some of the country's best medieval and Gothic landmarks.

Geneva

1 night. The excavations below the 12th-century Cathédrale St-Pierre, open to the public as the *site archéologique,* have yielded two 4th-century sanctuaries, Roman mosaics, and an 11th-century crypt. ⇨ *Chapter 13*

Montreux

1 night. The Château de Chillon, partially surrounded by the waters of Lac Léman, may be the most completely and authentically furnished in Switzerland. George Gordon, Lord Byron, signed the pillar where his "Prisoner of Chillon" was manacled. ⇨ *Chapter 12*

Gruyères

1 night. This magnificently beautiful castle-village draws crowds to its central street, souvenir shops, quaint inns, and frescoed castle, complete with dungeon and spectacular views. ⇨ *Chapter 8*

Fribourg

1 night. This bilingual city is the last Catholic stronghold of western Switzerland, rooted in its single-tower Cathédrale St-Nicolas. The cathedral's Last Judgment tympanum and art nouveau stained-glass windows deserve attention—but leave time to explore the Old Town, with its multilevel fortifications constructed for the ubiquitous Zähringens. ⇨ *Chapter 8*

Thun

1 night. If you're driving, cut across Fribourg toward Thun (by train, connect through Bern), where you'll see the Berner Alps in all their splendor. Schloss Thun, which dates from 1191, features a knights' hall, tapestries, local ceramics, and an intimidating collection of weapons. ⇨ *Chapter 10*

Bern

1 night. The Zähringens fortified this gooseneck in the River Aare; its 15th-century Münster features a restored (full-color, painted) main portal. ⇨ *Chapter 9*

Basel

1 night. In this historic, cosmopolitan city is a Münster with a lovely Romanesque portal and the tomb of the great humanist Erasmus. ⇨ *Chapter 7*

BY PUBLIC TRANSPORTATION

The complete itinerary works by rail, with most sites accessible on foot from the station; Gruyères has bus connections to the elevated castle and the Old Town.

Cantons of
Switzerland
GERMANY
FRANCE
AUSTRIA
LIECHTENSTEIN
ITALY
JURA MOUNTAINS
JURA
BASEL
SOLOTHURN
AARGAU
SCHAFF-
HAUSEN
ZÜRICH
THURGAU
APPENZELL
ST. GALLEN
NEUCHÂTEL
BERN
LUZERN
ZUG
SCHWYZ
GLARUS
UNTER-
WALDEN
URI
GRAUBÜNDEN
FRIBOURG
VAUD
GENEVA
VALAIS
TICINO
Basel
Porrentruy
Olten
Aarau
Brugg
Baden
Schaffhausen
Winterthur
Zürich
Küsnacht
Konstanz
Kreuzlingen
Frauenfeld
Wil
Arbon
Rorschach
St. Gallen
Appenzell
Buchs
Vaduz
Sargans
Glarus
Chur
Davos
Zernez
Scuol
St. Moritz
Solothurn
Biel
La Chaux-
de-Fonds
Neuchâtel
Lac de Neuchâtel
Murten
Payerne
Fribourg
Gruyères
Bern
Langnau
Thun
Interlaken
Meiringen
Grindelwald
Wengen
Luzern
Zug
Schwyz
Sarnen
Altdorf
Wassen
Andermatt
Biasca
Bellinzona
Locarno
Ascona
Lugano
Yverdon
Lausanne
Vevey
Montreux
Gstaad
Nyon
Lac Léman
Geneva
Villars-sur-Ollons
Sion
Sierre
Visp
Brig
Martigny
Verbier
Zermatt
Matterhorn
Grand St. Bernard Pass
Simplon Pass
Rhine
Bodensee
Rhône
Inn
BERNER ALPS
PENNINE ALPS
LEPONTINE ALPS
GLARNER ALPS
RHAETIAN ALPS
ENGADINE ALPS
0
20 mi
0
20 km

SCENIC TRAIN RIDES

AND DRIVES

Switzerland's scenic beauty has drawn visitors to its peaks for more than 150 years—and traders were crossing the mountains long before that. The result is an extensive road and rail network enabling you to discover each corner of the country, from glistening, mineral-rich rivers to the glaciers that feed them.

The efficient rail system provides speedy transport options, but the real treat is to slow down and turn your journey into an experience. Most scenic routes link big cities, making them easy to incorporate into your travels. Or take to the road yourself, and explore sites off the beaten path. We've scoured the countryside to find the best scenic routes, whether you are the driver or merely a passenger.

CLASSIC SWISS ROUTES

Vineyards in the Lavaux region

Whether you're riding the rails or behind the wheel, check out our favorite scenic routes in Switzerland. These rides and drives connect many popular Swiss destinations, and offer some unforgettable sights to see along the way. For more details on these routes, see the following pages.

SWISS TRAVEL PASS

If you'll be spending a week or more in Switzerland, and want to see as much of the country as possible, the Swiss Travel Pass or Swiss Travel Pass Flex could be the perfect ticket. Both allow unlimited travel on trains, buses, and boats nationwide, including scenic routes and local trams in 75 towns, as well as free entry to more than 480 museums. They also offer a 50% discount on most mountaintop trains and cable cars. The Swiss Travel Pass must be used on consecutive days. The Swiss Travel Pass Flex lets you choose your travel dates over the period of one month. The more days you buy, the better the deal becomes. *www.swisstravelsystem.ch*

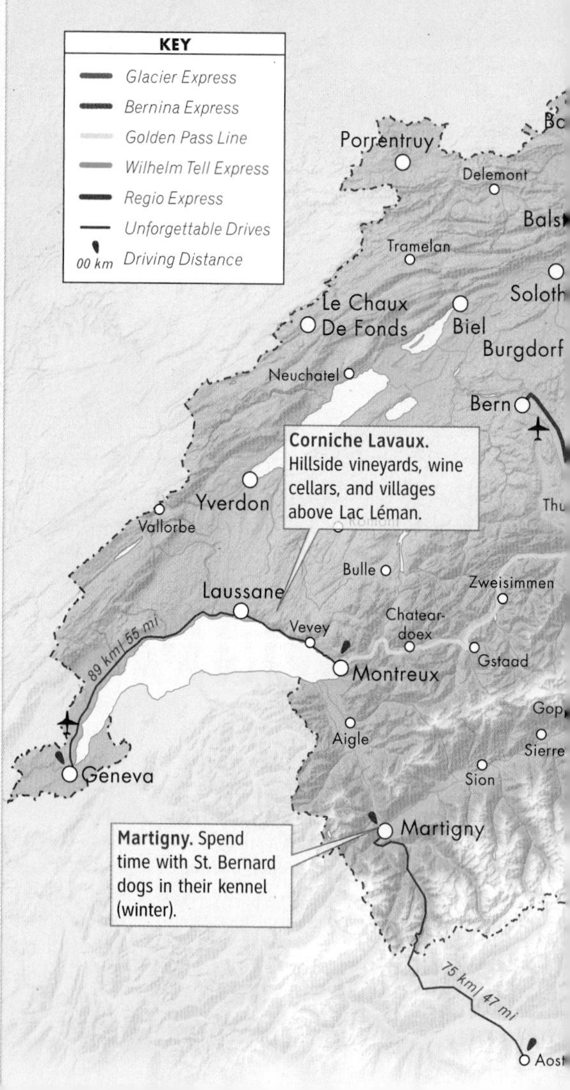

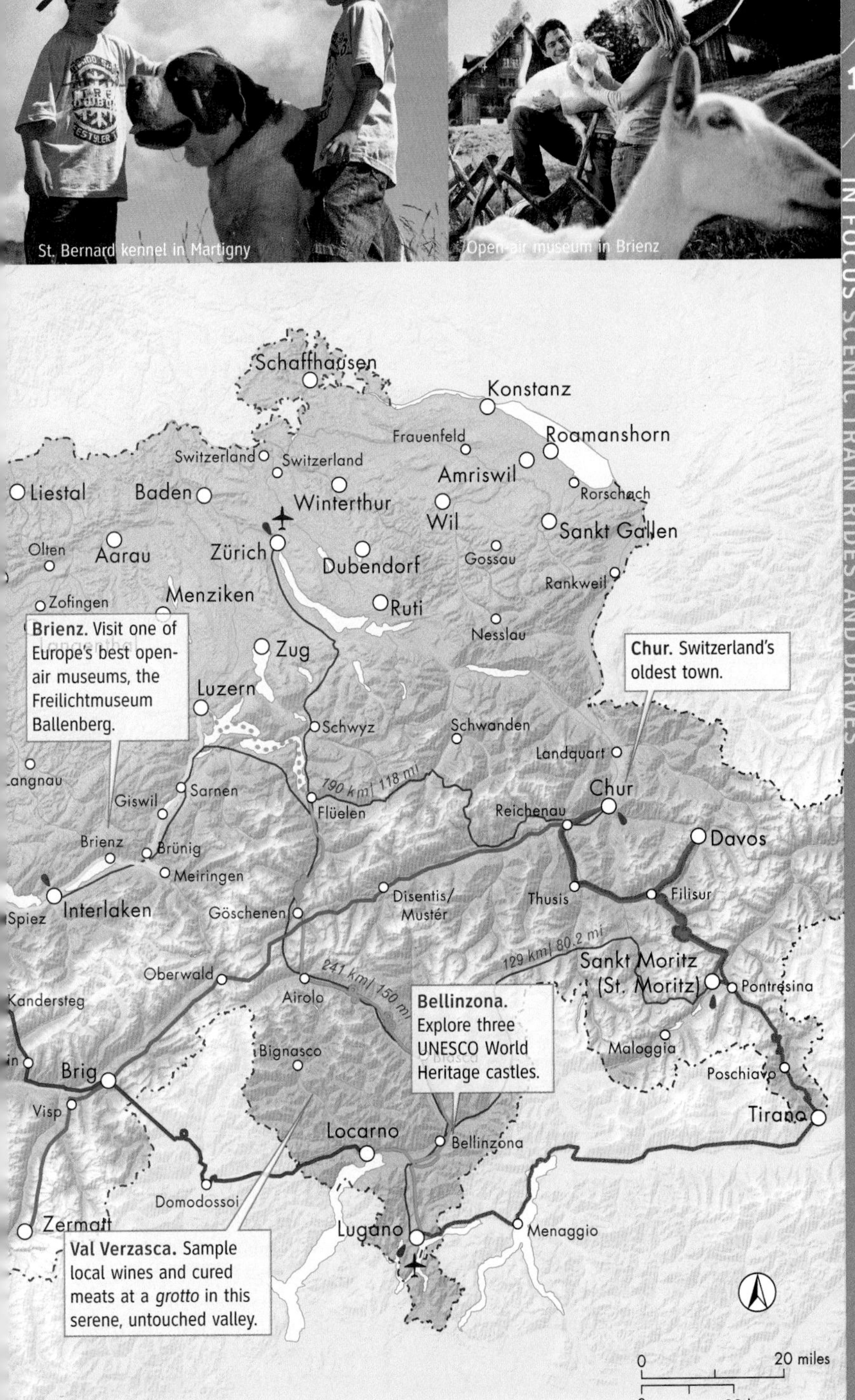

St. Bernard kennel in Martigny

Open-air museum in Brienz

TOP 5 SCENIC TRAIN RIDES

Glacier Express on the Landwasser Viaduct

GLACIER EXPRESS

Zermatt to St. Moritz

The queen of all scenic routes, the Glacier Express (also christened the world's slowest express train), begins and ends in two of Switzerland's most-frequented and fashionable resorts. But in between, it's the mountain landscape that people flock to see. Glaciated valleys, steep gorges, high meadows, and ancient townships are all viewed through panoramic cars, while the train passes over 291 bridges and through 91 tunnels.

Best For: Those who want to see the Alps, but aren't up for a lot of walking; food fanatics.

081/2886565 *www.glacierexpress.ch/en* *145 SF (plus 33 SF for seat reservation in summer; 13 SF in winter)* *7 hours, 30 min*

WILHELM TELL EXPRESS

Luzern to Locarno or Lugano (includes steamer ride)

Connecting Central Switzerland with the swaying palms of Ticino, this route takes you down the length of Lake Luzern, through the precipitous inner Alps, and on to the Swiss-Italian hubs of Locarno and Lugano. A historic paddle steamer carries you past the Rütli meadow (the birthplace of the Swiss Confederation). At the end of the lake, you'll step aboard an SBB panorama train to continue your journey south.

Best For: Lake enthusiasts; history buffs; families.

041/3676767 *www.wilhelmtellexpress.ch* *182 SF for boat and train (including seat reservation)* *5 hours Luzern–Locarno; Lugano is an additional 15 min*

GOLDENPASS/PANORAMIC EXPRESS

Montreux to Luzern

Travel in style in either a Belle Époque–inspired Orient Express train or a panoramic train from Lac Léman's "Swiss Riviera" into the cow-studded pastures and meadows of Central Switzerland. This journey squeezes through Vaud's vineyards to emerge in a higher valley strewn with chalets and farmsteads; later it scales the 1,000-meter-high Brünig Pass, before reaching Luzern. You must change trains twice, and with at least 10 trains plying this route per day, it's possible to hop on and off at any point along the itinerary.

Best For: Families (especially in the Orient Express cars); cow spotters; lake enthusiasts.

0900/245245 *www.goldenpass.ch* *72 SF (plus 17 SF seat reservation)* *5 hours, 20 min*

BERNINA EXPRESS

Chur to Tirano (Italy)

The highest Alpine railway crosses some of Graubünden's most famous bridges and viaducts. The leg from Chur to St. Moritz is part of the Glacier Express route, but as the little red train continues southeast towards Italy, it

Bernina Express

also passes Europe's highest concentration of hilltop castles, as well as imposing glaciers and icy blue lakes. Once at the Italian town of Tirano, travelers can continue on to Lugano, via a Bernina Express bus across northern Italy. Don't forget your passport.

Best For: Those who want a taste of both Switzerland and Italy; food fanatics

☎ *081/2886565* 🌐 *www.rhb.ch* 🎫 *Chur–Tirano 60 SF (plus 12 SF seat reservation); Chur–Lugano via Tirano 84 SF (plus 24 SF for seat reservation)* 🕓 *4 hours Chur–Tirano; 9 hours Chur–Lugano, via Tirano*

REGIOEXPRESS LÖTSCHBERGER

Bern to Brig

Jump aboard this scenic line to experience the beauty of the mountains between Bern and Brig. Rugged and romantic, the trip passes two picture-perfect spots for exploration: Kandersteg, with its cable car up to Oeschinensee, an otherworldly lake at the bottom of a sheer cliff face; and Goppenstein, the gateway to the Lötschen Valley, where you'll get a taste of classic Valaisan scenery. It's easy to hop on and off this train along the route.

Best For: Hikers and mountain enthusiasts; families; travelers en route to Zermatt

☎ *058/3272727* 🌐 *www.bls.ch/loetschberger* 🎫 *51 SF (no seat reservations)* 🕓 *1 hour, 50 mins*

OTHER SCENIC TRAIN JOURNEYS

Generally speaking, most Swiss rail lines pass something scenic, even if it's only lower-lying "hills," ferry-filled lakes, vineyards, or distinct local architecture. Trains through the vibrant, rolling hills in Eastern Switzerland, the journey between Bern and Interlaken, and the train line running above Lac Léman are very picturesque ways of getting from place to place. And, the GoldenPass' chocolate train from Montreux to Broc (May–Oct.) is a delicious way to combine chocolate tasting at Nestlé's Cailler factory with a visit to a cheese-making dairy in Gruyères. A new option is the Gotthard Panorama Express. After a steamer trip from Lucerne you board the train in Flüelen and go through the Gotthard Railway tunnel to Bellinzona.

UNFORGETTABLE DRIVES

PALM EXPRESS: ST. MORITZ TO LUGANO VIA ITALY

129 km/80.2 miles; 4 hours

This trip on the famed yellow Post Bus begins among the frozen glaciers of the Engadine, winding over the Maloja Pass into the picturesque Bregaglia Valley. From here, you travel to Menaggio, situated on Italy's villa-fringed Lake Como, then on to Lugano. The scenery is as varied as the views are spellbinding. ☎ *058/4483535* 🌐 *www.postbus.ch*

GENEVA TO MONTREUX, ALONG THE LAKESIDE ROAD

89 km/55 miles; about 2 hours

Lac Léman's shoreline road links the hubs of Geneva, Lausanne, and Montreux. With the French Alps towering above you from across the lake, and local vineyards tempting you to travel higher, it's easy to forget you are driving parallel to one of Switzerland's busiest highways, and in between some of its most frequented cities.

ZURICH TO LUGANO, OR ANY TWO DESTINATIONS IN BETWEEN

241 km/150 miles from Zurich to Lugano (3 hours, 15 mins)

When traveling from Germanic Switzerland to Ticino, you can avoid some of the holiday traffic jams at the Gotthard tunnel entrance by scaling the pass instead. The landscape is a bit bleak, but the hairpin turns and fresh mountain air make up for the time saved in the 16-km-long Gotthard Tunnel.

INTERLAKEN TO CHUR VIA THE GRIMSEL, FURKA, AND OBERALP PASSES

190 km/118 miles; 3 hours, 30 mins

This epic drive from the chalet-dotted Berner Oberland to the country's oldest town takes drivers over three winding mountain passes and past snow-capped peaks, glaciers, and gorges.

A Swiss Post Bus

MARTIGNY TO AOSTA, ITALY VIA THE GREAT ST. BERNARD PASS

75 km/47 miles; 1 hour, 30 mins

Switzerland's oldest and most famous pass, the Great St. Bernard, has served travelers (including Julius Caesar, Hannibal, and Napoleon) since Roman times. It links the country's forbidding, mountainous southwest region with historic Aosta and bustling Milan in Italy, including a photo-op with some St. Bernard dogs at the drive's summit.

PRACTICAL DRIVING TIPS

- Be sure to check when these routes are open, as most high passes close during winter.
- Include satellite navigation in your rental package to reduce stress during the journey.
- Control your speed: Switzerland is the land of speed cameras just waiting to catch—and heavily fine—unsuspecting speed racers.

2

ZÜRICH

WELCOME TO ZÜRICH

TOP REASONS TO GO

★ **A dip into the Middle Ages:** Museum-perfect in their leaded-glass and Gothic-wood details, a dozen medieval guildhalls have been transformed into time-burnished restaurants.

★ **Extreme shopping:** Luxury-encrusted with noted stores, Bahnhofstrasse is also lined with banks to refill your empty wallets—the nearby Altstadt has other "Ring bell to enter" boutiques, one of which may have that $10,000 belt you've been looking for.

★ **Amazing architecture:** The Old Town and the left bank's Oberdorf and Niederdorf have barely changed since the 18th century—savor their pedestrian-only cobblestone streets, medieval churches, and see-and-be-seen outdoor cafés.

★ **The "Great Church":** The Grossmünster lords over the city, both architecturally and psychologically, for here Ulrich Zwingli taught the city to buckle down, fear the Lord, and hail the Protestant work ethic in the 15th century.

1 Kreis 1: The Historic Core. Zürich's Altstadt (Old Town) is the main reason you're here. The east bank Niederdorf and Oberdorf neighborhoods are noted both for their cultural goodies and their lively bars and restaurants.

2 Kreis 2. This splendid neighborhood of leafy streets and 150-year-old villas is home to the Museum Rietberg, where Richard Wagner wrote his famed *Wesendonck Songs.*

3 Kreis 5: Zürich West. For something different, head here to check out the modern architecture—since the 1990s the area has made room for trendy lofts and hip clubs.

4 Kreis 7. Upscale houses crawl up the Zürichberg hill, which is topped with an elaborate zoo and the cemetery where James Joyce was interred in 1941—and still draws many fans to the Irish writer's grave.

5 Kreis 8. With its shoreline promenade and opportunities for swimming in the lake, this is especially a draw in summer, when the city's residents flock outdoors during their leisure hours.

6 Winterthur. Roughly 20 minutes from Zürich, this town is famed for its art collections.

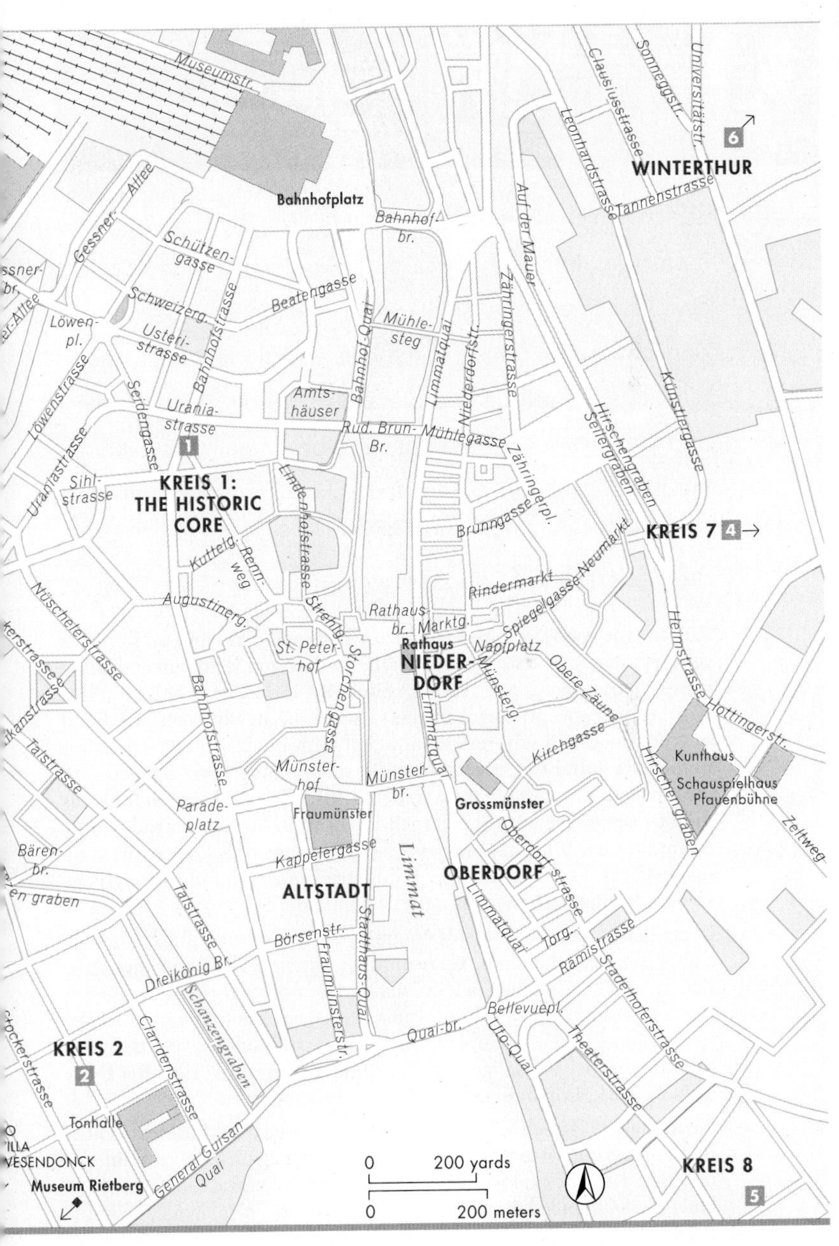
Museumstr.
Bahnhofplatz
Bahnhof-
br.
Gessner-Allee
Schützen-
gasse
Schweizerg.
Beatengasse
Löwen-
pl.
Usteri-
strasse
Bahnhofstrasse
Mühle-
steg
Bahnhof-Quai
Limmatquai
Niederdorfstr.
Zähringerstrasse
Auf der Mauer
Leonhardstrasse
Clausiusstrasse
Sonneggstr.
Universitätstr.
6
WINTERTHUR
Tannenstrasse
Künstlergasse
Löwenstrasse
Seidengasse
Amts-
häuser
Urania-
strasse
Rud. Brun-
Br.
Mühlegasse
Zähringerpl.
Hirschengraben
Seilergraben
1
Uraniastrasse
Sihl-
strasse
KREIS 1:
THE HISTORIC
CORE
Lindenhofstrasse
Brunngasse
KREIS 7
4
Kuttelg.
Renn-
weg
Augustinerg.
Nüschelerstrasse
Strehlg.
Rathaus-
br.
Marktg.
Rindermarkt
Spiegelgasse
Neumarkt
Heimstrasse
St. Peter-
hof
Storchengasse
Rathaus
NIEDER-
DORF
Napfplatz
Obere Zäune
Münsterg.
Hottingerstr.
Talstrasse
Kirchgasse
Kunthaus
Schauspielhaus
Pfauenbühne
Münster-
hof
Münster-
br.
Grossmünster
Parade-
platz
Fraumünster
Zeltweg
Bären-
br.
Kappelergasse
Limmat
OBERDORF
Oberdorfstrasse
ALTSTADT
Stadthaus-Quai
Limmatquai
Börsenstr.
Fraumünsterstr.
Torg.
Rämistrasse
Stadelhoferstrasse
Dreikönig Br.
Schanzengraben
Claridenstrasse
Bellevuepl.
Quai-br.
Utoquai
Theaterstrasse
KREIS 2
2
Tonhalle
General Guisan Quai
Museum Rietberg
0
200 yards
0
200 meters
KREIS 8
5

Updated by Kelly DiNardo

Zürich, which sits astride the Limmat River at the point where it emerges from the Zürichsee (Lake Zürich), is a beautiful city. Its charming Altstadt, which makes up a substantial part of the city center, is full of elegantly restored historic buildings as well as first-rate shopping, both in exclusivity and uniqueness. In the distance, snowy mountains overlook the lake, its shores dominated by centuries-old mansions. Few high-rise buildings disturb the skyline, and their heights are modest by U.S. standards.

Zürich was renowned as a center for commerce as early as the 12th century; many of its diligent merchants had made fortunes dealing in silk, wool, linen, and leather goods. By 1336 this privileged class had become too powerful in the view of the newly emerging band of tradesmen and laborers who, allied with a charismatic aristocrat named Rudolf Brun, overthrew the merchants' town council and established Zürich's famous trade guilds. Those 13 original guilds didn't lose power until the French Revolution—and even today they maintain their prestige. Every year Zürich's business leaders dress up in medieval costumes for the guilds' traditional march through the streets, heading for the magnificent guildhalls.

If the guilds defined Zürich's commerce, the Reformation defined its soul. From his pulpit in the Grossmünster, Ulrich Zwingli galvanized the region, and he ingrained in Zürichers a devotion to thrift and industriousness so successfully that it ultimately led them into temptation: the temptation to achieve global influence and tremendous wealth. Today the Zürich stock exchange is the fourth largest in the world, after those of New York, London, and Tokyo.

Nevertheless, Zürich is not your typical cold-hearted business center. In 1916 a group of artists and writers rebelling against the restraints of traditional artistic expression—among them Tristan Tzara, Jean Arp, and Hugo Ball—founded the avant-garde Dadaist movement here. The fertile atmosphere also attracted Irish author James Joyce, who spent years here while re-creating his native Dublin in *Ulysses* and *A Portrait of the Artist as a Young Man.* Today the city's extraordinary museums and galleries and luxurious stores along Bahnhofstrasse, Zürich's Fifth Avenue, attest to its position as Switzerland's cultural—if not political—capital.

In recent years "Züri," as it's known by the locals, has won a number of global accolades as one of the most "liveable" cities because of its green spaces, efficient and timely transportation system, and cleanliness. Swiss precision and eye for detail is visible everywhere, and no district is left untouched or forgotten. Even the so-called rougher areas are well kept by international standards. Zürich is a far cry from what it was thought to be 30 years ago: dull, closed to outsiders, and rigid. Today's city is a vibrant, multicultural metropolis that maintains the cool, modern, and international elegance that the Swiss pull off to perfection.

ZÜRICH PLANNER

WHEN TO GO

The temperate climate has four distinct seasons. Spring can be a maddening mix of brilliant sun and rain, which means colorful blossoms abound. Summers are humid and have been quite hot in the last several years, rivaling some Asian nations; evening thunderstorms are frequent.

Fall becomes crisp around the end of October, and winter brings a low fog ceiling (this is when locals head for any nearby peak over 5,000 feet) or light-to-slushy snow that tends to melt after a week or so.

FESTIVALS

If you see an elephant wandering around the streets of Zürich, don't worry: it just means the circus is in town. In the winter months a series of circuses—with acrobats, fire-eaters, and lion tamers—travel throughout the country in red-and-white caravans, each stopping along the way in Zürich. In addition to the usual opera, theater, and concert seasons, the city holds a variety of events throughout the year.

One of Zürich's most important festivals is **Sächsilüüte,** a kind of Groundhog Day. Descendants of medieval guild members march through town, then circle a bonfire containing a snowman topped with firecrackers. They march until the snowman's head blows off, and how long this takes is indicative of the coming summer's weather: the quicker the explosion, the warmer the summer.

When spring springs, so does **Jazznojazz,** with jazz musicians playing at venues all over town.

Summer is the time for the **Zurich Pride Festival,** a huge celebration of gay pride.

Even if you don't speak German, you should still attend the **Theater Spektakel,** a two-week outdoor theater festival, for the excellent food. Sensuous dancing marks the nine days in July of **Tangowoche,** and techno music is the sound track for August's three-day lovefest called **Street Parade.**

Fall arrives with the **Lange Nacht der Museen,** when museums leave their doors open all night. **Knabenschiessen,** a country fair held on the outskirts of the city, lets youngsters test their aim at shooting competitions. Toward the end of the year is **Expovina,** a wine exhibition, held on boats moored at Bürkliplatz.

PLANNING YOUR TIME

Despite its international stature, Zürich is a small city (some may argue "town"), which makes it ideal for a visit on foot. The historic center can easily be visited in a day, factoring in a nice lunch and a relaxing dinner or night at the opera. Add half a day for each museum you want to visit—and there are many—and one more for lakeside relaxation or hiking in the nearby hills.

GETTING HERE AND AROUND

AIR TRAVEL

Zürich Airport, 11 km (7 miles) north of the city, is Switzerland's most important airport and the 10th-busiest in the world. It's easy to take a Swiss Federal Railways feeder train directly from the airport to Zürich's Hauptbahnhof (main station), a 10-minute trip. A taxi into the center costs 50 SF to 60 SF and takes around 20 minutes. Most larger hotels have their own shuttles to and from the airport.

BOAT TRAVEL

Whether you feel like rowing out onto Lake Zürich, taking a cruise past waterfront villas, or zipping to one of the lakeside restaurants in a water taxi, there are all kinds of boats for rent in and around Zürich. Lago has a variety of boats for rent and operates a water-taxi service, and Zürichsee Schifffahrtsgesellschaft runs passenger ships between communities on the lake as well as round-trips.

Contacts Lago. ✉ *Utoquai 6, Kreis 8* ☎ *079/7753244* 🌐 *www.lago-zuerich.ch.* **Zürichsee Schifffahrtsgesellschaft.** ✉ *Bürklipl., Kreis 1* ☎ *044/4871333* 🌐 *www.zsg.ch.*

CAR TRAVEL

The A2 expressway from Basel to Zürich leads directly into the city. The A1 continues east to St. Gallen. Approaching from the south and the St. Gotthard route, take the A14 from Luzern (Lucerne). It feeds into the A3, which takes you through the Üetliberg Tunnel and into the city at its southwestern edge.

If Swiss drivers have a reputation throughout Europe for being unnecessarily impolite in their lead-footedness, Zürich must be where they're all hatched and trained. With a good number of streets in town marked "one-way" or "pedestrian-only" or with a speed limit of only 30 kph (18 mph), many drivers take out their frustrations on their fellow man. The rate of road rage is unnervingly high in Zürich, but road rules are very strict, and if you violate them, you run the risk of high fines.

TAXI TRAVEL

Taxis are very expensive, with a 6 SF minimum but no charge for additional passengers. An available taxi is indicated by an illuminated rooftop light. You can order a cab by calling Alpha Taxi or Züri Taxi.

Contacts Alpha Taxi. ☎ *044/7777777.* **Züri Taxi.** ☎ *044/2222222* 🌐 *www.zueritaxi.ch.*

TRAIN TRAVEL

There are straightforward connections and several express routes leading directly into Zürich from Basel, Geneva, Bern, and Lugano. All take you to the Zürich Hauptbahnhof in the city center.

TRAM TRAVEL

ZVV, the tram service in Zürich, is swift, punctual, and clean. It runs from 5:30 am to 12:30 am, every 7 minutes at peak hours and every 12 minutes at other times. All-day passes for the city center cost 8.40 SF and can be purchased from the same vending machines at the stops that post maps and sell one-ride tickets; you must buy your ticket before you board. Free route plans are available from VBZ Züri-Linie (Zürich Public Transport) offices, located at major crossroads (Paradeplatz, Bellevue, Central, Limmatplatz). Stops are clearly signposted.

Contacts ZVV. ☎ *0848/988988* 🌐 *www.zvv.ch.*

⇨ *For more information on getting here and around, see Travel Smart Switzerland.*

TOURS

Bicycle Tours. Year-round, Monday, Wednesday, and Friday at 10 am, you can take a three-hour bike tour from the Hauptbahnhof for around 50 SF (rates vary according to the number of people in the group). Tours are available in English; bikes are supplied. Reservations are advised.

Bus Tours. The Zürich Tourist office's daily Cityrama tour covers the main city sights; the trip lasts three hours, leaving at 11 am; it costs 58 SF. The Zürich Trolley Experience (34 SF) gives a good general idea of the city in two hours; it leaves at 9:45 am, noon, and 2 pm. The Combo Tour goes farther and includes a train trip to the top of the nearby Üetliberg. This is also a daily tour, given at 9:45 am, noon, and 2 pm; it takes four hours and costs 42 SF. All tours start from the Hauptbahnhof. The tourist office also offers a weekend Segway City Tour from 89 SF from April through October.

Walking Tours. Throughout the summer the tourist office offers daily two-hour walking tours (25 SF) that start at the Hauptbahnhof. In winter tours are offered three times a week. You can join a group with English-language commentary, but the times vary, so call ahead.

VISITOR INFORMATION

The **Zürich Card** (24 SF) gets you 24 hours of travel in the greater Zürich area on all trams, buses, trains, boats (with a 5 SF supplement), cable cars, and cogwheel trains, plus free entry into over 40 museums. It's available from the tourist information center.

Zürich Tourist Service. ✉ *Hauptbahnhof, Bahnhofpl., Kreis 1* ☎ *044/2154000* 🌐 *www.zuerich.com.*

EXPLORING

From the northern tip of the Zürichsee, the Limmat River starts its brief journey to the Aare and, ultimately, to the Rhine—and it neatly bisects Zürich at the starting gate. The city is crisscrossed by lovely, low bridges. On the left bank are the Altstadt, the grander, genteel pedestrian zone of the old medieval center; the Zürich Hauptbahnhof, the main train station; and Bahnhofplatz, a major urban crossroads and the beginning of the world-famous luxury shopping street Bahnhofstrasse. The right bank constitutes the livelier old section, divided into the Oberdorf (Upper Village) toward Bellevue, and the Niederdorf (Lower Village), from Marktgasse to Central and along Niederdorfstrasse, which buzzes on weekends. Most streets between Central and Bellevue are pedestrian-only zones, as is the Limmatquai from the Rudolf-Brun-Brücke to the Münsterbrücke.

Similar to the arrondissement system in Paris, Zürich is officially divided into a dozen numbered *Kreises* (districts), which spiral out clockwise from the center of the city. Kreis 1, covering the historic core, includes the Altstadt, Oberdorf, and Niederdorf. Zürich West is part of Kreis 5. Most areas in the city are commonly known by their Kreis, and a Kreis number is generally the most helpful in giving directions.

KREIS 1: THE HISTORIC CORE

Zürich's **Altstadt** (Old Town) is the main reason you're here, thanks to Gothic treasures like the Fraumünster, shopping galore, and an amazing collection of restaurants, and it's all right on the lake. Less elite but livelier, Zürich's east bank **Niederdorf and Oberdorf** neighborhoods are noted for both their cultural goodies, including the star-studded opera house and the Kunsthaus (Museum of Art), and their lively bars and restaurants.

LEFT BANK: THE ALTSTADT

The Altstadt is home to several of Zürich's most important landmarks—the Lindenhof, St. Peter's, the Fraumünster, and the Stadthaus—as well as the store-lined Bahnhofstrasse.

TOP ATTRACTIONS

Fodor's Choice ★ **Bahnhofstrasse.** Reputedly "the most expensive street in the world"—thanks to all of its extravagantly priced jewelry stores—Zürich's principal boulevard offers luxury shopping and hulking department stores, while much shifting and hoarding of the world's wealth takes place discreetly within the banks' walls. You can enjoy your window-shopping here in relative peace: the only vehicles allowed are the municipal trams. ✉ *Kreis 1* ✥ *Begins south of the Haupbahnhof.*

QUICK BITES

Sprüngli. Zürich's top confectionery, this landmark chocolatier and café for wealthy Bahnhofstrasse habitués concocts heavenly truffles and *Luxemburgerli*, small cream-filled cookies that require immediate eating. Good, plain hot lunches, sandwiches, and salads are also served. **Known for:** variety of desserts and chocolates; lively atmosphere; great people-watching. ✉ *Paradepl., Kreis 1* ☎ *044/2244711* 🌐 *www.spruengli.com* ⏲ *Closed Sun.*

Fodor's Choice ★ **Fraumünster** (*Church of Our Lady*). Of the church spires that are Zürich's signature, the Fraumünster's is the most delicate, a graceful sweep to a narrow point. It was added to the Gothic structure in 1732; the remains of Louis the German's original 9th-century abbey are below. Its Romanesque choir is a perfect spot for meditation beneath the ocher, sapphire, and ruby glow of the 1970 stained-glass windows by the Russian-born Marc Chagall, who loved Zürich. The Graubünden sculptor Alberto Giacometti's cousin, Augusto Giacometti, executed the fine painted window, made in 1930, in the north transept. ✉ *Stadthausquai, Kreis 1* 🌐 *www.fraumuenster.ch* 🎟 *5 SF.*

Kirche St. Peter (*Church of St. Peter*). Dating from the early 13th century, Zürich's oldest parish church was built on a site that has been occupied by a church since the 9th century. The existing building has been considerably expanded over the years, in styles ranging from a Romanesque choir to a baroque nave. The tower, for example, was extended in 1534, when the clock—which has the largest clockface in Europe—was added. Keep an eye out for inexpensive or even free classical concerts. ✉ *St. Peterhofstatt, Kreis 1* ☎ *044/2116057* 🌐 *www.st-peter-zh.ch/home.html.*

Paradeplatz (*Parade Square*). The hub of Bahnhofstrasse and a tram junction, this square is a great place to observe a microcosm of the local upper crust—furrowed-brow bankers striding to work while their fur-trimmed wives struggle with half a dozen bags and the dilemma of where to shop next. While you're at it, spoil your taste buds with incredible chocolate from the Sprüngli café. ✉ *Intersection of Bahnhofstr. and Poststr., Kreis 1.*

WORTH NOTING

Alfred Escher statue. Leave it to Zürich to have a statue that honors not a saint, not a poet or artist, but rather the financial wizard who single-handedly dragged Zürich into the modern age back in the mid-19th century. Escher (1819–82) established the city as a major banking center, championed the development of the federal railways and the city's university, and pushed through the construction of the tunnel under the St. Gotthard Pass. ✉ *In the middle of Bahnhofpl., Kreis 1.*

Hauptbahnhof (*Main Railway Station*). From the bustling main concourse of this immaculate 19th-century edifice you can watch crowds rushing to their famously on-time trains. Beneath lies a shopping mall, open daily (an exception to the closed-on-Sunday rule), with everything from grocery stores to clothing boutiques and bookstores. ✉ *Between Museumstr. and Bahnhofpl., Kreis 1.*

Haus Konstruktiv (*Museum of Constructivist Art*). Housed in a former electrical substation set by the River Sihl—an impressive 1930s modernist architectural statement in its own right—this collection traces the history of constructivist art, which became one of the vogues of the 1930s and '40s and had a big following in Switzerland (especially among its trailblazing graphic-art designers). The showpiece is the Rockefeller Dining Room, a 1963 salon designed by Swiss artist Fritz Glarner and looking very much like a pop-up Mondrian painting. Over the years the collection has broadened to include minimal art,

DID YOU KNOW?

Boats float on the Limmat River during Street Parade. The summer techno festival is Zürich's largest annual event.

CLOSE UP

Ulrich Zwingli, Freedom Fighter

Visitors to Zürich soon hear about Ulrich Zwingli, the no-nonsense (and, one suspects, humorless) religious reformer who taught the city to buckle down, work hard, and fear the Lord. But who was this much-revered man of the cloth, and why is he depicted holding a huge sword in the statue that stands in front of the Wasserkirche?

In 1484 Zwingli was born in the tiny village of Wildhaus in the canton of St. Gallen. He entered the priesthood, eventually rising to the head position at the Grossmünster in the city of Zürich. He had no problem declaring publicly where he differed with the teachings of the Catholic Church. His first quarrel, around 1512, was over the evils of the Swiss mercenary service propagated by the pope. A few years later, around 1519, he joined the fight against the church's growing practice of exacting payment for the forgiveness of sins.

Taking a closer look at the New Testament, Zwingli came up with his own very simple theology: if it's not in the Bible, it doesn't apply. This focus on both the Old and New Testaments soon spread throughout the Christian world, affecting Protestant congregations all the way to the English colonies in America. Whereas Martin Luther's form of protest was largely peaceful, Zwingli was not above getting into the fray. As people took up arms over their right to worship as they saw fit, Zwingli suited up and went to battle. He died in 1531, along with 500 of his compatriots, clutching that very big sword at the Battle of Kappel am Albis in the canton of Zürich.

concept art, and neo geo work. During the year there are several temporary shows. ✉ *Selnaustr. 25, Kreis 1* ☎ *044/2177080* 🌐 *www.hauskonstruktiv.ch* 🎫 *16 SF* ⏲ *Closed Mon.*

Lindenhof (*Linden Court*). On the site of this quiet square, overlooking both sides of the river, a Roman customhouse and fortress and a Carolingian palace once stood. The fountain was erected in 1912, commemorating the day in 1292 when Zürich's women saved the city from the Habsburgs. As the story goes, the town was on the brink of defeat as the Habsburg aggressors moved in. Determined to avoid this humiliation, the town's women donned armor and marched to the Lindenhof. On seeing them, the enemy thought they were faced with another army and promptly beat a strategic retreat. Today, the scene could hardly be less martial, as locals play boccie and chess under the trees. ✉ *Bordered by Fortunag. to the west and intersected by Lindenhofstr., Kreis 1.*

RIGHT BANK: NIEDERDORF AND OBERDORF

As soon as you step off the Quai Bridge on the right bank of the Limmat River, you'll notice a difference: the atmosphere is more casual. The area is also the center of Zürich's nightlife—both upscale and down—with the city's opera house and its historic theater, as well as plenty of bars and clubs. The area along Münstergasse to Marktgasse, parallel to the river, has a less Calvinistic bent. Each of the narrow streets and alleys that shoot east off Marktgasse (which quickly becomes Niederdorfstrasse) offers its own brand of entertainment. Niederdorfstrasse eventually empties onto the Central tram intersection, across the river from the main train station; from there it's easy to catch a tram along Bahnhofstrasse or the Limmatquai.

2

TOP ATTRACTIONS

Graphische Sammlung (*Graphics Collection*). The impressive collection of the Federal Institute of Technology includes a vast library of woodcuts, etchings, and engravings by such European masters as Albrecht Dürer, Rembrandt, Francisco Goya, and Pablo Picasso. Pieces from the permanent collection are often arranged in thematic exhibitions. ✉ *Rämistr. 101, Kreis 1* ✣ *Take Tram 6 or 10 from the Bahnhofpl. or Central stops or Tram 9 from Bellevue to the ETH/Universitätsspital stop* ☎ *044/6324046* 🌐 *www.gs.ethz.ch* 🎫 *Free* ⏲ *Closed between temporary exhibitions.*

Fodor's Choice ★ **Grossmünster** (*Great Church*). This impressive cathedral, affectionately known to English speakers as the "Gross Monster," features plump twin towers (circa 1781) on which are classical caricatures of Gothic forms bordering on the comical. The core of the structure was built in the 12th century on the site of a Carolingian church dedicated to the memory of martyrs Felix and Regula, who miraculously carried their own severed heads to the spot. Charlemagne is said to have founded the church after his horse stumbled over their burial site. On the side of the south tower an enormous stone Charlemagne sits enthroned; the original statue, carved in the late 15th century, is protected in the crypt. In keeping with what the 16th-century reformer Zwingli preached from the Grossmünster's pulpit, the interior is spare, even forbidding, with all luxurious ornamentation long since stripped away. The only artistic touches are modern: stained-glass windows in the choir by Augusto Giacometti, in the western nave by Sigmar Polke, and ornate bronze doors in the north and south portals dating from the late 1940s. ✉ *Zwinglipl., Kreis 1* ☎ *044/2513860* 🌐 *www.grossmuenster.ch* 🎫 *4 SF to visit the tower.*

Fodor's Choice ★ **Kunsthaus** (*Museum of Art*). With a varied and high-quality permanent collection of paintings—medieval, Dutch and Italian baroque, and impressionist—the Kunsthaus is Zürich's best art museum. The collection includes some fascinating Swiss works; others might be an acquired taste. Besides works by Ferdinand Hodler, with their mix of realism and stylization, there's a superb room full of Johann Heinrich Füssli paintings, which hover between the darkly ethereal and the grotesque. And then there's Pablo Picasso, Paul Klee, Edgar Degas, Henri Matisse, Wassily Kandinsky, Marc Chagall, and Edvard Munch, all satisfyingly represented. There are plans to expand the museum by adding a modern building across the street, with an underground tunnel in between; it should be finished in 2020. ✉ *Heimpl. 1, Kreis 1* ☎ *044/2538484* 🌐 *www.kunsthaus.ch* 🎫 *16 SF; additional charge for temporary exhibitions* ⏲ *Closed Mon.*

WORTH NOTING

Helmhaus. Changing exhibitions of contemporary, often experimental, art by Zürich-based artists are hosted at this museum, the open court of which once served as a linen market. In spring the museum hosts an exhibition of works from the city's annual competition for young artists. ✉ *Limmatquai 31, Kreis 1* ☎ *044/2516177* 🌐 *www.museums.ch/org/en/Helmhaus* 🎫 *Free* ⏲ *Closed Mon.*

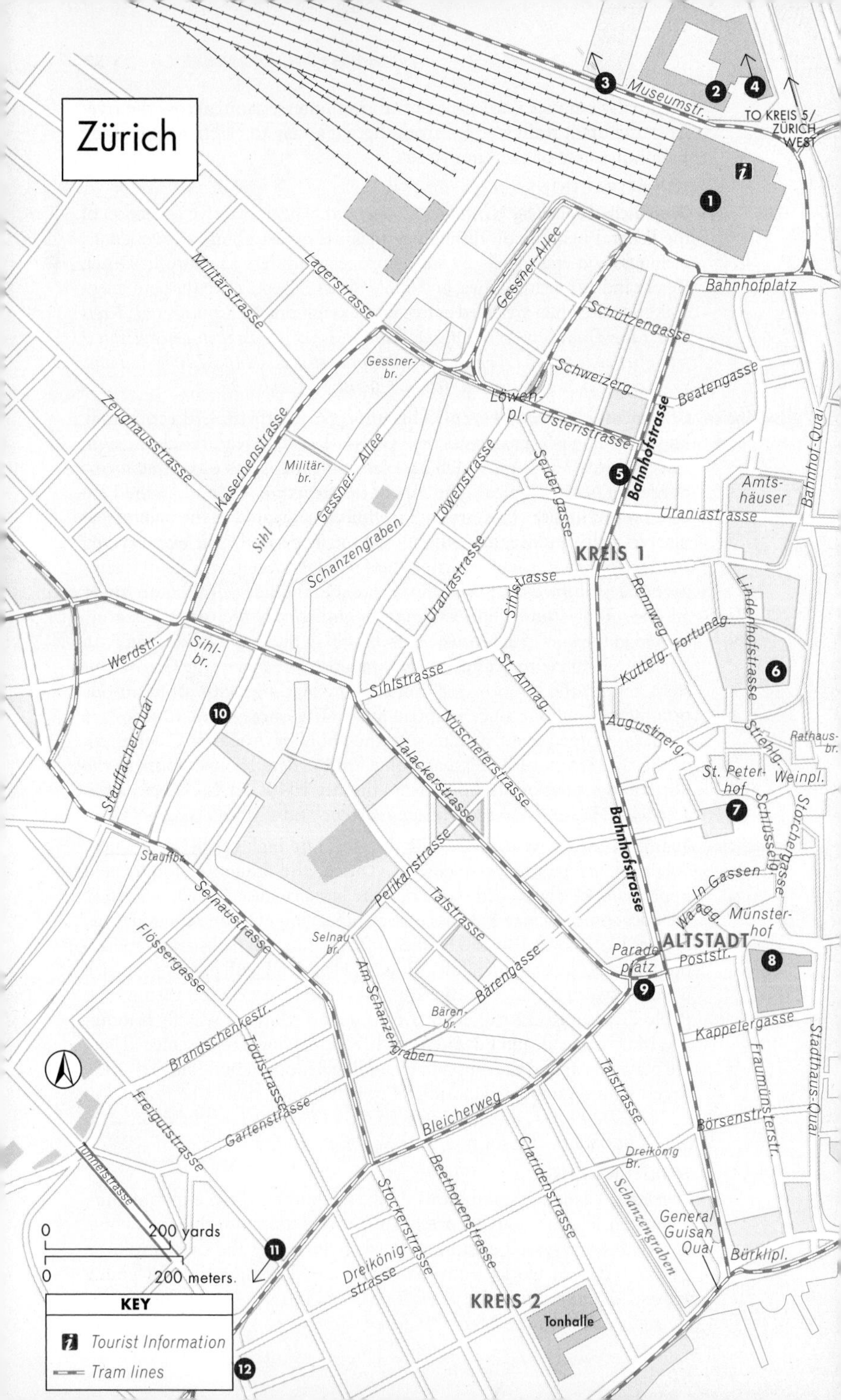
Zürich
Museumstr.
TO KREIS 5/ ZÜRICH WEST
Bahnhofplatz
Militärstrasse
Lagerstrasse
Gessner-Allee
Schützengasse
Schweizerg.
Beatengasse
Löwenpl.
Usteristrasse
Bahnhofstrasse
Gessner-br.
Zeughausstrasse
Kasernenstrasse
Militär-br.
Gessner-Allee
Sihl
Schanzengraben
Löwenstrasse
Seidengasse
Amts-häuser
Bahnhof-Quai
Uraniastrasse
KREIS 1
Uraniastrasse
Sihlstrasse
Rennweg
Lindenhofstrasse
Fortunag.
Kuttelg.
Werdstr.
Sihl-br.
Sihlstrasse
St. Annag.
Stauffacher-Quai
Nüschelerstrasse
Augustinerg.
Strehlg.
Rathaus-br.
Talackerstrasse
St. Peter-hof
Weinpl.
Schlüsselg.
Storchengasse
Stauffbr.
Pelikanstrasse
In Gassen
Selnaustrasse
Talstrasse
Waagg.
Münster-hof
Flössergasse
Selnau-br.
ALTSTADT
Parade-platz
Poststr.
Am Schanzengraben
Bärengasse
Bären-br.
Brandschenkestr.
Kappelergasse
Tödistrasse
Stadthaus-Quai
Fraumünsterstr.
Freigutstrasse
Gartenstrasse
Bleicherweg
Talstrasse
Börsenstr.
Claridenstrasse
Dreikönig Br.
Tunnelstrasse
Stockerstrasse
Beethovenstrasse
Schanzengraben
General Guisan Quai
Bürklipl.
0 200 yards
0 200 meters
Dreikönig-strasse
KREIS 2
Tonhalle
KEY
Tourist Information
Tram lines

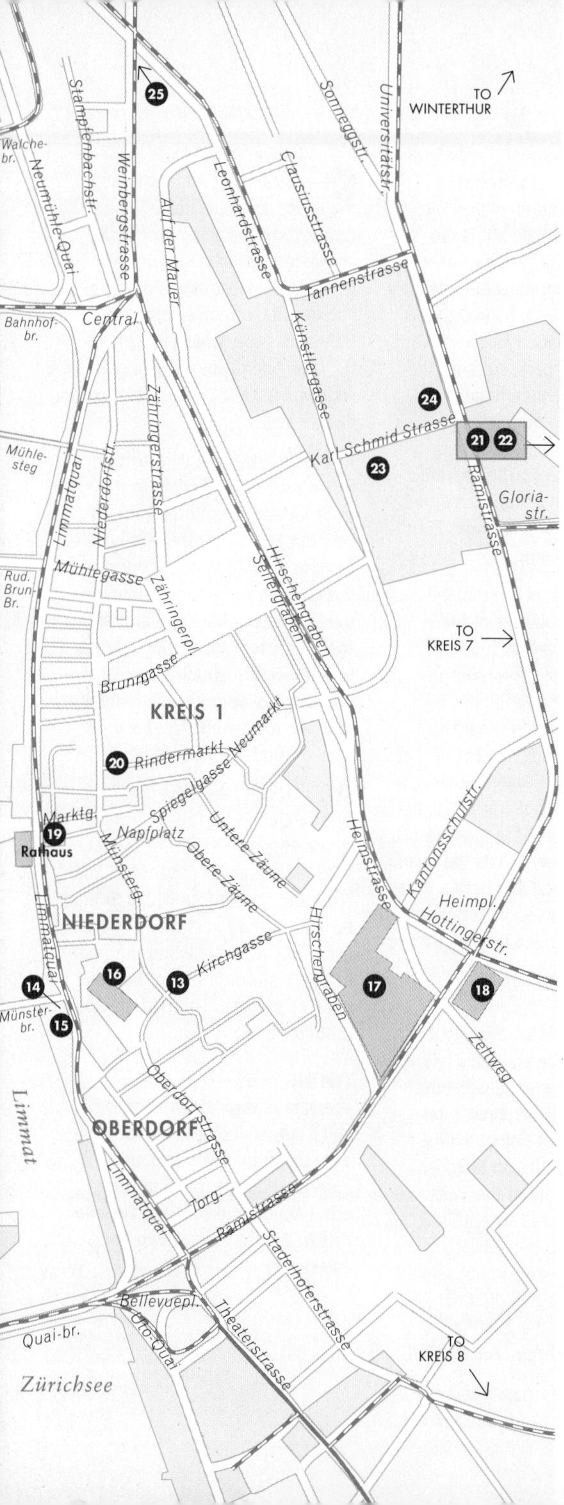

Alfred Escher Statue 12
Bahnhofstrasse 5
Fraumünster 8
Graphische Sammlung 24
Grossmünster 16
Hauptbahnhof 1
Haus Konstruktiv 10
Helmhaus 15
James Joyce's Grave 22
Kirche St. Peter 7
Kirchgasse 13
Kunsthalle 25
Kunsthaus 17
Lindenhof 6
Migros Museum für Gegenwartskunst 4
Museum für Gestaltung 3
Museum Rietberg 11
Paradeplatz 9
Rindermarkt 20
Schauspielhaus Pfauenbühne 18
Schweizerisches Landesmuseum 2
Wasserkirche 14
Zoologisches Museum 23
Zunfthaus zur Saffran 19
Zürich Zoo 21

A GOOD WALK

Begin at the **Hauptbahnhof**, a massive 19th-century edifice. Directly behind the Hauptbahnhof is the **Schweizerisches Landesmuseum**, housed in an enormous 19th-century neo-Gothic mansion; behind that is a shady green park. Walk northward to the tip of the park, cross on the left-hand side of the bridge, and turn north a bit along Sihlquai. Back at the train station, look across Bahnhofplatz and you'll see traffic careering around a statue of Alfred Escher, the man who brought Zürich into the modern age.

Cross the square to Bahnhofstrasse, Zürich's principal business and shopping boulevard. A quarter of the way up the street—about five blocks—veer left into Rennweg and left again on Fortunagasse, an atmospheric medieval street well removed from the contemporary elegance of Bahnhofstrasse. Climb up to the **Lindenhof**, a quiet, gravel square with a view across the river to the Niederdorf. From here a maze of medieval alleys leads off to your right. Nestled among them is **Kirche St. Peter**, whose tower has one of the largest clockfaces in Europe.

From Kirche St. Peter, bear right on Schlüsselgasse and duck into a narrow alley, Thermengasse, which leads left; you'll walk directly over excavated ruins of Roman baths. At Weinplatz, turn right on Storchengasse, where some of the most elite boutiques are concentrated, and head toward the delicate spires of the **Fraumünster**. In the same square you'll see two of Zürich's finest guildhalls, the Zunfthaus zur Waag and **Zunfthaus zur Meisen**.

Wind left up Waaggasse past the Hotel Savoy to **Paradeplatz**. From here you can take a quick side trip to the art collection at **Haus Konstruktiv** by going up Talackerstrasse to Sihlstrasse, turning left onto Selnaustrasse. Back at Paradeplatz, continue south on Bahnhofstrasse, which, as it nears the lake, opens onto a vista of boats, wide waters, and (on a clear day) distant peaks.

At Bürkliplatz, look to your right: those manicured parks are the front lawn of the Hotel Baur au Lac, the aristocrat of Swiss hotels. Beyond, you'll see the modern structure of the Kongresshaus and the Tonhalle, where the Zürich Tonhalle Orchestra resides. Across General-Guisan-Quai is one of the local swans' favorite hangouts: the boat dock, which is the base for trips around the Zürichsee.

Here you can take General-Guisan-Quai west to Seestrasse to the **Museum Rietberg** (about a 25-minute walk) or turn left and cross the Quaibrücke (Quay Bridge) for one of the finest views in town, especially at night, when the floodlit spires are mirrored in the inky river, its surface disturbed only by drifting, sleeping swans.

TIMING

The area is surprisingly compact; half a day is enough time for a cursory visit. If you plan on museum-hopping, the Schweizerisches Landesmuseum and Museum Rietberg merit at least two hours apiece.

Kirchgasse. Antiques, art, and book enthusiasts will delight in the shops on this street, and those interested in history or religion should note that No. 13 was Zwingli's last home before he was killed in battle (1531) while defending the Reformation. ✉ *Zürich.*

Rindermarkt. Fans of Gottfried Keller, commonly considered Switzerland's national poet and novelist, will want to visit this street. The 19th-century writer's former home, at No. 9, became famous thanks to his novel *Der Grüne Heinrich (Green Henry)*. Opposite is the restaurant Zur Oepfelchammer, where Keller ate regularly. ✉ *Between Marktg. and Neumarkt, Kreis 1.*

Schauspielhaus Pfauenbühne (*Peacock Theater*). During World War II this was the only German-language theater in Europe that wasn't muzzled by the Nazis, and it attracted some of the continent's bravest and best artists. It has been presenting plays ever since it was built in 1884; today its productions aren't always so risky, but they are stunningly mounted and performed, in German, of course. There are private tours, but the best way to see the interior is to catch a show. ✉ *Rämistr. 34, Kreis 1* ☎ *044/2587777* 🌐 *www.schauspielhaus.ch.*

Wasserkirche (*Water Church*). One of Switzerland's most delicate late-Gothic structures, this church displays stained glass by Augusto Giacometti. Both the church and the Helmhaus stand on what was once an island where martyrs Felix and Regula supposedly lost their heads. ✉ *Limmatquai 31, Kreis 1* ⏲ *Closed Sun. and Mon. and during services.*

FAMILY **Zoologisches Museum.** Engaging and high-tech, the Zoological Museum allows you a close look at its accessible displays on Swiss insects, birds, and amphibians. You can examine butterflies and living water creatures through microscopes and listen to birdcalls as you compare avian markings. ✉ *Karl Schmid-Str. 4, Kreis 1* ☎ *044/6343838* 🌐 *www.zm.uzh.ch* 🎟 *Free* ⏲ *Closed Mon.*

Zunfthaus zur Saffran. Portions of this guildhall for haberdashers date from as early as 1389. The modern restaurant downstairs has outdoor seating underneath medieval arches facing the river. ✉ *Limmatquai 54, Kreis 1* 🌐 *www.saffran.ch.*

KREIS 2

When Zürich's center got too cramped for 19th-century industrialists, they built themselves lakeside and hillside villas that still lend this neighborhood its quiet elegance.

TOP ATTRACTIONS

Museum Rietberg. Dancing Indian Shivas, contemplative Tibetan thangkas, late-18th-century literary paintings from China, and royal Benin bronzes from Nigeria—these are just a few of the treasures in the prodigious gathering of non-European art on view. This is the only museum of its kind in Switzerland, with the main focus on Asia, Africa, and ancient America. The main collection is on view in the huge underground Smaragd building. The Villa Wesendonck, the famous neoclassical jewel that was once a fabled home to Richard Wagner (it was for the lady of the house that he wrote his *Wesendonck Songs*) houses objects from India,

Overlooking the Limmat River, the Grossmünster is one of Zürich's most impressive churches.

the pre-Columbian Americas, Australia, and the Pacific Islands; there's more Indian, Islamic, and Asian art in an adjacent museum, the Park-Villa Rieter. ✉ *Gablerstr. 15, Kreis 2* ✣ *From the city center, follow Seestrasse south for nearly 2 km (1 mile) until you see signs for the museum; or take Tram 7 to the Rietberg Museum stop.* ☎ *044/2063131* 🌐 *www.rietberg.ch* 🎫 *14 SF for the collection; 18 SF for exhibition* 🕒 *Closed Mon.*

KREIS 5: ZÜRICH WEST

Zürich West is one of the city's most happening districts. Empty warehouses from the city's machine-industry days have been renovated, and others were torn down to make room for new glass-and-steel creations. The area is now chock-full of lofts, galleries, bars, restaurants, and dance clubs. The result is a swinging cultural center with a throbbing nightlife. The area is loosely bordered by Hardstrasse, Hardturmstrasse, and Pfingstweidstrasse; to get here by public transportation, take Tram 4, 13, or 17 to Escher Wyss Platz, or Tram 4 farther on to Schiffbau or Technopark. It's roughly a 10-minute trip from the Hauptbahnhof.

TOP ATTRACTIONS

Schweizerisches Landesmuseum (*Swiss National Museum*). An expansion in 2016 blends the original neo-Gothic building dating from 1889 with a new sculptural wing, and the expansion brings more flexibility in displaying the enormous collection of objects dating from the Stone Age to modern times. It has also added a library, bistro, and gift shop. Various parts of the museum will continue to be under renovation through 2019. ✉ *Museumstr. 2, Kreis 5* ☎ *044/2186511* 🌐 *www.nationalmuseum.ch* 🎫 *10 SF* 🕒 *Closed Mon.*

2

WORTH NOTING

Kunsthalle (*Center of Contemporary Art*). Set in West Zürich, this is one of two major modern art venues on the top floors of a former brewery. The gallery hosts exhibitions presenting new local and international artists, and works are always cutting-edge: you can say you saw it here first. ✉ *Limmatstr. 270, Kreis 5* ☎ *044/2721515* 🌐 *www.kunsthallezurich.ch* 🎫 *12 SF* ⏲ *Closed Mon.*

Migros Museum für Gegenwartskunst (*Migros Museum of Contemporary Art*). One floor below the Kunsthalle, this airy, white loft has the same focus—up-and-coming contemporary artists—but is privately funded by Switzerland's largest department store chain, Migros. Shows of recent work are interspersed with exhibitions from the extensive Migros collection, which includes works by Andy Warhol. The museum sponsors regular discussions with the artists. ✉ *Limmatstr. 270, Kreis 5* ☎ *044/2772050* 🌐 *www.migrosmuseum.ch* 🎫 *12 SF* ⏲ *Closed Mon.*

Museum für Gestaltung (*Design Museum*). The main repository for Switzerland's important legacy in graphic design, posters, and applied arts, this vast collection has been rehoused in a fully renovated former milk-products factory. The museum was originally envisioned as an academy devoted to design and applied arts, and while it has a robust series of education programs, it remains primarily a museum. Innovative temporary exhibitions focus on architecture, poster art, graphic design, and photography. This location also allows visitors, with a reservation, to admire not only the exhibitions but also the museum's collection of product and packaging design, graphics, and poster art (500,000 pieces). The core of the collection is in a freestanding high-bay warehouse on two floors, which operates as a display storage area. ✉ *Pfingstweidstr. 96, Kreis 5* ☎ *044/4466767* 🌐 *www.museum-gestaltung.ch* 🎫 *12 SF* ⏲ *Closed Mon.*

KREIS 7

Zürich's most luxurious residential neighborhood also is home to the zoo, wood-side walking paths with spectacular views of the Alps, and a cemetery that draws literary fans to James Joyce's grave.

TOP ATTRACTIONS

James Joyce's Grave. The inimitable Irish author not only lived and wrote in Zürich, but died here as well. The city's most famous literary resident is buried in the Friedhof Fluntern (Fluntern Cemetery). Atop his grave sits a contemplative statue of the writer, complete with cigar. A few steps away is the grave of another renowned author, Nobel Prize–winner Elias Canetti. The cemetery is adjacent to the Tram 6 terminus. ✉ *Zürichbergstr. 189, Zürich.*

FAMILY **Zürich Zoo.** This is one of Europe's outstanding zoos, with more than 1,500 animals, including Asian elephants, black rhinos, seals, and big cats. Two of the more unusual attractions are a huge dome stocked with flora and small free-range fauna you might encounter in a jungle in Madagascar, including lemurs and the endangered Bernier's teal; and the elephant park, Kaeng Krachan, which allows you to see the

The Kunsthaus houses a fascinating collection of art.

elephants swim underwater. Set in a tree-filled park, the zoo is just east of the city center and easily reached by Trams 5 and 6. ✉ *Zürichbergstr. 221, Kreis 7* ☎ *044/2542500* 🌐 *www.zoo.ch* 🎫 *26 SF.*

KREIS 8

This mainly residential area starts out as a long lakeside promenade dotted with swimming spots, rising up through several small parks to the Stiftung Sammlung E. G. Bührle, whose collection of impressionist art will be moving to a newly constructed wing of the Kunsthaus in 2020. Take a stroll down Seefeldstrasse for some upscale and, in some cases, one-off boutiques.

WHERE TO EAT

Since the mid-1990s, Zürich's restaurant trade has boomed. The new establishments, both Swiss and international, tend to favor lighter, leaner meals served in bright spaces that often open out to the street. The traditional cuisine, no longer ubiquitous but still easily found, is called *nach Zürcher Art,* meaning "cooked in the Zürich style." Think meat, mushrooms, potatoes, butter, cream—an extremely rich cuisine, perfectly suited to the leaded-glass and burnished-oak guildhalls.

In exploring Zürich's core, you will want to enter at least one of these famous medieval "union clubhouses" scattered along the riverfront neighborhoods; the best way is to dine in one, as all but the Zunfthaus zur Meisen, the Zunfthaus zur Saffran, and the Zunfthaus zur Schmide have restaurants open to the public. On your way to the restroom, sneak a peek into their other dining rooms—they are, for the most part, museum-perfect in their leaded-glass and Gothic-wood detail.

Zürich's signature dish, which you'll encounter throughout both French and German Switzerland, is *Geschnetzeltes Kalbfleisch*, or in French *émincé de veau*, bite-size slices of milky veal (and sometimes veal kidneys) sautéed in butter and swimming in a rich brown sauce thick with cream, white wine, shallots, and mushrooms. Its closest cousin is *Geschnetzeltes Kalbsleber* (calf's liver), served much the same way. You may also find *Rösti*, a kind of hash-brown potatoes, and *Spätzle*, egg noodles that are either pressed through a sieve or snipped, gnocchi-style, and served in butter.

ZÜRICHSEE (LAKE ZÜRICH)

It's a bit too busy for waterskiing, but every other activity is on offer on this end of the beautiful lake, from swimming to walking along the promenade and people-watching.

This may be the only major city in the world where you can actually swim in the heart of downtown—as hundreds do on hot summer days at its four beaches (called "Badeanstalte," or "Badis" for short—literally bathing installations—and subject to 7 SF admission). Expect to find changing rooms, lockers, restaurants, and either soft green grass or wooden docks to lie on.

Another culinary must is Zürich's favorite portable food, sausage and *Bürli* (a crunchy roll), eaten separately, two-fisted style. The best are to be had at Bellevue at the Sternen Grill; *Kalbsbratwurst* (veal) is mild, the smaller *Cervelat* (pork) saltier. Join the locals and munch away while waiting for a tram.

Zürichers also have a definite sweet tooth: refined cafés draw crowds for afternoon pastries, and chocolate shops vie for the unofficial honor of making the best chocolate truffles in town.

Restaurants in Zürich have been smoke-free by law since 2010. Some offer smokers' lounges; otherwise expect smoking at outdoor tables, where it is still allowed.

Use the coordinate (✣ B2) at the end of each listing to locate a site on the Where to Eat and Stay in Zürich map.

WHAT IT COSTS IN SWISS FRANCS

	$	$$	$$$	$$$$
At Dinner	Under 26 SF	26 SF–45 SF	46 SF–65 SF	Over 65 SF

Restaurant prices are the average cost of a main course at dinner or, if dinner is not served, at lunch.

KREIS 1

LEFT BANK: THE ALTSTADT

$$$ ECLECTIC **Baur au Lac Rive Gauche.** Its nondescript entrance off a noisy street corner belies the dark wood and mint-colored leather decor inside, which attracts crowds of hip young business executives and expense-account padders open to the concept of dining to thumping chill-out music. Part and parcel of the noted Hotel Baur au Lac, this spot offers specialties that are light, trendy, and off-the-grill, with names like "Dixie Chick"—grilled chicken breast—and "Found Nemo"—wild salmon with lime butter. "D for Two" offers mini-samples of the dessert menu. **Known for:** modern, sophisticated vibe; contemporary Swiss dining; attentive service. *Average main: 50 SF ✉ Hotel Baur au Lac, Talstr. 1, Kreis 1 ☎ 044/2205060 ⊕ www.agauche.ch ✣ D6.*

$$$ EUROPEAN Fodor's Choice ★ **George Bar & Grill.** Walking into George feels like stepping into a Don Draper–hosted cocktail party—the swanky penthouse space is decorated in vivid geometric patterns and warm wood, with pops of tangerine and turquoise, and the chic crowd is buzzing. The meat-centric menu is a mix of grilled fare and comfort dishes. **Known for:** lively, hip atmosphere; terrace and large windows with stunning views of the city below; midcentury modern interiors. *Average main: 55 SF ✉ Sihlstr. 50, Kreis 1 ☎ 044/4445060 ⊕ george-grill.ch/ ✣ B3.*

$$ VEGETARIAN **Hiltl.** Founded in 1898, when vegetarians were regarded as "grass eaters," this restaurant has more than proved its staying power, becoming an institution with a number of locations around the city. It was taken over in 1904 by Bavarian Ambrosius Hiltl, who married the cook; the current patron, Rolf Hiltl, is their great-grandson. **Known for:** extensive vegetarian buffet and à la carte menu; oldest vegetarian restaurant in the world, with the Guinness record to prove it; fun, relaxed vibe. *Average main: 27 SF ✉ Sihlstr. 28, Kreis 1 ☎ 044/2277000 ⊕ www.hiltl.ch ✣ C3.*

$$$ SWISS Fodor's Choice ★ **Kaiser's Reblaube.** Get the most out of the Altstadt experience by eating in one of its most beautiful medieval buildings, which dates back to 1260 and once hosted Johann Wolfgang von Goethe, who slept in a room now used as an extra dining room, the "Goethe Stübli." The restaurant offers an à la carte menu and two versions (one of which is for vegetarians) for each of the three-, four-, or five-course fixed-price menus. The menus change seasonally, but always include classic favorites like the duck liver and veal with Rösti. **Known for:** a modern approach to traditional Swiss fare; hearty vegetarian options; relaxed atmosphere in a charming medieval building. *Average main: 50 SF ✉ Glockeng. 7, Kreis 1 ☎ 044/2212120 ⊕ www.kaisers-reblaube.ch ⊗ Closed Sun. and Mon. ✣ E4.*

$$ ECLECTIC **Reithalle.** In a downtown theater complex behind Bahnhofstrasse, this old military riding stable now does its duty as a noisy and popular restaurant where its past is plain to see, with candles perched on the mangers and beams. Young locals share long tables to sample international specialties—from curry to ostrich tenderloin—many of them vegetarian, as well as an excellent list of open wines from all over the world listed on the blackboard. **Known for:** lively young crowd; good list of wines by the glass; summer beer garden. *Average main: 28 SF ✉ Gessnerallee 8, Kreis 1 ☎ 044/2120766 ⊕ restaurant-reithalle.ch ✣ C2.*

When the weather's nice, try one of Zürich's casual Right Bank cafés.

$$$ SWISS **Veltliner Keller.** Though its rich, carved-wood decor borrows from Graubündner Alpine culture, this dining spot is no tourist trap. There is a definite emphasis on the heavy and the meaty, but the kitchen is flexible and reasonably deft with more modern favorites as well: seafood in saffron sauce, chopped veal with mixed mushrooms, and delicious fruit sorbets. **Known for:** substantial dishes; charming Alpine decor; accommodating staff. *Average main: 50 SF ✉ Schlüsselg. 8, Kreis 1 ☎ 044/2254040 ⊕ www.veltlinerkeller.ch ⊙ Closed weekends ✣ E4.*

$$$ SWISS **Zunfthaus zur Waag.** With its magnificent Renaissance-inspired facade, this airy guildhall, with whitewashed woodwork and leaded-glass windows looking out to the Fraumünster, remains a lovely place to dine on such seasonal dishes as fillet of perch in almond butter with spinach, or sliced veal and Rösti. The Zunft-Saal (guildhall) is a pinewood showpiece, which greatly outshines the main restaurant—a rather dull Biedermeier room. **Known for:** impressive architecture; excellent service; Swiss classics. *Average main: 48 SF ✉ Münsterhof 8, Kreis 1 ☎ 044/2169966 ⊕ www.zunfthaus-zur-waag.ch ✣ E5.*

RIGHT BANK: NIEDERDORF AND OBERDORF

$$ SPANISH **Bodega Española.** The coats of arms of old Spanish provinces and garlands of onions and garlic line the dark-paneled interior of this upstairs Niederdorf restaurant, specializing in big steaks, seafood, omelets, and paella. Be sure to sample the excellent house Rioja (a Spanish wine specialty shop adjoins, so the choice is extensive). **Known for:** Spanish tapas and dishes like paella; lively downstairs bar; neighborhood feel. *Average main: 35 SF ✉ Münsterg. 15, Kreis 1 ☎ 044/2512310 ✣ F4.*

$$$ SWISS Fodor's Choice ★ **Haus zum Rüden.** The most ambitious of the city's many Zunfthaus dining places, this fine restaurant is also the most spectacular, with a wooden barrel-vaulted ceiling and 30-foot beams, beneath which you can enjoy such innovative entrées as lobster-coconut bisque with dried prawns and mango, or sautéed goose liver. Slick modern improvements—including a glassed-in elevator—manage to blend intelligently with the ancient decor and old-world chandeliers. **Known for:** old-world elegance; impeccable service; well-prepared Swiss and European fare. *Average main: 65 SF ✉ Limmatquai 42, Kreis 1 ☎ 044/2619566 www.hauszumrueden.ch Closed Sun. ✢ F4.*

$$$ SWISS Fodor's Choice ★ **Kronenhalle.** From Stravinsky, Brecht, and Joyce to Nureyev, Deneuve, and Saint Laurent, this beloved landmark has always drawn a stellar crowd. Every panel of gleaming wood wainscoting frames works by Picasso, Braque, Miró, Chagall, or Matisse, collected by Gustav Zumsteg, whose mother, Hulda, owned the restaurant from 1921 until her death in 1985. **Known for:** old-world charm and elegance; stunning art collection; traditional Swiss fare. *Average main: 65 SF ✉ Rämistr. 4, Kreis 1 ☎ 044/2629900 www.kronenhalle.com ✢ G6.*

EATS ON THE CHEAP

Zürich's inflated cost of living is reflected in its restaurants. There are few truly budget options, but daily prix-fixe menus are considerably cheaper, and even the glossiest places have business-lunch menus at lower rates. If you're on a tight budget, watch for posted *Tagesteller* offerings. These daily specials, with meat, potatoes, and possibly a hot vegetable, can still be found in the Niederdorf for under 25 SF, and in Kreis 5 for under 20 SF.

The local Migros or Coop are great places to load up on picnic food, and takeout stands can be found all over the city center.

$ SWISS FAMILY **Sternen Grill.** At lunchtime the line for its legendary take-out bratwurst sausages snakes out along a neighboring street, but it moves quickly, because the choice is relatively limited and most choose the freshly grilled veal sausage (bratwurst) or pork-based Cervelat. Once handed your order, grab a traditional large Bürli bread roll and some in-house spicy mustard from the front counter, then sit at the Sternen Grill's tables or wander across to the Sechseläutenplatz, with its wide-open space in front of the Opernhaus, before strolling to the lakefront. **Known for:** take-out bratwurst sausages and homemade mustard; friendly service; bustling vibe. *Average main: 16 SF ✉ Theaterstr. 22, Kreis 1 ☎ 44/2514949 www.sternengrill.ch No credit cards ✢ G6.*

$$ SWISS **Swiss Chuchi.** Right on the Niederdorf's main square, Hirschenplatz, this squeaky-clean Swiss-kitsch restaurant has an airy, modern decor, with Alpine-rustic chairs. It serves good home-cooked national specialties: Zürcher Geschnetzeltes, Rösti, Leberli, bratwurst, schnitzel, and battered fish with French fries and tartar sauce—the gang's all here. **Known for:** traditional Swiss dishes; central location; popular with tourists. *Average main: 35 SF ✉ Hotel Adler, Roseng. 10, Kreis 1 ☎ 044/2669696 www.hotel-adler.ch ✢ F3.*

$$ SWISS

✕ **Zur Oepfelchammer.** Dating from 1801, and once the haunt of Zürich's beloved writer Gottfried Keller, this lively restaurant serves traditional meat dishes—Geschnetzeltes Kalbfleisch—lightened up with fresh seasonal vegetables. One section is a dark and heavily graffitied wine bar, with sagging timbers and slanting floors; there are also two welcoming little dining rooms with coffered ceilings and plenty of carved oak and damask—choose the cozy, charming Gaststube (not the more staid Stübli). **Known for:** tongue-in-cheek attitude; traditional Swiss fare; lively, often crowded, atmosphere. *Average main: 40 SF* ✉ *Rindermarkt 12, Kreis 1* ☎ *044/2512336* *www.oepfelchammer.ch* *Closed Sun. and Mon.* ✣ *F4.*

2

KREIS 2

$$$ SWISS

✕ **Seerose.** As soon as it even vaguely looks like it'll be warm enough, the hip deck-shoe crowd drives, runs, cycles, or even sails to one of the best places on the lake, which not only has its own dock, but *is* its own dock, jutting far out and offering fabulous views. The food isn't bad either: seasonal ingredients make the difference in dishes such as beef tournedos with matchstick-thin French fries, or spaghetti with lobster. **Known for:** lakeside dining with stunning views; chic crowd; lively terrace. *Average main: 50 SF* ✉ *Seestr. 493, Kreis 2* ☎ *044/4816383* *seerose.dinning.ch* ✣ *D6.*

KREIS 3

$$$$ EUROPEAN

Fodor's Choice ★

✕ **Ecco.** Tucked inside the luxury hotel Atlantis, this intimate restaurant plays with textures—cool white marble floors, soft leather banquettes, and a modern, iciclelike glass chandelier. The same playfulness extends to the Michelin-starred menu, where the butter is frothed with buttermilk, the skins of Jerusalem artichokes crunch, and pickled mushrooms add some sharpness, creating an experience—and it is an experience—that is a creative but unfussy take on modern European fare. **Known for:** sublimely creative food; attentive service; chic interior. *Average main: 190 SF* ✉ *Atlantis by Giardino, 234 Doeltschiweg, Zürich* ☎ *044/4565533* *atlantisbygiardino.ch* *Closed Mon. and Tues.* ✣ *A5.*

KREIS 4

$$$ EUROPEAN

✕ **Caduff's Wine Loft.** In a 19th-century whitewashed former warehouse, industrial lighting, parquet floors, and the occasional strategically placed cactus set the minimalist tone for the kitchen's delicious, simple cuisine. The market determines the menu, which could be anything from veal shoulder to entrecôte to fish with tomato-basil gnocchi and seasonal vegetables. **Known for:** well-stocked wine cellar; regularly changing menu featuring Swiss and European fare; off the beaten path. *Average main: 55 SF* ✉ *Kanzleistr. 126, Kreis 4* ☎ *044/2402255* *www.wineloft.ch* *Closed Sun.* ✣ *A3.*

KREIS 5

$$ SWISS **Alpenrose.** It doesn't get more Swiss than this: the ingredients, the recipes, the wines, and the decor are all Helvetian. Enjoy seasonal dishes such as *Engadiner pizokel* (flour dumplings) with ham, or duck breast with dried-plum sauce and mashed potatoes; the owners' devotion to local ingredients means the menu often changes. **Known for:** Swiss specialties with local products; quaint Swiss decor; friendly service. *Average main: 35 SF Fabrikstr. 12, Kreis 5 044/2713919 www.restaurantalpenrose.ch Closed Mon. and mid-July–mid-Aug. E1.*

$$ ASIAN **Angkor.** A bit of Siem Reap in the middle of Zürich West: the lavish interior is full of stone carvings and wood latticework that seem right out of Ta Prohm, minus the jungle. The menu is huge and includes generous amounts of green curry, oyster sauce, and ginger, covering India, Thailand, Vietnam, and Japan. **Known for:** Pan-Asian fare; stylish environment that includes a koi pond; extensive outdoor seating. *Average main: 38 SF Giessereistr. 18, Kreis 5 043/2052888 www.restaurant-angkor.ch Closed Sun. in summer E1.*

$$ EUROPEAN **LaSalle.** This is a favorite haunt of theatergoers heading for the Schauspielhaus Schiffbauhalle—it conveniently shares the same building, where a glass, steel, and concrete interior mixes well with brick elements from the original factory building. Beneath an enormous Murano-glass chandelier, elegantly dressed patrons enjoy wines from a hefty list and delicate dishes that might feature black tiger prawns, langoustines, or beef fillet, all with innovative sauces. **Known for:** grand, glass-walled building in a former factory; extensive wine list; modern Swiss, French, and Italian fare. *Average main: 44 SF Schiffbaustr. 4, Kreis 5 044/2587071 www.lasalle-restaurant.ch E1.*

$ MEDITERRANEAN **Les Halles.** This old warehouse space in Zürich West has not so much been renovated as cleaned up and then highlighted with an eclectic mix of antiques and 1950s collectibles, all of which are for sale. Tapas and Mediterranean dishes, including their famous *moules frites* (mussels and fries) are available to order at the counter. **Known for:** casual, order-at-the-counter vibe; one of the few cash-only restaurants in Zürich; integrated market that sells fruit, vegetables, and meat. *Average main: 20 SF Pfingstweidstr. 6, Kreis 5 044/2731125 www.les-halles.ch No credit cards Closed Sun. E1.*

KREIS 6

$$ MODERN EUROPEAN **Mesa.** Prizewinning cuisine has won this restaurant its following and established it as a special-occasion favorite. Inside, the simple decor allows the attention to remain focused on the inventive modern dishes, presented with flair and including vegetarian options. **Known for:** excellent, creative European fare; extensive wine list; attentive, friendly service. *Average main: 32 SF Weinbergstr. 75, Kreis 6 043/3217575 www.mesa-restaurant.ch Closed Sun. and Mon.; Dec. 24–mid-Jan.; mid-July–mid-Aug. H1.*

2

WHERE TO STAY

A string of small boutique hotels has popped up in the last decade, all with a strong focus on design, sleeping comfort, and generous bathrooms—think large bed covered with a fluffy down comforter and soft pillows, looking onto an outsized flat-screen TV that invariably includes video games and a selection of movies, and a white-tiled bathroom with black slate floors and lots of mirrors. On our list we've included the Seefeld, Widder, and Zürichberg.

Another passion taking over the city—in fact, the country—is the trend toward so-called "wellness" vacations. Putting a new spin on the 19th- and early-20th-century tradition of the Swiss sanatorium—where convalescent patients from all over the world came to Switzerland to cleanse their lungs with Alpine air—hotels here are adding pools, saunas, steam rooms, and special areas for such ministrations as hot-stone massages or body wraps.

Smaller venues like the Hotel Seefeld have simply added a cosmetics studio to cover their customers' skin-care needs. Upscale houses cover everything from full-body peels, sports massages, and ice wraps (Park Hyatt) all the way through to the comprehensive spa services of the Dolder Grand Hotel, which also includes kotatsu footbaths, an aroma pool, and indoor and outdoor whirlpools. If you're still not feeling like a whole new you, there's even a clinic complete with a team of doctors for cosmetic surgery.

Hotel reviews have been shortened. For full information, visit Fodors.com. Use the coordinate (✣ B2) at the end of each listing to locate a site on the Where to Eat and Stay in Zürich map.

WHAT IT COSTS IN SWISS FRANCS

	$	$$	$$$	$$$$
For Two People	Under 201 SF	201 SF–300 SF	301 SF–500 SF	Over 500 SF

Hotel prices are the lowest cost of a standard double room in high season, including taxes.

KREIS 1

LEFT BANK: THE ALTSTADT

$$$$ HOTEL Fodor's Choice ★ **Baur au Lac.** Richard Wagner arrived and premiered the first act of his *Die Walküre* here, accompanied on the piano by his father-in-law, Franz Liszt. **Pros:** old-world luxury plus ultramodern comforts; within walking distance of much of the city; impeccable service. **Cons:** luxury has a hefty price tag; attracts those happy to show their money; those used to modern-day casualness will find the formality stuffy. $ *Rooms from: 870 SF* ✉ *Talstr. 1, Kreis 1* ☎ *044/2205020* 🌐 *www.bauraulac.ch* *126 rooms* *No meals* ✣ *D6.*

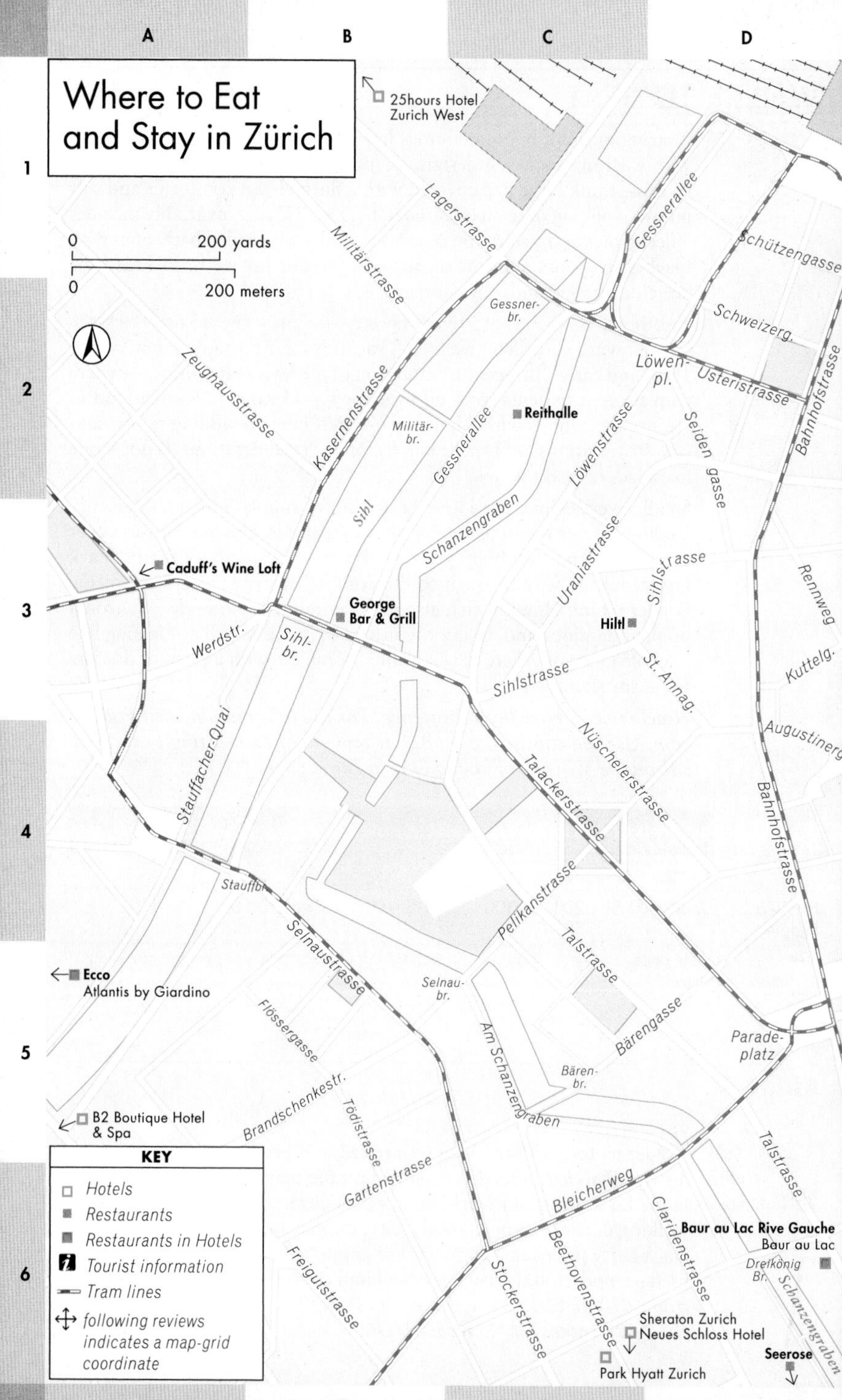

Where to Eat and Stay in Zürich
A
B
C
D
1
2
3
4
5
6
0
200 yards
0
200 meters
25hours Hotel Zurich West
Lagerstrasse
Militärstrasse
Gessnerallee
Schützengasse
Gessner-br.
Schweizerg.
Zeughausstrasse
Kasernenstrasse
Löwen-pl.
Usteristrasse
Bahnhofstrasse
Reithalle
Militär-br.
Gessnerallee
Löwenstrasse
Seiden gasse
Sihl
Schanzengraben
Uraniastrasse
Sihlstrasse
Rennweg
Caduff's Wine Loft
George Bar & Grill
Hiltl
Werdstr.
Sihl-br.
St. Annag.
Kuttelg.
Sihlstrasse
Augustinerg
Nüschelerstrasse
Talackerstrasse
Stauffacher-Quai
Bahnhofstrasse
Stauffbr.
Pelikanstrasse
Selnaustrasse
Talstrasse
Ecco
Atlantis by Giardino
Selnau-br.
Flössergasse
Am Schanzengraben
Bärengasse
Parade-platz
Bären-br.
Brandschenkestr.
B2 Boutique Hotel & Spa
Tödistrasse
Gartenstrasse
Talstrasse
Bleicherweg
Claridenstrasse
Baur au Lac Rive Gauche
Baur au Lac
Dreikönig Br.
Schanzengraben
Freigutstrasse
Stockerstrasse
Beethovenstrasse
Sheraton Zurich Neues Schloss Hotel
Park Hyatt Zurich
Seerose
KEY
Hotels
Restaurants
Restaurants in Hotels
Tourist information
Tram lines
following reviews indicates a map-grid coordinate

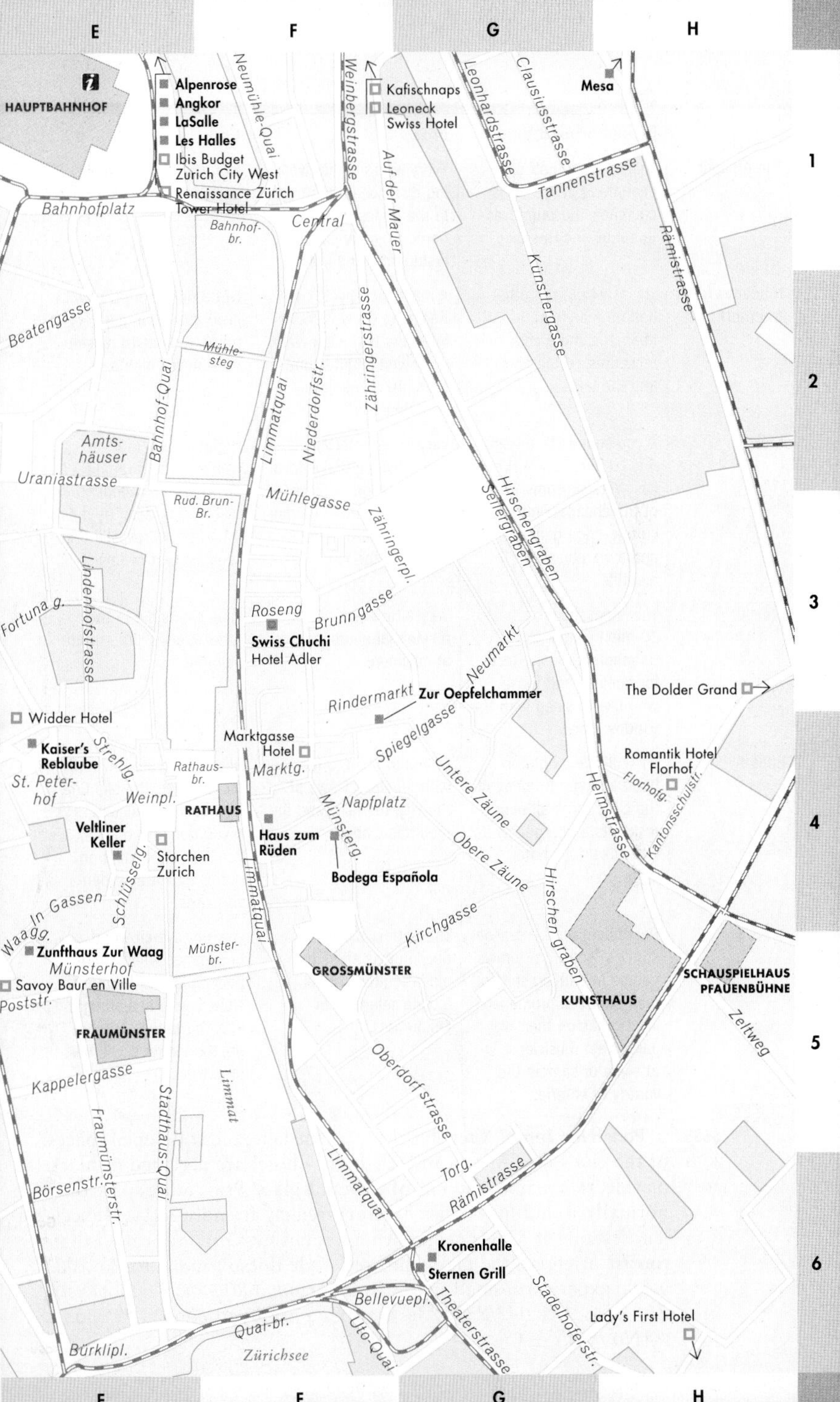
E
F
G
H
1
2
3
4
5
6
HAUPTBAHNHOF
Alpenrose
Angkor
LaSalle
Les Halles
Ibis Budget Zurich City West
Renaissance Zürich Tower Hotel
Kafischnaps
Leoneck Swiss Hotel
Mesa
Bahnhofplatz
Central
Bahnhofbr.
Neumühle-Quai
Weinbergstrasse
Auf der Mauer
Leonhardstrasse
Clausiusstrasse
Tannenstrasse
Rämistrasse
Künstlergasse
Beatengasse
Mühlesteg
Bahnhof-Quai
Limmatquai
Niederdorfstr.
Zähringerstrasse
Amtshäuser
Uraniastrasse
Rud. Brun-Br.
Mühlegasse
Zähringerpl.
Hirschengraben
Seilergraben
Lindenhofstrasse
Fortuna g.
Roseng
Swiss Chuchi
Hotel Adler
Brunngasse
Neumarkt
Rindermarkt
Zur Oepfelchammer
The Dolder Grand
Widder Hotel
Kaiser's Reblaube
Strehlg.
Marktgasse Hotel
Marktg.
Spiegelgasse
Romantik Hotel Florhof
Florhofg.
Kantonsschulstr.
St. Peterhof
Weinpl.
Rathausbr.
RATHAUS
Untere Zäune
Napfplatz
Heimstrasse
Veltliner Keller
Storchen Zurich
Haus zum Rüden
Münsterg.
Bodega Española
Obere Zäune
Schlüsselg.
In Gassen
Waagg.
Zunfthaus Zur Waag
Münsterhof
Münsterbr.
Kirchgasse
GROSSMÜNSTER
Hirschen graben
KUNSTHAUS
SCHAUSPIELHAUS PFAUENBÜHNE
Savoy Baur en Ville
Poststr.
FRAUMÜNSTER
Zeltweg
Kappelergasse
Limmat
Oberdorfstrasse
Stadthaus-Quai
Fraumünsterstr.
Börsenstr.
Torg.
Rämistrasse
Kronenhalle
Sternen Grill
Bellevuepl.
Theaterstrasse
Stadelhoferstr.
Lady's First Hotel
Quai-br.
Uto-Quai
Bürklipl.
Zürichsee

WHERE SHOULD I STAY?

	Neighborhood Vibe	Pros	Cons
The Altstadt	This is where half of everything in Kreis 1 is: churches, museums, restaurants, and the lake.	Everything's within walking distance (and often in the pedestrian zone); home to many elegant restaurants and hotels.	Not car-friendly; some parts are noisy; expensive.
Niederdorf and Oberdorf	This is where the other half of everything in Kreis 1 is: more churches, museums, restaurants, and the lake.	Almost exclusively car-free; very lively nightlife for every budget; a well-preserved architectural example of medieval "Mitteleuropa."	Not a good spot if you have a car; can get very noisy because of revelers on summer nights.
Kreis 5	If you squint, it's a teeny-tiny bit like New York's East Village. Home to one of the cheapest hotels, cutting-edge galleries, and a warehouse-style nightlife.	Very lively entertainment district; draws local hipsters; a great place for the budget-conscious interested in a more modern experience.	Nightlife gets raucous well into the morning on weekends; although ridiculously clean by most urban standards, still the seediest part of town.
Kreis 6	This quiet area is a 10-minute walk to Bahnhofstrasse. Perfect for families and those who like to sleep with the window open.	Very little noise; residential neighborhood atmosphere.	Main sights are in the other Kreises; little to no nightlife.
Kreis 7	This hillside neighborhood is home to many of the city's most affluent residents and arguably its most luxurious hotel.	Lush and quiet, often with fabulous views of the city, the lake, and the mountains beyond.	Restaurants are few and far between; the nightlife is almost nonexistent; if you don't have a car, you'll be depending on public transit or expensive taxis.
Kreis 8	Depending on the season, Zürich's "seashore" draws people in bathing suits or their smartest promenading clothes on their way past street musicians to swim or sample the variety of eateries.	The perfect place to decompress after "too much" culture; offers a wide selection of restaurants.	Can get overcrowded in summer, when street parking is next to impossible; basically a straight line: the farther out you go, the longer it will take to get back.

$$$$ HOTEL FAMILY **Park Hyatt Zurich.** A few blocks from the lake, the wide-open spaces of the city's first American-style luxury hotel are accented in black marble, rich maple, and lots of gleaming glass. **Pros:** more space than normally found in a Swiss hotel; extremely friendly service; excellent restaurant. **Cons:** neighborhood is business oriented rather than tourist oriented; the glass-and-steel style doesn't make for an old-world experience; small spa. *Rooms from: 680 SF* ✉ *Beethovenstr. 21, Kreis 1* ☎ *043/8831234* 🌐 *zurich.park.hyatt.ch* *138 rooms* *No meals* ✣ *C6.*

The Widder's historic location and room decor offer a glimpse into the city's past.

$$$ HOTEL **Savoy Baur en Ville.** Directly on Paradeplatz, at the hub of the banking, shopping, and sightseeing districts, this is one of Zürich's 19th-century landmarks. **Pros:** you can't get more downtown than this; Sprüngli, a must for chocolate-lovers, is across the street; classic, elegant vibe. **Cons:** conservative to the point of stuffiness; a business-minded atmosphere; street-side rooms can be noisy. *Rooms from: 450 SF* *Am Paradepl., Poststr. 12, Kreis 1* *044/2152525* *www.savoy-zuerich.ch* *104 rooms* *No meals* *E5.*

$$ HOTEL **Sheraton Zurich Neues Schloss Hotel.** Managed by the Sheraton chain, this intimate hotel in the business district, a few minutes from Paradeplatz and a block from the Tonhalle, offers a warm welcome, good service, and classic decor in earth tones. **Pros:** one block from the lake; excellent service; modern, comfortable rooms. **Cons:** kids are free, but only if they sleep with you in your bed; Wi-Fi is extra unless you're a member; breakfast is not included in all rates. *Rooms from: 250 SF* *Stockerstr. 17, Kreis 1* *044/2869400* *www.sheratonneuesschloss.com* *61 rooms* *Breakfast* *C6.*

$$$ HOTEL Fodor's Choice ★ **Storchen Zurich.** The central location of this airy 660-year-old structure—tucked between the Fraumünster and Kirche St. Peter on the gull-studded bank of the Limmat River—is stunning. **Pros:** expert and friendly service; charming Old Town location; the views. **Cons:** mosquitoes in summer (don't sleep with the window open); can be noisy during local festivals—and there are many; snagging a seat outside during the busy season is challenging. *Rooms from: 430 SF* *Weinpl. 2, Kreis 1* *044/2272727* *www.storchen.ch* *66 rooms* *Breakfast* *E4.*

The views don't get much better than from the riverfront Zum Storchen hotel.

$$$$ HOTEL Fodor's Choice ★ **Widder Hotel.** Zürich's most captivating hotel was created when 10 adjacent medieval houses were gutted and combined—now steel fuses with ancient stone and timeworn wood. **Pros:** the spectacular Room 210 and more modern Room 509; popular, lively bar; excellent location. **Cons:** expensive; rooms above the restaurant can be noisy; proximity to other apartments and offices can be unnerving for some. *Rooms from: 650 SF ✉ Rennweg 7, Kreis 1 ☎ 044/2242526 🌐 www.widder-hotel.ch 49 rooms Breakfast ✢ E4.*

RIGHT BANK: NIEDERDORF AND OBERDORF

$ HOTEL **Hotel Adler.** Smack in the middle of Niederdorf, this is a smart, state-of-the-art hotel where, from the gleaming lobby to the sleek, modular rooms, the ash-and-granite decor makes the most of tight spaces. **Pros:** free minibar with soft drinks; clean, bright rooms; hardwood floors. **Cons:** can get noisy on weekends; no a/c; the smell of raclette can permeate rooms above the restaurant. *Rooms from: 190 SF ✉ Roseng. 10, Kreis 1 ☎ 044/2669696 🌐 www.hotel-adler.ch 52 rooms Breakfast ✢ F3.*

$ HOTEL **Leoneck Swiss Hotel.** From cowhide-covered furniture to the edelweiss-print curtains, this budget hotel revels in its Swiss roots, but balances this indulgence with modern conveniences like the smartphones in each room, which you're welcome to take with you while exploring the city. **Pros:** very friendly service; close to the action but quiet; smartphones on loan with free calls to more than 30 countries. **Cons:** small rooms; breakfast not included in all room rates; some find the bells from the church next door too loud. *Rooms from: 180 SF ✉ Leonhardstr. 1, Kreis 1 ☎ 044/2542222 🌐 www.leoneck.ch 82 rooms Breakfast ✢ F1.*

2

$$ HOTEL Fodor's Choice ★ **Marktgasse Hotel.** Located in the heart of the cobblestone streets of Old Town, this boutique hotel smartly blends its 15th-century history with modern minimalism. **Pros:** in the heart of Old Town; casually hip vibe; friendly, knowledgeable staff. **Cons:** can be noisy; some rooms are small with low ceilings; not convenient for those with cars. *Rooms from: 275 SF ✉ Marketg. 17, Kreis 1 ☎ 044/2661010 🌐 www.marktgassehotel.ch/en/ 39 rooms Breakfast ✣ F4.*

$$ HOTEL **Romantik Hotel Florhof.** In a 17th-century merchant's mansion, this hotel offers the away-from-it-all atmosphere of a dreamily quiet residential area by the Kunsthaus, yet is just a few tram stops away from the main train station. **Pros:** close to everything, yet in a quiet oasis; friendly, accommodating service; cozy, familylike vibe. **Cons:** some rooms are small; some bathrooms are still being updated; no a/c. *Rooms from: 300 SF ✉ Florhofg. 4, Kreis 1 ☎ 044/2502626 🌐 www.hotelflorhof.ch/en/ 32 rooms Breakfast ✣ H4.*

KREIS 2

$$$ HOTEL FAMILY **B2 Boutique Hotel + Spa.** In a former brewery, this hotel melds its industrial past with sleek modern design—you can have fun looking for subtle industrial reminders hidden around the hotel and ask to visit the former engine room. **Pros:** luxury living with an industrial past; fun, hip vibe; excellent fitness and spa facilities. **Cons:** not downtown, requiring a tram ride to most sights; entrance to the spa costs extra; service can be inconsistent. *Rooms from: 310 SF ✉ Brandschenkestr. 152, Kreis 2 ☎ 044/5676767 🌐 www.b2boutiquehotels.com 60 rooms Breakfast ✣ A5.*

KREIS 3

$$$$ HOTEL Fodor's Choice ★ **Atlantis by Giardino.** At the foot of Zürich's Uetliberg mountain, this Y-shaped hotel was a 1970s playground for ABBA, The Who, and Freddie Mercury. **Pros:** modern, spacious rooms; unparalleled service; rich in amenities. **Cons:** 10-minute drive from most tourist sights; shuttle service to downtown could run longer, more frequently; small fitness area. *Rooms from: 560 SF ✉ 234 Doeltschiweg, Zürich ☎ 044/4565555 🌐 atlantisbygiardino.ch 95 rooms Breakfast ✣ A5.*

KREIS 5

$ HOTEL **Ibis Budget Zurich City West.** Working on the principle that cheap should only mean inexpensive, this chain hotel is a dependable, no-nonsense pick. **Pros:** great value; deep in the heart of Zürich West; efficient and clean. **Cons:** charmless; one side looks out onto an industrial park; no air-conditioning. *Rooms from: 150 SF ✉ Technoparkstr. 2, Kreis 5 ☎ 044/2762000 🌐 ibisbudgethotel.ibis.com 160 rooms No meals ✣ E1.*

$$ HOTEL **Renaissance Zurich Tower Hotel.** Towering above the nightclubs and galleries that surround it, this modern hotel offers a cutting-edge alternative to Zürich's historic gilded lodgings. **Pros:** sleek design; spacious rooms; friendly staff. **Cons:** neighborhood may be too industrial

Zürich's Old Town is charming under a coat of snow in winter.

for some; not walking distance to most attractions; breakfast is not included in all room rates. *Rooms from: 249 SF* ✉ *Turbinenstr. 20, Kreis 5* ☎ *044/6303030* 🌐 *www.renaissancezurichtower.com* *300 rooms* *Breakfast* ✣ *E1.*

$ HOTEL **25hours Hotel Zurich West.** Despite the nondescript building and charmless entrance, this hotel is awash with color and original design elements inside, and although the address screams hip-appeal, the atmosphere remains fresh and charming. **Pros:** fair-priced design hotel; in the middle of the hip Kreis 5 district; lively, quirky vibe. **Cons:** not in the historical center; can be noisy; some may find staff are trying too hard to be too hip. *Rooms from: 190 SF* ✉ *Pfingstweidstr. 102, Kreis 5* ☎ *044/5772525* 🌐 *www.25hours-hotels.com* *126 rooms* *Breakfast* ✣ *B1.*

KREIS 6

$ B&B/INN **Kafischnaps.** Away from the throb of downtown but only a 15-minute walk back, this is the best deal in town for anyone on a budget and willing to share a bathroom. **Pros:** beautifully designed rooms; hip café; great value. **Cons:** far from city center; check-in can be slow if the café is busy; shared bathroom. *Rooms from: 90 SF* ✉ *Kornhausstr. 57, Kreis 6* ☎ *043/5388116* 🌐 *www.kafischnaps.ch* *5 rooms* *No meals* ✣ *F1.*

KREIS 7

$$$$ HOTEL Fodor's Choice ★ **The Dolder Grand.** Set atop the Zürichberg mountain, this sprawling resort hotel, which began life as a Victorian-era Kurhaus (health spa resort), blends the Corinthian capitals and crystal chandeliers of the original structure with two modern glass-and-steel wings that mirror the natural surroundings. **Pros:** gorgeous views; high-end service; very good restaurants, including Michelin-starred The Restaurant. **Cons:** off the beaten path; a bit pricey; standard rooms are small, considering the cost. *Rooms from: 800 SF* ✉ *Kurhausstr. 65, Kreis 7* ☎ *044/4566000* 🌐 *www.thedoldergrand.com* *175 rooms* *No meals* ✣ *H3.*

KREIS 8

$ HOTEL **Lady's First Hotel.** Once a rooming house for country girls attending school in the big city, this boutique hotel has two floors that cater exclusively to women—a first in Switzerland. **Pros:** very pro-female, but also respectful of the "modern man"; quiet, but central location; excellent views from the roof deck. **Cons:** bathrooms were added as niches into each room, so there's less noise insulation; breakfast is not included; creaky floors. *Rooms from: 190 SF* ✉ *Mainaustr. 24, Kreis 8* ☎ *044/3808010* 🌐 *www.ladysfirst.ch* *28 rooms* *No meals* ✣ *H6.*

NIGHTLIFE AND PERFORMING ARTS

NIGHTLIFE

Of all the Swiss cities, Zürich has the liveliest nightlife. The Niederdorf is Zürich's nightlife district, with cut-rate hotels, strip joints, and bars crowding along Marktgasse, which becomes Niederdorfstrasse. On Thursday and weekend nights, the streets flow with a rowdy crowd of club- and bar-hoppers. In Zürich West, the locales are all a shade hipper. In winter, things wind down between midnight and 2 am, but come summer most places stay open until 4 am.

KREIS 1

BARS

Almodobar. A welcoming bar that tips a wink to Spain's most famous film director, Almodobar is an oasis for the young hipster crowd, set in a quiet neighborhood. ✉ *Bleicherweg 68, Kreis 1* ☎ *043/8444488* 🌐 *www.almodobar.com.*

Barfüsser. Established in 1956, Barfüsser claims to be one of the oldest gay bars in Europe. It has comfortable lounge chairs and space to mix and mingle. There's also excellent sushi. ✉ *Spitalg. 14, Kreis 1* ☎ *044/2514064* 🌐 *www.barfuesser.ch.*

Central 1. In the Hotel Central, the Central 1 bar is a popular neo–art deco café by day and a piano bar by night. ✉ *Central 1, Kreis 1* ☎ *044/2515555* 🌐 *www.central.ch.*

2

Set in a quiet hillside neighborhood, the elegant Dolder Grand Hotel resembles a fairy-tale castle.

Cranberry. This popular gay bar stocks a broad selection of rums and mixes up fine cocktails in an industrial-chic spot. ✉ *Metzgerg. 3, Kreis 1* ☎ *044/2612772* 🌐 *www.cranberry.ch.*

James Joyce Pub. This is a beautifully paneled Irish pub where the wood is as dark as the Guinness. ✉ *Pelikanstr. 8, off Bahnhofstr., Kreis 1* ☎ *044/2211828* 🌐 *www.jamesjoyce.ch.*

Jules Verne Panorama Bar. This wine bar boasts a wraparound view of downtown. ✉ *Uraniastr. 9, Kreis 1* ☎ *043/8886666* 🌐 *www.jules-verne.ch.*

Fodor's Choice ★ **Kronenhalle.** The narrow bar at the Kronenhalle draws crowds of well-heeled locals and internationals for its prizewinning cocktails. ✉ *Rämistr. 4, Kreis 1* ☎ *044/2511597* 🌐 *www.kronenhalle.ch.*

Metropol. Sit in the covered arcade at Metropol and select something from the extensive drinks list, which includes absinthe, elaborate cocktails, and a wide variety of whiskeys. ✉ *Fraumünsterstr. 12, Kreis 1* ☎ *044/2005900.*

Fodor's Choice ★ **Rimini Bar.** Located along the city's former 17th-century moat and ramparts, this bar is a bathing area during the day and then transforms into a hip bar in the evening. Chill out on cushions and enjoy grilled specialties and cool drinks. ✉ *Badweg 10, Kreis 1* ☎ *044/2119594* 🌐 *www.rimini.ch.*

Tao's. This Asian-accented lounge bar appeals to the young and well-heeled. It offers a nice garden in the summer and comfortable areas inside. Food is also available. ✉ *Augustinerg. 3, Kreis 1* ☎ *044/4481122* 🌐 *www.taos-lounge.ch.*

DANCE CLUBS

Fodor's Choice ★ **Kaufleuten.** This local landmark draws a well-dressed, upwardly mobile crowd. It's a popular performance space for established artists, such as Pink Martini and Angelique Kidjo, looking for an intimate venue. The Rolling Stones once showed up unannounced for an impromptu concert. ✉ *Pelikanstr. 18, Kreis 1* ☎ *044/2253333* 🌐 *www.kaufleuten.ch.*

Mascotte. Blasting everything from funk and soul to house and techno, Mascotte is popular with all ages. ✉ *Theaterstr. 10, Kreis 1* ☎ *044/2524481* 🌐 *www.mascotte.ch.*

KREIS 4

BARS

Dante Bar. This cool bar in an increasingly popular area offers a great selection of gins. ✉ *Zwinglistr. 22, Kreis 4* ☎ *043/3171918* 🌐 *www.dante-zurich.ch.*

DANCING

Plaza. Renovated from an old movie theater, this club has two dance floors where DJs play everything from R&B to disco to house. The club hosts regular concerts as well. ✉ *Badenerstr. 109, Kreis 4* ☎ *044/5429090* 🌐 *www.plaza-zurich.ch.*

KREIS 5

BARS

Basilica. Hipsters lounge here in an Italianate setting of red velvet and marble statues. ✉ *Heinrichstr. 237, Kreis 5* ☎ *043/3669383* 🌐 *www.basilica.ch.*

I.Q. Not just for intellectuals, I.Q. has a fully stocked whiskey bar. ✉ *Hardstr. 316, Kreis 5* ☎ *044/4407440* 🌐 *www.iqbar.ch.*

Spheres. This bar and bookstore stocks a great selection of international magazines and features a stage for regular readings and literary discussions ✉ *Hardturmstr. 66, Kreis 5* ☎ *044/4406622* 🌐 *spheres.cc.*

KREIS 8

BARS

Purpur. At this Moroccan-style lounge you can enjoy your drinks lying down on a heap of throw pillows while DJs mix ambient sounds. ✉ *Seefeldstr. 9, Kreis 8* ☎ *044/4192066* 🌐 *www.purpurzurich.ch.*

PERFORMING ARTS

Despite its small population, Zürich is a big city when it comes to the arts; it supports a top-rank orchestra, an opera company, and a theater. Check *Zürich News,* published weekly in English and German, or "Züri-tipp," a German-language supplement to the Thursday edition of the daily newspaper *Tages Anzeiger.*

Jecklin. This music store sells tickets for various music events. ✉ *Rämistr. 30, Kreis 1* ☎ *044/2537676* 🌐 *www.jecklin.ch.*

Musik Hug. Among other things, Musik Hug sells tickets to music events. ✉ *Limmatquai 28–30, Kreis 1* ☎ *044/2694100* 🌐 *www.musikhug.ch.*

Ticketcorner. Tickets for almost any event can be purchased in advance from Ticketcorner. ✉ *Zürich* ☎ *0900/800800* 🌐 *www.ticketcorner.ch.*

ARTS FESTIVALS

Theaterspektakel. During late August and early September the Theaterspektakel takes place, with circus tents housing avant-garde theater and experimental performances on the lawns by the lake. ✉ *Mythenquai, Zürich* ☎ *044/4123030* 🌐 *www.theaterspektakel.ch.*

Züricher Festspiele. The city's annual Züricher Festspiele—a celebration of opera, ballet, music, theater, and art—takes place in early summer at more than 20 venues in the city, including Opernhaus Zürich. ✉ *Zürich* ☎ *044/2699090* 🌐 *www.zuercher-festspiele.ch.*

FILM

Movies in Zürich are serious business, with many films presented in the original language. Check newspapers and the ubiquitous posters, and watch for the initials *E/d/f,* which means an English-language version with German (Deutsch) and French subtitles.

Metropol. The Metropol has a great sound system and the largest screen in Zürich. ✉ *Badenerstr. 16, Kreis 4* ☎ *0900/556789* 🌐 *www.kitag.com.*

Zürich Film Festival. The Zürich Film Festival takes place every year from late September to early October. ✉ *Zürich* ☎ *044/2866000* 🌐 *www.zff.com.*

MUSIC

Tonhalle. This concert hall was inaugurated by Brahms in 1895 and is the home of the Zürich Tonhalle Orchestra, which enjoys international acclaim. There are also solo recitals and chamber music programs. The season runs from September through July, and tickets sell out quickly. ✉ *Claridenstr. 7, Kreis 1* ☎ *044/2063434* 🌐 *www.tonhalle.ch.*

OPERA

Opernhaus. The permanent company at the Opernhaus is widely recognized and difficult to drop in on if you haven't booked well ahead, but single seats sometimes can be secured at the last minute. Performances are held from September through July. ✉ *1 Sechseläutenpl., Kreis 1* ☎ *044/2686666* 🌐 *www.opernhaus.ch.*

THEATER

Schauspielhaus. The venerable Schauspielhaus has a long history of cutting-edge performances—during World War II it was the only German-language theater in Europe that remained independent. Nowadays its main stage presents finely tuned productions, and experimental works are presented in the Keller (cellar). ✉ *Rämistr. 34, Kreis 1* ☎ *044/2587777* 🌐 *www.schauspielhaus.ch.*

Schauspielhaus Schiffbauhalle. The sister stage of Schauspielhaus Pfauenbühne, the Schauspielhaus Schiffbauhalle is home to large-scale productions in German. ✉ *Schiffbaustr. 4, Kreis 5* ☎ *044/2587777* 🌐 *www.schauspielhaus.ch.*

SHOPPING

Many of Zürich's designer boutiques lie hidden along the narrow streets between Bahnhofstrasse and the Limmat River. Quirky bookstores and antiques shops lurk in the sloping cobblestone alleyways leading off Niedorfstrasse and Oberdorfstrasse. The fabled Bahnhofstrasse—famous because it's reputedly the most expensive street in the world—is dominated by large department stores and extravagantly priced jewelry shops.

Bahnhofstrasse. The store-lined Bahnhofstrasse concentrates much of Zürich's most expensive (from elegant to gaudy) goods at the Paradeplatz end. ⊠ *Zürich.*

Löwenstrasse. There's a pocket of good stores around Löwenstrasse, southwest of the Hauptbahnhof. ⊠ *Zürich.*

Niederdorf. The Niederdorf, a car-free section of Old Town that gets its name from the main street, offers inexpensive fashions that appeal to young people, as well as antiques and antiquarian bookstores. ⊠ *Zürich.*

Storchengasse. The west bank's Altstadt, along Storchengasse near the Münsterhof, is a focal point for high-end designer stores. ⊠ *Zürich.*

Many city-center stores are open weekdays 9–8, Saturday 8–5. Most close on Sunday, with the exception of the shops at the Hauptbahnhof, the Stadelhofen train station, and the airport. Many smaller shops, particularly in the Niederdorf area, open later in the morning or the early afternoon and are closed entirely on Monday.

KREIS 1

BOOKS

Biblion. The antiquarian bookstores in the upper streets of the Niederdorf area are rich with discoveries—and most have selections of books in English. Biblion specializes in antique books and bindings. ⊠ *Kirchg. 40, Kreis 1* ☎ *044/2613830* 🌐 *www.biblion.ch.*

EOS Buchantiquariat Benz. This is a superb general bookstore spread over two storefronts. Both sell secondhand books as well as antiquarian tomes. ⊠ *Kirchg. 17, Kreis 1* ☎ *044/2615750* 🌐 *www.eosbooks.ch.*

Medieval. This eclectic store sells books, music, and replicas of medieval artifacts, including reproduction medieval shoes, jewelry, and water bottles. ⊠ *Spiegelg. 29, Kreis 1* ☎ *044/2524720* 🌐 *www.lemaroc.ch.*

CHOCOLATE

Teuscher. Teuscher is as famous for its extravagantly wrapped packages as it is for its amazing chocolates and candies. There are two other locations in town. ⊠ *Storcheng. 9, Kreis 1* ☎ *044/2115153* 🌐 *www.teuscher.com.*

DEPARTMENT STORES

COOP City. Popular with locals, COOP is cheap and cheerful. ⊠ *Theaterstr. 18, Kreis 1* ☎ *043/2688700* 🌐 *www.coop.ch.*

Globus. Globus sells men's and women's designer clothes and housewares. There is also a pricey but irresistible delicatessen in the basement. ✉ *Schweizerg. 11, Kreis 1* ☎ *044/2266060* 🌐 *www.globus.ch.*

Grieder. Zürich's most elegant department store, Grieder carries designs by Armani and Zegna, among others. ✉ *Bahnhofstr. 30, Kreis 1* ☎ *044/2243636* 🌐 *www.bongenie-grieder.ch.*

Jelmoli. Switzerland's biggest department store, Jelmoli has top-notch brand-name merchandise and swarms of staffers. ✉ *Bahnhofstr. and Seideng., Kreis 1* ☎ *044/2204411* 🌐 *www.jelmoli.ch.*

Manor. This store is both dependable and affordable. ✉ *Bahnhofstr. 75, Kreis 1* ☎ *044/2295699* 🌐 *www.manor.ch.*

MARKETS

Bürkliplatz. There's a flea market from 7 to 5 every Saturday from May to October on the lake end of Bahnofstrasse. ✉ *Bürklipl., Kreis 1.*

Fodor's Choice ★ **Christmas market.** The main train station and Niederdorfstrasse are each the site of a Christmas market, starting in early December. ✉ *Zürich.*

Rosenhof. There's a curio market on the Rosenhof every Thursday from 10 to 8 and Saturday from 10 to 5 between March and October. ✉ *Niederdorfstr. and Marktg., Kreis 1.*

MEN'S CLOTHES

Trois Pommes. Trois Pommes is the central boutique of a series of designer shops scattered through the Storchengasse area. The racks are heavily stacked with such high-profile international designers as Jil Sander, Versace, Donna Karan, and Dolce & Gabbana. There are locations throughout Switzerland, including several others within Zürich. ✉ *Weggeng. 1, Kreis 1* ☎ *044/2124710* 🌐 *www.troispommes.ch.*

TOYS

FAMILY **AHA.** AHA sells hypnotic optical-illusion gifts in styles and sizes to suit all ages. ✉ *Spiegelg. 14, Kreis 1* ☎ *044/2510560* 🌐 *www.aha-zurich.ch.*

WOMEN'S CLOTHES

En Soie. This boutique stocks sometimes gleaming, sometimes raw-textured silks. Although the fabrics are sophisticated, there's still an element of whimsy. ✉ *Strehlg. 26, Kreis 1* ☎ *044/2115902* 🌐 *www.ensoie.com.*

Miu Miu. Check out Miuccia Prada's latest designs at Miu Miu. ✉ *Storcheng. 16, Kreis 1* ☎ *044/2128318* 🌐 *www.miumiu.com.*

RAZZO. For high-quality vintage clothing, go to the place where Zürich's well-heeled ladies sell their "old" things. ✉ *Romerg. 8, Kreis 1* ☎ *044/2622859* 🌐 *razzo2ndhand.ch.*

SPAS

Zürich's spas are known as "wellness centers" and focus more on baths, saunas, and massages than on beauty treatments. Mostly attached to hotels, wellness centers can include everything from outdoor pools with views of the city to private treatment rooms where you can order a relaxing rubdown. Some also offer medical procedures, including plastic surgery.

Fodor's Choice ★ **The Dolder Grand Spa.** Zürich's most extravagant spa does everything from manicures to cosmetic surgery. Part of The Dolder Grand hotel, the 43,000-square-foot spa has a classic look with plenty of Japanese touches. It uses products by Kerstin Florian, La Prairie, Amala, and Horst Kirchberger to pamper guests in private suites equipped with treatment couches, soaking tubs, and fireplaces. Personal trainers are on hand to get you into shape. A "medical wellness" team can assess your health and develop a regimen to balance your physical and mental well-being. Doctors offer advice and treatment for "fine-tuning your physical features" in a medical facility attached to the hotel. ✉ *The Dolder Grand, Kurhausstr. 65, Kreis 7* ☎ *044/4566000* 🌐 *www.thedoldergrand.com.*

Fitnesspark Hamam Münstergasse. The highlight of this wellness center in the middle of the Niederdorf is a luxurious underground Turkish-style hammam. The treatment includes a warm herbal steam bath, a body scrub with a traditional *kese* glove, a hot herbal steam bath, a hot-stone relaxation space, and finally a relaxation room with herbal drinks and snacks. There are women-only rooms for the more intimate stops on the circuit; the rest of the areas are mixed. A massage treatment using rhassoul clay from the Atlas Mountains in Morocco is a specialty. ✉ *Blaufahnenstr. 3, Kreis 1* ☎ *058/5688182* 🌐 *www.fitnesspark.ch.*

Hammam Basar. Built on the edge of the delightful (in name and location) Patumbah Park in the upscale Kreis 2, this hammam is a feast for the eyes and senses. The interior is lined with a beautiful pale stone that reflects the geometric shards of light emanating from the Moroccan-inspired ceiling lights. The hammam also offers the chance to lunch on North African delicacies in an interior courtyard. The use of the hammam steam room includes all necessities—towel, wooden clogs, exfoliating glove, traditional Moroccan black soap, and rhassoul. Full-body massages and neck and back massages are also available. ✉ *Mühlebachstr. 157–159, Kreis 2* ☎ *044/3829060* 🌐 *www.hammambasar.ch.*

Labo. One of Zürich's classic day spas offers the full package of face, skin, and body treatments for her and him. Centrally located for quick pit stops, the ambience is quiet and relaxing. Asian accents in the minimalist space enhance the experience. With friendly, professional therapists, the spa does everything from the usual mani-pedis and facials to special treatments for expectant mothers to sybaritic rituals like the "Cocoon," which includes an aroma bath, leg and foot peeling, and a full-body massage. The massage menu boasts 15 different techniques from all over the world. ✉ *Talacker 41, Kreis 1* ☎ *043/4973440* 🌐 *www.labospa.ch.*

Thermalbad & Spa Zurich. Off the beaten track but a big draw with hipsters and locals, this extensive collection of different saunas and steam rooms includes a rooftop pool. Benefiting from the same natural spring as the brewery that used to operate on this site, the spa focuses on bathing, and offers massages, scrubs, and body wraps. The rooftop pool has a great view over the city and is therefore very popular—expect crowds on sunny days and evenings. Tuesday is reserved for women. ✉ *Brandschenkestr. 150, Kreis 2* ☎ *044/2059650* 🌐 *www.thermalbad-zuerich.ch*.

EASTERN SWITZERLAND AND LIECHTENSTEIN

WELCOME TO EASTERN SWITZERLAND AND LIECHTENSTEIN

TOP REASONS TO GO

★ **A bibliophile's paradise:** Admire the UNESCO-inscribed library at the Abbey of St. Gallen, which features an Egyptian mummy and over 100,000 ancient books.

★ **The cows finally come home:** Take part in an Appenzell Alpfahrt festival, when cows are herded up into the nearby mountain slopes (in spring) and back down (in fall).

★ **Colorful medieval architecture:** St. Gallen, Schaffhausen, and Stein-am-Rhein are teeming with colorful frescoes, half-timber buildings, dragon-clad steeples, and ornate bay windows.

★ **The Rhine maidens:** See Europe's third-largest river as it snakes its way to Germany. Take a lunch-boat ride, swim in the pristine river, or cycle along the river's grassy banks, lorded over by storybook castles.

★ **Swiss cheese:** Pungent Appenzeller is beloved by the Swiss. Using a 700-year-old recipe, this cow's milk cheese is aged and washed with a secret herbal brine.

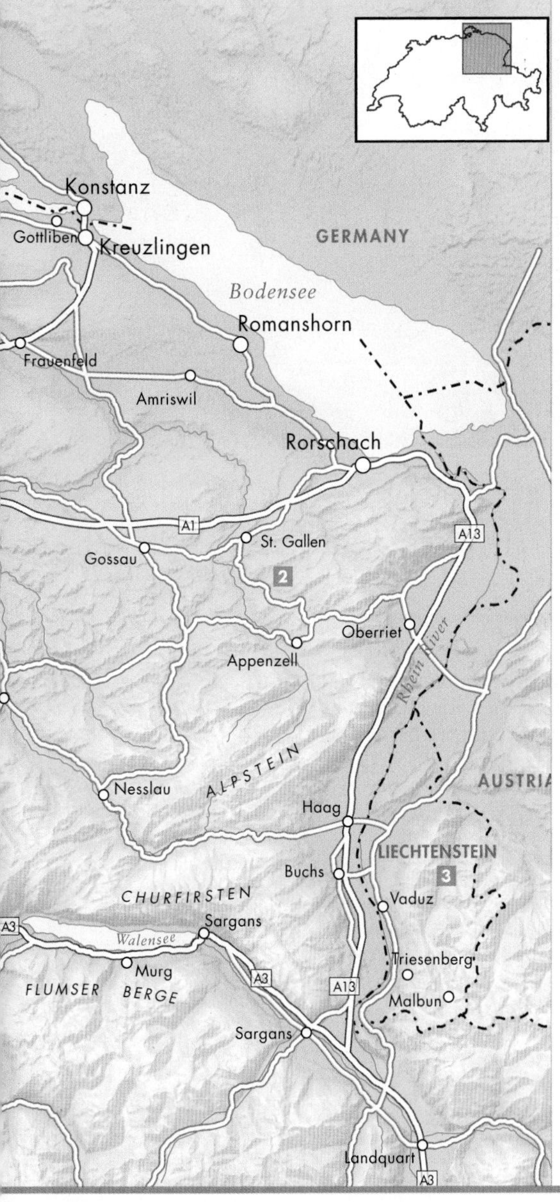

3

1 Schaffhausen and the Rhine. A trip from the Rhine Falls through Schaffhausen and upriver to the more tranquil village of Stein-am-Rhein transports you back to medieval and Renaissance times. The house facades, alive with colorful frescoes and bay windows, attract tourists by the busload.

2 Bodensee to Walensee. Vast and windy, the Bodensee—also known as Lake Constance—is a favorite of visiting Swiss and Germans who come for its mellow vibe. Creative and hardworking St. Gallen's biggest draw is its manuscript-stuffed Abbey Library (as well as a picturesque Old Town full of great public arts, tasty restaurants, and a thriving theater scene). Walensee's gorgeous, tranquil, cobalt-blue lake is backed by the dramatically steep Churfirsten range.

3 Liechtenstein. The last remnant of the Holy Roman Empire, this tiny castle-topped principality offers an excellent contemporary art museum and breathtaking hikes.

EATING WELL IN EASTERN SWITZERLAND

Eastern Switzerland's cuisine is the country's least cosmopolitan but includes some of its heartiest and tastiest dishes.

Don't leave without trying a regional sausage variety (above). Treat yourself to some of the country's most popular traditional dishes, from Spätzle (above, right) to Rösti (below, right).

Specialties from Appenzell, St. Gallen, Thurgau, and Schaffhausen bear names that defy pronunciation, like *Chäs Tschoope* (fried bread cubes with cheese and cream) and *Chäshappech* (cheese-and-beer batter funneled into snail-shell shapes, then deep-fried). *St. Galler Kalbsbratwurst* is a popular sausage made from veal, milk, and bacon, and *Mostbröckli* is a gamey air-dried beef worth sampling.

Regional wines from Thurgau and Shaffhausen are notable, but so is Appenzeller beer, which is found across Switzerland. For once, vegetarians have something to celebrate in otherwise meat-loving Switzerland. Appenzeller cheese has a robust flavor that comes from a secret herbal brine that reportedly includes roots, leaves, flowers, seeds, and bark. *Chääsflade* (cheese pie) and silky cheese soup are a few other must-try dishes, whether or not you're a vegetarian.

SPECIAL TREATS

Head to **Böhli** (✉ *9 Engelg., Appenzell* ☎ *071/7881570* 🌐 *www.boehli-appenzell.ch*) for *biber*, molded honey, spice, and almond-paste bakes, and for *chrempfli*, turnovers with hazelnut filling. *St. Galler Fladen*, locally produced fruit tarts, are available in the tearoom and shop at **Chocolaterie am Klosterplatz** (✉ *20 Gallusstr., St. Gallen* ☎ *071/2225770* 🌐 *www.chocolateriesg.ch*).

CHEESES
The earthy and pungent Appenzeller cheese dates back more than 700 years and is known as the "spiciest" cheese in Switzerland, but really it's just herbal. It adds a nice addition to the local fondue. If you're in the mood for something milder and creamier, Tilsit is your best bet. Unique to Thurgau, the cheese takes its name from the town of Tilsit, Russia, where an immigrant Swiss cheese maker helped develop the recipe before coming home to set up shop.

SAUSAGES
In St. Gallen, specialty sausages abound. Try the St. Galler Bratwurst, also known as the St. Galler Kalbsbratwurst, a white, unsmoked variety that custom dictates must be made with pork, at least 50% veal, and milk or milk powder. When ordered in St. Gallen, the legendary Olma-Bratwurst must be eaten with a hard piece of bread known as a *Bürli,* and never with mustard.

RÖSTI
These aren't your average hash browns. Deemed the national dish of Switzerland, *Rösti* is a dinner or lunch dish that is essentially grated, fried potatoes, covered with a variety of deliciously greasy toppings—bacon, bits of lard, ham, eggs, and cheese, or served alongside favorite regional main dishes. Although Rösti can be found all over Switzerland, it is especially loved by Swiss-Germans,

so much so that the border between the French- and German-speaking areas of Switzerland is known as the Röstigraben, which literally means Rösti ditch.

DUMPLINGS
Popular throughout Central and Eastern Europe, dumplings have been elevated to an art form in Switzerland. These tender egg noodles come in many forms and are known as *Spätzle,* or if in a smaller, rounded form as *Chnöpfli* (literally, little sparrows or little buttons, respectively). Eat them boiled, then fried in butter until golden brown and crispy, or oozing with melted cheese, a preparation known as *Chäschnöpfli.*

SWEETS
Don't let all the cheese and sausages fool you: eastern Switzerland has sweet treats to finish off any meal. Fruit and nuts reign supreme in Switzerland, and you'll be hard-pressed to find a dessert without either. Thurgau is famous for its apple orchards, and there's no better way to enjoy a healthful dessert than to snack on the region's lightly dried apple rings. Those who yearn for a buttery treat can delight in *Hüppen*—these long, crisp waffle cookies are sometimes filled with chocolate and are thought to take their name from the Greek *hopyes,* meaning wafer.

Updated by Chantal Panozzo

Switzerland's Germanic region bordering Germany and Austria should scream authenticity. Instead, it moos. With almost more cows (and alphorns) than people, Zürich's quiet neighbor offers landscapes and villages of an idyllic variety: its north is dominated by the rushing Rhine; the countryside is as lush with orchards as its towns are rich in history; and there is also a generous share of mountains (including Mt. Säntis, at roughly 8,200 feet) to climb. Take a swim in the Bodensee (Lake Constance), too, and you've got an itinerary for the real Switzerland.

Because the east draws fewer crowds, those who do venture here find a pleasant surprise: this is Switzerland sans kitsch, sans the hard sell, where the people live out a natural, graceful combination of past and present. And although it's a prosperous region, with its famous history of textile manufacturing and agriculture, its inns and restaurants cost noticeably less than those in adjoining areas. They can also lack the amenities found in more cosmopolitan parts of the country.

The cantons of Glarus, Schaffhausen, Thurgau, St. Gallen, and Appenzell harbor some of Switzerland's oldest traditions. In the northern part of the region are the old Rhine city of Schaffhausen, the dramatic Rheinfall, and the preserved medieval village of Stein-am-Rhein. The Bodensee occupies the northeastern corner of Switzerland, just below Germany. Farther south is the textile center of St. Gallen, where lace is created for high-profile designers like Karl Lagerfeld. A magnificent baroque cathedral lords over the valley. The hilly Appenzell region and the resort area of the Toggenburg Valley are lower-key destinations. The tiny principality of Liechtenstein lies just across the eastern border, within easy driving distance.

Although the cities have plenty of energy, the countryside in these parts has changed little over the years. In the plateau valley of Appenzell, women were prohibited from voting in cantonal elections until the federal court intervened on their behalf in 1991 (federal law had granted women the national vote in 1971). On the last Sunday in April in Appenzell, you still can witness the *Landsgemeinde*, an open-air election on cantonal issues counted by a show of hands.

Architecture along the Rhine resembles that of Old Germany and Austria, frequent features being half-timbers and rippling red-tile roofs. In cities like Schaffhausen, masterpieces of medieval frescoes decorate town houses, many of which have ornately carved bay windows called oriels. In the country, farmhouses are often covered with fine, feathery wooden shingles as narrow as Popsicle sticks, which weathering has turned to chinchilla gray. Appenzell has its own famous architecture: tidy, narrow boxes painted cream, with repeated rows of windows and matching wood panels. The very countryside itself—conical green hills, fruit trees, belled cows, neat yellow cottages—resembles the naive art it inspires.

EASTERN SWITZERLAND AND LIECHTENSTEIN PLANNER

WHEN TO GO

The four seasons are clearly defined here: nicely balanced periods of sun and rain bring springtime blossoms and flowers with a vengeance, thanks to the many orchards and fields; summer temperatures zoom upward to between 21°C (70°F) and 32°C (90°F), depending on whether it's a dry or wet one; the abundance of deciduous trees in this region means splashes of color in a crisp-aired, windy fall; and winter dumps lots of snow and brings temperatures hovering around –5°C (23°F) in town, down to –25°C (–13°F) on some mountaintops.

Summers in eastern Switzerland provide the best weather and activities; spring and fall are good alternatives. Although most places in this region are not too terribly crowded even in summer, Schaffhausen can become thick with tour buses and Stein-am-Rhein choked with spandex-clad cyclists looping around the Bodensee. Go earlier in the day or on a weekday when crowds are a bit thinner.

PLANNING YOUR TIME

This is the more tranquil slice of Switzerland; a great place to enjoy the scenery while tooling down back roads or gazing out the train window at the cow-dotted meadows on the way to the next quaint town. Take along a stack of books to read on the hotel balcony or a picnic lunch for your stop in a field en route. In winter, pick a ski resort or a large town such as Schaffhausen or St. Gallen as your home base—unless you're looking for complete, peaceful seclusion. In summer, swimming, kayaking, hiking, and cycling opportunities abound near the Rhine and the Bodensee, so pack a bathing suit and your cycling shorts, and take a leisurely lunch-boat ride.

GETTING HERE AND AROUND

As in all parts of Switzerland, the trains are superb—punctual, dependable, and comfortable—and offer stunning mountain views you won't see from behind the wheel of a rental car. Another great way to see the region is by the boats that ply the Rhine and the Bodensee.

AIR TRAVEL

Zürich Airport, just north of Zürich, is about 48 km (30 miles) south of Schaffhausen, about 75 km (46 miles) west of St. Gallen, and 130 km (81 miles) northwest of Liechtenstein.

BOAT AND FERRY TRAVEL

There's regular year-round service on the Bodensee through Schweizer Bodensee Schifffahrtsgesellschaft, though fewer boats run in winter. The Schweizerisches Schifffahrtgesellschaft Untersee und Rhein ship company offers a boat ride on the Rhine with romantic views of storybook castles, citadels, and monasteries. Boats run regularly up- and downstream, docking at Schaffhausen, Stein-am-Rhein, Gottlieben, Konstanz, and Kreuzlingen. Prices vary according to the distance traveled. A one-way trip from Schaffhausen to Kreuzlingen takes about 4½ hours. On both boat lines, you'll travel free if you have a Swiss Travel Pass.

Contacts Schweizer Bodensee Schifffahrtsgesellschaft. ✉ *Friedrichshafnerstr. 55, Romanshorn* ☎ *071/4667888* 🌐 *www.sbsag.ch.* **Schweizerische Schifffahrtsgesellschaft Untersee und Rhein.** ✉ *Freierpl. 8, Schaffhausen* ☎ *052/6340888* 🌐 *www.urh.ch.*

BUS TRAVEL

The famous yellow postbuses travel to every single town and village in Switzerland. The ride is comfortable, and the trip is free with your Swiss Travel Pass. Bus schedules are usually posted outside town post offices, but you can also obtain information from any train station. The smallest towns have one bus in the morning and one in the evening, and larger towns are served several times a day.

CAR TRAVEL

Driving in eastern Switzerland doesn't give you the same amazing views as the trains, which chug over the meadows so close to cows you can practically hear them munching grass. If you decide to drive, Highway 13 goes along the south shores of the Untersee and Bodensee and continues up through the hills to Appenzell. In cities, such as St. Gallen and Schaffhausen, you'll find it easiest to head directly for the center and abandon the car for the duration of your visit. Try to get into a parking lot, because finding a spot on the street can be difficult.

TRAIN TRAVEL

The narrow-gauge trains in Appenzell set it apart. The picture windows can be opened so you can lean out as you career over green hills and sniff wildflowers and fresh-cut grass. At St. Gallen, the main hub for regional trains, you can transfer to the Gossau–Appenzell–Wasserauen line. To see more of the territory, you may return to St. Gallen by way of Herisau. The Swiss Travel Pass includes St. Gallen and Schaffhausen city transit, as well as overall rail privileges throughout Switzerland.

⇨ *For more information on getting here and around, see Travel Smart Switzerland.*

HOTELS

During the summer high season, Stein-am-Rhein and Gottlieben swell with tourists because there's no town around to catch the overflow. St. Gallen has a large convention center, so you should make your reservation in advance. Other destinations will usually still have a room or two on short notice. For romantic getaways, consider the castellated Drachenburg und Waaghaus in Gottlieben, a teeny-tiny village on the misty bank of the Rhine, or something along the shore of Stein-am-Rhein, which quiets down in the evening when many of the bikers depart. For an adventurous getaway, try the Berggastaus Aescher-Wildkirchli, nestled high above Appenzell on the rocky face on Ebenalp. More and more hotels in this region are throwing away their Formica and commissioning hand-painted furniture to complement the beams they've so carefully exposed. The prices are somewhat lower on average here, with only slight variations from high to low season. Half-board is rarely included, but hearty cheese-and-meat-laden breakfast buffets almost always are. Warm, good service is a given.

RESTAURANTS

Restaurants in this region are often in centuries-old structures that have been home to some kind of eatery (in a few occasions under the same name) for 200 or even 300 years. This is especially true of Schaffhausen's Wirtschaft zum Frieden, which dates back to 1789, or St. Gallen's Schlössli, inside a small castle built in 1586. But architecture doesn't determine the style; you'll find everything from formal linen-tablecloth service to a laid-back country-kitchen atmosphere in eastern Switzerland's restaurants. The same dress code applies as in the rest of the country: jeans and a tucked-in shirt are preferable to a jacket and tie.

Restaurants typically fill up around 7 pm, slightly earlier than most of Switzerland. The Swiss have impeccable table manners, and the same is expected from visitors. Point your silverware away from you on the plate when finished, always look dinner companions in the eye when clinking glasses to say *prostli!*, and always, always add *en guete!*, the Swiss-German equivalent of *bon appétit.* Don't be surprised if you're charged for tap water, as this custom is tolerated throughout Switzerland.

Hotel and restaurant reviews have been shortened. For full information, visit Fodors.com.

WHAT IT COSTS IN SWISS FRANCS

	$	$$	$$$	$$$$
Restaurants	Under 26 SF	26 SF–45 SF	46 SF–65 SF	Over 65 SF
Hotels	Under 201 SF	201 SF–300 SF	301 SF–500 SF	Over 500 SF

Restaurant prices are the average cost of a main course at dinner or, if dinner is not served, at lunch. Hotel prices are the lowest cost of a standard double room in high season, including taxes.

VISITOR INFORMATION

The tourist office for all of eastern Switzerland is based in St. Gallen. There are small regional visitor information offices throughout eastern Switzerland. Liechtenstein's office is in its capital.

Contacts Ostschweiz Tourismus (*Tourist Association of Eastern Switzerland*). ✉ *Fürstenlandstr. 53, St. Gallen* ☎ *071/2749900* 🌐 *www.ostschweiz.ch.*

SCHAFFHAUSEN AND THE RHINE

Known to many Swiss as Rheinfallstadt (Rhine Falls City), Schaffhausen is the seat of the country's northernmost canton, which also shares its name. To gaze on the grand mist-sprayed Rheinfall is to look straight into the romantic past of Switzerland. Johann Wolfgang von Goethe and William Wordsworth were just two of the world's best-known wordsmiths to immortalize the falls' powerful grandeur.

SCHAFFHAUSEN

48 km (29 miles) northeast of Zürich, 20 km (12 miles) west of Stein-am-Rhein.

A city of about 37,000, Schaffhausen was from the early Middle Ages on an important depot for river cargoes, which—because of the rapids and waterfall farther along—had to be unloaded there. The name *Schaffhausen* is probably derived from the skiff houses along the riverbank. The city has a small but beautiful Altstadt (Old Town), whose charm lies in its extraordinary preservation; examples of late-Gothic, baroque, and rococo architecture line the streets. Though the town can sometimes feel like a museum, these buildings are very much in use, often as shops or restaurants, and lively crowds of shoppers and strollers throng the streets. Many streets (including Vorstadt, Fronwagplatz, Vordergasse, and Unterstadt) are pedestrian-only.

GETTING HERE AND AROUND

The fastest connection from Zürich is the commuter train, which takes 38 minutes. There are also trains to and from St. Gallen that connect through Winterthur (travel time 56 minutes).

To reach Schaffhausen by car from Zürich, take the A1 to Winterthur, then head north on the A4 motorway. In Schaffhausen, there's underground parking at the Stadttheater underneath Herrenacker.

VISITOR INFORMATION

Contacts Schaffhauserland. ✉ *Herrenacker 15, Schaffhausen* ☎ *052/6324020* 🌐 *www.schaffhauserland.ch.*

EXPLORING

TOP ATTRACTIONS

Fronwagplatz. Lined with shops and cafés, this square is a favorite place for young people to stroll, especially in the evening. A large 16th-century fountain-statue of a prosperous burgher, the Metzgerbrunnen, watches over the marketplace. The clock tower's astronomical clock (1564) records not only the time but also solar eclipses, seasons, and

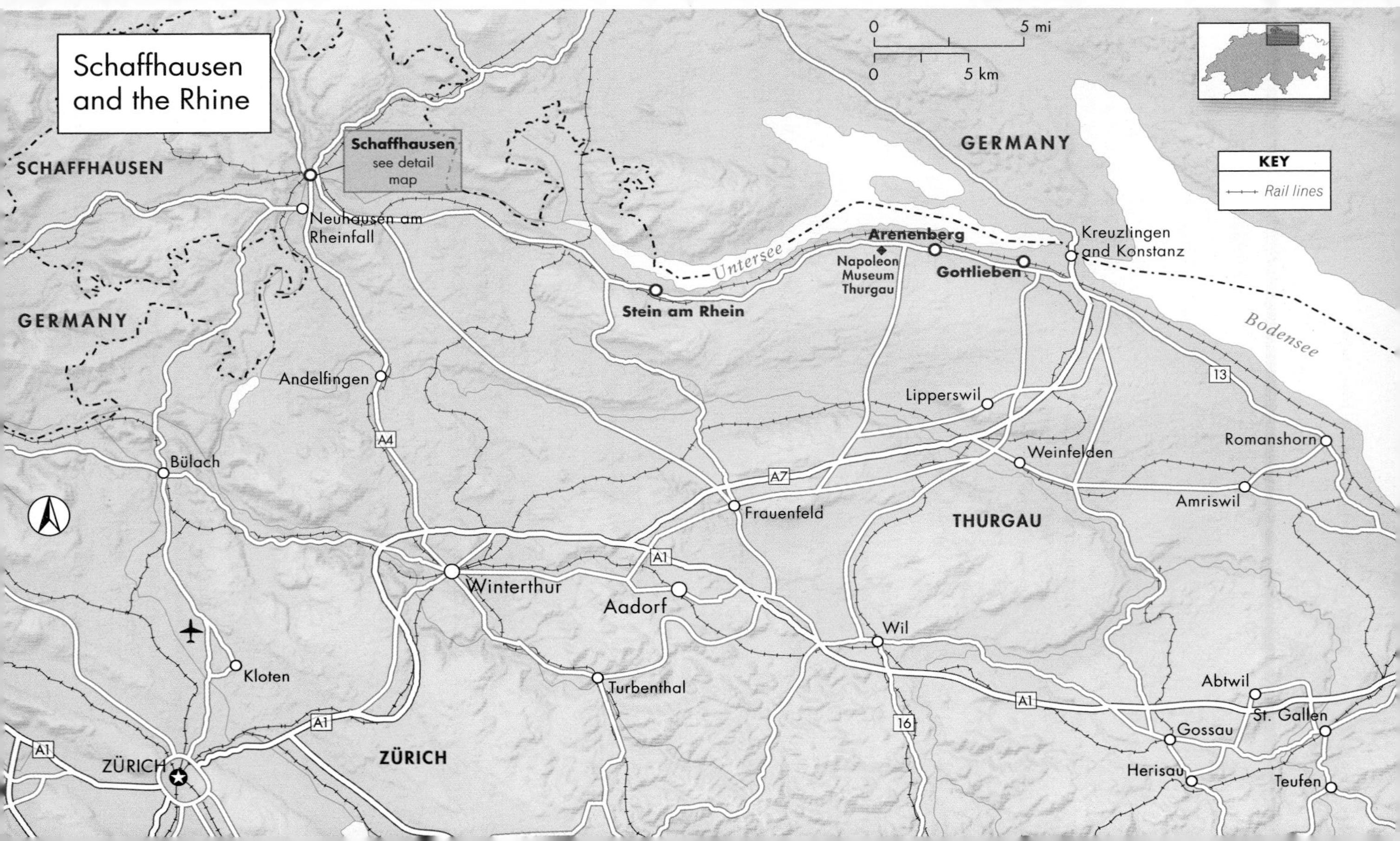

Schaffhausen and the Rhine
SCHAFFHAUSEN
Schaffhausen
see detail map
Neuhausen am Rheinfall
GERMANY
Andelfingen
Bülach
Kloten
ZÜRICH
ZÜRICH
Winterthur
Aadorf
Turbenthal
Stein am Rhein
Untersee
Arenenberg
Napoleon Museum Thurgau
Gottlieben
Kreuzlingen and Konstanz
GERMANY
Bodensee
Lipperswil
Weinfelden
Frauenfeld
THURGAU
Romanshorn
Amriswil
Wil
Abtwil
St. Gallen
Gossau
Herisau
Teufen
A1
A4
A7
13
16
0
5 mi
0
5 km
KEY
Rail lines

the course of the sun through the zodiac. Across the square, a reproduction of the 1535 Mohrenbrunnen (Moor's Fountain) represents Kaspar of the Three Kings. The original fountain is stored in the Museum zu Allerheiligen. ✉ *Fronwagpl., Schaffhausen.*

WALKING TOURS

The Schaffhausen tourist office gives guided walking tours with English commentary on the Old Town, the monastery, and the Munot. The tours leave from the tourist office on Saturday at 2 pm from May to October.

Munot. Built between 1564 and 1589 in full circle form based on an idea by Albrecht Dürer, the massive stone ramparts served as a fortress allowing for the defense of the city on all sides. From its top are splendid Schaffhausen and Rhine Valley views. ✉ *Munotstieg, Schaffhausen* 🎟 *Free.*

Fodor's Choice ★ **Münster zu Allerheiligen** (*All Saints Cathedral*). This beautiful cathedral, along with its cloister and grounds, dominates the lower city. Founded in 1049, the original cathedral was dedicated in 1064, and the larger one that stands today was built in 1103. Its interior has been restored to Romanesque austerity with a modern aesthetic (hanging architect's lamps, Scandinavian-style pews). The cloister, begun in 1050, combines Romanesque and later-Gothic elements. Memorial plates on the inside wall honor noblemen and civic leaders buried in the cloister's central garden. You'll also pass through the aromatic herb garden, so beautiful that you may feel you've stepped into a tapestry.

The centerpiece of the main courtyard, the cathedral's enormous Schiller Bell, was cast in 1486; it hung in the tower of the cathedral until 1895. Its inscription, *vivos—voco/mortuos—plango/fulgura—frango* ("I call the living, mourn the dead, stop the lightning"), allegedly inspired the German poet Friedrich von Schiller to write his "Lied von der Glocke" ("Song of the Bell"). ✉ *Klosterpl. 1, Schaffhausen* 🎟 *Free.*

Museum zu Allerheiligen (*All Saints Museum*). This excellent museum on the cathedral grounds houses an extensive collection of ancient and medieval historical artifacts. The period rooms are definitely worth a look; they cover 15th- to 19th-century interiors. The best of these is the 15th-century refectory, which was rented out and all but forgotten until its rediscovery in 1924. Museum literature is mainly available in German. ✉ *Klosterpl. 1, Schaffhausen* ☎ *052/6330777* 🌐 *www.allerheiligen.ch* 🎟 *12 SF* ⏲ *Closed Mon.*

FAMILY Fodor's Choice ★ **Rheinfall.** The Rheinfall is 492 feet wide, drops some 82 feet in a series of three dramatic leaps, and is split at the center by a bushy crag straight out of a 19th-century landscape painting. The effect—mist, roaring water, jutting rocks—is positively Wagnerian. Goethe saw in the falls the "ocean's source," although today's jaded globe-trotters have been known to find them "cute." A visitor center at the nearby Schloss Laufen includes a souvenir shop, restaurant, playground, and new bridge walkway that lets you see, hear, and get sprayed by the falls. ✉ *Rheinfallquai 32, Neuhausen am Rheinfall* 🌐 *www.rheinfall.ch* 🎟 *5 SF to hike down the falls under Schloss Laufen; otherwise free* ☞ *From Schaffhausen, the S33 or S9 train takes you to the Rheinfall in 5 mins.*

The best way to reach the dramatic Rhine Falls is to follow the Rhine Bank Trail from Schaffhausen.

WORTH NOTING

Gerberstube (*Tanners' Guildhall*). A pair of lions frames the doorway of the remarkable baroque building, which is the former drinking spot of the Tanners' Guild. A two-handled tanner's knife stretches between the lions. A restaurant now occupies the building. ✉ *Bachstr. 8, Schaffhausen.*

Haus zum Ritter (*Knight's House*). The city's finest mansion dates from 1492. Its fresco facade was commissioned by the resident knight, Hans von Waldkirch. Tobias Stimmer covered all three stories with paintings on classical themes, which are now displayed in the Museum zu Allerheiligen; the reproduction of the original was made in the 1930s. ✉ *Vorderg. 65, Schaffhausen.*

Schmiedstube (*Smiths' Guildhall*). With its spectacular Renaissance portico and oriel dating from 1653, this building is an embodiment of Schaffhausen's state of suspended animation. Framed over the door are the symbols of the tongs and hammer for the smiths, and that of a snake for doctors, who depended on the smiths for their tools and thus belonged to the guild. ✉ *Vorderg. 61, Schaffhausen.*

Schwabentorturm (*Swabian Gate Tower*). Once a part of the city wall, the tower dates from 1361. Inside the arch on the keystone is a relief from 1933 that bears a wise caution for anyone crossing the street: *Lappi tue d'auge uf* ("Open your eyes, you idiot!"). The tower's counterpart, the Obertorturm, lies just off the Fronwagplatz. ✉ *Vorstadt, Schaffhausen.*

Zum Goldenen Ochsen (*At the Golden Ox*). This late-Gothic building had a Renaissance-style portico and oriel window added to it in 1608. Flanking the windows are three floors of exterior frescoes depicting

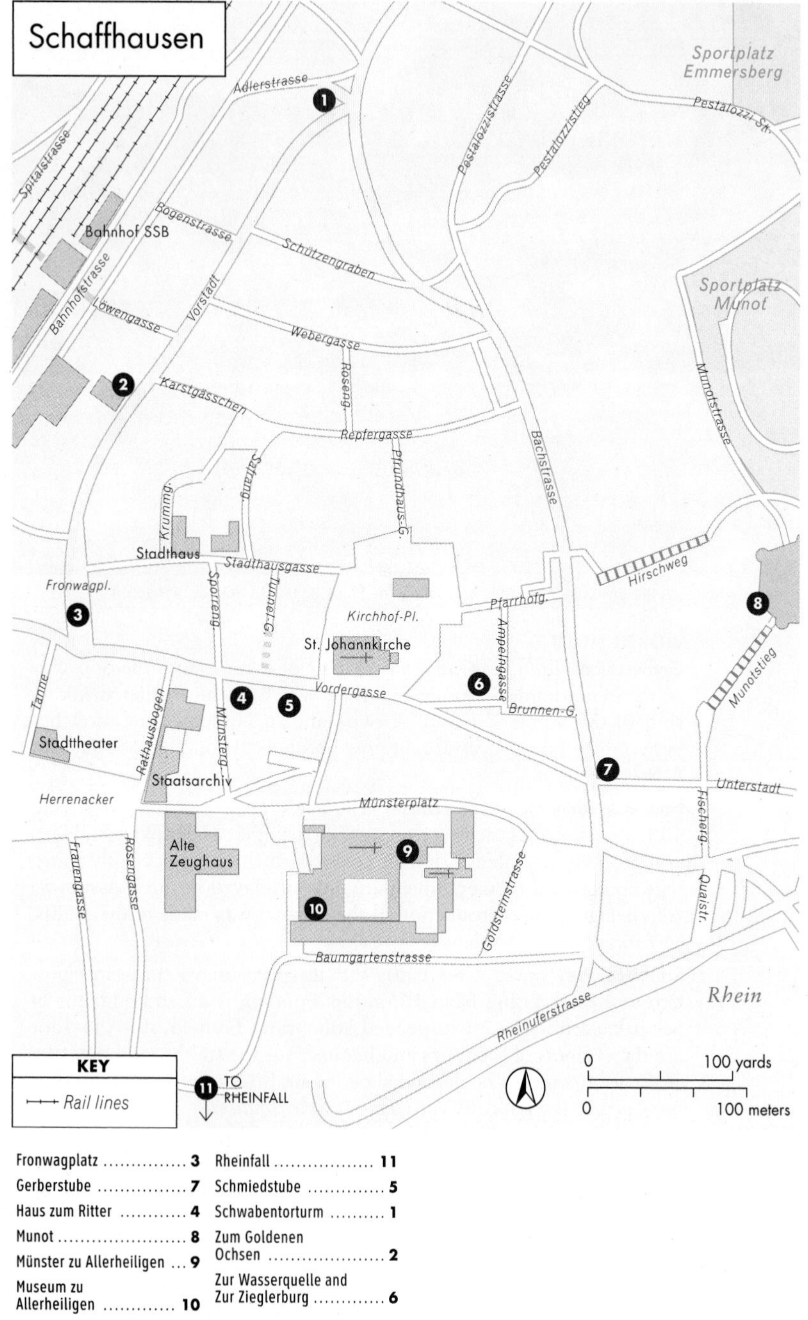

Fronwagplatz **3**	Rheinfall **11**
Gerberstube **7**	Schmiedstube **5**
Haus zum Ritter **4**	Schwabentorturm **1**
Munot **8**	Zum Goldenen Ochsen **2**
Münster zu Allerheiligen **9**	Zur Wasserquelle and Zur Zieglerburg **6**
Museum zu Allerheiligen **10**	

historic and mythological figures, most from the Trojan War. Sadly, an advertising billboard has also been added to the building. ✉ *Vorstadt 17, Schaffhausen.*

Zur Wasserquelle and Zur Zieglerburg (*At the Spring and At the Brick Castle*). This rococo duplex dates from 1738; since they are now private residences, you can see them only from the outside. Across the street are the Tellenbrunnen, a fountain-statue of Wilhelm Tell copied from the 1522 original, and the St. Johannkirche (St. John's Church), whose Gothic exterior dates from 1248. ✉ *Vorderg. 26/28, Schaffhausen.*

WHERE TO EAT

$$ INTERNATIONAL

Beckenburg. Well-heeled locals flock to this historic restaurant to sample innovative twists on classic Swiss and European staples, such as pike perch saltimbocca with lemon risotto or sliced veal with mushrooms. Using regional ingredients, the constantly evolving menu reflects both creativity and seasonality. **Known for:** fresh ingredients; continuous innovation; historical ambience. *Average main: 45 SF* ✉ *Neustadt 1, Schaffhausen* ☎ *052/6252820* *www.beckenburg.ch* *Closed Sun. and Mon.*

$ SWISS FAMILY

Restaurant Falken. This busy restaurant caters to crowds with a palate for simple local fare—Rösti (hash-brown potatoes), *Geschnetzeltes* (sliced veal in cream sauce), burgers, and spaghetti. The *Tagesteller* (daily special) is an especially good deal at lunchtime, and English-language menus are available. **Known for:** nice variety of food offerings; solid Swiss staples; good value. *Average main: 20 SF* ✉ *Vorstadt 5, Schaffhausen* ☎ *052/6253404* *www.falken-schaffhausen.ch.*

$$ EUROPEAN Fodor's Choice ★

Wirtschaft zum Frieden. Dating back to 1789, this cozy and centrally local favorite offers three delightful settings: a small *Stübli* (Swiss pub) full of waxed and weathered wood, a graceful tile-stove dining room with antiques, and a private garden thick with wisteria and luxuriant trees. Specialties include hearty dishes such as beef with white asparagus, and buttered Rösti with goat cheese. **Known for:** fresh ingredients; traditional dishes; first-class service. *Average main: 40 SF* ✉ *Herrenacker 11, Schaffhausen* ☎ *052/6254767* *www.wirtschaft-frieden.ch* *Closed Sun. and Mon.*

WHERE TO STAY

$ HOTEL

Hotel Kronenhof. This fine, quiet city hotel in the heart of Schaffhausen's Old Town has a traditional shutter- and flower-trimmed facade; inside, all is modern, with tidy, well-constructed rooms cheered by birch furniture, cherry-stained paneling, and abstract prints. **Pros:** central location; cobblestone terrace café; spa is free for hotel guests. **Cons:** the variation in style is a bit incoherent; service sometimes hurried; church bells can be loud. *Rooms from: 190 SF* ✉ *Kirchhofpl. 7, Schaffhausen* ☎ *052/6357575* *www.kronenhof.ch* *41 rooms* *Breakfast.*

$$ HOTEL

Hotel Park Villa. Except for the no-nonsense elevator tacked onto the exterior, this belle époque mansion has been transformed into a small hotel with little disruption to its grand but familial style. **Pros:** you can pretend you live in an old mansion; beautiful garden eating area;

park right outside the door. **Cons:** Wi-Fi not always reliable; noise from the railway station; very small reception area. *$ Rooms from: 229 SF ✉ Parkstr. 18, Schaffhausen ☎ 052/6356060 🌐 www.parkvilla.ch 25 rooms 🍽 Breakfast.*

$ HOTEL **Sorell Hotel Rüden.** Close to the train station, this former guild house turned hotel impresses with its grand staircase, glass elevator, and ornate ballroom where Johannes Brahms and Clara Schumann once entertained. **Pros:** central location; historic charm; modern (albeit utilitarian) bathrooms. **Cons:** modern lobby doesn't match other decor; some rooms don't have views; rooms on top floor can be hot in the summer. *$ Rooms from: 180 SF ✉ Oberstadt 20, Schaffhausen ☎ 052/6323636 🌐 www.rueden.ch 30 rooms 🍽 Breakfast.*

SPORTS AND THE OUTDOORS

Bahnhof Schaffhausen. Bicycles are a popular mode of transportation. They can be rented at the train station in Schaffhausen. It's also possible to return your rented bike to another train station. Reservations can be made online but are generally not necessary, unless you would like to rent an e-bike. *✉ Bahnhofstr., Schaffhausen ☎ 051/2234217 🌐 www.rentabike.ch From SF 27.*

STEIN AM RHEIN

20 km (13 miles) east of Schaffhausen.

Fodor's Choice ★ The riverside Stein am Rhein is one of Switzerland's loveliest (and wealthiest) communities. It lies at a pivotal point where the Rhine leaves the Bodensee, marked by three small leafy islands, one of which is still inhabited by monks. Crossing the bridge over the river, you see the village spread along the waterfront, its foundations and docks rising directly out of the water. Restaurants, hotels, and shops occupy 16th- and 17th-century buildings covered with ancient frescoes. Hovering over the walled town is a medieval castle surrounded by vineyards, home to an excellent restaurant with views.

GETTING HERE AND AROUND

The least complicated route from Schaffhausen is via train; the trip takes 24 minutes.

VISITOR INFORMATION

Contacts Tourismus Stein am Rhein. *✉ Oberstadt 3, Stein am Rhein ☎ 052/6324032 🌐 www.tourismus.steinamrhein.ch.*

EXPLORING

Hohenklingen. Directly above the town stands the 12th-century hilltop castle of Hohenklingen, which offers broad views of the Rhine Valley and the lake beyond. If you need sustenance after your trip up the hill, the castle houses an excellent restaurant. The tranquil vineyard trails up to the castle are a worthwhile diversion. *✉ Hohenklingenstr. 1, Stein am Rhein ☎ 052/7412137 🌐 www.burghohenklingen.com Free ⏲ Closed Mon. and late Dec.–early Mar.*

Kloster St. Georgen (*Monastery of St. George*). The Benedictine Kloster St. Georgen, a half-timber structure built in 1007, houses a cloister and a small museum devoted to examples of woodwork and local paintings.

Stein am Rhein celebrates Christmas by decking its streets with festive flair.

✉ *Fischmarkt 3, Stein am Rhein* ☎ *052/7412142* 🌐 *www.klostersankt-georgen.ch* 🎟 *5 SF* ⏲ *Closed Mon. and Nov.–Mar.*

KrippenWelt Stein-am-Rhein. Monika Amrein and Alfred Hartl's private collection of *krippen* (Nativity scenes) from around the world are tastefully displayed on two floors in their 14th-century home. There are more than 550 pieces in the collection, many made from paper, wood, metal, or even mushrooms. There is also a café and gift shop on the main floor. ✉ *Oberstadt 5, Stein am Rhein* ☎ *052/7210005* 🌐 *www.krippenwelt-ag.ch* 🎟 *10 SF* ⏲ *Closed Mon.*

Rathaus (*Town Hall Square*). Stein-am-Rhein's Rathaus (Town Hall) is flanked by tight rows of shingled, half-timber town houses, each rivaling the next for the ornateness of its oriels, the flamboyance of its frescoes. The elaborate decor usually illustrates the name of the house: Sonne (Sun), Ochsen (Ox), Weisser Adler (White Eagle), and so on. Most of the artwork dates from the 16th century. The Rathaus itself was built between 1539 and 1542, with the half-timber upper floors added in 1745; look for its fantastical dragon waterspouts, typical of the region. ✉ *Rathauspl., Stein am Rhein.*

WHERE TO EAT

$$ SWISS Fodor's Choice ★

Le Bateau. At one of eastern Switzerland's best restaurants, the seasonal menu includes dishes like pan-seared scallops bathed in a rich lemon sauce, sliced veal amped up with ruby-red chunks of seared tuna, and lobster tail in a buttery tarragon sauce so delicious that the waiter doesn't think twice before giving you a spoon. Surrounded by so much wood that it resembles a cruise ship's dining room, the restaurant's international cuisine is best enjoyed on the terrace overlooking the

Rhine's three leafy islands, one of which is still inhabited by monks. **Known for:** locally sourced beef; asparagus dishes; large regional wine list. *Average main: 40 SF Hotel Chlosterhof, Oehningerstr. 2, Stein am Rhein 052/7424242 www.chlosterhof.ch.*

$$ ITALIAN **Restaurant Schiff.** Perched on a gentle bend in the Rhine at the end of a colorful string of half-timber buildings, this family-friendly Italian restaurant offers an inviting riverside terrace and a wide variety of pasta options such as spaghetti with pesto sauce, Gorgonzola gnocchi, and risotto with mushrooms. The large menu also offers pizzas, meats, and fish—all served with a side of Swiss hospitality. **Known for:** pasta; picturesque riverside location; large pizza menu. *Average main: 26 SF Hotel Schiff, Schiffländi 10, Stein am Rhein 052/7412273 www.hotel-restaurant-schiff.ch.*

$ BAKERY **Zuckerbäckerei Ermatinger's Café Späth.** Small bakeries abound in Switzerland, but this one, run by Schaffhausen-based Ermatinger, offers such specialties as homemade pralines, fruit tortes, and other butter-laden confections. The locals also stop here for light snacks (the muesli is tasty), lunch (tomato-mozzarella sandwiches are the way to go), or a scoop of homemade ice cream. **Known for:** fruit tarts and cakes; ice cream; cash only. *Average main: 6 SF Rathauspl. 21, Stein am Rhein 052/6253940 www.zuckerbeck.ch No credit cards Closed Sun. No dinner.*

WHERE TO STAY

$ HOTEL **Hotel Adler.** With one of the most elaborately frescoed 15th-century facades on the Rathausplatz, this hotel has a split personality: colorful on the outside, no-nonsense on the inside. **Pros:** secure bicycle storage room; excellent service; central location. **Cons:** decor is in need of attention, with noticeably absent frills; church bells can be loud; rooms facing main square can be noisy late at night. *Rooms from: 185 SF Adlergaessli 4, Stein am Rhein 052/7426161 www.adlersteinamrhein.ch Closed late Jan.–early Feb. 23 rooms Breakfast.*

$ HOTEL Fodor's Choice ★ **Hotel Rheinfels.** Almost every room has a Rhine view at this waterfront landmark, which was built between 1508 and 1517. **Pros:** medieval atmosphere is a thrill; locals come from miles away for the fish dishes; waterfront location. **Cons:** slightly old-fashioned room decor; proximity to a busy thoroughfare; no reception desk. *Rooms from: 198 SF Rhig. 8, Stein am Rhein 052/7412144 www.rheinfels.ch Closed Jan. and Feb. 17 rooms Breakfast.*

$ HOTEL **Hotel-Restaurant Zur Rheingerbe.** Right on the busy waterfront promenade, this small inn has a delightful half-timber facade with green shutters and some lovely views of the Rhine, including from some of the rooms. **Pros:** centrally located; excellent rates; some rooms have river views. **Cons:** rooms are a bit sparse; steep steps; dated decor. *Rooms from: 160 SF Schifflände 5, Stein am Rhein 052/7412991 www.rheingerbe.ch 8 rooms Breakfast.*

ARENENBERG

40 km (25 miles) east of Schaffhausen, 20 km (12 miles) east of Stein-am-Rhein.

East of Stein-am-Rhein the Rhine opens up into the Untersee, the lower branch of the Bodensee. In its center lies the German island of Reichenau. Charles the Fat, great-grandson of Charlemagne, is buried here. Castles dominate the villages on either side of the Untersee.

EXPLORING

Fodor's Choice ★ **Napoleon Museum Thurgau** (*Napoleon Museum Arenenberg*). In the village of Salenstein, the Napoleon Museum is housed in a magnificent villa given to the municipality by Empress Eugénie of France in homage to her husband, Napoléon III, who grew up here with his mother, Hortense, sister-in-law of Napoléon I. Today the Schloss Arenenberg serves as a museum, and lovers of decorative arts will prize its ravishing period rooms dating from the Second Empire. Outside is a glorious park studded with ancestral statues as well as a separate seminar center with a small café. ✉ *Schloss und Park Arenenberg, off Arenenbergstr., Salenstein* ☎ *058/3457410* 🌐 *www.napoleonmuseum.tg.ch* 🎟 *12 SF* ⏲ *Closed Mon. mid-Oct.–Mar.*

GOTTLIEBEN

5 km (3 miles) east of Arenenberg, 45 km (28 miles) east of Schaffhausen.

The village of Gottlieben has a Dominican monastery-castle, where the Protestant reformers Jan Hus and Jerome of Prague were imprisoned in the 15th century by order of Emperor Sigismund and Antipope John XXIII, who was himself confined in the same castle a few years later. Although the castle can be viewed only from the outside, Gottlieben offers a romantic half-timber waterfront promenade—and two fine old hotels—before you reach the urban complex of Kreuzlingen and Germany's Konstanz.

WHERE TO STAY

$$ HOTEL Fodor's Choice ★ **Hotel Drachenburg und Waaghaus.** On the Rhine between the Bodensee and the Untersee, these two half-timber apparitions of onion domes, shutters, and gargoyles were first built in 1715 and retain their historic air despite modern expansions. **Pros:** extremely quiet; tons of character; right on the Rhine. **Cons:** in an isolated town; overtly theme-parkish; some beds are squeaky. $ *Rooms from: 274 SF* ✉ *Am Schlosspark 7 and 10, Gottlieben* ☎ *071/6667474* 🌐 *www.drachenburg.ch* *60 rooms* *Breakfast.*

BODENSEE TO WALENSEE

Along the shores of the Bodensee, orchards stripe rolling hills that slowly rise to meet the foothills of the Alps around St. Gallen. About 2,000 years ago this region lay on the northeastern border of the Roman Empire, Arbon (Arbor Felix) being the first stop on the trade route for goods coming into the empire from points east. Today, the region is mostly rural, with clusters of farmhouses dotting the grassy slopes. In summer the lake teems with vacationers, but in other seasons it remains a distinctly tranquil area.

BODENSEE

Known in English as Lake Constance, the Bodensee is about 65 km (40 miles) long and 15 km (9 miles) wide, making it second in size in Switzerland only to Lac Léman (Lake Geneva). The strong German flavor of the towns on its Swiss edge is seasoned with a resort-village mellowness; palm trees fringe the waterfront. This isn't the Mediterranean, though; because the lake is not protected by mountains, it can be windy in spring and fall and quite humid in summer. European vacationers come here during the warmer months for swimming, windsurfing, and fishing. Small vacation homes alternate with opulent villas along the lakefront.

FLEA MARKET FINDS

Some of the least developed land is in eastern Switzerland, which means there are still old houses stuffed with plenty of old furnishings, art pieces, and trinkets. This being Switzerland, commerce has responded: outdoor-indoor flea markets abound, as do secondhand thrift shops called *Bröckenhäuser* (*Brockenhaus* in the singular)—every town has at least one. Antiques dealers regularly troll the area, but it's still possible to find a bargain here and there, especially in out-of-the way villages. Let the hunt begin!

BEACHES

The Bodensee is the region's local swimming hole; there are several public beaches, usually more grass than sand. Most have changing rooms and concession stands.

FAMILY **Arbon.** With a gravel beach, Strandbad Buchhorn in Arbon makes getting into the water a little rough on tender feet; the nearby swimming pool is much smoother. **Amenities:** food and drink; showers; toilets; water sports. **Best for:** sunsets; swimming ✉ *Philosophenweg 11, Arbon* ☎ *071/4461333* 🌐 *www.strandbad-arbon.ch* 🎫 *7 SF.*

FAMILY **Kreuzlingen.** This beach has some sand at the water's edge, though you'll be spreading your towel on the grass. If you don't want to swim in the lake, you can also swim in the lakeside 50-meter swimming pool. **Amenities:** food and drink; parking (free); showers; toilets. **Best for:** sunsets; swimming. ✉ *Schwimmbadstr. 2, Kreuzlingen* ☎ *071/6881858* 🌐 *www.schwimmbadhoernli.ch* 🎫 *7 SF.*

FAMILY **Romanshorn.** The lakeside beach in Romanshorn includes a pool and a waterslide, as well as wide swaths of grass to lie on. **Amenities:** food and drink; parking (fee); showers; toilets. **Best for:** sunsets; swimming. ✉ *Badstr. 50, Romanshorn* ☎ *071/4631147* 🌐 *www.romanshorn.ch* 🎫 *7 SF.*

SPORTS AND THE OUTDOORS

BIKING

There's a great cycling path that starts outside Sargans, runs along the Rhine down to the Bodensee, and goes all the way to Schaffhausen, with views of the water on one side and some of Switzerland's most beautiful agricultural land on the other. Rent bikes at the train station in Sargans, St. Margrethen, Romanshorn, Kreuzlingen, Stein-am-Rhein, or

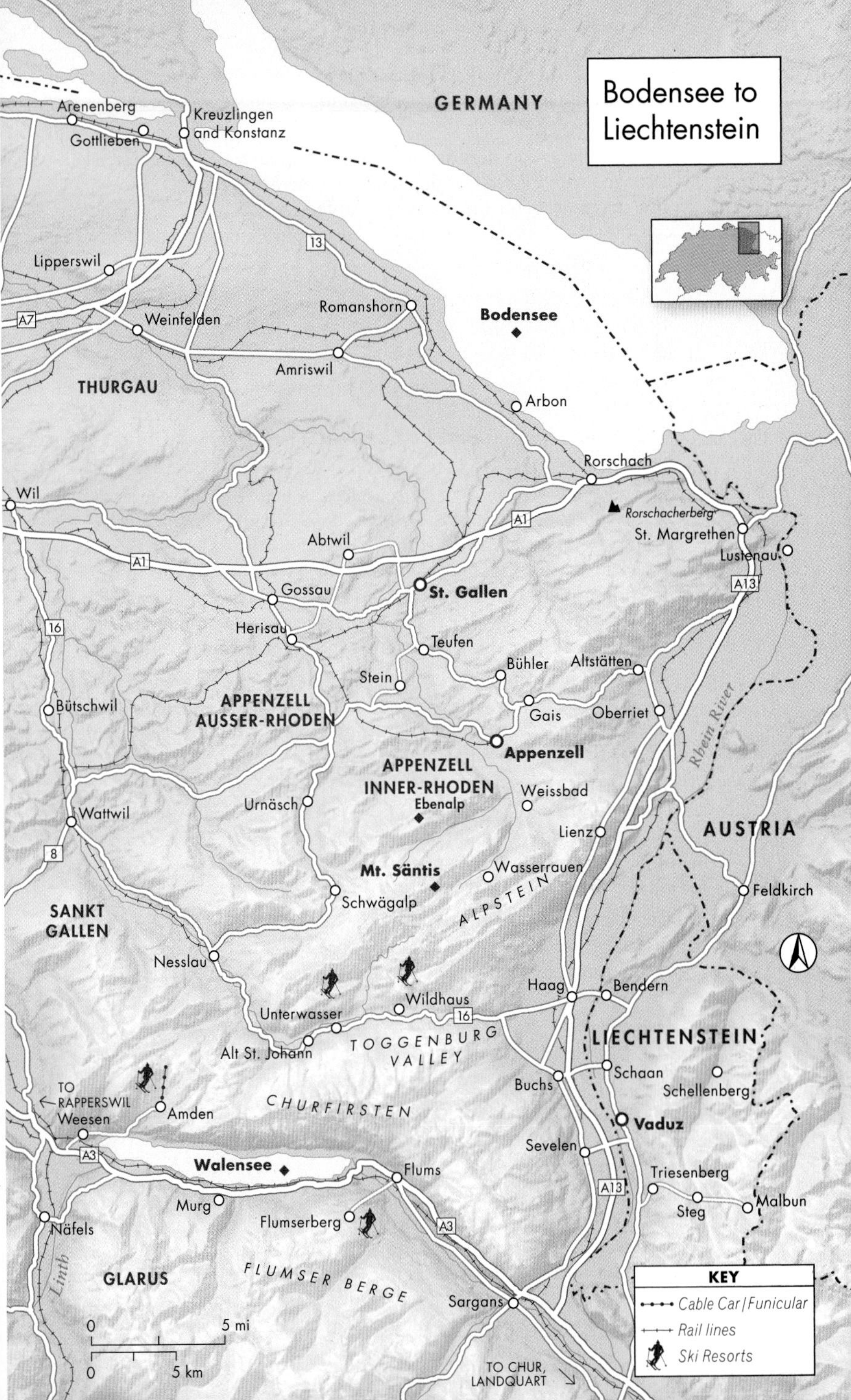

Bodensee to Liechtenstein
GERMANY
Bodensee
Arenenberg
Gottlieben
Kreuzlingen and Konstanz
Lipperswil
Weinfelden
Romanshorn
Amriswil
THURGAU
Arbon
Rorschach
Rorschacherberg
St. Margrethen
Lustenau
Wil
Abtwil
Gossau
St. Gallen
Herisau
Teufen
Bühler
Altstätten
Stein
Gais
Oberriet
Bütschwil
APPENZELL AUSSER-RHODEN
Appenzell
Rhein River
APPENZELL INNER-RHODEN
Ebenalp
Weissbad
Urnäsch
Wattwil
Lienz
AUSTRIA
Mt. Säntis
Wasserrauen
Schwägalp
ALPSTEIN
Feldkirch
SANKT GALLEN
Nesslau
Haag
Bendern
Wildhaus
Unterwasser
Alt St. Johann
TOGGENBURG VALLEY
LIECHTENSTEIN
Schaan
Schellenberg
Buchs
TO RAPPERSWIL
Weesen
Amden
CHURFIRSTEN
Vaduz
Sevelen
Walensee
Flums
Triesenberg
Steg
Malbun
Murg
Näfels
Flumserberg
Linth
GLARUS
FLUMSER BERGE
Sargans
0
5 mi
0
5 km
TO CHUR, LANDQUART
KEY
Cable Car/Funicular
Rail lines
Ski Resorts
A7
13
A1
16
8
A3
A13

Schaffhausen. One-way rentals are possible for a surcharge. For detailed route information, see ⊕ *www.veloland.ch.*

HIKING

As a summer resort destination, the area around the Bodensee is usually thronged with hikers. For timed hiking itineraries, topographical maps, and suggestions on the areas best suited to your style of wandering, consult the Tourismusverband Ostschweiz at ⊕ *www.ostschweiz-i.ch.*

ST. GALLEN

38 km (24 miles) southeast of Kreuzlingen, 94 km (59 miles) southeast of Schaffhausen.

Switzerland's largest eastern city, bustling St. Gallen is dominated by students during the school year. The narrow streets of the Altstadt (Old Town) are flanked by a wonderful variety of boutiques and antiques shops.

St. Gallen has been known for centuries as an intellectual center as well as the source of some of the world's finest needlework, including the embroidery that embellished the gown worn by Michelle Obama at President Barack Obama's inauguration ceremony in 2008. But today its commitment to the latest trends in art, design, and architecture marks a new direction for the city, which seems to be competing against Zürich, Basel, and Winterthur as a contemporary art destination.

St. Gallus, an Irish monk, came to the region in 612 to live in a hermit's cell in the Steinach Valley. In 719 an abbey was founded on the site where he died. Soon a major cultural focus in medieval Europe, the abbey built a library of awesome proportions.

GETTING HERE AND AROUND

Trains run to St. Gallen from Zürich, clocking in at just over an hour. The S8 commuter runs from Schaffhausen to St. Gallen every half hour, stopping at almost every town along the way. The trip takes almost two hours.

The A1 expressway from Zürich heads for St. Gallen through Winterthur. From the south, the A13 expressway leads from Chur along Liechtenstein to the east end of the Bodensee; from there, take the A1 into St. Gallen. The Altstadt is surrounded by underground parking lots. You'll find entrances on Burggraben, Oberergraben, and Spisertor.

VISITOR INFORMATION

Contacts St.Gallen-Bodensee Tourismus. ✉ *Bankg. 9, St. Gallen* ☎ *071/2273737* ⊕ *www.st.gallen-bodensee.ch.*

EXPLORING

TOP ATTRACTIONS

Altstadt. The grounds of the abbey and the cathedral border the Altstadt, which demonstrates a healthy symbiosis between scrupulously preserved Renaissance and baroque architecture and a thriving modern shopping scene. The best examples of oriel windows, half-timbering, and frescoes can be seen along Gallusstrasse, Schmiedgasse, Marktgasse, and Spisergasse, all pedestrian streets. ✉ *St. Gallen.*

The opulent Abbey Library in St. Gallen holds more than 100,000 books; you can also see an ancient Egyptian mummy here.

Fodor's Choice ★ **Kathedrale.** The cathedral is an impressive sight. Begun in 1755 and completed in 1766, it is the antithesis of the decadent Abbey Library nearby, although the nave and rotunda are the work of the same architect, Peter Thumb. The scale is outsized and the decor light, bright, and open, despite spectacular excesses of wedding-cake trim. ✉ *Klosterhof 6a, St. Gallen* ☎ *071/2273381*.

QUICK BITES

Café Vivendi. Healthful and delicious fare is served at Café Vivendi, a bistro in the pedestrian zone of the Old Town. Light meals, salads, and pastries from the restaurant's own bakery are local favorites. Known for: vegetarian and vegan offerings; homemade beverages; fresh ingredients. ✉ ***Bankg. 2, St. Gallen*** ☎ ***071/2221806*** ⏲ ***No dinner Sun.***

Fodor's Choice ★ **Stiftsbibliothek** (*Abbey Library*). Although the abbey was largely destroyed in the Reformation and closed down altogether in 1805, its library, built between 1758 and 1767, still holds a collection of more than 100,000 books and manuscripts. To visit the library hall, one of Switzerland's treasures, you are given gray felt slippers to protect the magnificently inlaid wood flooring. The hall is a gorgeous explosion of gilt, frescoes, undulating balconies, and luminously burnished woodwork, mostly walnut and cherry. Its contents, including 1,200-year-old manuscripts, constitute one of the world's oldest and finest scholarly collections. Also on display, incongruously, is an Egyptian mummy dating from about 650 BC. Not to be missed is the giant globe representing the world in 1570, with grossly misproportioned continents. The original was stolen by Zürich about 300 years ago, and in 2009 this reproduction was given to St. Gallen in lieu of the original. ✉ *Klosterhof 6d, St. Gallen* ☎ *071/2273416* 🌐 *www.stibi.ch* 🎫 *12 SF* ⏲ *Closed mid-Nov.–early Dec.*

Textilmuseum (*Textile Museum*). St. Gallen's history as a textile capital dates from the Middle Ages, when convent workers wove linen toile of such exceptional quality that it was exported throughout Europe. The industry expanded into cotton and embroidery before collapsing in 1918. Today St. Gallen dominates the small luxury market for fine handmade textiles, and magnificently historic finery is on view at the Textilmuseum. ✉ *Vadianstr. 2, St. Gallen* ☎ *071/2280010* 🌐 *www.textilmuseum.ch* 🎫 *12 SF.*

WORTH NOTING

FAMILY **Drei Weieren.** Atop Freudenberg Hill you'll find Drei Weieren, a relaxing park and swimming area with several refreshing ponds. Swimming is free at the largest pond and each is surrounded by grassy fields, lifeguard stations, and handsome striped changing cabins built in the 1920s. This lofty perch offers a fantastic lookout over the soaring steeples, tiled rooftops, and cow-grazed valleys below. ✉ *Bitzistr. 65, St. Gallen* 🎫 *Swimming in the Mannenweiher is free. Admission is charged to the family pond, the Frauenweiher* ☞ *Take Bus 2 or 8 to Mühlegg from the St. Gallen train station or take the Mühleggbahn.*

Mühleggbahn. Just a few steps from the abbey, at the end of the Old Town, is the Mühleggbahn, a self-service funicular that runs up the hillside, offering lovely views of St. Gallen and the Bodensee. Once at the top, take two immediate right turns to the wooden stairs leading to a paved path with park benches. ■ **TIP→ For a single ride only, choose the "Kurzstrecke" button when you buy your ticket.** ✉ *Steinachstr. 42, St. Gallen* ☎ *071/2439511* 🌐 *www.muehleggbahn.ch* 🎫 *2.40 SF.*

Mühlenenschlucht. A 30-minute walk up the steep Mühlenenschlucht takes you past the mossy Steinach Gorge, where St. Gallus allegedly befriended a bear in 612. To commemorate St. Gallus's 1,400th birthday in 2012, the city installed a public art exhibit here that includes a self-opening time capsule embedded in a river rock (by German artist Maria Eichhorn) and a haunting neon sign atop the gorge's railroad viaduct (by Welsh artist Bethen Hews). ✉ *Galluspl., St. Gallen.*

Stadt Lounge. Native-born artist Pipilotti Rist's *Stadt Lounge,* created with artist Carlos Martinez, is a public artwork project that has bathed an entire chunk of the city center under a coat of red paint, creating what they call a "red-carpet effect." It has transformed the neighborhood into a sultry "public living room" and has been so successful, it has been enlarged. ✉ *Raiffeisenpl., St. Gallen* 🌐 *www.raiffeisen.ch/web/stadtlounge.*

WHERE TO EAT

$$ SWISS ✕ **Am Gallusplatz.** The menu at this culinary landmark is based on market-fresh ingredients and may include such ample fare as a triumvirate of fillets (beef, veal, lamb) with fresh vegetables and potatoes, but can also be more inventive, in the form of veal Provençal. Vegetarians are asked to please contact the restaurant in advance so something special can be prepared. **Known for:** excellent service; historic atmosphere; fine

food. $ *Average main: 38 SF* ✉ *Gallusstr. 24, St. Gallen* ☎ *071/2300090* 🌐 *www.amgallusplatz-sg.ch* ⏲ *Closed Sun. and Mon.*

$ SWISS ✕ **Blumenmarkt.** Wood-and-steel furniture mixes with black painted walls and a fully stocked bar at this trendy St. Gallen café near the farmers' market. The house coffee (*Huuskafi*) here includes Appenzeller caramel vodka and whipped cream, and the tea comes from La Théirère in St. Gallen. **Known for:** local gathering place; delicious coffee; modern yet cozy atmosphere. $ *Average main: 6 SF* ✉ *Marktpl. 25, St. Gallen* ☎ *071/5354801* 🌐 *www.blumenmarktbar.ch.*

3

$$$$ SWISS Fodor's Choice ★ ✕ **Jägerhof.** This light and airy room in a 19th-century town house is St. Gallen's top address for organic ingredients, light, innovative cuisine, and heartfelt service. Local foodies and hipsters alike enjoy the prix-fixe menu that might include rabbit stuffed with truffles, chicken liver with brioche and quince compote, or pike perch with risotto and celery. **Known for:** haute cuisine; fresh and local ingredients; gracious service. $ *Average main: 80 SF* ✉ *Brühlbleichestr. 11, St. Gallen* ☎ *071/2455022* 🌐 *www.jaegerhof.ch* ⏲ *Closed Sun.*

$$ MODERN EUROPEAN ✕ **Lagerhaus.** Prosecco-boiled risotto, octopus salad, tender pork steak—the Swiss-Italian fusion dishes make Lagerhaus well worth a visit. The spacious and elegant eatery attracts a stylish and chatty crowd that appreciates the giant outdoor terrace and the epic list of local and international wines. **Known for:** steaks and seafood; attentive service; lively atmosphere. $ *Average main: 36 SF* ✉ *Davidstr. 42, St. Gallen* ☎ *071/2237007* 🌐 *www.restaurantlagerhaus.ch* ⏲ *Closed Sun. and Mon. No lunch Sat.*

$ ASIAN FUSION ✕ **Lansin.** What this restaurant lacks in decor it makes up for with tasty Vietnamese and Southeast Asian specialties. Noodle salads, noodle soups, and main courses like chicken with mango chutney served with homemade spicy sauce make for a nice change of pace from the usual Swiss fare. **Known for:** good value; no-frills authentic Asian cuisine; cash only. $ *Average main: 18 SF* ✉ *Weberg. 16, St. Gallen* ☎ *071/2232000* 💳 *No credit cards* ⏲ *Closed Sun. No dinner Mon.*

$$ SWISS ✕ **Lokal.** The service at Lokal comes across as arrogant, but the food—savory carrot ginger soup, cordon bleu heaped with *pomme frites,* coq au vin, and mounds of fresh green salads—is surprisingly affordable and always excellent. Sunday brunch shouldn't be missed. **Known for:** luxurious and unique decor; trendy atmosphere; fish and meat dishes. $ *Average main: 39 SF* ✉ *Lokremise, Grünbergstr. 7, St. Gallen* ☎ *071/2722570* 🌐 *www.lokremise.ch.*

$$ SWISS Fodor's Choice ★ ✕ **Schlössli.** Tidy, bright, and modern, this second-floor restaurant may lack the historic feel of some of its neighbors, but it features remarkable cooking from a well-regarded chef. Look for inventive dishes such as local *Bloderchäs* (sour cheese) fried in sage butter, or local lamb shanks with chanterelle mushrooms, seasonal vegetables, and bread dumplings. **Known for:** regional and seasonal ingredients; attentive service; creative menu. $ *Average main: 40 SF* ✉ *Zeughausg. 17, St. Gallen* ☎ *071/2221256* 🌐 *www.schloessli-sg.ch* ⏲ *Closed weekends and midsummer.*

$$ SWISS **Zum Goldenen Schäfli.** Of the second-story restaurants that are St. Gallen's trademark, this is the most popular—its slanting floors groan under crowds of locals and tourists. The menu offers regional standards lightened up for modern tastes such as sirloin steak with peppercorn sauce, Spätzle, and seasonal vegetables. **Known for:** steaks and sausages; courteous service; historic atmosphere. *Average main: 32 SF* *Metzgerg. 5, St. Gallen* *071/2233737* *www.zumgoldenenschaefli.ch* *Closed Sun.*

WHERE TO STAY

$$ HOTEL Fodor's Choice ★ **Einstein St. Gallen Hotel Congress Spa.** On the edge of the Old Town, this former embroidery factory is now an upscale hotel with sleek interiors (polished cabinetry, subdued floral fabrics), a uniformed staff, and a five-star attitude. **Pros:** St. Gallen's grand hotel; wonderful views from the top-floor restaurant; central location. **Cons:** focus on business clients; breakfast is expensive and not included in rate; all-white reception area feels stark. *Rooms from: 290 SF* *Berneggstr. 2, St. Gallen* *071/2275555* *www.einstein.ch* *113 rooms* *No meals.*

$$ HOTEL **Hotel Dom.** This warm, modern-design hotel in the heart of the Klosterviertel district puts you just steps from the Abbey Library. **Pros:** central location; friendly service; 24/7 coffee and tea. **Cons:** some rooms are small; street-facing rooms have some street noise; budget rooms have no in-room shower or toilet. *Rooms from: 255 SF* *Weberg. 22, St. Gallen* *071/2277171* *www.hoteldom.ch* *Closed 2 wks in Dec.* *40 rooms* *Breakfast.*

$ HOTEL **Hotel Vadian.** A narrow town house tucked behind half-timber landmarks in the Old Town, this is a discreet and tidy little place. **Pros:** high-quality personal service; central location; good value. **Cons:** rooms in the front have some street noise; no reception service after 9 pm; reception area very small. *Rooms from: 162 SF* *Gallusstr. 36, St. Gallen* *071/2281878* *www.hotel-vadian.com* *22 rooms* *Breakfast.*

$$$ HOTEL **Radisson Blu Hotel, St. Gallen.** A 10-minute walk from the Old Town, this glass-and-steel business hotel has crisp, stylish rooms with spacious baths. **Pros:** large rooms; friendly service; excellent breakfast (though not always included). **Cons:** expensive parking; business-guest focused; not much character. *Rooms from: 324 SF* *St. Jakobstr. 55, St. Gallen* *071/2421212, 071/2421200* *www.radissonblue.com/en/hotel-stgallen* *123 rooms* *No meals.*

$$ HOTEL **Sorell Hotel City Weissenstein.** This clean, comfortable, and centrally located hotel near the St. Gallen train station has a friendly staff and offers free Wi-Fi. **Pros:** 21st-century styling, which is rare in this region; very quiet; comfy pillows. **Cons:** about a 10-minute walk from the Old Town; breakfast room is part of the lobby; no restaurant. *Rooms from: 250 SF* *Davidstr. 22, St. Gallen* *071/2280628* *www.sorell-hotels.com* *20 rooms* *Breakfast.*

SPORTS AND THE OUTDOORS

FAMILY **Säntispark.** This sprawling water park and wellness center just outside St. Gallen also includes a tranquil spa, making it an ideal place for both families and couples who want peace and quiet. There's something to please (and exhaust) everyone, including bowling, billiards,

DID YOU KNOW?

St. Gallen's Abbey District joined the UNESCO World Heritage list in 1983, thanks in part to the Abbey Library's impressive collection of books and manuscripts.

and miniature golf. Young people love diving into the wave pool and zipping down a slide that corkscrews around the entire facility. Adults enjoy half a dozen varieties of saunas and steam rooms where they can relax au naturel in a kid-free environment. ✉ *Wiesenbachstr. 9, Abtwil* ☎ *071/3131515* 🌐 *www.saentispark.ch* 🎫 *28 SF for 2 hrs, 5 SF each additional hr.*

SHOPPING

Akris. This local couture house has gained international acclaim by selling its own line of luxury clothing, all of it manufactured in Switzerland. Designer Albert Kriemler has dressed many luminaries, including Michelle Obama, Nicole Kidman, and Princess Charlene of Monaco. ✉ *Felsenstr. 40, St. Gallen* ☎ *071/2277722* 🌐 *www.akris.ch.*

Fodor's Choice ★ **St. Galler Bauernmarkt.** St. Gallen's Friday Farmers' Market—full of farmers hawking tubes of local rapeseed mayonnaise, regional cheeses, fruit preserves, cured meats, and wine—opens at 7:30 am and ends promptly at 1 pm, so be sure to get there early. A Wednesday and Saturday general market in the same square is equally busy, but the food isn't necessarily from local sources. ✉ *Marktpl., St. Gallen* 🌐 *www.bauernmarkt-sg.ch* ⊗ *Closed Dec.–Mar.*

Stich-Galerie Osvald. An outstanding assortment of antique prints of Swiss landscapes and costumes is sold at a broad range of prices at Stich-Galerie Osvald. The pictures are cataloged alphabetically by canton for easy browsing. ✉ *Marktg. 26, St. Gallen* ☎ *071/2235016* 🌐 *www.graphica-antiqua.ch.*

APPENZELL

20 km (12 miles) south of St. Gallen, 98 km (60 miles) southeast of Schaffhausen.

Isolated from St. Gallen by a ridge of green hills, Appenzell is divided into two sub-cantons, Appenzell Ausserrhoden and Appenzell Innerrhoden. Both make up one of Switzerland's least-explored regions. The Appenzellers are known for their quirky senses of humor, old-fashioned costumes (including hoop earrings for most men), and good-natured *anstand*, which loosely translates as "decorum" or "decency." But more than anything, Appenzell is cheese and beer country, and you would be remiss to leave without a taste of either.

Named Appenzell after the Latin *abbatis cella* (abbey cell), the region served as a sort of colony to the St. Gallen abbey, and its tradition of fine embroidery dates from those early days. The perfect chance to see this embroidery is during a local festival, such as the Alpfahrten, when cows are herded up or down the mountains. Women's hair is coiffed in tulle, and their dresses have intricate embroidery and lace, often with an edelweiss motif; men wear embroidered red vests and suspenders decorated with edelweiss or cow figures. These traditional costumes are taken very seriously; they can cost thousands of francs, but in this case, pride supersedes economy.

To get your bearings in Appenzell, head to the Landsgemeindeplatz, the town square where the famous open-air elections (men-only until 1991) take place the last Sunday in April. The streets are lined with brightly painted homes, bakeries full of *Birnebrot* (pear bread) and souvenir *Biber* (almond-and-honey cakes). Embroidery is big business, but it's rare to find handmade examples of the local art; though women still do fine work at home, it's generally reserved for gifts or heirlooms. Instead, large factories have sprung up in Appenzell country, and famous fine-cotton handkerchiefs sold in specialty shops around the world are made by machine here at the Dörig, Alba, and Lehner plants.

DISCOUNTS AND DEALS

Available free to travelers staying for three or more nights in a local hotel, the Appenzell Card gives you complimentary admission to five museums, transport on three cable car lifts, a complimentary bike rental, and a self-guided tour of the factory where Appenzeller cheese is made, along with several other perks. It could save you hundreds of dollars.

GETTING HERE AND AROUND

The direct train from and to St. Gallen takes 48 minutes, or if you want a change of scenery, an alternative route goes via Herisau. A small highway (No. 3) leads into the hills through Teufen; the quaint Appenzell–Teufen–Gais rail line also serves the region.

VISITOR INFORMATION

Contacts Appenzellerland. ✉ *Hauptg. 4, Appenzell* ☎ *071/7889641* 🌐 *www.appenzell.ch.*

EXPLORING

TOP ATTRACTIONS

Brauquöll Appenzell. The locally brewed Appenzeller Quöllfrisch—just one of the high-quality beers made by Appenzell's family-owned Brauerei Locher—is an iconic drink in an old-fashioned flip-top bottle and found everywhere across Switzerland. The brewery's excellent shop and visitor center on the Sitter River let you sample local beers, including sweet dunkels, hoppy pilsners, malty chestnut and hemp beers, and even a special beer brewed under a full moon. An interactive English tour offers insight into the unique brewing processes. The company also makes fantastic whiskeys with peat from a bog just outside Appenzell. The staff is exceptionally friendly and will gladly arrange a flight of beers or whiskeys for you. ✉ *Brauereipl. 1, Appenzell* ☎ *071/7880176* 🌐 *www.brauquoell.ch* 🎫 *Free* 🕒 *Closed Jan. Closed Sun. and Mon. in Nov., Dec., Feb., and Mar.*

Fodor's Choice ★ **Ebenalp.** The northernmost peak of the Appenzeller Alps, the 5,380-foot Ebenalp is accessible via cable car from Wasserrauen, 7 km (4 miles) south of Appenzell. At the top is an easy hike that connects to other trails that lead to a mountain lake or loop back to the cable car. Also here is the Wildkirchli, a cave that was home to humans in the Paleolithic era and today houses a large bear skeleton that dates back 90,000 years. Five minutes farther along the trail is the Berggastaus Aescher-Wildkirchli, a mountainside restaurant with eye-popping views of the valley below. ✉ *Schwendetalstr. 82, Wasserauen* ☎ *071/7991212* 🌐 *www.ebenalp.ch* 🎫 *31 SF round-trip.*

FAMILY **Schaukäserei.** Modern cheese-making methods are demonstrated at the Schaukäserei, a combination of a factory and a museum. Cheese is made until 3. A self-guided tour (free with the Appenzell Card) reveals the history of the local cheese, and a movie about the region is a surefire way to whet your appetite. The attached restaurant is one of the best places to sample some traditional dishes made with Appenzeller cheese, including a silky cheese soup, gooey fondues and *raclettes* (melted cheese served with small potatoes in their skins, pickled pearl onions, and gherkins), and a savory *chääsflade* (cheese pie). A playground keeps children happy, too. ✉ *Dorf 711, Stein* ☎ *071/3685070* 🌐 *www.schaukaeserei.ch* 🎟 *Free.*

APPENZELL EMBROIDERY

True, the demanding embroidery technique for which the name Appenzell became famous can no longer be found in the town of its birth. Though this makes for a somewhat faux souvenir, the imports do a fine job of capturing the intricacies of Appenzell embroidery. In a sign-of-the-times switcheroo, **Margreiter** (✉ Hauptg. 29/31 ☎ *071/7873313*) carries a large stock of handkerchiefs turned out in the local factories. Very popular are ones embroidered with motifs of edelweiss. **Trachtenstube** (✉ Hauptg. 23 ☎ *071/7871606*) offers high-quality lace, embroidery, and crafts.

WORTH NOTING

Appenzeller Volkskunde Museum (*Folklore Museum*). This museum displays local arts and crafts, regional costumes, and hand-painted furniture. ✉ *Dorf, Stein* ☎ *071/3685056* 🌐 *www.appenzeller-museum.ch* 🎟 *7 SF* ⏲ *Closed Mon.*

Museum Appenzell. Showcasing handicrafts and local traditions, regional history, and an international embroidery collection, the Museum Appenzell provides a good general overview of the area's history and culture. The building itself dates from 1560. An English-language guide is available. ✉ *Hauptg. 4, Appenzell* ☎ *071/7889631* 🌐 *www.museum.ai.ch* 🎟 *7 SF* ⏲ *Closed Mon. Nov.–Mar.*

Museum für Appenzeller Brauchtum (*Museum of Appenzeller Tradition*). Costumes, cowbells, and a cheese wagon are on display at the Museum für Appenzeller Brauchtum, along with examples of farmhouse living quarters. ✉ *Dorfpl., Urnäsch* ☎ *071/3642322* 🌐 *www.museum-urnaesch.ch* 🎟 *6 SF* ⏲ *Closed Sun. Nov.–Mar.*

WHERE TO EAT

$$ SWISS ✕ **Adlerkeller.** The 450-year-old cellar underneath the Adler Hotel on the edge of Appenzell town is *the* place for fondue in the winter. Carved-wood-paneled walls, a dark medieval room, and ancient glassed-over cobblestones are a bit chilly and museumlike, but the friendly service and excellent local wine list will warm you right back up. ⚠ **Credit cards aren't accepted for bills under 40 SF.** **Known for:** fondue in winter; homemade ice cream; light summertime lunches. 💲 *Average main: 27 SF* ✉ *Weissbadstr. 2, Appenzell* ☎ *071/7871389* 🌐 *www.adlerhotel.ch* ⏲ *Closed Wed. No dinner summer.*

Dressed in traditional garb, these men prepare for a cattle show in Appenzell.

$$ SWISS Fodor's Choice ★ **Berggasthaus Aescher-Wildkirchli.** This is a mountain restaurant where you come for the views and stay for the Rösti, Appenzell cheese dishes, and *cervelat* (Swiss sausage). Since it's accessible only by cable car plus a 20-minute hike, you'll have earned your meal at this cliff-side café, which sits at the top of the Appenzeller Alps. **Known for:** breathtaking views; local cheese dishes; delicious Swiss Rösti. *Average main: 35 SF* *Weissbad* *20-minute hike from the top station of the Ebenalp cable car* *071/7991142* *www.aescher-ai.ch* *Closed Nov.–Apr.*

$$ SWISS **Gasthaus Hof.** One of Appenzell's most popular restaurants serves hearty regional meats and cheese specialties, such as *Käseschnitte* (cheese toast) and *Käsespätzli* (Spätzle with cheese), to locals and tourists who crowd elbow to elbow along shared tables and talk over the clatter from the bar. The rustic-wood decor, ladderback chairs, and display of sports trophies add to the local atmosphere. **Known for:** local specialties; Appenzell cheese dishes; big portions. *Average main: 28 SF* *Engelg. 4, Appenzell* *071/7872210* *www.gasthaus-hof.ch.*

WHERE TO STAY

$ HOTEL FAMILY **Freudenberg Hotel.** This is a cookie-cutter modern chalet, but its setting on a velvety green hillside overlooking town is the most scenic and tranquil you'll find in the area. **Pros:** child-friendly surroundings, including private playground; excellent value; good base camp for hikers. **Cons:** the trek from town is uphill; some bathrooms are small; isolated location. *Rooms from: 160 SF* *Riedstr. 57, Appenzell* *071/7871240* *www.hotel-freudenberg.ch* *Closed Nov.* *10 rooms* *Breakfast.*

$$ B&B/INN Fodor's Choice ★ **Hotel Appenzell.** Although built only in 1983, this warm, comfortable lodging has all the gabled coziness of its neighbors, with a view over the Landsgemeindeplatz and beyond to the mountains. **Pros:** central location; pastry shop on the ground floor; helpful service. **Cons:** restaurant is filled to capacity in summer; street noise; rooms can get warm in the summer. *Rooms from: 230 SF* *Landsgemeindepl., Appenzell* *071/7881515* *www.hotel-appenzell.ch* *Closed Nov.* *16 rooms* *Breakfast.*

$$$ RESORT **Hotel Hof Weissbad.** A popular destination among locals seeking a massage or other spa treatment, the sprawling and leafy Hotel Hof Weissbad is on a quiet street in the village of Weissbad. **Pros:** quiet retreat; great service; spa and fitness area included. **Cons:** also a rehab center; unfocused decor; train ride from most tourist sights. *Rooms from: 460 SF* *Im Park 1, Weissbad* *071/7988080* *www.hofweissbad.ch* *87 rooms* *Breakfast.*

$ HOTEL **Hotel Löwen.** Wising up to travelers' quests for "typical" local decor, the owners of this renovated 1780 guesthouse furnished several rooms in authentic Appenzeller style, with embroidered linens and built-in armoires painted with bright designs and naive local scenes—some actually reflecting the views from the window. **Pros:** friendly service; cozy atmosphere; central location. **Cons:** street-side rooms can be noisy; reception closes at 8 pm; proximity to church bells. *Rooms from: 160 SF* *Hauptg. 25, Appenzell* *071/7888787, 071/7888788* *www.loewen-appenzell.ch* *28 rooms* *Breakfast.*

$$ HOTEL **Romantik Hotel Säntis.** With a crisp and formal ambience, this prestigious hotel has been in business since 1835. **Pros:** large and comfortable with all the amenities; a good choice for both loungers and the activity-happy; central location. **Cons:** front view is onto the Landsgemeinde, which is a parking lot; can be noisy and smoky; rooms can be warm in the summer. *Rooms from: 240 SF* *Landsgemeindepl. 3, Appenzell* *071/7881111* *www.saentis-appenzell.ch* *Closed mid-Jan.–mid-Feb.* *36 rooms* *Breakfast.*

SHOPPING

Butchers, bakers, and liquor shops up and down the streets offer souvenir bottles of Appenzeller Bitter (Alpenbitter), an ironically very sweet aperitif made in town. A well-balanced eau-de-vie called Appenzeller Kräuter, made with blended herbs, is another specialty. Shops also sell *Mostbröckli*, an air-dried beef, *Landjäger*, a smoky dried sausage, regional cheeses, locally produced beer and wine, and bottles of peaty Swiss whiskey.

Chaeslade. Picnickers can sample the different grades of Appenzeller cheese and its unsung mountain rivals as well as purchase other local specialties at this centrally located shop. *Hauptg. 13, Appenzell* *071/7871317* *www.chaeslade.com.*

Chäs-Sutter. This shop has a good selection of locally made cheeses. *Marktg. 8, Appenzell* *071/7871333* *www.chaes-sutter.ch.*

MT. SÄNTIS

Schwägalp cable car is 33 km (21 miles) southwest of Appenzell, 121 km (75 miles) southeast of Schaffhausen.

Mt. Säntis bills itself as "the mountain," and it's hard to argue with that. Soaring 8,209 feet, it offers Alpine views as stunning as its jagged peak.

GETTING HERE AND AROUND

From Appenzell, take the train to Urnäsch or Nesslau and continue on postbus to Schwägalp, where a cable car does the heavy lifting those last 4,400 feet up to the peak.

EXPLORING

Fodor's Choice ★ **Mt. Säntis.** For a pleasurable high-altitude excursion out of Appenzell southwest to the hamlet of Schwägalp, you can ride a cable car that departs every 30 minutes up to the peak of Mt. Säntis. At 8,209 feet, it is the highest in the region, with beautiful views of the Bodensee as well as of the Graubünden and Bernese Alps. The very shape of the summit—an arc of jutting rock that swings up to the jagged peak housing the station—is spectacular. ✉ *Schwägalp* ☎ *071/3656565* 🌐 *www.saentisbahn.ch* 🎫 *45 SF round-trip.*

WALENSEE

40 km (24 miles) northwest of Vaduz, 65 km (36 miles) southeast of Zürich, 127 km (78 miles) southeast of Schaffhausen.

Between Liechtenstein and Zürich, the spectacular, blue-green lake called the Walensee stretches 16 km (10 miles) through the mountains, reflecting the jagged Churfirsten peaks. Once bypassed by Zürich residents en route to family chalets in Graubünden and Valais, this area is seeing new life as a weekend getaway because of a new tunnel that has discreetly hidden the cars in a pipeline of half tunnels. Walenstadt is the region's biggest town and has the most dining options, and the strand of other lakefront villages are picturesque and read like a Harry Potter witchcraft spell: Weesen, Quinten, Quarten, and Murg.

EXPLORING

Weesen. At the western end of the Walensee, Weesen is a quiet, shady resort noted for its mild climate and lovely lakeside walkway. ✉ *Weesen* 🌐 *www.amden-weesen.ch.*

WHERE TO STAY

$ HOTEL **Loft Hotel.** In the quiet town of Murg, this mod lodging is a high-concept, low-budget boutique hotel overlooking the sparkling Lake Wallen. **Pros:** incredible lake views; steps from the train station; exceptionally friendly staff. **Cons:** weak Wi-Fi in some areas; not many places to eat in the area; breakfast options are limited. $ *Rooms from: 180 SF* ✉ *Alte Spinnerei, Murg* ☎ *081/7203575* 🌐 *www.lofthotel.ch* *19 rooms* 🍽 *Breakfast.*

SKIING

Amden. Despite its small size, Amden is a major winter sports center, offering modest skiing in a ruggedly beautiful setting. Easy and medium slopes with unspectacular drops and quick, short-lift runs provide good weekend getaways for crowds of local Swiss families. The highest trails start at 5,576 feet; there are two chairlifts, three T-bars, one children's lift, 25 km (16 miles) of downhill runs, and 7 km (4½ miles) of cross-country trails. You can also take advantage of the ski school, a natural ice rink, and walking paths. ✉ *Sportbahnen Amden, Hinterbergstr. 2* ☎ *055/6111275* 🌐 *www.amden-weesen.ch* 🎫 *35 SF for one-day lift ticket; 165 SF for six-day pass.*

LIECHTENSTEIN

When you cross the border from Switzerland into the principality of Liechtenstein, you will see license plates marked "FL": this stands for Fürstentum Liechtenstein (Principality of Liechtenstein). You are leaving the world's oldest democracy and entering a monarchy that is the last remnant of the Holy Roman Empire—all 160 square km (59 square miles) of it. If you don't put the brakes on, you'll wind up in Austria.

Made up of 11 communes called *gemeinden,* this pint-sized principality was created at the end of the 17th century, when a wealthy Austrian prince, Johann Adam von Liechtenstein, bought out two bankrupt counts in the Rhine Valley and united their lands. In 1719 he obtained an imperial deed from Emperor Karl VI, creating the principality of Liechtenstein. The noble family poured generations of wealth into the new country, improving its standard of living, and in 1862 an heir, Prince Johann the Good, helped Liechtenstein introduce its first constitution as a "democratic monarchy" in which the people and the prince share power equally. Today the principality's 37,000 citizens enjoy one of the world's highest per-capita incomes—prosperous (though discreet) local industries range from making jam to molding false teeth—and pay virtually no taxes.

It's hard to not be curious about this little vestige of royalty, but you may find yourself disappointed in the rather sterile capital city of Vaduz. Its one must-see attraction is the bold and beautiful contemporary art museum, housed in a dazzling black terrazzo box and filled with works by lesser-known contemporary greats like Bill Bollinger and Günter Fruhtrunk. You won't be alone, as the streets are packed with package tourists climbing out of tour buses. Quite a few of the newcomers are from Asia, particularly China, and many of Vaduz's restaurants now offer overpriced sweet-and-sour chicken and other dishes.

Outside the capital you'll find some attractive views, including vineyards climbing up the hillsides. Hiking trails and ski slopes provide ample opportunity to glance, perhaps longingly, back at Switzerland.

Vaduz Castle is home to the reigning prince of Liechtenstein.

VADUZ

31 km (18 miles) southeast of Appenzell, 159 km (98 miles) southeast of Schaffhausen.

The best reason to go to Vaduz? To get a stamp from Liechtenstein in your passport. Vaduz is an experience unto itself—which makes sense since it's in another country. In what is possibly the world's smallest capital, almost all the attractions are on the same street, with the exception of Vaduz Castle, where the prince of Liechtenstein still lives.

GETTING HERE AND AROUND

From Zürich, take the A1 expressway to Sargans, then change to the A13 heading north and take the Vaduz exit. From St. Gallen, follow the A1 northeast to the Bodensee, where it changes into the A13. Follow this south approximately 50 km (31 miles) to the Vaduz exit.

There are no direct trains to Vaduz, Liechtenstein's capital city; you have to stop on the Swiss side of the Rhine and take a bus across the river. From St. Gallen via Buchs, by train and bus, the trip takes 75 minutes. If you're traveling from Zürich, take the 55-minute train to Sargans, where a connecting bus takes you to Vaduz (travel time approximately 80 minutes).

VISITOR INFORMATION

You can have your passport stamped for 3 SF at the tourist office's hard-to-miss Liechtenstein Center.

Contacts Liechtenstein Center. ✉ *Städtle 39, Vaduz* ☎ *423/2396363* 🌐 *www.tourismus.li.*

EXPLORING

Fodor's Choice ★ **Kunstmuseum Liechtenstein** (*Liechtenstein Museum of Art*). The gorgeous black box that is the Kunstmuseum Liechtenstein offers frequently changing exhibitions of modern art. Don't come expecting Old Dutch Masters, because this collection embraces Peter Fischli & David Weiss, Andy Warhol, and Donald Judd, as well as lesser-known rising stars like Bill Bollinger and Günter Fruhtrunk. The casual café is one of Vaduz's cooler spots, a great place to relax with a volume from the well-curated bookshop. ✉ *Städtle 32, Vaduz* ☎ *423/2350300* 🌐 *www.kunstmuseum.li* 🎫 *15 SF* ⏲ *Closed Mon.*

Liechtensteinisches Landesmuseum (*National Museum*). Housed in a former tavern and customhouse, the Liechtensteinisches Landesmuseum includes a modern annex built into the cliff. The collection covers the geology, history, and folklore of the principality. ✉ *Städtle 43, Vaduz* ☎ *423/2396820* 🌐 *www.landesmuseum.li* 🎫 *10 SF* ⏲ *Closed Mon.*

Postmuseum. Liechtenstein's postage-stamp-sized postal museum demonstrates the principality's history as a maker of beautifully designed, limited-edition postage stamps. ✉ *Städtle 37, Vaduz* ☎ *423/2366846* 🌐 *www.landesmuseum.li/postmuseum* 🎫 *Free.*

Vaduz Castle. At the top of a well-marked hill road (you can climb the forest footpath between Restaurant Ratskeller and Café Burg) stands Vaduz Castle. Here, His Serene Highness Hans-Adam II, prince of Liechtenstein, reigns in a romantic fortress-home with red-and-white medieval shutters, massive ramparts, and a broad perspective over the Rhine Valley. Originally built in the 12th century, the castle was burned down by troops of the Swiss Confederation in the Swabian Wars of 1499 and partly rebuilt during the centuries that followed. A complete overhaul that started in 1905 gave it its present form. It is not open to the public, as Hans-Adam II enjoys his privacy. He is the son of the late beloved Franz Josef II, who died in November 1989 after a more than 50-year reign. Franz Josef's birthday, August 15, is still celebrated as the Liechtenstein national holiday. Heir to the throne Prince Alois increasingly has taken over daily business while Hans-Adam II travels to Vienna several times a year, where the family museum is one of the city's finest cultural jewels. ✉ *Vaduz.*

WHERE TO EAT

$$ SWISS Fodor's Choice ★ ✕ **Wirtschaft zum Löwen.** Though there's plenty of French, Swiss, and Austrian influence, Liechtenstein has a cuisine of its own, and this is the place to try it. In a wood-shingle landmark farmhouse on the Austrian border, the friendly Biedermann family serves tender homemade *Schwartenmagen* (the pressed-pork mold unfortunately known as headcheese in English), tripe in white wine, lovely meats, and the local crusty, chewy bread. **Known for:** fresh regional ingredients; cheese dumplings with sour cheese; steaks. $ *Average main: 33 SF* ✉ *Im Winkel 5, Schellenberg* ✥ *10 km (6 miles) north of Vaduz off Rte. 16. Also accessible by bus; the restaurant is about 100 yds from the Hinterschellenberg stop* ☎ *423/3731162* 🌐 *www.loewen.li* ⏲ *Closed Wed., Thurs., and 3 wks in Aug.*

3

WHERE TO STAY

$$$ HOTEL **Park Hotel Sonnenhof.** With pleasant views of the valley below and mountains beyond, this hillside retreat offers a leafy respite from the crowds. **Pros:** views of the valley; peace and quiet; excellent service. **Cons:** stuffy decor; a hike from town; open balconies offer little privacy. *Rooms from: 395 SF* *Mareestr. 29, Vaduz* *423/2390202* *www.sonnenhof.li* *Closed late Dec.–early Jan.* *29 rooms* *Breakfast.*

$$$ HOTEL **Residence Hotel.** At Residence, rice-paper screens and down duvets mingle in a simple Japanese-European style. **Pros:** 21st-century design with modern conveniences; centrally located; excellent service and restaurant. **Cons:** a little sleek for the Holy Roman Empire experience; the reception desk is hidden away upstairs; rooms facing street can be noisy. *Rooms from: 330 SF* *Städtle 23, Vaduz* *423/2392020* *www.residence.li* *29 rooms* *Breakfast.*

SPORTS AND THE OUTDOORS

BIKING

Bike Garage. In Triesen, about 4 km (2½ miles) south of Vaduz, bikes can be rented from Bike Garage. *Landstr. 1, Triesenberg* *423/3900390* *www.bikegarage.li* *Closed Sun. and Mon.*

Liechtenstein Center. The tourist office has e-bikes for rent. They can exchange batteries for e-bikes as well. Reservations can be made by phone or through the website via email. *Staedlte 39, Vaduz* *423/2396363* *www.tourismus.li.*

SHOPPING

Liechtenstein is sometimes called the unofficial, per-capita world champion of stamp collecting. To buy some of its famous stamps, whether to send a postcard to a philatelist friend or to invest in limited-issue commemorative sheets, you must line up with the tour-bus crowds at the popular post office on the Städtle. A sharp crumbly cheese called Liechtensteiner Käseräss can be found while visiting its agriculture commune Ruggell, and wines like Chardonnay, Riesling, and Gewürztraminer are an ideal souvenir upgrade from postage stamps. The country's Hofkellerei "Princely Cellars" in Vaduz is a great place to sample some local varietals. There's also an excellent beer brewery in the commune of Schaan, and the brewmeister is happy to arrange tours in English or offer flights of their flavorful ales and pilsners.

Der Hofladen vom Bangshof. If you're looking for the real-deal Liechtenstein cheese, this farm shop in Ruggell is the best place to buy it. You can also get homemade jams, sausages, and pastas, as well as products from other area farms. Their beautifully packaged gift baskets make a fantastic souvenir. The farm store is a 16-minute drive (or a 37-minute bus ride) from Vaduz. *Fallagass 41* *423/3734930* *www.bangshof.li/hofladen.*

Hofkellerei des Fürsten von Liechtenstein. For the finest local wines bottled by the royal family themselves, head to the Hofkellerei just outside of Vaduz and try a Pinot Noir or Chardonnay. Other varietals, including Riesling and Merlot, are offered here, too, but they come from a winery in Austria, which also belongs to the royal family. If you'd like your wine to accompany a fine meal, the property also has a restaurant, Torkel, in a medieval building with a beautiful terrace overlooking the Herawingert vineyards. ✉ *Fürstliche Domaene, Feldstr. 4, Vaduz* ☎ *423/2321018* 🌐 *www.hofkellerei.at.*

Philatelie Liechtenstein. This shop, in Schaan, is the best place to buy stamps in Liechtenstein. It's a 9-minute drive from Vaduz (or a 13-minute bus ride). ✉ *Zollstr. 58* ☎ *423/3994466* 🌐 *www.philatelie.li.*

Schaedler Keramik. Though shops on the main street of Vaduz carry samples of the local dark-glaze pottery painted with folksy flowers and figures, the central source is 8 km (5 miles) north of Vaduz at Schaedler Keramik. Simple household pottery as well as traditional and often ornate hand-painted pieces are available for sale. Pottery making is demonstrated here, but it's open only on weekdays. ✉ *Churerstr. 60, Nendeln* ☎ *423/3731414* 🌐 *www.schaedler-keramik.com.*

GRAUBÜNDEN

WELCOME TO GRAUBÜNDEN

TOP REASONS TO GO

★ **Chic, chicer, chicest:** From Arosa to Pontresina, every mountain resort is a place to be seen by the ski elite. Sparkling St. Moritz, Davos, and Klosters are perfect for chilling out, but don't forget your Gucci sunglasses.

★ **Heidi's hideaway:** Shirley Temple immortalized the just-too-cute orphan, but find out just how much her 1937 film differed from Johanna Spyri's beloved book with a visit to Maienfeld's Heidi Village.

★ **Beautiful sgraffiti:** The Lower Inn Valley is home to some picture-perfect villages, famous for their folkloric dwellings graced with sgraffiti wall decorations. For the best close-ups, head to Guarda—so beautiful, it is under federal protection.

★ **Keeping body and soul together:** Palatial spa hotels and a landscape that inspired great painters and philosophers is what Graubünden is about.

Covering about 2,800 square miles, Graubünden is the largest canton in Switzerland, occupying more than one-sixth of the country. With high mountains nestling chic resorts like St. Moritz, Davos, and Klosters, the Grisons (to use the French name) offers as much attitude as altitude. Cross any of the passes southeast to the Engadine Valley for quaint sgraffiti-covered villages and more fresh air than you can imagine.

1 Heidiland. Everybody's favorite little Swiss miss lived here, and today the village of Maienfeld pays homage to the legendary character with a Heidi Village, Heidi Path, and Heidihof Hotel. To the south lies Chur, the capital of Graubünden—largely modern, it has, in fact, nearly 11,000 years of history exhibited in the local museums, churches, even the streets. Then strike southeast for Arosa, a high-altitude village perfect for those who find the winter elegance of St. Moritz just a trifle overbearing.

2 Prätigau and Davos. The fertile Prätigau Valley with its abundance of meadows, forests, and panoramic Alpine vistas is home to Klosters, an attractive, chaleted resort perfect for those seeking fantastic skiing in a quieter atmosphere. Lively, neighboring Davos—Europe's highest city—is as renowned for its winter sports as it is for hosting the World Economic Forum.

3 The Lower Engadine. Bustling Scuol has maintained its ancient feel despite modern amenities. Nature lovers will have all wishes fulfilled in the famed Swiss National Park, and art lovers will adore flower-boxed Guarda and the magnificent fortress at Tarasp, which seems lifted from the pages of a medieval illuminated manuscript.

4 The Upper Engadine and St. Moritz. Take New York luxury, Paris fashion, a bit of London and Milan, a drop of Munich, a handful of Rome, large swaths of premium ski slopes and crystalline lakes, then add a perfect "champagne climate" of crisp, dry air and plenty of sunshine, mix well, and pour onto a few acres in a gorgeous high-altitude valley. How can anything compare to St. Moritz?

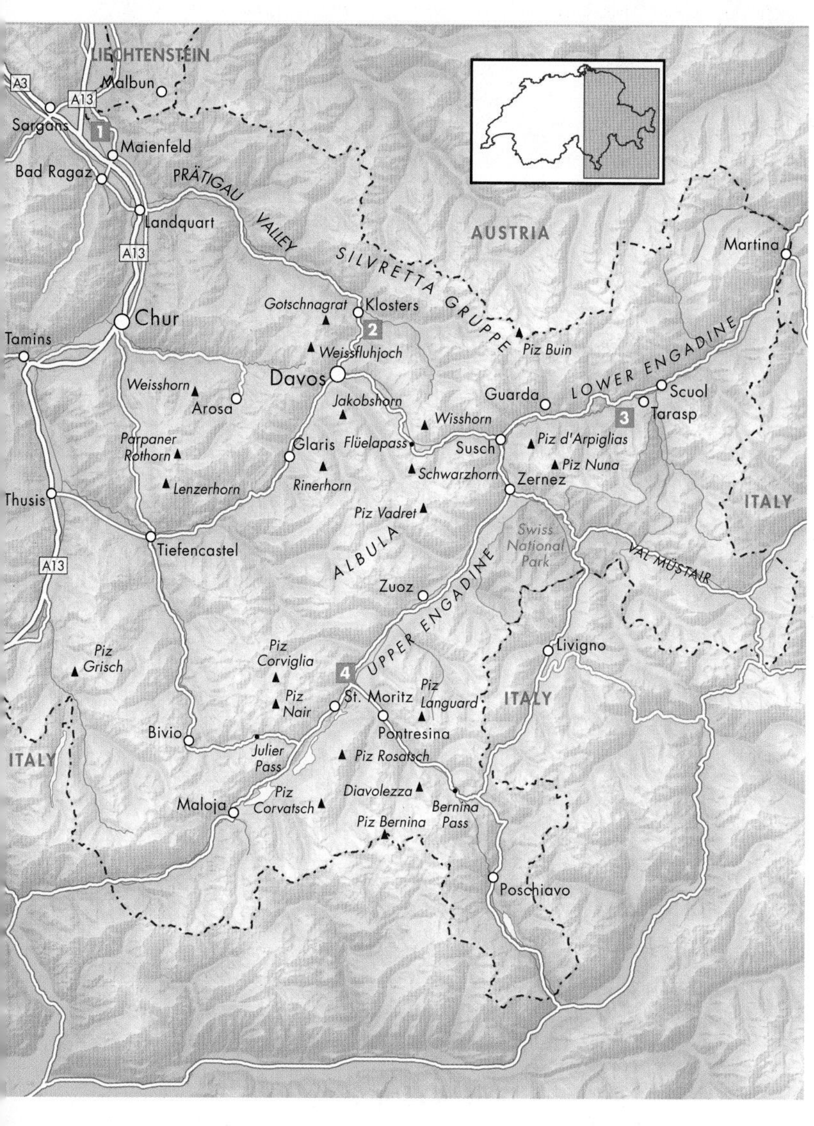
LIECHTENSTEIN
Malbun
A3
A13
Sargans
1
Maienfeld
Bad Ragaz
PRÄTIGAU VALLEY
Landquart
A13
AUSTRIA
SILVRETTA GRUPPE
Martina
Gotschnagrat
Klosters
Chur
2
Piz Buin
Tamins
Weissfluhjoch
LOWER ENGADINE
Davos
Weisshorn
Arosa
Guarda
Scuol
Jakobshorn
Tarasp
3
Wisshorn
Parpaner Rothorn
Glaris
Flüelapass
Susch
Piz d'Arpiglias
Piz Nuna
Schwarzhorn
Zernez
Thusis
Lenzerhorn
Rinerhorn
ITALY
Piz Vadret
Swiss National Park
Tiefencastel
ALBULA
VAL MÜSTAIR
A13
UPPER ENGADINE
Zuoz
Livigno
Piz Grisch
Piz Corviglia
4
Piz Languard
ITALY
Piz Nair
St. Moritz
Pontresina
Bivio
Julier Pass
ITALY
Piz Rosatsch
Diavolezza
Piz Corvatsch
Maloja
Bernina Pass
Piz Bernina
Poschiavo

4

Updated by
Liz Humphreys

Although the names of its biggest resorts, such as St. Moritz and Davos, register almost automatic recognition, the region wrapped around them remains surprisingly unsung, untouched by the fur-clad celebs who make stages out of its sports centers, aloof to the glamour trends—quirky, resilient, and decidedly set apart. Nowhere in Switzerland will you find a sharper contrast than the one between the bronzed seven-day citizens who jet into St. Moritz and the stalwart native farmers who nurse archaic dialects and gather their crops by hand, as their Roman-Etruscan ancestors did. Resort life in winter is quite different from everyday existence in Graubünden.

As it straddles the continental divide, its rains pour off northward into the Rhine River, eastward with the Inn River to the Danube River and Black Sea, and south to the River Po. The landscape here is thus riddled with bluff-lined valleys. The southern half basks in crystalline light and, if it weren't for the Italian-speaking Ticino, would receive the most sunshine in the country. Its 150 valleys and 615 lakes are flanked by 937 peaks, among them Piz Buin (10,867 feet) in the north and Piz Bernina (13,307 feet), the canton's highest mountain, in the south.

Like many Swiss cantons, Graubünden is culturally diverse. To the north it borders Austria and Liechtenstein, and in the east and south it abuts Italy. Swiss-German and Italian are widely spoken, and about one-sixth of the local residents speak Romansh, an ancient regional language. Even the name *Graubünden* itself comes in a variety of forms: Grisons (French), Grigioni (Italian), and Grischun (Romansh). It originates from the "Gray Confederation," one of three leagues that joined together in 1471 to resist the feudal Habsburg rulers. After a period as a "free state," Graubünden became a Swiss canton in 1803. With these dialects and their derivatives cutting one valley culture neatly off from another, it's no wonder the back roads of the region seem so removed from the modern mainstream.

GRAUBÜNDEN PLANNER

WHEN TO GO

Graubünden has essentially two climatic regions. In the lower Rhine Valley (Chur, Heidiland, and so on), there are normally four distinct seasons. Up in the Engadine, there are four seasons as well, but their distribution is heavily skewed toward winter. Snow can remain until May, and after a brief spring and summer, you may experience flurries or frozen dew in August. So even if you're traveling in summer, pack some warm clothing, like a sweater and a windbreaker.

PLANNING YOUR TIME

In Switzerland's largest canton, you can party with the in crowds at Davos or St. Moritz, chill out someplace remote like Guarda or Tarasp, or hit the highlights in between. Decide which towns or areas you most want to visit, and then pick one or two hubs. It is certainly possible to embark on a whirlwind tour of many different valleys, but if you want to really experience the unique local culture, feel, and food of Graubünden, then slow down and take your time to explore a place or two in more depth.

GETTING HERE AND AROUND

For more information on getting here and around, see Travel Smart Switzerland.

AIR TRAVEL

Engadine Airport is mainly used by private planes. At 5,600 feet, it's the highest airport in Europe. The closest international airports are Zürich (about 2 hours from Chur) and Lugano (about 2½ hours from St. Moritz).

BUS TRAVEL

You can take the Swiss postbus (postauto) system's Palm Express from Lugano in the Ticino to St. Moritz. The four-hour trip passes through a corner of Italy and over the Maloja Pass. Though owners of a Swiss Pass do not need to purchase an additional ticket, reservations are essential. Postbuses are a good way to wind your way up Alpine switchbacks over the region's great passes—that is, if you're not inclined toward motion sickness. The main ski resorts have "sport bus" shuttles, which connect the villages and mountain stations. The service is usually included in the price of your lift ticket or on presentation of a "guest card" (check to see if your hotel offers these discount booklets).

Contacts Palm Express. ☎ *058/3413492* 🌐 *www.postauto.ch/en/excursion-tips/palm-express.*

CAR TRAVEL

Unless you intend to explore every nook and cranny of Graubünden or some of the more remote valleys, you will not really need a car. In fact, a car might cost more time and irritation than simply using public transportation, although driving a convertible along the mountain roads can be a breathtaking, if pricey, experience.

Graubünden is mountainous, with few major highways. Drivers can enter either by way of the San Bernardino Pass from the south or from the north on A13, the region's only expressway, which follows a north–south route. Coming from Austria and Munich, the A27 leads into the Lower Engadine; roads over the Ofen and Bernina passes lead into the Engadine from the South Tyrol and Veltline areas of Italy respectively, and the approach to the Upper Engadine from Italy is over the Maloja Pass. The Oberalp and Lukmanier passes lead from Uri and Ticino respectively to the Surselva region to join A13.

If you're traveling in winter, make sure to check the status of the passes beforehand. Trains through the Vereina Tunnel shuttle cars between Klosters and Sagliains (Susch–Lavin). The tunnel has made the Lower Engadine quickly accessible during the winter, when the Flüela Pass is seldom open.

TRAIN TRAVEL

Thanks to the Swiss Railways (SBB/CFF/FFS) and the affiliated UNESCO World Heritage–status narrow-gauge Rhätische Bahn (the Rhaetian Railway, commonly referred to as the "Rhätibahn"), most destinations mentioned here are reachable by train, and Swiss postbuses stop in places where there is no train service.

The Bernina Express runs from Chur to St. Moritz via the Albula route and on to Italy past the spectacular Bernina peaks, lakes, and glaciers. The Engadine Star makes its way from Klosters to St. Moritz in a couple of hours. The glamorous Glacier Express, billed as "the slowest express in the world," connects St. Moritz with Zermatt via the Oberalp Pass, crossing 291 bridges during its 7½-hour journey. The train includes an antique burnished-wood dining car; you can book a table along with your reservation.

Reservations for these trains are mandatory and can be made at almost any European rail station. As on the federal railways, a variety of reduced-price passes are available.

Contacts Rhätische Bahn. ☎ *081/2886565* 🌐 *www.rhb.ch.*

HOTELS

Hoteliers in Graubünden invest fortunes in preserving Alpine coziness on both the outside and inside of their lodgings, which is not always the case in other parts of Switzerland. Therefore, prices in this popular region are comparatively high. Even higher prices are charged for the winter holiday period and in February, when most schools are on their winter breaks; during the rest of winter you may find special lower-priced packages that include ski passes. Summer rates are lower. Many hotels close between seasons, from April to mid-June and from mid-October to mid-December, but the dates and months vary each year, so be sure to check. In a few winter resorts there are hotels that stay closed all summer; we have not included these in our listings.

Hotels publish tariffs in various ways; double-check to see whether you're paying per person or per room, as well as whether you have

Halbpension (demipension, or half-board). If you plan to stay in one place for more than a day or two, half-board can cut costs. You may also want to ask about GästeKarte (guest cards), small booklets given by hotels that provide various deals on local transit or attractions. Many places are packed between Christmas and about January 15—so make reservations well in advance for this time. Keep in mind that all taxes are included in the price.

If you are interested only in sports, you may wish to budget less for hotels by staying in more out-of-the-way villages and commuting to the more expensive areas, such as St. Moritz and Pontresina.

RESTAURANTS

Thanks to all those tourists, restaurants tend to stay open throughout the day for the hungry visitor, especially in the winter season. The way to be sure is to look for a sign that bears the word *durchgehend*, meaning "without a stop." Some places, however, will serve only snacks—or close entirely—between 2:30 and 5:30. If you're traveling in the low season (November or April), you may encounter quite a few closed doors. Remember, the rugged mountainscape can be deceiving. Hikers and skiers will frequently encounter a cozy *Bergbeizli* ("mountain inn"), where fine locally grown food is served up in a most congenial atmosphere.

Many restaurants in resort towns close from the end of April to mid-June and October to December; there are variations and exceptions, of course, so if you plan a visit during the off-season, check in advance.

Hotel and restaurant reviews have been shortened. For full information, visit Fodors.com.

WHAT IT COSTS IN SWISS FRANCS

	$	$$	$$$	$$$$
Restaurants	Under 26 SF	26 SF–45 SF	46 SF–65 SF	Over 65 SF
Hotels	Under 201 SF	201 SF–300 SF	301 SF–500 SF	Over 500 SF

Restaurant prices are the average cost of a main course at dinner or, if dinner is not served, at lunch. Hotel prices are the lowest cost of a standard double room in high season, including taxes.

TOURS

Arosa, Davos, and Lenzerheide-Valbella offer special hiking packages. You can walk from Davos to Arosa one day and from Arosa to Lenzerheide the next.

The Arosa tourist office offers a variety of activities from June through October; you can visit a cheese maker, a regional museum, or a 15th-century chapel. The Davos and Klosters tourist office "active" daily program allows tourists to visit a brewery, tour the town, and take a guided walk from the end of June to October. The Chur tourist office arranges guided tours of the Old Town from April to October every Wednesday at 2 in

German only. To explore on your own, download the audio tour from the Chur tourist office site (🌐 *www.churtourismus.ch*) to your mobile phone.

The Pontresina tourist office offers free guided walking tours of its Old Town on Wednesday at 3:30 from early June to mid-October, and Wednesday at 2:15 from mid-December to early April. It also offers guided botanical excursions (mid-June to mid-October) and glacier treks (May to October), both free of charge.

Heidiland Tourist Office. The Heidiland Tourist Office offers culinary hiking and biking tours of the region, which include stops at restaurants. ✉ *Valenserstr. 6, Bad Ragaz* ☎ *081/7200820* 🌐 *www.heidiland.com/en* 🎫 *From 50 SF.*

Wine Tours Switzerland. This company leads wine tours through Heidiland and nearby. Packages include half-day or whole-day tours, and ones that focus on the food of the region and visiting Heidi's childhood home. English-language tours are available. ✉ *Postfach 48, Maienfeld* ☎ *078/7350042* 🌐 *www.wine-tours.ch* 🎫 *From 115 SF.*

VISITOR INFORMATION

Contacts Graubünden Holidays. ✉ *Alexanderstr. 24, Chur* ☎ *081/2542424* 🌐 *www.graubuenden.ch.*

HEIDILAND

The Maienfeld region, with its hills and craggy peaks sloping down to sheltered vineyards, is the gateway from the north into Graubünden, but its claim to fame is that the legendary Heidi lived here. To the west in Surselva, the villages of Flims, Laax, and Falera together form the Alpine Arena, Graubünden's largest connected ski area. Arosa, to the east in the Schanfigg Valley, is a quieter resort village that lies in a bowl at the end of a spectacular, steep, winding road. The transportation hub of the region is Chur, the district capital.

MAIENFELD

102 km (63 miles) southeast of Zürich, 50 km (32 miles) south of Appenzell.

Above this graceful little village full of fountains, vineyards, and old stucco houses, the Zürich author Johanna Spyri set *Heidi,* the much-loved children's story of an orphan growing up with her grandfather on an isolated Alpine farm. Taken away to accompany the invalid Clara in murky Frankfurt, she languishes until returning to her mountain home. Spyri spent time in Maienfeld and was inspired by the mountains, but it's unknown whether actual people inspired her tale.

EXPLORING

FAMILY **Heididorf** (*Heidi Village*). Fans of Heidi can visit the area that inspired the legend along the circular Heidi-Weg (Heidi Path). Here you can find the house that was used as a model for the illustrations in the original *Heidi* books. It now houses Heidi-appropriate furnishings and life-size models of Heidi, Grandfather, and Peter. You can also take a

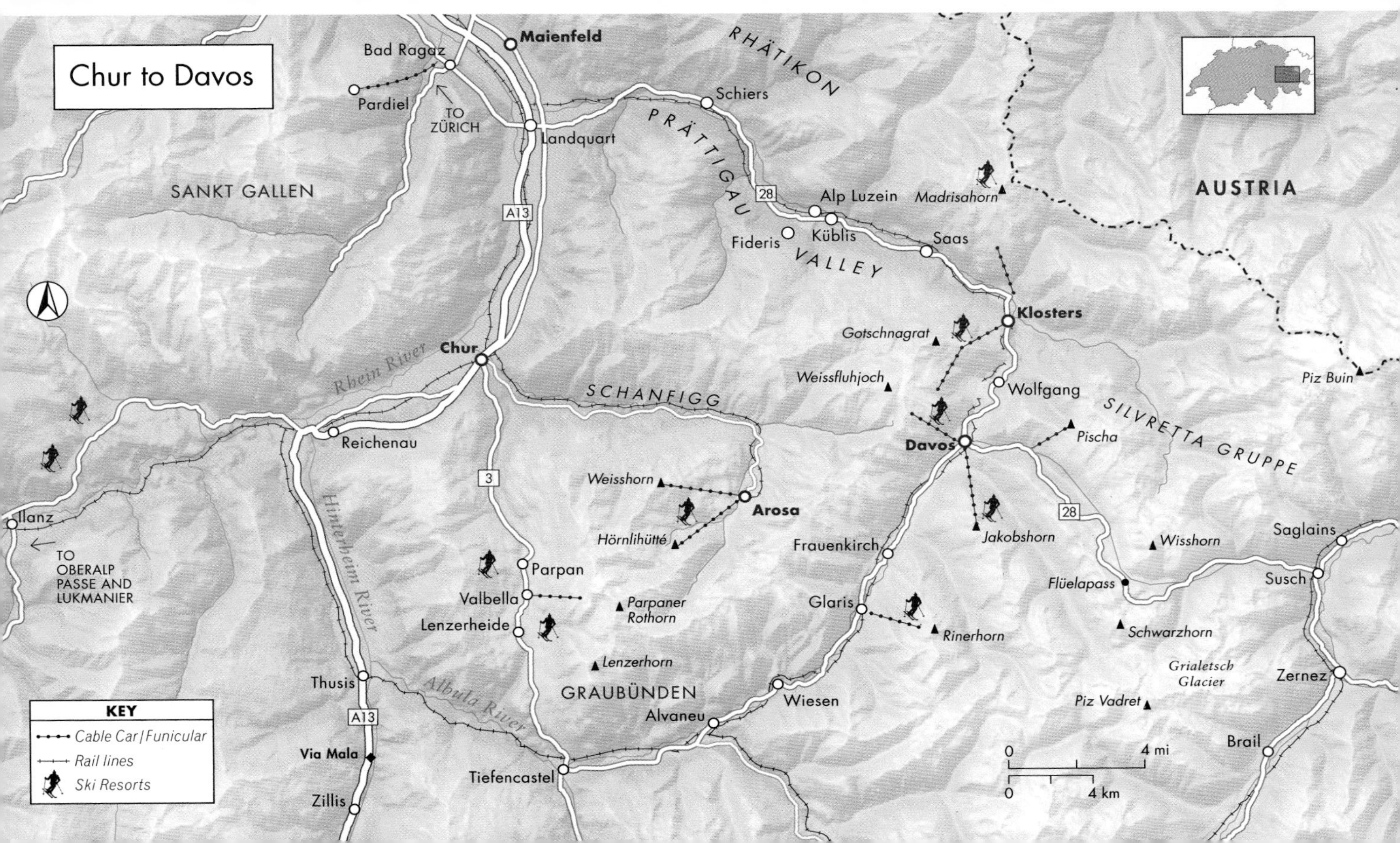

Chur to Davos
Bad Ragaz
Pardiel
TO ZÜRICH
Maienfeld
Landquart
RHÄTIKON
Schiers
PRÄTTIGAU
VALLEY
SANKT GALLEN
AUSTRIA
A13
28
Alp Luzein
Küblis
Fideris
Saas
Madrisahorn
Klosters
Gotschnagrat
Weissfluhjoch
Wolfgang
Piz Buin
SILVRETTA GRUPPE
Pischa
Davos
Chur
Rhein River
SCHANFIGG
Reichenau
3
Weisshorn
Arosa
Hörnlihütte
Jakobshorn
Frauenkirch
Wisshorn
Saglains
Susch
Flüelapass
Ilanz
TO OBERALP PASSE AND LUKMANIER
Hinterheim River
Parpan
Valbella
Lenzerheide
Parpaner Rothorn
Lenzerhorn
Glaris
Rinerhorn
Schwarzhorn
Grialetsch Glacier
Zernez
Thusis
Albula River
GRAUBÜNDEN
Wiesen
Alvaneu
Piz Vadret
Brail
KEY
Cable Car/Funicular
Rail lines
Ski Resorts
Via Mala
Tiefencastel
Zillis
0
4 mi
0
4 km

somewhat-challenging hike up to Heidi's Alp Hut, get a Heidi stamp at the Heidi post office, and meet Heidi and Peter's goats at the petting zoo. ✉ *Maienfeld* ☎ *081/3301912* 🌐 *www.heididorf.ch* 🎫 *13.90 SF for Heidi's House and Heidi's Alp Hut.*

FAMILY **Heidi-Weg** (*Heidi Path*). From Maienfeld you can hike along the Heidi-Weg (Heidi Path), either on the short circular route or, for more energetic hikers, continuing across steep open meadows and through thick forests to what now have been designated Peter the Goatherd's Hut, the Alm-Uncle's Hut, and Heidi's Alp Hut. The short version of the route begins at the train station and passes through the cobblestone alleyways of Maienfeld's Old Town. It continues up to the enclave of Rofels, where the Heididorf (Heidi Village) is situated. After passing through most of the attractions there, the trail leads back to Maienfeld through picturesque vineyards. You might meet today's versions of the characters, who can answer Heidi-related questions in English. Along the way you'll take in awe-inspiring Rhine Valley views from flowered meadows that would have suited Heidi beautifully. ✉ *Maienfeld.*

Fodor's Choice ★ **Schloss Salenegg.** The Castle Salenegg in Maienfeld presides regally over the oldest vineyards in the region—and some of the oldest in Europe. The privately owned castle and wine cellar, now a study in contrasts, have been inseparable since 1068. An intricately painted portal leads through the pristine, cyprus-lined grounds to the stone-clad, arched wine "Torkel" (old winepress). Despite the winery's history, there's nothing old-fashioned about the products—all wines are made from Blauburgunder (Pinot Noir) or Chardonnay—or the environmentally friendly ideas. Though registration is required for cellar tours, English-speaking wine tastings are available on a drop-in basis. ✉ *Steigstr. 21, Maienfeld* ☎ *081/3021151* 🌐 *www.schloss-salenegg.ch* ⊙ *Closed Sat. (except the 1st weekend of each month).*

WHERE TO EAT

$$$ SWISS Fodor's Choice ★ ✕ **Schloss Brandis.** The Knight's Hall of Schloss Brandis, a castle whose earliest portions date from the 10th century, is the atmospheric setting for its namesake restaurant, which serves up Maienfeld specialties along with local wine, including from its own vineyards. The beamed ceilings and candlelit tables create a romantic ambience worthy of the rich and satisfying fare: you'll always find chateaubriand, Maienfelder Riesling soup, house-made Grisons dumplings (with meat or vegetables), and local pike perch, along with seasonal specialties, including venison in the fall. **Known for:** charming historic setting; well-prepared local dishes; good choice of wines from the region. $ *Average main: 46 SF* ✉ *Maienfeld* ☎ *081/3022423* 🌐 *www.schlossbrandis.ch.*

$$ SWISS ✕ **Weinstube Alter Torkel.** This homey wine bar offers both simple and more elaborate gourmet meals, depending on your interest. Inside, the massive wooden winepress is the star; outside, it's the beautiful garden terrace with views of the surrounding vineyards. **Known for:** vineyard views; great wine selection; somewhat high prices. $ *Average main: 32 SF* ✉ *Jeninserstr. 3* ☎ *081/3023675* 🌐 *www.torkel.ch.*

The classic children's story of Heidi was set in the peaceful countryside around Maienfeld.

WHERE TO STAY

$ HOTEL **Heidihof Hotel.** At the kitsch-happy farmhouse that's been expanded to a small inn, you can have a snack and take in the view or spend the night. **Pros:** short walk to Heidi Village and hiking trails; fun setting for Heidi fans; peaceful location. **Cons:** very simple rooms; extra charge for breakfast; a bit pricey overall for what you get. *Rooms from: 124 SF* *Bovelweg 16, Maienfeld* *081/3004747* *www.heidihof.ch* *15 rooms* *No meals.*

$ B&B/INN Fodor's Choice ★ **Schlaf-Fass Riesling-Silvaner Maienfeld.** For a unique experience, you can sleep in an 8,000-liter wine barrel amid the vineyards below Heidi Village; there's a second location nearby in Jenins (Schlaf-Fass Blauburgunder Jenins). **Pros:** unique location; short walk to Heidi Village; tasty fondue dinner and hearty breakfast. **Cons:** no showers; toilets in the farmer's house; must book far in advance. *Rooms from: 180 SF* *Bündte 1, Maienfeld* *079/2800262* *www.schlaf-fass.ch* *2 rooms* *Breakfast.*

$ HOTEL **Swiss Heidi Hotel.** An easy-to-get-to location off the motorway and near the train station makes this a practical base for discovering the region or conducting business. **Pros:** ample, free parking; buffet breakfast included; rooms are clean and comfortable. **Cons:** 20-minute walk to town; no air-conditioning; no particular charm. *Rooms from: 175 SF* *Werkhofstr. 1, Maienfeld* *081/3038888* *www.swissheidihotel.ch* *81 rooms* *Breakfast.*

CLOSE UP

Romansh

The ancient Romansh (literally, "Roman") language is still predominant in the Lower Engadine and Surselva; roughly 20% of Graubünden residents can speak it. The language dates back to the 1st century BC, when the area was conquered by the Romans and became a province called Rhaetia Prima. An alternative view on this point says the tongue predates the Romans and originated as long ago as 600 BC, when an Etruscan prince named Rhaetus invaded the region.

Anyone versed in a Latin language can follow Romansh's simpler signs (*abitaziun da vacanzas*, for example, is a vacation apartment), but Romansh is difficult to pick up by ear. Nor do the Graubündners smooth the way: Rhaetian Romansh is fragmented into five dialects, which developed separately in formerly isolated valleys, so that depending on where you are, the word for *house* can be seen written on the facades of homes as *casa, chasa, chesa, tga/tgesa,* or *tgea.*

SPAS

Tamina Therme. Welcome to the ultimate spa and wellness location in Switzerland, featuring a breathtaking range of treatments and courses designed to relax and invigorate. There are the usual suspects like thermal baths, massages, skin care, saunas, and fitness classes, and for those who have been working or playing hard, their signature "haki" treatments, a combination of stretching and massage that can be done in or out of the water. Reservations for the bathing and sauna areas are not necessary, but are required for the treatments. All the facilities are in a luxurious, immaculately kept resort complex, with stunning mountain views, two hotels, seven restaurants, an 18-hole and a 9-hole golf course, and a casino. You can get a day ticket for the thermal baths, but there's an additional cost to use the saunas. ✉ *Hans Albrecht Str., Bad Ragaz* ☎ *081/3033030* 🌐 *www.taminatherme.ch/en.*

CHUR

17 km (11 miles) south of Maienfeld.

Narrow streets, cobblestone alleys, hidden courtyards, and ancient shuttered buildings hint that this Alpine city is the oldest city in Switzerland. The biggest little town in Switzerland is the capital of Graubünden and a contemporary transportation hub, in keeping with its Middle Ages past as a trading route to the south. Discoveries of Stone Age tools place Chur's origins back to roughly 11,000 BC. The Romans founded Curia Raetorium on the rocky terrace south of the river; from here, they protected the Alpine routes that led to Lake Constance. By AD 284 the town served as the capital of a flourishing Roman colony, Rhaetia Prima. Its heyday was during the Middle Ages, when it was ruled by bishops and bishop-princes. Today, many of the hotels have been upgraded in Alpine-chic style and offer great value.

GETTING HERE AND AROUND

The Swiss Federal Railway trains that enter Graubünden travel only as far as Chur. From here the local Rhätische Bahn (RhB) takes over. Frequent trains arrive in Chur from Zürich (1¼ hours away), Klosters (1 hour), Davos (1½ hours), and Liechtenstein (1 hour).

VISITOR INFORMATION

Contacts Chur Tourism Office. ✉ *Bahnhofpl. 3, Chur* ☎ *081/2521818* 🌐 *www.churtourismus.ch.*

EXPLORING

TOP ATTRACTIONS

Fodor's Choice ★ **Bündner Kunstmuseum Chur.** Graubünden's art museum reopened in 2016 with a striking, ultramodern extension where newer works and rotating exhibitions are shown; the majestic neoclassical Villa Planta building, erected in 1875 as a private residence, houses the core of the museum's collection. It includes works by well-known artists who lived or worked in the canton, including Angelika Kauffmann; Ferdinand Hodler; Giovanni Segantini; Ernst Kirchner; H. R. Giger; and Giovanni, Augusto, and Alberto Giacometti. ✉ *Bahnhofstr. 35, Chur* ☎ *081/2572870* 🌐 *www.buendner-kunstmuseum.ch* 🎫 *15 SF* ⊙ *Closed Mon.*

Hof-Torturm (*Citadel Gate Tower*). Opposite the Rätisches Museum, a stone archway under this tower leads into the court of the strong bishop-princes of Chur, once hosts to Holy Roman emperors—sometimes with whole armies in tow—passing through on their way to Italy or Germany. The bishops were repaid for their hospitality by imperial donations to the people. The thick fortifications of the residence aren't for show: they reflect the tendency of inhabitants to dispute the bishops' powers. By the 15th century those who rebelled could be punished with excommunication. ✉ *Hofstr. 1, Chur* ☎ *081/2523230.*

Obere Gasse. Once the main street through Chur and a major route between Germany and Italy, Obere Gasse is now lined with small shops and cafés. At the end stands the 16th-century Obertor (Upper Gate), guarding the bridge across the Plessur River. ✉ *Old Town, between the Obertor and Arcaspl., Chur.*

FAMILY **Rätisches Museum.** Displayed in a 1675 mansion, this collection provides a thorough, evocative overview of the canton's development. It includes not only furnishings and goods from that period, but also archaeological finds from the region, both Roman and prehistoric. Display texts are in German, but an English-language guidebook is available for purchase. There are also exhibitions of special interest on display most of the time. ✉ *Hofstr. 1, Chur* ☎ *081/2574840* 🌐 *www.raetischesmuseum.gr.ch* 🎫 *6 SF* ⊙ *Closed Mon.*

WORTH NOTING

Kathedrale St. Maria Himmelfahrt. The Cathedral of the Assumption was built between 1151 and 1272, drawing on stylistic influences from all across Europe. On this same site have stood a Roman castle, a bishop's house in the 5th century, and a Carolingian cathedral in the 8th century. Inside, the capitals of the columns are carved with fantastical beasts; clustered at their bases are less threatening animals, such as sheep and marmots. In the choir is a magnificent late-15th-century

A hike through Heidiland offers rewarding views of steep meadows and dense forests.

altar of gilded wood with nearly 150 carved figures created by Jakob Russ from Ravensburg, Germany. ✉ *Hofstr. 14, Chur* ☎ *081/2522076* 🌐 *www.kathkgchur.ch.*

Kirche St. Martin. St. Martin's was rebuilt in 1491 after a fire destroyed the 8th-century original. Since 1526 it has been Protestant. On your right as you enter are three stained-glass windows created in 1919 by Augusto Giacometti, the father of the Graubünden sculptor Alberto Giacometti. The steeple dates from 1917; with permission from the sacristan, you can climb to the top to see the bells. Of note, too, is the 1716 fountain beside the church, whose basin features the signs of the zodiac (the figure on top is a replica of the original). ✉ *Evangel. Kirchgemeinde, Kirchg. 12, Chur* ☎ *081/2522292* 🌐 *www.chur-reformiert.ch.*

Rathaus. Chur's Town Hall was built as two structures in 1464, which were connected in 1540. At ground level, under the arches, is the old marketplace. In the open hall on the second floor is a model of the Old Town, which can help you plan a tour of the city. The Grosser Ratsaal (Council Chamber) has a timber ceiling dating from 1493; the Bürgerratskammer (Citizens' Council Chamber) has wall panels from the Renaissance. Both chambers have old ceramic stoves, with the one in the Ratsaal depicting the seven deadly sins. Embedded in the wall beside the door on Reichsgasse 64 is a rod of iron about a foot long—the standard measure of a foot or shoe before the metric system was introduced. Although both chambers are generally closed to the public, very small groups can contact the tourist office to arrange a visit. ✉ *Poststr. 33, Chur* 🕓 *Closed weekends.*

OFF THE BEATEN PATH

Via Mala and St. Martin Zillis. Heading south toward the San Bernardino pass on the A13, turn off at Thusis and follow the sign for the Via Mala. This "bad road" was used by Romans and traders over centuries. It runs about 6 km (3½ miles) alongside the narrow Hinterrhein gorge. Shortly after the start of the gorge, climb down 359 steps to view the river, rock formations, a mid-18th-century bridge, and the old road itself. Continue to Zillis (*Postpl., www.zillis-st-martin.ch*) to see the St. Martin church's renowned 12th-century painted wood ceiling, whose 153 panels mostly depict stories from the Bible. It is one of the world's oldest original artistic works from the Romanesque era. *Chur 081/6509030 www.viamala.ch Gorge 6 SF; Church of St. Martin Zillis 5 SF Gorge closed Nov.–Mar.*

WHERE TO EAT

It may not be Vienna or Budapest, but Chur celebrates the pre-Starbucks coffee culture, taking the time to relax over a cup of coffee and something sweet. Coffee shops are sprinkled throughout the city, most with a delicious assortment of homemade cakes, pastries, and ice cream. All of the cafés offer seasonal light lunches.

$ ECLECTIC

Calanda. Young and old meet in this friendly, trendy place with a great big mural featuring the restaurant's specialty: chicken. The special dishes change daily, and the popular lunchtime menu and Sunday brunch are reasonably priced. **Known for:** Swiss free-range chicken; cherry cordon bleu, with cheese, cherry tomatoes, and bacon; a large beer selection. *Average main: 25 SF Postpl., Chur 081/2530880 www.calanda-chur.ch.*

$$$$ CONTEMPORARY

Schauenstein Schloss Restaurant Hotel. For one of Graubünden's—if not Switzerland's—top food experiences, make a beeline to world-renowned chef Andreas Caminada's tasting-menu-only restaurant, within a charming castle in the mountain town of Fürstenau. Diners can choose from three- to six-course menus at lunch and dinner, with two optional "surprise" dishes, all featuring seasonal, local ingredients presented in beautiful and imaginative ways. **Known for:** elaborate tasting menus; relaxed and friendly atmosphere; somewhat remote though charming location. *Average main: 230 SF Schlossg. 77, Chur 081/6321080 www.schauenstein.ch Closed Mon. and Tues. No lunch Wed.*

WHERE TO STAY

$$ HOTEL

Hotel ABC. Just yards from the train station, you can enjoy the convenience of a central location at this boutique hotel without worrying about getting a good night's rest, as there are no night trains. **Pros:** great for catching a morning train; free business center; modern rooms with hardwood floors and granite bathrooms. **Cons:** hotel has no restaurant; somewhat sterile feel; not right in the center of the Old Town. *Rooms from: 225 SF Ottostr. 8, off Bahnhofpl., Chur 081/2541313 www.hotelabc.ch 54 rooms Breakfast.*

$$ HOTEL Fodor's Choice ★

Romantik Hotel Stern. Like many of the good vintages on the wine list of its notable restaurant, this historic inn, built in 1677, just keeps getting better. **Pros:** intimate ambience; renowned restaurant, with seasonal dishes; welcoming hosts. **Cons:** church bells can be a little too close for comfort during the day; some rooms are smaller than average; some interiors could do with a makeover. *Rooms from: 220 SF Reichsg. 11, Chur 081/2585757 www.stern-chur.ch 65 rooms Breakfast.*

NIGHTLIFE

Giger Bar. The futuristic Giger Bar is a strange space created by Academy Award winner H. R. Giger, a Chur native who designed the monsters and sets for the film *Alien.* ✉ *Comercialstr. 23, Chur* ☎ *081/2537506* 🌐 *www.hrgiger.com/barchur.*

SPAS

7132 Therme & Spa Vals. Designed by Swiss architect Peter Zumthor, the 7132 Therme is built from local Valser gneiss stone into the side of a mountain in a remote Graubünden valley. Focusing on the serene, primal experience of bathing, the therapies and treatments offered are designed to relieve tension and pamper; think masks, exfoliation, baths, wraps, and massages. Seven different pools in a range of temperatures are available, including an exclusive sound bath resonance room linking the rejuvenating powers of water and sound. The special water shiatsu massage combines the positive elements of water therapy with the advantageous properties of shiatsu; while floating weightlessly in warm water, your body will experience reflexive lengthening and stretching, inducing deep relaxation. The on-site hotel has been completely revamped in a luxurious style, and includes rooms designed by renowned architects—though a night's stay may break the bank. ✉ *Vals* ✣ *51 km (31½ miles) southwest of Chur* ☎ *058/7132010 baths, 058/7132011 spa treatment reservations* 🌐 *7132therme.com.*

AROSA

29 km (18 miles) southeast of Chur.

Thanks to its altitude of 5,900 feet, the picturesque village of Arosa is a well-known year-round sports center, offering brisk hiking, paragliding, and other activities in summer, and a long skiing or snowboarding season with a guarantee of snow. Its modest size, isolated location, quiet atmosphere, and natural beauty set it apart. There is little of the rush of Davos or the pretension of St. Moritz: this is a friendly, family-oriented spot staffed by upbeat, down-to-earth people. On a winter walk you are more likely to be overtaken by sleds and horse-drawn carriages than by cars.

The town has two sections. Inner-Arosa, where the Walsers (immigrants from the Valais) built their wooden chalets in the 14th century, is at the end of the valley. Ausser-Arosa is near the train station and the Obersee (Upper Lake). Between the two is the impossible-to-miss casino, with its mosaic facade of screaming colors (it has been converted into a theater-cinema). A convenient free bus shuttles through the town, and traffic is forbidden between midnight and 6 am. After you deliver your luggage to your hotel, you probably won't be using your car again while in town.

GETTING HERE AND AROUND

Arosa lies at the end of a beautiful, winding 29-km (19-mile) road with grades of more than 12% and more than 360 turns. Taking the train from Chur is a lot less nerve-racking than driving. The Rhätische Bahn (RhB) has frequent departures to and from Arosa. Within town, you can ride the municipal buses for free if you have the Arosa Card, which is available in the summer. At that time, the card is included in all overnight stays. **TIP→ The Arosa Card (free for overnight guests; 18 SF for day-trippers) gives summer visitors access to many attractions, as well as round-trip rides on the Rhätische Bahn railway between Arosa and Luen-Castiel and trips on local mountain lifts and railways, which is great for hikers.**

VISITOR INFORMATION

Contacts Arosa Tourism Office. ✉ *Sport- und Kongresszentrum Arosa, Arosa* ☎ *081/3787020* 🌐 *www.arosa.ch.*

4

EXPLORING

Schanfigger Heimatmuseum (*Local History Museum*). This museum is in one of the oldest and best-kept buildings from Arosa's past—it was first mentioned in a 1550 document. Besides exhibiting the tools of the mountain farmer's difficult trade, this little museum has put together a slide show on local history. The museum building, a mid-16th-century wooden farmhouse also known as the Eggahaus, is a sight in itself. ✉ *Poststr., Arosa* ☎ *081/3771731* 🌐 *www.arosa-museum.ch* *3 SF; free with Arosa Card in summer* ⏲ *Mid-June–mid-Oct., closed Tues., Thurs., Sat., and Sun.; late Dec.–mid-Apr., closed Mon., Wed., Thurs., Sat., and Sun.*

WHERE TO EAT

$$$$ SWISS Fodor's Choice ★

La Vetta. The traditional atmosphere (flowered wallpaper, beamed ceilings, red-and-gold chairs) at the Tschuggen Grand Hotel's centerpiece Michelin-starred restaurant gives no hint about the ultramodern and imaginative dishes deftly prepared by the kitchen. Mainly Swiss ingredients, along with a smattering of Asian flavors, are combined and presented in unexpected ways; for instance, even a simple-sounding farmer's salad includes olive oil ice cream. **Known for:** elegant setting; creative cuisine; extensive wine selection. *$ Average main: 102 SF* ✉ *Tschuggen Grand Hotel, Sonnenbergstr., Arosa* ☎ *081/3789999* 🌐 *tschuggen.ch/en/restaurants/la-vetta* ⏲ *Closed Mon. and Tues., early Apr.–early July, and late Sept.–late Nov. No lunch.*

$$ FRENCH

Le Bistro. The decor fits the name, with a tile floor, old French posters, dried flower bouquets hanging from the ceiling, and newspaper cuttings on the walls. The menu leans French, with fillet of French Charolais beef or sirloin steak from Limousin beef, but there is relatively lighter fare, including such fish creations as Scottish salmon smoked on-site. **Known for:** an elegant setting; good choice of beef, fish, and vegetarian dishes; extensive wine list. *$ Average main: 45 SF* ✉ *Hotel Cristallo, Poststr., Arosa* ☎ *081/3786868* 🌐 *www.cristalloarosa.ch/Restaurant/Le-Bistro/* ⏲ *Closed early Apr.–late June and late Sept.–early Dec.*

WHERE TO STAY

$$$$ HOTEL Fodor's Choice ★

Arosa Kulm Hotel & Alpin Spa. What was once a 19th-century wooden chalet has expanded to become a full-fledged "Alpine lifestyle" destination, and its position on the farthest edge of town, at the base of the slopes, is its biggest draw. **Pros:** cheaper rates in summer; perfect location for views and skiing (ski-in, ski-out); spa packages for a mind, body, and soul revamp. **Cons:** shopping opportunities not as classy as this hotel merits; expensive on-site restaurants; rooms could use a bit of a refresh. *Rooms from: 540 SF* *Innere Poststr., Arosa* *081/3788888* *www.arosakulm.ch* *Closed mid-Sept.–Nov. and early Apr.–June* *119 rooms* *Breakfast.*

$$ HOTEL **Hotel Alpensonne.** About 200 yards from the ski lifts of Inner-Arosa, this family-owned and family-run hotel is perfect for those seeking a homey feel that is clean and comfortable. **Pros:** stunning views; accommodating hosts; close to village and ski slopes. **Cons:** some room interiors and balcony furniture need an upgrade; situated on main road through village; busy during the day, but traffic is forbidden at night. *Rooms from: 290 SF* *Poststr., Arosa* *081/3771547* *www.hotel-alpensonne.ch* *Closed late Apr.–late June and mid-Oct.–Nov.* *30 rooms* *Breakfast.*

$$$ HOTEL FAMILY **Hotel Astoria.** Genuine, warmhearted service is the key to this small, traditional house that offers great value. **Pros:** huge breakfast buffet and dinner included in room price; lovely spa area; children's playroom. **Cons:** a steep walk there; no bathrobes in the room; limited parking, so must reserve in advance. *Rooms from: 318 SF* *Alteinstr., Arosa* *81/3787272* *www.astoria-arosa.ch* *34 rooms* *Breakfast.*

$$ HOTEL **Hotel Vetter.** About 20 yards from the Weisshorn cable car and the Tschuggen chairlift, the Hotel Vetter makes a perfect overnight stop for skiers and hikers, and rewards guests with superior lake views from some rooms. **Pros:** excellent and popular restaurant; great location for skiing; convenient walk from the train station. **Cons:** breakfast buffet is basic; rooms are on the small side; lower-floor rooms don't have great views. *Rooms from: 300 SF* *Seeblickstr., Arosa* *081/3788000* *www.arosa-vetter-hotel.ch* *Closed Easter–June* *28 rooms* *Breakfast.*

$$ HOTEL **Sonnenhalde.** The sensor-touch heavy pine door that welcomes you to this *garni* (without a restaurant) chalet-hotel is your first sign of the happy marriage between charm and modern comfort here, followed by the welcoming family and small staff offering energetic and reliable service in a cozy space. **Pros:** proximity to ski lifts and village; cheaper rates during the low and summer seasons; friendly atmosphere. **Cons:** more gourmet dining requires venturing out; surcharge if guests don't stay at least three nights; extra fee to use the sauna. *Rooms from: 236 SF* *Sonnenbergstr., Arosa* *081/3784444* *sonnenhalde-arosa.ch* *Closed mid-Apr.–late June; mid-Oct.–Nov., closed Mon.–Thurs.* *25 rooms* *Breakfast.*

$$$$ HOTEL Fodor's Choice ★ **Tschuggen Grand Hotel.** Luxury seekers looking for a friendly vibe are in seventh heaven as they step into the welcoming environs of this mountainside hotel, which offers impressive amenities such as a wonderful spa and direct access to the ski slopes. **Pros:** well-regarded spa; private mountain railway delivering guests to the heart of the ski area; wonderful restaurants. **Cons:** colorful, eclectic decor not to everyone's taste; rates can be expensive; service, although friendly, can be distracted. *Rooms from: 625 SF* *Sonnenbergstr., Arosa* *081/3789999* *tschuggen.ch* *Closed early Apr.–late June and mid-Sept.–early Dec.* *130 rooms* *Breakfast.*

Designed by Swiss architect Mario Botta, the sail-shaped skylights of Tschuggen Grand Hotel's Bergoase spa are a colorful beacon against Arosa's snowy backdrop.

$$$ **HOTEL** **Valsana Hotel and Appartements.** The luxe Tschuggen Grand Hotel's hip little sister has ultra-contemporary rooms of wood, stone, and glass, complete with cool touches like record players and complimentary minibars. **Pros:** first cool boutique hotel in Arosa; all rooms have balconies; gym open 24 hours, rare for Switzerland. **Cons:** some bathrooms on the small side; only one restaurant; no Jacuzzi in the spa. *Rooms from: 400 SF ✉ Oberseepromenade 2, Arosa ☎ 081/3786363 🌐 valsana.ch ⏲ Closed early Apr.–mid-June and mid-Sept.–early Dec. 49 rooms 🍽 Breakfast.*

NIGHTLIFE AND PERFORMING ARTS

BARS

Lindemann's Overtime Bar and Lounge. Tourists and locals alike gather to have a beer or special cocktail and watch that night's hockey games. In summer, sip a drink on the terrace lounge and enjoy the view of the lake. DJs spin on the weekends. *✉ Am Postpl., Arosa ☎ 081/3775555 🌐 www.overtimearosa.ch.*

LOS Café Bar. If you're looking to play a lively game of foosball or rock the weekend away with a live band or DJ, head to LOS Café Bar, a chill snowboarders' hangout where locals and tourists mix 'n' mingle. *✉ Haus Madrisa, Arosa ☎ 081/3565610 🌐 www.losbar.ch.*

Strumpf Bar. Located in the Arosa Vetter Hotel, this popular après-ski bar (open Dec.–Mar.) turns into a smokers' lounge at night and serves a selection of rum, whiskey, and cigars from around the world. *✉ Seeblickstr., Arosa ☎ 081/3788000 🌐 www.arosa-vetter-hotel.ch.*

MUSIC

Bergkirchli. During various months throughout the year, concerts are given at 5 pm on Tuesday on the hand-painted organ in Arosa's 500-year-old, wooden-roof Bergkirchli mountain chapel. Check the Arosa Kultur website for details. ✉ *Über dem Schanfigg-Tal, Arosa* 🌐 *arosakultur.ch.*

Kultursommer Arosa. At venues throughout Arosa, classical music and jazz concerts, theater, and children's programs begin in mid-June and last through mid-October. Get the program from Arosa Kultur. ✉ *Arosa* ☎ *081/3538747* 🌐 *arosakultur.ch.*

SPORTS AND THE OUTDOORS

GOLF

Arosa Golf Club. Europe's highest tee (6,209 feet) is on the 8th hole of Arosa's 18-hole course at Maran. ✉ *Arosa* ☎ *081/3774242* 🌐 *www.golfarosa.ch* 🎫 *85 SF* 🏌 *18 holes, 4809 yards, par 65.*

HIKING AND BIKING

Arosa Tourism Office. Over 200 km (124 miles) of trails are maintained by the Arosa Tourism Office, which also has maps, offers advice on routes, and can arrange hiking or biking trips (including a five-day trek from Davos to Arosa). ✉ *Sports and Conference Centre, Arosa* ☎ *081/3787020* 🌐 *www.arosa.ch.*

SKATING AND CURLING

Eissporthalle. At the indoor Eissporthalle you can watch ice hockey as well as take skating or curling lessons; there's an open-air rink alongside it. ✉ *Sports and Conference Centre, Arosa* ☎ *081/3787020.*

SKIING

Though Arosa's ski area is small compared with those of the Upper Engadine, Davos-Klosters, and the Alpine Arena (Flims-Laax), a cable car connects it to neighboring Lenzerheide, resulting in 225 km (140 miles) of trails—and creating the largest ski region in the Graubünden, with 43 transport systems (cable cars and chairlifts). Closely screened in by mountains, the 5,900-foot-high resort has runs suitable for every level of skier. The Arosa slopes can be accessed directly from the valley at three points: the top of the village, behind the train station, and the Prätschli, a "feeder" lift to the main ski area. The black piste on the **Weisshorn** (8,700 feet) is challenging, but most of the runs there, as well as on **Hörnli** (8,200 feet), range from easy to intermediate. The **Urdenbahn**, with its panoramic windows, zips from Hörnli to Urdenfürggli in Lenzerheide, where an additional 125 km (78 miles) of slopes await.

All ski schools have English-speaking instructors. At this writing, a one-day lift ticket costs 75 SF; a six-day pass costs 340 SF (incremental increases are likely each season). For cross-country skiing or snowshoeing, the Maran and Isla trails have 30 km (18 miles) of groomed trails. There are three official sled runs: Tschuggen, Prätschli, and Litzirüti.

ABC Snowsport School. Ski lessons are available at the ABC Snowsport School. ✉ *Arosa* ☎ *081/3565660* 🌐 *www.abcarosa.ch.*

Langlauf- und Schneeschuhzentrum Geeser. Cross-country skiers or Nordic walkers will find instruction, guided tours, equipment, and information at the Langlauf- und Schneeschuhzentrum Geeser, the Cross-Country and Snowshoe Center. ✉ *Arosa* ☎ *081/3772215* 🌐 *www.geeser-arosa.ch.*

Schlittenkönig. You can rent sleds at the train station or at Schlittenkönig. ✉ *Seeblickstr., Arosa* ☎ *081/7250440* 🌐 *www.schlittenkoenig.ch.*

Swiss Ski and Snowboard School. You can get snow-sports instruction at the official Swiss Ski and Snowboard School. ✉ *Seeblickstr., Arosa* ☎ *081/3787500* 🌐 *www.skischule-arosa.ch.*

PRÄTTIGAU AND DAVOS

4

The name Prättigau means "meadow valley," and it's just that—a lush landscape of alternating orchards, pastures, and pine-covered mountains (though the main highway is very busy). The predominant language is German, introduced by immigrants from the Valais in the 13th century, though most villages still have Romansh names. Prättigau's most renowned ski resort is Klosters. Its perhaps-even-more-famous neighbor, Davos, lies in the Landwasser Valley, over the Wolfgang Pass. If you prefer something urban, head to Davos; for a quieter village experience, look to Klosters.

KLOSTERS

79 km (49 miles) northeast of Arosa, 49 km (29 miles) east of Chur.

At one time simply a group of hamlets, Klosters has become a small but chic resort, made up mostly of weathered-wood and white-stucco chalets. The village has two districts: Platz, which is older and busier, and Dorf, which lies on the main road toward Landquart. Klosters is famed for its skiing—British royal family members are faithful visitors—and makes the most of its access to the slopes of the Parsenn, above Davos.

GETTING HERE AND AROUND

The Rhätische Bahn (RhB), or a combination of Swiss railways and the RhB, covers the distance to Klosters in around one hour from Chur.

VISITOR INFORMATION

Contacts Information Klosters. ✉ *Alte Bahnhofstr. 6, Klosters Platz* ☎ *081/4102020* 🌐 *www.davos.ch.*

EXPLORING

Nutli-Hüschi. A brief visit to the folk museum Nutli-Hüschi shows the resort's evolution from its mountain roots. This pretty wood-and-stone farmhouse with a stable was built in 1565. It shows how people lived and worked in the Prättigau in centuries past through exhibits of kitchen utensils, handcrafts, tools, and the spare regional furniture, including a child's bed that could be expanded as the child grew. ✉ *Monbielerstr. at Talstr., Klosters Platz* ☎ *079/4406948* 🌐 *www.museum-klosters.ch* 🎫 *5 SF* ⏲ *Closed Sat.–Tues. and Thurs., and mid-Oct.–mid-June.*

St. Jacob. In Klosters Platz the church of St. Jacob, dating from 1492, is the only remnant of the medieval monastery from which the village took its name. Its windows were painted by Augusto Giacometti. ✉ *Klosters Platz.*

WHERE TO EAT

$$ INTERNATIONAL **Restaurant Gotschna.** A homey, rustic eatery slightly outside Klosters offers up an eclectic menu of traditional Swiss dishes,international plates, and—a rarity in this region—Asian recipes, all family-friendly and without fuss or fanfare. Stone-clad floors and wall-to-ceiling *Arvenholz* (the traditional pinewood interior of the region) ensconce you in the warmth and comfort of a true mountain abode. **Known for:** Asian specialties; reasonable prices for the region; charming, cozy atmosphere. *Average main: 28 SF Serneuserstr. 63, Klosters Serneus 081/4221428 www.restaurant-gotschna.com Closed Mon. and Tues.; late Nov.–mid-Dec.; and Easter–mid-June.*

$$ SWISS **Restaurant Höhwald.** This friendly, touristy restaurant up the hill from Klosters stands proud in its majestic setting, with a large, open terrace offering incredible valley and mountain views. As for the food, there is a wide selection of dishes to choose from—most using regional and sustainable ingredients—but be sure to try their seasonal game specialties. **Known for:** awe-inspiring vistas; local products; autumn game menu. *Average main: 34 SF Monbielerstr. 171, Monbiel 081/4223045 www.hoehwald-klosters.ch Closed Mon. and Tues.; mid-Apr.–May; and mid-Oct.–mid-Dec. No dinner Sun.*

WHERE TO STAY

$$$ HOTEL **Hotel Alpina.** Conveniently located across from the train station on one side and the Gotschna cable car on the other, this family-owned and family-run property made up of three buildings with south-facing balconies is rustic yet comfortable. **Pros:** good on-site restaurants; convenient to the main ski lift; nice wellness area. **Cons:** no minibar; view of the mountainscape is marred by the train station; no dedicated area for kids. *Rooms from: 314 SF Bahnhofstr. 1, Klosters-Pl., Klosters Platz 081/4102424 www.alpina-klosters.ch Closed early Apr.–early June and mid-Oct.–late Nov. 43 rooms Breakfast.*

$ HOTEL FAMILY Fodor's Choice ★ **Hotel Silvapina.** This delightful hotel in an old chalet-style building is family run and welcoming of other families, with apartments featuring small kitchens and fireplaces perfect for a small clan. **Pros:** comfy and clean budget accommodations for families; four-minute walk to Madrisa cable car; lovely hosts. **Cons:** next to train track, which can be noisy during the day; dated dining area; no spa amenities except sauna. *Rooms from: 188 SF Silvapinaweg 6, Klosters Dorf 081/4221468 www.silvapina.ch Closed mid-Apr.–early June and mid-Oct.–mid-Dec. 14 rooms Breakfast.*

$$ HOTEL Fodor's Choice ★ **Romantik Hotel Chesa Grischuna.** Located directly in the town center and renovated from a farmhouse in 1938, the family-run Chesa Grischuna has one of the most charming settings—and, arguably, the friendliest owners—in Switzerland. **Pros:** full of character and a vibrant eclectic social scene; famed restaurant; wonderful, helpful service. **Cons:** some rooms are on the small side; no wellness facilities; no elevator. *Rooms from: 234 SF Bahnhofstr. 12, Klosters Platz 081/4222222 www.chesagrischuna.ch Closed early Apr.–late June and mid-Oct.–early Dec. 23 rooms Breakfast.*

SKIING IN GRAUBÜNDEN

With Davos, site of the world's first ski lift; St. Moritz, arguably the world's ritziest resort; and other hot spots within its confines, Graubünden has earned its reputation as the ultimate winter destination. You'll find downhill skiing and snowboarding for all skill levels, as well as miles of *Langlauf* (cross-country skiing) trails prepared for both the classic and skating techniques.

Sports shops can outfit you with the necessary equipment; in Davos, you can even rent ski clothing. If you plan to spend a few days in one resort, check with local tourist offices for special packages. If you want to spend a day in a different resort within Graubünden, buy the lift ticket with your train ticket and the return fare will be reduced. Remember that accidents do occur, especially in unmarked zones. Avoid such areas unless you are suitably equipped and led by a qualified guide.

4

NIGHTLIFE

Casa Antica. Revelers dance late into the night at Casa Antica, a centuries-old converted barn. ✉ *Landstr. 176, Klosters Platz* ☎ *081/4221621* 🌐 *www.casaantica-klosters.ch.*

Chesa Bar. A popular after-dinner spot, Chesa Bar has piano music and several intimate bar areas. ✉ *Bahnhofstr. 12, Klosters Platz* ☎ *081/4222222* 🌐 *www.chesagrischuna.ch.*

Gaudy's Graströchni. Located at the bottom of Run 21, near the Gotschnabahn, the Graströchni is a lively place to end a day of skiing with a pint. ✉ *Rütipromenade 2, Klosters Platz* ☎ *081/4221793* 🌐 *www.grastroechni.ch.*

SPORTS AND THE OUTDOORS

BIKING AND HIKING

The Klosters area has plenty of trails for exploring the countryside. The 250 km (155 miles) of summer hiking routes are reduced to 35 km (22 miles) of prepared paths in winter. There are 120 km (74½ miles) of mountain-biking routes, including a steep, free-ride track running from the Gotschnabahn midstation (Gotschnaboden) back down into Klosters Platz—for serious riders only.

Bardill Sport. To rent mountain bikes, try Bardill Sport. ✉ *Talstation Gotschnabahn, Landstr. 185, Klosters Platz* ☎ *081/4221040* 🌐 *www.bardill-sport.ch.*

Bertram's Bike Shop. This bike shop is an excellent source for mountain bikes in Klosters. ✉ *Doggilochstr. 64, Klosters Serneus* ☎ *076/3184264.*

GOLF

Golf Klosters. Not to be outdone by its neighbors, Klosters has added a relatively tough 9-hole Golf Klosters, including a driving range. An electric golf cart is included in the greens fee, and the 7th hole provides the additional handicap of a jaw-dropping view of Klosters. The course is closed from late October through April. ✉ *Selfrangastr. 44, Klosters Platz* ☎ *081/4221133* 🌐 *www.golf-klosters.ch* 💳 *60 SF weekdays, 75 SF weekends* 🏌 *9 holes, 3976 yards, par 62.*

SKATING

Arena Klosters. Klosters's Arena has rinks for skating, hockey, and curling. Skate rentals are available. ✉ *Doggilochstr. 51, Klosters-Pl., Klosters Platz* ☎ *081/4102131* 🌐 *www.arena-klosters.ch.*

SKIING

Klosters is known for its vast range of downhill runs, which, together with those of Davos, total 300 km (186½ miles). These are divided almost equally among easy, moderate, and difficult pistes. From the Gotschnagrat (7,494 feet), skiers can connect to the Parsenn slopes and try, for example, the famous Weissflüh run down to the village of Küblis. The sunny Madrisa slopes above Klosters Dorf offer relatively easy skiing and snowboarding, as well as free-ride opportunities.

Lift tickets to the combined Davos–Klosters area cost 143 SF for two days and 342 SF for six days. KeyCards, which give you access to all cable cars, funiculars, and ski lifts, are required for lift tickets of more than two days; you can purchase them for 5 SF at any ticket office (🌐 *www.davosklosters.ch*). Train or bus transport back to Klosters from other villages within the ski area is included in the price of the regional ski ticket.

■ TIP→ When booking your hotel, it is worth asking if it offers any special ski-pass deals during your desired travel period. Early- or late-season offers are frequently available.

Swiss Ski + Snowboard School. For instruction or to go on a snowshoe trek, contact the Swiss Ski + Snowboard School, in Platz. ✉ *Bahnhofstr. 4, Klosters Platz* ☎ *081/4102828* 🌐 *www.sssk.ch/en.*

Swiss Ski & Snowboard School Saas. The Swiss Ski & Snowboard School Saas, in Dorf, offers standard instruction plus special courses in carving, slalom skiing, and more. ✉ *Landstr. 15, Klosters Dorf* ☎ *081/4202233* 🌐 *www.ski-snow-fun-klosters.ch.*

SLEDDING

Klosters–Davos is big on sledding, with eight sled runs crisscrossing resort mountains. The 3.7-km (2.3-mile) Rinerhorn run, up the valley from Davos, is lighted up at night. A day card costs 53 SF, and a sled can be rented for 13 SF at the cable-car valley station with a 50 SF deposit; most shops will also accept your passport as a deposit. Evening runs on the lighted slope are open Wednesday and Friday, 7–11 pm, from January to March. They cost 26 SF for an evening.

Day tickets for Schatzalp to Davos Platz cost 30 SF, and night sledding (6–10:30 pm) costs 24 SF. Day cards at Madrisa mountain cost 39 SF. The run here is 8½ km (5 miles) long and ends in Saas, from which you can return by bus to Klosters (buses leave every hour or so until 7:24 pm). Sled rentals at the Madrisa cable-car station are 10 SF. Another sled run begins at the midway station of the Parsenn Klosters (Gotschna) cable car. Day passes cost 39 SF; sled rentals at the station cost 10 SF.

Andrist Sport. Sleds are available for rental at Andrist Sport. ✉ *Alte Bahnhofstr. 4, Klosters Platz* ☎ *081/4102080* 🌐 *www.andrist-sport.ch.*

DID YOU KNOW?

Although Klosters is best known for its superb downhill skiing, the resort also has notable sled runs, including a 3½-km (2-mile) track that's lighted after dark for nighttime thrills.

Gotschna Sport. Gotschna Sport rents sleds during snowy months in Klosters. ✉ *Alte Bahnhofstr. 5, Klosters Platz* ☎ *081/4221197* 🌐 *www.gotschnasport.ch/en.*

DAVOS

11 km (7 miles) southwest of Klosters.

At 5,116 feet, this highest "city" (stretching the definition) in Europe is good for cold-weather sports even in the soggiest of winters. Davos is famous for its ice sports and skiing, and almost more celebrated for hosting the annual World Economic Forum every January. The town and its lake lie in the Landwasser Valley, which runs parallel to the Upper Engadine, though they're separated by the vast Albula chain, reaching to more than 9,840 feet. On the opposite side of the valley stands the Strela chain, dominated by the Weissfluhgipfel.

This is a capital for action-oriented sports enthusiasts and not necessarily for anyone seeking a peaceful, rustic mountain retreat (especially at the end of December, when there's an invasion of ice-hockey fans for the international Spengler Cup).

Davos is divided into Platz and Dorf (village), which together are one noisier-than-average urban strip, though Dorf is the calmer of the two. The town's first visitors came to take cures for lung disease in the bracing mountain air. Now, except for a few token historic structures and brightly painted buildings, the town is modern and architecturally undistinguished, and its center sometimes fills with the exhaust of city traffic. But no matter how densely populated and fast paced the town becomes, the slopes are still spectacular, and the regulars return.

GETTING HERE AND AROUND

Davos is 30 minutes from Klosters, 1½ hours from Chur, and 2½ hours from Zürich. When traveling from Zürich or Chur, you'll have to change trains at Landquart. The journey from St. Moritz takes 1½ hours, with a transfer at Filisur. From Scuol, it takes 1 hour 15 minutes, with a change in Klosters Platz. In case you accidentally ski down to the wrong resort, or your après-ski lasts longer than anticipated, it's worth noting that there is at least one train an hour from Klosters to Davos between 5 am and at least 10 pm, though it tends to be 11:30 pm during the ski season.

The Vereina Tunnel provides year-round train service from Klosters to Sagliains, near Susch–Lavin. Car-carrying trains leave from just above Klosters—road signs indicate a train carrying cars and the name Vereina.

Once in Davos, there is one train per hour covering the 3 km (1¾ miles) between the villages of Davos Dorf and Platz. Much more convenient is the bus line through town, along the Promenade; it's free for overnight guests in summer and for winter guests in possession of a valid lift pass.

VISITOR INFORMATION

Contacts Information Davos Platz. ✉ *Talstr. 41, Davos* ☎ *081/4152121* 🌐 *www.davos.ch.*

Even if you don't ski, Graubünden has fun outdoor activities for the whole family.

EXPLORING

Kirche St. Johann (*Church of St. John the Baptist*). Among the town's few architectural highlights, the late-Gothic Kirche St. Johann stands out by virtue of its windows by Augusto Giacometti. Nearby is the 17th-century Rathaus (Town Hall). ✉ *Rathausstutz 2, Davos.*

Kirchner Museum. This museum has the world's largest collection of works by the German artist Ernst Ludwig Kirchner, whose off-kilter lines and unnerving compositions inspired the expressionist movement. He traveled to Davos in 1917 for health reasons and stayed until his suicide in 1938. ✉ *Promenade 82, Davos-Platz, Davos* ☎ *081/4106300* 🌐 *www.kirchnermuseum.ch* 🎟 *12 SF* ⏲ *Closed Mon.*

Wintersportmuseum Davos. Showcasing the history of winter sports, from their relatively primitive infancy to the modern day, this museum has a large collection of well-preserved equipment, including sleds, skis, skates, bindings, and costumes. ✉ *Promenade 43, Davos-Platz, Davos* ☎ *081/4132484* 🌐 *www.wintersportmuseum.ch* 🎟 *Free* ⏲ *Closed Wed. and Fri.–Mon.*

WHERE TO EAT

$$ ECLECTIC ✕ **Bar-Bistro Angelo.** If you're a meat lover who's had enough Bündner specialties, try this restaurant for a diverse menu of cordon bleu (meat-wrapped cheese, breaded and fried), *Rösti* (hash browns), and exotic meats, such as kangaroo, cooked on hot stone. The vibrant artwork, live piano music, and a well-stocked bar create a cool, modern feel. **Known for:** eight varieties of cordon bleu; grilled meats; welcoming, casual atmosphere. $ *Average main: 30 SF* ✉ *Promenade 119, Davos* ☎ *079/2479779* 🌐 *www.bistro-angelo.ch* ⏲ *Closed Tues. Oct. and Nov., and Sun. and Mon. year-round. No lunch.*

$$ SWISS Fodor's Choice ★ **Bistro Gentiana.** A cozy bistro and the region's top place for fondue, this "café des artistes" dates back to the late 1880s, when it served as the town firehouse. After an art deco overhaul, it became a long-standing haunt for those seeking out snails, regional mushrooms, and age-old recipes for cheese and meat fondues. **Known for:** superlative fondue; delicious snails, in soup, garlic butter, puff pastry, and more; cozy art deco atmosphere. *Average main: 37 SF* *Promenade 53, Davos* *081/4135649* *www.gentiana.ch* *Closed Easter–late June and mid-Oct.–early Dec. Closed Sun. and Mon. in summer.*

$$$$ SWISS Fodor's Choice ★ **GLOW by Armin Amrein.** Swiss celebrity chef Armin Amrein helms the kitchen at this innovative Michelin-starred eatery, by far the most sophisticated place to dine in (surprisingly) restaurant-challenged Davos. The restaurant is connected to the Escher Raumdesign modern interior design showroom and reflects its sleek, sophisticated look in its lighting and designer furniture. **Known for:** creative seasonal cuisine; refined contemporary ambience; comprehensive and informed wine selection. *Average main: 115 SF* *Promenade 115, Davos* *081/4164343* *www.glow-davos.ch/en/home* *Closed Mon. and Tues., early Apr.– late June, mid-Oct.–early Dec., and during the World Economic Forum. No lunch Wed. in summer.*

WHERE TO STAY

$ HOTEL **arthaus HOTEL.** This striking red building exudes a mysterious pull: inside, the walls are brightened by lively abstract paintings created by the owner, and the guest rooms are little works of art unto themselves. **Pros:** unique and quirky, with original art throughout; owner welcomes guests with personal service; highly regarded restaurant. **Cons:** not a high-style hotel with requisite amenities; no sauna or après-ski facilities; no elevator. *Rooms from: 138 SF* *Platzstr. 5, Davos* *081/4100510* *www.arthaushotel.ch* *19 rooms* *Breakfast.*

$ HOTEL FAMILY **Bünda Davos.** In a typical chalet-style building, this hotel is perfectly located right by the children's and beginners' slope, and the cross-country ski track; in addition, the Parsenn funicular is only a few minutes' walk away. **Pros:** direct access to beginner and kids' skiing; great for families; very inexpensive for the area. **Cons:** slightly outside the center; lacks character; parking costs extra. *Rooms from: 169 SF* *Museumstr. 4, Davos* *081/4171819* *www.buendadavos.ch* *41 rooms* *Breakfast.*

$$ HOTEL Fodor's Choice ★ **Hotel Schatzalp.** About 950 feet above town on a quiet, car-free slope, this magnificent, if a tad faded, hotel will transport you back to the grand spa days of Davos. **Pros:** peaceful, awe-inspiring location; historic charm; boundless activities for all ages. **Cons:** those seeking amazing amenities or modern rooms might be disappointed; no TVs; could use a gentle refresh. *Rooms from: 242 SF* *Schatzalp, Davos* *081/4155151* *www.schatzalp.ch* *Closed early Apr.–mid-June and mid-Oct.–mid-Dec.* *93 rooms* *Breakfast.*

$$$ HOTEL FAMILY Fodor's Choice ★ **InterContinental Davos.** A welcome ultramodern hotel in a sea of older-style accommodations, the InterContinental Davos, near the edge of Lake Davos at the northern end of town, boasts a distinctive "cone"-shaped facade on the outside and a sophisticated, streamlined design on the inside. **Pros:** atmosphere of understated luxury; spacious guest

rooms; complimentary minibar (for nonalcoholic beverages). **Cons:** extra charge for Wi-Fi; breakfast not usually included in rates; staff can be hard to find off-season. *Rooms from: 468 SF* *Baslerstr. 9, Davos* *081/4140400* *davos.intercontinental.com* *Closed late Sept.–early Dec. and early Mar.–early July* *216 rooms* *No meals.*

$$ HOTEL **Steigenberger Grandhotel Belvédère.** For an appealing mix of traditional and modern in a central city location, the Hotel Belvédère provides old-fashioned Swiss charm in its woodsy guest rooms and a more contemporary look in its inviting public spaces. **Pros:** prime central location; outstanding personal service; lovely, welcoming public spaces. **Cons:** can be overrun by tour groups; some guest rooms are a bit faded; quality of food is mixed. *Rooms from: 299 SF* *Promenade 89, Davos* *081/4156000* *en.steigenberger.com* *Closed mid-Apr.–mid-June and late Sept.–late Nov.* *126 rooms* *Breakfast.*

NIGHTLIFE AND PERFORMING ARTS

BARS

Ex Bar. In the Hotel Europe, the Ex Bar is where hipsters gather to listen to bands and DJs, and have a bite to eat along with their beer. *Promenade 63, Davos-Platz, Davos* *081/4135645* *ex-bar-davos.ch.*

CASINO

Casino. The bright, glassed-in Casino is one of the main socializing places in Davos. It opens at 2 pm daily and does not require formal dress. *Hotel Europe, Promenade 63, Davos-Platz, Davos* *081/4100303* *www.casinodavos.ch.*

DANCING

Cabanna Club. This hot spot lures an energetic crowd with techno music—those on the older side usually head to the "Cava" (under the Cabanna) for more acoustic fare. *Promenade 63, Davos-Platz, Davos* *081/4154141.*

Pöstli Club. In the Morosani Posthotel, the Pöstli Club is the party place in Davos. Rock and oldies are at home here, as are well-dressed visitors. Put your dancing shoes on and hit the dance floor. Note that patrons must be 23 years of age or older to enter. *Promenade 42, Davos-Platz, Davos* *081/4155500* *www.morosani.ch/en/bars-and-night-club/poestli-club.*

Rotliechtli Music Club. In the Hotel Davoserhof, the Rotliechtli Music Club attracts a young—or at least young at heart—crowd with somewhat traditional taste in music. *Berglistutz 2, Davos-Platz, Davos* *081/4149443* *www.rotliechtli.ch.*

MUSIC

The annual **Young Artists in Concert festival** (*www.davosfestival.ch*) is held in August. Young musicians from all over the world practice and perform classical music in churches, the Hotel Morosani Schweizerhof, and other venues throughout town.

SPORTS AND THE OUTDOORS

HIKING AND BIKING

Davos is threaded with more than 700 km (435 miles) of well-marked hiking trails and 1,300 km (807 miles) of biking trails in winter and summer. The Bike Touring Map is available at the tourist office.

Bike Academy Davos. Mountain bikes and equipment such as helmets can be rented at Bike Academy Davos, in the Davos Dorf Train Station. ✉ *Bahnhofstr. 8, Davos* ☎ *081/4207220* 🌐 *www.bike-academy.ch.*

SAILING AND WINDSURFING

Segelschule Davosersee. Sailing and windsurfing are popular on Davos Lake, where there's always a stiff breeze. To rent boats or take a lesson with a sailing school, call Segelschule Davosersee. ✉ *Flüelastr. 4, Davos* ☎ *079/4746722* 🌐 *www.davossail.ch.*

SKATING

Sports Center Davos. Davos has a long reputation as an important ice-sports center, with its enormous Sports Center Davos and speed-skating rink, the biggest natural ice track in Europe. The Ice Stadium maintains one indoor and two outdoor rinks. The Davos World of Ice adventure ice playground features themed ice rinks and is open in winter only. ✉ *Talstr. 41, Davos-Platz, Davos* ☎ *081/4153600.*

SKIING

Davos can accommodate some 24,000 visitors on 300 km (186½ miles) of runs. The fairly steep slopes of the **Parsenn-Gotschna** are accessed from town by the Parsenn funicular. For an alternative, try the **Rinerhorn,** a 15-minute ride by bus or train. Here the slopes lead to the hamlet of **Glaris,** 7 km (4½ miles) from Davos. A must for the skilled skier is the descent from **Weissfluhgipfel** (9,330 feet) to **Küblis,** in the Prättigau. This magnificent 13-km (8-mile) piste has a vertical drop of 6,560 feet and is classified as difficult at the top but moderate for most of its length. A real challenge for experts is the three-hour tour across the mountains to Arosa—which requires a guide and good weather conditions. An easy 2-km (1-mile) run is No. 11, the Meierhofer Tälli. **Jakobshorn,** a ski and snowboard area on the west-facing side, is reached by a cable car and lift from Davos Platz. The **Pischa** ski area, on the Flüela Pass road, is a free-ride paradise, and especially suitable for children and families—as is the **Bünda** slope in Davos Dorf.

Lift tickets to the combined Davos–Klosters area cost 143 SF for two days, 342 SF for six days, and include transport between the ski areas.

PaarSenn. If you need to get outfitted for skiing, including clothing, go to PaarSenn. There are four locations, including Promenade 63, Promenade 79, and the railway station in Davos Platz, as well as Promenade 159 in Davos Dorf. ✉ *Promenade 159, Davos* ☎ *081/4101010* 🌐 *www.paarsennsport.ch.*

Schweizer Schneesportschule Davos (*Swiss Snowsports School Davos*). There are 78 km (48 miles) of prepared cross-country ski trails in Davos and Klosters, for which there is no charge. The Swiss Snowsports School Davos offers group and private lessons for cross-country skiing, as well as downhill skiing, snowboarding, and more. ✉ *Promenade 157, Davos* ☎ *081/4162454* 🌐 *www.ssd.ch.*

Top Secret Ski & Snowboard Company. For the expert skier (freestyle, off-piste, and the like), the place to go is Top Secret Ski & Snowboard Company for equipment rentals and sales as well as lessons. ✉ *Talstation Jakobshorn, Brämabüelstr. 11, Davos* ☎ *081/4137374* 🌐 *www.topsecretdavos.ch.*

THE LOWER ENGADINE

This is the most picturesque of Graübunden's many valleys, and like Dorothy landing in Oz, you might be a bit shocked by what you find here. You'll hear people talk of *Schellenursli* (a legendary little boy with a bell), and there's even a sort of Scarecrow—during the *Hom Strom* holiday on the first Saturday in February, the children of Scuol make a figure out of hay to scare winter away. Festivals and folklore abound, as do dense forests and quaint village settings. "Allegra!" is the proper greeting on the street, reflecting the Romansh language and Latinate culture here. The outer walls of houses are decorated using the sgrafitto technique—a signature of the Engadine. (First a layer of dark stucco is whitewashed, and then symbols and drawings of local fauna are scraped into the paint, revealing the dark stucco beneath—usually the name of the original builder appears with a quote or a poem, and the extent and quality of the sgraffiti suggests the wealth and station of the owner.) Although the Lower Engadine is more enclosed than its upper counterpart, both have a dry, crisp "champagne" climate.

4

GUARDA

37 km (23 miles) east of Davos.

The former main road through the Inn Valley (Engadine) was higher up on the slopes than today's road. It passed through Guarda, one of a pleasant chain of small villages that includes Ardez and Ftan. Each has fine sgraffitied homes, but Guarda, where the architecture is government protected, is particularly well suited for a leisurely exploration along its ancient cobbled streets. The dark-on-light etchings on the facades (contrasting sharply with the bright flowers on the windowsills) draw pedestrians from one photo op to the next. As its name implies, Guarda ("watch") sits high on a hillside looking out over the valley and the peaks to the south, which reach up to 9,840 feet.

WHERE TO STAY

$$ HOTEL **Hotel Meisser.** This picturesque, family-owned hotel, made up of two 17th-century farmhouses, has sgraffiti and flower boxes on the outside, antiques and honey-color pine on the inside, and a luxurious restaurant serving tasty local dishes. **Pros:** unique ambience and style of the renovated farmhouses; special local cuisine; very convenient for walking and hiking excursions. **Cons:** restaurants and shops are a 20-minute drive; no spa; no elevator. $ *Rooms from: 205 SF* ✉ *Dorfstr. 42, Guarda* ☎ *081/8622132* 🌐 *www.hotel-meisser.ch* ⏲ *Closed early Apr.–early May and Nov.* *20 rooms* *Breakfast.*

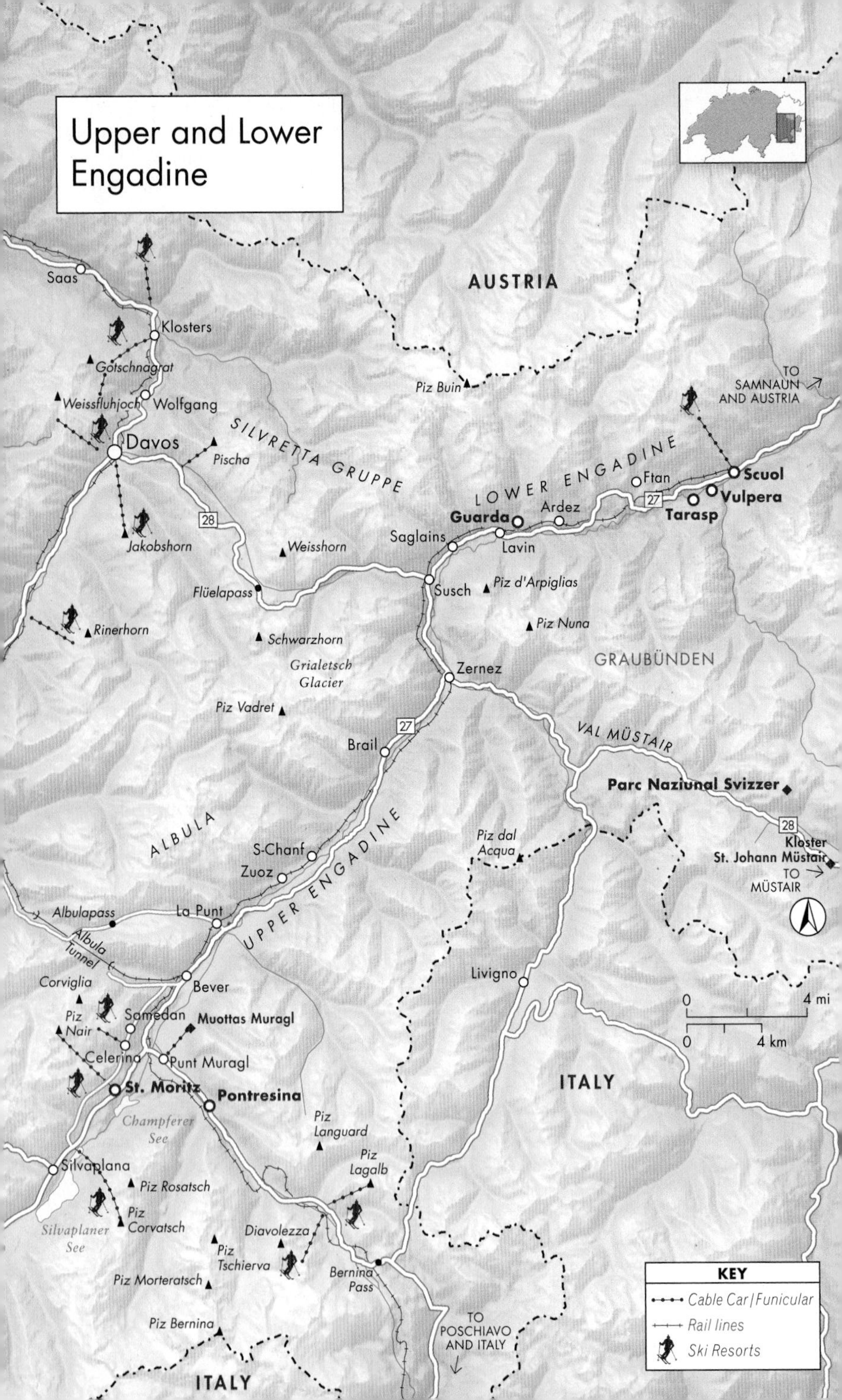
Upper and Lower Engadine
AUSTRIA
ITALY
ITALY
GRAUBÜNDEN
SILVRETTA GRUPPE
LOWER ENGADINE
UPPER ENGADINE
VAL MÜSTAIR
ALBULA
Saas
Klosters
Gotschnagrat
Weissfluhjoch
Wolfgang
Davos
Pischa
Jakobshorn
Rinerhorn
Flüelapass
Weisshorn
Schwarzhorn
Grialetsch Glacier
Piz Vadret
Piz Buin
TO SAMNAUN AND AUSTRIA
Scuol
Vulpera
Tarasp
Ftan
Ardez
Guarda
Lavin
Saglains
Susch
Piz d'Arpiglias
Piz Nuna
Zernez
Brail
S-Chanf
Zuoz
La Punt
Albulapass
Albula Tunnel
Bever
Corviglia
Piz Nair
Samedan
Muottas Muragl
Celerina
Punt Muragl
St. Moritz
Pontresina
Champferer See
Silvaplana
Silvaplaner See
Piz Rosatsch
Piz Corvatsch
Piz Languard
Piz Lagalb
Diavolezza
Piz Tschierva
Piz Morteratsch
Piz Bernina
Bernina Pass
TO POSCHIAVO AND ITALY
Livigno
Piz dal Acqua
Parc Naziunal Svizzer
Kloster St. Johann Müstair
TO MÜSTAIR
27
28
0
4 mi
0
4 km
KEY
Cable Car/Funicular
Rail lines
Ski Resorts

Guarda's preserved sgraffitied houses and vibrant flowering window boxes produce great photo ops.

SCUOL AND TARASP-VULPERA

13 km (8 miles) east of Guarda.

The villages of Scuol and Tarasp-Vulpera effectively form one large resort, although a car or bus is needed to travel between the two. The area owes its popularity to the 20 mineral springs (traditionally used for liver cures), the beautiful surroundings (mountains and dense forests), and the proximity of the Parc Naziunal Svizzer. Previously popular only in summer, the villages now fill up in winter, thanks to skiing on the south-facing slopes of Motta Naluns.

A small town, Scuol has a petite but exemplary Old Town, with five fountains from which you can do a taste-test comparison of normal tap water against spring water.

GETTING HERE AND AROUND

Scuol is connected to Chur (2 hours away) and Klosters (45 minutes) by train. To get here from St. Moritz (1 hour 21 minutes), change at Samedan.

ESSENTIALS

Visitor Information Engadin Scuol Tourist Information. ✉ *Stradun 403a, Scuol* ☎ *081/8618800* 🌐 *www.engadin.com.*

EXPLORING

Two other villages lie on the opposite side of the river from Scuol. **Vulpera,** whose permanent residents number around 50, has an 1876 Trinkhalle (pump house) with its spring pumping out mineral-rich water that's said to be good for the digestive tract; you can enjoy this water at the nearby Bogn Engiadina spa, since the Trinkhalle is no longer open to the public. From Vulpera, take a 10-minute bus ride up to **Tarasp,** a cluster of houses, inns, and farms around a tiny lake. The Vulpera golf course straddles the road, so if you are traveling by car you may want to close your windows.

Fodor's Choice ★ **Schloss Tarasp.** The village is dominated by the magnificently picturesque stronghold Schloss Tarasp, perched 500 feet above. This grand castle lords over the valley with an impressive main tower. The oldest sections date from the 11th century, when the castle was built by the leading family of Tarasp. Tarasp became part of Austria in 1464; the imperial eagle still can be seen on the castle walls. In the early 1800s Napoléon gave Tarasp to Canton Graubünden, newly part of the Swiss federation. In 2016, the castle was bought by Swiss artist Not Vital, with plans to add contemporary art inside and a sculpture park outside. You must join a tour (German-language) to see the interiors, which range from the Romanesque chapel to the opulent 19th-century reception rooms; the schedule varies, but there are at least two tours a day (except Monday) from May to October, with up to four tours a day in July and August, and special late-night tours during the full moon. Call ahead for times. The bus from Vulpera departs roughly every hour, or it's a 1½-hour walk from Scuol, following a well-marked path that goes over the Punt'Ota (high bridge). ✉ *Tarasp* ☎ *081/8649368* 🌐 *www.schloss-tarasp.ch* 🎟 *20 SF* ⏲ *Closed Mon. mid-May–mid-Oct. Closed Sat.–Thurs. mid-Oct–mid-Dec. and Easter–mid-May. Closed Wed. and Fri.–Mon. mid-Dec–Easter.*

WHERE TO STAY

$ HOTEL FAMILY **Hotel Belvédère Scuol.** If you're in Scuol primarily to visit the Bohn Engiadina Scuol, you can't do better than to stay at this centrally located family-owned hotel—there's a covered pathway that leads directly to the spa, so you can discreetly head over in your robe and slippers any time you like—and room prices include unlimited spa access. **Pros:** unbeatable access to the spa; central location, on main shopping street and close to Old Town; open year-round. **Cons:** restaurant food could be better; room information (menus, room details, etc.) only in German; rooms lack a certain charm. $ *Rooms from: 195 SF* ✉ *Stradun 330, Scuol* ☎ *081/8610606, 081/8610620 reservations* 🌐 *www.belvedere-scuol.ch* *81 rooms* 🍽 *Breakfast.*

$$ HOTEL **Hotel Engiadina.** This typical 16th-century Engadine house is in the heart of Scuol's Old Town and has inviting rooms decorated with Swiss pine, carved ceilings, and exposed beams. **Pros:** enchanting location; service with a smile; delicious food. **Cons:** a bit of an uphill hike into town; no views from rooms; no elevator. $ *Rooms from: 244 SF* ✉ *Rablüzza 152, Scuol* ☎ *081/8641421* 🌐 *www.hotel-engiadina.ch* ⏲ *Closed early Apr.–early June and late-Oct.–mid-Dec. Restaurant closed Sun. and Mon.* *16 rooms* 🍽 *Breakfast.*

$ HOTEL **Hotel Villa Post.** Marked by its distinctive turret topped with a Swiss flag, this former post office provides simply and tastefully decorated guest rooms and a familial atmosphere ideal for those seeking a peaceful home away from home. **Pros:** sense of history; grand natural setting; free shuttle to Motta Naluns ski area. **Cons:** staid social atmosphere; there's only one public-transport bus per hour; restaurant not open for dinner. $ *Rooms*

CLOSE UP

The Rhätibahn

The Rhätibahn (Rhätische Bahn) is not simply a means of transport but a journey that thousands love to experience every year. In July 2008 it won UNESCO World Heritage status in recognition of its feats of engineering and the wondrous landscapes that it passes through. The track winds its way across glaciers, over viaducts and gorges, and past stupendous Alpine scenery—along the way revealing scenes from a centuries-old way of life that's been all but forgotten in the bigger towns and cities.

The tracks of this wondrous travel experience thread a large section of Graubünden but also reach to other cantons in Switzerland and can even transport you southward across the border to Italy. The network offers special services with named prestige trains—the top three are the Arosa Express, the Bernina Express, and the Glacier Express. Each follows its own route, and prebooking is essential. Doing a little research to see which lines fit with your itinerary is well worth it. To ensure your chosen outpost is on one of the varied lines and to avoid disappointment, it is best to check online or call ahead. For more details, call ☎ *081/2886565* or visit 🌐 *www.rhb.ch.*

4

from: 175 SF ✉ *Vulpera* ☎ *081/8641112* 🌐 *www.villa-post.ch* ⊙ *Closed late Mar.–early June and mid-Oct.–late Dec.* *25 rooms* *Breakfast.*

$$ HOTEL Fodor's Choice ★ **Schlosshotel Chastè.** Although many Swiss hoteliers can claim a second generation of family ownership, this hidden treasure boasts 500 years under the Pazeller family's care, who have preserved the bulging, sgraffitied stucco exterior and modernized much of what's behind the magnificently carved Arvenholz wood door. **Pros:** superb cuisine; enchanting rooms; untouched magical surroundings. **Cons:** not a convenient location for those coming by train; not very lively; rooms in the front can be a bit noisy. $ *Rooms from: 300 SF* ✉ *Tarasp* ☎ *081/8613060* 🌐 *www.schlosshoteltarasp.ch* ⊙ *Closed late Mar.–late May and mid-Oct.–mid-Dec.* *18 rooms* *Breakfast.*

SPAS

Fodor's Choice ★ **Bogn Engiadina Scuol.** For the inside-and-out spa experience, head to the Bogn Engiadina Scuol, one of Europe's most famous spas. Standing in the middle of town tucked against the mountainside, an elevator and a staircase in a silo-like modern construction lead you down to the entrance, and the calming blue interior, fantastic aquatic murals, and shifting reflections from backlit pools start relaxing you before your toes even touch the water. Six pools, both indoor and outdoor, range in temperature from 60°F to 90°F. There are also saunas, solariums, steam rooms, and a massage area. A special Roman-Irish ritual treatment alternates between moist and dry heat, massage, and mineral baths, and lasts 3½ hours; it's best to reserve 24 hours in advance. A therapy center offers mud baths, gymnastics, thalassotherapy (using seawater), and electrotherapy (if you have a doctor's prescription). In addition to steeping in mineral water, you can fill a glass with the water from four different sources near the entrance. There's a basic entry fee plus additional fees for therapies. ✉ *Town center, Scuol* ☎ *081/8612600* 🌐 *www.bognengiadina.ch.*

The majestic Tarasp Castle lords over this part of the valley.

SPORTS AND THE OUTDOORS

BIKING

Rental bicycles are available at sports shops in Scuol. For the adventurous, bikes can be taken on the cable car; once on the mountain, you can explore on your own or join a guided tour. Contact the tourist office for details.

ICE SPORTS

Sportanlage Trü. Open-air ice rinks for hockey, curling, and skating are available in Scuol from early December to early March at Sportanlage Trü. A swimming pool and mini-golf course are open in summer. ⊠ *Scuol* ☏ *081/8612606.*

SKIING AND SNOWBOARDING

The region's ski area centers around 14 gondolas and lifts going up Scuol's **Motta Naluns,** at elevations between 4,100 and 9,184 feet. The 70 km (43½ miles) of trails include the 10-km (6-mile) Traumpiste (Dream Run), a good run of medium difficulty with a few tough areas. There is a wide range of ski passes available for an equally wide range of prices, beginning at 57 SF for a one-day pass. Tarasp has one short ski lift for beginners. Bus transport between Scuol–Sent and Scuol–Tarasp-Vulpera is free of charge if you have a ski pass.

Snowboarding is extremely popular on these broad, sunny slopes. There are also 77 km (48 miles) of prepared cross-country tracks around Scuol. Rental equipment is available at sports shops in Scuol and next to the Motta Naluns cable-car station.

Element Snowboard School. Conveniently located close to the train station and valley gondola station, the Element Snowboard School can rent you gear *and* teach you how to shred the pistes. ✉ *Talstation Bergbahnen, Scuol* ☎ *081/8600777* 🌐 *www.element-scuol.ch.*

Kinderland Nalunsin. Children can find snowy excitement at the Kinderland Nalunsin, a combination ski school and day care center. ✉ *Scuol* ☎ *081/8611723* 🎫 *From 8 SF per hour; 40 SF per day; additional 10 SF for lunch.*

Schweizer Skischule Scuol-Ftan. You can sign up with Schweizer Skischule for instruction in Alpine and cross-country skiing, as well as snowboarding. ✉ *Talstation Bergbahnen, Scuol* ☎ *081/8641723* 🌐 *www.snowsportscuol.ch.*

4

SLEDDING

There are three main sled runs, between 2½ and 7 km (1½ and 4½ miles) long.

Sport Heinrich. You can rent a sled at the Motta Naluns mountain station or from Sport Heinrich in Scuol. ✉ *Hauptstr. 400, Scuol* ☎ *081/8641956* 🌐 *www.sport-heinrich.ch.*

WHITE-WATER RAFTING

Swissraft. Swissraft organizes daily white-water rafting expeditions in rubber dinghies on the Inn River from June to late September. ✉ *Scuol* ☎ *081/9115250* 🌐 *www.swissraft.ch.*

PARC NAZIUNAL SVIZZER

1 km (½ mile) east of Zernez.

This Swiss National Park is a magnificent federal preserve of virtually virgin wilderness teeming with local wildlife.

GETTING HERE AND AROUND

There are access roads from Zernez, Scuol, S-chanf, and the Ofen Pass.

EXPLORING

Kloster St. Johann Müstair. If you walk through the Swiss National Park over the Ofen Pass to the Münster Valley and Italy, you can visit the Benedictine Convent of St. John at Müstair, a UNESCO World Heritage Site on the Italian border. The convent is still active and has fasting weeks in spring and fall. Take time to wonder at the Romanesque frescoes from AD 800–1170; more paintings are being uncovered using laser technology, including at the adjacent 8th-century Chapel of the Holy Cross, accessible only by guided tour. The appealingly simple convent complex also houses a small museum with baroque statues and Carolingian works. ✉ *Müstair* ☎ *081/8586189* 🌐 *www.muestair.ch* 🎫 *Abbey free (10 SF with guided tour), museum 12 SF, Chapel of the Holy Cross 12 SF (with guided tour).*

Fodor's Choice ★ **Parc Naziunal Svizzer** (*Swiss National Park*). Established in 1914, the Parc Naziunal Svizzer covers 173 square km (67 square miles), including the Macun lakes near Lavin. Although small compared with a U.S. or Canadian national park, it has none of the developments that typically hint of "accessibility" and "attraction": no campgrounds, no picnic sites, no residents, and few rangers. This is genuine wilderness, every leaf protected from anything but nature itself. Rangers see that rules are

DID YOU KNOW?

The Swiss National Park is a wonderful place to be one with nature—there are no campgrounds, no picnic sites, and few park rangers. It's a great place to try to spot an ibex, the horned goatlike animal on Graubünden's flag.

obeyed—no fires, dogs, bikes, skis, or tents are allowed, and picking plants is forbidden. The park is home to large herds of ibex (the heraldic animal on the Graubünden flag), chamois (a distant relative of the goat), red and roe deer, and marmots. Don't forget binoculars; without them you might not see much fauna—the animals give a wide berth to the 80 km (50 miles) of marked paths. If big game fail to appear, you can just enjoy the scenery and watch out for a bearded vulture overhead. Before heading into the park, visit the three-story **National Park Centre** in Zernez, where you can view the permanent exhibition with the help of your English audio guide, stock up on maps, and enjoy the natural-history exhibit. Special exhibitions change once or twice each year. Guided walks in German are available Tuesday through Thursday; reserve one to two days in advance to join a group or book a private guided walk in English. Trails start out from parking lots off the park's only highway (visitors are encouraged to take buses back to their starting point)—a series of wild, rough, and often steep paths. Visitors are restricted to the trails except at designated resting places. Download the digital hiking app iWebPark, which has park maps and other info, to ensure you don't get lost. ✉ *Nationalpark-Haus, Zernez* ✣ *Leaving the village toward Ofen Pass* ☎ *081/8514141* 🌐 *www.nationalpark.ch* 🎫 *Park 7 SF, guided walks (German only) 25 SF–40 SF, private guided walks (English) 350 SF.*

WHERE TO STAY

$ HOTEL **Hotel Parc Naziunal, Il Fuorn.** This century-old mountain inn in the Swiss National Park makes an ideal base for hikers. **Pros:** only hotel in the national park; nice outdoor dining terrace; idyllic location for nature lovers, hikers, and bike enthusiasts. **Cons:** rooms are basic; shared bathrooms for some rooms; not all rooms have views. $ *Rooms from: 196 SF* ✉ *Zernez* ☎ *081/8561226* 🌐 *www.ilfuorn.ch* ⏲ *Closed late Oct.–mid-May* 🛏 *37 rooms* 🍽 *Breakfast.*

THE UPPER ENGADINE

Stretching from Brail to Maloja and with a gate to the Swiss National Park at S-chanf, this is one of the country's highest regions—the highest settlement is at 6,710 feet—and one of its most dazzling. From mountain peaks, such as Piz Corvatsch or Piz Nair, you can swoosh down some of Switzerland's best slopes or simply take in the dizzying views over the lakes and mountains. In addition to sports, winter and summer are both packed tight with cultural programs and events. Summer is also when the lowland farmers send their cows up to the high Alpine pastures to graze.

PONTRESINA

38 km (24 miles) southwest of Zernez.

On a south-facing shelf along the Flaz Valley, Pontresina is a beautiful resort town. It grew by converting its farmhouses to pensions and hotels for use by summer tourists. Today its climbing school has made a name for itself, and the village has become a popular hiking center. From here

Pontresina is a popular hub for climbing and hiking.

you can see clear across to the Roseg Valley, once filled with a glacier that has retreated to the base of Piz Roseg itself. The River Flaz winds through the valley from the Morteratsch glacier, which oozes down from Piz Bernina. Although the main street is built up with restaurants and shops, the resort still has a relaxed atmosphere. Every second Thursday from the end of June until the middle of August, there's a street market in the lower part of the village, with locals selling fresh produce and handmade crafts. The altitude of Pontresina (6,000 feet) ensures wintry weather, and skiers have easy access to the slopes of Diavolezza (9,751 feet). In the off-seasons between Easter and mid-June and mid-October through Christmas, many hotels are closed.

GETTING HERE AND AROUND

Trains connecting with Pontresina by and large follow the same schedule as those to and from St. Moritz, with a change in Samedan. Pontresina–Chur trains take two hours, with a change at Samedan. The Scuol–St. Moritz trains also take you to Pontresina, with a transfer at Samedan. Direct trains from Scuol to Pontresina are also possible.

VISITOR INFORMATION

Contacts Pontresina Tourist Information. ✉ *Via Maistra 133, Pontresina* ☎ *081/8388300* 🌐 *www.pontresina.ch.*

EXPLORING

Museum Alpin. This museum documents local history and life in the region over the centuries. It also exhibits local flora, fauna, and minerals; be sure to check out the room full of birds whose recorded songs can be heard at the push of a button. The summer and winter seasons bring a revolving schedule of exhibitions. ✉ *Via Maistra 199, Pontresina* ☎ *081/8427273* 🌐 *www.pontresina.ch/museumalpin* 🎟 *8 SF* ⏲ *Closed Sun. Closed mid-Oct.–mid-Dec. and mid-Apr.–early June.*

EN ROUTE **Muottas Muragl.** At Punt Muragl, off the train line and highway between St. Moritz and Pontresina, you'll find the funicular to reach Muottas Muragl, at 8,058 feet. Up here, in the winter, walkers can take the Philosophers' Path, which is dotted with quotations from famous minds as well as more modern observations about life. Following the three circular paths takes about two to three hours. From Muottas Muragl, you can also embark on a 2½-hour-long traverse to Alp Languard, where you can take a chairlift down to Pontresina. The Segantini Hut (approximately halfway along) offers possibly the most spectacular (and photographed) views of the Upper Engadine and its series of five terraced, serenely azure lakes. Expect moderate difficulty, since parts are rocky and steep; hiking boots are a must. Instead of the funicular, an alternative way back down to the valley is the 4.2-km (2.6-mile) sled run. This, together with a large playground, makes Muottas a good excursion for children. ✉ *Punt Muragl, Pontresina* ☎ *081/8428308 Station Muottas Muragl, 081/8300000* 🎟 *Funicular (round-trip): 35 SF during daytime, 18 SF after 6 pm. Sled rental (at the valley station): 15 SF, with a 50 SF deposit or ID* ⏲ *Closed early Apr.–late May and mid-Oct.–mid-Dec.*

WHERE TO EAT

$$ SWISS ✕ **Colani Stübli.** For seasonal Engadine specialties served in a charming setting, try lunch or dinner at the Colani Stübli, inside the Hotel Steinbock. The restaurant serves regional dishes such as barley soup, Rösti, and Capuns (meat-filled dumplings wrapped in Swiss chard), but really shines in the autumn, when the kitchen prepares exceptional game and chestnut dishes. **Known for:** Engadine-style polenta; fall game dishes; central location. 💲 *Average main: 35 SF* ✉ *Hotel Steinbock, Via Maistra 219, Pontresina* ☎ *081/8393626* 🌐 *www.hotelsteinbock.ch* ⏲ *Closed mid-Oct.–early Dec.*

$ SWISS ✕ **Grond Café Pontresina.** This café offers fantastic views down the Roseg Valley, as well as a menu that satisfies all kinds of cravings—from bowls of breakfast muesli to a wide selection of sandwiches, pastas, risotto, and plates of Rösti. Locals know to ask for the homemade Engadiner *Nusstorte* (shortbread crust with a dense nut-and-caramel filling) or a strudel—as well as for a seat on the terrace. **Known for:** yummy desserts; terrace seating; lovely mountain views. 💲 *Average main: 18 SF* ✉ *Via da Mulin 28, Pontresina* ☎ *081/8388030* 🌐 *www.grond-engadin.ch* ⏲ *No dinner.*

$$$ SWISS Fodor's Choice ★ ✕ **Panorama Restaurant Muottas Muragl.** For a candlelit, romantic Swiss meal with a truly spectacular view, take the funicular up to the restaurant at the Romantik Hotel Muottas Muragl. The rustic-chic setting and expansive terrace provide perfect outlooks to the lakes and mountains as you dine on local and seasonal specialties. **Known for:** some of the best views around; friendly, efficient service; well-prepared renditions of classic local dishes. 💲 *Average main: 46 SF* ✉ *Romantik Hotel Muottas Muragl, Samedan* ☎ *081/8428232* 🌐 *www.muottasmuragl.ch* ⏲ *Closed mid-Apr.–early June and mid-Oct.–mid-Dec.*

The spa at the Grand Hotel Kronenhof is a relaxing place to soak in the mountain views.

WHERE TO STAY

$$$ HOTEL Fodor's Choice ★ **Grand Hotel Kronenhof.** A grand Versailles set amid mountain peaks, the Kronenhof is the pinnacle for rest, relaxation, and pampering, with gorgeous designs inside and out, a keen attention to detail, and a sprawling lawn perfect for admiring the views of Roseg Valley. **Pros:** beautiful grounds and location; excellent dining options; top-of-the-line children's facility. **Cons:** expensive for this area; hotel checkout could be more streamlined; more modern rooms lack character of the traditional ones. *Rooms from: 485 SF* ✉ *Via Maistra 1, Pontresina* ☎ *081/8303030* 🌐 *www.kronenhof.com* ⏲ *Closed early Apr.–mid-June and mid-Oct.–early Dec.* *112 rooms* *Breakfast.*

$ HOTEL **Hotel Roseg Gletscher.** This isolated hotel is reachable only on foot or by horse-drawn carriage/sleigh (it's about 7½ km [4½ miles] up the ruggedly beautiful Roseg Valley), but its location in this untouched valley at the foot of a majestic glacier makes for a unique hiking or relaxing point. **Pros:** unique, gorgeous location; good food; great spot for hiking. **Cons:** remote; can be noisy before dawn during hunting season; simple rooms. *Rooms from: 180 SF* ✉ *Roseg Valley, Pontresina* ☎ *081/8426445* 🌐 *www.roseg-gletscher.ch* ⏲ *Closed early Apr.–mid-June and mid-Oct.–early Dec.* *15 rooms* *Breakfast.*

$$ HOTEL **Hotel Station.** Next to the Roseg Valley entrance, the cross-country skiing center, and the train station, this handy hotel offers dependable, low-key accommodations with simple, tasteful guest rooms decked out in traditional wooden furniture. **Pros:** open year-round; easily accessible; relatively affordable. **Cons:** a short, uphill walk into town; guest rooms on the small side; rooms on ground floor can be noisy. *Rooms from:*

230 SF ✉ Cuntschett 2, Pontresina ☎ 081/8388000 🌐 www.station-pontresina.ch *21 rooms* *Breakfast.*

NIGHTLIFE

BARS AND LOUNGES

Bar Pitschna Scena. This bar has live music Thursday nights in summer and winter seasons. *✉ Hotel Saratz, Via de la Staziun 2, Pontresina ☎ 081/8394000.*

Gianottis Wilderei. This elegant wine bar with its wood, stone, and fur seat cushions serves a wide range of wines, along with small plates and larger grilled dishes, and is conveniently located on the main street. *✉ Via Maistra 140, Pontresina ☎ 081/8427090.*

Pöstli Bar. The Pöstli serves up cocktails, long drinks, and shooters, and has live music on occasion. *✉ Hotel Post, Via Maistra 160, Pontresina ☎ 081/8389300.*

SPAS

Bellevita. In the center of Pontresina, Bellavita (meaning "good life") features indoor and outdoor hot pools, cold plunge pools, and a range of wet and dry saunas. Views of the surrounding mountains are epic, and the wellness area is complemented by a decent range of massage options (reservations required). The spa is family-friendly, with a diving board and 245-foot black-hole slide to keep younger (and in some cases, not so young) guests occupied. Prices are reasonable and the baths are open into the evening, giving visitors the opportunity to watch the sun dip behind the mountains from the comfort of a relaxing thermal pool. *✉ Via Maistra 178, Pontresina ☎ 081/8370037 general, 081/8370038 appointments 🌐 www.pontresina-bellavita.ch.*

SPORTS AND THE OUTDOORS

BIKING

Cross-Country Ski and Bike Center. Rent a bike next to the train station, and you can return it at one of 80 railway stations throughout Switzerland. *✉ Cuntschett 1, Pontresina ☎ 081/8388388 🌐 www.pontresina-sports.ch/bikezentrum/bikezentrum_en.*

Fähndrich Sport. Touring and mountain bikes can be rented at the Fähndrich Sport. *✉ Via Maistra 169, Pontresina ☎ 081/8427155 🌐 www.faehndrich-sport.ch.*

CARRIAGE RIDES

Horse-drawn carriages and sleighs in Pontresina are very popular in both summer and winter, when there is scheduled service. They should be booked in advance.

Kutschenbetrieb H. Riedberger. In summer (roughly June through October) you can take a one-hour carriage ride. In winter (December 20 through Easter), you can take a sleigh ride. *✉ Chesa Cuntschett, Pontresina ☎ 079/6812980 🌐 www.kutschenbetrieb-riedberger.ch.*

Wohlis Kutschenfahrten & Gina's Reitschule. In addition to carriage rides, this company offers horseback riding and instruction. Regularly scheduled group rides (June through October) travel between the Hotel Roseg and the Hauptbahnhof in Pontresina; you can also book private carriage rides. Reservations are required. *✉ Hof Suot Spuondas,*

Cuntschett 9, Pontresina ☎ *078/9447555 carriage rides and reservations, 078/6521332 horseback riding* 🌐 *www.engadin-kutschen.ch* 🎫 *Group rides from 20 SF; private carriage rides from 120 SF.*

HIKING

Pontresina and the top of the Alp Languard chairlift (open only in summer) are good starting points for hikers.

The Muottas Muragl funicular near Pontresina carries you to a high Alpine perch to begin the 9-km (5½-mile) trek to Alp Languard. You're bound to break a sweat; the trail climbs 912 vertical feet and drops 3,038. The chairlift at Alp Languard brings you back to the valley.

The Diavolezza cable car, which runs in the summer, and the Rhaetian Railway also bring you to good hiking trails. For information on a variety of guided excursions and glacier hiking, contact the tourist office. If you're staying overnight in Pontresina, some of the tours are free.

ICE SPORTS

Eisplatz Roseg. There's a large natural ice-skating rink at the Eisplatz Roseg. Rental skates (complimentary) and instruction (for a fee) are available. There are also curling rinks, with introductory lessons. ✉ *Via Maistra 62, Pontresina* ☎ *081/8426346* ☞ *Closed Mar.–mid-Dec.*

MOUNTAIN CLIMBING

Bergsteigerschule Pontresina. The biggest mountain-climbing school in Switzerland, Bergsteigerschule Pontresina offers instruction in rock and ice climbing for people of all skill levels. The company also leads guided tours and ski tours in English. ✉ *Via Maistra 163, Pontresina* ☎ *081/8428282* 🌐 *bergsteiger-pontresina.ch.*

SKIING

There's a small beginners' slope in the village at San Spiert. The compact ski areas of Diavolezza (9,768 feet) and, on the other side of the road, Lagalb (9,705 feet), on the Bernina Pass, complement the much more extensive ones at St. Moritz. All three are about 20 minutes away by bus. Lift tickets cost 156 SF for two days, 376 SF for a six-day regional ticket. Individual day passes for Diavolezza and Lagalb cost 67 SF, or 38 SF if you stay more than one night in a participating hotel in the region. Rides on the Engadine bus service are included in the price of a regional ski ticket.

Cross-Country Ski and Bike Center. Below the village, on the Engadine Marathon Trail, is the Cross-Country Ski and Bike Center. ✉ *Cuntschett 1, Pontresina* ☎ *081/8388388* 🌐 *www.pontresina-sports.ch.*

Ski and Snowboard School. Newcomers can learn the basics at the Ski and Snowboard School. ✉ *Rondo/Kongresszentrum Pontresina, Via Maistra 133, Pontresina* ☎ *081/8388383* 🌐 *www.pontresina-sports.ch.*

ST. MORITZ

5 km (3 miles) west of Pontresina, 85 km (53 miles) southeast of Chur.

Fodor's Choice ★

Who put the *ritz* in St. Moritz? Undoubtedly, St. Moritz's reputation was made by the people who go there and who have been going there, generation after generation, since 1864, when hotelier Johannes Badrutt dared a group of English tourists—already summer regulars—to brave

Funiculars and cable cars whisk hikers and walkers to magnificent trails above St. Moritz.

the Alpine winter as his guests. They loved it, delighted in the novelty of snowy mountain beauty—until then considered unappealing—and told their friends. By the turn of the century St. Moritz, Switzerland, and snow were all the rage.

The first historical reference to the town dates from 1139, and in 1537 Paracelsus, the great Renaissance physician and alchemist, described the health-giving properties of the St. Moritz springs. St. Moritz gets busy with celebs and socialites around the winter holidays—some New Year's Eve events have guest lists closed a year in advance—but the glitter fades by spring. Very ordinary people fill the streets come summer—the same hikers you might meet in any resort—and hotel prices plummet.

Then visitors see St. Moritz for what it really is: a busy, built-up old resort city that sprawls across a hillside above an aquamarine lake, the St. Moritzersee, surrounded by forested hills and by graceful, though not the region's most dramatic, peaks. Piz Rosatsch, with its glacier, dominates the view, with Piz Languard (10,699 feet) on the east and Piz Güglia (7,492 feet) on the west.

St. Moritz-Dorf is the most like a downtown, with busy traffic, but outlawing cars in the center of town and building the Serletta parking lot near the train station has alleviated competitive parking. Other than that, don't expect a picturesque village.

Even a hundred years of hype have not exaggerated its attraction as a winter sports center. The place that twice hosted the Olympic games (1928 and 1948)—and trademarked the shining sun as its logo—is still well set up for sports, with excellent facilities for ice-skating, bobsledding, ski jumping, and horseback riding. But it hardly has a lock on fine skiing: St. Moritz shares a broad complex of trails and facilities with Sils, Silvaplana, Celerina, and Pontresina; only the slopes of Corviglia, Marguns, and Piz Nair are directly accessible from town.

GETTING HERE AND AROUND

Between Chur and St. Moritz, direct trains take about two hours. To get to St. Moritz from Scuol you must change trains in Samedan.

VISITOR INFORMATION

Contacts St. Moritz Tourist Information. ✉ *Via Maistra 12, St. Moritz* ☎ *081/8373333* 🌐 *www.stmoritz.ch.*

EXPLORING

Museum Engiadinais (*Engadiner Museum*). One of the few reminders that flashy, contemporary St. Moritz was not so very long ago a simple Engadine village is the Engadiner Museum, a reproduction of the traditional sgraffitied home. In a building dating from 1906, the fully renovated museum has displays of furniture, tools, and pottery in rooms decorated in styles from different periods, as well as an exhibit explaining the Romansch language. Visitors receive an iPad that acts as an electronic guide as they make their way through the museum. ✉ *Via dal Bagn 39, St. Moritz* ☎ *081/8334333* 🌐 *www.museum-engiadinais.ch* 🎫 *13 SF* 🕒 *Closed Tues. and mid-Oct.–late Nov.*

Segantini Museum. The somewhat forbidding stone structure that houses the Segantini Museum showcases the work of Italian artist Giovanni Segantini (1858–99). His huge triptych *La Vita, La Natura, La Morte* hangs in the domed upper floor. Take a seat on the bench to take in the work of this fine impressionist artist. ✉ *Via Somplaz 30, St. Moritz* ☎ *081/8334454* 🌐 *www.segantini-museum.ch* 🎫 *10 SF* 🕒 *Closed Mon.; mid-Oct.–mid-Dec.; and mid-Apr.–mid-May.*

WHERE TO EAT

$$$ INTERNATIONAL

✕ **Chesa Veglia.** In a 17th-century rustic-luxe *Bauernhof* (farmhouse) whose raw beams, aged wood, and native carvings have been self-consciously restored, the Chesa Veglia (run by Badrutt's Palace hotel, which is just up the street) is divided into three restaurants: an upscale grill (Grill Chafaö), which uses an original stone oven; a cozy Stübli (Patrizier Stublen); and a pizzeria (Pizzeria Heuboden). Menus include a good range of Continental and local cuisine—with sky-high St. Moritz prices, except for the more casual, family-friendly pizzeria (which, true to St. Moritz style, still uses premium ingredients like truffles and Grison air-dried meat in addition to the classics). **Known for:** rustic yet extremely upscale setting; choice of dining options (though all expensive); truffle pizza at the pizzeria. 💲 *Average main: 60 SF* ✉ *Via Veglia 2, St. Moritz* ☎ *081/8372800* 🌐 *www.badruttspalace.com/en/restaurants-bars-club/chesa-veglia* 🕒 *Closed Apr.–mid-June and mid-Sept–late Nov. Grill Chafaö: Closed in summer. No lunch. Pizzeria Heuboden: No lunch.*

$$ SWISS

✕ **Engiadina.** With its pine-paneled interior and crackling log fire, this traditional Engadine restaurant has all the coziness of Grandma's house: it's more homespun than glitz and glamour, and reasonably priced and low-key for couples or a small group of friends. The specialty is a decadent champagne fondue, though other favorites are steak with french fries and, in winter, escargots. **Known for:** lovely lake views; champagne fondue; charming and friendly atmosphere. *Average main: 38 SF* ✉ *Via Dimlej 1, St. Moritz* ☎ *081/8333000* 🌐 *www.restaurant-engiadina.ch.*

$$ SWISS Fodor's Choice ★ **Meierei.** On a winding, private forest road partway around the lake, this 17th-century *Landgasthof* (country inn) is sought out for its light meals and delicious combinations using fresh, local ingredients, along with tempting house-made baked goods for dessert. It was formerly both a farm and a dairy, and its sun terrace attracts day hikers, cross-country skiers, and horseback riders. **Known for:** pasta and risotto dishes made with local ingredients; meat and game, including lamb and deer; outdoor seating with lovely lake vistas. *Average main: 36 SF* ✉ *Via Dimlej 52, St. Moritz* ☎ *081/8387000* 🌐 *meierei.ch/en/gastronomy* *Closed Apr.–mid-June and late Oct.–early Dec.*

$$$$ MEDITERRANEAN **Talvò by Dalsass.** With a focus on the highest-quality ingredients and a simplistic, Mediterranean cooking style that allows each individual taste to shine, dining here is a true culinary experience, though be prepared to spend almost as much on a meal as on a hotel room. Though the menu changes seasonally, it always includes a tempting mix of fish, game, meat, and poultry dishes, with a blend of local and international ingredients. **Known for:** refined Mediterranean cuisine; historic 17th-century farmhouse setting; olive oil chocolate mousse. *Average main: 78 SF* ✉ *Via Gunels 15, Champfèr* *3 km (2 miles) southwest of St. Moritz, about 330 feet from the postbus stop* ☎ *081/8334455* 🌐 *www.talvo.ch* *Closed Apr.–late June and mid-Oct.–early Dec. Closed Mon., Tues., and Wed. in summer. No lunch Mon. and Tues. in winter.*

WHERE TO STAY

$$$$ HOTEL FAMILY Fodor's Choice ★ **Badrutt's Palace Hotel.** From the moment your Rolls-Royce whisks you from the train station to the hotel, you'll see why Badrutt's Palace is Switzerland at its most glitzy and glamorous, complete with magnificent public spaces, an exclusive spa, and a high-society pedigree. **Pros:** amazing concierge services; fabulous lake and mountain views; wonderful kids' club. **Cons:** sky-high prices; some rooms on the small side; not all rooms have lake views. *Rooms from: 830 SF* ✉ *Via Serlas 27, St. Moritz* ☎ *081/8371000* 🌐 *www.badruttspalace.com* *Closed Apr.–mid-June and mid-Sept.–early Dec.* *157 rooms* *Breakfast.*

$$$$ HOTEL FAMILY Fodor's Choice ★ **Giardino Mountain.** This Alpine-chic design hotel—within seven 18th-century buildings that formerly housed a boarding school—brings a younger, fresher vibe to often-traditional St. Moritz. **Pros:** stylish, contemporary feel; friendly, personalized service; free extra room for kids age six and above when you stay at least five nights. **Cons:** limited restaurant options near the hotel; some rooms on the small side; a bit far removed from the St. Moritz action. *Rooms from: 587 SF* ✉ *Via Maistra 3, Champfèr* ☎ *081/8366300* *Closed mid-Mar.–late June and mid-Sept.–mid-Dec.* *giardino-mountain.ch* *Breakfast.*

$$$ HOTEL **Hotel Corvatsch.** This family-run hotel in the middle of St. Moritz-Bad will make you feel right at home, as the friendly service and a drink by the crackling fire in the cozy "living room" are often all one needs at the end of a long day of hiking or skiing. **Pros:** family hosts are welcoming and helpful; the food is delicious; easy walk to lake or town. **Cons:** those who need a "room with a view" should stay elsewhere;

beds are not large; no spa. *Rooms from: 340 SF* *Via Tegiatscha 1, St. Moritz-Bad* *081/8375757* *www.hotel-corvatsch.ch* *Closed mid-Oct.–Dec. and late Apr.–late May* *31 rooms* *Breakfast.*

$$ B&B/INN **Hotel Languard.** Set in the town center, this delightful little hotel shares the Kulm's lovely mountain views, but not its prices. **Pros:** affordable (for St. Moritz) with five-star views; central location; charming wood interiors. **Cons:** no spa or restaurant; bathrooms are a bit dark; steep climb up from the train station. *Rooms from: 281 SF* *Via Veglia 14, off Via Maistra, St. Moritz* *081/8333137* *www.languard-stmoritz.ch* *Closed late Apr.–early June and mid-Oct.–early Dec.* *22 rooms* *Breakfast.*

$$$ HOTEL **Hotel Schweizerhof.** This big-city hotel in the center of town was built in 1896 and still offers grand public areas with carved wood and moldings alongside refined, if a tad faded, guest rooms with truly wondrous views. **Pros:** central location; views over lake from top floor; lively bars. **Cons:** old-world grandeur feels a tad faded; bathrooms have the newest amenities, but are a bit tight; small spa area open only upon request in summer. *Rooms from: 430 SF* *Via dal Bagn 54, St. Moritz* *081/8370707* *www.schweizerhofstmoritz.ch* *82 rooms* *Breakfast.*

$$$ HOTEL **Hotel Waldhaus am See.** As the hotel in St. Moritz closest to the lake, this charming property geared to leisurely stays emphasizes its superlative views with a big, sunny balcony and dining rooms with enormous windows. **Pros:** peaceful location with stunning views; amazing whiskey bar; free parking. **Cons:** dated in places; small wellness area; a bit of a hike to the train station and into town. *Rooms from: 351 SF* *Via Dimlej 6, St. Moritz* *081/8366000* *www.waldhaus-am-see.ch* *50 rooms* *Breakfast.*

$$$ HOTEL FAMILY **Hotel Waldhaus Sils.** With old-fashioned style and inviting public spaces, this charming grande dame in the neighboring village of Sils ticks all the boxes, from elegant restaurants to a surprisingly modern and architecturally stunning spa. **Pros:** hasn't lost its old-world charm; high-quality food; unique spa area. **Cons:** some rooms are still decorated in a 1980s style; reception can be a bit harried; far from the St. Moritz train station. *Rooms from: 364 SF* *Via de Fex 3, Sils* *081/8385100* *waldhaus-sils.ch/en* *Closed mid-Apr.–early June and mid-Oct.–mid-Dec.* *140 rooms* *Breakfast.*

$$$$ HOTEL FAMILY Fodor's Choice ★ **Kulm Hotel St. Moritz.** This luxury hotel can claim its share of St. Moritz superlatives: it was the first hotel here (1856) *and* the first house to have electricity in all of Switzerland (1878), but modern comfort has come a long way, as seen in top-quality facilities like a 9-hole golf course and putting green, and ice-skating and curling in winter. **Pros:** excellent location in the center of town; no desire is too big or too small; amazing spa, particularly the outdoor pool, with wondrous views. **Cons:** exterior is not the most attractive; very expensive; food quality can vary. *Rooms from: 675 SF* *Via Veglia 18, St. Moritz* *081/8368000* *www.kulm.com* *Closed early Apr.–mid-June and early Sept.–early Dec.* *172 rooms* *Breakfast.*

$$$ HOTEL FAMILY Fodor's Choice ★ **Nira Alpina.** Across from the Corvatsch cable car that transports guests up 3½ km (2 miles) to the highest peak in the surrounding area, this boutique design hotel, quite different from most other "traditional" St. Moritz–area accommodations, is an ideal choice for skiing, sledding, and hiking on Silvaplana Lake—along with just hanging out in its cool environs. **Pros:** ski-in ski-out to Corvatsch; friendly service; free underground parking. **Cons:** spa can get a bit crowded; no swimming pool; need to drive or cab to St. Moritz proper. *Rooms from: 337 SF* ✉ *Via dal Corvatsch 76, St. Moritz* ☎ *081/8386969* 🌐 *www.niraalpina.com* *Closed early Apr.–mid-June and late Sept.–early Dec.* *70 rooms* *Breakfast.*

$$$$ HOTEL Fodor's Choice ★ **Suvretta House.** Outside St. Moritz, with stupendous views of Piz Corvatsch and Silvaplana Lake, the Suvretta House encourages visitors to take advantage of the indoor ski center, rental facilities, and ski school, with private access to the Corviglia slopes just outside the front door—or just to lounge by the indoor pool or outdoor hot tub. **Pros:** beautiful location and views; state-of-the-art ski facilities; 25-meter pool. **Cons:** a bit far out of town; some common areas seem dated; ultraformal atmosphere at Grand Restaurant not to everyone's taste. *Rooms from: 660 SF* ✉ *Via Chasellas 1, St. Moritz* ☎ *081/8363636* 🌐 *www.suvrettahouse.ch* *Closed early Apr.–June and Sept.–early Dec.* *181 rooms* *Breakfast.*

NIGHTLIFE AND PERFORMING ARTS

To find out what's happening, check the English-language section in the biweekly *Engadine Information* brochure, available at the tourist office, hotels, and shops, or find information online (🌐 *www.engadin.stmoritz.ch*).

BARS AND LOUNGES

Cava. The après-ski clique favors the Steffani Hotel's Cava. ✉ *Via Traunter Plazzas 6, St. Moritz* ☎ *081/8369696* 🌐 *www.steffani.ch/en/cava-bar.*

Devil's Place. Choose from the world's largest selection of whiskeys (2,500 at last count) at the Devil's Place, in the Waldhaus am See. It has been mentioned in the *Guinness Book of World Records.* ✉ *Via Dimlej 6, St. Moritz* ☎ *081/8366000* 🌐 *www.waldhaus-am-see.ch/en-us/Whisky-Wine.*

QN Bar. Lively, late-night action in the center of town can be found downstairs in the Hotel Schweizerhof's QN Bar, which serves cocktails, champagne, wine, and snacks, along with cigars. ✉ *Via dal Bagn 54, St. Moritz* ☎ *081/8370707* 🌐 *www.schweizerhofstmoritz.ch/en/party-bars-and-nightlife/bars/.*

Sunny Bar. Midnight jazz and rock concerts make this venue in the Kulm Hotel—the oldest sports bar in the Alps—a lively weekend option in summer and winter. ✉ *Via Veglia 18, St. Moritz* ☎ *081/8368000* 🌐 *www.kulm.com/en/culinary-art/bars-lobby.*

CASINOS

Casino St. Moritz. In the Kempinski Grand Hôtel des Bains in St. Moritz-Bad, the Casino St. Moritz offers roulette, poker, blackjack, and slot machines with a "fantasy jackpot." ✉ *Via Mezdi 29, St. Moritz* ☎ *081/8375454* 🌐 *www.casinostmoritz.ch.*

DANCING

Anton's Bar. Open year-round, Anton's Bar is a winter-season hot spot at the Suvretta House known for its live music and large selection of gin. ✉ *Via Chasellas 1, St. Moritz* ☎ *081/8363636* 🌐 *www.suvrettahouse.ch.*

King's Club. In Badrutt's Palace, the King's Club—the oldest nightclub in Switzerland—has a Moorish decor. Open only in winter, it has a steep cover charge on weekends. ✉ *Via Serlas 27, St. Moritz* ☎ *081/8372638* 🌐 *www.badruttspalace.com/en/restaurants-bars-club/kings-club.*

Pampa St. Moritz. This come-as-you-are club, with no dress code, showcases national and international music, including house, hip-hop, and Latin. ✉ *Plazza dal Mulin 2, St. Moritz* ☎ *081/8344273.*

Vivai. In the basement of the Steffani Hotel, Vivai is open during the winter season. ✉ *Via Traunter Plazzas 6, St. Moritz* ☎ *079/7154262* 🌐 *www.steffani.ch/en/bars/vivai-dance-club.*

MUSIC

Engadin Festival. The Engadin Festival takes place from late July to mid-August, with smaller-scale performances throughout the Upper Engadine. ✉ *St. Moritz* ☎ *081/8373333* 🌐 *www.engadinfestival.ch.*

Festival da Jazz St. Moritz. International jazz acts play in intimate venues, from the rustic Dracula's Ghost Riders Club to hotels to open-air stages, every July. ✉ *St. Moritz* 🌐 *www.festivaldajazz.ch.*

St. Moritz Salon Orchestra. The St. Moritz Chamber Orchestra gives free daily concerts in summer at 10:30 am in the spa center's hall or park. Contact the tourist office for more information. ✉ *St. Moritz* 🌐 *www.salonorchester-stmoritz.ch.*

SPAS

Medizinisches Therapiezentrum Heilbad. As a break from all those sports, the town offers relaxation at the Medizinisches Therapiezentrum Heilbad. The local mineral springs have been known for more than 3,000 years; in 1535 the physician and alchemist Paracelsus praised the water, which is the richest in iron and carbonic acid in Europe. Massages and most treatments are done in individual cabins with private baths. Choose from a St. Moritz peat pack, a mineral bath, or an aroma bath with scents such as rosemary or lavender. ✉ *Plazza Paracelsus 2, St. Moritz* ☎ *081/8333062* 🌐 *www.heilbad-stmoritz.ch* ⏲ *Closed Sun.*

SPORTS AND THE OUTDOORS

This is the place to see winter sports that were, or still are, found only here, such as polo and cricket played on snow, bobsledding on natural ice, and horse racing on snow, which includes *skijöring* (skiers pulled by riderless horses). The frozen lake acts as the "white arena" for some events and provides the backdrop for others. A tent village complete with grandstands, palm trees, restaurants, bars, and art exhibitions is installed on the lake in February during the White Turf, which includes horse racing and skijöring.

4

BIKING

Free maps of biking routes are available at the tourist office.

Engadin Bikes. Engadin Bikes rents all types of bikes, along with helmets and locks, and can suggest bike routes. ✉ *Via del Bagn 1, St. Moritz* ☎ *081/8289888* 🌐 *engadinbikes.com.*

BOBSLEDDING

In 1890 and 1891 the first bobsled races were held on the road between St. Moritz and Celerina. The present-day run, built each year from natural ice, follows roughly the same course; it's the only one of its kind in the world.

Olympia Bob Run. There is no entry fee if you want to watch the regular Olympia Bob Run races. Or you can tear along the run yourself by riding behind an experienced pilot. Book well in advance. The run is open from late December through early March. ✉ *Plazza Gunter Sachs, St. Moritz* ☎ *081/8300200* 🌐 *www.olympia-bobrun.ch.*

GOLF

Engadine Golf Course. Samedan's 18-hole Engadine Golf Course, the oldest on the continent, is about 10 minutes by car from St. Moritz. It's open from mid-May to early October. ✉ *A l'En 14, Samedan* ☎ *081/8510466* 🌐 *www.engadin-golf.ch/en* 🎫 *90–120 SF (depending upon season and day)* ⛳ *18 holes, 6239 yards, par 72.*

Kulm Golf St. Moritz. Kulm Golf St. Moritz has a 9-hole course in the Kulm Park. ✉ *St. Moritz* ☎ *081/8368236* 🌐 *www.stmoritz-golfclub.ch* 🎫 *35 SF; free for Kulm Hotel and Grand Hotel Kronenhof guests* ⛳ *9 holes, 1017 yards, par 27.*

HIKING

There are dozens of hiking and walking routes around St. Moritz, all well signposted. Maps are available at the tourist office. All cable cars, funiculars, and some chairlifts run in summer, providing access to higher trails, including the magnificent Via Engiadina path (moderate difficulty), which runs along the mountainside at roughly 6,560 feet to the beginning of the valley. The full walk takes about six hours, but you can descend to valley level earlier if you're tuckered out.

ICE SPORTS

Cresta Run. On the world's one and only Cresta Run, riders on skeletons (metal toboggans) rush headfirst down a winding ice channel from St. Moritz to Celerina, accelerating to about 90 mph. You can watch the runs every morning from the path or the roof of the Junction Hut. If you'd like to try the run, contact the St. Moritz Tobogganing Club. It's a private club, but they do allow temporary memberships that will give you five runs. The Cresta is open from late December to early March. Note that the run is not open to women, except during special Ladies' Events. ✉ *St. Moritz* 🌐 *www.cresta-run.com.*

Kulm Hotel St. Moritz Rinks. The skating and curling rinks at the Kulm Hotel are open to the public in winter; rental skates and curling lessons are also available. ✉ *Klum Hotel St. Moritz, St. Moritz* ☎ *081/8368000* 🌐 *www.kulm.com/en/activities-events/winter.*

DID YOU KNOW?

St. Moritz is arguably the ritziest ski resort in Switzerland. If you're staying at a different resort within Graubünden but still want to try the famed slopes here, buy the lift ticket with your train ticket and the return fare will be reduced.

Ludains Ice Arena. The outdoor Ludains Ice Arena, along the lake, is open from mid-July to late April. Skate rentals are available. ✉ *Via Ludains 5, St. Moritz-Bad* ☎ *081/8335030* 🎫 *5.50 SF.*

SKIING

Don't let the whirlwind of activities at St. Moritz make you forget that its raison d'être is skiing. You can reach the **Corviglia–Piz Nair, Suvretta,** and **Marguns** slopes, immediately above St. Moritz, from the Chantarella–Corviglia funicular in Dorf, the Signal cableway in Bad, the Suvretta chairlift, and the Marguns gondolas in Celerina. There are 80 km (50 miles) of difficult, intermediate, and easy runs and a half pipe for snowboarders. The Upper Engadine ski region offers 350 km (217 miles) of prepared trails. The views from Corviglia, Piz Nair, and the Suvretta Paradise run are magnificent.

Descents behind Piz Nair (10,026 feet) eventually lead down to Marguns; they are often in shadow in early winter but have the best snow up to the end of the season. With the help of snowmaking equipment, conditions usually remain excellent until late April. The sunny Suvretta slopes are usually less crowded, but they don't have snowmaking equipment. You can join a group and go with an instructor on a free "snow safari" offered by any ski school, which begin in Sils and end in Morteratsch. One-day tickets for St. Moritz are 79 SF; six-day regional passes cost 376 SF. Prices include transportation between ski stations on the Engadine bus service.

■ TIP→ In an effort to attract more visitors, St. Moritz's top hotels have banded together to offer an unbeatable lift-ticket deal: book a minimum two-night stay, and pay 38 SF per person per day. The rest of the ticket price is covered by the hotel, which means three-star properties are less likely to participate. The deal is available only when you make your booking, so be sure to inquire up front.

Ski Service Corvatsch. Rental equipment is available at Ski Service Corvatsch in St. Moritz and Silvaplana. ✉ *Via Stredas 11, St. Moritz* ☎ *081/8387788* 🌐 *www.skiservice-corvatsch.com.*

St. Moritz Ski School. This ski school in St. Moritz is the oldest, and still one of the best, in Switzerland. ✉ *Via Stredas 14, St. Moritz* ☎ *081/8300101* 🌐 *www.skischool.ch.*

Suvretta Snowsports School. For instruction on an array of winter sports, a good bet is Suvretta Snowsports School. ✉ *Via Chasellas 1, St. Moritz* ☎ *081/8366161* 🌐 *www.suvrettasnowsports.ch.*

5

TICINO

WELCOME TO TICINO

TOP REASONS TO GO

★ **Luscious Lugano:** Nowhere in Ticino do Italian chic and Swiss quality mingle so perfectly. But there is more going on here than people-watching and ice-cream tasting; churches, museums, and the restored Old Town also demand attention.

★ **Land o' Lakes:** Gaze at the verdant mountains, cozy villages, and palm-fronted shores from the vantage point of the elegant old ferryboats that ply the waters of Lago Maggiore and Lago di Lugano.

★ **Castle-topped Bellinzona:** Old cobblestone streets, shady arcades, and three fortresses that once held the line between Italy and Switzerland turn the clock back to a time when this region belonged to Milan.

★ **Get a view:** Monte Brè (near Lugano) can be climbed on foot or by funicular, which is faster and far less tiring. Either way, the view from the top takes many a breath away.

The canton is geographically divided into two regions by the small mountain range (1,817 feet) called Monte Ceneri, which rises south of the valley below Bellinzona. Extending northeast and northwest of Monte Ceneri in the windswept Sopraceneri region are several mountainous valleys, including Valle di Blenio, Valle Maggia, Valle Verzasca, and Valle Leventina. Included in this region north of, or literally above, Monte Ceneri are Locarno and Ascona, which share a peninsula bulging into Lago Maggiore. The more developed southern region, Sottoceneri ("below Ceneri"), is home to business and resort towns, notably Lugano.

1 Sopraceneri. The capital of Ticino, Bellinzona has always been a famous crossroads thanks to three passes—the St. Gotthard, the Lukmanier, and the San Bernardino—from the north. The town's great castles—Castelgrande, Montebello, and Sasso Corbaro—prove that Bellinzona was always in the firing line. To the west along Lago Maggiore lies Locarno, Switzerland's sunniest town, with its bevy of baroque and Renaissance churches (including the cliff-top Santuario della Madonna del Sasso). Just beyond are the lakeside promenades of Ascona, so beloved by painters, and the Isole di Brissago (Brissage Islands), Switzerland's most beautiful botanical garden.

2 Sottoceneri. South of Monte Ceneri, Ticino changes. Whereas the countryside shelters many Italianate villages clustered around ancient bell towers, the bustling city of Lugano draws all eyes. There are really two Luganos. Sophisticated, modern Lugano is Switzerland's third-most-important financial center; Lugano of the old-world charm is another, its arcades and twisting streets reminiscent of a small Italian town. Fashionable boulevards and art-filled museums compete with the fabled waterside promenade, Il Lungolago, and lose out to its stupendous vistas of the blue lake and bluer peaks. On Lago di Lugano's shores lie a gaggle of gorgeous villages: Gandria, Campione, and Morcote.

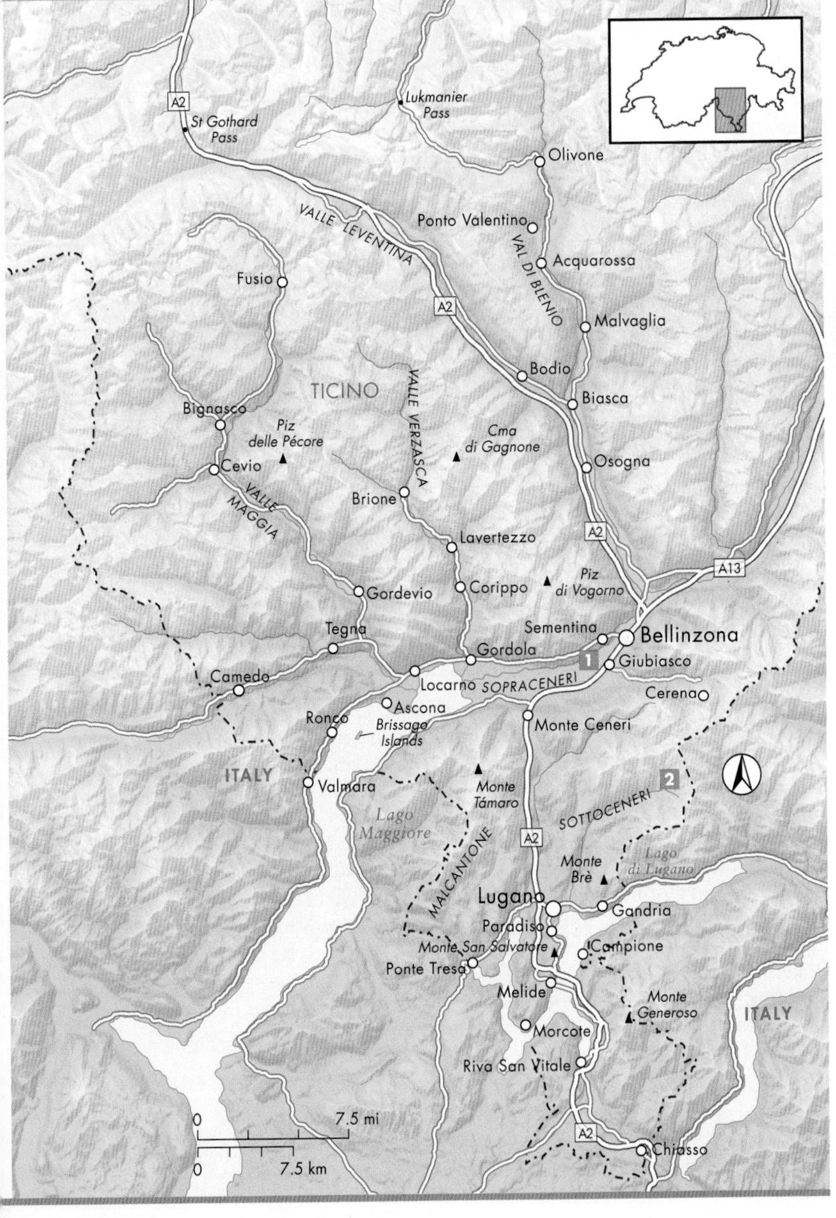

St Gothard Pass
Lukmanier Pass
Olivone
Ponto Valentino
Acquarossa
VAL DI BLENIO
VALLE LEVENTINA
Fusio
Malvaglia
Bodio
Biasca
TICINO
VALLE VERZASCA
Bignasco
Piz delle Pécore
Cma di Gagnone
Cevio
Osogna
VALLE MAGGIA
Brione
Lavertezzo
Gordevio
Corippo
Piz di Vogorno
Tegna
Sementina
Bellinzona
Gordola
Giubiasco
Camedo
Locarno
SOPRACENERI
Cerena
Ascona
Ronco
Brissago Islands
Monte Ceneri
ITALY
Valmara
Monte Támaro
Lago Maggiore
SOTTOCENERI
MALCANTONE
Monte Brè
Lago di Lugano
Lugano
Gandria
Paradiso
Monte San Salvatore
Campione
Ponte Tresa
Melide
Monte Generoso
ITALY
Morcote
Riva San Vitale
Chiasso
0
7.5 mi
0
7.5 km
A2
A13
1
2

TICINO LAKES

There's no need to travel so far south to "do as the Romans do" (and the wealthiest Italians and Swiss still do) for a taste of the good life. Simply vacation in this balmy corner of paradise.

There are many ways to explore Ticino's lovely lakes: hop on a bike for a leisurely cycle along the water (above), or head for higher ground on a hike with spectacular views (below, right).

Though it's often known as the Italian Lake Country, the shores of Lago Maggiore and Lago di Lugano are partly Swiss. You won't find white sands or waist-high waves, but its Mediterranean feel has nonetheless earned Ticino a reputation as a summer idyll. From the tall palms and semitropical vegetation gracing the coast to the rounded green mountains, which feel a little like Rio, the Ticino lakes are an ideal destination for beachcombers, photographers, and nature lovers. Sunbathe at Lugano's famous Lungolago, take a daylong cruise on Lago Maggiore, or hike the many trails that wind from the lakes to the mountains. No matter how you spend your free time, you'll probably want to spend most of it outdoors.

BEST TIME TO GO

In south-of-the-Alps Ticino, you can usually dine alfresco from March onward. By June, there are sunny skies day in, day out. July and August may be hot and crowded, but that means people-watching is at its best and that the water's fine. Autumn brings richly hued leaves and sparser crowds.

WAYS TO EXPLORE

BY WATER

Both Lago di Lugano and Lago Maggiore are crisscrossed by ferries. By day, choose the scenic tour that whisks you from Lugano around the lake, stopping at Campione d'Italia, Ponte Tresa, and Morcote. By night, a jazz or gin-soaked "booze" cruise on one of the many sleek party boats awaits. Feeling sporty? Rent a kayak or canoe, available in nearly every town on Lago Maggiore, and paddle your way across the gentle waves to Italy. Bring a picnic lunch and just drift before garnering the strength to make it home. For those who don't fancy a workout, most rental outfits also have less taxing paddleboats.

BY BIKE

Being so close to Italy means that car traffic can be intense; therefore, biking here is best suited to experienced riders. For a short adventure on two wheels, pedal through Lugano's Old Town and window-shop at the numerous art galleries or designer boutiques before stopping to indulge in creamy gelato.

Brave souls can rent a bike, or one of the hugely popular electrically assisted e-bikes, and pedal the roughly four-hour, 70-km (44-mile) Locarno–Camedo–Locarno loop. From the public beach, cross the Maggia River to Ascona and ride along the lake, with stunning views of the surrounding mountains and the Isole di Brissago. At Cannòbio, you can head back to Locarno along the same route, or continue through to Camedo and the picturesque Centovalli before arriving back where you began this tiring, thrilling journey.

BY FOOT

Begin in the Castagnola area of Lugano, following the Sentiero (Footpath) di Gandria, which passes by narrow cobblestone streets, manor houses, and silver-hued olive trees. Just past the Sasso (Rock) di Gandria, stairs lead up to the quaint fishing village of Gandria. Take time for a cool drink on a balcony overlooking the lake.

BEST PHOTOS

- Capture the magic of the Ticino lakes region by setting your lens on the following sights:
- Locarno's Casa dei Canonici and its medieval garden in the heart of the Old Town—and the Madonna del Sasso perched on the hillside above.
- Campione's otherworldly casino, visible from any point across Lago di Lugano.
- The more-than-900 varieties of camellia trees in bloom at the Camellia Park in Locarno.
- Glistening bathing beauties (of both sexes) in skimpy suits at Lugano's Lido.
- Tiny Gandria's winding streets and stately mansions.
- The crumbling stone houses and colorful frescoes in Vira, one of the tiny villages that line the Riviera del Gambarogno, a 10-km (6-mile) stretch of Maggiore lakeshore across from Locarno.
- Views of Monte San Salvatore rising lush above the morning fog.

5

Updated by Alexis Munier

Ticino is a canton apart: graceful, open, laissez-faire. This is the most glamorous of Swiss regions: the waterfront promenades of Lugano, Locarno, and Ascona contain a rich social mix of jet-set resorters among the tightly pruned trees, rhododendrons, and bobbing yachts. Yet a drive of a few miles brings the canton's impoverished past into view. Foothill and mountain villages are still scattered with low-roof stone cabins, although nowadays those cabins have been gentrified into chic vacation homes. The climate too is different, with an extraordinary amount of sunshine—much more than in central Switzerland and even sunny Italy, immediately across the border.

Hearing names like Lugano, Ascona, Locarno, and Bellinzona, it's quite natural for visitors to assume they're in Italy. Color photographs of the region might not even set them straight, because nearly every publicity shot shows palm trees, mimosas, azure waters, and indigo skies. Surely this is the Italian Mediterranean or the coast of the Adriatic. But behind the waving date palms are telltale signs: fresh paint, manicured gardens, and punctual trains. Make no mistake; it's a little bit of Italy, but the canton of Ticino is decidedly Swiss.

For the German Swiss, it's a paradise. They can cross over the St. Gotthard or San Bernardino passes and emerge into balmy sunshine, where they fill up on gnocchi and polenta in shaded grottos, drink Merlot from ceramic bowls, gaze at the waters of Lago Maggiore, and still know their lodging is strictly controlled by the Swiss Hotel Association. There's no need to even change currency. The combination is irresistible, and so in spring, summer, and fall they pour over the Alps to revel in low-risk Latin delights.

The Ticinese welcome them like rich, distant cousins, to be served, coddled, and—perhaps just a bit—tolerated. The Italian-speaking natives of Ticino—a lonely 8% of the Swiss population—are a minority in their own land, dominated politically by the German-speaking Swiss and set apart from them by language and culture.

Their Italian leanings make perfect sense. An enormous mountain chain blocks them from the north, pushing them inexorably toward their lingual roots. Most of the territory of Ticino belonged to the pre-Italian city-states of Milan and Como until 1512, when the Swiss Confederation took it by force. It remained a Swiss conquest until 1798, when from the confusion of Napoléon's campaigns it emerged a free canton. In 1803 it joined the confederation for good.

Although prosperous, with Lugano standing third in banking after Zürich and Geneva, the Ticinese hold on to their long-held mountain culture, which draws them to hike, hunt, and celebrate with great pots of risotto stirred over open outdoor fires. It's that contrast—contemporary glamour combined with an earthy past—that grants visits as balanced and satisfying as a good Merlot.

TICINO PLANNER

WHEN TO GO

No one complains about the weather in Ticino. Palm trees, magnolia, century plants, and full-bodied wines suggest why so many "northerners" come to the canton for vacation: the weather is milder in winter than elsewhere in Switzerland, and stark summer temperatures are moderated by the lakes and mountains.

There can be some surprises, though, since you are in the Alps. Sudden storms and drops in temperature are possible, so make sure you have some warm and waterproof clothing. If you intend to trek up the valleys or to the summit of a mountain, sturdy hiking boots and sunglasses are an absolute necessity.

Lush and Mediterranean, Ticino is gorgeous in springtime. The season starts as early as mid-March here, making the region a popular late-winter escape. In summertime, lakeside activity surges, and the weather can at times be hot.

PLANNING YOUR TIME

The important sights of Ticino are all fairly close to one another, but depending on the amount of time you have, you might want to choose one or two home bases. Locarno or Ascona allow easy and quick access to the Verzasca and Maggia valleys and Lago Maggiore, and Lugano opens the doors to Lago di Lugano and the gems of Gandria, Morcote, and Campione. From Bellinzona, just about everything is easy to reach. Shopping in Lugano, touring the lakes by ferry, hopping a funicular up a mountain, enjoying long meditative walks in the mountains or along the lakes, and dining on simple meals in a grotto give you some classic Ticinese moments. More active types have lots of sports options available: skiing and snowboarding in winter, and swimming, climbing, and golfing during the warmer months. If you need a big city, remember that Milan is at most 1½ hours away by train from Lugano.

GETTING HERE AND AROUND

AIR TRAVEL

The nearest international airport is in Malpensa, near Milan, Italy. Shuttle buses connect it and Linate airport (in the city of Milan) with Lugano. Swiss International Air Lines is Switzerland's domestic carrier and has direct connections to Lugano's airport, Aeroporto di Lugano-Agno.

To get to Lugano from Aeroporto di Lugano-Agno, take one of the frequent shuttle buses or a taxi.

Contacts Shuttle Bus. ☎ *091/9676030* 🌐 *www.shuttle-bus.com.*

BOAT AND FERRY TRAVEL

Lago di Lugano and Lago Maggiore are traveled by graceful steamers that carry passengers from one waterfront resort to another against the backdrop of the mountains. On Lago di Lugano, the Società Navigazione del Lago di Lugano (Navigation Company of Lake Lugano) runs excursions around the bay to Gandria and toward the Villa Favorita. Boats owned by Navigazione Lago Maggiore (Navigation Company of Lake Maggiore) cruise Lago Maggiore.

Contacts Navigazione Lago Maggiore. ✉ *1 Lungolago Motta, Locarno* ☎ *091/7516140* 🌐 *www.navlaghi.it.* **Società Navigazione del Lago di Lugano.** ✉ *Viale Castagnola 12, Lugano* ☎ *091/2221111* 🌐 *www.lakelugano.ch.*

BUS TRAVEL

The Palm Express scenic postbus route carries visitors from St. Moritz to Lugano via the Maloja Pass. It takes about four hours and can be arranged at any train station or tourist office.

You can also contact Railtour Suisse.

There's a convenient postbus sightseeing system here that you can use to get around the region, even into the backcountry. Booklets with suggested itineraries and prices are available through the Autopostale Ticino-Moesano or local tourist and post offices.

Postbus excursion prices are reduced with the Ticino Discovery Card. Even better, they are free with the Swiss Pass.

Contacts AutoPostale Svizzera SA. ✉ *19 Via Serafino Balestra, Lugano* ☎ *0840/852852* 🌐 *www.autopostale.ch.* **Railtour Suisse.** ☎ *031/3780101* 🌐 *www.railtour.ch.*

CAR TRAVEL

There are two major gateways into Ticino: the St. Gotthard Pass in the northwest and San Bernardino Pass to the northeast. From the St. Gotthard Pass, the swift A2 expressway leads down the Valle Leventina to Bellinzona, where it joins with A13, which cuts south from the San Bernardino. A2 directs traffic flow southward past Lugano to Chiasso and the Italian border, where the expressway heads directly to Como and Milan.

As an alternative, there's the St. Gotthard Tunnel. If traffic is light, it can cut an hour off your travel time, but if the passes are closed and it's during the vacation period, tunnel traffic can be nasty. A car is a real asset here if you intend to see the mountain valleys but a hindrance in the congested lakeside resorts.

TRAIN TRAVEL

The St. Gotthard route goes south from Zürich, cuts through the pass tunnel, and heads into Bellinzona and Lugano. Side connections lead into Locarno from Brig, crossing the Simplon Pass and cutting through Italy. Swiss Pass travelers do not have to pay Italian rail fares to cross from Brig to Locarno via Domodossola and the Centovalli. Trains connect out of Zürich's airport and take about three hours to Lugano, Locarno, and Ascona; from Geneva, catch the Milan express, changing at Brig or Olten. For information contact the Swiss Federal Railway, here called the Ferrovie Federali Svizzere.

Secondary rail connections here are minimal and can make all but the most mainstream rail sightseeing a complicated venture; most excursions require some postbus connections. Nevertheless, there is a regional discount pass called the Ticino Discovery Card, available from the Ferrovie Autolinee Regionali Ticinesi. The pass is valid for the Lugano and Locarno areas and provides unlimited free travel for any three days in a seven-day period on buses and trains, and a 30%–50% discount on other days.

Contacts Ferrovie Federali Svizzere. ☎ *0900/300300 1.19 SF per min* 🌐 *www.sbb.ch.*

⇨ *For more information on getting here and around, see Travel Smart Switzerland.*

HOTELS

The hotel industry of this Mediterranean region of Switzerland capitalizes on its natural assets, with lakeside views of Lago Maggiore and Lago di Lugano, and swimming pools and terraces that pay homage to the omnipresent sun. Because Ticino is at its best in spring and fall and packed with sunseekers in summer, many hotels close down for the winter. Tourist offices often publish lists of those remaining open, so if you're planning to visit in low season—even in January the lake resorts can be balmy—check carefully.

Keep in mind that most hotels are not air-conditioned, in spite of hot spells in July and August. Vacation resorts don't depend on the *demi-pension* (with some meals included) system like many of their mountain counterparts, but arrangements can be made. Remember, there are several regional and town festivals in summer, notably in Locarno and Lugano—so expect full hotels. Otherwise, Ticino is moderately well visited throughout most of the year, except in late fall and after the Christmas–New Year period.

RESTAURANTS

From rib-sticking local specialties like *pizzoccheri* to refined fare such as expertly grilled seafood and delicate homemade pasta, Ticino has it all. The Ticinese, like their Italian cousins, believe life is too short for bad food or bad wine. The result is a cuisine with simple ingredients that are delicious in any combination. Don't forget to wash it all down with local Merlot. Restaurants here run the gamut from highbrow four-star establishments to local pizzerias with wood-burning ovens.

⇨ *Hotel and restaurant reviews have been shortened. For full information, visit Fodors.com.*

WHAT IT COSTS IN SWISS FRANCS

	$	$$	$$$	$$$$
Restaurants	Under 26 SF	26 SF–45 SF	46 SF–65 SF	Over 65 SF
Hotels	Under 201 SF	201 SF–300 SF	301 SF–500 SF	Over 500 SF

Restaurant prices are the average cost of a main course at dinner or, if dinner is not served, at lunch. Hotel prices are the lowest cost of a standard double room in high season, including taxes.

TOURS

Original Tours Ticino. As this small company claims in its name, its tours are original. Combining the best of education and sightseeing, each tour begins with 60 to 90 minutes of Italian lessons and conversation. Once tongues are loosened, tours head out for an excursion. From a cable car ride up to Monte Brè to a risotto cooking class, director Patricia Carminati leads a variety of rotating daily activities. ✉ *Crocetta 23B, Lugano* ☎ *076/6166842* ✉ *tours-in-ticino@bluewin.ch* 🎫 *From SF 20.*

Swiss River Adventures. Ticino is called the "canyoning mecca of Europe" for a reason—a vast selection of gorges and lush vegetation make the canton a favorite for the sport. Follow a river down its narrow pathway, sliding over smooth rocks and rappelling down giant boulders. Tours are available for ages 12 and up, at all levels, from beginner to expert. ☎ *081/9360104* 🌐 *www.swissriveradventures.ch* 🎫 *From 150 SF.*

VISITOR INFORMATION

Contacts Ticino Turismo. ✉ *Via Canonico Ghiringhelli 7, Bellinzona* ☎ *091/8257056* 🌐 *www.ticino.ch.*

SOPRACENERI

The mountainous valleys of Valle di Blenio, Valle Maggia, Valle Verzasca, and Valle Leventina reach, like the fingers of a hand, south from the Alps into the basin of Lago Maggiore and Monte Ceneri, in the Sopraceneri. At the tips are the sun-kissed resorts of Locarno and Ascona, both on the northern edge of Lago Maggiore. Here the true spirit of the canton is still evident in the numerous small valley communities, many with fewer than 100 inhabitants, each of which was once politically autonomous. The Sopraceneri reveals a slower-paced, homier side of Ticino, leaving the flashier offerings to Lugano in the south.

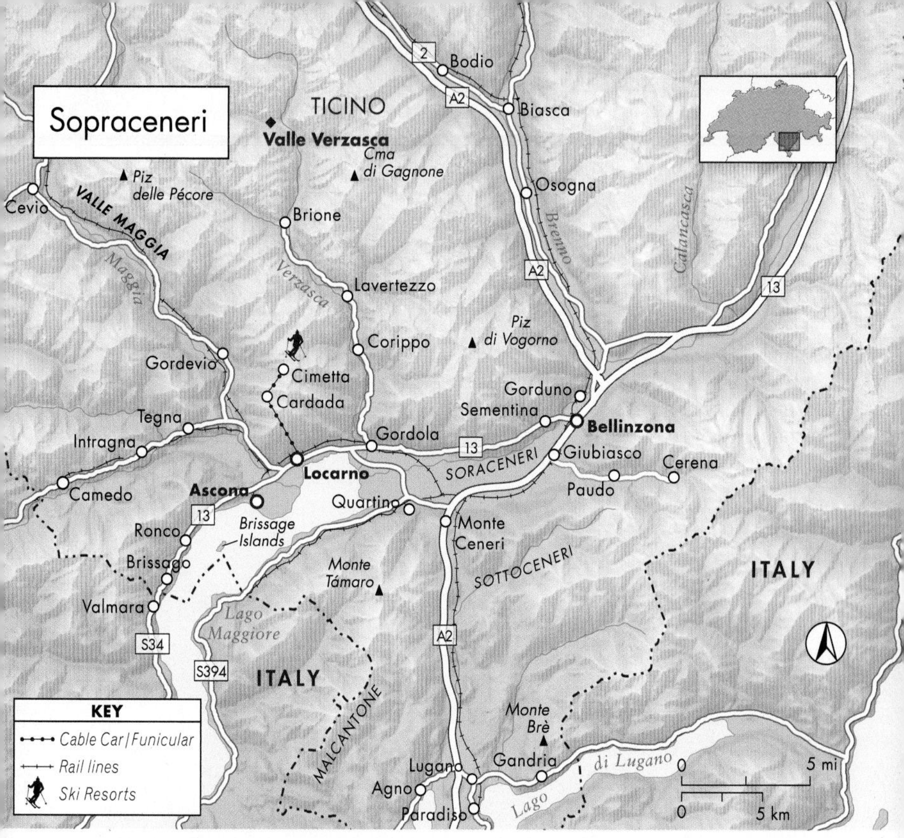

BELLINZONA

141 km (88 miles) south of Luzern, 150 km (93 miles) south of St. Moritz.

Fodor's Choice ★

All roads lead to Bellinzona, the fortified valley city that guards the important European crossroads of the St. Gotthard and San Bernardino routes. The capital of Ticino, its importance through the ages is evident in the three massive fortified castles that rise over its ancient center. As the only example of late-medieval military architecture preserved along the Alpine range, the castles and fortifications have been named a World Heritage Site by UNESCO. They were built by the Sforza and Visconti families, the dukes of Milan who ruled northern Italy and its environs for centuries. In the 15th century many of the surrounding valleys began falling into the hands of the expanding Swiss Confederation. Bellinzona, however, remained Italian until Milan itself—as well as Bellinzona—was occupied by the French in 1503. Bellinzona decided to cast its lot in with the confederation. Ironically, the names of the castles that had been built in part to keep the Swiss at bay were then changed to Schwyz, Uri, and Unterwalden—the three core cantons of the Swiss Confederation. Eventually the names were changed again, and the fortresses are known today as Castelgrande, Castello di Montebello, and Castello di Sasso Corbaro.

WORD OF MOUTH

Ticino's capital, Bellinzona, is distinguished by three medieval-era fortified castles and may make you feel as if you are in Italy rather than Switzerland, particularly when you visit the local Saturday produce market. The city remained under Italian control until the early 16th century, when it finally joined the Swiss confederation.

The three castles have been exceptionally well restored, and each merits a visit (a walk along the ramparts at night is particularly appealing), but the city itself should not be overlooked. It's a classic Lombard town, with graceful architecture, red cobblestones, and an easy, authentically Italian feel. Plus, it's relatively free of tourists and thus reveals the Ticino way of life, complete with a lively produce market on Saturday featuring boar salami, wild mushrooms, and local cheeses.

GETTING HERE AND AROUND

As the transportation gateway to Ticino, Bellinzona is not only on the Zürich–Milan route but also has frequent trains running to and from Locarno (25 minutes away) and Lugano (30 minutes). Buses to smaller villages leave from the bus depot at the train station. Remember, if you have a Swiss Pass or another rail-discount card, it applies to the buses.

VISITOR INFORMATION

Contacts Bellinzona Turismo. ✉ *Palazzo Civico, Via Camminata 2, Bellinzona* ☎ *091/8252131* 🌐 *www.bellinzonaturismo.ch.*

EXPLORING

TOP ATTRACTIONS

Castello di Montebello. The most striking of Bellinzona's three castles has a core section that dates from the 13th century. The palace and courtyard, both from the 15th century, are encircled by walls with spectacular walkways on top. The center structure houses an attractive, modern Museo Civico (Municipal Museum) and the Museo Archeologico (Archaeology Museum), with exhibits on local history and architecture, including an impressive collection of Gothic and Renaissance stone capitals. ✉ *Via Artore 4, Bellinzona* ☎ *091/8251342* 🌐 *www.bellinzonaturismo.ch/en/castles* 🎫 *10 SF, combination ticket 15 SF includes Castelgrande and Castello di Sasso Corbaro* ⏲ *Closed Feb. and Mar.*

Castello di Sasso Corbaro. This massive and forbidding fieldstone construction's almost complete absence of curves is typical of the Sforza style. It was designed by a Florentine military engineer and built in 1479 for the Duke of Milan, who insisted that the work be completed in six months, as indeed it was. Temporary art exhibitions are held in the belvedere and in the Emma Paglia Room. Ambitious walkers can reach the castle in about 45 minutes by treading uphill from Castello di Montebello along a switchback road through woods; if you're driving, follow the signs to Artore. ✉ *Via Sasso Corbaro, Bellinzona* ☎ *091/8255906* 🎫 *10 SF, 15 SF combination ticket includes Castelgrande and Castello di Montebello* ⏲ *Closed Nov.–Mar.*

Centro Storico. With its heavy-column arcades, wrought-iron balconies, and shuttered facades, Bellinzona's Old Town exhibits the direct influence of medieval Lombardy. The small area is distinguished by red cobblestones. ✉ *Bellinzona.*

Chiesa di Santa Maria delle Grazie. The earliest records of the Church of St. Mary of Grace date from the 15th century, when it was part of a Franciscan monastery. Now it's a retirement home. The church's most remarkable feature is the huge fresco painted by an unknown Lombard artist some time around 1500 on the wall segmenting the main nave. It

CLOSE UP

Ticino's Fossil Trove

Rooted firmly on the southern shores of Lago di Lugano, the 3,595-foot Monte San Giorgio has been an irresistible draw for paleontologists since the mid-19th century. Excavations in its five successive strata have regularly yielded extremely well-preserved fossils, allowing scientists to study the evolution of various groups of marine creatures of the Middle Triassic era (245–230 million years ago). Thousands of the reptiles, fish, and invertebrates found here—some of them unique specimens—have made their way into museums of paleontology in Zürich, Lugano, and Milan.

No wonder, then, that UNESCO added the entire region—an area measuring 2,098 acres and extending across the communities of Meride, Riva San Vitale, and Brusino Arsizio—to the list of World Heritage Natural Sites in 2003. This designation for Monte San Giorgio is Switzerland's second such honor, coming two years after the one for the glaciers spanning the Jungfrau, Aletsch, and Bietschhorn summits.

depicts the Crucifixion in the center, surrounded by 15 vignettes from the life of Christ. ✉ *Via Convento 5, Bellinzona* ☎ *091/8252663.*

Palazzo Civico. This splendid Renaissance structure was rebuilt in the 1920s. Its courtyard is framed by two stacked rows of delicate vaulted arcades decorated with sgraffiti (layered tinted plaster) depicting Bellinzona in the 19th century. The top floor consists of an airy loggia. ✉ *Piazza Nosetto, Bellinzona.*

WORTH NOTING

Castelgrande. Although this castle was first mentioned in a 6th-century document, the current structure dates from the 1200s. The massive exterior is dominated by two heavy, unmatched towers and the remaining portion of a crenellated wall that once stretched all the way to the river. Modern renovations have added an elaborate complex of restaurants and museums that include historical and archaeological exhibitions. The 14th-century ceiling murals, created to embellish the wooden ceiling of a local villa (now demolished), offer a peek at privately commissioned decorative art. A dramatic audiovisual history of Bellinzona and the Ticino Valley is shown in one room. ✉ *Salita al Castelgrande, Bellinzona* ☎ *091/8258145* 🎫 *Museum 10 SF, inner courtyard free, combination ticket 15 SF includes Castello di Montebello and Castello di Sasso Corbaro.*

Chiesa Collegiata di San Pietro e San Stefano. The sober, late-Renaissance facade of the Collegiate Church of St. Peter and St. Stephen, begun in the 16th century, stands across from the Castelgrande. Its baroque interior is richly decorated with frescoes and stuccowork by a host of Ticino artists. Of particular note is the late-18th-century Crucifixion attributed to Simone Peterzano that serves as the central altar painting. ✉ *Piazza Collegiata, Bellinzona* ☎ *091/8252131.*

Chiesa San Biagio. One of Bellinzona's two Italianate churches, St. Biagio is a spare medieval treasure guarded on the exterior by an outsize fresco of a soldierly Christ. The 12th-century late-Romanesque structure suggests a transition into Gothic style. Alternating natural red brick and gray stone complement fragments of exquisitely colored 14th-century frescoes. ✉ *Via San Biagio 13, Bellinzona* ☎ *091/8252131.*

Museo Villa dei Cedri. The city's art gallery sporadically mounts worthwhile exhibits of pieces from its collection, donated by private citizens. Behind the garden and grounds, the city maintains a tiny vineyard used to produce its very own Merlot, available for sale inside. ✉ *Piazza San Biagio 9, Bellinzona* ☎ *091/8218520* 🌐 *www.villacedri.ch* 🎫 *10 SF* ⏲ *Closed Mon. and Tues.*

WHERE TO EAT

$$$ MODERN ITALIAN Fodor's Choice ★

✕ **Castelgrande.** The oldest of the city's castles boasts a chic, modern restaurant that offers a serious experience, with daringly cool, postmodern decor, sophisticated cuisine from chef Davide Alberti, and a wine list that includes more than 70 Ticino Merlots. Downstairs, the more casual Grotto restaurant has a lighter atmosphere, and its stunning summer terrace is a great spot to soak up views and sunshine. **Known for:** excellent views; extensive selection of local wines; both fancy and casual dining areas. $ *Average main: 42 SF* ✉ *Salita al Castelgrande, Bellinzona* ☎ *091/8148781* 🌐 *www.ristorantecastelgrande.ch* ⏲ *Closed Sun., Mon., and July and Aug.*

$$ ITALIAN

✕ **Grotto Malakoff.** In this small family restaurant uphill from the town center, chef Rita Fuso prepares innovative Italian dishes and variations on regional fare from high-quality local ingredients—the pasta is homemade, the vegetables and meats often come from nearby farms, and some of the herbs come from Fuso's own garden. The best value (at around 32 SF) is the daily two-course special, with dishes such as monkfish carpaccio followed by a beef fillet with grilled seasonal vegetables. **Known for:** ultrafresh ingredients; simple yet refined cuisine; quaint hillside location. $ *Average main: 38 SF* ✉ *Carrale Bacilieri 10, Bellinzona* ☎ *091/8254940* ⏲ *Closed Sun. and Wed.*

$$ MEDITERRANEAN

✕ **Osteria Sasso Corbaro.** From the heights of the ancient Castello di Sasso Corbaro, this atmospheric restaurant serves meals inside a beautifully restored hall, and in the summer you can dine alfresco at sturdy granite tables in the shady, walled-in courtyard. The cooking, Mediterranean with French touches, includes fresh seafood, good local wines round out the experience, and the 45-minute walk up from the rail station is a virtuous prelude to indulging in desserts like creamy panna cotta and homemade tiramisu. **Known for:** ice cream–layered tiramisu; historic atmosphere; valley-wide views. $ *Average main: 38 SF* ✉ *Castello di Sasso Corbaro, Via Sasso Corbaro 44, Bellinzona* ☎ *091/8255532* 🌐 *www.osteriasassocorbaro.ch* ⏲ *No dinner Sun. Closed Mon. and Dec.–Feb.*

WHERE TO STAY

$ HOTEL FAMILY

🏨 **Hotel & SPA Internazionale.** Mixing the contemporary with the historic, the century-old hotel is furnished with black-and-white modern pieces set against a gray palette, which contrasts with original stained-glass windows and a wrought-iron staircase. **Pros:** central location; two wheelchair-accessible rooms; excellent, varied breakfast. **Cons:**

5

top floor not accessible by elevator; no room service; gray rooms could use a hint of color. *Rooms from: 200 SF* ✉ *Viale Stazione 35, Bellinzona* ☎ *091/8254333* 🌐 *www.hotel-internazionale.ch* *61 rooms* *Breakfast.*

$ B&B/INN **Locanda Osteria Brack.** Owners Marco and Gesa Brack run a very fine bed-and-breakfast in this converted farmhouse perched on the hillside of Gudo, between Bellinzona and Locarno. **Pros:** peaceful, beautiful surroundings; owners are passionate about sharing their unique philosophy; excellent osteria is the main draw for this property. **Cons:** remote location; besides the hotel's restaurant, there are limited dining choices; without a car it's a steep walk uphill. *Rooms from: 200 SF* ✉ *Via Malacarne 26, Progero* ☎ *091/8591254* 🌐 *www.osteriabrack.ch* *Closed Dec.–Feb. Restaurant closed Tues. and Wed.* *7 rooms* *Breakfast.*

LOCARNO

25 km (15 miles) west of Bellinzona, 45 km (28 miles) northwest of Lugano.

Superbly placed on the sheltered curve of the northernmost tip of Lago Maggiore and surrounded on all sides by mountains, Locarno is Switzerland's sunniest town. Subtropical flora flourishes here, with date palms and fig trees, bougainvillea and rhododendron, and even aloe vera burgeoning on the waterfront. Don't forget your sunglasses—you don't show your face in Locarno without a stylish set of shades, especially during August, when the town makes worldwide news with its film festival, showcasing the latest cinema on an outdoor screen in the Piazza Grande. It also hosts international artists in concert.

Modern Locarno is actually made up of three tiny communities—Locarno, Muralto, and Minusio—that are so close together that you often don't notice moving from one to another. The town's raison d'être is its waterfront, which has a graceful promenade curving around the east flank of the bay and a beach and public pool complex along the west. Its clear lake is often as still as glass, reflecting the Ticinese Alps to the south. Locarno's Lombard-style arcades and historic landmarks continually draw visitors inland as well. There are a few pedestrian-only streets in the heart of the Old Town.

GETTING HERE AND AROUND

From Bellinzona by rail it's a 20- to 30-minute ride. Trains from Bern are frequent, taking about four hours; they pass through Luzern and the Gotthard Pass or the Lötschberg Tunnel and Centovalli. From Geneva, the fastest and most scenic route passes through Domodossola and Centovalli on a trip that takes around 4½ hours. The Centovalli is all twists and turns, so if you suffer from motion sickness, avoid these routes. The town is best explored on foot, because the traffic can be stifling, especially in the summer. Buses run frequently to Ascona, next door.

VISITOR INFORMATION

Contacts Sportello Informativo di Locarno. ✉ *Via Largo Franco Zorzi 1, Locarno* ☎ *0848/091091* 🌐 *www.ascona-locarno.com.*

Crowds of movie buffs descend on Locarno in August for the town's international film festival.

EXPLORING

TOP ATTRACTIONS

Chiesa di San Francesco. Harmonious and almost delicate, the Church of St. Francis and its convent stand cheek by jowl with the painfully bulky, modern building that houses the city's Department of Education, Culture, and Sports. The history of the parish goes back to the early 13th century, when it was allegedly founded by St. Anthony of Padua. The current church was begun in 1538, however, on the remains of earlier constructions. Perhaps the most remarkable aspect of the interior is the series of frescoes, which have been restored to their original splendor. Note the fine marble carvings and paintings on the side altars. ✉ *Piazza San Francesco, Locarno.*

Chiesa Nuova (*New Church*). This exuberantly decorated baroque church, built in 1630, has a disproportionately large statue of St. Christopher on its facade. ✉ *Via Cittadella, Locarno.*

Piazza Grande. From underneath the crowded arcades of this piazza, shoppers spill onto the square to lounge in cafés and watch each other drink, chat, and pose. ✉ *Locarno.*

Fodor's Choice ★ **Santuario della Madonna del Sasso.** With a breathtaking view of Locarno, the Sanctuary of the Madonna of the Rock crowns the hilltop hamlet of Orselina. Pilgrims make the steep hike up to it, but most others opt for the short funicular ride that boards close to the train station. The church is open to visitors, but you must reserve ahead to see the rest of the convent, where Brother Bartolomeo da Ivrea had a vision of the Virgin Mary in 1480. Inside the sanctuary are several side chapels with statues depicting scenes from the New Testament, such as the

Last Supper. The church, which was given a neo-Renaissance facade in the late 19th century, is a lavish affair. Among its artistic treasures are Bramantino's 1520 *Flight into Egypt* and Ascona-born Antonio Ciseri's *Christ Carried to the Sepulcher,* a dramatic, Caravaggesque procession scene painted in 1870. ✉ *Via Santuario 2, Orselina* ☎ *091/7436265* 🌐 *www.madonnadelsasso.org* 🎫 *Funicular 7.50 SF round-trip.*

WORTH NOTING

Casa dei Canonici. The House of the Canons has a lovely interior courtyard. It's now a private house, so you'll have to just take a peek. ✉ *Via Cittadella, Locarno.*

Chiesa di Sant'Antonio. Built in the 17th century, the Church of St. Anthony stands on a small plaza in the midst of narrow streets lined with splendid old medieval and baroque houses. The baptismal font (1589) features the double coat of arms of the ancient community of Locarno, and was overlaid in bronze by local sculptor Remo Rossi. ✉ *Piazza Sant'Antonio, Locarno.*

Museo Civico e Archeologico. The city's Municipal and Archaeological Museum's collection is notable for its Roman relics, including a major collection of glass and Romanesque sculpture. It's housed in a heavily rebuilt version of what was once Castello Visconteo, erected in 1300 as a stronghold of the dukes of Milan. Soon after, it was virtually destroyed by the invading Swiss Confederates. ✉ *Via B. Rusca 5, Locarno* ☎ *091/7563180* 🎫 *7 SF* ⏲ *Closed Nov.–Mar.; Mon. and noon–2 Tues.–Sun. Apr.–Oct.*

Pinacoteca Comunale Casa Rusca. Immediately to the left of the Church of St. Anthony stands the city's art gallery, inside what was an 18th-century residence. Its permanent collection includes the work of Jean Arp, and temporary exhibits highlight both Swiss and international artists. ✉ *Piazza Sant'Antonio, Locarno* ☎ *091/7563185* 🌐 *www.museocasarusca.ch* 🎫 *12 SF* ⏲ *Closed mid-Jan.–Mar., all day Mon., and noon–2 Tues.–Sun. Apr.–mid-Jan.*

WHERE TO EAT

$$ ITALIAN

✕ **Casa del Popolo.** The politics lean left at this town classic, where the sprawling terrace spills out onto the square and the crowds come more for the ambience than the food. Among the Italian favorites, the amazingly delicate *piccata alla Milanese* (veal cutlets pounded thin, coated in egg, and sautéed) is a standout. **Known for:** nearly two dozen varieties of pizza; appearances by local celebrities and politicos; spicy penne all'arrabbiata is a classic. $ *Average main: 27 SF* ✉ *Piazza Corporazione, Locarno* ☎ *091/7511208.*

$$ ITALIAN Fodor's Choice ★

✕ **Osteria del Centenario.** Across from the waterfront, this unashamedly nouvelle restaurant east of the town center serves innovative Franco-Italian cuisine that's absolutely top quality. You can have an aperitif on the lakefront terrace before sitting down to a meal in a chic environment with warm terra-cotta tiles and dark-wood furniture. **Known for:** tender lamb steaks served with herb-infused vegetables; selection of menus from business lunch to lavish five-course sampling; intriguing display of modern art on the walls. $ *Average main: 45 SF* ✉ *Viale Verbano 17, Muralto* ☎ *091/7438222* ⏲ *Closed Nov. and Sun.; also Mon. in Jan. and Feb.*

WHERE TO STAY

$ B&B/INN **Hotel Cittadella.** Perched near Lago Maggiore, this Old Town restaurant-with-rooms has pleasant, fairly good-value accommodations tucked under the rafters, with classic tile floors in cream and red adding to the simple, rustic charm. **Pros:** surprisingly peaceful atmosphere; tasty local seafood from virtually at your feet; in the heart of Old Town. **Cons:** top-floor rooms can get stuffy in the summer; sometimes difficult to reach staff by phone; showers only, no bathtubs. *Rooms from: 150 SF ✉ Via Cittadella 18, Locarno ☎ 091/7515885 🌐 www.cittadella.ch 10 rooms Breakfast.*

$$ HOTEL **Hotel Garni Du Lac.** A terrific location, at the east end of the Piazza Grande, makes this friendly hotel a particularly good base for exploring Locarno, and, thanks to the pedestrian-only street and the nearby public gardens, it's relatively quiet. **Pros:** friendly, smiling staff; parking garage just steps away; outdoor breakfast option. **Cons:** no restaurant; tourists abound on Piazza Grande; piazza sometimes hosts concerts. *Rooms from: 210 SF ✉ Via Ramogna 3, Locarno ☎ 091/7512921 🌐 www.du-lac-locarno.ch 30 rooms Breakfast.*

$$ B&B/INN Fodor's Choice ★ **T3e Terre.** This gorgeously equipped bed-and-breakfast—perhaps the nicest in all of Ticino—has five chic rooms with burnished hardwood floors and tasteful contemporary furnishings. **Pros:** good value; multiple choices for foodie vegetarians; dramatic river and swimming holes close by. **Cons:** near a firing range that's in use one day a week; outside Locarno; limited dining options when restaurant is closed. *Rooms from: 215 SF ✉ Via Vecchia Stazione 2, Tegna ☎ 091/7432222 🌐 www.3terre.ch Restaurant closed Tues. and Wed. 5 rooms Breakfast.*

NIGHTLIFE AND PERFORMING ARTS

BARS

Bar Lungolago. This bar draws a young and style-conscious crowd. *✉ Via Bramantino 1, Locarno ☎ 091/7515246.*

Mono Bar. This laid-back bar has a great beer selection as well as classic cocktails. The crowd is youthful, and Mono Bar buzzes with energy, especially on nights when there is live music. *✉ Via Ciseri 19, Locarno ☎ 079/7537327 🌐 www.monobar.ch.*

CASINO

Casinò Locarno. With 150 slot machines and table games, the Casinò di Locarno has plenty of gambling options. *✉ Via Largo Zorzi 1, Locarno ☎ 091/7563030 🌐 www.casinolocarno.ch.*

FILM

Locarno International Film Festival. Held since 1946, the festival screens prestigious international movies every August on the Piazza Grande. *✉ Via B. Luini 3a, Locarno ☎ 0848/091091 🌐 www.pardo.ch.*

MUSIC

Moon and Stars. This series of evening concerts by international pop stars is held the second week of July. *✉ Piazza Grande, Locarno ☎ 0900/800800 🌐 www.moonandstarslocarno.ch.*

5

THEATER

Teatro di Locarno. Theatrical companies are hosted here September through May. ✉ *Palazzo Kursaal, Via Largo Zorzi 1, Locarno* ☎ *091/7597660* 🌐 *www.teatrodilocarno.ch.*

SHOPPING

Open Air Market. Locarno's weekly market is held every Thursday on the Piazza Grande from April to November. You'll find typical market wares like pots and pans alongside artisan crafts and antiques. ✉ *Piazza Grande, Locarno.*

VALLE VERZASCA

12 km (7½ miles) north of Locarno, 25 km (15½ miles) north of Lugano.

Ticino's mountain valleys, just a short distance from its major cities, are rugged reminders of the region's modest history. Stone homes, called *rustici,* dot the valleys, some of which are so deep that the sun never quite reaches bottom. Driving through these valleys can be disorienting. Time seems to have stopped, and whole villages seem perched on craggy mountainsides in apparent defiance of gravity. A short drive along Route 13 through the wild and rugged mountain gorge of the Valle Verzasca leads to Corippo, where a painterly composition of stone houses and a 17th-century church are all protected as architectural landmarks. The mountain village of Sonogno lies at the end of the 26-km (16-mile) valley.

GETTING HERE AND AROUND

Buses headed to the Verzasca Valley leave from both Ascona and Locarno; to get here you have to change in either Bignasco or Cavergno. The trip takes nearly two hours.

EXPLORING

Ponte dei Salti. About 12 km (7½ miles) north of Corippo, in the town of Lavertezzo, find this graceful double-arch stone bridge dating from the 16th or 17th century. The bridge was destroyed in a flood in 1906 and rebuilt in 1958.

SPORTS AND THE OUTDOORS

HIKING

The Verzasca River carved an impressive gorge from these jagged peaks, and you can weave along its banks through hardwood groves and tiny villages. When hunger strikes, stop for wild-mushroom risotto in one of the grotto restaurants along the 13-km (8-mile) trail that connects Sonogno and Lavertezzo.

ASCONA

3 km (2 miles) west of Locarno.

Although it's only a few minutes from Locarno, tiny Ascona has a life of its own. The town was little more than a fishing village until the end of the 19th century, when it was adopted by vegetarians, socialists, mystics, nudists, and other progressive sorts.

GETTING HERE AND AROUND

From Locarno, pick up the bus on the lake end of the Piazza Grande. You can also take the ferry over for a more romantic, 30-minute ride. No trains head to Ascona.

EXPLORING

Monte Verità. A hillside park behind the waterfront, Monte Verità was the site of a utopian, vegetarian artists' colony in the early 1900s. Influenced by Eastern and Western religions as well as new realms of psychology, its ideals attracted thousands of sojourners, including dancer Isadora Duncan, novelist Hermann Hesse, and psychologist Carl Jung. You can visit some of the Monte Verità buildings, including the unusual flat-roofed Casa Anatta, and the museum, which was renovated in 2017. The main park and grounds are open year-round. ✉ *Via Collina 84, Ascona* ☎ *091/7854040* 🌐 *www.monteverita.org* 🎟 *Park entrance free, museum SF 12* ⏲ *Museum closed Mon. and Nov.–May.*

Piazza Motta. On the waterfront, the pedestrian-only Piazza Motta is crowded with sidewalk cafés, and the water along the promenade swarms with boats. ✉ *Ascona.*

Via Borgo. A charming labyrinth of lanes behind Piazza Motta leads uphill past art galleries (not all showing very good works) to Via Borgo, lined with contemporary shops and galleries. ✉ *Via Borgo, Ascona.*

OFF THE BEATEN PATH

Isole di Brissago. Alpine drama and subtropical colors are wed in Brissago, yet another flowery lakefront resort at the lowest elevation in Switzerland. It's an easy excursion by car or bus from Ascona. The main attraction, the federally protected Brissago Islands, are set like jewels in the lake. Their botanical gardens teem with more than a thousand species of subtropical plants, identified by plaques in Italian, German, and French. An English guide to the plants is for sale for 8 SF at the gate. Have lunch or drinks at the restaurant in a beautifully restored 1929 villa. Boats bound for the islands depart regularly from Ascona (20 SF round-trip) and Locarno (34 SF round-trip). You must leave with the last boat back to the mainland—usually around 6 pm—so check the schedule carefully when planning your excursion. ✉ *Isola Grande, Ascona* ☎ *091/7914361* 🌐 *www.isolebrissago.ch/en* 🎟 *8 SF.*

WHERE TO EAT

$ ITALIAN Fodor's Choice ★

✕ **Grotto du Rii.** On your way to or from Italy, consider a visit to this beautiful stone grotto-house, where you can enjoy rosemary-infused wine on the terrace, followed by such dishes as *brasato* (beef shoulder) with polenta and the daring *dolce sorpresa* (surprise dessert). On Tuesday night the good-value four-course meal is accompanied by Ticinese musicians. **Known for:** traditional grotto dining; interiors jam-packed with antique collectibles; picture-perfect location in the Centovalli. Ⓢ *Average main: 25 SF* ✉ *Via Cantonale, Intragna* ✣ *A 15-min walk from the train station in Intragna, 9 km (5 miles) northwest of Ascona.* ☎ *091/7961861* 🌐 *www.grottodurii.ch* ▭ *No credit cards* ⏲ *Closed Wed. Sept.–June.*

$$ ITALIAN

✕ **Hostaria San Pietro.** If you're looking for a bite in the Old Town, take out your map and try your best to find this charming restaurant, tucked away in a maze of tiny streets. This little gem serves creative

Ascona's Piazza Motta is a popular spot for lakeside strolls and dining alfresco.

Italian-influenced pasta and fish dishes—sample its fresh local catch (often a fish fillet in lemon-basil sauce) or any of the grilled specialties. **Known for:** romantic setting; plump ravioli stuffed with vegetables and toasted almonds; being hard to find but worth the struggle. *Average main: 35 SF* ✉ *Passagio San Pietro 6, Ascona* ☎ *091/7913976* ⏲ *Closed Mon. and Jan.*

$$ ITALIAN ✕ **Osteria Nostrana.** The tables of this bustling restaurant spread onto the piazza overlooking the lake, while inside rough wooden ceilings, marble-top tables, chandeliers, and a hodgepodge of photos and posters add to its charm. Look for the spaghetti with porcini, bacon, and cream, along with daily and seasonal specials. **Known for:** extensive wine list; simple, tasty pizza Margherita; can be crowded. *Average main: 28 SF* ✉ *Piazza Motta, Ascona* ☎ *091/7915158* 🌐 *www.ristoranti-ff.ch.*

$$ ECLECTIC ✕ **Seven Easy.** The Seven Group has taken over little Ascona, with several locations spanning the promenade, including an upscale gastronomic restaurant, a dedicated seafood offering, an Asian-inspired sushi joint, and a casual bistro. If you're not in the mood for fine dining, head to the more relaxed Seven Easy, which serves tasty pizza and lighter fare. **Known for:** rollicking atmosphere; excellent selection of pizza; open year-round. *Average main: 27 SF* ✉ *Piazza Giuseppe Motta 61, Ascona* ☎ *091/7807777* 🌐 *www.seven.ch.*

WHERE TO STAY

$$$ HOTEL **Castello Seeschloss.** Dating from 1250, this hotel oozes romance, and that doesn't even take into account its garden setting and enviable address across from the waterfront. **Pros:** lakeside rooms have original details; deluxe tower rooms start not much higher than standard

doubles; charming, historic atmosphere. **Cons:** the tower loft can be reached only by spiral staircase; on the busy promenade; some rooms are exceptionally small. *Rooms from: 350 SF via Circonvallazione 26, Ascona 091/7910161 www.castello-seeschloss.ch Closed Nov.–Mar. 45 rooms Breakfast.*

$$$$ HOTEL Fodor's Choice ★ **Giardino Ascona.** The Great Gatsby would feel in his element in this Relais & Châteaux property that's as glamorous as a Mediterranean villa but still fabulously modern. **Pros:** Sunday frequently features ballet recitals or jazz performances; spectacular garden setting; good value for money for a five-star hotel. **Cons:** overflowing with German and Swiss-German tourists; room prices vary greatly—call ahead for rates; traditional guests may not appreciate the hotel's touch of whimsy. *Rooms from: 700 SF Via Segnale 10, Ascona 091/7858888 www.giardino-ascona.ch Closed mid-Nov.–Mar. 77 rooms Some meals.*

$$ HOTEL **Hotel Tamaro.** The shuttered windows of this 18th-century patrician house overlook the waterfront, and inside you can lounge in sitting rooms richly furnished with precious antiques, handsome books, and even a grand piano. **Pros:** personable staff isn't afraid to show a sense of humor; private terrace has fine lake views; tasty breakfast buffet. **Cons:** not all rooms have a/c; some rooms lack Internet access, but free Wi-Fi is available in the lobby; some bathrooms need updating. *Rooms from: 250 SF Piazza Giuseppe Motta 35, Ascona 091/7854848 www.hotel-tamaro.ch Closed mid-Nov.–Feb. 51 rooms Breakfast.*

NIGHTLIFE AND PERFORMING ARTS

The ideals that brought Isadora Duncan here still bring culture to Ascona: every year it hosts a series of excellent jazz and classical music concerts. Almost every day of the summer, the lakefront piazza serves as an open-air stage for entertainment, with mime, theater, and pop bands. Locarno's August film festival is only a cab ride away across the peninsula.

BARS AND DANCING

Eden Bar. At the luxurious Hotel Eden Roc, Eden Bar is the place to sip Bellinis and listen to live jazz, pop, and standards. *Hotel Eden Roc, Via Albarelle 16, Ascona 091/7857171 www.edenroc.ch.*

MUSIC

JazzAscona. This festival seeks out performers a cut above the standard jazz and swing groups. It attracts an amazing array of international performers to its open-air bandstands for one week in June, as well as winter concerts in various locations hosted by the Jazz Cat Club. *Piazza Giuseppe Motta, Ascona 091/7910091 www.jazzascona.ch, www.jazzcatclub.ch Some concerts free.*

Settimane Musicali. The Settimane Musicali bring in orchestras, chamber groups, and top-ranking soloists to Ascona and Locarno. Events run from late August to mid-October. *Ascona 091/7597665 www.settimane-musicali.ch.*

5

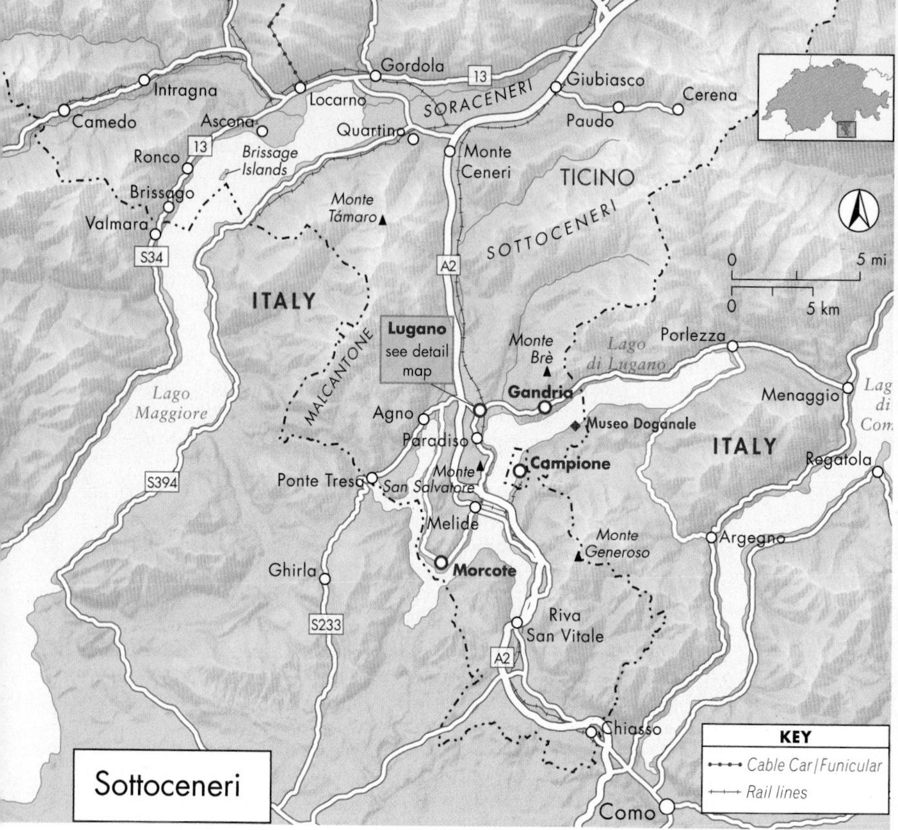

SOTTOCENERI

Although Monte Ceneri is no Everest, it marks the border between the Sopraceneri and its vastly different southern cousin, "below" the Ceneri. The Sottoceneri is Ticino with attitude, where culture and natural beauty join forces with business and commerce. The resort town of Lugano is an international glamour magnet, but even there the incredible scenery and traditional warmth haven't been completely upstaged.

LUGANO

45 km (28 miles) southeast of Ascona, 39 km (24 miles) southeast of Locarno.

Strung around a sparkling bay like Venetian glass beads, with dark, conical mountains rising out of its waters and icy peaks framing the scene, Lugano earns its nickname as the Rio of the Old World. Of the three world-class waterfront resorts, Lugano tops Ascona and Locarno for architecture, sophistication, and natural beauty. This isn't to say that it has avoided the pitfalls of a successful modern resort: there's thick traffic right up to the waterfront, much of it in manic Italian style, and it has more than its share of concrete waterfront high-rise hotels with balconies skewed to produce "a room with a view" regardless of aesthetic cost. Yet the sacred *passeggiata*—the afternoon stroll to see and be seen that winds down every Italian day—asserts the city's true personality as a graceful, sophisticated resort. It's not Swiss, not Italian ... just Lugano.

GETTING HERE AND AROUND

From Bellinzona, trains run frequently and take about 30 minutes. Trains from Locarno run at least once an hour (with a change usually in Bellinzona or Giubiasco); the trip lasts nearly one hour. Lugano is 1–1½ hours away from Milan, with frequent connections. Trains coming from Geneva pass either through Bern/Luzern or Zürich for five- to six-hour journeys. Postbuses spider out from Lugano to hamlets and main towns from the depot on Via Serafino Balestra. Lugano is particularly difficult to drive through, and the parking garages are usually packed.

Take the funicular from the station to the Old Town—unless you want to carry your suitcases down the steep hill and many steps. It's best to start your tour through the city in the morning, before it gets too hot. Note that museums are closed on Monday.

VISITOR INFORMATION

Contacts Ente Turistico del Luganese. ✉ *Palazzo Civico, Riva Albertolli, Lugano* ☎ *058/8666600* 🌐 *www.luganoturismo.ch.*

EXPLORING

TOP ATTRACTIONS

Chiesa di Santa Maria degli Angioli (*Church of St. Mary of the Angels*). The simple facade doesn't prepare you for the riches within. Begun in the late 15th century, the church contains a magnificent fresco of the *Passion and Crucifixion,* as well as the *Last Supper* and *Madonna with the Infant Jesus,* all by Bernardino Luini (1475–1532). ✉ *Piazza Luini, Old Town.*

Giardino Belvedere (*Belvedere Gardens*). This lakefront sculpture garden frames a dozen modern works with palms, camellias, oleanders, and magnolias. At the far west end there's a public swimming area. ✉ *Quai Riva Antonio Caccia, Old Town* ✣ *Near Piazza Luini* 🎫 *Free.*

Herman Hesse Museum. In the tower of the Casa Camuzzi, a fabulous jumble of old houses on a hilltop in Montagnola, the Herman Hesse Museum is tiny but impressive. The Nobel Prize–winning author lived here the last 43 years of his life, writing *Siddhartha* and *Steppenwolf.* His rooms have been meticulously preserved; you can see his papers, books, desk, glasses, even his straw hat. Take the postbus marked Agra-Montagnola from Lugano's train station. ✉ *Torre Camuzzi, 2 Ra Cürta, Montagnola* ☎ *091/9933770* 🌐 *www.hessemontagnola.ch* 🎫 *8.50 SF* ⏲ *Closed weekdays Nov.–Feb.*

Fodor's Choice ★ **Il Lungolago.** This 2-km (1-mile) lakefront promenade is lined with highly pruned lime trees, funereal cypresses, and graceful palm trees stretching from the Lido all the way to the Paradiso neighborhood. Il Lungolago is the place to see and be seen—while taking in the views, of course. At night luminous fountains turn the lake near the Parco Civico into a special attraction. ✉ *Lugano.*

To capture a photo of Lake Lugano's picturesque charm, hop aboard one of the many boats that ply the lake for mountain, town, and water views all at once.

Monte Brè. A funicular departs every 30 minutes from the east end of Lugano in Cassarate to the top of Monte Brè, where there are several well-marked hiking trails. An "art trail" in the summit village of Brè features a path studded with pieces of sculpture. The funicular costs 25 SF round-trip. ☎ *091/9713171* 🌐 *www.montebre.ch.*

Monte Generoso. Take a boat from Lugano across to Capolago, where you can take the 40-minute cogwheel train up to soaring Monte Generoso and its striking geometric observatory designed by Mario Botta. Fares vary, depending on the route taken, but are between 35 SF and 50 SF round-trip. At the top of the observatory are two restaurants, one self-service and the other fine dining, as well as a panoramic terrace. After lunch, head out on one of the many marked hiking trails. ✉ *Via Luerga, Capolago* ☎ *091/6305111* 🌐 *www.montegeneroso.ch* ⏲ *Closed Jan.–mid-Mar.*

Monte San Salvatore. Monte San Salvatore can be reached via the funicular in Paradiso. Departing every 30 minutes, it costs 30 SF round-trip. At the top is a huge relief model of the entire Sottoceneri region, with "nature itinerary" paths marked and signs pointing out flowers and trees. ✉ *Paradiso* ☎ *091/9852828* 🌐 *www.montesansalvatore.ch* ⏲ *Closed mid-Nov.–mid-Mar.*

Museo d'arte della Svizzera italiana, Lugano (MASI)—LAC (*Swiss-Italian Art Museum*). In 2015, the Museo Cantonale d'Arte and Museo d'Arte joined forces to create the new MASI, hosted in an enormous modern building on the lakeside. Dubbed the "LAC"—Lugano Art and Culture—building, it features over 27,000 square feet of 20th-century and contemporary art, emerging artists, and

A GOOD WALK: LUGANO

Begin at **Piazza della Riforma,** which is dominated by the **Palazzo Civico,** or Town Hall. Look up to the gable above the clock to see the city's coat of arms. (The building also houses the tourist office, whose entrance is lakeside.)

On the western side of the square, Piazza della Riforma bleeds into Piazza Rezzonico, which contains a large fountain by Otto Maraini dating from 1895.

Heading out of Piazza della Riforma on the north side, onto Via Luvini, you come to Piazza Dante, which is dominated by a large department store and a bank. From here, if you pop over one street east to the busy Via Pretorio, you can get a look at Lugano's oldest building, the Pretorio (1425), at No. 7. Back at Piazza Dante, turn left down Via Pessina, which leads you into Piazza Cioccaro, on your right. Here the funicular from the train station terminates and the typical *centro storico* (Old Town) begins, its narrow streets lined with chic clothing shops and small markets selling mushrooms and pungent local cheeses.

From Piazza Cioccaro, walk up the shop-lined staircase street of Via Cattedrale. The street curves left, ending at the **Cattedrale di San Lorenzo.** Take a moment to enjoy the view from the church square.

Head back and then south along the waterfront promenade known as **Il Lungolago,** and at the Imbarcadero Centrale (Central Wharf) take the underpass to cross the road, coming back up at Piazza della Riforma.

Leave the piazza at the northeast side through a portico onto Via Canova. After crossing over Via della Posta/Via Albrizzi, you come to the **Museo Cantonale d'Arte**, on your right.

Continue straight ahead to the 17th-century church of San Rocco, with its neo-baroque facade. Turn left onto Via Carducci before you reach the church and find the small orange-tile pedestrian entranceway into the Quartiere Maghetti—a town within a town. It's a tangle of streets full of porticoes, little squares, shops, and offices—a modern take on old forms, created in the early 1980s by the architects Camenzind, Brocchi, and Sennhauser.

Exit the Quartiere Maghetti onto Via Canova (behind the church) and continue east, crossing Via Stauffacher. On your left is the open Piazza dell'Independenza. Cross over the wide Corso Elvezia to enter the **Parco Civico.** Inside the grounds, in addition to the nearly 15 acres of greenery, is the **Museo Cantonale di Storia Naturale.**

From here you can spend the afternoon at the **Lido,** the city's public beach and pool, just east of the park across the River Cassarate.

Head back to town along the waterfront promenade and take in the stunning mountain views: straight ahead, the rocky top of Monte Generoso (5,579 feet), and flanking the bay at right and left, respectively, Monte San Salvatore and Monte Brè.

interdisciplinary exhibitions in collaboration with the theater and music departments of LAC. ✉ *Piazza Bernardino Luini 6, Old Town* ☎ *058/8664230* 🌐 *www.masilugano.ch* 🎫 *15 SF, includes admission to both sites* ⏲ *Closed Mon.*

Museo d'arte della Svizzera italiana, Lugano (MASI)—Palazzo Reali. This second location of the MASI is housed in the grand Palazzo Reali, a historic palace dating back to the Renaissance and the former site of the cantonal art museum. In contrast to the trendy LAC site, the atmosphere here is classic and refined. Its offerings are dedicated to the historic art of the region, with a permanent collection of local Ticinese artists. ✉ *Via Canova 10, Lugano* ☎ *091/8157971* ✉ *info@masilugano.ch* 🌐 *www.masilugano.ch* 🎫 *SF 15, includes admission to both sites* ⏲ *Closed Mon.*

THE PARKS OF CASTAGNOLA

For an idyllic daytime excursion, take a short tram trip out of Lugano's city center to the fabled Castagnola parks, which surround the Villa Favorita (the famous Thyssen-Bornemisza estate, now closed to the public). The Parco degli Ulivi (Olive Park) spreads over the lower slopes of Monte Brè and offers a romantic landscape of silvery olive trees mixed with wild rosemary. Enter from the Sentiero di Gandria (Gandria Footpath). Parco San Michele (St. Michael Park), also on Monte Brè, has a public chapel and a broad terrace that overlooks the city, the lake, and the Alps.

Fodor's Choice ★ **Piazza della Riforma** (*Reformation Square*). In the early 19th century, several buildings were torn down to enlarge the square, providing room for the present-day café tables. Commonly referred to simply as "La Piazza," it's the social and cultural heart of the city and the site of outdoor markets and open-air concerts. ✉ *Old Town.*

WORTH NOTING

Cattedrale di San Lorenzo (*Cathedral of St. Lawrence*). Behind this church's early-Renaissance facade is a baroque interior with carefully restored frescoes and a baptismal font dating from 1430. The church has premedieval origins, becoming a collegiate church in 1078 and a cathedral eight centuries later. ✉ *Via Cattedrale, Old Town.*

Lido. The city's public beach has two swimming pools and two restaurants. To reach it, you have to cross the River Cassarate. Heading east from the Parco Civico, cross Viale Castagnola and then turn toward the lake. The entrance to the main swimming area is ahead on the right. Everyone from families to scenesters comes here to cool off. ✉ *Via Cassarate 6, Lugano* ☎ *058/8666880* 🎫 *11 SF* ⏲ *Closed Oct.–Apr.*

Museo Cantonale di Storia Naturale (*Cantonal Museum of Natural History*). A museum since 1854, the Cantonal Museum of Natural History contains exhibits of fossils, animals, and plants, mostly those typical of the region, with all labels in Italian. There's a large section on local crystals, which is especially interesting for people planning long hikes in the mountains. ✉ *Viale Cattaneo 4, Parco Civico* ☎ *091/8154761* 🌐 *www.ti.ch/mcsn* 🎫 *Free* ⏲ *Closed Mon. all day and noon–2 Tues.–Sat.*

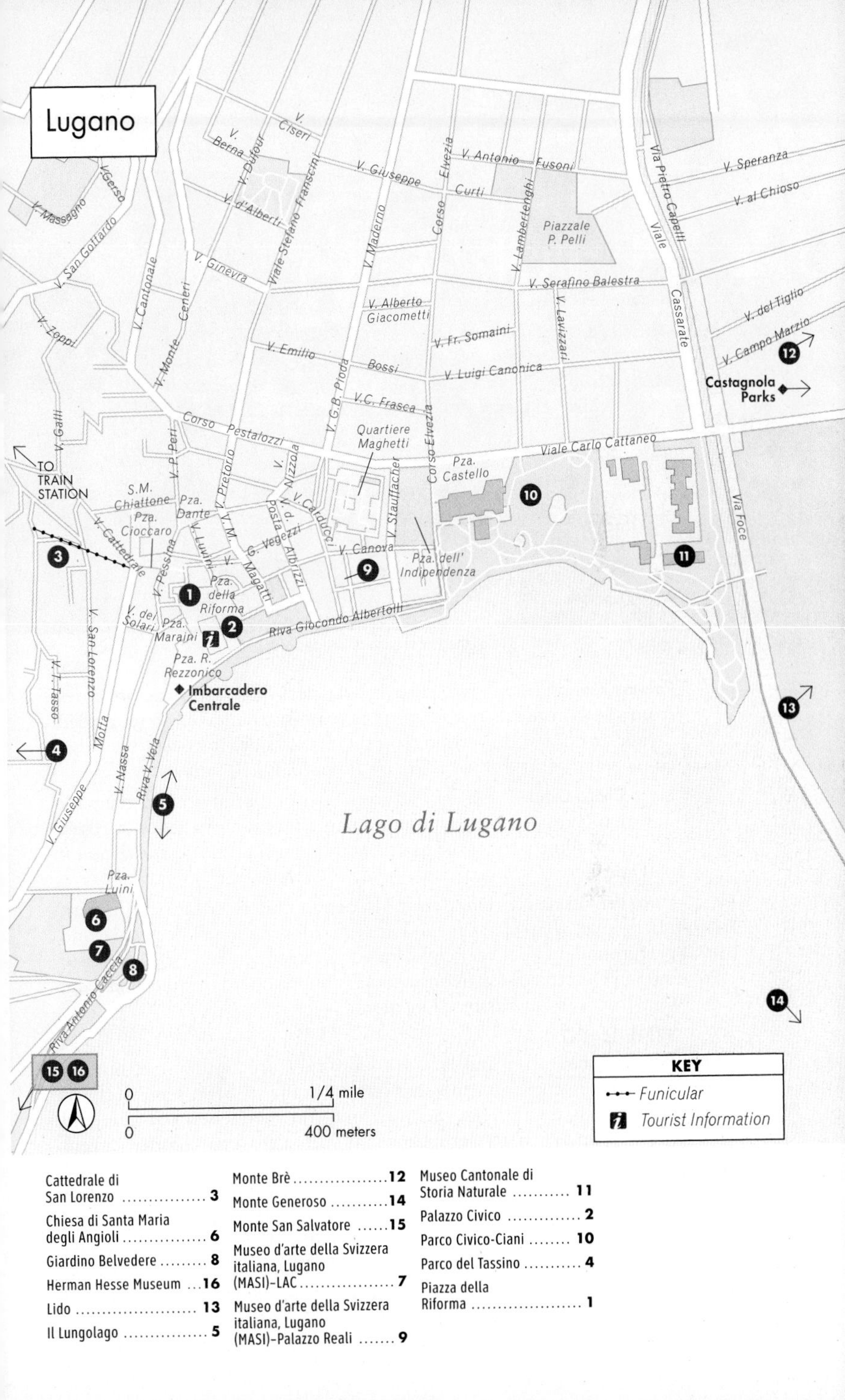

Lugano
V. Ciseri
V. Berna
V. Dufour
V. Gerso
V. Massagno
V. San Gottardo
V. d'Alberti
Viale Stefano Franscini
V. Giuseppe Curti
V. Antonio Fusoni
Corso Elvezia
V. Lambertenghi
Piazzale P. Pelli
Via Pietro Capelli
Viale Cassarate
V. Speranza
V. al Chioso
V. Ginevra
V. Cantonale
V. Monte Ceneri
V. Maderno
V. Serafino Balestra
V. Alberto Giacometti
V. Lavizzari
V. del Tiglio
V. Campo Marzio
V. Zoppi
V. Emilio Bossi
V. Fr. Somaini
V. Luigi Canonica
V. G. B. Pioda
V.C. Frasca
Castagnola Parks
Corso Pestalozzi
Quartiere Maghetti
V. Galli
V. P. Peri
V. Pretorio
V. Nizzola
Viale Carlo Cattaneo
Pza. Castello
TO TRAIN STATION
S.M. Chiattone
Pza. Dante
Pza. Cioccaro
V. Cattedrale
V. M. Magatti
V. d. Posta
V. Albrizzi
V. Carducci
V. Stauffacher
Corso Elvezia
Via Foce
V. Luvini
G. Vegezzi
V. Canova
Pza. dell' Indipendenza
V. Pessina
Pza. della Riforma
V. del Solari
Pza. Maraini
Riva Giocondo Albertolli
V. San Lorenzo
Pza. R. Rezzonico
Imbarcadero Centrale
V. T. Tasso
Motta
V. Nassa
Riva V. Vela
V. Giuseppe
Lago di Lugano
Pza. Luini
Riva Antonio Caccia
0
1/4 mile
0
400 meters
KEY
Funicular
Tourist Information
Cattedrale di San Lorenzo 3
Chiesa di Santa Maria degli Angioli 6
Giardino Belvedere 8
Herman Hesse Museum ... 16
Lido 13
Il Lungolago 5
Monte Brè 12
Monte Generoso 14
Monte San Salvatore 15
Museo d'arte della Svizzera italiana, Lugano (MASI)–LAC 7
Museo d'arte della Svizzera italiana, Lugano (MASI)–Palazzo Reali 9
Museo Cantonale di Storia Naturale 11
Palazzo Civico 2
Parco Civico-Ciani 10
Parco del Tassino 4
Piazza della Riforma 1

Lugano's Piazza della Riforma is the main site of the city's markets and festivals.

Palazzo Civico (*Town Hall*). This neoclassical Lombard structure dates from 1844. Inside there's a large inner yard surrounded by a four-sided arcade, with a wide vestibule on the piazza side. It houses the town council and tourist office. ✉ *Riva Albertolli, Old Town.*

Parco Civico-Ciani (*City Park*). A green oasis in the city center, the park has cacti, exotic shrubs, and more than a thousand varieties of roses, as well as a fine view of the bay from its peninsula. ✉ *Lugano ✣ South of Viale Carlo Cattaneo, east of Piazza Castello.*

FAMILY **Parco del Tassino** (*Tassino Park*). Just behind the train station, this park offers lovely bay views from its rose gardens. A small deer park and playground make it very child-friendly. To get here, take Bus 2 east to the San Domenico stop in Castagnola, or hop aboard the funicular from Old Town. ✉ *Via Tassino, Lugano* 🎫 *Free.*

WHERE TO EAT

$$$ ITALIAN Fodor's Choice ★ ✕ **Al Portone.** Silver and lace dress up the stucco and stone, but the ambience is cozy, and the chef-owner, Francis Carré, serves refined Franco-Italian cuisine at this true find—nowhere else in Switzerland can you find such an elegant meal at such a reasonable price. Inventive dishes like cardamom-poached pears with Gorgonzola mousse and roasted loin of lamb in a Provençale crust are served alongside vegetarian delights on the special meat-free menu. **Known for:** well-priced gourmet cuisine; small garden for alfresco dining; charming chef aims to please. [$] *Average main: 50 SF* ✉ *Viale Cassarate 3, Cassarate* ☎ *078/7229324* 🌐 *www.ristorante-alportone.ch* 🕓 *Closed Sun. and Mon., and in early Jan. and Aug.*

$$ ITALIAN **Antica Osteria del Porto.** Celebrity chef Silvio Galizzi pursues *nuova cucina* (contemporary Italian cuisine) with ambition and flair in this Lugano eatery, proving he still has the culinary dazzle that earned him his first accolades two decades ago, when he made waves in the world of Swiss gastronomy. After a few short-lived ventures, he has settled down here to a more casual backdrop, offering classic dishes as well as foreign favorites like barbecue-roasted chicken and fish-and-chips. **Known for:** renowned chef; outdoor dining in summer; Italian twists on foreign favorites like barbecue-roasted chicken. *Average main: 32 SF Via Foce 9, Lugano 091/9714200 www.anticaosteriadelporto.ch.*

$$ ITALIAN **Da Raffaele.** Having a meal in this family-run Italian restaurant feels like being let in on a neighborhood secret, and although the staff members don't speak much English, their warmth needs no translation. Start with a pasta, like the marvelous homemade orecchiette (ear-shaped pasta) or *mezzelune* (half moons) stuffed with ricotta and spinach, then try something from the grill, like *gamberoni alla griglia* (grilled shrimp). **Known for:** homey feel; filled with local diners; first-rate homemade pasta. *Average main: 32 SF Contrada dei Patrizi 8, Lugano Take Bus 8 or 9 from the train station to the last stop, Viganello 091/9716614 Closed Sun., last wk of July, and 1st 2 wks of Aug. No lunch Sat.*

$$ MODERN ITALIAN **Grotto della Salute.** This absolutely authentic, no-frills place pulls in a local crowd for a good bottle of Ticinese wine and a satisfying, contemporary spin on old favorites like homemade pasta, roasted meat, and fresh fish. The dedicated owners pride themselves on high-quality ingredients with absolutely no additives. **Known for:** gorgeous outdoor seating area; fresh steak tartare with white truffles; vibrant, traditional atmosphere. *Average main: 42 SF Via Madonna della Salute 10, Massagno 091/9660476 www.grottodellasalute.com No credit cards Closed Sun., 2 wks in mid-Aug. and 2 wks in mid-Jan.*

$ ITALIAN **La Tinera.** Tucked down an alley off Via Pessina, this cozy basement taverna squeezes loyal locals and tourists onto hard wooden chairs and benches for authentic regional specialties, hearty meats, and pastas. Ticinese wines are served in traditional ceramic bowls—try a strong red to cut through the thick *polenta taragna,* made of cornmeal and buckwheat (once you try it, you will never eat the bland yellow version again), served with *luganighe,* cumin-flavored local sausages. **Known for:** budget-friendly traditional meals; melt-in-your-mouth tiramisu; wine served in handmade boccalini. *Average main: 24 SF Via dei Gorini 2, Old Town 091/9235219 Closed Sun. and Aug.*

$$ SEAFOOD **Locanda del Boschetto.** The grill is the first thing you see in this grotto-style eatery specializing in pure and simple seafood *alla griglia* (grilled). Homemade pasta is another specialty, and when the two are combined, as in the house favorite—linguine *allo scoglio* (with shellfish)—plates are left cleaner than whistles. **Known for:** seafood specialties; quiet, residential location; friendly, down-to-earth staff. *Average main: 42 SF Via Boschetto 8, Paradiso 091/9942493 www.locandadelboschetto.ch Closed Mon. and last 2 wks of Aug.*

5

$$ ITALIAN **Ristorante Orologio Da Savino.** Snow-white tablecloths and chairs stand out against shiny, dark hardwood floors in this open, minimalist restaurant. The attentive staff and personable owner are quick to bring you modern Italian dishes and a fine selection of fresh fish, as well as vegetarian-pleasing delights like balsamic-marinated tofu with grilled vegetables. **Known for:** locals rather than tourists; courteous, friendly staff; elegant surroundings. *Average main: 45 SF* *Via Giovanni Nizzola 2, Old Town* *091/9232338* *www.ristoranteorologio.ch* *Closed Sun. and 2 wks in Aug.*

WHERE TO STAY

$ HOTEL **Hotel Pestalozzi Lugano.** Right in the middle of town, this renovated older hotel is a few steps away from the lake and offers excellent value in rooms that are simple, clean, and functional. **Pros:** a favorite among thrifty travelers; a stone's throw from the Old Town; restaurant caters to vegetarians. **Cons:** some rooms lack a/c; others lack TVs; simple, sparse decor. *Rooms from: 175 SF* *Piazza Indipendenza, Lugano* *091/9214646* *www.pestalozzi-lugano.ch* *55 rooms* *Breakfast.*

$ HOTEL **Hotel San Carlo Garni.** Ideally located on the main shopping street, this friendly hotel is owned and managed by one of the nicest families in town. **Pros:** uniquely crafted rooms; terrific prices; courteous staff. **Cons:** some decor is straight out of high-school wood shop; thin walls; small spaces can feel confined. *Rooms from: 170 SF* *Via Nassa 28, Old Town* *091/9227107* *www.hotelsancarlolugano.ch* *20 rooms* *Breakfast.*

$$$ HOTEL Fodor's Choice ★ **Hotel Splendide Royal.** This local landmark opened its doors in 1888, and much of the Victorian luster of its common areas—colorful frescoes, crystal chandeliers, ornate antiques—has been respectfully preserved. **Pros:** the historic suites are showstoppers; even the smallest rooms have heated bathroom floors; every detail displays refined luxury. **Cons:** the 1983 wing is less glamorous, more Miami Vice than Pride and Prejudice; grand interiors missing a bit of cozy warmth; could use a bit more color. *Rooms from: 490 SF* *Riva A. Caccia 7, Loreto* *091/9857711* *www.splendide.ch* *93 rooms* *Breakfast.*

$$ HOTEL **International au Lac Historic Lakeside Hotel.** Next to the Church of St. Mary of the Angels, this historic hotel's 1908 interiors are exuberantly decorated, with gilded paintings, ornate antiques, and heavy, sumptuous furniture. **Pros:** you forget you're downtown when lounging at the pool or in the back garden; live classical music; antique furnishings. **Cons:** some rooms feel dated; not the place for up-to-date amenities and luxury toiletries; in-town location is perfect for exploring but can get a bit noisy. *Rooms from: 275 SF* *Via Nassa 68, Old Town* *091/9227541* *www.hotel-international.ch* *Closed Nov.–Easter* *80 rooms* *Breakfast.*

$$ HOTEL **Lugano Dante Center Swiss Quality Hotel.** Friendly and well decorated, this lodging is rated by many travelers as the best deal in town, and the location, in the Old Town just steps from the funicular, could not be more convenient. **Pros:** affordable; exceptionally friendly staff; near the funicular. **Cons:** central location means throngs of tourists in the

immediate area; some rooms are small; no-frills amenities. *Rooms from: 240 SF* *Piazza Cioccaro 5, Old Town* *091/9105750* *www.hotel-luganodante.com* *No credit cards* *83 rooms* *Breakfast.*

$$$$ HOTEL **Villa Principe Leopoldo and Residence.** Spectacularly perched on a hillside overlooking Lake Lugano, this mansion offers an unparalleled location and old-world service. **Pros:** beautiful views of Lake Lugano and the surrounding mountains; worlds away from the noise and traffic of the city; world-famous risottos from head chef. **Cons:** staff as well as guests can be pretentious; unless you're driving a Ferrari, you may feel out of place; rooms are tasteful but with little patina. *Rooms from: 800 SF* *Via Montalbano 5, Collina d'Oro* *091/9858855* *www.leopoldohotel.com* *74 rooms* *Breakfast.*

$$ HOTEL **Villa Sassa Hotel, Residence & Spa.** Set on a hill overlooking Lugano, Villa Sassa's lake and mountain views are so pretty, you might find it hard to leave the hotel to make the trek into town. **Pros:** peaceful grounds; free arrival and departure shuttle; gorgeous views from the infinity pool. **Cons:** must prearrange kitchen use with apartment rental; not in town; wellness center can be crowded in peak season. *Rooms from: 300 SF* *Via Tesserete 10, Lugano* *091/9114111* *www.villasassa.ch* *No credit cards* *120 rooms* *No meals.*

NIGHTLIFE AND PERFORMING ARTS

BARS

Belle Epoque Bar. For a refined and uncrowded place to enjoy a cocktail, head to the palatial Belle Epoque Bar at the Splendide Royale. *Splendide Royal, Riva A. Caccia 7, Lungolago* *091/9857711.*

Bottegone del Vino. Just off the Piazza delle Riforma, Bottegone del Vino has a great selection of wine accompanied by good local cheeses and tapas. *Via Massimiliano Magatti 3, Old Town* *091/9227689.*

Cafè Retrò. This swanky piano bar features both local and international musicians. *Via Guisan 6, Paradiso* *091/9931654.*

CASINO

Casinò Lugano. In addition to slot machines and gaming tables, the three-floor Casinò Lugano has a bar and a first-rate restaurant. *Via Stauffacher 1, Old Town* *091/9737111* *www.casinolugano.ch.*

DANCING

Living Room. With a dance floor and lounge, the lively Living Room hosts some of the better European electro and rock up-and-comers. *Via Trevano 89a, Molino Nuovo* *091/9233281* *www.livingroomclub.ch* *16 SF* *Basic entry includes drink.*

Morandi. On Friday and Saturday night Morandi is the most popular club catering to the over-30 crowd. It's a great place to dance to songs from the 1970s and '80s. *Via Trevano 56, Molino Nuovo* *091/9211097.*

MUSIC FESTIVALS

Blues to Bop Festival. At the end of August, this festival livens up the Piazza della Riforma. *Piazza della Riforma, Lugano* *www.bluestobop.ch.*

5

Estival Jazz. Early July brings this jazz and world music festival to the Piazza della Riforma. ✉ *Piazza della Riforma, Lugano* 🌐 *www.estivaljazz.ch.*

Lugano Festival. From April to June, the city hosts the Lugano Festival, which draws world-class orchestras and conductors. ✉ *Lugano* 🌐 *www.luganofestival.ch.*

SHOPPING

Fox Town. If it's international designer clothing bargains you're after, explore this factory outlet store. It's open daily from 11 to 7. ✉ *Via Angelo Maspoli, Mendrisio* ☎ *0848/828888.*

Via Cattedrale. Cute novelty and antiques shops line the staircase street of Via Cattedrale. ✉ *Lugano.*

Via Nassa. All the top designers can be found in the stores lining the pedestrian-only Via Nassa. ✉ *Lugano.*

GANDRIA

7 km (4 miles) southeast of Lugano.

Fodor's Choice ★

Although its narrow waterfront streets are crowded with tourists, the tiny historic village of Gandria still merits a visit, either by boat or by car. Gandria clings vertiginously to the steep hillside; its many stairways and passageways lined with flower-filled balconies hang directly over open water. Souvenir and crafts shops now fill its backstreet nooks, but the ambience of an ancient fishing village remains.

EXPLORING

OFF THE BEATEN PATH

Museo Doganale. The thrilling subject of smuggling is brought to life at the Museo Doganale, on the shady southern shore of Lago di Lugano across from Gandria. Known as the "Smuggler's Museum," this place explores the romantic history of clandestine trade between Italy and Switzerland. It bristles with ingenious containers, illicit weapons, and other contraband. You can catch a boat from the jetty in Gandria. ✉ *Cantine di Gandria* ☎ *091/9239843* 🌐 *www.museodelledogane.admin.ch/* 🎫 *Free* ⊙ *Closed Nov.–Easter.*

SPORTS AND THE OUTDOORS

Olive Grove Trail. This easy 3-km (2-mile) trail runs from Gandria to Castagnola, passing groves of ancient olive trees along the way. The walk takes approximately two hours and has only slight changes in elevation. ✉ *Gandria.*

CAMPIONE

18 km (11 miles) south of Gandria, 12 km (7½ miles) south of Lugano.

In the heart of Swiss Italy lies Campione. Here, in this southernmost of regions, the police cars have Swiss license plates but the officers inside are Italian; the inhabitants pay their taxes to Italy but do so in Swiss francs. Its narrow streets are saturated with history, and the surrounding landscape is a series of stunning views of Lago di Lugano and Monte San Salvatore.

In the 8th century the lord of Campione gave the tiny scrap of land, less than a square kilometer (½ square mile) in area, to the monastery of St. Ambrosius of Milan. Despite all the wars that passed it by, Campione remained Italian until the end of the 18th century, when it was incorporated into the Cisalpine Republic. When Italy unified in 1861, Campione became part of the new Kingdom of Italy—and remained so. There are no frontiers between Campione and Switzerland, and it benefits from the comforts of Swiss currency, customs laws, and postal and telephone services. Despite its miniature scale, it has exercised disproportionate influence on the art world. In the Middle Ages a school of stonemasons, sculptors, and architects from Campione and the surrounding region worked on the cathedrals of Milan, Verona, Cremona, Trento, Modena, and even the Hagia Sophia in Istanbul.

NIGHTLIFE AND PERFORMING ARTS

Casino Campione. Campione is a magnet for gamblers, thanks to an eye-catching casino designed by star architect Mario Botta. It calls to mind a huge brown UFO landing on the little town. When you're not playing the tables, you can dine in the restaurant or enjoy a show. Men are required to wear a jacket, but they don't have to wear a tie in summer. ✉ *Piazza Milano 1, Campione* ☎ *091/6401111* 🌐 *www.casinocampione.it.*

5

EN ROUTE

Swissminiatur. If you wish to see all of Switzerland's monuments in a few hours, then stop in the town of Melide, 8 km (5 miles) south of Lugano. The Swissminiatur has all the sights and sites you could wish for, including pint-sized versions of the Château de Chillon, Basel's Münster, and Locarno's Madonna del Sasso. More than 3 km (2 miles) of miniature tracks have been laid out and are busily used by tiny passenger and freight trains. ✉ *Melide* ☎ *091/6401060* 🌐 *www.swissminiatur.ch* 🎫 *19 SF* ⏲ *Closed early Nov.–mid-Mar.*

MORCOTE

11 km (7 miles) northwest of Campione, 10 km (6 miles) south of Lugano.

Fodor's Choice ★

At the southernmost tip of the glorious Ceresio Peninsula is the atmospheric village of Morcote, its clay-colored houses and arcades looking directly over the waterfront.

GETTING HERE AND AROUND

A half-hour bus ride connects Morcote to Lugano.

EXPLORING

Chiesa Santa Maria del Sasso (*Church St. Mary of the Rock*). A steep and picturesque climb leads up to the Chiesa di Madonna del Sasso, with its well-preserved 16th-century frescoes. Its elevated setting affords wonderful views. ✉ *Morcote.*

Parco Scherrer. A remarkable garden, the Parco Scherrer was created over a period of decades by the Swiss business executive Arthur Scherrer (1881–1956). This folly rising from the lakeside brings together architectural samples from around the world—including an Egyptian sun temple, a Siamese teahouse, and an Indian palace—within the setting of a carefully landscaped garden. ✉ *Morcote* 🎫 *7 SF* ⏲ *Closed Nov.–mid-Mar.*

WHERE TO STAY

$$ HOTEL Fodor's Choice ★ **Dellago.** Combining a soothing atmosphere, personal service, and unpretentious savoir-faire, this stylish refuge on the lake not only pampers its guests, but is one of the hippest hotels in Ticino and one of the few in the canton to dare break from the traditional hotel mold. **Pros:** breakfast comes with homemade jams, fine teas, and unusual breads; there's a hotel paddleboat for excursions on the lake; the dockside lounge pours outstanding cocktails. **Cons:** rooms facing the busy street are noisy; most rooms do not allow children; some rooms are on the small side. *Rooms from: 240 SF* ✉ *Lago di Lugano, Melide* ☎ *091/6497041* *20 rooms* *Breakfast.*

6

LUZERN AND CENTRAL SWITZERLAND

WELCOME TO LUZERN AND CENTRAL SWITZERLAND

TOP REASONS TO GO

★ **Luzern:** The must-see spot on the tour, it offers not only famous sights—the Chapel Bridge, the Lion Monument—but also other treasures, like the Rosengart Picassos and that perfect table for two under the chestnut trees on the lakeside promenade.

★ **Mountain majesty:** Thanks to cable cars and cog railways, hill thrills—and some of the most staggering panoramas—can be yours atop Mts. Pilatus, Titlis, and Rigi.

★ **Wilhelm Tell country:** As with all good legends, the story of the famous archer who shot an apple from his son's head with a crossbow may have little basis in fact, but don't tell that to the crowds who visit his home turf in and around Altdorf.

★ **A paddle steamer ride:** Lake Luzern's smart white steamboats—including beautifully kept and picturesque old paddle steamers—offer a voyage back in time.

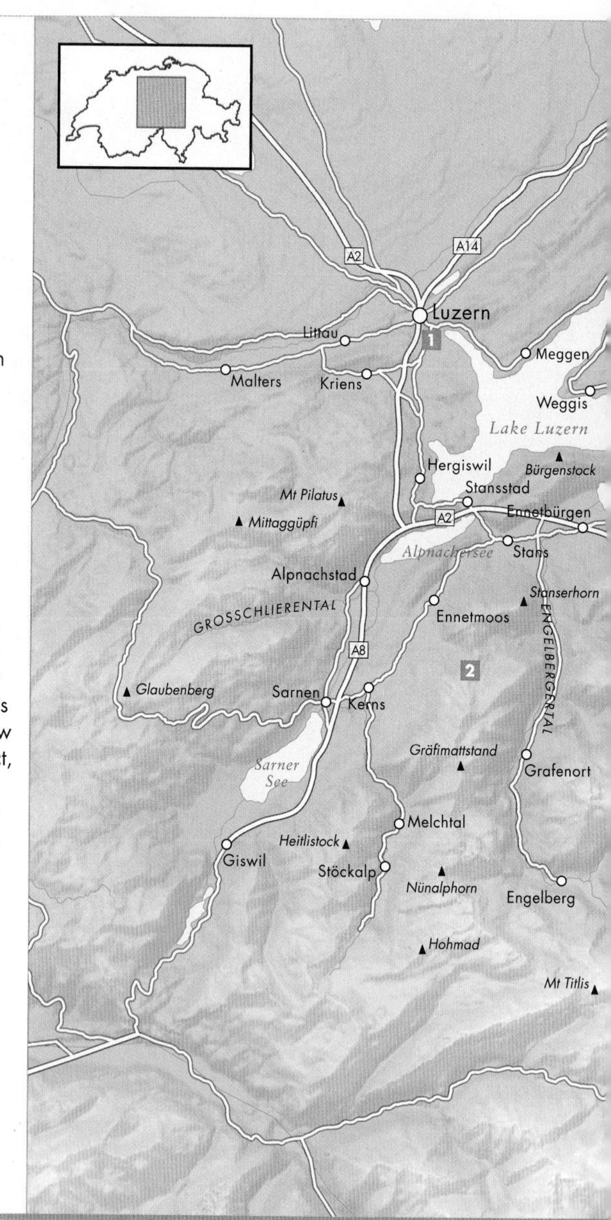

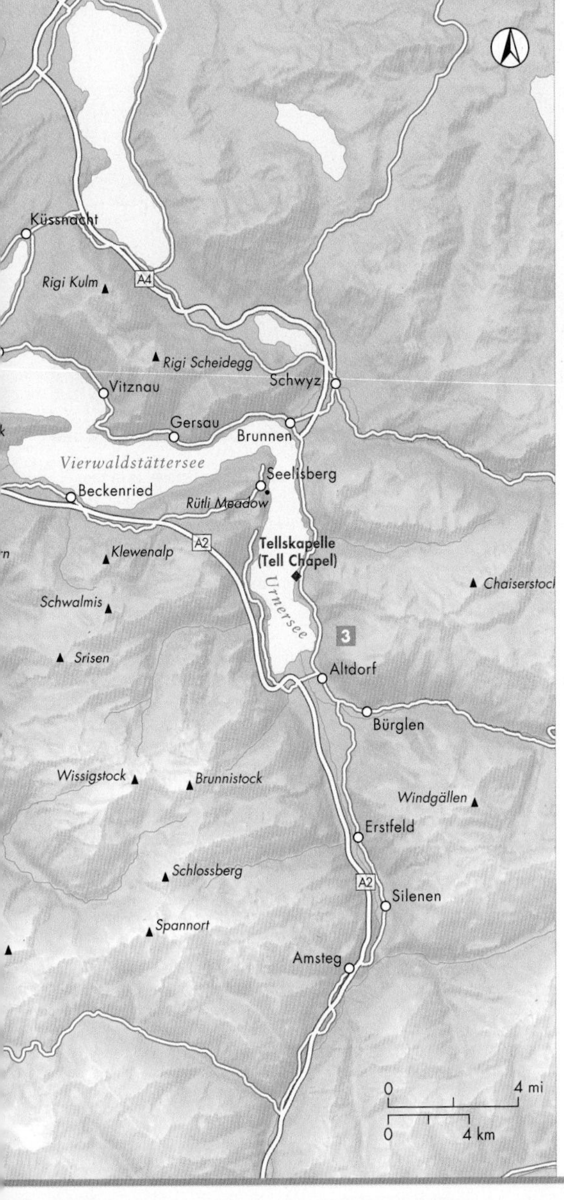

1 Luzern. This little big city offers a full cultural palette: wander through the medieval Old Town; shop at chic boutiques; take a boat cruise; and listen to a diva sing in Jean Nouvel's architectural wonder, the Kultur- und Kongresszentrum.

2 Around Luzern. Towering over Luzern, Mt. Pilatus is impressive, with a restaurant at the top. Take the "golden round-trip," which includes a bus from Luzern, a cable car trip to the top, a cogwheel train back down the other side, and a boat ride back to Luzern. Head south to Engelberg, where you can take the gondola up to the top of Mt. Titlis.

3 Urnersee. Hallowed by myths, the Urnersee is the southern leg of Lake Luzern. Weggis and Vitznau are the "Riviera" towns, sheltered by coves and beloved by the rich. Farther south, pay your respects to the historic Rütli Meadow; the picturesque Tell Chapel, just across the lake; and Altdorf, where Wilhelm Tell first became a legend.

LAKE LUZERN

Lake Luzern (above) is in the heart of Switzerland, both geographically and historically. Lake steamers cruise the water (below, right), and photo ops of the surrounding mountains abound (above, right).

Towns where travelers used to stop to brush the dust off their clothes have turned into full-service spas with culinary temples, hiking trails, and docks for pleasure boats. What was once a part of the long route from Germany to Italy is now a destination in its own right.

The many inlets of Lake Luzern that stretch all over the region vary in size, depth, and wind conditions. They are at some points flanked by gentle green hillsides and at others by steep mountain cliffs. The lake's lower end is home to gusting winds that thrill windsurfers, and the quiet middle basin is perfect for waterskiing. Boats steam along from the top of the lake to the bottom, carrying lunching locals and tourists snapping shots of imposing peaks that loom high above. Endless trails snake around the region, often with altitude differences of 1,000 feet over just a few miles, and secondary (and some primary) roads along its shores are narrow and winding—the perfect excuse to rent a convertible.

BEST TIME TO GO

Although misty spring or fall can be romantic, the low clouds that winter brings usually obscure the scenery. It's summer you want: hiking trails are free of snow, the lake is a comfortable 73°F (23°C), restaurant terraces are open, cowbells clang in the distance, and the sky is so blue you're suspicious.

WAYS TO EXPLORE

BY BOAT

If you have the time, the best way to see the sights is on the water. Short one-hour cruises offer a new angle on the area you're in, but to get the full Technicolor panorama of the lake's character, take the 3½-hour tour of the whole lake: it heads from the hilly and small-scale but busy series of inlets dotted with impressive villas near Luzern; through the quieter basin surrounded by the spa towns of Bürgenstock, Weggis, and Vitznau; to the wilder Urnersee between Brunnen and Flüelen, where the cliffs rise precipitously out of the depths of the lake and high into the sky.

BY BIKE

Whether you prefer an easy ride through the green pastures of cow country or are ready to tackle a steep mountain pass, you'll find both options here, and all levels in between. For easy trips, check out the good network of official bike paths off the main thoroughfares. For something with more altitude, you may have to share a narrow twisting road with a car or two from time to time.

BY FOOT

Switzerland has such an extensive network of hiking trails that you can be sure of getting to wherever you want. Thousands of official yellow *Wanderweg* (trail) signposts can be found all over the country, so you always know where you're going and how long it will take to get there. The map system is also very comprehensive and detailed, so feel free to go exploring up Mt. Pilatus, along the lake, or into the green fields of the lowlands. History buffs will appreciate the Swiss Path, which winds around the Urnersee and passes sites significant to the birth of the nation.

BEST PHOTO OPS

If you're in Luzern early in the morning on a clear day, head for the Seebrücke. The lighting will be ideal for postcard-perfect shots of the Chapel Bridge, the Water Tower, and Mt. Pilatus. You may even catch some fishers trying their luck in the River Reuss. For lake and mountain panoramas, wait until later in the day and walk along the National-quai for the best-lighted views. To get the Old Town rooftops in the picture, you can gain altitude via the old city ramparts, called the Museggmauer.

Updated by Susan Misicka

With the mist rising off the water and the mountains looming above in the morning sun, it's easy to understand why people are mesmerized by the inspiring terrain around Luzern. Where else can you sit and gaze at mountains, a river, and a lake plus architectural treasures like a late-medieval wooden bridge and a baroque church—all from the same sidewalk café seat? Central Switzerland's popularity with tourists has spawned an infrastructure of hotels, restaurants, museums, excursions, and transportation that makes it one of the easiest places to explore in Switzerland—and one of the most rewarding.

It was on Lake Luzern that Wilhelm Tell—the beloved Swiss national folk hero—supposedly leaped from the tyrant Gessler's boat to freedom. And it was in a meadow nearby that three furtive rebels and their cohorts swore an oath by firelight and planted the seed of the Swiss Confederation. The Rütli Meadow on the southern leg of Lake Luzern is the very spot where the confederates of Uri, Schwyz, and Unterwalden are said to have met on the night of November 7, 1307, to renew the 1291 Oath of Allegiance—Switzerland's equivalent of the U.S. Declaration of Independence. With this oath, one of the world's oldest modern democracies was born, as the proud charter territories swore their commitment to self-rule in the face of the Habsburgs' Holy Roman Empire.

Every August 1, the Swiss national holiday, citizens gather in the meadow in remembrance of the oath, and the sky glows with the light of hundreds of mountaintop bonfires. Wilhelm Tell played an important role in that early rebellion and his story, especially as told by German poet and playwright Friedrich von Schiller in his play *Wilhelm Tell* (1805), continues to stir those with a weakness for civil resistance. Here, around the villages of Altdorf, Bürglen, and the stunningly picturesque lakeside Tell Chapel, thousands come to honor the memory of the rebellious archer.

Yet for all its potential for drama, central Switzerland and the area surrounding Lake Luzern are tame enough turf: neat little towns, accessible mountains, smooth roads, virtually glamour-free resorts—with modest, graceful Luzern astride the River Reuss much as it has been since the Middle Ages. An eminently civilized region, Zentralschweiz (Central Switzerland) lacks the rustic unruliness of the Valais, the spectacular extremes of the Berner Oberland, and the eccentricity of Graubünden. It's also without the sophistication and snob appeal of jet-set resorts or the cosmopolitan mix of Geneva, Basel, and Zürich. Instead, villages here range neatly around their medieval centers; houses are tidy, pastel, picture-book cottages, deep-roofed and symmetrical, each rank of windows underscored with flowers. Luzern, the capital, hosts arts festivals and great shopping, but little native industry. Serene and steady as the Reuss that laps at the piers of its ancient wooden bridges, it's an approachable city in an accessible region.

LUZERN PLANNER

WHEN TO GO

The geographic heart of Switzerland enjoys four distinct seasons, which are temperate in the valleys and more extreme in the mountains. Spring, summer, and fall are perfect for warm-weather outdoor activities.

Fall becomes crisp around October, and winter brings snow to the highlands. Keep in mind that snow can stay as late as May and come as early as August over 6,500 feet.

Avoid walking in creek beds: a hidden rainstorm high in the mountains can turn a trickling brook into a rushing torrent in a matter of seconds and has swept away many a hiker.

If you're going up and down mountains, dress like an onion: in layers. The warmth of the valley can be quickly replaced by a cold breeze 5,000 feet higher.

GETTING HERE AND AROUND

AIR TRAVEL

The nearest airport is Zürich Airport, which is approximately 54 km (33 miles) northeast of Luzern.

BOAT AND FERRY TRAVEL

One of the joys of traveling in this region is touring Lake Luzern on one of its time-stained 20th-century paddle steamers. These are a slow but extremely scenic and therefore worthwhile mode of transportation; you'll find locals on day trips traveling along with you.

Lake Luzern boasts five historic paddle steamers built between 1901 and 1928, and they connect virtually every community on the lakeside. The larger boats have full restaurant facilities, and even the smaller ones offer refreshments. As elsewhere in Switzerland, they link, where practical, with both the train and postbus services. The round-trip/excursion tickets offer the best value for the money.

In stark contrast to the old steamers is the modern and massive MS *Diamant*, a luxury pleasure cruiser built in Luzern's shipyard and inaugurated in 2017. Its features include a marvelous glass dome, two elegant cabins, and a lake-water footbath. The four-level vessel can carry up to 1,100 passengers on a regularly scheduled cruise or 400 banquet guests for a private event.

Services are frequent in the peak season, but in the off-season, services are limited, so check on availability when you arrive. Schifffahrtsgesellschaft des Vierwaldstättersees offers culinary and sightseeing cruises around the lake daily from May to October. Rides on these are included in a Swiss Pass, Swiss Boat Pass, or the discount Tell Pass. Individual tickets can be purchased at Luzern's departure docks; the fee is based on the length of your ride.

Contacts Schifffahrtsgesellschaft des Vierwaldstättersees. ✉ *Landungsbrücke 1, Luzern* ☎ *041/3676767* 🌐 *www.lakelucerne.ch.*

BUS TRAVEL

The postbus network carries travelers faithfully, if slowly, to the farthest corners of the region. It also climbs the St. Gotthard and Furka passes (remember, these are closed in winter).

CAR TRAVEL

Although Mt. Rigi and Mt. Pilatus aren't accessible by car, nearly everything else in this region is.

The descent from Andermatt past the Devil's Bridge, which once carried medieval pilgrims from the St. Gotthard Pass and drew thrill-seekers during the 19th century, now exemplifies awe-inspiring Swiss mountain engineering: from Göschenen, at 3,627 feet, to the waterfront, it's a four-lane expressway.

Keep in mind, many of the towns in this region are scattered around the unusually shaped Vierwaldstättersee, so sometimes a ferry will be faster than a freeway.

TRAIN TRAVEL

Swiss National Railways is enhanced here by a few private lines (to Engelberg, Pilatus, the Rigi Kulm) that make it possible to get to most sights.

HOTELS

In the mountains, high season means the winter ski season; in the valleys, summer is more expensive. The terrain and climate vary radically between balmy lakefronts and icy heights, so check carefully for high and low seasons before booking ahead. Resorts such as Weggis and Vitznau cut back service considerably in winter, just when Engelberg comes alive. Book early for ever-popular Luzern. Prices drop by as much as 25% in winter, approximately November through March. Rates are often calculated on a per-person basis, so it's wise to confirm rates, particularly if you're traveling as anything other than a couple. Hotel reviews have been shortened. *For full information, visit Fodors.com.*

THE TELL PASS

If you don't have a Swiss Travel Pass, there's a central Switzerland regional discount pass, called the Tell Pass, on sale from April to October. The Tell Pass is good for unlimited train, bus, boat, and aerial cableway travel, and it also entitles the holder to discounts on many other attractions. Passes are valid for 2, 3, 4, 5, or 10 consecutive days, and range in price from 180 SF to 300 SF. A pass for an accompanying child is just 30 SF for the whole period. Buy your pass at rail or boat ticket offices, on cruise boats, from travel agencies, or from tourist offices, or order it online and take advantage of the print-at-home option.

For more information go to 🌐 *www.tellpass.ch*.

RESTAURANTS

In this heavily visited region, most restaurants are open all day, sometimes with a more limited menu between lunch and dinner. You'll find outside seating wherever it's possible to create any, including huge gravel-strewn terraces shaded by magnificent chestnut trees as well as tiny sidewalk tables fighting for space with pedestrians. Unless you're eating in one of the upscale hotels where "smart casual" clothing is a must, the unofficial dress code of the rest of the country applies: if you're clean, you're in. Fresh, nonsloppy jeans are preferable to a dirty suit.

6

WHAT IT COSTS IN SWISS FRANCS

	$	$$	$$$	$$$$
Restaurants	Under 26 SF	26 SF–45 SF	46 SF–65 SF	Over 65 SF
Hotels	Under 201 SF	201 SF–300 SF	301 SF–500 SF	Over 500 SF

Restaurant prices are the average cost of a main course at dinner or, if dinner is not served, at lunch. Hotel prices are the lowest cost of a standard double room in high season, including taxes.

VISITOR INFORMATION

A good online resource for ideas and orientation can be found at 🌐 *www.lakeluzern.ch*.

LUZERN

57 km (35 miles) southwest of Zürich.

Luzern city is a convenient base for excursions all over central Switzerland. The countryside here is tame, and the vast Vierwaldstättersee offers a prime opportunity for a lake steamer cruise. Where the River Reuss flows out of Lake Luzern, Luzern's Old Town straddles the narrowed waters.

There are a couple of discount passes available for museums and sights in the city. **■TIP→ The Lucerne Museum Card, which costs 36 SF, grants admission to several museums over a two-day period.** If you're staying in a hotel, pick up a special visitor's card; once stamped by the hotel, it entitles you to discounts at most museums and other tourist-oriented businesses. Both passes are available at the tourist office, which will give you a free public transit pass if you make your hotel booking through them.

DRESS CODE

Although residents appreciate the value of comfortable clothes, this is definitely not the place to let it all hang out: droopy T-shirts, ill-fitting shorts, and baseball caps will get you looks of disdain, service nowhere but McDonald's, and difficulty gaining admission to most churches. Of course we don't mean you in particular, it's those other guys ...

GETTING HERE AND AROUND

Luzern's centrally located train station functions as a rail crossroads, with express trains connecting from Zürich, a 46-minute trip, and Geneva, a three-hour trip. Trains enter from the south via the St. Gotthard Pass from the Ticino and via the Furka Pass from the Valais. Directly outside the station's entrance is the quay where lake boats that form part of the public transit system can take you to a variety of towns along the Vierwaldstättersee, including Weggis, Vitznau, Flüelen (with a bus connection to Altdorf), and Brunnen.

It's easy to reach Luzern from Zürich by road, approaching from national expressway A3 south, connecting to A4 via the secondary E41 in the direction of Zug, and continuing on A4, which turns into the A14, to the city. From Basel in the northwest, it's a clean sweep by the A2 to Luzern.

Approaching from the south, take the A2 to Altdorf, where a tunnel takes you through to the shores of the lake. If you're heading for resorts on the north shore, leave the expressway at Flüelen and follow the scenic secondary route.

Parking is limited, and Luzern's Old Town is pedestrians-only; it's best to park your car and walk. All the destinations in this region mentioned here are small, reachable by train or boat, and can easily be traveled on foot once you get there.

The main tourist office for the hub city of Luzern is in the Bahnhof, off Track 3.

VISITOR INFORMATION

Contacts Luzern Tourism. ✉ *Zentralstr. 5, Luzern* ☎ *041/2271717* 🌐 *www.luzern.com.*

Don't miss the elaborate frescoes inside the Jesuitenkirche (Jesuit Church) in Luzern.

EXPLORING

The Luzern tourist office offers English-language walking tours of the city. The usual schedule is daily from May to October and Wednesday and Saturday from November to March. In April there are tours on Wednesday and weekends. Tours take about two hours and cost 18 SF.

TOP ATTRACTIONS

Altes Rathaus (*Old Town Hall*). In 1606 the town council held its first meeting in this late-Renaissance-style building, constructed between 1602 and 1606. It still meets here today. ✉ *Kornmarkt 3, Luzern.*

Bourbaki-Panorama. The panorama was the IMAX theater of the 19th century; its sweeping, wraparound paintings brought to life scenes of epic proportions. The Bourbaki is one of only 30 remaining in the world. Painted by Édouard Castres between 1876 and 1878 (he was aided by many uncredited artists, including Ferdinand Hodler), it depicts the French Army of the East retreating into Switzerland at Verrières, a famous episode in the Franco-Prussian War. As you walk around the circle, the imagery seems to pop into three dimensions; in fact, with the help of a few strategically placed models, it does. There's a recorded commentary in English. A modern glass cube filled with stores, movie theaters, and a restaurant surrounds its conical wooden structure. ✉ *Löwenpl. 11, Luzern* ☎ *041/4123030* 🌐 *www.bourbaki-panorama.ch* 🎫 *12 SF.*

Historisches Museum (*History Museum*). Housed in the late-Gothic armory dating from 1567, this stylish institution exhibits numerous city icons, including the original Gothic fountain that stood in the

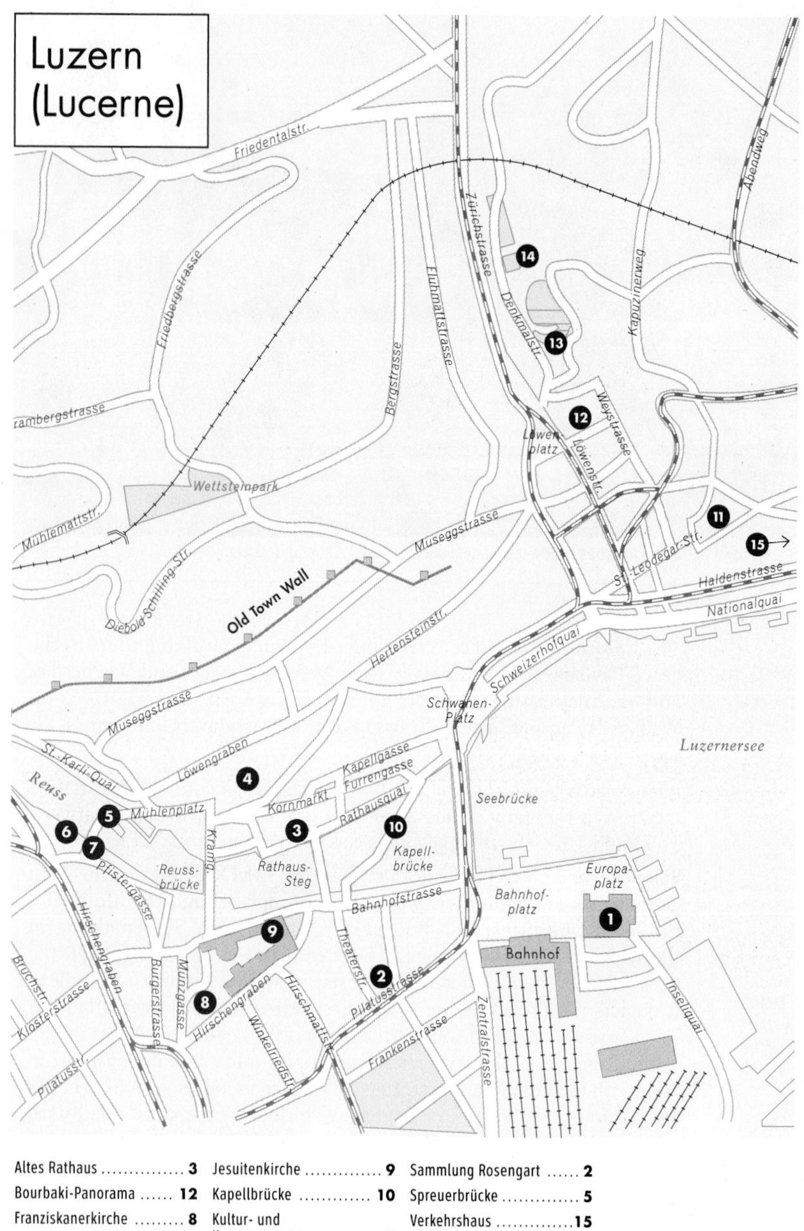

Luzern (Lucerne)
Friedentalstr.
Friedbergstrasse
Bergstrasse
Fluhmattstrasse
Zürichstrasse
Denkmalstr.
Kapuzinerweg
Abendweg
Weystrasse
Löwenplatz
Löwenstr.
rambergstrasse
Wettsteinpark
Mühlemattstr.
Diebold-Schilling-Str.
Museggstrasse
Old Town Wall
Hertensteinstr.
St.-Leodegar-Str.
Haldenstrasse
Nationalquai
Schweizerhofquai
Schwanen-Platz
Luzernersee
Museggstrasse
St.-Karli-Quai
Reuss
Löwengraben
Kapellgasse
Furrengasse
Kornmarkt
Rathausquai
Mühlenplatz
Seebrücke
Kramg.
Rathaus-Steg
Kapell-brücke
Reuss-brücke
Pfistergasse
Europa-platz
Bahnhof-platz
Bahnhofstrasse
Bahnhof
Hirschengraben
Burgerstrasse
Munzgasse
Hirschengraben
Hirschmattstr.
Theaterstr.
Pilatusstrasse
Zentralstrasse
Inseliquai
Bruchstr.
Klosterstrasse
Winkelriedstr.
Frankenstrasse
Pilatusstr.
Altes Rathaus 3
Bourbaki-Panorama 12
Franziskanerkirche 8
Gletschergarten 14
Historisches Museum 7
Hofkirche 11
Jesuitenkirche 9
Kapellbrücke 10
Kultur- und Kongresszentrum 1
Löwendenkmal 13
Natur-Museum 6
Sammlung Rosengart 2
Spreuerbrücke 5
Verkehrshaus 15
Weinmarkt 4

A GOOD WALK

Start at the **Kultur- und Kongresszentrum**, near the train station, which gives you a beautiful view of all the places you'll see in Luzern. Walk down Pilatusstrasse to see the impressive modern-art collection at the **Sammlung Rosengart.**

Cut north to Bahnhofstrasse, taking a left to the modern bridge, the Rathaus-Steg, and head north to the **Altes Rathaus,** across the bridge. This late-Renaissance building is on Rathausquai, the city's main avenue.

Turn left and climb the stairs past the ornately frescoed Zunfthaus zur Pfistern, a guildhall dating from the late-15th and early-16th centuries, to the Kornmarkt, where the grinding din of the grain market was once heard. Cut left to the **Weinmarkt,** a fountain square.

Leave the square from its west end, turn right on Kramgasse, and head west across the Mühlenplatz to the **Spreuerbrücke,** an unlikely exhibition space for dark paintings of the plague.

Crossing the bridge to the left bank you'll find a pair of museums, the **Natur-Museum** and the **Historisches Museum.**

From the end of the Spreuerbrücke, cut back upriver along Pfistergasse, veer left on Bahnhofstrasse, and turn right into Münzgasse to the **Franziskanerkirche.**

Return to Bahnhofstrasse and head to the **Jesuitenkirche.** Continuing east past the Rathaus-Steg Bridge, you'll see the **Kapellbrücke,** the oldest bridge of its kind in Europe.

After crossing the Kapellbrücke, break away from Old Town through thick pedestrian and bus traffic at Schwanenplatz to Schweizerhofquai.

Double back and take the first right, St. Leodegarstrasse, to the **Hofkirche.**

Go back down the church steps, doubling back on St. Leodegarstrasse, turn right, and continue on to Löwenstrasse.

Turn right and walk up to Löwenplatz and the **Bourbaki-Panorama,** which dominates the square with its mix of Victorian and modern architecture.

Beyond the plaza, up Denkmalstrasse, is the **Löwendenkmal,** called by Mark Twain "the most mournful and moving piece of stone in the world."

Immediately adjoining the small park that shades the lion lies the **Gletschergarten.**

Return down Denkmalstrasse and, at Löwenplatz, turn right on Museggstrasse, which cuts through an original city gate and runs parallel to the watchtowers and crenellated walls of Luzern, constructed around 1400.

TIMING

The Old Town is easy to navigate and ideal for walking. You can take in the sights on this route in about three hours; to this add another hour each to see the Natur-Museum and Historisches Museum, and time to linger at the Kapellbrücke and the Löwendenkmal. Both the Natur-Museum and the Historisches Museum are closed on Monday.

The Chapel Bridge is the oldest wooden bridge in Europe.

Weinmarkt. In the permanent exhibit, guests can use a handheld scanner to learn about the thousands of barcoded items on display. ✉ *Pfisterg. 24, Luzern* ☎ *041/2285424* 🌐 *historischesmuseum.lu.ch* 🎫 *10 SF* ⊙ *Closed Mon., except some holidays.*

Fodor's Choice ★ **Jesuitenkirche** (*Jesuit Church*). Constructed in 1666–77, this baroque church with a symmetrical entrance is flanked by two onion-dome towers, added in 1893. Inside, its vast interior, restored to its original splendor, is a dramatic explosion of gilt, marble, and epic frescoes. Nearby is the Renaissance **Regierungsgebäude** (Government Building), seat of the cantonal government. ✉ *Bahnhofstr. 11a, Luzern* ☎ *041/2100756* 🌐 *www.jesuitenkirche-luzern.ch.*

Fodor's Choice ★ **Kapellbrücke** (*Chapel Bridge*). The oldest wooden bridge in Europe snakes diagonally across the Reuss. When it was constructed in the early 14th century, the bridge served as a rampart in case of attacks from the lake. Its shingle roof and grand stone water tower are to Luzern what the Matterhorn is to Zermatt, but considerably more vulnerable, as a 1993 fire proved. Almost 80% of this fragile monument was destroyed, including many of the 17th-century paintings inside. Nevertheless, a walk through this dark, creaky landmark will take you past polychrome copies of 110 gable panels, painted by Heinrich Wägmann in the 17th century and depicting Luzern and Swiss history; stories of St. Leodegar and St. Mauritius, Luzern's patron saints; and coats of arms of local patrician families. ✉ *Luzern* ✥ *Between Seebrücke and Rathaus-Steg, connecting Rathausquai and Bahnhofstr.*

Fodor's Choice ★ **Kultur- und Kongresszentrum** (*Culture and Convention Center*). Architect Jean Nouvel's stunning glass-and-steel building manages to stand out from as well as to fuse with its ancient milieu. The lakeside center's roof is an oversized, cantilevered, flat plane; shallow water channels thread inside, and immense glass plates mirror the surrounding views. The main draw is the concert hall, which opened in 1998. Although the lobbies are rich in blue, red, and stained wood, the hall itself is refreshingly pale, with brilliant acoustics. Among the annual music events is the renowned International Music Festival. A museum focuses on rotating exhibits of new international artists. ✉ *Europapl. 1, Luzern* ☎ *041/2267070* 🌐 *www.kkl-luzern.ch.*

Löwendenkmal (*Lion Monument*). The Swiss guards who died defending Louis XVI of France at the Tuileries in Paris in 1792 are commemorated here. Designed by Danish sculptor Berthel Thorwaldsen and carved out of a sheer sandstone face by Lucas Ahorn of Konstanz, this 19th-century wonder is a simple, stirring image of a dying lion. The Latin inscription translates "To the bravery and fidelity of the Swiss."✉ *Denkmalstr. 4, Luzern* 🌐 *www.luzern.com/en/sightseeing-fuehrungen/sightseeing/lion-monument.*

6

Sammlung Rosengart (*Rosengart Collection*). A father-and-daughter team amassed this amazing group of works by major late-19th- and 20th-century artists. Now housed in a former bank building, the collection reveals their intensely personal approach; the Rosengarts acquired according to their own tastes instead of investment potential. Here you can see Joan Miró's *Dancer*, Fernand Léger's *Contraste de formes*, and works by Paul Cézanne, Claude Monet, Henri Matisse, Paul Klee, and Marc Chagall. There's an especially rich selection of works by Pablo Picasso; the artist painted the daughter, Angela Rosengart, five times. ✉ *Pilatusstr. 10, Luzern* ☎ *041/2201660* 🌐 *www.rosengart.ch* 🎫 *18 SF.*

Weinmarkt (*Wine Market*). What is now the loveliest of Luzern's several fountain squares was famous across Europe for the passion plays staged here in the 15th to 17th centuries. Its Gothic central fountain depicts St. Mauritius (patron saint of soldiers), and its surrounding buildings are flamboyantly frescoed in 16th-century style. ✉ *West of Kornmarkt, Luzern.*

WORTH NOTING

Franziskanerkirche (*Franciscan Church*). Since its construction in the 13th century, this church has been persistently remodeled. It still retains its 17th-century choir stalls and carved wooden pulpit. The barefoot Franciscans once held a prominent social and cultural position in Luzern, which took a firm stance against the Reformation and today remains approximately 70% Roman Catholic. ✉ *Franziskanerpl. 1, off Münzg., Luzern* ☎ *041/2299600.*

Gletschergarten (*Glacier Garden*). This tourist attraction, excavated between 1872 and 1875, shows stones that have been dramatically pocked and polished by Ice Age glaciers. A private museum on the site, the **Alpineum**, displays impressive relief maps of Switzerland and an elaborate 19th-century hall of mirrors. ✉ *Denkmalstr. 4, Luzern* ☎ *041/4104340* 🌐 *www.gletschergarten.ch* 🎫 *15 SF.*

Hofkirche. This sanctuary of St. Leodegar was first part of a monastery founded in 750. Its Gothic structure was mostly destroyed by fire in 1633 and rebuilt in late-Renaissance style, so only the towers of its predecessor were preserved. The carved pulpit and choir stalls date from the 17th century, and the 80-rank organ (1650) is one of Switzerland's finest. Outside, Italianate loggias shelter a cemetery for patrician families of Old Luzern. ✉ *St. Leodegarstr. 6, Luzern* ☎ *041/2299500* ⏲ *Call for hrs.*

FAMILY **Natur-Museum** (*Natural History Museum*). Unusually modern display techniques bring nature lessons to life here. The museum focuses on local natural history, with panoramas of early Luzern settlers and live animals for children to meet. ✉ *Kasernenpl. 6, Luzern* ☎ *041/2285411* 🌐 *www.naturmuseum.ch* 🎟 *8 SF* ⏲ *Closed Mon.*

Spreuerbrücke (*Chaff Bridge*). This narrow covered bridge dates from 1408. The weathered wood structure's interior gables hold a series of eerie, well-preserved 17th-century paintings of the *Dance of Death* by Kaspar Meglinger. Medieval in style and inspiration, they chronicle the plague that devastated all of Europe in the 14th century. ✉ *Luzern* ✥ *Between Geissmattbrücke and Reussbrücke, connecting Zeughaus Reuss-Steg and Mühlenpl.*

OFF THE BEATEN PATH

Verkehrshaus (*Swiss Museum of Transport*). Almost a world's fair in itself, the complex of buildings and exhibitions—both indoors and out—includes live demonstrations, dioramas, and a 1:20,000 scale photo of Switzerland that you can walk on in special slippers. Every mode of transit is discussed, from stagecoaches and bicycles to jumbo jets and space capsules. The museum also houses a planetarium and an IMAX theater. It's easily reached by steamer, car, train, or Bus 6, 8, or 24. If you're driving, head east on Haldenstrasse at the waterfront and make a right on Lidostrasse. Signs point the way. ✉ *Lidostr. 5, Luzern* ☎ *041/3704444* 🌐 *www.verkehrshaus.ch* 🎟 *30 SF.*

WHERE TO EAT

$$ ITALIAN

✕ **Bellini Locanda Ticinese.** This sleek restaurant brings a taste of Ticino to Luzern's New Town with hearty and reasonably priced Swiss-Italian dishes like spinach gnocchi, sausage with polenta, and all sorts of pizzas. In addition to beautiful mosaic tiles and a crackling fireplace, the dining room features the work of young local artists, and the lounge hosts live piano music some evenings. **Known for:** romantic atmosphere in the evenings; Sunday brunch, including a glass of Spumante, for 52 SF; summer patio well sheltered from traffic. [$] *Average main: 33 SF* ✉ *Hotel Continental, Murbacherstr. 4, Luzern* ☎ *041/2289050* 🌐 *www.continental.ch.*

$$ FRENCH

✕ **Bodu.** A touch of Paris in the heart of Luzern—advertising posters from the 1920s and 1930s, simple wooden tables, and a green-and-yellow-checkered floor—is the setting for sumptuous dishes based on fresh market ingredients. Steamed sea bass or rack of lamb are typical offerings. **Known for:** full menu all day; riverside terrace and balcony seating; separate dining room/bar for smokers. [$] *Average main: 41 SF* ✉ *Kornmarkt 5, Luzern* ☎ *041/4100177* 🌐 *www.brasseriebodu.ch.*

Luzern's position on the River Reuss and Lake Luzern offers lakeside dining options galore.

$$ SWISS

Galliker. Step past the ancient facade and into a room roaring with local action, where brisk waitresses deliver the dishes that *Mutti* (Mom) used to make: fresh *Kutteln* (tripe) in rich white-wine sauce with cumin seeds; real *Kalbs-kopf* (chopped fresh veal head) served with heaps of green onions and warm vinaigrette; and authentic Luzerner *Kügelipaschtetli* (puff-pastry nests filled with finely ground beef, savory herbs, and cream sauce). Occasional experiments in a modern mode—such as steak with wasabi sauce—prove that Peter Galliker's kitchen is no museum. **Known for:** being a Luzern institution; simple, authentic atmosphere; its specialty, pot-au-feu. *Average main: 36 SF* *Schützenstr. 1, Luzern* *041/2401002* *Closed Sun., Mon., and mid-July–mid-Aug.*

$$$ SWISS Fodor's Choice ★

Old Swiss House. This popular establishment has been feeding travelers since 1931 in what was originally built as a farmhouse in 1858, now containing a beautifully contrived collection of 17th-century antiques, leaded glass, and an old-world style, pleasantly burnished by more than 80 years of service. The standing menu includes specialties from around the country: cubed fillet of beef in a green-pepper mustard sauce, pike perch with ratatouille, and chocolate mousse. **Known for:** more than 30,000 bottles of wine in stock; plush and elegant atmosphere; kitchen that's open all day. *Average main: 56 SF* *Löwenpl. 4, Luzern* *041/4106171* *www.oldswisshouse.ch* *Closed Mon., and Sun. Jan. and Feb.*

$$ SWISS

Pfistern. One of the architectural focal points of the Old Town waterfront, this floridly decorated guild house provides an authentic medieval setting in which to sample reasonably priced local fare (the guild's origins can be traced to 1341). Lake fish or *pastetli* (meat pies with puff pastry) are worthy local options. **Known for:** lovely riverside views; fondue served in a festive outdoor setting; good-value lunch specials. *Average main: 35 SF* *Kornmarkt 4, Luzern* *041/4103650* *www.restaurant-pfistern.ch.*

$$ SWISS **Rebstock/Hofstube.** Formerly a 16th-century tavern, this lively brasserie is a favorite meeting place for Luzern's art and media crowd, humming with locals lunching by the bar, while the more formal old-style restaurant glows with wood and brass under a low-beamed parquetry ceiling. Fresh market ingredients are combined for modern, international fare, including chicken simmered in white wine, rabbit stew, and classic garlic snails. **Known for:** hearty food and generous portions; architecturally attractive location; Vogelheu: batter-fried croissants sprinkled with sugar and cinnamon. *Average main: 38 SF* *St. Leodegarstr. 3, Old Town* *041/4171819* *www.rebstock-luzern.ch.*

$ ITALIAN **Valentino.** This simple Italian spaghetteria has been charming its guests for over three decades, and some staff members have held similarly long tenures. Tables of varying sizes are packed close together, giving it a lively, family-style atmosphere, and Valentino's menu is full of hearty pasta and pizza as well as some meat and fish dishes. **Known for:** cozy and convivial atmosphere; plaza seating in summer; good value for the money. *Average main: 24 SF* *Metzgerrainle 3, Luzern* *041/4103193* *www.valentinos-luzern.ch* *Closed Sun.*

WHERE TO STAY

$$$ HOTEL **Art Deco Hotel Montana Luzern.** The luxurious original woodwork, parquet floors, and shining terrazzo are all in superb condition at this 1910 palace, where public rooms flank the ground floor's south side, and on a clear day offer a magnificent view of the lake and the mountains. **Pros:** breathtaking views; large terrace hovers over the lake; jazz concerts in a you-are-there venue. **Cons:** not convenient for quick jaunts into center; somewhat difficult to find; "day spa" means treatments, not a spa. *Rooms from: 330 SF* *Adligenswilerstr. 22, Luzern* *041/4190000* *www.hotel-montana.ch* *61 rooms* *No meals.*

$$ HOTEL **Boutique Hotel Weisses Kreuz.** In the bustling heart of the Old Town, this adults-only hotel has a tongue-in-cheek combination of sleek modern lines and gilded frames and fat cherubs, and though the rooms are small, they are well designed, with dark hardwood floors, white linens, and pastel accents. **Pros:** free Wi-Fi; hotel guests get discounts at in-house pizzeria; in-room coffeemakers. **Cons:** some room views are limited; can be noisy at night; no a/c. *Rooms from: 260 SF* *Furreng. 19, Luzern* *041/4188220* *www.altstadthotelluzern.ch* *21 rooms* *Breakfast.*

$$$ HOTEL **Grand Hotel National Luzern.** This monumental landmark, founded in 1870, was once home base to Cesar Ritz, the man who invented the world's first modern luxury hotel. **Pros:** glorious views on lake side; promenade restaurant under chestnut trees; large indoor pool, sauna, and massage and cosmetic treatments. **Cons:** constant street noise on city side; breakfast buffet expensive and not that grand; casino next door can mean overly boisterous guests. *Rooms from: 465 SF* *Haldenstr. 4, Luzern* *041/4190909* *www.grandhotel-national.ch* *41 rooms* *No meals.*

$$$ HOTEL **Hotel Des Balances.** Built in the 19th century on the site of two ancient guildhalls, this waterfront lodging is full of style, and one of the best addresses in the heart of the Old Town makes this the slickest in its price class. **Pros:** most rooms have great views; the river terrace is exceptional; excellent location. **Cons:** top-floor rooms are very small; revelers outside can be noisy; no a/c. *Rooms from: 350 SF* ✉ *Weinmarkt, Luzern* ☎ *041/4182828* 🌐 *www.balances.ch* *56 rooms* *No meals.*

$$ HOTEL **Hotel Hofgarten.** This gracious 12th-century house close to the Hofkirche and the Löwendenkmal has been artfully modernized with an eclectic mix of colors and themes. **Pros:** lots of character; convenient and attractive location; leafy garden terrace in summer. **Cons:** some rooms quite small; surroundings can be noisy; no a/c. *Rooms from: 240 SF* ✉ *Stadthofstr. 14, Luzern* ☎ *041/4108888* 🌐 *www.hofgarten.ch* *19 rooms* *Breakfast.*

$$$ HOTEL **Hotel Krone Luzern.** Spotless and modern, this hotel softens its edges with white linens and walls; look in the recessed niche of one of the interior walls for a stone shrine retained from the original structure. **Pros:** very friendly and helpful staff; good central location; in-room coffeemakers. **Cons:** restaurant doesn't serve alcohol; square can be noisy on weekends; no a/c. *Rooms from: 320 SF* ✉ *Weinmarkt 12, Luzern* ☎ *041/4194400* 🌐 *www.krone-luzern.ch* *29 rooms* *Breakfast.*

$$$ HOTEL **The Hotel Lucerne - Autograph Collection.** Award-winning French architect Jean Nouvel, who also designed Luzern's Kultur- und Kongresszentrum, focuses on ultrahip design here; parquet floors are this lodging's only remaining old-world touch. **Pros:** heaven for style junkies; hip restaurant and lounge; adjacent to a park. **Cons:** larger-than-life movie stills and black walls might not appeal; some rooms rather dark; next-door church bells might wake you. *Rooms from: 365 SF* ✉ *Sempacherstr. 14, Luzern* ☎ *041/2268686* 🌐 *www.the-hotel.ch* *30 rooms* *No meals.*

$$ HOTEL **Hotel Wilden Mann.** One of the city's best-known hotels, the gracious and atmospheric Wilden Mann has stone walls, coffered ceilings, brass fittings, and burnished wood everywhere. **Pros:** medieval architecture straight out of Middle Earth; lovely common areas; guest rooms with character. **Cons:** some ceilings are a bit low; rather high bathtub walls; no a/c. *Rooms from: 300 SF* ✉ *Bahnhofstr. 30, Luzern* ☎ *041/2101666* 🌐 *www.wilden-mann.ch* *48 rooms* *Breakfast.*

6

NIGHTLIFE AND PERFORMING ARTS

For information on goings-on around town, go to the tourist office for a copy of the German-English *Luzern City Guide,* published quarterly by the city. Get it stamped by your hotel for discounts on museums, public transit, and special events.

NIGHTLIFE

BARS AND LOUNGES

Louis Bar. This bar offers live jazz in the style of its namesake, Louis Armstrong. While you're there, sip one of the 130 Scotch whiskies on hand. ✉ *Hotel Montana, Adligenwilerstr. 22, Luzern* ☎ *041/4190000* 🌐 *www.hotel-montana.ch.*

A Carnival party atmosphere takes over Luzern for the seven days of Fasnacht.

Opus. This place specializes in fine wines, many served by the glass. ✉ *Bahnhofstr. 16, Luzern* ☎ *041/2264141* 🌐 *www.restaurant-opus.ch*.

Pacifico. Reds dominate the murals and furnishings at this high-ceilinged Mexican cantina, where young locals come for its variety of fancy cocktails. ✉ *Pilatusstr. 15, Luzern* ☎ *041/2268787* 🌐 *www.pacifico-luzern.ch*.

Penthouse. With three rooftop terraces, Penthouse has outstanding views and an extensive drink menu. DJs do their thing on Friday and Saturday nights, when the bar is open until 3:30 am. ✉ *Pilatusstr. 29, Luzern* ☎ *041/2268888* 🌐 *www.penthouse-luzern.ch*.

Roadhouse. Spread over three levels and spilling onto the sidewalk across from the train station, this place hosts lots of DJs and theme parties. ✉ *Pilatusstr. 1, Luzern* ☎ *041/2202727* 🌐 *www.roadhouse.ch*.

CASINO

Grand Casino Luzern. Some of the most elegant nightlife in Luzern is found in the Grand Casino Luzern, an early-20th-century building on the lake's northern shore near the grand hotels. You can play *boule* (a type of roulette) in the Gambling Room; dance in the Club; watch the cabaret in the Casineum; or have a meal in Olivo, a Mediterranean restaurant with views of the mountains and the lake. In summer, sit outside under the palm trees at the loungelike Seecafe. ✉ *Haldenstr. 6, Luzern* ☎ *041/4185656* 🌐 *www.grandcasinoluzern.ch*.

CARNIVAL: SEVEN DAYS OF MADNESS

Although Carnival (called *Fasnacht* in German) is celebrated throughout the country, the party aspect is taken most seriously in Luzern. On the first Thursday seven weeks before Easter each year, seven days of madness follow, alive with parades, confetti, dancing, singing, and, of course, drinking. The parades begin with an orderly procession of Guggä—elaborately costumed brass and drums bands that can turn any pop tune into a festive event—that soon devolves into a writhing, rowdy, Old Town festival that goes more or less nonstop throughout the week. Visitors are encouraged, if not downright expected, to join in. Many locals take the week off—there's no getting any work done anyway.

PERFORMING ARTS

MUSIC

Blue Balls Festival. In July, the eclectic (and badly named) **Blue Balls Festival** brings nine days of indoor and outdoor concerts, plus a lakeside market and a host of food and drink vendors. ✉ *Schweizerhofquai, Luzern* ☎ *043/2437323* 🌐 *www.blueballs.ch.*

Lucerne Festival. The cultural hub of central Switzerland, the city hosts the annual Lucerne Festival from mid-August to mid-September in the Kultur- und Kongresszentrum. Outstanding classical performers come from all over the world; past guests have included tenor Jonas Kaufmann and superstar pianist Lang Lang. The Lucerne Festival also has an Easter version as well as a series of piano concerts in November. ✉ *Europapl. 1, Luzern* ☎ *041/2264400* 🌐 *www.lucernefestival.ch.*

Luzerner Symphonieorchester. Performing at the Kultur- und Kongresszentrum, this symphony orchestra has a season that runs from October through June. ✉ *Europapl. 1, Luzern* ☎ *041/2260510* 🌐 *www.sinfonieorchester.ch.*

Stadtkeller. Summer performances at the Stadtkeller come with yodelers, dirndled dancers, and more. In the winter, the stage features contemporary sounds, including blues, jazz, and rock. Meals are also available. ✉ *Sternenpl. 3, Luzern* ☎ *041/4104733* 🌐 *www.stadtkeller.ch.*

THEATER

Luzerner Theater. Across from the Kapellbrücke, the Luzerner Theater hosts plays in German and operas in their original languages. ✉ *Theaterstr. 2, Luzern* ☎ *041/2281414* 🌐 *www.luzerner-theater.ch.*

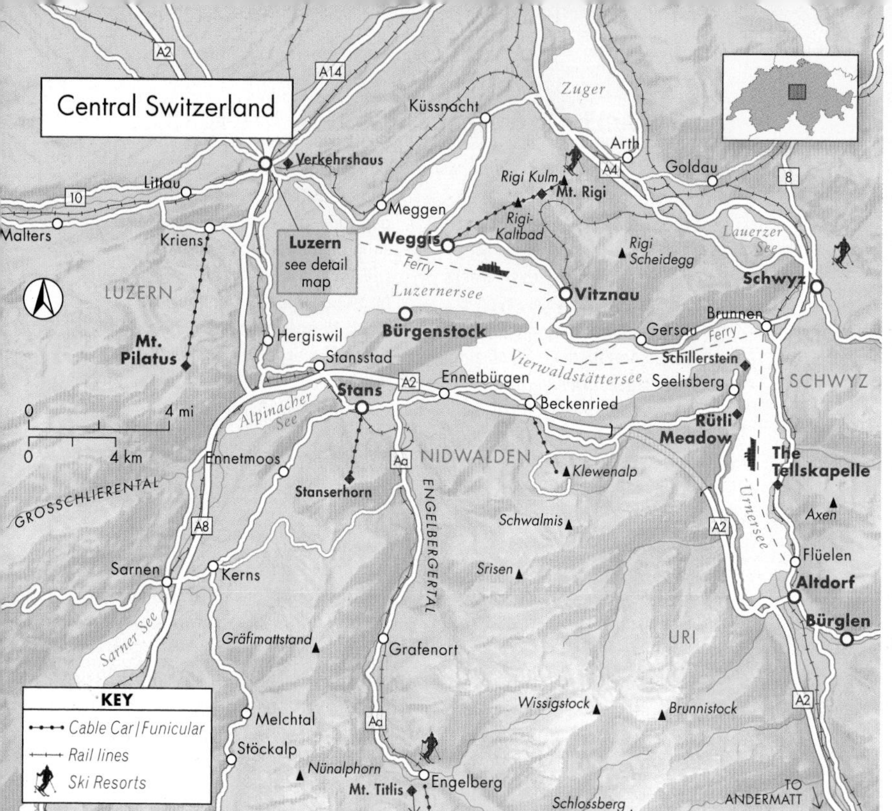

SPORTS AND THE OUTDOORS

BIKING

The Swiss practice of renting bicycles from the train station comes in handy here, because the lake-level terrain offers smooth riding. Alternatively, Nextbike offers bicycles all over Luzern and in the countryside for 2 SF per hour or 20 SF per day.

Nextbike. ✉ *Bahnhofpl., Luzern* ☎ *041/5080800* 🌐 *www.nextbike.ch.*

Rent a Bike. ✉ *Bahnhofpl., Luzern* ☎ *051/2273261* 🌐 *www.rentabike.ch* 🎫 *From 31 SF.*

BOATING

Marina Charter. Pedal-, motor-, and sailboats are available through Marina Charter. ✉ *Alpenquai 13, Luzern* ☎ *041/3607944* 🌐 *www.bootsvermietung.ch.*

SNG Luzern. This company offers fair-weather boat rentals from April to October and a variety of boat tours throughout the year, some of which include tasty meals. ✉ *Alpenquai 11, Luzern* ☎ *041/3680808* 🌐 *www.sng.ch.*

Werft Herzog AG. Motorboats that accommodate up to eight passengers are available from this company. ✉ *Nationalquai, Luzern* ☎ *041/4104333* 🌐 *www.herzog.ch.*

SWIMMING

FAMILY **Lido Luzern.** Near the Verkehrshaus, the Lido Luzern lets you swim in the lake from May to September. If the lake is too cold, there's a heated pool that's popular with families. Other amenities include a playground and a restaurant with an attractive patio overlooking the waterfront. ✉ *Lidostr. 6a, Luzern* ☎ *041/3703806* 🌐 *www.lido-luzern.ch* 🎟 *7 SF.*

SHOPPING

The best shopping in the region is concentrated in Luzern, which has a wide variety of Swiss handicrafts (embroidery, wood figurines, clocks) as well as the luxury goods appropriate to its high profile. The pedestrian-only zone along Hertensteinstrasse is packed with boutiques and department stores. In Luzern, stores are generally open until 6:30 pm, except on Thursday and Friday, when many stay open until 9 pm. On Saturday, most shut their doors at 4 pm and don't reopen until Monday.

From May to October, a **Flohmärt,** or flea market, takes place every Saturday from 8 to 4 at Untere Burgerstrasse, not far from the Franziskanerkirche. For locally made crafts, there's a **Handwerksmarkt** on the Weinmarkt. It takes place on the first Saturday of every month from April through December.

6

DEPARTMENT STORES

Globus. The city's most fashionable department store, Globus has a wonderful gourmet supermarket in the basement. ✉ *Pilatusstr. 4, Luzern* ☎ *058/5785555* 🌐 *www.globus.ch.*

Manor. A good bet for sporting goods, Manor has a cafeteria-style restaurant on the top floor, a rooftop terrace with great views of Luzern, and free Wi-Fi. ✉ *Weggisg. 5, Luzern* ☎ *041/4197699* 🌐 *www.manor.ch.*

Migros. This store specializes in groceries and inexpensive items. ✉ *Hertensteinstr. 9, Luzern* ☎ *041/4170740* 🌐 *www.migros.ch.*

HANDICRAFTS AND GIFTS

Aux Arts du Feu. High-end china and crystal are on offer at Aux Arts du Feu. ✉ *Schweizerhofquai 2, Luzern* ☎ *041/4101401* 🌐 *www.auxartsdufeu.ch.*

Bookbinders Design. An upscale stationer, Bookbinders Design stocks high-quality pens, pencils, rubber stamps, and brightly colored recycled-paper products. ✉ *Hertensteinstr. 3, Luzern* ☎ *041/4109506* 🌐 *www.bookbindersdesign.ch.*

Schmid-Linder. With an extensive line of Swiss embroidery and linen, Schmid-Linder also stocks cuckoo clocks, cowbells, and a large range of wood carvings from Brienz, in the Berner Oberland. ✉ *Denkmalstr. 9, Luzern* ☎ *041/4104346.*

WATCHES

Bucherer. One of the city's poshest jewelry and watch stores, Bucherer sells Audemars Piguet, Piaget, and Rolex. ✉ *Schwanenpl. 5, Luzern* ☎ *041/3697700* 🌐 *www.bucherer.com.*

Gübelin. A high-end watch shop, Gübelin is the place for Breguet, Patek Philippe, and its own house brand. ✉ *Schwanenpl. 7, Luzern* ☎ *041/4170010* 🌐 *www.guebelin.ch.*

WOMEN'S CLOTHING

Caroline. This shop sells wild, one-of-a-kind hats for all seasons. Even if you're not in the market for one, it's fun to peek in the window and watch Caroline Felber and her apprentices at work. ✉ *Stiftstr. 4, Luzern* ☎ *041/2105363* 🌐 *www.huete.ch.*

De Boer Plus. This exclusive plus-size boutique has a vast selection of labels and styles. ✉ *Weggisg. 29, Luzern* ☎ *041/4106239* 🌐 *www.maisondeboer.ch.*

Rive Gauche. This store stocks a wide variety of styles, from feminine to trendy to business. ✉ *Pilatusstr. 14, Luzern* ☎ *041/2108916.*

SPAS

Fitnesspark National Luzern. This chain of wellness centers extends throughout the country, but the one in Luzern stands out for its extensive pool area, which includes thermal baths, hot tubs, and great views of Mt. Pilatus. Swimsuits are required in the pool, but the men's and women's saunas and steam rooms are textile-free. The Fitnesspark National is good value, especially if you bring along your own soap, towel, and indoor footwear; otherwise you can buy or rent what you need. You can also book a massage, a fitness class, or a session with a personal trainer. ✉ *Haldenstr. 23, Luzern* ☎ *041/4170202* 🌐 *www.fitnesspark.ch/luzern* 🎫 *35 SF.*

Palace Spa. Though petite, the Palace Spa manages to feel grand thanks to its clever layout, elegant fixtures, and generous amenities. On the third floor of the Palace Hotel, the spa has separate men's and women's saunas, steam rooms, and relaxation areas that are free for hotel guests and anyone who books a treatment. Especially relaxing is the signature Palace Massage, which combines long strokes with gentle pressure. Couples can book the spa suite to enjoy side-by-side massages while gazing out at the lake and mountains. There's also a small gym. The day spa packages are good value. Be sure to ask about the giant singing bowl ceremony. ✉ *Palace Hotel, Haldenstr. 10, Luzern* ☎ *041/4161515* 🌐 *www.palace-spa.ch.*

AROUND LUZERN

Since Luzern doesn't have the sprawling suburbs associated with most cities, bucolic landscapes are just a short day trip away. Craggy mountaintops, lush hills dotted with grazing cows, and peaceful lakeside villages—along with one of the most famous mountains in Switzerland—are easily reached by boat, train, or car.

Reach for the sky with a hike around Mt. Pilatus, 10 km (6 miles) from Luzern.

MT. PILATUS

10 km (6 miles) southwest of Luzern.

Unlike Queen Victoria, who rode to the summit of this 6,953-foot mountain by mule in 1868, you can travel to Mt. Pilatus via cable car. At the top, a grand 19th-century "mountaineer's" hotel is the centerpiece of the surprisingly stroller-friendly mountain peak.

The mountain was named either from the Latin *pileatus* (wearing a cap), to refer to its frequent cloud covering, or, more colorfully, for the ghost of Pontius Pilate, who supposedly haunts the summit. (His body, it was said, was brought here by the devil.) For centuries it was forbidden to climb the mountain and enrage the ghost, who allegedly unleashed deadly storms.

GETTING HERE AND AROUND

If you don't have time for the four-hour hike, there are two ways to get to the top of Mt. Pilatus from Luzern: either a bus and a cable car or a boat ride and a cogwheel train will take you there.

VISITOR INFORMATION

Contacts Pilatus Tourist Information. 🌐 *www.pilatus.ch.*

EXPLORING

FAMILY Fodor's Choice ★ **Mt. Pilatus.** To reach the mountain by cable car, get a bus from the train station in Luzern to the suburb of Kriens, where you catch a tiny, four-seat cable car that flies silently up to Fräkmüntegg (4,600 feet). From there, change to the sleek, multilevel 55-passenger cable car that sails through open air up the rock cliff to the summit station (5,560 feet). A 10-minute walk takes you to **Esel**, one of the central peaks that make up Pilatus. From

DID YOU KNOW?

The world's steepest cog railway carries visitors to the summit of Mt. Pilatus (6,953 feet). At times, the car travels on gradients inclined 48%, and the track punches through sheer rock in a series of tunnels. The views at the top are truly stunning.

a platform here, views unfold over the Alps and the sprawling, angular Lake Luzern. Once you reach the top, glorious views are everywhere. The flat main trail on the top leads in and out of the mountain, and comes replete with striking cavern windows that offer drop-dead-gorgeous vistas. The main view takes in Luzern, which looks like a toy village. The refurbished Hotel Pilatus-Kulm, once graced by Queen Victoria, features 27 rooms and three suites in Alpine-chic style. Meanwhile, it still feels like the 19th century in the restaurant, where the food is spiced up by the views just outside the elegant sash windows. There's also the simpler Hotel Bellevue in a more modern building; it has 20 rooms.

A super variation for the trip from Mt. Pilatus to Luzern involves riding one of the steepest cogwheel trains in the country—often down gradients inclined nearly 48%—through four tunnels that pierce sheer rock, to Alpnachstad. From there, take the train or the ferry, which leaves from the jetty across from the train station, back to Luzern. The trip to Mt. Pilatus costs 72 SF regardless of whether you start in Kriens or Alpnachstad. To go on to Engelberg, get off the Luzern-bound train at Hergiswil, where you can cross the tracks and climb aboard the small, private Stans–Engelberg train that heads up the Engelbergertal (Engelberg Valley). ☎ *041/3291111* 🌐 *www.pilatus.ch.*

STANS

10 km (6 miles) southeast of Mt. Pilatus, 10 km (6 miles) south of Luzern.

In the heart of lush valley terrain and mossy meadows, Stans is an old village whose appealing Old Town center is dotted with the deep-roof houses typical of central Switzerland. This was the home of the beloved Heinrich Pestalozzi, the father of modern education. After the French army invaded the village in 1798, slaughtering nearly 2,000 citizens, it was Pestalozzi who gathered the orphaned children into a school, where he applied his progressive theories in the budding science of psychology to the practice of education. Instead of rote memorization and harsh discipline, Pestalozzi's teaching methods emphasized concrete examples (using plant specimens to teach botany, for example) and moral as well as intellectual development. He also championed the idea of fostering a child's individuality.

VISITOR INFORMATION

Contacts Nidwalden Tourism. ☎ *041/6108833* 🌐 *www.nidwalden.com.*

EXPLORING

Monument to Arnold von Winkelried. On the town square, facing the Pfarrkirche St. Peter und St. Paul, stands this 19th-century monument to Arnold von Winkelried, a native of Stans who died while leading the Swiss Confederates to victory over the Austrians at the battle of Sempach in 1386. The Austrians, armed with long spears, formed a Roman square so that the Swiss, wielding axes and halberds, couldn't get in close enough to do any damage. Shouting, "Forward, confederates, I will open a path!" von Winkelried threw himself on the spears, clasping as many of them as he could to his breast and creating an opening for his comrades. ✉ *Rathauspl., Stans.*

Pfarrkirche St. Peter und St. Paul (*Church of Sts. Peter and Paul*). The bell tower of the Pfarrkirche St. Peter und St. Paul is in Italian Romanesque style, with increasing numbers of arched windows as it rises. The incongruous steeple was added in the 16th century. ✉ *Knirig. 1, Stans* ☎ *041/6109261*.

FAMILY **Stanserhorn.** A two-part journey on a nostalgic 1893 funicular and an ultramodern cable car takes you to the Stanserhorn (6,200 feet), and from its peak you can see the Titlis, the highest point in central Switzerland. A "convertible" version of the cable car lets you feel the wind in your hair. ✉ *Stansstaderstr. 19, Stans* ☎ *041/6188040* 🌐 *www.stanserhorn.ch* 🎫 *74 SF round-trip* 🕑 *Closed mid-Nov.–mid-Apr.*

OFF THE BEATEN PATH

Mt. Titlis. Set 19 km (12 miles) south of Stans, this is perhaps the most spectacular of the many rocky peaks that surround the Obermatt's long, wide bowl. Thanks to a sophisticated transportation system that benefits skiers, hikers, climbers, and sightseers alike, it's possible to ride a small cable car up to the tiny mountain lake (and famous ski area) called Trübsee (5,904 feet). From there, change and ascend to Stand to catch the famous Rotair cable car, which rotates to give 360-degree panoramas on its way up to the summit station on the Titlis. At the top is a multilevel structure that seems to conjure up Disney's Space Mountain: four rock-embedded, fortress-thick floors lead to stores, an ice grotto (serving drinks from a solid-ice bar), and a restaurant with views that take in the Jura Mountains, the Graubünden, and Bernese Alps. Mt. Titlis looms over the village of Engelberg (3,280 feet), which is an hour from Luzern by train. Engelberg clusters at the foot of its Benedictine Kloster (monastery), founded in 1120. The monastery grounds are open to the public daily and include a dairy. ✉ *Gerschnistr. 1, Engelberg* ☎ *041/6395050* 🌐 *www.titlis.ch* 🎫 *92 SF round-trip*.

WEGGIS

20 km (12 miles) northeast of Luzern.

With a pretty waterfront park and promenade, Weggis is a summer resort town known for its mild, almost subtropical climate—little wonder that it is a magnet for Switzerland's retirees. It's far from the highway and accessible only by the secondary road, so you get a pleasant sense of isolation. At 5,900 feet, the famed **Mt. Rigi** is just a cable car ride away. Or consider climbing to the top, staying in the hotel, and getting up early to see the sun rise over the Alps—a view that astounded both Victor Hugo and Mark Twain. With Lake Luzern on one side and Lake Zug on the other, Mt. Rigi can feel like an island.

GETTING HERE AND AROUND

During daylight hours, boats arrive here every hour from Luzern (19.60 SF one way) and Flüelen (41 SF one way). There are also bus and train connections, which are considerably cheaper.

Contacts SGV boat station. ✉ *Seestr. 7, Weggis* ☎ *041/3901133* 🌐 *www.lakelucerne.ch.*

VISITOR INFORMATION

Contacts Weggis Tourist Information. ✉ *Seestr. 5, Weggis* ☎ *041/2271800* 🌐 *www.wvrt.ch.*

EXPLORING

Mt. Rigi. Weggis has a cable car up to the top of the Rigi, and neighboring Vitznau has a cogwheel train. You can also approach Rigi via the cogwheel train from Arth-Goldau; the two lines were built by competing companies in the 1870s in a race to reach the top and capture the lion's share of the tourist business. The line rising out of the lakefront resort of Vitznau won, but the Arth-Goldau line gets plenty of business, as its base terminal lies on the mainstream St. Gotthard route. Rigi is one of the few mountains covered by the Swiss Travel Pass. Otherwise, a day card from Weggis, Vitznau, or Arth-Goldau is 72 SF. If you're approaching from Weggis, follow signs for the Rigibahn, a station high above the resort (a 15-minute walk). From here you can ride a large cable car to Rigi-Kaltbad, a small resort on a spectacular plateau; walk across to the electric rack-and-pinion railway station and ride the steep tracks of the Vitznau–Rigi line to the summit of the mountain. Take an elevator to the Rigi Kulm hotel to enjoy the views indoors or walk to the crest (45 minutes) to see as far as the Black Forest in one direction and Mt. Säntis in the other. ☎ *041/3998787* 🌐 *www.rigi.ch.*

WHERE TO STAY

$$ RESORT **Hotel Beau Rivage.** Built in 1908, this attractive business-class resort concentrates its comforts on a small but luxurious waterfront site, with a large restaurant above the manicured lawn, a small swimming pool with mountain views, and comfortable lounge chairs at the lake's edge. **Pros:** lovely location; spa facilities; wonderful views from lakeside rooms. **Cons:** backs onto the main road; rooms can get hot in summer; no kettle or coffeemaker in room. [$] *Rooms from: 298 SF* ✉ *Gotthardstr. 6, Weggis* ☎ *041/3927900* 🌐 *www.beaurivage-weggis.ch* *Closed Oct.–Mar.* *39 rooms* *Breakfast.*

$$ HOTEL **Rigi Kulm Hotel.** Some parquet floors remain, but this 19th-century lodging now has a modern look and feel and more modern conveniences than some city hotels. **Pros:** a sunny perch above the fog that can dim Luzern; unique site for sunrises and sunsets; good restaurant on-site. **Cons:** once you're here, you're here; poor weather can ruin the view; lots of day-trippers. [$] *Rooms from: 228 SF* ✉ *Kulmweg 7, Rigi Kulm* ☎ *041/8801888* 🌐 *www.rigikulm.ch* *33 rooms* *Breakfast.*

VITZNAU

4 km (2½ miles) southeast of Weggis, 26 km (16 miles) east of Luzern.

For a quintessentially scenic spot, stop over in Vitznau, a tiny waterfront resort that competes with Weggis for the balmiest weather. Small as this village may be, it looms large on the tourist radar. Not only is Vitznau the home of the magnificently palatial Park Hotel, but it's also the site of Switzerland's first-ever cog railway (opened in 1871); the Mülefluh fortress (the first artillery fortress in the country); and the shipyards where Lake Luzern's fabled paddle steamers were first built. Today it's the best place to see the world's largest Swiss flag, proudly displayed in summer on a face of Mt. Rigi overlooking Vitznau.

GETTING HERE AND AROUND

Vitznau is easily reached by SGV Boat from Luzern.

Contacts SGV Boat Station. ✉ *Seestr., Vitznau* ☎ *041/3971430* 🌐 *www.lakelucerne.ch.*

VISITOR INFORMATION

Contacts Vitznau Tourism Information. ✉ *Bahnhofstr. 1, Vitznau* ☎ *041/2271810* 🌐 *www.wvrt.ch.*

WHERE TO STAY

$ HOTEL **Hotel Rigi Vitznau.** This solid lodging has a delightfully old-fashioned facade, modern interiors, and a welcoming atmosphere that comes from being family owned and run. **Pros:** centrally located; friendly service; calm atmosphere. **Cons:** some traffic noise in daytime; parking is limited; could use a slight face-lift. *$ Rooms from: 150 SF* ✉ *Seestr., Vitznau* ☎ *041/3998585* 🌐 *www.rigi-vitznau.ch* *35 rooms* *Breakfast.*

$$ RESORT **Hotel Vitznauerhof.** With its own lakefront garden, a full-service spa, and a restaurant in the former boathouse serving delicacies like spicy lobster with oranges or veal with artichokes and truffles, you're likely to be tempted to stay a little longer, no matter how many days you booked. **Pros:** exquisite setting; myriad outdoor seating options; spa. **Cons:** backs onto a main road; bold decor won't suit everyone; no a/c. *$ Rooms from: 217 SF* ✉ *Seestr. 80, Vitznau* ☎ *041/3997777* 🌐 *www.vitznauerhof.ch* *Closed late Oct.–Apr.* *58 rooms* *Breakfast.*

$$$$ RESORT Fodor's Choice ★ **Park Hotel Vitznau.** Set in a fairy-tale lakefront palace, this isolated but lavish retreat dates back to 1902. **Pros:** glorious lakeside location with ample space to enjoy it; large spa, including pool with a view of the mountains; mechanical beds, tablets to control the blinds, and other gadgets. **Cons:** white stone floors seem cold and clinical; adjacent to a real clinic you might wander into; finance theme is a crass reminder of the expense. *$ Rooms from: 1,000 SF* ✉ *Seestr. 18, Vitznau* ☎ *041/3996060* 🌐 *www.parkhotel-vitznau.ch* *47 rooms* *Breakfast.*

SPAS

Mineralbad & Spa. The region's mineral springs have been attracting visitors for hundreds of years, and this spa, which opened in 2012, represents the latest wave. Perched at 4,757 feet above sea level, the Mineralbad & Spa offers stunning mountain views and delightful pools both inside and out. Designed by Swiss architect Mario Botta, it's fashioned mostly from Italian granite. The adults-only spa has a steam room, a unisex sauna, and a so-called crystal bath, which is pretty but only a few inches deep. Despite its lofty location, the spa is easy to reach by cable car from Weggis or cogwheel train from Vitznau. There's a day rate, and spontaneous visitors can rent a swimsuit and towel for an additional charge. ✉ *Rigi Kaltbad* ☎ *041/3970406* 🌐 *www.mineralbad-rigi-kaltbad.ch.*

EN ROUTE

From Vitznau, a boat tour will take you across Lake Luzern to **Beckenried,** from which a cable car leads to Klewenalp (5,250 feet), a small resort overlooking the lake. The area is excellent for hiking, with breathtakingly panoramic views of the lake and mountains on clear days. If you're driving, you could also follow the north shore to Gersau, a tiny lake resort that was an independent republic—the world's smallest—from 1332 to 1798. From Gersau the boat snakes around the sharp peninsula of the Seelisberg; the 1980 completion of a 9¼-km

A steam train heads to the summit of Mt. Rigi on the Vitznau–Rigi railway.

(nearly 6-mile) tunnel through the peninsula, south of the lake, opened the way for even swifter north–south travel between Luzern and points north and the St. Gotthard route and points south.

URNERSEE

Perhaps it was destiny that Switzerland was born right here. Take one look at the spectacular mix of snowy peaks, sapphire lakes, and picturesque meadows surrounding the Urnersee—the southern leg of Lake Luzern—and you'll wonder if all this beauty inspired the pact signed in 1291 between the clans of Schwyz, Unterwalden, and Uri. This Oath of Eternal Alliance announced the creation of a new realm—the world's longest-running continuous democracy.

This is not the only iconic historical event in the region. Although Wilhelm Tell is considered by some to be mere myth, this is the hallowed ground where he may have been born and where he became a legend. Every year, thousands of Swiss make a pilgrimage here, taking a lake steamer from Luzern all the way down to the Urnersee (or driving the same route along the northern lakefront highway to Brunnen) to find their way to the Rütli Meadow—the birthplace of Switzerland—and to then trace the story of Tell in neighboring lakeside villages. If you want to get a bird's-eye view of the area, opt for the excursion up to the top of majestic Rigi Kulm, the summit of Mt. Rigi, by cogwheel train or cable car.

Lake cruises depart from the main docks by the train station (schedules are available at the ticket and tourist offices); the boat will be marked for Flüelen. First-class seats are on top; each level has a restaurant-café. The exterior seats are only slightly sheltered; if you want to sit inside, you may feel obligated to order a drink. Take advantage of the boat's many stops—you can get on and off at will.

BÜRGENSTOCK

20 km (13 miles) southeast of Luzern.

The rich have always headed to Lake Luzern, thanks, in good part, to the famous Bürgenstock hotel resort. This high-end hideaway, perched atop its own Alp, has lured many celebs to these parts—Audrey Hepburn, Sophia Loren, Sean Connery, and Shirley MacLaine once colonized the chalets around here. A resort shuttle boat as well as most Flüelen-bound boats go to the base of the Bürgenstock, where you can take a funicular to the isolated resort at the top of a ridge. Though the plateau isn't terribly high—only about 2,800 feet—it rises dramatically above the water and offers striking views of the region. Bürgenstock also can be approached by car, up a steep, sometimes dangerous road that connects Luzern and the town of Stansstad. Drive carefully: it was designed with many switchbacks to prevent Ferrari-driving playboys from speeding. For another kind of adrenaline rush, stroll along the cliff walk and take Europe's highest outdoor elevator to the resort's 3,658-foot peak. The Hammetschwand Lift is built into the side of the cliff and leads to hiking trails and an informal restaurant with stunning views.

6

GETTING HERE AND AROUND

It takes about 45 minutes to get to Bürgenstock from Luzern via boat and funicular. If you're driving from Luzern, the journey should take about 30 minutes.

WHERE TO STAY

$$$$ RESORT Fodor's Choice ★ **Bürgenstock Resort Lake Lucerne.** Glorious views of Lake Luzern, the mountains. **Pros:** well designed, with many attractive design touches; amazing views, especially from the infinity pool; getting there via boat and funicular is part of the fun. **Cons:** long walk from Palace Hotel to the spa; spa's textile-free area has a stark atmosphere and odd layout; boat and funicular schedule requires disciplined timing. *$ Rooms from: 510 SF ✉ Bürgenstockstr., Obbürgen ☎ 041/6126000 ⊕ www.buergenstock.ch 383 rooms Breakfast.*

RÜTLI MEADOW

14 km (8½ miles) southeast of Vitznau, 15 km (9½ miles) northwest of Altdorf on Urnersee, 35 km (22 miles) southeast of Luzern.

Fodor's Choice ★ At the south end of Lake Luzern, past the gorgeously scenic Seelisberg Peninsula, the narrow, majestic Urnersee accesses some of the most legendary landmarks in the region.

GETTING HERE AND AROUND

The lake steamers from the Luzern-based Schifffahrtsgesellschaft des Vierwaldstättersees (SGV) make frequent stops here. Check online for schedules. ⊕ *www.lakelucerne.ch.*

The Rütli Meadow is the birthplace of modern Switzerland, and the world's oldest democracy.

EXPLORING

The **Schillerstein,** on the right as you cruise past the peninsula, is a spectacular natural rock obelisk extending nearly 85 feet up out of the lake, onto which has been carved a gigantic dedication: "To the author of Wilhelm Tell, Friedrich von Schiller. 1859." About 10 minutes beyond the rock, the lake steamer pulls up at the quaint, 19th-century landing dock for perhaps the most historically significant site in central Switzerland: the Rütli Meadow.

Rütli Meadow. This is where the confederates of Schwyz, Unterwalden, and Uri are said to have met in 1307 to renew the 1291 Oath of Eternal Alliance. A five-minute walk up the hillside brings you to a grassy plateau where a rock and flagpole mark the historic location. Nearby is a medieval rock bench nestled by towering trees—the perfect spot to think about another monumental event that took place here centuries later: amid threats of a 1940 German invasion, General Guisan, Swiss army commander in chief, summoned hundreds of officers to the meadow to reaffirm their commitment to the Swiss Confederation in a secret, stirring ceremony. Afterward, head back down the hill to study the small video presentation (perhaps also take a photo of a costumed historical interpreter) and be sure to stop in the time-burnished, 19th-century chalet snack shop, with its lovely stained-glass salons and picturesque wood verandas. For a more substantial meal, stop at the Rütlihaus restaurant above the meadow. ✉ *Rütli.*

CLOSE UP

The Swiss Path

Central Switzerland is well suited to experiencing the country's history, with landmarks representing facts and legends going back more than 700 years. You can see the sights below in a day by boat, bus, and train; on foot or by bicycle it will take you at least two days. Start at Switzerland's birthplace: take the boat from Luzern to the Rütli Meadow, where representatives from the three original cantons swore their Oath of Eternal Alliance against the Habsburgs in 1291. A short boat trip down the lake to Flüelen and the bus to Altdorf will take you to the statue of Wilhelm Tell, Switzerland's legendary symbol of independent spirit.

Back in Flüelen, walk the *Weg der Schweiz* (the Swiss Path), which you can locate on the shore right by the train station, and head north along the lake. The path dates from 1991, when it was created to commemorate the 700th anniversary of the signing of the oath of allegiance. The historic footpath covers 35 km (22 miles) of lakefront lore in 26 sections, each honoring one of Switzerland's cantons. In 14 hours, or better yet spread out over several days, you can trace the mythical steps of Wilhelm Tell and the genuine steps of medieval forerunners, climb through steep forests and isolated villages, and visit the holiday resort of Brunnen.

As you walk along it, you'll find yourself going through a series of hand-hewn tunnels that form part of the original Axenstrasse, a road built into the mountainside in 1865. This amazing feat of engineering shortened the long voyage from north to south over the Alps. You can walk to the romantic 19th-century lakeside chapel, the Tellskapelle (one hour each way) or all the way to Brunnen (on foot 5½ hours; by bike 2½ hours) or turn around and head back to Flüelen if you run out of steam.

A side trip to Schywz from Brunnen takes you to the Bethlehemhaus, a wooden structure built in 1287. From Brunnen or Flüelen, you can take the train back to Luzern, where the Bourbaki Panorama depicts the French army's retreat through Switzerland in 1870–1871. Up the street, see the moving *Löwendenkmal*, a dying lion sculpted into a cliff in 1821 in memory of Swiss mercenaries who died defending Louis XVI during the French Revolution; and the Gletschergarten, an outdoor park incorporating an expanse of rock shaped by passing Ice Age glaciers.

ALTDORF

20 km (12½ miles) south of Rütli Meadow, 35 km (22 miles) southeast of Luzern.

Schiller's play *Wilhelm Tell* sums up the tale for the Swiss, who perform his play religiously in venues all over the country—including the town of Altdorf, just up the road from the Rütli Meadow. Leave the steamer at Flüelen, the farthest point of the boat ride around the lake, and connect by postbus to Altdorf, the capital of the canton Uri and, by popular if not scholarly consensus, the setting for the famous scene in which Tell was forced to use his crossbow to shoot an apple off his own son's head.

Though there are no valid records of Wilhelm Tell's existence, and versions of the legend conflict with historical fact, no one denies the reality of his times, when central Switzerland—then a feudal dependent of Austria but by its own independent will not yet absorbed into the Holy Roman Empire—suffered brutal pressures and indignities under its local rulers. The mythical Gessler was one of those rulers, and his edict—that the proud Swiss should bow before his hat suspended from a pole in the village square at Altdorf—symbolizes the cruel oppression of the time. Schiller's Tell was a consummate hero: brisk, decisive, a highly skilled helmsman as well as marksman, and not one for diplomatic negotiations. He refused to kneel and provoked his famous punishment: to shoot an apple off his young son's head before a crowd of fellow townsmen. If he refused, both would be killed. Tell quietly tucked an arrow in his shirt bosom, loaded another into his crossbow, and shot the apple clean through. When Gessler asked what the second arrow was for, Tell replied that if the first arrow had struck his child, the second arrow would have been for Gessler and he would not have missed.

For this impolitic remark, Tell was sentenced to prison. While deporting him across Lake Luzern, the Austrians (including the ruthless Gessler) were caught in a violent storm and turned to Tell, the only man on board who knew the waters, to take the helm. Unshackled, he steered the boat to a rocky ridge, leaped free, and pushed the boat back into the storm. Later he lay in wait in the woods near Küssnacht and shot Gessler in the heart. This act inspired the people to overthrow their oppressors and swear the Oath of Eternal Alliance around a roaring bonfire, laying the groundwork for the Swiss Confederation.

GETTING HERE AND AROUND

On the main train and car route linking the area south of the Alps with the north, Altdorf was a main stop on the journey when it took weeks, not hours, to get from Zürich to Milan. As a consequence, there are hourly train connections from Zürich, Luzern, or Lugano (stop in Flüelen and take the five-minute bus ride to the Telldenkmal stop in Altdorf's center). The lake steamers from Luzern take about three hours to Flüelen.

VISITOR INFORMATION

Contact Uri Tourismus. ✉ *Schützeng. 11, Altdorf* ☎ *041/8748000* 🌐 *www.altdorftourismus.ch.*

EXPLORING

Wilhelm Tell Monument. This often-reproduced monument in the village center shows a proud father with crossbow on one shoulder, the other hand grasping his son's hand. It was sculpted by Richard Kissling in 1895. ✉ *Rathauspl., Altdorf.*

Across the lake from the Rütli Meadow sits the Tellskapelle, a beautiful shrine to Wilhelm Tell.

THE TELLSKAPELLE

14 km (9 miles) north of Altdorf, 41 km (25½ miles) southeast of Luzern.

Have your camera ready for this magnificently picturesque lakeside chapel, set at the foot of the Axen mountain.

GETTING HERE AND AROUND

The lake steamer from Luzern stops here as well as at the Rütli Meadow (directly across the lake), making it convenient to see both sites in one shot. Boats leave Luzern hourly in summer, less frequently in winter. You can also take a taxi from Brunnen (about 50 SF each way), but set a time for your driver to pick you up again: there is no stand at the Tellskapelle. The steamer also stops in Brunnen.

EXPLORING

Fodor's Choice ★ **Tellskapelle.** A shrine to Wilhelm Tell, the church is adjacent to the **Tellsplatte,** which was the rocky ledge onto which Tell, the rebellious archer, leaped to escape from Gessler's boat, pushing the boat back into the stormy waves as he jumped. Built in 1500, it was restored in High Victorian fashion in 1881. It contains four frescoes of the Tell legend (painted at the time of restoration), showing the taking of the oath at Rütli Meadow, Tell shooting the apple on his son's head, Tell's escape, and Gessler's death. ✣ *South of Sisikon by boat (10 mins) or on foot (about 35 mins)* 🌐 *www.uri.info.*

BÜRGLEN

3 km (2 miles) southeast of Altdorf, 40 km (25 miles) southeast of Luzern.

Wilhelm Tell was supposedly from the tiny, turreted town of Bürglen, just up the road from Altdorf.

EXPLORING

Tell-Museum. Documents and art related to the legendary man are displayed in this museum. ✉ *Postpl., Bürglen* ☎ *041/8704155* 🌐 *www.tell-museum.ch* 🎫 *8 SF* ⏲ *Closed Nov.–Apr., except groups by appointment.*

SCHWYZ

35 km (22 miles) southeast of Luzern.

This historic town is the capital of the canton Schwyz, root of the name Switzerland and source of the nation's flag. Switzerland's most precious archives are stored here as well. Traces of an independent settlement at Schwyz have been found from as far back as the Bronze Age (2500 BC–800 BC), but it was its inhabitants' aid in the 1291 Oath of Eternal Alliance that put Schwyz on the map.

Many of Schwyz's splendid houses owe their origin to the battlefield. The men of Schwyz had a reputation as fine soldiers and were in demand in other countries as mercenaries during the 16th and 17th centuries. They built many of the houses you can see today with their military pay.

VISITOR INFORMATION

Contacts Schwyz Tourismus. ✉ *Zeughausstr. 10, Schwyz* ☎ *041/8555950* 🌐 *www.schwyz-tourismus.ch.*

EXPLORING

Bundesbriefmuseum (*Federal Charter Museum*). See the beautifully scripted and sealed original Oath of Allegiance, as well as battle flags and paintings of the period, in Schwyz's Bundesbriefmuseum. ✉ *Bahnhofstr. 20, Schwyz* ☎ *041/8192064* 🌐 *www.bundesbriefmuseum.ch* 🎫 *5 SF* ⏲ *Closed Mon.*

Fodor's Choice ★ **Ital-Redinghaus.** Schwyz has several notable baroque churches and a large number of fine old patrician homes dating from the 17th and 18th centuries, not least of which is the Ital-Redinghaus with its magnificent interior, antique stoves, and fine stained glass. A visit to this grand house includes a peek inside the neighboring **Bethlehemhaus,** the oldest wooden house in Switzerland, dating from 1287. There is no parking on the grounds; park on the nearby town square and walk 50 yards to the entrance off Reichstrasse. ✉ *Rickenbachstr. 24, Schwyz* ☎ *041/8114505* 🌐 *www.irh.ch* 🎫 *5 SF* ⏲ *Closed Mon. and Nov.–May.*

Rathaus (*Town Hall*). Schwyz's most famous landmark is the Rathaus; its richly frescoed exterior (1891) depicts the Battle of Morgarten, the 1315 conflict in which the Swiss defeated the Austrian army. The building is still used as the Town Hall, and the interior is accessible only on a group tour (in German). ✉ *Hauptpl. 1, Schwyz.*

7

BASEL

WELCOME TO BASEL

TOP REASONS TO GO

★ **Three corners:** Not many cities offer a more cosmopolitan mix. Here Switzerland merges with Germany and France, and Basel is home to some 150 nationalities.

★ **Art old and new:** This city of the arts has galleries full of Old Master paintings and some pictures so contemporary the paint is still drying—nearly 40 museums cater to every taste.

★ **Fasnacht:** Each spring during its three-day Lenten celebration the city's streets are filled with spectacularly costumed revelers, bands, and pipers.

★ **Münster madness:** Not only is this cathedral an amazing piece of architecture, but it also offers fabulous views of the city and the River Rhine.

★ **Noble dust:** A short boat ride from Basel, the Colonia Augusta Raurica is the oldest Roman settlement on the Rhine, complete with a restored 1st-century-BC theater.

Shouldering the Swiss Jura Mountains, the German Black Forest, and the French Vosges, Basel is Switzerland's third-largest city and the central conurbation (extended urban area) for the northwest part of the country. Bordering both banks of the Rhine, Basel is 730 feet above sea level—the lowest altitude of any Swiss city north of the Alps. From here the river turns 90 degrees north and widens into a majestic waterway.

1 Altstadt. Bordering the marketplace, the Altstadt (Old Town) lies in front of the majestic red Town Hall and is host to a thriving market. Winding alleyways lead off to a maze of shopping possibilities.

2 Kleinbasel. East of the Rhine on the German side of town, Kleinbasel (Small Basel) is a lively blue-collar center that includes the huge Messe Basel complex, where Art Basel is held every June.

3 St. Alban. Narrow quiet streets wind around patrician houses downhill to the Rhine, where a medieval paper mill is just steps from the Art Museum Basel | Contemporary.

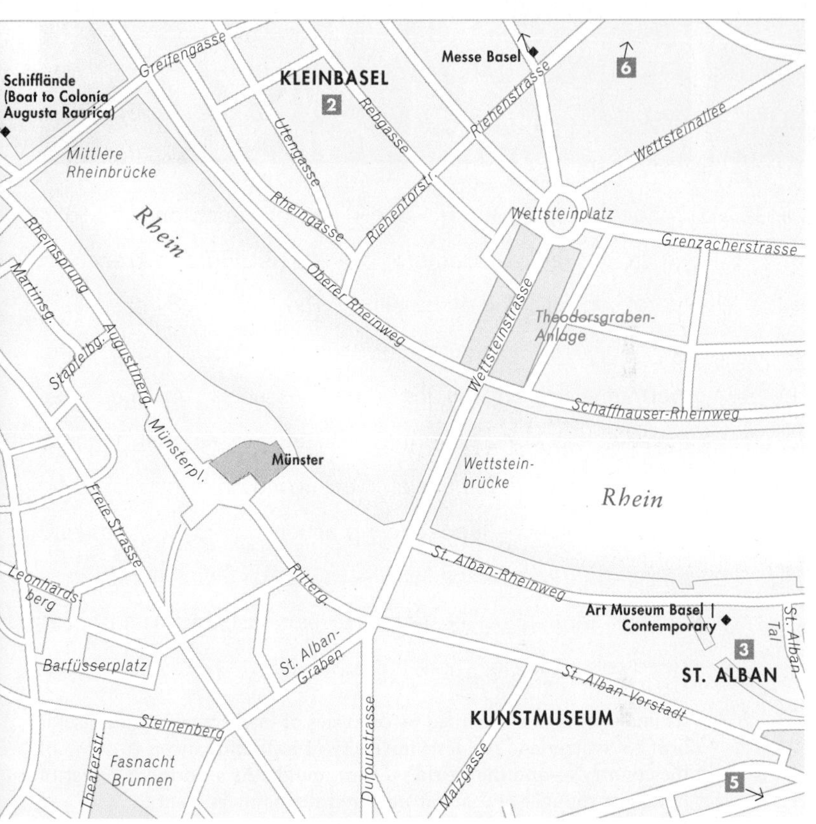

4 Zoo. A hollow nestled behind the SBB train station is home to more than 600 kinds of animals and offers experiences such as penguin walks (in winter), elephant baths, and pelican feedings.

5 Colonia Augusta Raurica (Augst). Painstakingly restored over the past 50 years, this former Roman town includes the original amphitheater and a re-creation of a typical villa, along with a museum of artifacts found during archaeological digs.

6 Greater Basel. Technically not part of Basel but so close that it hardly matters—even if one is just across the German border—the surrounding towns are home to museums and historic sites worth a visit.

Updated by
Liz Humphreys

Although it lacks the gilt and glitter of Zürich and the Latin grace of Geneva, in many ways Basel (Bâle in French) is more sophisticated than either. The hub of Switzerland's vibrant pharma industry, wedged between France and Germany, this city on the Rhine has nearly 40 museums, including the world-class Kunstmuseum, the Museum Tinguely, and the Fondation Beyeler. Baselworld in spring and Art Basel in summer—the world's premier fairs for watches and contemporary art respectively—as well as Switzerland's most famous carnival, or Fasnacht, gives midsized Basel an outsized role as an international destination.

Its imagination has been fed by centuries of intellectual input: Basel is host to Switzerland's oldest university (1460) and patron to some of the country's—and the world's—finest minds. As a northern center of humanist thought and art, it nurtured the painters Konrad Witz and Hans Holbein the Younger, as well as the great Dutch scholar Erasmus. And it was Basel's visionary lord mayor Johann Rudolf Wettstein who, at the end of the Thirty Years' War, negotiated Switzerland's groundbreaking—and lasting—neutrality.

As high culture breeds good taste, Basel has some of the most varied, even quirky, shopping in Switzerland, all within walking distance. But you can still get a beer and a bratwurst here: natives primarily speak German or their own local version of *Schwyzerdütsch,* called *Baseldytsch*.

Each day more than 70,000 French and German commuters cross into Basel, working at leading banks and pharmaceutical firms. Yet Basel's population remains modest, hovering just above 175,000; its urban center lies gracefully along the Rhine, though now two skyscrapers, the 32-floor Trade Fair Tower and Switzerland's highest building, pharma giant Roche's headquarters, dominate views across the Rhine. Two blocks from the heart of the thriving shopping district you can walk along medieval residential streets cloaked in perfect, otherworldly silence to Münsterhügel (cathedral mount), where the Romanesque-Gothic cathedral offers superb views over the wonderfully preserved Altstadt.

BASEL PLANNER

WHEN TO GO

Basel is in the Rhine Valley, which affords it an agreeably mild climate. Warm Mediterranean air also wafts this way from the Rhône Valley. The average temperature in January, the coldest month, is 2°C (36°F); in July, the warmest, 20°C (68°F). Fog is more rare than in regions farther south, and the average rainfall is the lowest north of the Rhône.

PLANNING YOUR TIME

If you are in town for just a day, your best bet is to take a stroll through Basel's Altstadt, making sure to see the Münster and the sweeping views from the terrace overlooking the Rhine. Art enthusiasts could decide to circle from here directly to the Kunstmuseum, and shoppers may want to head down one of the winding alleyways into the Freie Strasse or the Marktplatz. A leisurely late-afternoon walk across the Mittlere Rheinbrücke and upstream along the sunny Kleinbasel riverside promenade (Oberer Rheinweg) is a good way to see the town in its best light.

If you are sticking around for longer, then take in some of the city's smaller museums, perhaps in the picturesque St. Alban quarter. From here take a ferry across the river and head east to the Museum Tinguely. Or organize your day around a trip to Riehen; the Fondation Beyeler's stunningly well-rounded (and beautifully presented) collection of 20th-century art can be reached in a mere 20 minutes by tram.

In summer you could opt to take a boat trip to the Roman ruins of Augusta Raurica in Augst, east of Basel. Or take a driving tour of, or catch a local train to, some of the small villages scattered south of the city, such as Balsthal, Holderbank, Oberer Hauenstein, Langenbruck, and Liestal to experience the more rural delights of the area. Cool off in very hot weather like the locals by taking a dip in the Rhine. Dive in after the Wettsteinbrücke and float down to one of several popular refreshment stands where you can watch a seemingly endless stream of locals doing the same.

GETTING HERE AND AROUND

Hotel guests in Basel receive a complimentary Basel Mobility Ticket, which allows free use of all public transportation within the city during their stay. Holders of the Swiss Pass also travel free on all Basel public transport systems.

AIR TRAVEL

Basel uses EuroAirport, one of the world's only binational airports (Geneva is the other). Arriving travelers can exit customs directly to Switzerland or to France. Direct flights link Basel to most major European cities as well as the Middle East, North Africa, and Canada.

Regular bus service runs between EuroAirport and the Bahnhof SBB in the center of Basel. The trip takes about 15 minutes and costs 4.70 SF per person.

One-way taxi fare from the airport to the Basel center is approximately 40 SF; it takes about 15 minutes in light traffic and up to 30 minutes at rush hour. There are normally cabs at the taxi stand, but if you need to call one from the airport, make sure you leave the building on the Swiss side.

CAR TRAVEL

The German autobahn A5 enters Basel from the north and leads, as the E25, directly to the Rhine and the center of the city. From France the autoroute A35 (E9) continues through Basel via a tunnel linking to the E25. The E25 feeds into the A2 autobahn leading to the rest of Switzerland. Since most of the city's sights are within walking distance of downtown, it's advisable to park your car for the duration of your visit. Expect to pay around 25 SF per day for parking at an all-day garage.

TAXI TRAVEL

Unless you need transportation in the middle of the night, taking taxis makes little sense in Basel: most sights are clustered in the pedestrian zone along tram lines or within a maze of one-way streets. Taxis are costly, less efficient, and less available than the ubiquitous tram.

Contacts Mini Cab. ☎ *061/7777777.* **Taxi-Zentrale.** ☎ *061/2222222.* **33er Taxi.** ☎ *061/3333333.*

TRAIN TRAVEL

There are three main rail stations in Basel. The Bahnhof SBB in Grossbasel connects to destinations in Switzerland and with the Intercity Express to Germany. Trains from France leave from the SNCF, within the same station. The Badischer Bahnhof in Kleinbasel runs services to Germany. If you're coming from Germany and staying in the Old Town, make sure your train goes all the way to the SBB station on Centralbahnstrasse; many a weary traveler has walked an hour from the German side of town.

Contacts Badischer Bahnhof. ✉ *Schwarzwalderstr. 200, Kleinbasel* ☎ *061/6901215.* **Bahnhof Basel SBB.** ✉ *Centralbahnstr., Zoo* ☎ *0900/300300* 🌐 *www.sbb.ch.* **Basel SNCF.** ✉ *Centralbahnstr., Basel* ☎ *0900/300300* 🌐 *www.sncf.com/en/passengers.*

TRAM TRAVEL

Most Basel trams run every 6 to 8 minutes all day, and every 15 minutes in the late evening. Tickets must be bought at the automatic machines at every stop. Stops are marked with green-and-white signs; generally the trams run from 5:30 or 6 in the morning until midnight, and several lines carry on through the night on weekends. *Mehrfahrtenkarten* (multijourney cards) allow you six trips, saving you 10% on each trip. *Tageskarten* (day cards), also available from the ticket machines at the tram stops, allow unlimited travel all day within the central zones for 9.90 SF or through all the areas mentioned for 18.70 SF.

⇨ *For more information on getting here and around, see Travel Smart Switzerland.*

Kids will love watching the Jean Tinguely–designed Carnival Fountain.

TOURS

Basel Tourismus organizes walking tours of the city, which start from the tourist information office in the Stadt Casino and cater to both German and English speakers. Tours take place from May to October, daily at 2:30. From November to April the walking tours are held every Saturday at 2:30. The cost is 18 SF.

VISITOR INFORMATION

The main tourist information desk in Basel is in the Stadt Casino at Barfüsserplatz and is open weekdays 9–6:30, Saturday 9–5, Sunday and holidays 10–3; there is also a branch in the Bahnhof SBB train station on Centralbahnstrasse.

Contacts Basel Tourismus (*Basel Tourism*). ✉ *Stadt Casino, Steinenberg 14, Altstadt* ☎ *061/2686868* 🌐 *www.basel.com.*

EXPLORING

The Rhine divides the city into two distinct sections: on the southwestern bank lies Grossbasel (Greater Basel), the commercial, cultural, and academic center, which encompasses the Altstadt (Old Town) and, directly upriver, the quiet winding medieval streets of St. Alban, where you can stroll along the Rhine, peek into antiques shops, then dine in a cozy bistro. Also in Grossbasel is the upscale and leafy residential neighborhood of Bruderholz, home to one of Switzerland's best restaurants, Stucki. The opposite bank, to the northeast, is Kleinbasel (Lesser Basel), a Swiss enclave on the "German" side of the Rhine that is the blue-collar quarter of the city. Here are the convention center, chain stores galore, artsy boutiques, and hotels with terraces that afford glorious views of the Münster (cathedral).

The best way to see Basel is on foot or by tram, as the landmarks, museums, and even the zoo radiate from the Old Town center on the Rhine, and the network of rails covers the territory thoroughly.

ALTSTADT

If you stand in the middle of the Marktplatz, or even just watch river traffic from the Mittlere Rheinbrücke, it's easy to envision the Basel of centuries ago. On a bend of the Rhine, Basel's historic center is full of half-timber houses that appear, from the outside, largely unchanged since the 1600s. Still, woven through its delicately preserved architecture are impressive state-of-the-art museums and miles of shop-lined pedestrian zones.

To reach the center of the Altstadt from the SBB, head north (left) on Heuwaage-Viadukt, turn right on Steinenvorstadt, and continue until you reach the central square, Barfüsserplatz.

TOP ATTRACTIONS

Fodor's Choice ★ **Basler Münster** (*Basel Cathedral*). Basel's cathedral evolved into its current form through a combination of the shifts of nature and the changing whims of architects. A 9th-century Carolingian church, it was consecrated as a cathedral by Henry II in 1019. Additions, alterations, and reconstructions in late Romanesque and early Gothic style continued through the 12th and 13th centuries. When Basel's devastating earthquake destroyed much of the building in 1356, subsequent reconstruction, which lasted about a century, adhered to the newly dominant Gothic style. The facade of the north transept, the *Gallusp-forte* (St. Gall's Door), is a surviving remnant of the original Romanesque structure. It's one of the oldest carved portals in German-speaking Europe—and one of the loveliest. Each of the evangelists is represented by his symbol: an angel for Matthew, an ox for Luke, a lion for Mark, and a bulbous-chested eagle for John. Above, around the window, a wheel of fortune flings little men off to their fates.

Inside on the left, following a series of tombs of medieval noblemen whose effigies recline with their feet resting on lions or their loyal dogs, stands the strikingly simple **tomb of Erasmus.** North of the choir, you can see the delicately rendered death portraits on the double **tomb of Queen Anna of Habsburg** and her young son, Charles, from around 1285. The vaulted **crypt** was part of the original structure and still bears fragments of murals from 1202. Both towers can be climbed, offering stunning, but dizzying, views over the city. ✉ *Münsterpl., Altstadt* ☎ *061/2729157* 🌐 *www.baslermuenster.ch* 🎫 *Towers: 5 SF.*

FAMILY **Fasnacht-Brunnen** (*Carnival Fountain*). Created by the Swiss artist Jean Tinguely, known for his work in mechanized media, this delightful, animated construction was inaugurated by the city in 1977. Its whimsically styled metal figures busily churn, lash, and spray with unending energy. It is especially impressive in winter when the jets of water freeze, creating unique airborne sculptures. ✉ *Theaterpl., Altstadt.*

FAMILY **Historisches Museum** (*History Museum*). Housed within the 13th-century Barfüsserkirche (Church of the Shoeless Friars), this museum has an extensive collection of Basel's cathedral treasury, wooden sculptures, coins, armor, and other vestiges of the city's past. An underground gallery displays fully reconstructed medieval and Renaissance guild rooms, complete with stained glass, ceramic stoves, and richly carved wood. Upstairs, next to the choir, the Münster Treasury contains priceless reliquaries in gold. Despite its status as one of the finest examples of Franciscan architecture north of the Alps, the church was deconsecrated in the 19th century and turned into a warehouse until it was rescued in 1894 and converted to its present-day use as a museum. General descriptions are in German, French, and English. See the website for information in English about special exhibits. ✉ *Barfüsserpl., Altstadt* ☎ *061/2058600* 🌐 *www.hmb.ch* 🎫 *12 SF* ⏲ *Closed Mon.*

Kunsthalle (*Basel Art Gallery*). A must-see for lovers of contemporary art, this museum has hosted landmark, precedent-setting exhibits of contemporary art since 1872. In addition to showing the work of several modern masters early in their careers (Paul Klee and Pablo Picasso), the gallery was the first in Europe to display works by American abstract expressionists. It's renowned as one of the world's most active institutions dedicated to the presentation of contemporary art. Programs include video installations, performances, and artist talks. ✉ *Steinenberg 7, Altstadt* ☎ *061/2069900* 🌐 *www.kunsthallebasel.ch* 🎫 *12 SF includes admission to Architekturmuseum, which is housed in the same building.* ⏲ *Closed Mon.*

Fodor's Choice ★ **Kunstmuseum Basel** (*Museum of Fine Arts*). In a city known for its museums, the Kunstmuseum is Basel's heirloom jewel. It was built in 1936 to house one of the world's oldest public art collections, owned by the city since 1661. The imposing facade of the main building, called the Hauptbau, gives way to an inner courtyard studded with statues. Inside is the world's largest assemblage of paintings by members of the Holbein family, an exceptional group of works by Konrad Witz, and, in fact, such a thorough gathering of the works of their contemporaries that the development of painting in the Upper Rhine is strikingly documented. Other Swiss artists are well represented, from Basel's own Arnold Böcklin to Gustav Klimt–like Ferdinand Hodler. A newer second building across the street, called the Neubau, houses both temporary exhibits and other items from the Kunstmuseum's permanent modernist collection (art from after 1950); it's accessible from the original museum by a tunnel. A third building, the Gegenwart, contains contemporary art and is about a five-minute walk away. ✉ *St. Alban-Graben 16, Altstadt* ☎ *061/2066262* 🌐 *www.kunstmuseumbasel.ch* 🎫 *16 SF; 26 SF for special exhibitions plus permanent collection. Free Tues., Wed., Fri., and Sat. 5 pm–6 pm and first Sun. of the month 10 am–6 pm (not including special exhibitions).*

Marktplatz (*Marketplace*). Flowers, fruits, and vegetables are sold most mornings from open stands in this central square. In fall and winter passersby purchase bags of hot roasted chestnuts, the savory scent of which wafts through the square. ✉ *South of Marktg., Altstadt* ⏲ *Closed Sun.*

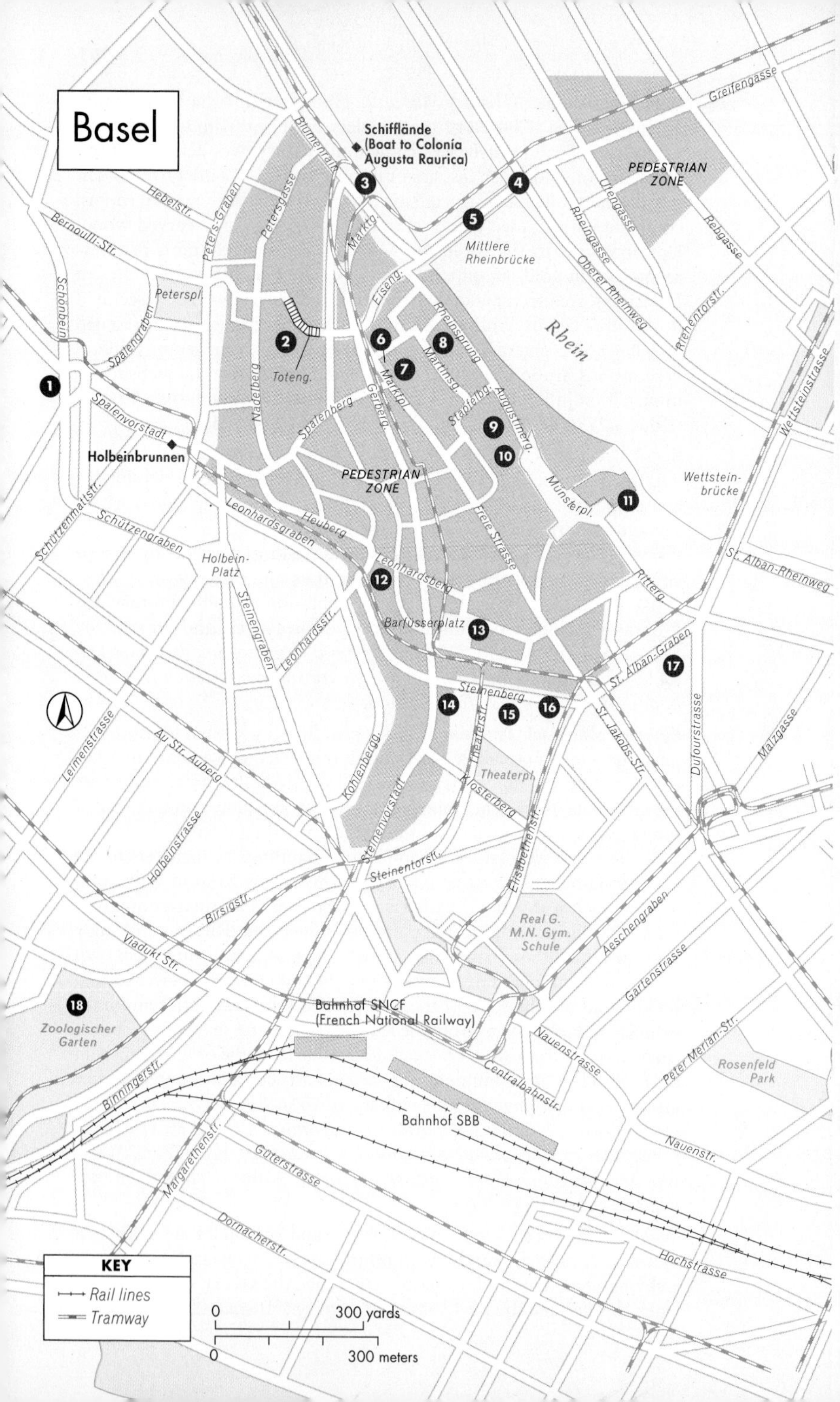
Basel
Schifflände
(Boat to Colonía
Augusta Raurica)
PEDESTRIAN
ZONE
Mittlere
Rheinbrücke
Rhein
Wettstein-
brücke
Holbeinbrunnen
Toteng.
PEDESTRIAN
ZONE
Holbein-
Platz
Barfüsserplatz
Theaterpl.
Real G.
M.N. Gym.
Schule
Bahnhof SNCF
(French National Railway)
Bahnhof SBB
Zoologischer
Garten
Rosenfeld
Park
KEY
Rail lines
Tramway
0
300 yards
0
300 meters

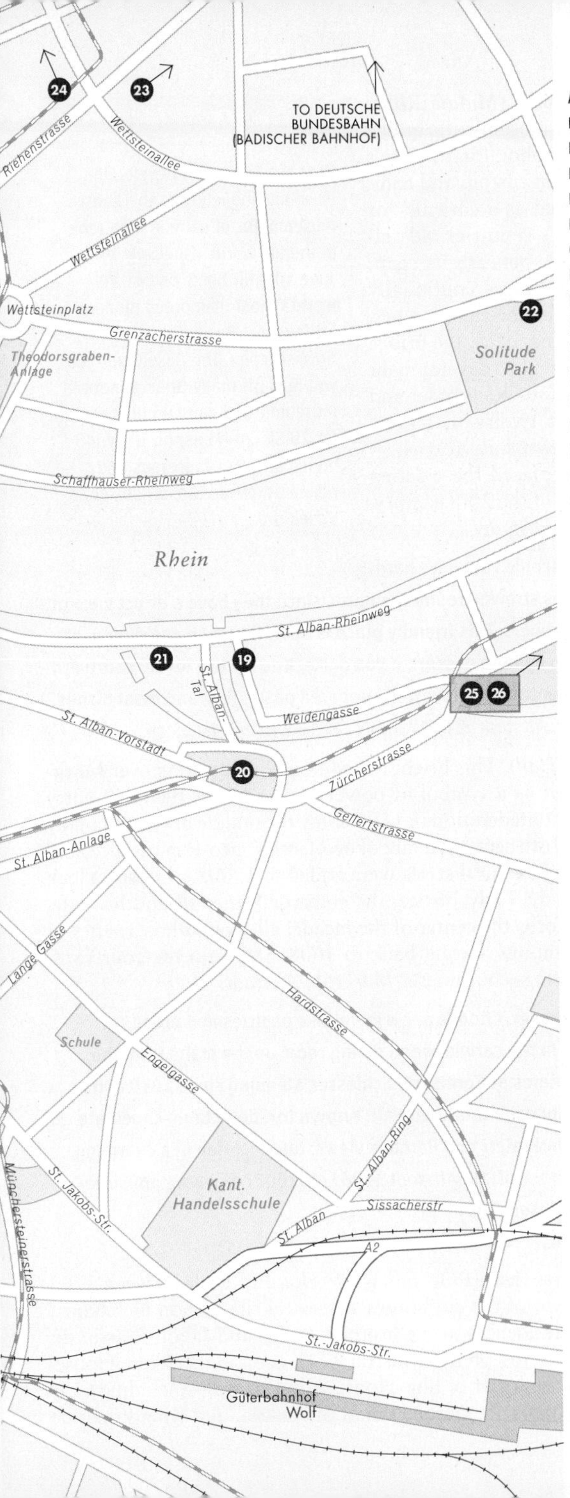

Augusta Raurica 25
Basler Münster 11
Basler Papiermühle 19
Blaues und Weisses Haus 8
Fasnacht-Brunnen 15
Fondation Beyeler 23
Grand Hotel Les Trois Rois 3
Historisches Museum 13
Kunsthalle 16
Kunstmuseum Basel 17
Kunstmuseum Basel | Gegenwart .. 21
Leonhardskirche 12
Marktplatz 6
Mittlere Rheinbrücke 5
Museum der Kulturen Basel 10
Museum Tinguely 22
Naturhistorisches Museum 9
Pharmazie-Historisches Museum 2
Rathaus 7
Römermuseum 26
St. Alban-Tor 20
Spalentor 1
Spielzeug Welten Museum Basel ... 14
Statue of Helvetia 4
Vitra Design Museum 24
Zoologischer Garten 18

Mittlere Rheinbrücke (*Middle Rhine Bridge*). Basel's most historic bridge is a good metaphor for the city's successful mix of custom and commerce. It is used as a catwalk for many of Basel's centuries-old celebrations, while beneath its span, processions of barges continually glide through its low-slung arches. First built around 1225, the bridge made possible the development of an autonomous Kleinbasel and the consequent rivalry that grew between the two half towns. A stone bridge replaced the wooden one at the turn of the 20th century. ✉ *Schifflände, Altstadt.*

BASEL'S ART SCENE

With the Fondation Beyeler, the Museum Tinguely, and the Kunstmuseum, Basel earns a high rank in the art world, especially each June when it hosts one of the world's most glamorous modern art fairs, Art Basel (🌐 *www.artbasel.com*). The BaselCard gives you 50% off many (though not all) museums, and can be purchased for 20 SF (24 hours) or 30 SF (48 hours) at Basel Tourismus and online at 🌐 *www.basel.com/en/BaselCard.*

QUICK BITES

Zum Isaak. For scenic value, it's hard to beat the tables strewn around the plaza, since they have a direct view of the cathedral's towers. This friendly place is open for lunch and dinner, or you can just stop by for a dessert, if you'd like. **Known for:** lovely courtyard seating; prime central location; well-prepared pasta, fish, and meat dishes. ✉ *Münsterpl. 16, Altstadt* ☎ *061/2614712* 🌐 *www.zum-isaak.ch.*

Rathaus (*Town Hall*). This bright red edifice, which towers over Marktplatz, was built as a symbol of power and to honor the city's entry into the Swiss Confederation in 1501. Only the middle portion actually dates from the 16th century; a mix of neo-Gothic, neo-Renaissance, and art nouveau architectural styles were added in 1900. A massive clock with figures of the Lady Justice, the emperor Henry II, and his wife, Kunegunde, adorns the center of the facade; all around it is a series of colorful oil paintings, dating back to 1608. Step into the courtyard, where the paintings continue. ✉ *Marktpl., Altstadt.*

QUICK BITES

Confiserie Schiesser. Choose a few jewel-like pastries and order leaf-brewed tea in the carved-wood dining room up the stairs from the vitrines of chocolates at Confiserie Schiesser, steeping since 1870 in its prime location opposite the Town Hall. **Known for:** delectable chocolate truffles; prime Marktplatz and Rathaus views; tea or coffee in a charming atmosphere. ✉ *Marktpl. 19, Altstadt* ☎ *061/2616077* 🌐 *www.confiserie-schiesser.ch* ⏲ *Closed Sun.*

WORTH NOTING

Blaues und Weisses Haus (*Blue and White Houses*). Built between 1763 and 1775 for two of the city's most successful silk-ribbon merchants, these were the residences of the brothers Lukas and Jakob Sarasin. In 1777 the emperor Joseph II of Austria was a guest in the White House. Adding that to the roster of Blue House visitor names—including Czar Alexander of Russia, Emperor Francis of Austria, and King Friedrich

A GOOD WALK

Six bridges link the two halves of the city; the most picturesque is the **Mittlere Rheinbrücke.** On the corner at Schifflände, you can see a facsimile of the infamous **Lällekönig,** a 17th-century gargoyle mechanized to stick out his tongue and roll his eyes at his rivals across the river. Walking across the bridge, you'll see Basel's peculiar, gondola-like ferryboats (you can ride one for a small fee).

Back across the Mittlere Rheinbrücke in the Altstadt, turn left up a steep alley called the **Rheinsprung,** banked with 15th- and 16th-century houses. Turn right at Archivgässlein, and you'll come to the **Martinskirche,** the city's oldest parish church, dating from 1287.

Continue along Martinsgasse to the elegant neighboring courtyards of the **Blaues und Weisses Haus,** meeting place of kings. Just beyond, turn left and head past the basilisk fountain into Augustinergasse; No. 2 is the **Naturhistorisches Museum,** and just beyond, around the corner on the Markplatz, is the **Museum der Kulturen Basel,** both of which house great natural-history and prehistory collections.

Augustinergasse leads into the Münsterplatz, dominated by the striking red-sandstone 12th-century **Münster,** burial place of Erasmus. Walk around to the cathedral's riverside to the Pfalz terrace for wide views of the river, the Altstadt, Kleinbasel, and the Black Forest.

From the Münsterplatz, head down Rittergasse to the first busy cross street. Ahead of you is St. Alban-Vorstadt, which leads to the **St. Alban-Tor,** one of the original 13th-century city gates. St. Alban-Tal leads from St. Alban-Vorstadt down to St. Alban-Rheinweg on the Rhine to the **Kunstmuseum Basel | Gegenwart** (Art Museum Basel | Contemporary).

Take St. Alban-Rheinweg back down the riverside, ascend the Wettstein Bridge stairways, and head left onto St. Alban-Graben to find the **Kunstmuseum,** home of one of Europe's oldest public collections. Continue down St. Alban-Graben to the intersection of Steinenberg. To circle back into the center of the Altstadt, veer right on Steinenberg, which goes by the **Kunsthalle.**

Continue on Steinenberg until it opens out onto the bustling Barfüsserplatz and the **Historisches Museum.** Behind the tram concourse on Barfüsserplatz, follow the pedestrian zone to Leonhardsberg, which leads left up the stairs to the late-Gothic **Leonhardskirche.** Continue along the church walk into Heuberg Street, the spine of one of the loveliest sections of Old Basel. On Spalenvorstadt perches the **Holbeinbrunnen,** styled from a drawing by Hans Holbein. The Spalenvorstadt stretches to the 14th-century **Spalentor** gate, carefully refurbished in 2014.

The Kunstmuseum is renowned worldwide for its excellent collection of statues and paintings.

Wilhelm III of Prussia, who met for dinner here in 1814—brings the guest book over the top. The restored buildings now house part of the city government and are clearly labeled for curious passersby. ✉ *Rheinsprung 16/18, Altstadt.*

Grand Hotel Les Trois Rois (*Three Kings Hotel*). The statues on the facade depict the biblical three wise men and are thought to date from 1754. The young general Napoléon Bonaparte lunched here in 1797, and an opulently decorated suite is named after him. Noteworthy guests have included Queen Elizabeth II, Charles Dickens, and Picasso. In 1897 the great Hungarian-born Jewish writer Theodor Herzl stayed here during the first Zionist Congress, which laid the groundwork for the founding of the state of Israel. ✉ *Blumenrain 8, Altstadt* 🌐 *www.lestroisrois.com.*

Leonhardskirche (*St. Leonard's Church*). Like virtually all of Basel's churches, this one was destroyed in the 1356 earthquake before being rebuilt in the Gothic style, although its original Romanesque crypt remains. Its High Gothic wooden pulpit is distinctive. Free organ concerts are often held on Friday evenings. ✉ *Leonardskirchpl., Altstadt* 🌐 *www.orgelspielzumfeierabend.ch.*

Museum der Kulturen Basel (*Basel Museum of Cultures*). After a radical renovation by star architects Herzog & de Meuron, the ethnographic museum did away with its dusty scenes of indigenous cultures; it now presents a hands-on investigation of what "culture" means. The museum includes more than 300,000 ethnographic artifacts from around the world, as well as 50,000 historic photographs. Permanent exhibitions, as well as three to five rotating exhibitions on topics such as migration and the sun, moon, and stars, explore the history

CLOSE UP

Fasnacht

Dating from the Middle Ages, Fasnacht, Switzerland's best-known festival, draws people from all over the world. Beginning at 4 am on the Monday after Ash Wednesday, all lights are turned off and the city is illuminated by the lanterns of the *Cliques* (carnival associations). The early-morning event features a blast of fifes and drums, joined later in the day by boisterous *Guggemusik* (played by enthusiastic, rather than talented, marching bands). The streets are packed with zillions of onlookers who have fortified themselves against the cold nights with a bowl of the traditional *Mehlsuppe* (flour soup). Each day features a different candy-and-confetti-strewn parade as well as nighttime revelry, which, despite the amount of beer and *Glühwein* (mulled wine) that is consumed, remains tame enough for tourists.

of Switzerland and its neighbors. Descriptions are available in German, French, and English. ✉ *Münsterpl. 20, Altstadt* ☎ *061/2665600* 🌐 *www.mkb.ch* 🎫 *16 SF* ⏲ *Closed Mon.*

FAMILY **Naturhistorisches Museum** (*Natural History Museum*). All aspects of the natural sciences—from the history of the earth to extinct mammals to interesting insects—are featured here. Kids will love the saber-toothed tigers, mammoths, and skeletons of several dinosaurs, while adults will enjoy the rotating exhibits investigating the natural world in a state of change. Most descriptive materials are in German only in the permanent collection. ✉ *Augustinerg. 2, Altstadt* ☎ *061/2665500* 🌐 *www.nmbs.ch* 🎫 *7 SF; extra charge for special exhibitions* ⏲ *Closed Mon.*

Pharmazie-Historisches Museum (*Museum of Pharmaceutical History*). This museum showcases original and re-created pharmacy counters and all kinds of beakers and flacons, and old remedies—from preserved crocodiles to mummy paste. Though labels are in German, audio guides are available in English, as well as several other languages. All kinds of herbs and teas can be purchased at the lovely shop. The museum is housed in Zum Vorderen Sessel, a home once frequented by Paracelsus. ✉ *Totengässlein 3, Altstadt* ☎ *061/2074811* 🌐 *www.pharmaziemuseum.ch* 🎫 *8 SF; 2 SF for audio guide; 2 SF for headphones* ⏲ *Closed Sun. and Mon.*

Spalentor (*Spalen Gate*). Refurbished in 2014, the Spalentor once served as Basel's most important medieval city gate. More imposing than graceful, the 14th-century structure has a toothy wooden portcullis; note Basel's coat of arms atop the gate. ✉ *Spalenvorstadt, Altstadt.*

FAMILY **Spielzeug Welten Museum Basel** (*Toy Worlds Museum Basel*). Bordering on the Barfüsserplatz, this museum has several floors filled with 18th-, 19th-, and 20th-century toys, including a cast of 2,500 teddy bears. The dollhouses, on a 1:12 scale, are all artistically displayed. ✉ *Steinenvorstadt 1, Altstadt* ☎ *061/2259595* 🌐 *www.spielzeug-welten-museum-basel.ch* 🎫 *7 SF* ⏲ *Closed Mon. Jan.–Nov.*

DID YOU KNOW?

The Rathaus (Town Hall), which dominates the Marktplatz, was built to honor the city's entry into the Swiss Confederation in 1501. Many of the building's exterior architectural features are actually paintings, added to the facade by artist Hans Bock.

KLEINBASEL

More down-to-earth than its "big brother" across the river, Kleinbasel is where you'll see people living rather than visiting. Immigrants from India, Turkey, the Balkans, and beyond mix well with young people on a budget in the narrow streets, which are lined with small shops, corner bars, and eateries. Warm weather attracts a crowd along the banks of the Rhine and the green riverside promenade, and in June the neighborhood is completely transformed into hipster central as the rich and famous flock to Art Basel.

TOP ATTRACTIONS

FAMILY Fodor's Choice ★ **Museum Tinguely.** As you circle the innovative and quirky installations at Museum Tinguely, you may have a few questions. How do they work? What do they mean? And where did the artist find this stuff? Born in Fribourg, 20th-century master Jean Tinguely is best known for his whimsical *métamécaniques* (mechanical sculptures), which transform machinery, appliances, and items straight from the junk heap into ironic and often macabre statements. For instance, *Le Ballet des Pauvres,* from 1961, suspends a hinged leg with a moth-eaten sock, a horse tail and a fox pelt, a cafeteria tray, and a blood-soaked nightgown, all of which dangle and dance on command. The wing of the museum projecting over the Rhine has a splendid river view of Basel. Many of the sculptures are activated at preset times, typically every 5 to 15 minutes, and it pays to wait and see them in action. Admission to temporary exhibitions is included in the entrance fee. Information sheets are available in English. ✉ *Paul Sacher-Anlage 2, Kleinbasel* ☎ *061/6819320* 🌐 *www.tinguely.ch* 🎫 *18 SF* ⏲ *Closed Mon.*

WORTH NOTING

Statue of Helvetia. What would the woman pictured on most Swiss coins do if freed from the confines of currency? With spear and shield set aside (and with a packed suitcase in hand), this humanistic interpretation shows her seemingly contemplating the possibilities from a perch not far from the border of her homeland and the wide world beyond. ✉ *On the edge of Mittlere Rheinbrücke, Kleinbasel.*

ST. ALBAN

Just off the very busy crossing of Sankt Alban Graben and Durfourstrasse is quiet St. Alban, also known as Dalbe to locals. A neighborhood of old patrician town houses and villas, it's still home to Basel's oldest affluent families and a pleasant mix of museums and restaurants.

TOP ATTRACTIONS

FAMILY Fodor's Choice ★ **Basler Papiermühle** (*Basel Paper Mill*). In a beautifully restored medieval mill with a still functioning waterwheel, this museum honoring paper, writing, and printing is wonderfully accessible. The museum is entirely hands-on, and visitors leave with paper they have made and wax seals they have pressed, as well as various writing and printing samples. In addition there is a wonderful permanent collection, from ancient scrolls to 20th-century newspaper-printing presses. Exhibits are in German, French, and English. ✉ *St. Alban-Tal 37, St. Alban* ☎ *061/2259090* 🌐 *www.papiermuseum.ch* 🎫 *15 SF* ⏲ *Closed Mon.*

WORTH NOTING

Kunstmuseum Basel | Gegenwart (*Art Museum Basel | Contemporary*). Bringing the city's art collections up to the present, this museum focuses on works from the 1960s onward. The fittingly modern building looks as though it has shouldered its way in between the street's half-timber houses. The language of the exhibition materials typically corresponds to the nationality of the artists. ✉ *St. Alban-Rheinweg 60, St. Alban* ☎ *061/2066262* 🌐 *www.kunstmuseumbasel.ch* 🎫 *16 SF with Kunstmuseum; 26 SF with Kunstmuseum and special exhibitions. Free Tues., Wed., Fri., and Sat. 5 pm–6 pm and first Sun. of the month 10 am–6 pm* ⏲ *Closed Mon.*

St. Alban-Tor (*St. Alban's Gate*). This original medieval city gate is set amid a lovely garden near remnants of the town's ramparts. Parts of the gate date from the end of the 14th century. ✉ *St. Alban-Vorstadt, St. Alban.*

ZOO

At this zoo with a conscience, the management makes an effort to both educate the public and help save rare species from extinction, making visits an exciting experience, especially for children.

TOP ATTRACTIONS

FAMILY **Zoologischer Garten** (*Zoological Garden*). Referred to by Baslers as *Zolli*, this zoo is famed for its rhinoceroses, hippopotamuses, gorillas, and fabulous vivarium filled with fish and reptiles. A monkey house allows the gorillas and chimps access to the outdoors. A combined elephant enclosure and restaurant makes an unusual location from which to watch the majestic animals while dining on contemporary cuisine. ✉ *Binningerstr. 40, Zoo* ☎ *061/2953535* 🌐 *www.zoobasel.ch* 🎫 *21 SF.*

GREATER BASEL

A trip outside Basel is worth it, whether you visit the spectacular grounds of the Fondation Beyeler or cross the border to visit Germany's famous Vitra Design Museum, where private foundations enhance the area's reputation as a center for art.

Basel's Roman history can seen in nearby Augst. Founded in 44–43 BC, Augst is the oldest Roman settlement on the Rhine, and today has been largely reconstructed as a noted museum of ancient Roman antiquities. The site is reachable by car from Basel in 15 minutes or in summer via a leisurely boat trip up the river. From the Bahnhof SBB take train S1 to Kaiseraugst, or Bus 81 from Basel-Aeschenplatz to Augst; thereafter it takes approximately 10 minutes from either of these stops to walk uphill to the Roman Museum. To view the restoration areas scattered around the almost suburban neighborhood, be prepared for a fair bit of walking.

TOP ATTRACTIONS

Augusta Raurica. The remains of this 2,000-year-old Roman settlement have been extensively rebuilt, with substantial portions of the ancient town walls and gates, streets, water pipes, and heating systems all in evidence. The 1st-century-BC theater, described as the best-preserved ancient complex north of the Alps, has been gloriously restored in the last few years. ✉ *Giebenacherstr. 17, Augst* ☎ *061/5522261* 🌐 *www.augustaraurica.ch* 🎫 *Free.*

Fodor's Choice ★

Fondation Beyeler. For decades, the world's most prestigious art collectors would journey to Basel to worship at the feet of one of modern art's greatest gallery owners, Ernst Beyeler, the founder of Art Basel, who died in 2010. At the end of his phenomenal career, he left his incomparable collection to the public and commissioned the noted architect Renzo Piano to build a museum in the town of Riehen, on the outskirts of Basel. The Fondation Beyeler presents an astonishingly well-rounded collection of modern art, and Piano's simple lines direct attention to more than 200 great works. The collection's catalog reads like a who's who of modern artists—Cézanne, Matisse, Lichtenstein, and Rauschenberg.

In this bright and open setting, Giacometti's wiry sculptures stretch toward the ceiling and Monet's water lilies seem to spill from the canvas into an outdoor reflecting pool. Indigenous carved figures from New Guinea and Nigeria stare into the faces on canvases by Klee and Dubuffet. A stellar selection of Picassos is juxtaposed with views of blue skies. Besides the permanent collection, several prestigious art exhibits every year attract art lovers from around the globe. To accommodate even more space for art, as well as for events, an extension designed by Swiss architect Peter Zumthor is expected to begin construction in 2018. The tram trip from Schifflände takes about 20 minutes. Public tours in English are offered on occasional Sundays, or private tours can be arranged. ✉ *Baselstr. 101, Riehen* ☎ *061/6459700* 🌐 *www.fondationbeyeler.ch/en* 🎫 *25 SF; 20 SF Mon. 10 am–6 pm and Wed. 5–8 pm.*

Römermuseum (*Roman Museum*). Roman daily life is vividly depicted in this carefully rebuilt home. Everything, from the thermal baths to the ancient board games in the sitting rooms, has been completely re-created. The museum also exhibits the largest trove of Roman silver known to exist, which was unearthed in 1962. The objects, dating mostly from the 4th century, are believed to have been buried by the Romans in 350 to protect them from the ravages of the Alemanni, the German tribes who drove the Romans out of Switzerland. English, French, and German brochures are available. ✉ *Giebenacherstr. 17, Augst* ☎ *061/5522261* 🌐 *www.augustaraurica.ch* 🎫 *8 SF.*

OFF THE BEATEN PATH

Vitra Design Museum. In the German town of Weil am Rhein, this renowned design museum's main building is a startling white geometric jumble designed by famed architect Frank Gehry that hosts large-scale temporary exhibits that put architecture, art, and everyday design on display. The neighboring Vitra Schaudepot, designed by Swiss architects Herzog & de Meuron, displays more than 400 objects from the museum's permanent collection, as well as smaller temporary exhibitions. There's also the striking Vitra Slide Tower by German artist Carston Höller—a viewing point, art piece, and slide all in one. During guided tours, buildings by architectural masters, including the exquisitely angular Fire Station by Zaha Hadid and the curved symmetry of the Conference Pavilion by Tadao Ando, can be visited. To get here by car,

The Fondation Beyeler is an incredible collection of contemporary and modern art housed in a museum designed by Renzo Piano.

take A5/E35 north from Basel toward Karlsruhe; turn right onto Route 532, then turn left after exiting at Weil am Rhein. The museum is 1½ km (about 1 mile) ahead on the right. Or from either Claraplatz or the Badischer Bahnof train station in Basel, take Bus 55 toward Kandern to the Vitra stop (20 minutes) or Tram 8 to the Weil am Rhein stop, from which the museum is a 10-minute walk. Architecture tours are held in English twice daily (11:30 and 1), and tours of the Schaudepot are from Friday to Sunday only at 2 pm. ✉ *Charles-Eames-Str. 1, Weil am Rhein* ☎ *07621/7023200* 🌐 *www.design-museum.de* 🎫 *Museum €11, Schaudepot €8, combination ticket for both €17. Architecture tour €14; Schaudepot tour €7.*

WHERE TO EAT

Classic but boundary pushing, bank-breaking but exquisite gourmet cuisine has long been one of Basel's fortes. New trends are appearing and disappearing in the blink of an eye. Snuggled between three countries, Basel has inherited the culinary interests of each, and excels with offering its own specialties and those of its neighbors—and beyond.

Eating out here, as anywhere in Switzerland, can be a costly delight, and top of the range. Michelin-starred restaurants are plentiful. At the other end of the scale, you will never have to go far for a German-style sausage, Italian pasta, or mouthwatering desserts, as reliable local restaurants and cafés can be found on practically every street. Basel is, in fact, full of comfortable haunts. The city's down-to-earth fare owes its roots to the Germanic hordes who arrived here to rout the ancient

Romans, bringing with them homey dishes like schnitzel and *Spätzle* (tiny dumplings), all to be washed down with beer.

As for dining specialties, the proximity of the Rhine means that most Basel restaurants serve a variety of freshwater fish. If the city could claim a regional specialty, it would be salmon. (These days much of it is shipped in from elsewhere, but the Rhine variety is making a comeback.) The meaty fish is best served *nach Basler Art* (Basel-style), meaning in a white-wine marinade with fried onions on top. Try it with a bottle of the fruity local Riesling.

If you're on the Marktplatz, join other hungry shoppers standing in front of mobile kitchens, holding bare *Wienerli* (hot dogs) and dipping them into thick golden mustard. You should also indulge in *Kaffee und Kuchen*—the late-afternoon coffee break the neighboring Germans live for. But locals have their own version: instead of a large slice of creamed cake, they select tiny sweet pastries—two or three to a saucer—and may opt for a delicate Chinese tea instead of a Kaffee.

Beyond local specialties, Basel's strengths are Thai and Middle Eastern cuisines, whether you choose the ubiquitous kebab (a Turkish gyro), a spicy bowl of green curry, or one of the fusion dishes that appear even in Basel's most traditional dining rooms.

For a satisfying and budget-friendly lunch, many restaurants offer lunch specials (*Tagesmenu*) that include a dish of the day, a starter or salad, and maybe even a dessert. They are the best way to eat well on a budget. Smoking is banned in all restaurants in Basel—except on terraces.

7

WHAT IT COSTS IN SWISS FRANCS

	$	$$	$$$	$$$$
At Dinner	Under 26 SF	26 SF–45 SF	46 SF–65 SF	Over 65 SF

Restaurant prices are the average cost of a main course at dinner or, if dinner is not served, at lunch.

ALTSTADT

$$ SWISS — **Atelier.** The Teufelhof hotel's less expensive dining option, the artsy Atelier serves modern cuisine made with regional ingredients. Daily specials are written on chalkboards, and the unfussy à la carte menu always features lighter fare like soups and salads along with seasonal pasta, vegetarian, and meat plates. **Known for:** relaxed, welcoming vibe; large selection of wines by the glass; good choice of vegetarian and gluten-free options. *Average main: 43 SF* *Der Teufelhof Basel, Leonhardsgraben 49, Altstadt* *061/2611010* *www.teufelhof.com/en/eating-drinking/restaurant-atelier*.

$$$ FRENCH Fodor's Choice ★ — **Bel Étage.** The formal Bel Étage showcases chef Michael Baader's masterly culinary inventions, with seasonal dishes using a mix of Swiss and international ingredients. The restaurant takes up four rooms of the historic Teufelhof hotel and is jazzed up with modern art on the walls. **Known for:** tasting menus with wine pairings; amazing service;

elegant but friendly atmosphere. *Average main: 60 SF* ✉ *Der Teufelhof Basel, Leonhardsgraben 49, Altstadt* ☎ *061/2611010* 🌐 *www.teufelhof.com/en/eating-drinking/restaurant-bel-etage* 🕓 *Closed Sun. and Mon. No lunch Sat.*

$$$$ FRENCH Fodor's Choice ★ **Cheval Blanc by Peter Knogl.** In a grand, chandelier-bedecked dining room with sweeping views of the Rhein, chef Peter Knogl prepares sophisticated, beautifully presented French creations (with touches of Mediterranean and Asian flavors) using decadent ingredients. The intimate three-Michelin-star restaurant within the Grand Hotel Les Trois Rois—one of Switzerland's best—has only 10 tables, perfect for people-watching. **Known for:** sublime tasting menus; lovely yet laid-back setting; interesting wine selection. *Average main: 80 SF* ✉ *Grand Hotel Les Trois Rois, Blumenrain 8, Altstadt* ☎ *061/2605007* 🌐 *www.lestroisrois.com/en/restaurants/cheval-blanc* 🕓 *Closed Sun. and Mon., 1st wk in Jan., mid-Feb.–early Mar., and late July–late Aug.*

$$$ ITALIAN **Chez Donati.** Under ownership of the Grand Hotel Les Trois Rois, and just a five-minute stroll away, this much-loved establishment has been serving up a selection of the finest Piedmont cuisine for more than 60 years and is well known for its antipasti and wonderfully decadent desserts. Don't come here for modern Italian food—the menu is quite traditional, with a fine selection of classic pasta, fish, and meat dishes. **Known for:** solid Italian classics like osso buco and scampi with a special house sauce; somewhat stuffy service; fantastic dessert trolley. *Average main: 56 SF* ✉ *Grand Hotel Les Trois Rois, St. Johanns-Vorstadt 48, Altstadt* ☎ *061/3220919* 🌐 *www.lestroisrois.com/en/restaurants/chez-donati* 🕓 *Closed Sun. and Mon., mid- to late Feb., and early July–early Aug.*

$ ITALIAN **Manger & Boire.** In this quiet little bistro right in the middle of the shopping mayhem of Gerbergasse, the friendly staff will bring you tasty inventions with an Italian slant, including what some claim is Basel's best fresh pasta. The daily menus always include a vegetarian, fish, and meat option, and à la carte menu items are clearly labeled as vegetarian or vegan (though there are plenty of delectable nonvegetarian options, too). **Known for:** unusual (and delicious) house-made ravioli; friendly, helpful service; young and trendy atmosphere. *Average main: 25 SF* ✉ *Gerberg. 81, Altstadt* ☎ *061/2623160* 🌐 *www.mangerboire.ch* 🕓 *Closed Sun.*

$$ INTERNATIONAL **ONO.** With its floor-to-ceiling windows, vaulted ceilings, and wide-open spaces, this eclectic eatery on the edge of the Old Town offers a cosmopolitan atmosphere where you can find cuisine from around the world. The market-fresh lunch menu changes daily and the dinner menu rotates monthly, but the Thai curries are always a good bet, and the *salade de chevre chaud croustillant* (warm and crispy goat cheese salad) with truffle oil and honey is a tasty classic with a twist. **Known for:** international, wide-ranging menu; modern versions of Thai dishes; interesting specialty cocktails. *Average main: 38 SF* ✉ *Leonhardsgraben 2, Altstadt* ☎ *061/3227070* 🌐 *www.ono-lifestyle.ch* 🕓 *Closed Sun.*

$$ INTERNATIONAL **Schlüsselzunft.** This extremely popular historic guildhall has been transformed into an airy and elegant dining room, and is famous for its traditional and beautiful ceramic stove. Though the

Swiss-international food can hold its own, many visit just for the atmosphere: arched doorways, beamed ceilings, mural-covered walls, and a charming courtyard. **Known for:** wonderful romantic atmosphere; extensive wine list; international cuisine with a twist. *Average main: 45 SF Freie Str. 25, Altstadt 061/2612046 www.schluesselzunft.ch Closed Sun. in June–Aug.*

KLEINBASEL

$$ SWISS **Restaurant Fischerstube.** The restaurant part of the Fischerstube, a famous local brewery, has a simple look, with whitewashed walls and sanded wooden tables, and offers a range of tasty snacks like oven-fresh pretzels to heartier meat-heavy dishes of steak, schnitzel, and burgers. The brewery produces its own lagers and ales in the copper tanks you see at the back of the room; if you're serious about sampling the local color, stop in here for a cold one. **Known for:** beer brewed on the premises; simple but satisfying pub food; service on Sunday, rare for Basel. *Average main: 30 SF Rheing. 45, Kleinbasel 061/6929200 www.restaurant-fischerstube.ch.*

$$ SWISS **Zum Goldenen Fass.** Zum Goldenen Fass (the Golden Barrel) is one of the most interesting restaurant options in Lesser, with the emphasis on the unique rather than the traditional. Come not for tablecloths or thick menus—you won't find them—but instead for the focus on local ingredients and an excellent wine list. **Known for:** simple-sounding dishes, done with a twist; cozy and classy surroundings; quiet location in off-the-beaten-path neighborhood. *Average main: 35 SF Hammerstr. 108, Kleinbasel 061/6933400 www.goldenes-fass.ch No lunch. Closed Sun. and Mon.*

7

ST. ALBAN

$ CAFÉ FAMILY **Restaurant Café Papiermühle.** With the splashing of the paper mill's waterwheel in the background, this is a restful spot for lunch or afternoon coffee (it's open only until 6 pm), whether in the medieval house or the streamside courtyard. The hand-scrawled chalkboard lists daily specials—generally salads, quiches, soups, and pasta dishes. **Known for:** daily-changing lunch menus; ingredients from small, local producers; family-friendly brunch, where meals for kids under 12 cost 1 SF per year. *Average main: 20 SF St. Alban-Tal 35, St. Alban 061/2724848 www.papiermuehle.ch Closed Mon.*

ZOO

$ ECLECTIC FAMILY **Markthalle Basel.** The multimillion-dollar renovation of Basel's vast cupola of a covered market was a total disaster—no shoppers came, and the designer shops all fled. But the Altemarkthalle has a third life as Basel's best poor-weather lunch destination, with several dozen food carts offering everything from Thai curries to wood-fired pizza. **Known for:** a large variety of international cuisines; cheap eats in an expensive town; late-night hours. *Average main: 25 SF Steinentorberg 20, Zoo www.altemarkthalle.ch.*

BRUDERHOLZ

$$$$ CONTEMPORARY Fodor's Choice ★ **Restaurant Stucki.** Chef Tanja Grandits gives her guests a delightful culinary experience in a refined—but not uptight—setting, using a cuisine style that the German-born chef calls "aroma kitchen." Contrasting flavors, colors, and textures shine through in fanciful creations of fish, seafood, and Swiss meats combined with unusual touches such as wasabi mousse or green tea guacamole. Exciting seasonal choices can be sampled in the 8- or 12-course "Aroma Menu," or in the more affordable three- or four-course lunchtime menus. **Known for:** extremely modern cuisine; artful food presentations; only expensive prix-fixe menus. *Average main: 200 SF* *Bruderholzallee 42, Bruderholz* *061/3618222* *www.tanjagrandits.ch/en/restaurant-stucki/restaurant* *Closed Sun. and Mon., 2 wks in Oct., and last wk of Dec.*

WHERE TO STAY

Grand as a palace? Way-cool as a converted prison? An art-lover's paradise? Or cozy and comfortably lived-in? The hotel scene in Basel is definitely varied. But with its busy convention center offering a different trade fair most months, this is a city that prides itself on being especially business-friendly. Many hotels pamper their business clientele (a never-ending supply), with leisure travelers taking second place. Signs pointing to meeting rooms and business centers are often more prominent than any paintings on the wall. But don't write off the city's business-oriented hotels—these often drop their prices significantly on weekends and offer superb amenities.

Depending upon your taste and budget, you can find hotels ranging from historic grandes dames, with wonderful restaurants and lots of character, to original and artsy boutique properties, to basic cheap and cheerful places with few amenities. Many hotels offer a river view and a calm, relaxed, designer interior, and Swiss service is, more often than not, helpful and efficient.

When there's a trade fair in town, prices shoot through the roof, and every bed for miles can be filled. This is also true during Fasnacht, Art Basel, and many of the other festivals. Most hotels do not include breakfast in their rates, though it's almost always available for an extra fee. All Basel hotels equip their guests with free travel passes for use in the city during their stay.

Hotel reviews have been shortened. For full information, visit Fodors.com.

	WHAT IT COSTS IN SWISS FRANCS			
	$	$$	$$$	$$$$
For Two People	Under 201 SF	201 SF–300 SF	301 SF–500 SF	Over 500 SF

Hotel prices are the lowest cost of a standard double room in high season, including taxes.

ALTSTADT

$$ HOTEL Fodor's Choice ★ **Der Teufelhof Basel.** Basel's top boutique hotel, the Teufelhof is actually two hotels in one. **Pros:** great location—only three tram stops away from the main station; excellent service; breakfast included in the rates. **Cons:** no air-conditioning; no elevator in the Art Hotel; some noise in rooms facing the tram. *Rooms from: 228 SF ✉ Leonhardsgraben 49, Altstadt ☎ 061/2611010 🌐 www.teufelhof.com 33 rooms 🍴 Breakfast.*

$$$$ HOTEL FAMILY Fodor's Choice ★ **Grand Hotel Les Trois Rois.** Basel's leading rendezvous for the rich and famous, the Trois Rois—the oldest city hotel in Switzerland, and one of the oldest in Europe—has long been an integral part of Basel history, though it also includes up-to-date accoutrements like flat-screen TVs and top-notch restaurants. **Pros:** regal prices are reflected in regal service; complimentary minibar; wide array of dining choices. **Cons:** can hear tram noise from some rooms; less expensive rooms can be on the small side; breakfast not included in all rates. *Rooms from: 550 SF ✉ Blumenrain 8, Altstadt ☎ 061/2605050 🌐 www.lestroisrois.com 101 rooms 🍴 No meals.*

$ HOTEL **Hotel Brasserie Au Violon.** Housed in a 12th-century building looming over the Altstadt that served as a cloister and then a prison, the hotel now captivates its clientele with subdued elegance, a peaceful location, and a terrific restaurant. **Pros:** unique and charming concept; highly rated restaurant; fresh breakfast favorites are included and served in a cozy dining room. **Cons:** some small rooms; safes available only at reception; no TVs in cell rooms. *Rooms from: 160 SF ✉ Im Lohnhof 4, Altstadt ☎ 061/2698711 🌐 www.au-violon.com ⊙ Closed Christmas–New Year's 20 rooms 🍴 Breakfast.*

$ HOTEL **Hotel D - Basel.** This affordable, centrally located hotel offers well-lighted modern rooms and Italian-made rainfall showerheads, as well as a sauna and fitness studio in the cellar. **Pros:** tasteful modern design; convenient location across from upscale Les Trois Rois; some rooms have views of the Rhine. **Cons:** neighborhood can be busy; breakfast not always included in rates; lower-priced rooms are small. *Rooms from: 168 SF ✉ Blumenrain 19, Altstadt ☎ 061/2722020 🌐 www.hoteld.ch 48 rooms 🍴 No meals.*

$ HOTEL Fodor's Choice ★ **Nomad Design & Lifestyle Hotel.** This urban-chic, centrally located hotel (from the same owners as the Krafft) with a young and lively vibe offers design-conscious rooms and a casual eatery with cocktail bar that attracts stylish locals and visitors. **Pros:** fun, cool vibe; rooms less expensive than others in Basel; very convenient to the train station and Altstadt attractions. **Cons:** no views from rooms; only some rooms have balconies; restaurant food gets mixed reviews. *Rooms from: 198 SF ✉ Brunngässlein 8, Altstadt ☎ 061/6909160 🌐 www.nomad.ch 65 rooms 🍴 No meals.*

$ HOTEL Fodor's Choice ★ **The Passage.** Modern with a gleaming white facade and an airy foyer, the Passage offers the best fitness studio of Basel's hotels. **Pros:** an economical option for expensive Basel; arguably the best hotel gym in town; cool modern vibe. **Cons:** no on-site restaurant; walls a bit thin; staff can be harried at times. *Rooms from: 185 SF ✉ Steinengraben 51, Altstadt ☎ 061/6315151 🌐 www.thepassage.ch 56 rooms 🍴 No meals.*

KLEINBASEL

$ HOTEL — **easyHotel Basel.** Less is definitely more at the easyHotel, where guest rooms are compact, minimalist, and decorated with up-to-date (though basic) decor and vivid colors. **Pros:** central location (close to the convention center where Art Basel and Baselworld are held); impeccably clean rooms; unbeatable prices. **Cons:** no restaurant; charge for lockers to hold luggage; five-floor hotel has no elevator. *Rooms from: 79 SF ✉ Riehenring 109, Kleinbasel ⊕ www.easyhotel.com 24 rooms No meals.*

$$ HOTEL Fodor's Choice ★ — **Hotel Krafft Basel.** In an elegant, waterfront mansion, the art deco Krafft has a can't-get-any-better location that makes it perfect for people-watching. **Pros:** refreshment station on each floor with tea, water, and fruit; very friendly staff; charming, design-conscious look. **Cons:** waterfront location can be noisy; no air-conditioning; only a few rooms have balconies. *Rooms from: 257 SF ✉ Rheing. 12, Kleinbasel ☎ 061/6909130 ⊕ www.krafftbasel.ch 60 rooms No meals.*

ZOO

$ HOTEL — **Hotel City Inn.** If you'd rather do without all the pomp and circumstance, consider one of the brightly colored, crisply furnished rooms at the City Inn. Under the same management as Hotel Euler (where you pick up your room key), this hotel gives you the same service as its sister property at a much lower price. **Pros:** you can use the excellent facilities of Hotel Euler; convenient location near the main train station; very good value. **Cons:** elevator doesn't reach all levels; rooms have a spartan feel; pricey breakfast not included in the rates. *Rooms from: 137 SF ✉ Centralbahnpl. 14, Zoo ☎ 061/2758000 ⊕ www.cityinn.ch 44 rooms No meals.*

$$ HOTEL — **Hotel Euler.** This 150-year-old landmark has been tastefully renovated throughout to bring out the best of its original features, including elaborate gilt-edged mirrors and stucco ceiling moldings. **Pros:** near the train station and close to the center of town; oversized terrace great for people-watching; pillow menu to choose the ones you like best. **Cons:** glazed windows reduce noise from the trams outside, but sometimes not enough; no gym; standard rooms on the small side. *Rooms from: 225 SF ✉ Centralbahnpl. 14, Zoo ☎ 061/2758000 ⊕ www.hoteleuler.ch 66 rooms No meals.*

NIGHTLIFE AND PERFORMING ARTS

For tips on events, subscribe to Basel Tourism's monthly email newsletter. If you'd like to play it by ear, the Steinenvorstadt is crowded with bars filled with young people, and on the Kleinbasel side there are late-night bars along Oberer Rheinweg.

TICKETS

Ticketcorner. You can purchase tickets to all sorts of events here, from pop concerts to ballet, at numerous locations within Basel, as well as online. ☎ *0900/800800* 🌐 *www.ticketcorner.ch.*

ALTSTADT

BARS AND LOUNGES

Baragraph. With its back-to-the-1970s feel, the centrally located Baragraph attracts a mixed crowd for its beer and cocktails. ✉ *Kohlenberg 10, Altstadt* ☎ *061/2618864* 🌐 *www.baragraph.ch.*

Campari Bar. Behind the Kunsthalle, Campari Bar pulls in an artsy crowd with its pop-art interior and tree-shaded terrace. Toward the end of each month, guests can dance to a DJ. ✉ *Steinenberg 7, Altstadt* ☎ *061/2724233* 🌐 *www.restaurant-kunsthalle.ch/campari-bar-5.*

Das Café des Arts. The extremely popular Café des Arts draws an interesting mix of patrons with its leather stools, grand piano (often complete with a musician), and elegant spiral staircase. ✉ *Barfüsserpl. 6, Altstadt* ☎ *061/2735737* 🌐 *rhyschaenzli.ch/de/des-arts.*

Fodor's Choice ★ **Hinz und Kunz Bar.** Some say the bartenders here make the best cocktails in town. There's also a large selection of rum and whiskey. ✉ *Steinentorberg 20, Altstadt* ☎ *061/4030404* 🌐 *hinzundkunz.bar.*

Fodor's Choice ★ **Kaserne.** The several stages and bars of Basel's former barracks are the center of Basel's indie music scene, with local and international shows several nights a week, as well as theater and dance performances. ✉ *Klybeckstr. 1b, Altstadt* ☎ *61/6666000* 🌐 *www.kaserne-basel.ch.*

Sperber. With the feel of an English pub, Sperber presents live jazz music some evenings. ✉ *Hotel Basel, Münzg. 12, Altstadt* ☎ *061/2646800* 🌐 *www.hotel-basel.ch/en/restaurants/sperber.*

CLASSICAL MUSIC

Musik Akademie Basel. This important music academy draws top-drawer international performers—though most of the regular shows are given by students. However, the concerts in the lovely rooms are often free. ✉ *Leonhardsstr. 6, Altstadt* ☎ *061/2645757* 🌐 *www.musik-akademie.ch.*

Stadt-Casino. The Stadt-Casino hosts the Basel Symphony Orchestra and the Basel Chamber Orchestra. This is also the city's top address for a wide range of visiting musicians. At the time of this writing, the venue is undergoing renovations led by Swiss architects Herzog & de Meuron and expected to be completed by summer 2019. In the meantime, all events are being held at the Musical Theater. ✉ *Steinenberg 14, Altstadt* ☎ *061/2263600* 🌐 *www.stadtcasino.ch.*

DANCE CLUBS

Atlantis. The tables at this well-loved restaurant give way to a dance floor later in the evening at what was once Basel's hottest club, but now offers a more low-key evening. ✉ *Klosterberg 13, Altstadt* ☎ *061/2289696* 🌐 *www.atlan-tis.ch.*

Club 59. Enjoy the three floors of music at Club 59, where the DJ rages through disco to reggae. ✉ *Steinenvorstadt 33, Altstadt* ☎ *061/2815950* 🌐 *www.club59.ch*.

THEATER

Theater Basel. Theater Basel hosts opera, operetta, and dance performances, as well as dramas, usually in German—though visiting companies occasionally perform in English. The season runs from August to June. ✉ *Theaterstr. 7, Altstadt* ☎ *061/2951133* 🌐 *www.theaterbasel.ch*.

KLEINBASEL

BARS AND LOUNGES

Bar Rouge. Basel's highest bar, on the top floor of Basel's second-highest building, has the best views over the city before dark, but offers mostly overpriced drinks and run-of-the-mill techno later on. ✉ *Messepl. 10, 31st fl., Kleinbasel* ☎ *061/3613031* 🌐 *www.barrouge.ch*.

Sud. This bar in Basel's stately old brewery is off the beaten path, but most of those who come for the concerts like it that way. ✉ *Burgweg 7, Kleinbasel* ☎ *061/2722323* 🌐 *rhyschaenzli.ch/de/sud*.

THEATER

Musical Theater Basel. The modern Musical Theater is a popular venue for touring companies, with shows ranging from musicals to circus performances. ✉ *Feldbergstr. 151, Kleinbasel* ☎ *061/6998899* 🌐 *www.musicaltheaterbasel.ch*.

SHOPPING

The major downtown shopping district stretches along Freie Strasse, Spalenberg, and Gerbergasse, where you can find many one-of-a-kind boutiques. More reasonably priced shops along Steinenvorstadt cater to a younger crowd.

ALTSTADT

BOOKS

Bider & Tanner. Bider & Tanner is Basel's largest international bookstore, with a large selection of English books. You can also book tickets to arts events here. ✉ *Aeschenvorstadt 2, Altstadt* ☎ *061/2069999* 🌐 *www.biderundtanner.ch*.

Erasmushaus. Erasmushaus has one of the city's largest collections of fine antique manuscripts, books, and autographs, mostly in German but including a large selection of multilingual publications. If they cannot help you in the search for a particular tome, they will be happy to supply the names of the other specialist shops in the Basel area. ✉ *Bäumleing. 18, Altstadt* ☎ *061/2289944* 🌐 *www.erasmushaus.ch*.

Orell Füssli Basel. This shop on one of the city's main shopping strips sells music, movies, toys, and books. There's a decent English section. ✉ *Freie Str. 32, Altstadt* ☎ *061/2642626* 🌐 *www.orellfuessli.ch*.

WORD OF MOUTH

Basel is known for its Christmas traditions, including it's popular Christmas Market, one of the largest in Switzerland. Houses and store windows in the Old Town are also lovingly decorated.

CALLIGRAPHY

Abraxas. A great source for fine writing instruments, Abraxas also stocks everything from thick paper and delicate fountain pens to luxurious sealing waxes and reproductions of antique silver seals. The store is open only limited days and hours, so check the website for details. ✉ *Rheinsprung 6, Altstadt* ☎ *061/2616070* 🌐 *www.abraxas-switzerland.com.*

Scriptorium am Rheinsprung. Dedicated to the art of calligraphy, Scriptorium am Rheinsprung even mixes its own ink. ✉ *Rheinsprung 2, Altstadt* ☎ *061/2613900* 🌐 *www.kalligraphie.com.*

CLOTHING FOR WOMEN AND MEN

Beldona. This boutique stocks classy Swiss lingerie. There are three other locations in Basel. ✉ *Freie Str. 103, Altstadt* ☎ *061/2731170* 🌐 *www.beldona.ch.*

Classic Herrenmode. This shop carries everything for the well-dressed man: formal and casual shirts, cashmere pullovers, and underwear. ✉ *Fischmarkt 5, Altstadt* ☎ *061/2610755* 🌐 *www.classic-mode.ch.*

SET & SEKT. This trendsetting concept store stocks clothes for women (and men) from both small and more established designers, as well as shoes and jewelry. ✉ *Rümelinspl. 5, Altstadt* ☎ *061/2710765* 🌐 *www.setandsekt.com.*

Trois Pommes. This boutique dominates the high end of fashion, with Jil Sander, Stella McCartney, Gucci, and Saint Laurent. There's also a men's shop at the same location. ✉ *Freie Str. 74, Altstadt* ☎ *061/2729255* 🌐 *www.troispommes.ch.*

CRAFTS AND GIFTS

Heimatwerk. This large shop sells a selection of exquisite Swiss crafts. It's the perfect stop for anyone looking to bring unique gifts home. ✉ *Schneiderg. 2, Altstadt* ☎ *061/2619178* 🌐 *www.heimatwerk.ch.*

Johann Wanner. Highly specialized handiwork comes from Johann Wanner, which sells handblown, hand-painted, and hand-molded Christmas ornaments, Victorian miniatures, tartan ribbons, cards, and calendars. ✉ *Spalenberg 14, Altstadt* ☎ *061/2614826* 🌐 *www.johannwanner.ch.*

DEPARTMENT STORES

Globus. This upscale department store on four floors stocks everything from gourmet edibles to chic clothing. ✉ *Marktpl. 2, Altstadt* ☎ *058/5784545* 🌐 *www.globus.ch.*

FOOD

Confiserie Bachmann. This shop carries a Basel specialty called *Leckerli,* a chewy cookie made of almonds, honey, dried fruit, and kirsch. There are also branches of Confiserie Bachmann on Blumenrain and Centralbahnplatz. ✉ *Gerberg. 51, Altstadt* ☎ *061/2609999* 🌐 *www.confiserie-bachmann.ch.*

Fodor's Choice ★ **Confiserie Schiesser.** A convivial tearoom that opened in 1870, Schiesser sells carefully crafted (and costly) confections in its downstairs shop. ✉ *Marktpl. 19, Altstadt* ☎ *061/2616077* 🌐 *www.confiserie-schiesser.ch.*

Glausi's. This fine selection of more than 250 types of cheeses comes from the Swiss Alps, the neighboring Jura and Vosges mountains, and beyond. ✉ *Spalenberg 12, Altstadt* ☎ *061/2618008* 🌐 *www.kaese-glausis.ch.*

Läckerli-Huus. The famous Läckerli-Huus sells a variety of sweets, including wonderful Leckerli, and also has a café. A large selection of gift canisters and a shipping service make getting gifts home a cinch. There are also branches of Läckerli-Huus on Greifengasse and Centralbahnplatz. ✉ *Gerberg. 57, Altstadt* ☎ *061/2642205* 🌐 *www.laeckerli-huus.ch.*

LINENS

Schlossberg Boutique. All manner of household linens for the bedroom, dining room, and kitchen are for sale at Schlossberg Boutique. ✉ *Gerberg. 26, Altstadt* ☎ *061/2610900* 🌐 *www.schlossberg.ch.*

Sturzenegger. This shop specializes in household items, including table decorations edged with St. Gallen lace. It also carries a selection of women's clothing with labels such as Hanro. ✉ *Theaterstr. 4, Altstadt* ☎ *061/2616867* 🌐 *www.sturzeneggerbasel.ch.*

TOYS

Bercher & Sternlicht. For the young (or young at heart), Bercher & Sternlicht is one of the top stores in all of Europe for model trains and accessories. ✉ *Spalenberg 45, Altstadt* ☎ *061/5609060* 🌐 *www.bercher-sternlicht.ch.*

Spielegge. With an emphasis on wooden toys, Spielegge stocks chisel-carved puppets and whimsical watercolor puzzles of fairy-tale scenes. ✉ *Rümelinspl. 7, Altstadt* ☎ *061/2614488* 🌐 *spielegge.ch.*

KLEINBASEL

CLOTHING FOR WOMEN AND MEN

Riviera. Clothes and accessories from exciting new designers (for women and men) are the focus at this well-curated boutique. ✉ *Feldbergstr. 43, Kleinbasel* ☎ *061/5342914* 🌐 *www.rivierabasel.ch.*

GREATER BASEL

SPAS

Spas are gaining in popularity all over Switzerland, and new ones seem to be popping up all the time. Basel is no exception, and spas cater to customers who want the latest fitness equipment, a pampering massage, or even waterslides and a wave pool.

FAMILY **Aquabasilea.** While you enjoy the purifying effects of a mud bath or the serenity of a steam bath, the kids will have a ball zooming around the Turbo Tube slide or free-falling down the nearly vertical Cliff Drop. "Something for everyone" is not an exaggeration at Aquabasilea, outside Basel in the town of Pratteln. The huge facility houses waterslides, a wave pool, a swimming pool, indoor and outdoor saunas, a full-service spa, and several restaurants and cafés, as well as a Turkish-style hammam. No bathing suits are allowed in the mixed-gender separate sauna complex (many wrap themselves in the large towels), though no nudity is permitted elsewhere. Look for the spa changing rooms on the second floor to avoid the locker-room feel of the main changing area. ✉ *Hardstr. 57, Pratteln* ☎ *061/8262424* 🌐 *www.aquabasilea.ch.*

Dampfbad Basel. An urban oasis tucked inside a former train station, this Turkish-style hammam has a quaint and cozy feel. True to the traditional spa experience in the Middle East, guests are invited to relax in one of two steam rooms, cleanse and exfoliate their skin using a bath mitt and mild olive oil soap, and then relax in a warm-water basin. Unlike many Swiss spas, the Dampfbad does not require you to be nude and provides bath sheets to be worn throughout the hammam. Much-appreciated perks include high-end health and beauty products as well as complimentary herbal tea, fresh fruit, and water in the resting lounge. The Dampfbad offers an extensive menu of excellent massage services, including deep-tissue and reflexology. Reservations are essential. ✉ *Vogesenpl. 1, St. Johann* ☎ *061/3221505* 🌐 *www.dampfbadbasel.ch.*

Fodor's Choice ★

Sole Uno. The incredibly relaxing saltwater pool at Sole Uno mimics the sensation of floating in the Dead Sea, with the added advantage of soft music that's audible underwater. About 20 minutes outside Basel, Rheinfelden became known as a healing haven after natural salt deposits were discovered here in the late 19th century. Wellness seekers still come for the soothing waters, which they can enjoy in peaceful surroundings at the all-season outdoor pool that spirals into a bubbling whirlpool. The sprawling facility includes Finnish-style saunas, an authentic Russian banya, and several steam baths—the sauna complex does not allow bathing suits (whereas the pools require them). To get here by car, take A3 toward Zürich, then get off at the Rheinfelden East exit. ✉ *Roberstenstr. 31, Rheinfelden* ☎ *061/8366763* 🌐 *www.parkresort.ch/en/sole-uno.*

FRIBOURG AND NEUCHÂTEL

WELCOME TO FRIBOURG AND NEUCHÂTEL

TOP REASONS TO GO

★ **Stir the melting pot:** Fondue famously originated in the Neuchâtel area—try the two-cheese fondue *neuchâteloise* that honors Switzerland's fabulous Gruyère and Emmental cheeses, or opt for fondue *fribourgeoise,* a delicious Vacherin Fribourgeois delight.

★ **Switzerland's largest lake:** Lac de Neuchâtel is a great place for a boat trip, wakeboarding, or savoring the fine fish served on its shores.

★ **You say Schloss:** And I say Château. In either language, this area has some of Switzerland's most impressive castles, from Grandson to Gruyères.

★ **Homegrown talent:** Whether it's the clockwork extravaganzas of Tinguely or the disturbing alienlike creations of Giger, these two sculptors are true knockouts.

★ **Gorgeous Gruyères:** Step into a postcard in this perfect specimen of a medieval stronghold, with its single main street cozy within the ramparts.

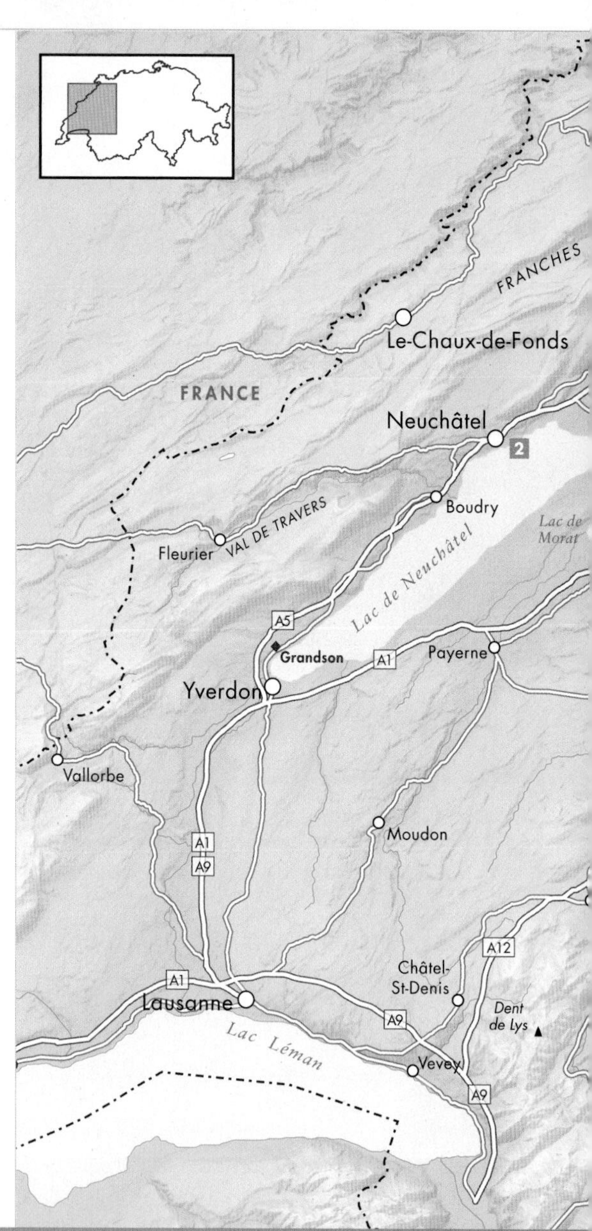

1 Fribourg. Gateway town to the region, Fribourg is one of Switzerland's best-kept secrets. Have your camera ready for its picturesque, medieval Old Town and many bridges. To the south is pretty-as-a-picture Gruyères, with a lovely square and spectacular hilltop castle. After touring this car-free village, take in modern and traditional cheese-making demonstrations of the famed regional cheeses, Vacherin Fribourgeois and Gruyère. North of Fribourg lies time-burnished Murten, a peaceful lakeside resort.

2 Lac de Neuchâtel and Nearby. In the heart of "Watch Valley" and flanked by vineyards, this French-accented city on the shores of Lac de Neuchâtel celebrates the grape each fall with a weekend of parades and feasting. Enjoy its architecture—Romanesque to rococo—and discover the Bronze Age lifestyle of stilt-house dwellers at Laténium. South, along the shores of Lac de Neuchâtel, discover the grand castle at Grandson.

CHEESE: FRIBOURG'S CALLING CARD

La Maison du Gruyère (above) is the starting point for many dairy tours. Here you can watch the production of the region's namesake cheese (below, right), or enjoy a pot of fondue (above, right).

A traveler cruising Switzerland's emerald hills and villages far from industrial turf can't help but notice the damp, fresh, earthy ephemera of the dairy that hangs in the air—a mild, musky tang that scents the cream, thickens the chocolate, and alchemizes the cheese.

Nowhere else will you smell this as strongly as in the region of Fribourg—the area that gave birth to the famous cheese Gruyère, a main component of fondue. This region also sits shoulder to shoulder with two other areas that give us great cheeses: Emmental (near Bern) and the Jura Mountains, where Tête de Moine comes from.

As always, Swiss cheese is most delightfully experienced in that most satisfying of all Swiss dishes, fondue, which first became fashionable in America during the 1950s ski craze. Those who have not acquired the habit may feel uncomfortably replete after only a few mouthfuls.

CRÈME-DOUBLE DE LA GRUYÈRE

In the Fribourg countryside is another dairy delight. Crème-double, a Gruyère specialty, rivals Devonshire cream. The rich, extra-thick, high-fat cream—without whipping—almost supports a standing spoon; it is served in tiny carved-wood *baquets* (vats), to be spooned over bowls of berries and meringues.

DAIRY TRAIL

In the Gruyère region and surrounding mountains, cattle head uphill in summer, and production of local cheeses—the firm, fragrant Gruyère and Vacherin—soars. They are sold at various stages: young and mild, ripe and savory, or aged to a heady tang. The great commercial cheese factory of Gruyère may have an automated, cheese-turning robot, but the hills of Fribourg still prefer old copper pots sizzling over wood fires.

The Sentier des Fromageries is an excellent walking path that connects the dairies in Pringy-Moléson. Two routes are available, but each begins at the **Maison du Gruyère** (✉ *3 pl. de la Gare* ☎ *026/9218400* 🌐 *www.lamaisondugruyere.ch*) and ends at the lofty **Fromagerie d'Alpage** (✉ *Moléson-sur-Gruyères* ☎ *026/9211044* 🌐 *www.fromagerie-alpage.ch*) in Moléson-Village. The Maison du Gruyère stands in the meadows that lie below the Château de Gruyères. It's both a museum and a demonstration dairy, and you can learn the history of the famous cheese and how it retains its AOC (*appellation d'origine contrôlée*) standing. Several times a day, from 9 to 11 and 12:30 to 2:30, the cheese makers open their doors and welcome you to their wonderfully pungent world. At the end of the trail at Fromagerie d'Alpage, you can assist in the cheese-making process if you reserve in advance (May to September only). Cheese-making demonstrations are held at 10 am daily. For more information on the Sentier des Fromageries, see the Gruyère Tourism site at 🌐 *www.la-gruyere.ch*.

OFF THE BEATEN PATH

Halfway between the mountain pass that connects Schwarzsee with Charmey, **Alp Balisa** (*Schwarzsee* ☎ *026/4121295* 🌐 *www.alpbalisa.ch*) is a small family-run dairy that operates all summer long. It may be out of the way, but it has a reputation as one of the most charming in Switzerland.

FONDUE

Though fondue is de rigueur in any Alpine setting, Fribourg has a fanatical stronghold. The recipe is surprisingly simple—cheese melted together with white wine, garlic, and a dash of kirsch (brandy distilled from cherries). Aficionados debate the perfect blend of cheeses and whether to include mushrooms or tomatoes. Fribourg is the source of *fondue fribourgeoise*, the combination of the canton's two greatest cheeses—Gruyère and Vacherin Fribourgeois—into a creamy *moitié-moitié* (half-and-half) blend. The Vacherin can be melted alone for an even creamier fondue, and potatoes can be dipped instead of bread. Eat like a local and head to Fribourg's **Café du Midi** (✉ *25 rue de Romont* ☎ *026/3223133* 🌐 *www.lemidi.ch*), Bulle's **Café de la Gare** (✉ *6 av. de la Gare* ☎ *026/9127688*), or **Café Tivoli** (✉ *18 pl. d'Armes* ☎ *021/9487039* 🌐 *www.cafetivoli.ch*) in Châtel-St-Denis, all of which are famous for their hospitality, decor, and, most of all, their fabulous fondue.

Updated by Alexis Munier

Shouldered by the more prominent cantons of Bern and Vaud, Fribourg and Neuchâtel are easily overlooked by hurried visitors. If they do stop, it is usually for a quick dip into the environs of Fribourg and Gruyères, leaving the rest of this largely untouched area to the Swiss, who enjoy its relatively unspoiled and relaxed approach to life. Natural delights take pride of place here. From bird-watching at La Grande Cariçaie, the largest marshland in Switzerland, to waterskiing on Lac de Neuchâtel, there's no shortage of opportunities to work up an appetite for the region's famous fondue.

Although the strict cantonal borders are a messy reflection of historic power struggles, the regional boundaries are unmistakable, even to an outsider. Fribourg starts in the pre-Alpine foothills above Charmey and rolls down across green hills, tidy farms, and ancient towns until it reaches the silty shores of the Murten, Neuchâtel, and Biel lakes. The region of Neuchâtel begins in these silt-rich fields (which grow everything from lettuce to tobacco), sweeps across Lac de Neuchâtel to its château- and vineyard-lined western shore, and rises up to the Jura Mountains.

The Röstigraben (or "Rösti Divide," named after the buttery, panfried potato cakes Swiss Germans are particularly fond of) is the tongue-in-cheek name for the linguistic border where French meets German. It runs through Fribourg and butts up against the northern borders of Neuchâtel. In some towns you can walk into a *boulangerie* (bread bakery) selling dark *Vollkornbrot* (whole-grain bread) or find a family named Neuenschwand that hasn't spoken German for generations.

But no matter what aspect of history interests you, you should find something to please you: prehistoric menhirs and the lifestyle of stilt-house people at Laténium, near Neuchâtel; the Roman amphitheater in

Avenches; or imagining the Battle of Murten from the city's ramparts. Perhaps you'd prefer Grandson Castle, with Charles the Bold's ridiculously bejeweled hat and life-size, fully armored replicas of jousting knights. If you love Gothic churches and religious art, you can have your fill, especially in Fribourg, Neuchâtel, and Romont.

FRIBOURG AND NEUCHÂTEL PLANNER

WHEN TO GO

Spring and fall are beautiful times to visit this region. During the summer, temperatures reach an average of 18°C–20°C (65°F–68°F), which is comfortable, but crowds tend to pick up, especially in Gruyères. During a heat wave it's not unusual for temperatures to soar to 30°C (86°F). In winter the average temperature is 0°C–3°C (32°F–38°F). In the pre-Alps region there can be long periods of snowfall. January is great for winter sports, but you can't be sure of snow in December. In February, some cantons (not to mention Germans, English, Dutch, and Italians) invariably have school vacations, so slopes get pretty crowded. If the snow lasts, March can also be great for skiing.

PLANNING YOUR TIME

Though the major sights themselves don't require too much time to visit, they are scattered throughout the region, so it takes a while to get to them. If you have only one or two days, try to take in one or more of the cities. Neuchâtel and Fribourg have very different characters, and a day can easily be spent walking around the city centers, visiting a few museums, and sampling restaurants.

8

If you aren't interested in museums, the cities could be combined with a trip to one of the smaller nearby towns. More time allows you to tour the area and take in its subtle differences. If you start at Fribourg, cut south to the castle at Gruyères, then circle northwest through the ancient town of Murten on your way to Neuchâtel.

From Neuchâtel, head south along the Route du Vignoble (Wine Route) to the château town of Grandson and on to Yverdon-les-Bains. It's also a good idea to spend some time pursuing the many sporting opportunities available each season. Summer is the perfect time to take a long trip on Lac de Neuchâtel or to enjoy a hike.

GETTING HERE AND AROUND

AIR TRAVEL

Fribourg lies between Geneva International Airport, 138 km (86 miles) to the southwest, and Zürich Airport, 180 km (112 miles) to the northeast. Train connections to both are good.

The Bern-Belp Airport is a small international airport 34 km (21 miles) northeast of Fribourg, near Bern.

BIKE TRAVEL

Biking is popular here, and itineraries are varied. You can huff and puff uphill, bounce over mountain-bike trails, or coast along the flatlands around the lakes. Route maps can be picked up in most tourist offices or train stations. Swiss Federal Railways has reasonably priced rentals at most train stations. Bikes must be reserved at least one day in advance, three in summer. Check with tourist offices for a map of over 20 different biking itineraries called La Broye à Vélo. At Estavayer-le-Lac and Payerne, cyclists (and hikers) can also book a "Safari Nature" package with one overnight stay (reserve at least one week in advance).

Contacts Estavayer-le-Lac Tourisme. ☎ *026/6606161* 🌐 *www.estavayer-payerne.ch.*

BOAT AND FERRY TRAVEL

There are frequent boat trips on the lakes of Neuchâtel and Murten in summer, plus usually a host of themed evening trips. Contact La Navigation Lacs de Neuchâtel et Morat for more information.

Contacts Navigation Lacs de Neuchâtel et Morat. ☎ *032/7299600* 🌐 *www.navig.ch.*

BUS TRAVEL

Postbus connections, except in the principal urban areas, can be few and far between.

Consequently, you should plan excursions carefully using the bus schedules available at the train station, or phone the local tourist office for advice.

CAR TRAVEL

An important and scenic trans-Swiss artery, the A12 expressway cuts from Bern to Lausanne, passing directly above Fribourg. A parallel route to the northwest extends the A1 between Zürich and Bern, connecting Bern to Murten, Payerne, and Lausanne.

The A5 expressway runs between Neuchâtel and Yverdon but passes through a lot of tunnels. If you have the time, take the national road for a more scenic view of the lakeshore. The charms of this varied region can be experienced easily by car, and there are scenic secondary highways throughout. Keep in mind that some towns, like Gruyères, are car-free or have pedestrian-only centers; in these cases, parking lots are easy to find.

TRAIN TRAVEL

The main train route connecting Basel, Zürich, and Geneva passes through the Fribourg station between Bern and Lausanne. Neuchâtel has hourly connections to main Swiss cities. Regional train services to smaller destinations leave from the larger towns of Fribourg and Neuchâtel, though buses may take a more direct route.

HOTELS

As they become more tourist oriented, Fribourg and Neuchâtel are developing better hotel infrastructures. Fribourg is the best equipped, though there's still only a handful of choices in the Old Town. In Neuchâtel most lodgings sit along the lake. Many hotels don't have air-conditioning but do offer more than one meal plan.

RESTAURANTS

Both Fribourg and Neuchâtel have a plethora of top-quality, French-influenced restaurants. They have far cheaper lunch menus (three or more courses) and sometimes even a plat du jour, although it costs more than it does in simpler establishments, where the price is typically under

20 SF. No one here lays down strict dress codes: the more upscale the restaurant, the fancier the attire, but you won't be thrown out for not wearing a tie. Restaurants open for dinner at about 6 in the evening, though diners tend to arrive closer to 7:30, and kitchens wind down between 9:30 and 10. Lunch is usually served from 11:30 to 2, but you can often get simple fare even after that. For a quick, cheap meal that still has local flavor, try a crêperie. The closer you are to France, the more of these there are.

Hotel and restaurant reviews have been shortened. For full information, visit Fodors.com.

WHAT IT COSTS IN SWISS FRANCS

	$	$$	$$$	$$$$
Restaurants	Under 26 SF	26 SF–45 SF	46 SF–65 SF	Over 65 SF
Hotels	Under 201 SF	201 SF–300 SF	301 SF–500 SF	Over 500 SF

Restaurant prices are the average cost of a main course at dinner or, if dinner is not served, at lunch. Hotel prices are the lowest cost of a standard double room in high season, including taxes.

FRIBOURG

8

With its landscape of green hills against the craggy peaks of the pre-Alps, Fribourg is one of Switzerland's most rural cantons. Its famous Fribourgeois cows—the Holsteins (black and white, the colors of the cantonal coat of arms)—provide the canton with its main income, although light industry is gradually replacing the cows. Fondue has a long history here, as does Gruyère cheese and Switzerland's famous crème-double (double cream, with a fat content of at least 45%).

FRIBOURG

34 km (21 miles) southwest of Bern, 74 km (46 miles) northeast of Lausanne.

Between the rich pasturelands of the Swiss plateau and the Alpine foothills, the Sarine River (called the Saane by German speakers) twists in an S-curve, its sandstone cliffs joined by webs of arching bridges. In one of the curves of the river is the medieval city of Fribourg. The city of overlapping layers is an astonishing place of hills and cobblestones, ramparts and Gothic fountains, ancient passageways, and worn wooden stairs. Only on foot can you discover its secret charm as one of the finer ensembles of medieval architecture in Europe.

Historic Fribourg is a stronghold of Catholicism, and its citizens remained staunch believers even during the Reformation. The evidence is everywhere, from the numerous chapels and religious orders to the brown-robed novitiates walking the sidewalks. Fribourg University, founded in 1889, remains the only Catholic university in Switzerland.

It is also the only bilingual institution of its kind and reflects the region's peculiar linguistic agility. Two-thirds of the people of Canton Fribourg are native French speakers, one-third are native German speakers, and many switch easily between the two. In the Basse-Ville neighborhood, old-timers still speak a unique mixture of the two languages, called Boltz. Officially, the city is bilingual, although French predominates.

GETTING HERE AND AROUND

Direct trains connect Fribourg to major Swiss cities: Geneva is 1 hour 25 minutes away, Lausanne is 45 to 50 minutes, Bern is 22 to 35 minutes, and Zürich is 1 hour 24 minutes on a direct train. Buses leave from behind Fribourg's train station for villages in the surrounding canton. If your knowledge of French or German is good, then the Fribourg and Neuchâtel transportation websites are useful.

From the Place de Tilleul in Fribourg, the Rue de Lausanne climbs upward. Like Rue des Alpes, it, too, is shop lined, with tightly spaced 18th-century buildings hiding terraced gardens of surprising size. The 19th- and 20th-century section of the city begins at the top of Rue de Lausanne; nearby are the main buildings of the university. The 21st century has arrived in the form of the Fribourg Center shopping mall, close to the station.

VISITOR INFORMATION

Contacts Fribourg Tourisme. ✉ *1 av. de la Gare, Fribourg* ☎ *026/3501111* 🌐 *www.fribourgtourism.ch.*

EXPLORING

TOP ATTRACTIONS

Basse-Ville (*Lower City*). At Fribourg's very core is the Basse-Ville, tucked into a crook of the river. Here you'll find the 11th- through 16th-century homes of the original village, as well as a lively café and cellar-theater scene. ✉ *Fribourg.*

Fodor's Choice ★ **Cathédrale St-Nicolas** (*St. Nicholas Cathedral*). Fribourg's grand cathedral rears up from the surrounding gray, 18th-century buildings. Its massive tower was completed in the 15th century, two centuries after construction began in 1283. Above the main portal, a beautifully restored tympanum of the Last Judgment shows the blessed few headed toward Peter, who holds the key to the heavenly gates; those not so fortunate are led by pig-faced demons into the cauldrons of hell. Inside you can see the famous 18th-century organ, as well as the restored 1657 organ. The exceptional stained-glass windows, installed between 1873 and 1983, are executed in a number of styles, including Pre-Raphaelite and art nouveau. In the **Chapelle du St-Sépulcre** (Chapel of the Holy Sepulchre), a group of 13 figures dating from 1433 portrays the entombment of Christ. If you can handle the 368 steps, climb to the tower for a panoramic view. During services, entry is not allowed. ✉ *Rue St-Nicolas, Fribourg* 🎫 *Free, tower 3.50 SF* ⏲ *Tower closed Nov.–Mar.*

Église des Cordeliers (*Church of the Franciscan Friars*). This imposing 13th-century church is attached to a Franciscan friary. Its pale walls and the rose-, gray-, and alabaster-colored ceiling contrast with the Gothic darkness of the interior. A 16th-century polyptych by an anonymous Nelkenmeister, or *Maître à l'Oeillet* (one of a group of painters who

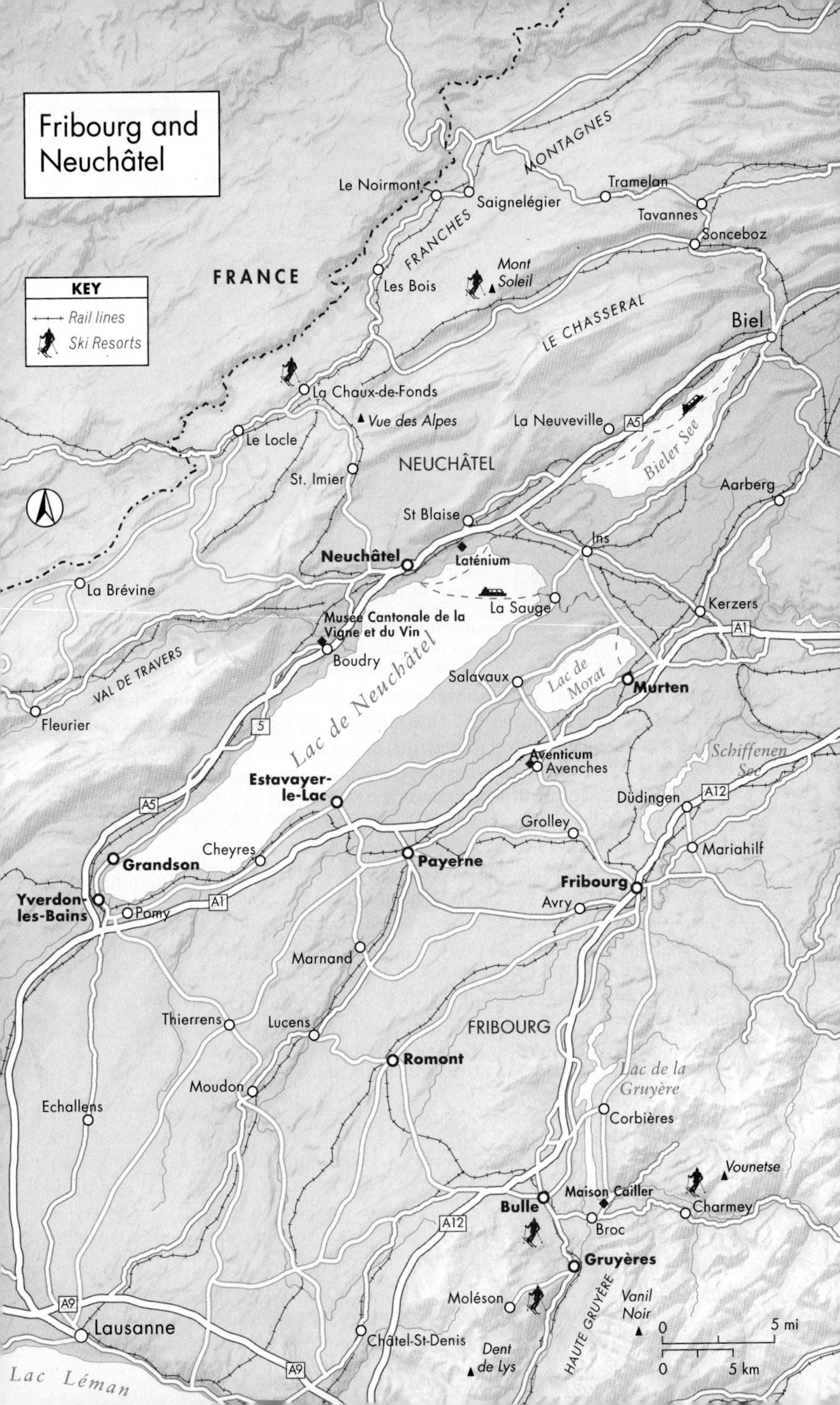

Fribourg and Neuchâtel
KEY
Rail lines
Ski Resorts
FRANCE
FRANCHES MONTAGNES
Le Noirmont
Saignelégier
Tramelan
Tavannes
Sonceboz
Les Bois
Mont Soleil
LE CHASSERAL
Biel
La Chaux-de-Fonds
Vue des Alpes
La Neuveville
A5
Bieler See
Le Locle
NEUCHÂTEL
St. Imier
Aarberg
St Blaise
Ins
Neuchâtel
Laténium
La Brévine
La Sauge
Kerzers
Musée Cantonale de la Vigne et du Vin
A1
Boudry
VAL DE TRAVERS
Lac de Neuchâtel
Salavaux
Lac de Morat
Murten
Fleurier
5
Aventicum
Avenches
Schiffenen See
Estavayer-le-Lac
Düdingen
A12
A5
Grolley
Cheyres
Grandson
Payerne
Mariahilf
Fribourg
Yverdon-les-Bains
Pomy
A1
Avry
Marnand
Thierrens
Lucens
FRIBOURG
Romont
Moudon
Lac de la Gruyère
Echallens
Corbières
Vounetse
Maison Cailler
Bulle
Charmey
Broc
A12
Gruyères
Vanil Noir
Moléson
HAUTE GRUYÈRE
A9
Lausanne
Châtel-St-Denis
Dent de Lys
0
5 mi
0
5 km
A9
Lac Léman

All that cheese comes from right here: herds of cows dot the Fribourg countryside, and at the end of every summer, they are bedecked with flowers and paraded in the streets during the *Désalpes* celebrations.

signed their works only with red and white carnations), hangs over the high altar. A carved-wood triptych, believed to be Alsatian, and a 15th-century retable of the temptation of St. Anthony painted by the Fribourg artist Hans Fries decorate the side walls. At the entrance to the cloister leading to the friary is a 13th-century five-panel fresco depicting the birth of the Virgin Mary. ✉ *Pl. de Notre-Dame, Fribourg* ☎ *026/3471160* 🎫 *Free.*

FAMILY **Espace Jean Tinguely–Niki de Saint Phalle.** Once the city's tram terminal, this is one of the premier modern-art spaces in Switzerland. It houses a selection of whirring, tapping, spinning metal sculptures by Jean Tinguely and a wall full of the voluptuous, colorful work of his wife, Niki de Saint Phalle. After working in the Dadaist movement, Tinguely (1925–91) made headlines as a pioneer of the "kinetic art" movement. Kids (16 and under free) are often fascinated by Tinguely's work, which is full of fantastical elements: skis are walking, a potted plant is turning, and a toy rabbit is being hit on the head. ✉ *2 rue de Morat, Fribourg* ☎ *026/3055140* 🌐 *www.mahf.ch* 🎫 *7 SF* ⏲ *Closed Mon. and Tues.*

Hôtel de Ville (*Town Hall*). The Hôtel de Ville (Rathaus in German) is the seat of the cantonal parliament, built on the foundations of the château of Berthold IV of Zähringen, who founded the town of Fribourg in 1157. The symmetrical stairways were added in the 17th century, as were the clockworks in the 16th-century clock tower. A vibrant produce market sets up on the square in front of the Town Hall on Saturday mornings. ✉ *Pl. de l'Hôtel de Ville, Fribourg* ⏲ *Closed Sun.*

Musée d'Art et d'Histoire de Fribourg (*Fribourg Museum of Art and History*). This important museum is housed in the Renaissance Ratzé

Mansion and, incongruously, an old slaughterhouse connected to the mansion proper by an underground passage. The mansion displays 12th- to 19th-century art, including several works by Hans Fries. The 19th-century slaughterhouse, a stark stone structure modernized with steel-and-glass blocks, provides the setting for a provocative mix of sacred sculptures and the kinetic, scrap-iron whimsies of native son Jean Tinguely. The attic gallery displays 19th- and 20th-century paintings from Swiss artists, as well as from Delacroix, Courbet, and others. Take a breather in the quiet sculpture garden overlooking the river. Limited descriptive material in English is available upon request, and guided tours in English can be booked in advance. ✉ *12 rue de Morat, Fribourg* ☎ *026/3055140* 🌐 *www.mahf.ch* 🎫 *10 SF* ⏲ *Closed Mon.*

Planche-Supérieure. As Fribourg expanded from the Basse-Ville, it crossed the river over the Pont du Milieu (Middle Bridge) to a narrow bank, the Planche-Inférieure, where picturesque, terraced houses abound. As the town prospered, it spread to the statelier 16th- and 17th-century Planche-Superiéure, a large, sloping, open triangular *place* (square) that was once the busy livestock market. It is now lined with several upscale restaurants and cafés. From here you can walk up to the Chapelle de Lorette (Loreto Chapel), once a favored pilgrimage site, for the best view of Fribourg. ✉ *Fribourg.*

Pont de Zähringen (*Zähringen Bridge*). From St. Nicholas Cathedral, slip through the Rue des Épouses to the Grand-Rue, lined with 18th-century patrician homes. Near the end of this street is the historic and now pedestrianized Zähringen Bridge, with views over the Pont de Berne, the Pont de Gottéron, and the wooden remains of the ancient towers that once guarded the entrance to the city. You're now in the area where Duke Berthold IV first established his residence and founded the city in 1157. ✉ *Fribourg.*

8

NEED A BREAK

✗ Le Café du Belvédère. The terrace of Le Café du Belvédère has a fabulous view up the river to the Planche-Supérieure. The friendly staff serves a selection of teas, coffees, and homemade syrups as well as alcohol, and you can enjoy platters of local cheese and smoked meats in addition to Asian delights from the excellent Tam's Kitchen restaurant upstairs. Known for: Sunday brunch is a very good value; frothy, steamed hot caramel milk; eclectic ambience, which makes it a favorite for the city's artists. ✉ ***36 Grand-Rue, Fribourg*** ☎ ***026/3234407.***

WORTH NOTING

Musée Suisse de la Machine à Coudre et Objets Insolites (*Swiss Museum of Sewing Machines and Other Objects*). Examples of almost every sewing machine ever built (more than 250) are on exhibit here. There's also a collection of contraptions created to ease the life of handworkers and housewives before the age of electricity, including useful household firsts such as vacuum cleaners and washing machines. A side room is packed with curiosities from bygone days, such as chestnut-hulling boots. Second-generation owner and half-American Marc Wassmer charms with anecdotes and history—he alone is worth the visit. ✉ *58 Grand-Rue, Fribourg* ☎ *026/4752433* 🌐 *www.museewassmer.com* 🎫 *7 SF.*

EATING WELL IN THE REGION

The cuisines of these two regions all use robust, seasonal food: perch from the lakes, game and mushrooms from the forested highlands, and, of course, the dairy products of Fribourg and the Gruyère region. In the lake towns, menus are thick with *perche* (perch), *sandre* (a large cousin of the perch), *bondelle* (a pearly-fleshed trout found exclusively in Lac de Neuchâtel), or *silure* (catfish). Mushrooms are another strong suit, from the delicate *schwämli* (*chanterelles* in French) to robust *steinpilze* (*bolets* in French), fat, fleshy mushrooms with a meaty texture and taste. These are particularly wonderful when sautéed and served with slices of dark bread or with local rabbit or venison, along with a glass of Neuchâtel Pinot Noir.

Many regions of Switzerland are known for fondue, but Neuchâtel is where it all began. The fondue mix bearing the Neuchâtel name is made of Gruyère and Emmental cheeses. Fribourg is the source of *fondue fribourgeoise*, a creamy single-cheese fondue made from Vacherin Fribourgeois. Potatoes can be dipped in fondue instead of bread.

Those familiar cows dotting the green landscape of the Fribourg countryside yield more than cheese, however. An additional debt of gratitude is owed them for producing crème-double, a Gruyère region specialty that rivals Devonshire cream.

A rich, extra-thick, high-fat cream that—without whipping—almost supports a standing spoon, it is served in tiny carved-wood baquets (tubs), to be spooned over berries and meringues.

Neuveville (*New Town*). When the Pont de St-Jean was built in the 17th century, making the northern bank of the river readily accessible, the merchant houses and walled cloisters of the Neuveville popped up. ✉ *Fribourg.*

Pont de Berne (*Bern Bridge*). In this city of bridges, the Pont de Berne is the oldest. Set to the north of the Basse-Ville, it is made entirely of wood and was once the only access to the city. ✉ *Fribourg.*

EN ROUTE

Maison Cailler. On the way from Fribourg to Gruyères, chocoholics should consider stopping at this tantalizing chocolate factory in the otherwise unassuming town of Broc. A name in Swiss chocolate since 1819, Cailler offers a 90-minute tour complete with chocolate tasting. ✉ *7 rue Jules Bellet, Broc* ☎ *026/9215960* 🌐 *www.cailler.ch* 🎫 *12 SF.*

WHERE TO EAT

$$ FRENCH

✕ **Café de la Fonderie.** *MasterChef* TV series participants Benoît Waber and Leonard Gamba are earning top honors with their newly opened gastronomic café, set in a spacious, renovated warehouse near the university. The chefs create a unique, limited menu each week, with the goal of titillating the senses using unusual or unexpected ingredients. **Known for:** brainchild of TV cooking stars Ben and Léo; unfussy yet decidedly tasty gourmet dishes; locally sourced products make up the ever-changing menu. [$] *Average main: 30 SF* ✉ *11 rte. de la Fonderie, Fribourg* ☎ *026/3012033* 🌐 *www.benandleo.ch* ⏲ *Closed Sun. and Mon.*

$$ SWISS Fodor's Choice ★ **Café du Midi.** This classic spot has been serving fondue since 1877. With rich wooden paneling and a historic decor, the Café du Midi is one of the oldest and best-preserved restaurants in town. **Known for:** excellent fondue that draws hordes; quaint dining room interiors; friendly, English-speaking waitstaff. *Average main: 28 SF* *25 rue de Romont, Fribourg* *026/3223133* *www.lemidi.ch.*

$$$ FRENCH Fodor's Choice ★ **Des Trois Tours.** If you have a penchant for innovative food that's superbly presented, try Alain Bächler's well-regarded restaurant just outside town. Enjoy your meal in the sunny bistro, the main dining room, or on the chestnut-tree-shaded terrace in summer. **Known for:** superb foie gras and lobster paté; well-priced wine-pairing menu du marché; high ratings from respected dining reviewers. *Average main: 65 SF* *15 rte. de Bourguillon, Bourguillon* *026/3223069* *www.troistours.ch* *Closed Sun. and Mon.*

$$ FRENCH **Hôtel de Ville.** Centrally located, this is one of the top Fribourg restaurants, thanks to owner-chef Frédérik Kondratowicz's superlative take on seasonal cuisine. The ambience in this one-floor-up spot is bourgeois bistro with artsy notes, and there are some great views of Fribourg from the windows. **Known for:** creative dishes with unusual ingredients; fine dining with a good quality-to-price ratio; occasional live entertainment and art exhibitions. *Average main: 45 SF* *6 Grand-Rue, Fribourg* *026/3212367* *www.restaurant-hotel-de-ville.ch* *Closed Sun. and Mon.*

$ FRENCH **Xpresso Café.** On the fourth floor of the Fribourg Centre, this café does waffles and crêpes—both savory and sweet—as well as panini and pizza. The outpost of a popular Swiss chain offers a perfect time-out from heavy-duty retail therapy. **Known for:** vast choice of teas and coffees; American-style stacks of pancakes; copious breakfast platters. *Average main: 15 SF* *12 av. de la Gare, Fribourg* *026/3417808* *Closed Sun.*

8

WHERE TO STAY

$$ B&B/INN Fodor's Choice ★ **Auberge aux 4 Vents.** Guests reserve months ahead for this quirky, high-style country inn noted for its fabulous gardens and fanciful themed rooms. **Pros:** individuality and quirky character of venue; beautifully appointed rooms mix antiques with modern touches; glamorous restaurant feels like a film set. **Cons:** traditionalists may feel out of place here; outside central Fribourg but easily reached by bus; difficult to secure a reservation last minute. *Rooms from: 260 SF* *124 rte. de Grandfey, Fribourg* *026/3215600* *www.auberge4vents.ch* *Closed Mon. and Tues.* *9 rooms* *Breakfast.*

$ HOTEL **Hôtel de la Rose.** In a typical 17th-century sandstone house, this hotel is within walking distance of museums, churches, the cathedral, and Old Town. **Pros:** excellent central location; high-quality service; friendly staff. **Cons:** lack of air-conditioning; noise from the street below can be bothersome; pricey parking. *Rooms from: 180 SF* *1 rue Morat, Fribourg* *026/3510101* *www.hoteldelarose.ch* *40 rooms* *Breakfast.*

$ HOTEL **Hotel du Faucon.** At this attractive seven-story hotel, guests are treated to modern, quiet, and spacious studiolike rooms at very good prices. **Pros:** friendly staff; pedestrian zone means no traffic noise; calm, quiet ambience. **Cons:** overpriced breakfast; unstaffed reception desk at night; parking adds to the tab. *Rooms from: 125 SF* *76 rue de Lausanne, Fribourg* *026/3213790* *www.hotel-du-faucon.ch* *23 rooms* *No meals.*

$$ HOTEL **Romantik Hotel Restaurant Au Sauvage.** A cloister in the 17th century and an inn during the cattle-market days of the 18th and 19th centuries, this sophisticated auberge now has a striking blend of minimalist furnishings and medieval details. **Pros:** enchantingly steeped in medieval history; central location; fine-dining restaurant serves fresh, inventive cuisine. **Cons:** staff does not always speak English well; typically neutral Swiss color scheme; walls may feature uninspiring paintings. *Rooms from: 280 SF* *12 Planche-Supérieure, Fribourg* *026/3473060* *www.hotel-sauvage.ch* *17 rooms* *Breakfast.*

NIGHTLIFE

BARS

Café de L'Ancienne Gare. This trendy café retains all the airy splendor of its location, the former train station. With a mixed crowd of students, young professionals, and artsy types of all ages, L'Ancienne Gare shakes up classic cocktails and a good selection of beer and wine—all at prices slightly lower than the Swiss average. The carefully curated cultural calendar of concerts, events, comedy nights, and more provides a variety of intriguing entertainment. *3 Esplanade de l'Ancienne Gare, Fribourg* *026/3225772* *www.cafeanciennegare.ch.*

La Cave de la Rose. To get a feel for Fribourg's nightlife, try one of the cellar bars scattered throughout the Old Town, such as La Cave de la Rose. This convivial place stays open into the wee hours of the morning. *1 rue de Morat, Fribourg* *026/322244.*

Planet Edelweiss. Seemingly in the middle of nowhere, this 19th-century inn has been transformed into a lively late-night dining spot and disco. The diverse crowd (ranging from bankers to farmers) at this haven of rural hipsterdom doesn't arrive until after 10 pm, but stays until 2 am during the week and 4 am on weekends. The 12-minute taxi ride from town runs about 25 SF. *1 Mariahilf, Düdingen* *026/4920505* *www.planet-edelweiss.ch.*

GRUYÈRES

35 km (21 miles) south of Fribourg.

Fodor's Choice ★ Rising above the plain on a rocky crag against a backdrop of Alpine foothills, the castle village of Gruyères seduces from afar. This perfect specimen of a medieval stronghold comes complete with a cobbled main street, stone fountains, and well-preserved houses, whose occupants try to outdo each other with picturesque facades and geranium displays in summer. The town was once the capital of the Alpine estates of the Burgundian counts of Gruyères, and its traditional crest bears a stylized crane (*grue*), a motif that adorns countless pieces of the town's famed blue-and-white or dark-red-and-white pottery. Gruyères is car-free, so you'll have to park in one of three lots outside town and walk up from the Maison du Gruyère.

CLOSE UP

La Désalpe

When the Alpine grass thins out in the fall, the cows of Haute Gruyère are led down to the village stables—in style, with huge bells around their necks and flowers and pine branches wound through their horns. Not to be outdone by their beasts, the cowherds wear their Sunday best: typically, a dark blue jacket embroidered with edelweiss motifs and puffy short sleeves that optically double the width of the wearers' shoulders. With their black-trimmed straw caps, fancy pipes, and bushy beards, the men are the real stars of the day. The women, in red-checked aprons and flat straw hats, stay in the background. To avoid two weeks of continual congestion on the roads, the foothill villages of Charmey (last Saturday in September) and Albeuve (first Saturday in October) have the herds descend together, making a folk festival of it. Decorated cows, heifers, sheep, goats, and even pigs are paraded through the streets from 9 am until about 3 pm. The partying goes on all day, with flag throwing, marching bands, alpenhorn playing, and stalls selling Bénichon specialties. (Originally a benediction of the church, Bénichon has become a harvest celebration.) Watch for the *poyas* adorning the front walls of Gruyères farmhouses. These are naive-style paintings of cows filing up to the high pastures in spring. They advertise which breed the farmer owns and symbolize hope for a productive summer. (Before the 1820s, cheese was made only up on the Alps, where the cows had the lushest grass, so farmers had four months a year to make their living.)

GETTING HERE AND AROUND

To connect with Gruyères via public transport, buses from Fribourg are best. Take a bus to Bulle, and change to another bus that heads directly to Gruyères (a trip of 1 hour, 15 minutes). Alternatively, take the bus to Bulle, change to a train, and get off at the town of Gruyères in front of the cheese dairy La Maison du Gruyère. Walk up to the town (approximately 15 minutes). This option takes 1 hour, and there are hourly connections. If traveling from Lausanne or Zürich, transfer to a local train at Palézieux—this rail journey takes up to about 5 hours.

VISITOR INFORMATION

Contacts Gruyère Tourisme. ✉ *Village center, Gruyères* ☎ *848/424424* 🌐 *www.la-gruyere.ch.*

EXPLORING

Fodor's Choice ★ **Château de Gruyères.** Crowning the storybook village of Gruyères is the town's famed château. Between 1080 and 1554, 19 counts held political power over this region, and they built and expanded this medieval castle. Little is known about them except for the last one, Michel. A lover of luxury and big spending, he expanded the estates and then fled his creditors in 1555. In 1849 a wealthy Geneva family bought the castle and encouraged painter friends to decorate a room now known as Corot's Room, because it features four of Jean-Baptiste-Camille Corot's landscapes. Also worth seeing is the Knights' Room with its impressive 19th-century fresco cycle depicting local legends, and the aptly named Fantastic Art Room, hung with contemporary work. An 18-minute multimedia show called *Gruyères,* which brings to life the history of the castle in animated form (available in eight languages), shown daily in the old caretaker's lodge, is worth your time. ✉ *Gruyères* ☎ *026/9212102* 🌐 *www.chateau-gruyeres.ch* 🎫 *10 SF.*

Giger Museum. This museum houses the world's largest collection of paintings, sculpture, furniture, and film designs by the enormously talented but equally tormented H. R. Giger. The Swiss surrealist, who died in 2014, won an Academy Award for his set design for the horror film *Alien*; he was not likely to win any prizes for his cheerful, healthy outlook on life (or women). That said, a few of his sculpture-furniture pieces are very good. Most people get enough of an idea about the artist just by sitting in the Giger Bar, opposite the museum. Here you can admire ceiling buttresses that look like elongated backbones with ribs, and his ingenious trademark chairs: yet more spines and ribs, with pelvises for headrests. ✉ *Château St. Germain, Gruyères* ☎ *026/9212200* 🌐 *www.hrgigermuseum.com* 🎫 *12.50 SF* ⏲ *Closed Mon. and Tues. Nov.–Mar.*

Maison du Gruyère. Before going up to town, you can visit the very touristy Maison du Gruyère, a demonstration *fromagerie* (cheese dairy) where the famous cheese is produced with fully modernized equipment. Demonstrations are given two to four times a day, depending on the season. There's also a shop and a restaurant that sells every variation on a cheese dish you ever dreamed of (including three-course "Gruyère cheese menus"). ✉ *Pringy-Gruyères, Gruyères* ☎ *026/9218400* 🌐 *www.lamaisondugruyere.ch* 🎫 *7 SF.*

Tibet Museum. Housed in an artfully converted chapel, this museum run by the Alain Bordier Foundation boasts an important collection of some 300 Buddhist sculptures, paintings, and ritual objects, mainly Tibetan or otherwise Himalayan, and also some from northern India and Myanmar. ✉ *4 rue du Château, Gruyères* ☎ *026/9213010* 🌐 *www.tibetmuseum.ch* 🎫 *10 SF* ⏲ *Closed Mon. Nov.–Mar.*

WHERE TO EAT

$$ SWISS

✕ **Auberge de la Halle.** Set amid Gruyères's most historic buildings, the exterior of this medieval structure welcomes guests with cheerful flower boxes and green-and-white-striped awnings. Inside, a warm woody interior with raftered ceiling and smooth stone floors offers an appealing setting in which to enjoy traditional dishes such as a moitié-moitié (half Gruyère, half Vacherin Fribourgeois) fondue. **Known for:** great views from the veranda; house specialty Soupe du Chalet (with vegetables, cheese, and croutons); lively ambience in a historic setting. 💲 *Average main: 28 SF* ✉ *24 rue de Bourg, Gruyères* ☎ *026/9212178* 🌐 *www.aubergehalle.ch* ⏲ *Closed Tues. Oct.–Apr.*

$$ SWISS

✕ **La Fleur de Lys.** Traditional Swiss fare (local fish, cheese specialties, Rösti, ham off the bone called *jambon à l'os*) and some French classics are served in this inviting restaurant set in a pink-hued historic building that doubles as a hotel. The plain, spacious guest rooms have a wonderful view of the mountains and town castle, and there's an ample breakfast buffet. **Known for:** central location on the cobbled main street; seasonal game dishes in autumn; tender steaks that hit the spot when you've had enough cheese. *Average main: 28 SF* ✉ *14 rue du Bourg, Gruyères* ☎ *026/9218282* 🌐 *www.hotelfleurdelys.ch* *No credit cards* *Closed Mon. and Tues. Oct.–Mar.*

WHERE TO STAY

$ B&B/INN **Hostellerie St-Georges.** Delicious views make this hotel a treat—breathtaking mountain and valley views are definitely the main attractions. **Pros:** copious breakfasts; atmospheric dining with both pizza and traditional dishes; stunning views. **Cons:** flies can be a problem during summer months; no elevator; small and noisy rooms are at front of house. *Rooms from: 180 SF* ✉ *22 rue du Bourg, Gruyères* ☎ *026/9218300* 🌐 *www.hostelleriesaintgeorge-gruyere.com* *Closed Nov.–Mar.* *14 rooms* *Breakfast.*

$ HOTEL **Hôtel de Gruyères Wellness & Seminaires.** Standing outside the gates of Gruyères, this family-friendly hotel shares the same views of the valley and castle as in-town lodgings, but without the noise. **Pros:** quiet location; spa, sauna, hammam, and fitness on-site; a haven from the throngs of tourists. **Cons:** no restaurant in-house; lack of an elevator makes it difficult with luggage; no accessible rooms. *Rooms from: 175 SF* ✉ *1 ruelle des Chevaliers, Gruyères* ☎ *026/9218030* 🌐 *www.gruyereshotels.ch* *37 rooms* *Breakfast.*

$ B&B/INN **Hôtel De Ville.** Right on cobblestoned Rue du Bourg, this beckoning small hotel has large, airy rooms that tastefully mix bright Tuscan colors with traditional pine furnishings. **Pros:** traditional country hotel in enchanting medieval setting; sidewalk terrace for fair-weather dining; charming staff go the extra mile. **Cons:** rich fondue smell in the restaurant may be too pungent for the fainthearted; no elevator; lack of air-conditioning. *Rooms from: 160 SF* ✉ *29 rue du Bourg, Gruyères* ☎ *026/9212424* 🌐 *www.hoteldeville.ch* *8 rooms* *Breakfast.*

SPORTS AND THE OUTDOORS

SKIING

Moléson. At 3,609 feet, Gruyère's' "house mountain" of Moléson offers skiing and wraparound views of the pre-Alps and Lake Geneva. There are 30 km (18 miles) of downhill runs. Ascend via funicular, cable car, or T-bar. Sledding and snowshoeing are also popular here. ✉ *Gruyères.*

BULLE

5 km (3 miles) northwest of Gruyères, 31 km (19 miles) southwest of Fribourg.

With more than 17,000 inhabitants, the town of Bulle has many attractions worthy of a larger destination: a castle (not open to the public), three-story patrician houses lining the cobblestone main street, and a scenic backdrop so perfect you might think it a painting. Bulle is also the site of the annual Salon Suisse des Goûts et Terroirs, a big-deal food fair held in October.

DID YOU KNOW?

Gruyères is worth visiting for more than its namesake cheese. It's a charming village with beautiful views and the hometown of famed artist of the macabre H.R. Giger, who you may know more for his work designing the creature from *Alien*.

HOTEL DE VILLE

GETTING HERE AND AROUND

Trains from Fribourg to Bulle change in Romont and take 45 minutes. There is direct bus service from Fribourg station, which takes 37 minutes.

EXPLORING

Musée Gruérien. Learn about regional traditions at the Musée Gruérien, which contains displays of folk costumes, handicrafts, and farm tools. It even has full reconstructions of the interiors of rural dwellings and a mountain cheese-making facility. The museum boasts reserves of more than 25,000 items. ✉ *25 rue de la Condémine, Bulle* ☎ *026/9161010* 🌐 *www.musee-gruerien.ch* 🎫 *12 SF* ⏲ *Closed Mon.*

ROMONT

15 km (9 miles) northwest of Bulle, 49 km (30 miles) southwest of Fribourg.

The best way to approach this 13th-century town of two broad streets is to leave the highway and drive up to its castle terrace. The fortress's 13th-century ramparts surround the town, forming a belvedere from which you can see the Alps—from Mont Blanc to the Berner Oberland. There's also a 12th-century Cistercian convent, 17th-century Capuchin monastery, and lovely 13th-century Collégiale, one of the purest examples of a Gothic church in Switzerland, with period (and modern) windows, sculptures, choir stalls, a screen, and an altarpiece.

GETTING HERE AND AROUND

By train, it takes 17 minutes to reach Romont from Fribourg.

EXPLORING

Vitromusée (*Stained-Glass Museum*). Inside the castle, the Vitromusée shimmers with crisscrossing shafts of colored light from its glass panels, both ancient and contemporary. A slide presentation traces the development of the craft, and a workshop area demonstrates current techniques. The museum now includes a donated collection of reverse painting on glass. ✉ *Rte. de Romont, Romont* ☎ *026/6521095* 🌐 *www.vitromusee.ch* 🎫 *12 SF* ⏲ *Closed Mon.*

PAYERNE

15 km (9 miles) north of Romont, 18 km (11 miles) west of Fribourg.

The meandering streets in this market town are filled with pastel-painted 18th-century buildings, now converted to shops and restaurants. The star attraction, however, remains the town's celebrated abbey church, a landmark of the Swiss Romanesque style.

GETTING HERE AND AROUND

The train from Fribourg to Payerne takes 26 minutes; from Neuchâtel to Payerne, change at Yverdon (52 minutes).

VISITOR INFORMATION

Contacts Payerne Tourisme. ✉ *10 pl. du Marché, Payerne* ☎ *026/6769922* 🌐 *www.payerne.ch.*

EXPLORING

Église Abbatiale (*Abbey Church*). The magnificent 11th-century Église Abbatiale, built on the site of an ancient Roman villa, is one of the finest examples of Romanesque art in Switzerland. Of particular note in its austere, restored interior is the impressively engineered barrel vaulting; the frescoes and primitive carvings on the capitals of stone pillars are also of interest. Organ concerts are frequent attractions, and exhibitions are staged in both the church and an adjoining museum. ✉ *Pl. du Marché, Payerne* ☎ *026/6626704* 🌐 *www.abbatiale-payerne.ch* 🎫 *7 SF* ⏲ *Closed Mon.*

ESTAVAYER-LE-LAC

7 km (4 miles) northwest of Payerne, 30 km (19 miles) northwest of Fribourg, 51 km (32 miles) southeast of Neuchâtel.

Along with its history-soaked and highly picturesque Old Town (in summer, don't miss the Saturday morning market bursting with local produce), lakeside Estavayer is a haven for walkers, cyclists, boaters, and water-sports enthusiasts. In addition, it is a beloved base for nature lovers who head here to enjoy Grande Cariçaie, one of Europe's premier nature reserves, along the southern flank of Lac de Neuchâtel.

The tiny town can still be navigated using a map drawn in 1599. It has retained much of its medieval architecture, from the arcades of the town center to the gracious, multitowered medieval **Château de Chenaux,** which now houses its government offices.

8

GETTING HERE AND AROUND

Estavayer-le-Lac is 35 minutes from Fribourg by train; from Neuchâtel, change trains at Yverdon (41 minutes).

VISITOR INFORMATION

Contacts Estavayer-le-Lac Tourisme. ✉ *16 rue de L'Hôtel de Ville, Estavayer-le-Lac* ☎ *026/6631237* 🌐 *www.estavayer-payerne.ch.*

EXPLORING

Musée des Grenouilles (*Frog Museum*). For something completely different, visit the quirky Musée des Grenouilles. Here are displays of 108 embalmed frogs posed like people in scenes of daily life from the 19th century. Other exhibits include an authentic 17th-century kitchen, military artifacts, and household objects dredged from Lac de Neuchâtel. ✉ *13 rue du Musée, Estavayer-le-Lac* ☎ *026/6648065* 🌐 *www.museedesgrenouilles.ch* 🎫 *5 SF* ⏲ *Closed Mon. Mar.–Oct., weekdays Nov.–Feb.*

MURTEN

19 km (12 miles) northeast of Estavayer-le-Lac, 17 km (11 miles) north of Fribourg.

The ancient town of Murten, known in French as Morat, is a popular resort on the Murtensee/Lac de Morat (Lake Murten). The bilingual town has a boat-lined waterfront, windsurfing rentals, a lakeside public pool complex, grassy picnic areas, and a promenade as well as a superbly preserved medieval center. From the town's 13th-century gates,

Climb to Murten's ramparts for a nice view of Lake Murten over the town's rooftops.

take a stroll through the fountain-studded cobblestone streets. Climb up the worn wooden steps to the town ramparts for a view of the lake over a charming montage of red roofs and stone chimneys.

Although a small town, Murten looms large in the history of Switzerland. Its most memorable moment came on June 22, 1476, when the Swiss Confederates—already a fearsomely efficient military machine—attacked with surprising ferocity and won a significant victory over the Burgundians, who were threatening Fribourg under the leadership of Duke Charles the Bold. Begun as a siege 12 days earlier, the battle cost the Swiss 410 men and the Burgundians 12,000. The defeat at Murten prevented the establishment of a large Lotharingian kingdom and kept Switzerland's autonomy unchallenged for decades. Legend has it that a Swiss runner, carrying a linden branch, ran from Murten to Fribourg to carry the news of victory. He expired by the town hall, and a linden tree grew from the branch he carried. Today, to commemorate his dramatic sacrifice, some 15,000 runners participate annually on the first Sunday in October in a 17-km (11-mile) race up the steep hill from Murten to Fribourg. As for the linden tree, it flourished in Fribourg for some 500 years until 1983, when it was ingloriously felled by a drunk driver. It has been replaced with a steel sculpture.

GETTING HERE AND AROUND

Murten is 29 minutes from Fribourg by train; from Neuchâtel, change at Kerzers (37 minutes). If arriving by car, leave it in the parking area in front of the town's 13th-century gates (the town center is car-free).

VISITOR INFORMATION

Contacts Murten Tourismus. ✉ *6 Franz-Kirchg., Murten* ☎ *026/6705112* 🌐 *www.regionmurtensee.ch.*

EXPLORING

Aventicum. One of the most notable ancient Roman settlements of Switzerland's "Roman era" is Aventicum, which dates from 58 BC to AD 400. In the famous Musée et Théâtre Romain (Roman Museum and Theater), you can still see the remains of an ancient Roman forum, a bathhouse, and an amphitheater where bloodthirsty spectators once watched the games. The collection of Roman antiquities at the town museum is noteworthy, particularly the gold bust of emperor Marcus Aurelius. To get here from Murten, head 8 km (5 miles) southwest to Avenches. ✉ *Rue Centrale, Murten* ☎ *026/6751727* 🌐 *www.aventicum.org* 🎫 *Free* ⏲ *Closed Mon. Nov.–Mar., Mon. and Tues. Apr.–Oct.*

Musée de Morat (*Murten Museum*). Complete with two water-powered mill wheels, the Musée de Moratis is the town's old mill. On view are prehistoric finds from the lake area, military items, and trophies from the Burgundian Wars. ✉ *4 Ryf, Murten* ☎ *026/6703100* 🌐 *www.museummurten.ch* 🎫 *6 SF* ⏲ *Closed Mon. Dec.–Mar.*

WHERE TO EAT

$$ FRENCH Fodor's Choice ★ ✕ **Auberge des Clefs.** This is a very special restaurant, so if you're traveling by car and can book well ahead, definitely stop by to see why it gets such high praise from top critics. The atmosphere is laid-back, staff are on the ball and friendly, and views of the lake and mountains from the terrace are divine. **Known for:** prix-fixe menus in the upstairs section, à la carte options in the bistro; seemingly simple dishes deliver surprisingly complex flavors; hilltop location above Lake Murten in Lugnorre. $ *Average main: 44 SF* ✉ *4 rte. de Chenaux, Lugnorre* ☎ *026/6733106* 🌐 *www.aubergedesclefs.ch* ⏲ *Closed Wed. and Thurs.*

$$ INTERNATIONAL ✕ **Restaurant Hotel Murten.** Whether you choose to dine in the chic, velvet-cushioned dining room or the high-tabled, fashionable bar section, this stylish eatery is one of the most happening in town. Eschewing the typical bland hotel restaurant cuisine, the menu is on the small side but boasts fresh, local fish as well as more exotic European specials. **Known for:** sleek and stylish interiors with a neon bar; thin, crispy Wiener schnitzel, sometimes available as a special; glass walls open for breezy summer dining. $ *Average main: 32 SF* ✉ *7 Bernstr., Murten* ☎ *026/6788181* 🌐 *www.hotelmurten.ch.*

WHERE TO STAY

$$ HOTEL FAMILY Fodor's Choice ★ 🏨 **Hotel de l'Ours.** Talk about having it all: this converted 19th-century winegrower's home has stylish rooms with marble bathrooms, a lakefront location, a to-die-for terrace and garden, and even an indoor pool. **Pros:** near train station and boat landing; kid-friendly atmosphere—under 16s stay free; refined, romantic ambience on a canal bridging two lakes. **Cons:** hard to leave; need a car or must take a bus to access; restaurant can be busy at mealtimes—best to reserve. $ *Rooms from: 240 SF* ✉ *5 rte. de l'Ancien Pont, Sugiez* ☎ *026/6739393* 🌐 *www.hotel-ours.ch* ⏲ *Closed 3 wks in mid-Oct. and late Dec.–early Jan.* 🛏 *8 rooms* 🍽 *Breakfast.*

$ HOTEL **Hotel Murtenhof & Krone.** In the heart of Murten's Old Town, this cluster of patrician houses dating back to 1428 conjures images of centuries gone by. **Pros:** individuality and heritage of establishment cherished; in the heart of the peaceful Old Town; kindly and quirky staff. **Cons:** some say the walls are a tad too thin; room design varies greatly; busy restaurant below can be overwhelming in summer. *Rooms from: 200 SF* ✉ *1–3 Rathausg., Murten* ☎ *026/6729030* 🌐 *www.murtenhof.ch* *62 rooms* *Breakfast.*

SPORTS AND THE OUTDOORS

Known locally as Lac de Morat or Murtensee, this charming little lake is beloved by swimmers and fishers alike. From the picturesque town of Murten, explore the lakefront promenade and participate in the many water sports available. The lake's shallow depth has given it the reputation of being one of the warmest in Switzerland.

LAKE CRUISES

King Boat. King Boat offers live music and DJs every Friday and Saturday night in July and August. The lake cruise takes several hours and stops at Neuchâtel, where you may board the vessel. ✉ *Quai du Port 10, Neuchâtel* ☎ *032/7299600* 🌐 *www.kingboat.ch* *From 15 SF.*

LAC DE NEUCHÂTEL AND NEARBY

The region of Neuchâtel belonged to Prussia from 1707 to 1857, with a brief interruption caused by Napoléon and a period of dual loyalty to Prussia and the Swiss Confederation between 1815 and 1857. Yet its French heritage remains untouched by Germanic language, diet, or culture. Some boast that the inhabitants speak "the best French in Switzerland," which is partly why so many summer language courses are taught here.

NEUCHÂTEL

28 km (17 miles) northwest of Murten, 48 km (30 miles) northwest of Fribourg.

At the foot of the Jura Mountains, flanked by vineyards and facing southeast, the city of Neuchâtel enjoys panoramic views of Lac de Neuchâtel and the range of the middle Alps, including the majestic mass of Mont Blanc and the Berner Oberland. Lac de Neuchâtel, at 38 km (24 miles) long and 8 km (5 miles) wide, is the largest lake entirely within Switzerland. (The much larger lakes of Geneva and Constance are shared with France and Germany, respectively.) A prosperous city, Neuchâtel has a reputation for precision work, beginning with watchmaking in the early 18th century. In fact, the region is often referred to by locals as "Watch Valley." The city itself lies on the Watchmaking Route—a 200-km (125-mile) heritage trail with 27 stops running from Geneva to Basel. There are traditional workshops, museums, and countless other insights into the ingenuity of this craftsmanship and time itself.

Visitors to Neuchâtel city note the neo-Romanesque yellow-sandstone buildings along the broad avenues in the lower part of town bordering the lake, which inspired author Alexandre Dumas to call Neuchâtel "a city with the appearance of an immense *joujou* [toy] dressed in butter." The Collegiate Church and the 12th-century castle, which today houses the cantonal government, sit gracefully above the city's bustling old marketplace. Stroll (or cycle) along the lakeside promenade as far as Hauterive, the next village to the north.

Neuchâtel's biggest annual festival is the winemakers' three-day celebration of the grape harvest, the *fête des vendanges*. It's celebrated the last weekend of September (🌐 *www.fete-des-vendanges.ch*) with parades and fanfare throughout the city. Also of note are the many absinthe distilleries in the area. Absinthe originated in Val-de-Travers, 26 km (16 miles) to the west of Neuchâtel city, in the 18th century, and since 2005 (when Switzerland relegalized absinthe), the regional distillers have become famous for brewing some of the best absinthe in the world. At a restaurant in town, it's worth ordering this local specialty just to observe the elaborate serving ritual.

GETTING HERE AND AROUND

Neuchâtel has direct trains to and from major Swiss cities: Geneva is 1 hour, 10 minutes away, Lausanne is 41 minutes, Bern is 33–50 minutes, Basel and Zürich are both 1½ hours away. Trains run frequently between Fribourg and Neuchâtel (with transfers) and take at least 1 hour.

Take Bus No. 7 to Place Pury to get Littoral Neuchâtel buses to countryside villages. Bus information can be found on the town website.

8

VISITOR INFORMATION

Contacts Neuchâtel Tourisme. ✉ *Hôtel des Postes, Neuchâtel* ☎ *032/8896890* 🌐 *www.neuchateltourisme.ch.*

EXPLORING

TOP ATTRACTIONS

Église Collégiale (*Collegiate Church*). The French influence in Neuchâtel is revealed in many monuments and in its architecture, most notably the Église Collégiale. The handsome Romanesque and Burgundian Gothic structure, with a colorful tile roof, dates from the 12th century. The church contains a strikingly realistic and well-preserved grouping of life-size painted figures called *le cénotaphe,* or monument, which is closed for renovation until 2019. Dating from the 14th and 15th centuries, this is considered one of Europe's finest examples of medieval art. From April through September there are guided tours (usually between 10 and 4) of the Château de Neuchâtel (Neuchâtel Castle) adjoining the church; check at the château entrance to learn when the English one starts. Anyone not wanting to climb steep streets can reach the church from the Promenade Noire off the Place des Halles by an inconspicuous elevator—*ascenseur publique.* ✉ *3 rue de la Collégiale, Neuchâtel* 🌐 *www.collegiale.ch* 🎫 *Free.*

FAMILY **Laténium.** Located at water's edge, this interactive archaeological museum is the largest in Switzerland. In the nearby community of Hauterive, it displays artifacts found in and around Lac de Neuchâtel and explains how they were recovered. The lifestyles of Bronze Age lake dwellers are skillfully depicted, with pride of place going to a sculpted standing stone that resembles a man, from Bevaix, a village southwest of Neuchâtel. Inside the museum, see the remains of a 60-foot-long Gallo-Roman barge; outside in the park, its reconstruction is moored near a full-scale wooden Bronze Age house on stilts. There is a pamphlet in English, and for 5 SF you can rent an hour-long audio guide in English. There is a free shuttle-boat service to Hauterive from the port in Neuchâtel that runs Friday–Sunday in April and May and Tuesday–Sunday from June to September. ✉ *Espace Paul Vouga, Hauterive* ☎ *032/8896917* 🌐 *www.latenium.ch* 🎫 *9 SF* ⏲ *Closed Mon.*

Fodor's Choice ★ **Musée d'Art et d'Histoire** (*Museum of Art and History*). Thanks to a remarkable curator, the Musée d'Art et d'Histoire displays a striking collection of paintings gathered under broad themes—nature, civilization—and mounted in a radical, evocative way. The 15th-century allegories, early impressionist paintings, and contemporary abstractions pack the walls from floor to ceiling, interacting, conflicting, and demanding comparison. You may climb a platform (itself plastered with paintings) to view the higher works. This aggressive series of displays is framed by the architectural decorations of Neuchâtel resident Clement Heaton, whose murals and stained glass make the building itself a work of art.

This novel museum also has the honor of hosting three of this watchmaking capital's most exceptional guests: the **automates Jaquet-Droz,** three astounding little androids, created between 1768 and 1774, that once toured the courts of Europe like young mechanical Mozarts. Pierre Jaquet-Droz and his son Henri-Louis created them, and they are moving manifestations of the stellar degree to which watchmaking had evolved by the 18th century. Le Dessinateur (the Draughtsman) is an automated dandy in satin knee pants who draws graphite images of a dog, the god Eros in a chariot pulled by a butterfly, and a profile of Louis XV. La Musicienne (the Musician) is a young woman playing the organ. She moves and breathes subtly along with the music and actually strikes the keys that produce the organ notes. L'Écrivain (the Writer) dips a real feather into real ink and writes 40 different letters. Like a primitive computer, he can be programmed to write any message simply by the change of a steel disk. The automatons come alive only on the first Sunday of the month, at 2, 3, and 4 (more often in summer; days and times are posted on the museum's website), but the audiovisual show re-creates the thrill. ✉ *1 esplanade Léopold-Robert, Neuchâtel* ☎ *032/7177925* 🌐 *www.mahn.ch* 🎫 *8 SF* ⏲ *Closed Mon.*

WORTH NOTING

Centre Dürrenmatt. Named after the Swiss writer and artist Friedrich Dürrenmatt (1921–90), the Centre Dürrenmatt, perched high above Neuchâtel, houses an exhibition devoted to modern literature and visual arts. One of Switzerland's (and the world's) top architects, Mario Botta, designed a curving, skylit underground space connected to Dürrenmatt's former home (now a private library and offices). Many of Dürrenmatt's paintings are disturbing, reflecting a bleak worldview that tends to be softened by the humor, albeit acerbic, in his writing. Letters and excerpts of his books are also on display, with each artwork accompanied by a quote. ✉ *74 chemin du Pertuis-du-Sault, Neuchâtel* ☎ *032/7202060* 🌐 *www.cdn.ch* 🎫 *8 SF* ⏲ *Closed Mon. and Tues.*

Château de Neuchâtel. Perched on a rocky hill at the center of the city, the relatively modest château is one of a cluster of historic buildings that made up the ancient royal court of Neuchâtel, including the Collegiale and Tour des Prisons. Until the canton joined the Swiss Confederation in 1848—uniquely, the only monarchy to do so—it was inhabited by various branches of Prussian royalty. Today, it serves as the main administrative offices of the canton, but a selection of the castle's rooms and fittings can be viewed on a guided tour, which is offered four times daily on days that the château is open to visitors. Taking the tour is the only way to visit the fascinating Roman-built Tour des Prisons,where visitors may enter the original wooden prison cells and take in stunning views from its panoramic terrace. ✉ *Rue du Château, Neuchâtel* 🌐 *www.neuchateltourisme.ch* 🎫 *SF 5 for the guided tour* ⏲ *Closed Oct.–Mar. Closed weekdays Apr. and May. Closed Mon. June–Sept.*

Galeries de l'Histoire (*History Gallery*). This gallery houses scale models of Neuchâtel from the year 1000 to 2000. ✉ *7 av. du Peyrou, Neuchâtel* ☎ *032/7177925* 🌐 *www.mahn.ch* 🎫 *Free* ⏲ *Closed Mon., Tues., Thur.–Sat.*

Old Town. The architecture of the Old Town presents a full range of French styles. Along Rue des Moulins are two perfect specimens of the Louis XIII period, and—at its opposite end—a fine Louis XIV house anchors the Place des Halles (market square), also notable for its turreted 16th-century Maison des Halles. The Old Town has several fine patrician houses, such as the magnificent Hôtel DuPeyrou, home of the friend, protector, and publisher of Jean-Jacques Rousseau, who studied botany in the nearby Val-de-Travers. Most of the Old Town is pedestrian-only, though public buses do rumble through. You can stroll as far as Marin-Epagnier (east side) and Vaumarcus (west side). ✉ *Neuchâtel.*

8

EN ROUTE

Musée Cantonale de la Vigne et du Vin. Neuchâtel is part of the Three Lakes wine region, the smallest of Switzerland's six wine-growing areas. The famous Pinot Noir rosé wine, Oeil de Perdrix, originated in Neuchâtel, and the canton produces many other excellent wines, including traditional-method sparkling wine made by the Mauler winery in an old Benedictine monastery in Val-de-Travers. Amid the vineyards that fan out to the west of Neuchâtel city and slope gently down to the lake sits Château Boudry, which houses the Musée Cantonale de la Vigne et du Vin (Cantonal Museum of Vine and Wine). ✉ *Château Boudry, Sentier du Château, Boudry* ☎ *032/8421098* 🌐 *www.chateaudeboudry.ch* 🎫 *Museum 7 SF* ⏲ *Closed Mon. and Tues.*

WHERE TO EAT

$ FRENCH Fodor's Choice ★

✕ **Bach & Buck.** This simply furnished crêperie-cum-tearoom opposite the Jardin Anglais is an ideal spot to grab a cheap but tasty meal. Its location close to the university ensures a young crowd, many of whom head here to enjoy a choice from more than 120 types of crêpes: sweet or savory, meat or vegetarian. **Known for:** gluten-free crêpe options; a

Set on an eponymous lake, Neuchâtel is a bustling city with a strong French influence.

vast tea selection; comic books and video games for guests. *Average main: 12 SF* ✉ *29 av. du 1er-Mars, Neuchâtel* ☎ *032/7256353* 🌐 *www.bachetbuck.ch* ⏲ *Closed Sun.*

$$ FRENCH Fodor's Choice ★

Le Bocca. Despite its proximity to the lake, there's neither a terrace nor a view at Le Bocca, and charming owner-chef Claude Frôté wants it that way: customers should come to this spot for his innovative food. Just north of Neuchâtel, the restaurant has an array of menus in its brasserie and main dining room. If you're a fan of organ meats such as tripe—long popular in Neuchâtel—you can eat for a lot less: Le Bocca's contemporary takes on these traditional dishes run you only 32 SF to 47 SF. **Known for:** massive wine cellar with over 25,000 bottles; organ meats served in creative fashion; fine dining in restaurant, casual atmosphere in brasserie. *Average main: 44 SF* ✉ *11 av. Bachelin, St-Blaise* ☎ *032/7533680* 🌐 *www.le-bocca.com* ⏲ *Closed Sun. and Mon.*

$$ FRENCH

Le Bureau. This smartly styled restaurant with a calm interior serves surprising gourmet creations, finding the balance between fine dining and trendy fare. Le Bureau—literally "The Office"—promotes a hybrid experience that goes beyond food; you can easily converse with other guests, some of whom are there for coworking over a coffee or meal. **Known for:** well-priced, midday three-course meals; savory terrine of foie gras with fresh, seasonal fruit; guests conversing with other guests, unlike in most Swiss restaurants. *Average main: 37 SF* ✉ *4 rue de l'Orangerie, Neuchâtel* ☎ *032/7244868* 🌐 *www.resteaubureau.ch* ⏲ *Closed Sun.*

$$ FRENCH

Le Cardinal Brasserie. Enjoy a perfect café crème or a whole meal along with the Neuchâtelois at one of the most authentic cafés in the Old Town. This place models itself on a traditional Parisian brasserie, and the striking art nouveau interior certainly helps: the molded ceiling, etched windows, and blue-and-green decorative tiles all date from 1905. **Known for:** excellent coffee; any of the fish specialties; reasonably priced menu of the day. *Average main: 35 SF* *9 rue du Seyon, Neuchâtel* *032/7251286* *www.lecardinal-brasserie.ch* *Closed Sun.*

WHERE TO STAY

$$$ HOTEL **Beau-Rivage Hotel.** This thoroughly elegant, gracefully restored 19th-century hotel has a perfect perch on the lakeshore; on a clear day there's a splendid view of the Alps. **Pros:** high standard of service and facilities rare in region; outstanding views; lakeside location. **Cons:** too corporate and lacking in character for some; fourth-floor rooms are darker and smaller than the rest; only two-thirds of rooms have a lake view. *Rooms from: 410 SF* *1 esplanade du Mont Blanc, Neuchâtel* *032/7231515* *www.beau-rivage-hotel.ch* *66 rooms* *No meals.*

$ HOTEL **Café-Hôtel de L'Aubier.** In the pedestrian zone at the foot of the château, this delightful, entirely environmentally friendly hotel offers light, modern, spacious guest rooms with warm color schemes inspired by the spices for which they are named. **Pros:** central location in pedestrian zone; bright, light, and modern atmosphere; organic fare on offer in the restaurant. **Cons:** sometimes noisy on weekends; not well suited to those traveling by car; limited terrace seating. *Rooms from: 180 SF* *1 rue du Château, Neuchâtel* *032/7101858* *www.aubier.ch* *9 rooms, 3 with bath* *No meals.*

$ HOTEL **Hotel Alpes et Lac.** This modest 19th-century hotel across from the train station overlooks the tile rooftops, sparkling lake, and white-capped Alps. **Pros:** welcoming staff helps you with your French; just steps from the station; cheerful red-and-gold decor in the rooms. **Cons:** some rooms are on the small side; rooms facing the station can be noisy; unpleasant smells from the nearby McDonald's can be a problem. *Rooms from: 180 SF* *2 pl. de la Gare, Neuchâtel* *032/7231919* *www.alpesetlac.ch* *30 rooms* *Breakfast.*

$$$$ HOTEL Fodor's Choice ★ **Hôtel Palafitte.** Unique in Europe, this one-level hotel is partly built on piles on Lac de Neuchâtel, giving it unbeatable clear-day views that include the distant Alps. **Pros:** some rooms have ladders so you can descend directly into the lake for a swim; golf-cart-style vehicle shuttles guests to rooms; unique structure with loads of character. **Cons:** despite air-conditioning, strong sun may heat your room up; some glitches in maintenance; breakfast is expensive. *Rooms from: 560 SF* *2 rte. des Gouttes d'Or, Monruz* *032/7230202* *www.palafitte.ch* *40 suites* *No meals.*

$ B&B/INN **Hotel-Restaurant La Maison du Prussien.** In the gorge of Vauseyon, 10 minutes from Neuchâtel, this restored 18th-century brewery sits alongside a roaring woodland stream. **Pros:** traditional old-world charm; a romantic, countryside vibe prevails; restaurant rated one of the top in the region. **Cons:** no elevator. *Rooms from: 175 SF* *Au Gor du Vauseyon, 11 rue des Tunnels, Neuchâtel* *032/7305454* *www.hotel-prussien.ch* *10 rooms* *Breakfast.*

Lac de Neuchâtel is the largest lake entirely within Switzerland's borders.

NIGHTLIFE

Neuchâtel has an ever-changing selection of restaurants *de nuit* and *bars musicaux,* establishments that pulse with hot sounds until the wee hours of the morning and sometimes serve food—along the lines of steak frites—to keep you going.

Casino Neuchâtel. The small casino has 150 slot machines as well as favorite table games like roulette, blackjack, and Ultimate Texas Hold'em Poker. ✉ *14 faubourg du Lac, Neuchâtel* ☎ *032/7244848* 🌐 *www.casino-neuchatel.ch.*

Chauffage Compris. This simple, cozy wine bar is proud to offer dozens of Swiss wines from the region and beyond, as well as a few European vintages. ✉ *37 rue des Moulins, Neuchâtel* ☎ *032/7214396* 🌐 *www.chauffagecompris.ch.*

SPORTS AND THE OUTDOORS

The largest lake entirely within Switzerland, Lac de Neuchâtel has a variety of water sports, beaches, and boat excursions to quaint lakeside villages. La Grande Cariçaie, a marshy nature preserve spanning 40 km (25 miles) on the southern shore, is a bird-watcher's paradise.

LAKE CRUISES

FAMILY **Navigation Lacs de Neuchâtel et Morat.** Boats ply the lakes year-round, but choices are more plentiful in the warm season. Take a four-hour cruise of the Three Lakes Region, spanning Neuchâtel, Morat, and Biel, or bring a bike and hop between cycling routes, beaches, and historic sites. ☎ *026/3501111* 🌐 *www.navig.ch.*

GRANDSON

29 km (18 miles) southwest of Neuchâtel.

A tour of the Old Town of Grandson is eminently worthwhile. The church, tower, fountains, and narrow streets lined with extraordinary facades make this a truly time-burnished spot. For guided strolls, stop in at the tourist office in the Maison des Terroirs (open daily 11–6). This lakeside village in Canton Vaud has a long history. It is said that in 1066 a member of the Grandson family accompanied William of Normandy (better known as William the Conqueror) to England, where he founded the English barony of Grandson. Otto I of Grandson took part in the Crusades.

GETTING HERE AND AROUND

Trains from Yverdon-les-Bains to Grandson take less than 5 minutes; buses from the station take 20. From Neuchâtel to Grandson the trip is approximately 30 minutes by train, with a change in Yverdon-les-Bains.

EXPLORING

FAMILY
Fodor's Choice
★

Château de Grandson (*Grandson Castle*). When the Burgundian Wars broke out in the late 15th century, the Château de Grandson, built in the 11th century and much rebuilt during the 13th and 15th centuries, was in the hands of Charles the Bold of Burgundy. In 1475 the Swiss won it by siege, but early the next year their garrison was surprised by Charles, and 418 of their men were captured and hanged from the apple trees in the castle orchard. A few days later the Swiss returned to Grandson and, after crushing the Burgundians, retaliated by stringing up their prisoners from the same apple trees. After being used for three centuries as a residence by the Bernese bailiffs, the castle was bought in 1875 by the de Blonay family, who restored it to its current impressive state, with high, massive walls and five cone turrets. Inside, you can see reproductions of Charles the Bold's Burgundian war tent and two jousting knights astride their horses—in full armor. There are also oubliettes (dungeon pits), torture chambers, and a model of the Battle of Grandson, complete with a 20-minute slide show (in English if you get in quickly enough to push the right button). The dungeons now house an extensive vintage-car museum, displaying the prized beauties of Greta Garbo and Winston Churchill. ✉ *Pl. du Château, Grandson* ☎ *024/4452926* 🌐 *www.chateau-grandson.ch* 🎫 *12 SF.*

YVERDON-LES-BAINS

6 km (4 miles) southwest of Grandson, 38 km (24 miles) southwest of Neuchâtel.

With a center closed to traffic, Yverdon-les-Bains is a charming, bustling place. Located at the southernmost tip of Lac de Neuchâtel, this pastel-colored lakefront town has been appreciated for its thermal waters and sandy, willow-lined shore since the Romans first invaded and set up thermal baths here. In the 18th century its fame spread across Europe. Today, along the waterfront are parks, promenades, a shady campground, and a 2-km (1¼-mile) stretch of little beaches.

8

GETTING HERE AND AROUND

Trains from Fribourg to Yverdon-les-Bains take 54 minutes; from Neuchâtel to Yverdon-les-Bains the trip is 18 minutes.

VISITOR INFORMATION

Contacts Yverdon-les-Bains Tourisme. ✉ *2 av. de la Gare, Yverdon-les-Bains* ☎ *024/4236101* 🌐 *www.yverdonlesbainsregion.ch.*

EXPLORING

Château de Yverdon-les-Bains. In the center of the Old Town sits the turreted, mid-13th-century Château de Yverdon-les-Bains. Most of the castle is now a museum, with exhibits on locally discovered prehistoric and Roman artifacts, Egyptian art, natural history, and, of course, local history. A special room is dedicated to the famous Swiss educator Johann Heinrich Pestalozzi (1746–1827), who spent 20 years here. His influential ideas on education led to school reforms at home and in Germany and England. ✉ *1 pl. Pestalozzi, Yverdon-les-Bains* ☎ *024/4259310* 🌐 *www.musee-yverdon-region.ch* 🎟 *10 SF* ⏲ *Closed Mon.*

Hôtel de Ville (*Town Hall*). In front of Yverdon's Hôtel de Ville—an 18th-century building notable for its French-inspired neoclassical facade—stands a bronze statue of Swiss educator Johann Heinrich Pestalozzi, grouped with two children. ✉ *1 pl. Pestalozzi, Yverdon-les-Bains.*

Maison d'Ailleurs. Although Yverdon has a lot of history, it also has a special place in its heart for the future, thanks to this fanciful "museum of science fiction, utopia, and extraordinary journeys." Although mainly a research center and library for scholars, the House of Elsewhere mounts fascinating exhibitions for the general public, including such recent shows as the ones devoted to the popular Return to Dinotopia books and H. P. Lovecraft. ✉ *14 pl. Pestalozzi, Yverdon-les-Bains* ☎ *024/4256438* 🌐 *www.ailleurs.ch* 🎟 *12 SF* ⏲ *Closed Mon.*

Thermal Center. The municipal Thermal Center is completely up-to-date, with indoor and outdoor pools, whirlpools, and massage jets, as well as numerous massage, beauty, and relaxation treatments. Swim caps are mandatory, and children under three are not permitted. ✉ *22 av. des Bains, Yverdon-les-Bains* ☎ *024/4230232* 🌐 *www.bainsyverdon.ch* 🎟 *19 SF.*

9

BERN

WELCOME TO BERN

TOP REASONS TO GO

★ **Lived-in history:** UNESCO made Bern a World Heritage Site in 1983, but the city's cobblestone arcades and clock towers have been beautifully preserved since the 1400s.

★ **Feats of Klee:** The spectacular Zentrum named for Paul Klee—the prolific painter who hopscotched across art—is a tour de force of vibrant creativity.

★ **Undercover shopping:** Bern's got it all—from couture fashion to artisan chocolatiers—and, thanks to those famous arcaded streets, you can even enjoy window-shopping in rainy weather.

★ **The Zibelemärit:** Think of an object—a train car, an alarm clock, a teddy bear—and you will likely see it rendered in onions at November's citywide celebration of the vegetable.

★ **Those sunbathing Swiss:** Warm summer days lure swimmers to the Marzili's sweeping lawns and swift stretch of river below the Federal Parliament Building.

Few capital cities are as charming and compact as Bern, Switzerland's political nerve center. Alluring medieval streets, frolicsome fountains, and palpable history coexist so easily with outdoor markets and traditional cheese-and-potatoes that it's easy to forget this is actually a fully wired, surprisingly young, 21st-century urban center.

1 Altstadt (Old Town) and City Center. Today the historic Rathaus, Münster, painted fountains, and 18th-century guildhalls rub shoulders with arcades and cellars full of restaurants and quirky boutiques. The swath of land between the Zytglogge and the Hauptbahnhof is Bern's most commercially vibrant, a dense warren of narrow streets and pedestrian passageways studded with stores, hidden alleys, grand architecture, and the Swiss Federal Government complex.

2 Bärengraben and Rosengarten. The eastern end of Bern's Old Town houses the BearPark on the slopes of the River Aare. Up the hill is the Rose Garden, with an impressive collection of flora and stunning views over the city.

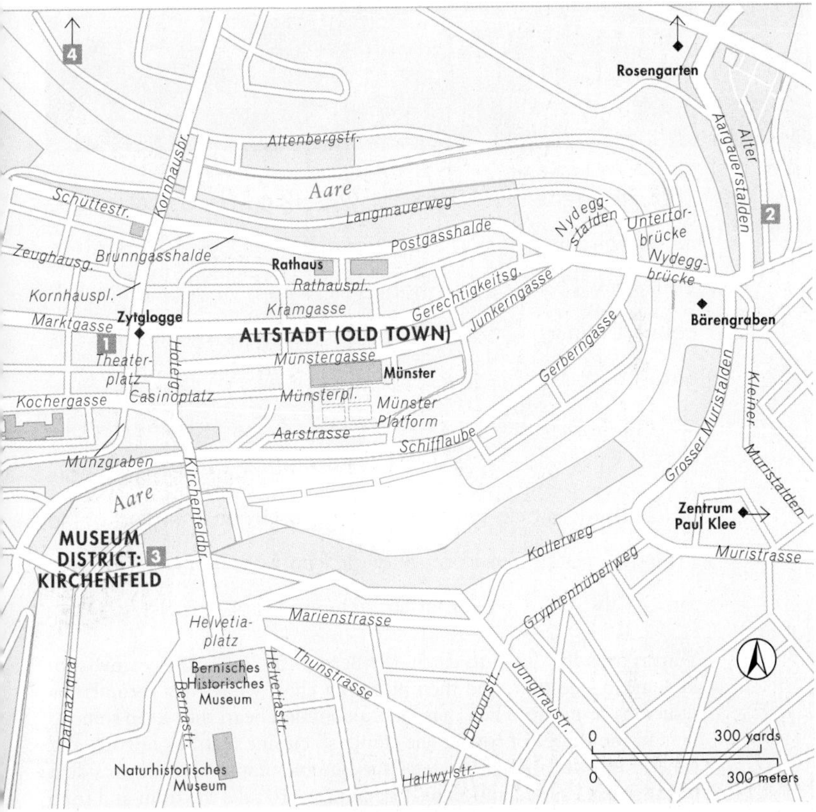

Rosengarten
Altenbergstr.
Aare
Schüttestr.
Kornhausbr.
Langmauerweg
Postgasshalde
Nydegg-stalden
Untertor-brücke
Nydegg-brücke
Alter Aargauerstalden
2
4
Zeughausg.
Brunngasshalde
Rathaus
Rathauspl.
Kornhauspl.
Kramgasse
Gerechtigkeitsg.
Junkerngasse
Marktgasse
Zytglogge
ALTSTADT (OLD TOWN)
Bärengraben
1
Theater-platz
Hotelg.
Münstergasse
Münster
Gerberngasse
Kochergasse
Casinoplatz
Münsterpl.
Münster Platform
Grosser Muristalden
Kleiner Muristalden
Aarstrasse
Schifflaube
Münzgraben
Kirchenfeldbr.
Aare
Zentrum Paul Klee
MUSEUM DISTRICT: 3 KIRCHENFELD
Kollerweg
Muristrasse
Gryphenhübeliweg
Helvetia-platz
Marienstrasse
Bernisches Historisches Museum
Thunstrasse
Jungfraustr.
Dalmaziquai
Bernastr.
Helvetiastr.
Dufourstr.
Naturhistorisches Museum
Hallwylstr.
0 300 yards
0 300 meters

3 Museum District: Kirchenfeld. The Kirchenfeld neighborhood is a masterpiece of late-19th-century urban planning, where a top array of Bern's museums is grouped together in a tight, easy-to-visit cluster on the south bank of the River Aare.

4 Greater Bern. Just north of the center are neighborhoods that stray from the medieval feel of the Old Town. Be it modern, funky, or artistic, each is charming in its own way. The Paul Klee Center, an easy bus ride away, is in the eastern suburbs and well worth the detour.

Updated by
Susan Misicka

Bern, the federal capital of Switzerland, is a picturesque medieval city whose creators had a keen eye for detail—a trait shared by today's inhabitants, who lovingly maintain its colorful fountains, frescoes, and window boxes. Turn a corner and you might gasp at stunning views of the River Aare down below or the Alps in the distance. For indoor entertainment, check out one of the excellent museums or quirky boutiques. Bern is also full of food begging to be sampled at the farmers' market, in traditional or trendy restaurants, and in the candy stores with their seductive window displays.

Warm, friendly, down-to-earth, the Bernese are notoriously slow-spoken; ask a question, and then pull up a chair while they formulate a judicious response. Their mascot is a common bear; they keep some as pets in the center of town. The standard cuisine features fatback and sauerkraut, the annual fair fetes the humble onion, and the president of the Swiss Confederation has been known to take the train and tram to work. Walking down broad medieval streets past squares crowded with markets and cafés full of shirt-sleeved politicos, you might forget that Bern is the geographic and political hub of a sophisticated, modern, and prosperous nation.

In fact, at first glance you might take the city (Berne in French) for a thriving country town rather than a major European capital. Arriving in the city center, either by car or by train, most visitors see only its Old Town and miss altogether the modern sprawl of banking and industry that surrounds it. Although Bern is full of patrician houses and palatial hotels, there is no official presidential residence: the seven members of the coalition government, each of whom serves a year as president, have to find their own places to live when in Bern.

Bern wasn't always so self-effacing. It earned its pivotal position through a history of power and influence that dates from the 12th century, when

Berchtold V, Duke of Zähringen, expanded his fortress at the tip of a sharp meander in the River Aare. He named his new city for the first animal he killed in the local woods (an unlucky but now immortalized brown bear). Over the years Bern stayed on top, and when the Swiss Confederation took its contemporary, federal form in 1848, Bern was a natural choice for its capital.

Yet today it's not the massive Bundeshaus (Federal Parliament Building) that dominates the city, but instead its perfectly preserved arcades, fountains, and thick, sturdy towers—all remnants of its heyday as a medieval power. Bern owes its architectural unity to a major fire that swept through town in 1405, destroying most of the houses, then mainly of wood. It was rebuilt in sandstone, and its arcades stretch on for some 6 km (4 miles). They're the reason UNESCO granted Bern World Landmark status.

BERN PLANNER

WHEN TO GO

Architecture can be a big tip-off: covered stone arcades, dark underground cellars, small windows, and thick stone walls were all medieval coping tactics in the face of bad weather. Bern can be cold and wet and miserable in winter, its indoor spaces warmed with fires and packed with people.

But it is mild and sunny from spring through autumn, when every restaurant that can sets up camp in the street, windows are thrown open, and people take to the river by the Marzili with unrestrained glee. Summer is warm, and July through mid-August is vacation season. Note that many restaurants close up shop for a few weeks during the summer season.

PLANNING YOUR TIME

The Bernese do not scurry around their city, and neither should you—its considerable charms are best discovered at a slow, steady pace with a plan to get from A to B but no fixed idea how. The most efficient, flexible, cheap, and enjoyable way to navigate Bern's cobblestones is on foot. The city is easy to navigate: count on 15 minutes to walk at a steady clip from the Hauptbahnhof to the Bärenpark; about 5 to take the bus.

It is technically possible to see the major sights in a day, but you'd miss watching the sun set over medieval rooftops, you wouldn't be able to linger in restaurants—and this is a city that comes out at night. Do pace yourself as you wander the streets, do take the time to get the most out of your museum admission fees, and do get a running start on the narrow curved steps up the Münster steeple. Indulge any urges to explore Marzili or Matte, to pursue your curiosity at the markets, to take a sudden chocolate break, to watch the bears, or to admire the fountains—although it is indeed strange to find the latter sitting in the middle of main-street traffic.

GETTING HERE AND AROUND

AIR TRAVEL

Bern Airport is 10 km (6 miles) from the city center. A shuttle-bus ride to the Hauptbahnhof takes 30 minutes and costs 10 SF; reservations are required at *www.busdriver-bern.ch* or *076/3251961*. Costing about 6 SF, another option is go via train and bus, which takes about the same amount of time. A taxi to the Hauptbahnhof costs about 50 SF.

CAR TRAVEL

Bern sits squarely on the map of Swiss expressways. The A1 connects the city with Basel and Zürich to the north, with Lac Léman and Geneva to the south, and via Lausanne with the Valais. The A6 to the Berner Oberland runs just east of the city. Downtown pedestrian-only zones make parking in city garages a virtual necessity; electric signs on major incoming roads post current numbers of available spaces.

BUS AND TRAM TRAVEL

Trams and buses are handy for getting outside the Altstadt. Service by Bernmobil is extensive, with city center fares costing between 2 SF and 5 SF. An unlimited day ticket is about 13 SF. Buy tickets from the dispensers, located at every stop, by finding the name of the stop closest to your destination on the map, then selecting the fare listed for it. Hotel guests receive a free Bern Ticket for transportation, which covers the city as well as Bern Airport and Gurten's funicular. Swiss Pass holders also travel free.

Contacts Bernmobil. *031/3218844* *www.bernmobil.ch.*

TAXI TRAVEL

Bernese taxis are clean and plentiful, but circuitous downtown traffic routing renders them cumbersome and expensive; a ride from the Hauptbahnhof to the Bärengraben costs about 20 SF.

Contacts Bären Taxi. *031/3711111* *www.baerentaxi.ch.* **Nova Taxi.** *031/3313313* *www.novataxi.ch.*

TRAIN TRAVEL

Bern is a train-based city with high-speed connections to Berlin, Paris, and Milan. Bern's Hauptbahnhof is also a major hub for trains within Switzerland. Count on an hour to reach Zürich or Basel, less than two for Geneva, and four hours to Lugano. A tight network of local and regional trains keeps Bern connected to surrounding communities.

VISITOR INFORMATION

Bern Tourismus, based in the Hauptbahnhof, distributes free brochures and maps, publishes *Bern Guide*, and operates a 3-D multimedia history presentation called *BernShow* at its satellite information center next to the Bärengraben.

Its guides also lead 90-minute English-language walking tours of the Altstadt at 11 am daily between April and October, and on Saturday the rest of the year. Upon request they also organize group tours conducted by bus or down the Aare in rafts. Reserve at the tourist center in the Hauptbahnhof.

Contacts Bern Tourismus. *Hauptbahnhof, Bahnhofpl. 10a, City Center* *031/3281212* *www.bern.com.*

The best way to explore Bern is to take your time meandering through the city's markets and arcades.

EXPLORING

From the time it was built on a high, narrow peninsula above the rushing Aare, Bern's streets have followed the river's flow. The original town began by what is now the Nydegg Bridge—it controlled the ferry crossing there—and spread westward, uphill to the *Zeitglockenturm* (known locally as the *Zytglogge*), a clock tower constructed in 1191 to mark Bern's first significant western gate. Further expansion in 1256 stretched the city to where the Käfigturm now stands; one last medieval growth spurt, hot on the heels of a resounding victory over the Burgundians in 1339, moved the city walls west yet again to the present-day train station, the Hauptbahnhof.

The bustling, commercial city center radiates out from that train station. To get to the Altstadt, follow the trams across Bärenplatz and through the Käfigturm. Marzili and Matte, former working-class and still flood-prone neighborhoods, lie together along the riverbed of the Aare. All these areas are easily explored on foot, but in Marzili and Matte you may want to take your cue from the locals: walk down, ride the funicular up. The cluster of museums in Kirchenfeld, on the south side of the river, is a short (spectacular) walk or tram ride away.

ALTSTADT (OLD TOWN) AND CITY CENTER

Fire destroyed the original, predominantly wooden structures that composed the Altstadt, the historical heart of the city that perches above the Aare. The Bernese rebuilt using local sandstone, and today's arcaded, cobblestone streets radiate medieval appeal. Eclectic upscale boutiques

A GOOD WALK

Bern's downtown is not large, but it can be steep, and there's a lot to absorb. To begin the walk, exit the main hall of the Hauptbahnhof, following signs for the Altstadt.

On the far side of Spitalgasse is the **Heiliggeistkirche.** Duck inside for a peek at its colorful baroque ceiling, then follow the trams left past the cheerful Pfeiferbrunnen (Bagpiper Fountain) to the first intersection, Bärenplatz.

Keep following the trams (carefully) through the **Käfigturm,** a 17th-century prison tower built on the site of the city's 13th-century main gate, and continue down Marktgasse. At the end, follow the trams to the left to the Kindlifresser-brunnen, atop which an ogre (most likely a Fasnacht character) sits munching on several small children.

Dominating the town center is the mighty **Zytglogge,** Bern's original western gate and communal horological reference point since 1530. Continue down Kramgasse, the medieval main street. The painted figures and insignia above some houses indicate their connections to specific guilds; others date from the city's 18th-century height of prosperity.

At No. 49, the **Einsteinhaus** is where a young man named Albert struggled to make his name in physics. Take nearby Kramgasse (called Gerechtigkeitsgasse from this point on) and continue down the hill. The Gerechtigkeitsbrunnen (Justice Fountain), considered the jewel of Bern's fountains, depicts the emperor, the pope, the sultan, and the mayor of Bern.

As you pass the Hotel zum Goldenen Adler, the 18th-century successor to the city's oldest guesthouse, veer left where the main street becomes Nydeggasse and aim downhill into Nydeggstalden.

The **Nydeggkirche,** set back from the road on your right, occupies the site of Duke Berchtold's original fortress and thus represents the oldest part of the city.

From the church courtyard, head for the far end of the church and take the covered Burgtreppe stairs down to Mattenenge, turning left then right when you get to the bottom.

You will be facing Bern's oldest river crossing, the Untertorbrücke, or Lower Gate Bridge, with the Läuferb-runnen (Messenger Fountain) and its bear-human duo sheltering under a tree to your left.

Cross the swift, blue-green Aare and head left past the Landhaus to the paved footpath marked "Rosengarten" and zigzag to the right on Lerberstrasse. When you reach Aargauerstalden, you will be rewarded with a fetching view of the Altstadt. From here, head back down the hill to the traffic circle and cut directly across it to the **BearPark.**

Walk straight through the carefully tended **Rosengarten** to see the best view of all—the city's bridges, rooftops, and the tree-covered **Gurten**, Bern's local hill.

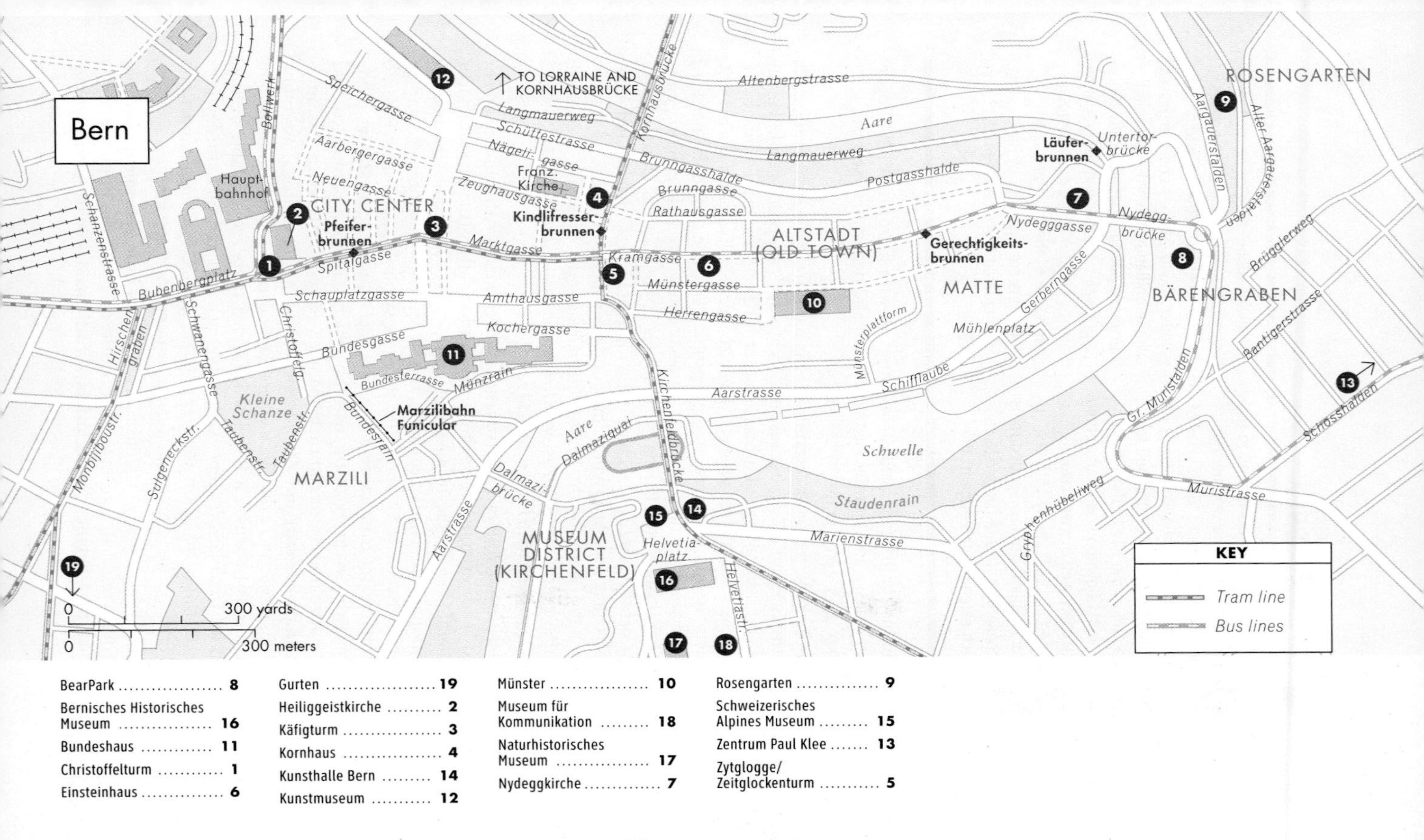

BearPark 8
Bernisches Historisches Museum 16
Bundeshaus 11
Christoffelturm 1
Einsteinhaus 6
Gurten 19
Heiliggeistkirche 2
Käfigturm 3
Kornhaus 4
Kunsthalle Bern 14
Kunstmuseum 12
Münster 10
Museum für Kommunikation 18
Naturhistorisches Museum 17
Nydeggkirche 7
Rosengarten 9
Schweizerisches Alpines Museum 15
Zentrum Paul Klee 13
Zytglogge/Zeitglockenturm 5

CLOSE UP

Bern's Arcades

As Albert Einstein discovered to his delight in 1902, the weather has been bested in Bern. "Both sides of the road are completely lined by old arcades so that one can stroll from one end of the city to the other in the worst downpour without getting noticeably wet," he wrote to his fiancée in 1902. Sturdy 15th-century pillars support the low vaulted roofs of these picturesque *Lauben* (arcades), which extend to the edge of the sidewalk along miles of Altstadt streets. Steeply angled cellar doors at street level lead down to additional underground eateries and businesses, while brilliantly colored and carved *Brunnen* (fountains), historically the city's water sources and congregation points, punctuate the main thoroughfares. Ten of the most prominent fountains are the work of Hans Gieng, who created them between 1542 and 1549.

inhabit some of the oldest buildings downhill from the Zytglogge; Marktgasse and Spitalgasse favor chain and department stores.

TOP ATTRACTIONS

FAMILY Fodor's Choice ★ **BearPark.** Bern almost certainly gets its name from the local contraction of the German *Bären,* because of Berchtold V's supposed first kill in the area, and the image of a bear is never far away, from the official coat of arms to chocolate morsels. The city has kept live bears since 1513, when victorious Bernese soldiers brought one back from the Battle of Novara and installed it in a hut on what is now Bärenplatz. Björk, Finn, and their daughter, Ursina, seem to feel at home in this closed-in area just off the Aare River, complete with quasi forest, shrubs, and cave, where they can play, swim, climb, and sleep all day. Photos and plaques in English describe the bears and their lifestyle. The park is open all hours, every day. ✉ *Grosser Muristalden 6, Altstadt* ☎ *031/3571515* 🌐 *www.baerenpark-bern.ch* 🎫 *Free.*

Bundeshaus (*Houses of Parliament*). Conceived as a national monument and the beating heart of the Swiss Confederation (the seven-member Federal Council, the 46-member Council of States, and the 200-member National Council all meet here), this massive, majestic domed complex built between 1852 and 1902 takes its symbolism seriously. The 26 fountains out front represent the Swiss cantons; solemn statues inside depict the swearing of the oath on which the union is founded; and two huge murals, one in each chamber, represent the Vierwaldstättersee (Lake Luzern) and a Landsgemeinde (outdoor cantonal assembly) scene, respectively the place where Swiss democracy was founded and the means by which it flourished. Guided tours are available in English on weekdays (except Wednesday) at 2 pm and on Saturday at 4 pm. ✉ *Bundespl. 3, City Center* ☎ *058/3229022* 🌐 *www.parlament.ch* 🎫 *Free* ⏲ *Closed Sun. and during parliamentary sessions.*

Einsteinhaus (*Einstein's House*). This genteel little apartment has been lovingly re-created to evoke the world of 1905, the miracle year in which then-tenant Albert Einstein, a badly paid, newly married young

Carved figures of angels stand above the main door of the Bern Münster.

clerk in Bern's Patent Office, developed and published his *Special Theory of Relativity.* All signage is in German and English. Downstairs, the **Einstein café** with its separate smokers' lounge serves drinks, lunch, and snacks. ✉ *Kramg. 49, Altstadt* ☎ *031/3120091* 🌐 *www.einstein-bern.ch* 🎫 *6 SF* ⏲ *Closed Jan.*

Heiliggeistkirche (*Church of the Holy Ghost*). Built in the shadow of the huge Christoffelturm on the site of a disused monastery hospital, this baroque church, laid out like a Huguenot temple, turned out to be a survivor as town walls, houses, gates, and fountains crashed down around it to create today's busy transportation hub. Serenity does still reign within, where natural light floods the green sandstone supporting a magnificent vaulted stucco ceiling. ✉ *Spitalg. 44, City Center* ☎ *031/3701552* 🌐 *www.heiliggeistkirche.ch* 🎫 *Free* ⏲ *Closed Mon. and Sat.*

Fodor's Choice ★

Kunstmuseum (*Museum of Fine Arts*). The permanent collection here, one of the largest and most diverse in Switzerland, begins with the Italian Trecento (notably Duccio and Fra Angelico), then follows Swiss art from Niklaus Manuel in the 15th century through Albert Anker and Ferdinand Hodler in the 19th and on to Giovanni Giacometti and Cuno Amiet in the 20th. The impressionists are covered, from Manet through Monet; the Nabis, by Bonnard. Picasso bridges the gap between Toulouse-Lautrec and Braque; Kirchner, Kandinsky, and Klee represent German expressionism through Blue Rider to Bauhaus. Mondrian and Meret Oppenheim round out the 20th century. Temporary exhibits often take it from there. ✉ *Hodlerstr. 8–12, City Center* ☎ *031/3280944* 🌐 *www.kunstmuseum-bern.ch* 🎫 *10 SF (permanent collection only)* ⏲ *Closed Mon.*

Fodor's Choice ★ **Münster** (*Cathedral*). Master builder Matthäus Ensinger already had Strasbourg's cathedral under his belt when he drew up plans for what became the largest and most artistically important church in Switzerland. The city broke ground in 1421 on the site of a smaller church that was dismantled once the cathedral's choir could accommodate Sunday worshippers, and work continued, with minor interruptions, for about 180 years. The finishing touch, the tip of the open, octagonal, 328-foot **steeple,** was added almost 200 years after that, in 1893. Today Switzerland's highest church tower houses a tower keeper (in an apartment below the spire) and presents wraparound views of Bern and the surrounding mountains.

The Reformers dismantled much of the Catholic Münster's interior decoration and paintings (dumping them in the Münsterplattform, next door), but the exterior 15th-century representation of the Last Judgment above the **main portal** was deemed worthy and spared. The archangel Michael stands between ivory-skinned angels with gilt hair (heaven) on the left and green demons with gaping red maws (hell) on the right; painted images of the Annunciation and the Fall of Man flank the carved figures as you pass through the doors. Elaborately carved pews and choir stalls within are crowned by 15th-century **stained-glass** windows that show an easy mix of local heraldry and Christian iconography. The organ, above the main entrance, is often used for concerts. ✉ *Münsterpl. 1, Altstadt* ☎ *031/3120462* 🌐 *www.bernermuenster.ch* 🎫 *Steeple 5 SF.*

QUICK BITES

Restaurant Rosengarten. This restaurant serves light snacks and sandwiches as well as hearty Mediterranean dishes and Swiss classics like fondue against a backdrop of panoramic Altstadt views. Known for: cheese fondue on the veranda in winter; freshly squeezed orange juice; beef tartare with local bakery bread. ✉ ***Alter Aargauerstalden 31b, Altstadt*** ☎ ***031/3313206*** 🌐 ***www.rosengarten.be.***

FAMILY **Rosengarten** (*Rose Garden*). The lower Altstadt's hilltop cemetery was converted into a public park in 1913, and today, its lawns, arbors, playground, and formal gardens draw leisurely couples and families with young children. The gardens are planted with azaleas, irises, rhododendron, and rose varieties such as Ingrid Bergman (deep velvet red), Maria Callas (bright magenta), Christopher Columbus (peach), Cleopatra (red tips, orange interior), and Lady Di (small and pink). ✉ *Alter Aargauerstalden and Laubeggstr., Altstadt* ☎ *031/3281212* 🎫 *Free.*

Zytglogge/Zeitglockenturm (*Clock Tower*). Though its exterior dates from 1771, the internal walls of Bern's first western gate reach back to the 12th century and represent the city's core. The calendar clock on the Kramgasse side began keeping Bern's official time in 1530; the gilded rooster to the left of the mechanical figures crows four minutes before every hour to begin the sequence of marching bears, fools, and gilded knights who strike the bells. The astronomical clock to the rooster's right keeps track of the day, the month, the zodiac, and the moon. Tours of the horological masterpiece behind it all are conducted in English, German, and French. ✉ *Kramg. at Hotelg., Altstadt* ☎ *031/3281212* 🌐 *www.zeitglockenturm.ch* 🎫 *Tour 15 SF* ☞ *Reservations recommended (essential Nov.–Mar.).*

WORTH NOTING

Christoffelturm (*Christoffel Tower*). The 14th-century maps, 19th-century photographs, and St. Christopher's huge limewood head give context to the thick stone foundations of Bern's third city gate. The tower was built between 1344 and 1366 and destroyed in 1865 after a tight vote in favor of the train station. Its ruins have been incorporated into the underground shopping mall of the train station. ✉ *Christoffel-unterführung, City Center.*

Käfigturm (*Prison Tower*). This tower, completed in 1643, served as the city's prison until 1897. Reconfigured as the Confederation's Political Forum in 1999, it now hosts political events and exhibitions. ✉ *Marktg. 67, City Center* ☎ *058/4627500* 🌐 *www.kaefigturm.ch* 🎫 *Free* 🕓 *Closed Sun. and public holidays.*

Kornhaus (*Granary*). Wine stocked the cellar and grain filled the top three floors of this granary for 100 years during Bern's golden age. Then the 1814 Vienna Congress separated the city from its territories, and this monumental baroque storage depot lost its function overnight. The cellar was renovated in 1893 and painted four years later; today it houses a restaurant and bar. The **Kornhausforum** (Media and Design Center) upstairs organizes contemporary design, architecture, video, photography, and applied art exhibits. ✉ *Kornhauspl. 18, Altstadt* ☎ *031/3129110* 🌐 *www.kornhausforum.ch* 🎫 *Free; occasional charge for special events* 🕓 *Closed Sun. and Mon.*

QUICK BITES

Kornhaus Café. Outdoor tables, a sunny central location, light meals, homemade pastries, several kinds of coffee, and open doors from 8 am (9 am on Sunday) until midnight give the Kornhaus Café a constant, market-like buzz. Known for: vast hot beverage menu; evening drinks; convenient location. ✉ ***Kornhauspl. 18, Altstadt*** ☎ ***031/3277270*** 🌐 ***www.bindella.ch/de/kornhauscafe.html.***

Nydeggkirche (*Nydegg Church*). A plaque on the outside wall of the church indicates where vestiges of Duke Berchtold's 12th-century Nydegg Castle (destroyed about 1270) still poke through the landscape; the church itself was begun in 1341, and its wooden pulpit dates from 1566. ✉ *Nydeggstalden 9, Altstadt* ☎ *031/3520443* 🌐 *www.nydegg.ch.*

9

MUSEUM DISTRICT: KIRCHENFELD

Kirchenfeld is a quiet, leafy neighborhood due south of the Altstadt, with radial streets and unexpected vistas. It was constructed in 1881 according to a district plan and quickly filled with embassies, consulates, and the bulk of Bern's museums.

TOP ATTRACTIONS

Bernisches Historisches Museum (*Bern History Museum*). Indonesian shadow puppets, Japanese swords, Polynesian masks, Indian figurines, and Celtic jewelry fill the ground floor, and the Islamic collection is exquisite, but head to the basement for the real focus: Bern and its place in Swiss history. Armor and arms, lavish church treasure (including sculptures from the Münster), magnificent silver, tapestries "acquired"

DID YOU KNOW?

The Zähringer Fountain, in front of Bern's Clock Tower, portrays an armored bear. The Duke of Zähringen established Bern in the 12th century, naming the city after a bear he killed in the forest nearby. Bern's association with the animal is evident today in the statues, flags, and live bears that live in the city's BearPark.

in 1476–77 when the Bernese pushed Charles the Bold back into France, and several of Hans Gieng's original fountain statues lead the charge. The second floor is devoted to Einstein. Major signage is in English, and there are audio guides in nine languages. ✉ *Helvetiapl. 5, Kirchenfeld* ☎ *031/3507711* 🌐 *www.bhm.ch* 🎫 *13 SF* 🕓 *Closed Mon.*

FAMILY Fodor's Choice ★ **Museum für Kommunikation** (*Museum of Communication*). This resolutely interactive museum keeps its focus on the act of communication rather than the means. Exhibits examine body language across cultures, the views of Switzerland's minority populations, the history of the Swiss postal service, and the evolution of telecommunication through to the Internet. One of the world's largest collections of postage stamps is also here. All signage is in English. ✉ *Helvetiastr. 16, Kirchenfeld* ☎ *031/3575555* 🌐 *www.mfk.ch* 🎫 *15 SF* 🕓 *Closed Mon.*

FAMILY **Naturhistorisches Museum** (*Museum of Natural History*). The biggest draw here is the stuffed body of Barry, a St. Bernard who saved more than 40 people in the Alps between 1800 and 1812. But start with the Alpine minerals, diamonds, and fossils in the basement, working up to wild animals in the city. Birds' nests, skeletons large and small, interactive temporary exhibits, and more than 200 wildlife dioramas round out the highlights. Basic signage is in English. ✉ *Bernastr. 15, Kirchenfeld* ☎ *031/3507111* 🌐 *www.nmbe.ch* 🎫 *8 SF* 🕓 *Closed Mon. (am only).*

WORTH NOTING

Kunsthalle Bern (*Bern Art Gallery*). A completely different animal from the Kunstmuseum across town, this groundbreaking contemporary art venue built in 1918 by and for artists (among them Ernst Ludwig Kirchner, Paul Klee, and Alberto Giacometti) seeks to confront, provoke, and engage viewers with the artistic phenomena of today. This translates each year to several exhibits of work by living artists; they become part of a history that includes Wassily Kandinsky, Henry Moore, Jasper Johns, Sol LeWitt, Bruce Nauman, Christo, and Grandma Moses. ✉ *Helvetiapl. 1, Kirchenfeld* ☎ *031/3500040* 🌐 *www.kunsthalle-bern.ch* 🎫 *8 SF* 🕓 *Closed Mon.*

Schweizerisches Alpines Museum (*Swiss Alpine Museum*). This is the place for an in-depth look at the world of mountaineering and its passionate participants and followers. Regularly changing exhibitions focus on topics like climbers in the Himalayas and their media presence, surveying techniques in the Andes, and humble but nourishing Alpine cuisine. All signage is in English. ✉ *Helvetiapl. 4, Kirchenfeld* ☎ *031/3500440* 🌐 *www.alpinesmuseum.ch* 🎫 *16 SF* 🕓 *Closed Mon.*

GREATER BERN

Just north of the center are neighborhoods that stray from the medieval feel of the Old Town, be it modern, quirky, or artistic, and each is charming in its own way. The Paul Klee Center, an easy bus ride away, is in the eastern suburbs and well worth the detour.

CLOSE UP

Paul Klee: Bern's Artistic Son

It's ironic that expressionist painter Paul Klee (1879–1940), one of Switzerland's most prolific and talented artists, wasn't a Swiss citizen during his life. Though he was born near Bern and spent most of his life in the country, his nationality was determined by the lineage of his father, who was German.

Born into a family of musicians, Klee filled his schoolbooks with caricatures and images copied from magazines. At age 19 he left Bern to study drawing in Munich, but he couldn't support himself with his art and returned to his parents in 1902. Four years later he had saved enough from his work as a violinist with the Bern Music Society to marry pianist Lily Stumpf and move to Munich, where they lived until 1926.

A trip to Tunisia in 1914 clarified Klee's artistic calling. "Color has taken possession of me," he wrote, upon encountering desert light. "I am a painter." His signature became color—rendered in oil, watercolor, ink, or all three—and almost childlike paintings with a highly developed sense of poetry, music, and dreams. Recognition followed in the 1920s, with exhibitions in Paris and New York and a teaching position at the Bauhaus from 1921. In 1933 the Nazis labeled him a degenerate, his academic position in Düsseldorf was terminated, and he and Lily moved to Switzerland. The apartment they took the following year in Bern's Elfenau district became his studio for the rest of his life.

In 1935 Klee began to show symptoms of severe fatigue, and what was misdiagnosed as the measles turned out to be scleroderma (determined after his death). He continued to paint, however, and produced more than 1,000 works the year before his death in the Ticino, where he had gone to convalesce. His ashes are buried in Bern's Schosshalde cemetery, next to today's Zentrum Paul Klee.

TOP ATTRACTIONS

FAMILY Fodor's Choice ★ **Zentrum Paul Klee** (*Paul Klee Center*). Engaged creativity are the watchwords in this undulating, light-filled complex inspired by the life and art of Paul Klee and designed by Renzo Piano. The permanent collection is the world's largest of works by Klee (about 200 are on display at any given time); temporary exhibits focus on his artistic environment and legacy. The Ensemble Paul Klee performs regular, varied, and colorful short concerts in the auditorium; guest artists from the worlds of theater and dance present productions, readings, and workshops (mainly in German) with a pictorial slant. The Kindermuseum Creaviva, a sunny, paint-spattered area visible from the Restaurant Schöngrün on the north end of the interior Museum Street, is open to children over four and anyone else who would like to make art. A sculpture garden and multilingual audio tours of the permanent collection round out the possibilities—come early and plan to spend the day. Basic signage is in English. ✉ *Monument im Fruchtland 3, Schöngrün* ✣ *From Hauptbahnhof, take No. 12 bus (10 mins) to the end of the line* ☎ *031/3590101* 🌐 *www.zpk.org* 💳 *20 SF* ⏲ *Closed Mon.*

OFF THE BEATEN PATH

Gurten. Bern's very own hill rises 1,000 feet above the city and presents a delightful alternative to the city on clear afternoons. The view moves from the Jura Mountains in the west to the Alps in the east by way of Bern itself; multiple lawns, terraces, and restaurants allow for picnics, cafeteria service, or formal dining as you gaze. The funicular to the top takes three minutes; head left to the east for a diagram labeling more than 200 distant peaks or right for a 360-degree view from the top of the Gurtenturm. The playground includes bumper cars and a kiddie train. You can also walk up from Wabern, or in winter, whiz down on a rented sled. ✉ *Wabern* ✣ *Tram No. 9 to Gurtenbahn* ☎ *031/9612323 funicular* 🌐 *www.gurtenpark.ch* 🎫 *Funicular 10.50 SF round-trip.*

WHERE TO EAT

Traditionally, dining in Bern has been a pretty grounded affair, characterized by Italian home cooking and German-style meat and potatoes. Two favorite local dishes are the *Bernerplatte*—great slabs of salt pork, beef tongue, smoked bacon, pork ribs, and mild pork sausage cooked down in broth, then heaped on top of juniper-scented sauerkraut, green beans, and boiled potatoes—and *Berner Rösti,* shredded potatoes panfried with onions, butter, and chunks of bacon. But newer options include creative vegetarian cuisine, refined gastronomic delicacies, fresh fish—often caught in the nearby River Aare—and myriad international foods. Most menus change with the seasons, featuring asparagus in spring, berries in summer, and wild game in fall. Food presentation can be sophisticated, and service is almost universally friendly.

Many of Bern's established restaurants are dark, often underground, and accessible through a kind of cellar storm door that looks much like the one Dorothy just missed getting to when the tornado hit her Kansas farm. But once you're down there, you'll find the atmosphere cozy and warm, with a hint of the medieval—especially in the simpler, beer-hall-type venues. Another option is sitting at one of the few tables that are usually outside each restaurant, but under the famous Bernese arches, so you're sheltered from summer showers on a hot July evening, say, or a biting spring breeze. As soon as the weather permits, indoor restaurants are abandoned—but still open—as diners flock outdoors.

Be sure to make reservations, especially if you want to eat outside in warm weather. Popular garden restaurants that attract both tourists and locals will be packed at lunch, so you might try arriving a little before noon—but don't try the other extreme and come late, because most kitchens switch to the snack menu after 2 pm—if they're still open. Bärenplatz and Waisenhausplatz are good bets for all-day dining options, with some restaurants open 365 days a year.

Fans of Paul Klee's colorful paintings should not miss the extensive collection of his work at Zentrum Paul Klee.

	WHAT IT COSTS IN SWISS FRANCS			
	$	$$	$$$	$$$$
At Dinner	Under 26 SF	26 SF–45 SF	46 SF–65 SF	Over 65 SF

Restaurant prices are the average cost of a main course at dinner or, if dinner is not served, at lunch.

ALTSTADT (OLD TOWN) AND CITY CENTER

$$ SWISS **Altes Tramdepot.** A beer hall at heart, this restaurant brews dark, light, and "normal" varieties in copper vats behind the bar. Filling dishes like Bernerplatte with homemade Spätzli, cordon bleu, Weisswurst, and warm pretzels filled with ham pair perfectly with the house brews. **Known for:** specialty beers at Easter, in October, or during the full moon; hearty burgers, including a vegetarian version; in the garden, cheeky sparrows that beg for pretzels. *Average main: 26 SF* *Grosser Muristalden 6, Altstadt* *031/3681415* *www.altestramdepot.ch.*

$$ SWISS **Della Casa.** Beloved by Swiss politicians, this 125-year-old institution is affectionately nicknamed "Delli" and has been operating nearly as long as the Federal Parliament Building down the street. It specializes in traditional dishes like Bernerplatte, luscious veal liver with Rösti, and hearty oxtail stew with fried macaroni. **Known for:** traditional and hearty Swiss fare; local patrons, some of them prominent; generous portions. *Average main: 36 SF* *Schauplatzg. 16, City Center* *031/3112142* *www.della-casa.ch* *Closed Sun.*

$$ MODERN ASIAN ✕ **Fugu-Nydegg.** Modern Thai and Japanese cuisine are the two pillars of this sleek two-level restaurant in the Old Town, with shady sidewalk seating in summer; in winter, try to get a seat upstairs where it's brighter. In addition to curry, noodle, beef, and fish dishes, the menu offers innovative desserts like bananas in fried dough smothered in chocolate sauce. **Known for:** high-quality Asian food; unusual drink menu; fashionable look and feel. *Average main: 31 SF ✉ Gerechtigkeitsg. 16, Altstadt ☎ 031/3115125 🌐 www.fugu-nydegg.ch.*

$$ SWISS ✕ **Harmonie.** Fondue is Harmonie's raison d'être. Whether classic (Gruyère), *moitié-moitié* (half Gruyère, half Vacherin), or gussied up with truffles and champagne, pots of hot cheese arrive trailing copious amounts of bread and, ideally, a carafe of Vaudois white. *Käseschnitte* (open-face sandwiches with melted cheese), traditional pork sausage, veal, beef, lamb, and sides of crispy brown Rösti or *Spätzle* (dumplings) complete the picture of a nation well fed. **Known for:** classic Swiss food; single portions of fondue; burgers for under 20 SF. *Average main: 32 SF ✉ Hotelg. 3, Altstadt ☎ 031/3131141 🌐 www.harmonie.ch ⊙ Closed weekends.*

$$$ FRENCH ✕ **Jack's Brasserie.** Time moves a little more slowly here amid the civilized elegance of chandeliers and china teapots, gilt ceiling details, grapevine motifs, and striped banquettes, and the day's papers hang from lampposts at discreet intervals between tables. The menu changes seasonally, but the classic French theme is constant—expect tartares and minestrone in summer, cassoulet or veal liver in winter, and Jack's giant Wiener schnitzel year-round. **Known for:** elegant, old-world vibe; Wiener schnitzel that dwarfs the plate; lobster breakfast omelet. *Average main: 48 SF ✉ Hotel Schweizerhof Bern, Bahnhofpl. 11, City Center ☎ 031/3268080 🌐 www.schweizerhof-bern.ch.*

$$ ECLECTIC Fodor's Choice ★ ✕ **Klösterli Weincafé.** The focus here is on local and seasonal ingredients, served with a flourish on slates and in miniature Dutch ovens, and the impressive Swiss and European wine list includes 20 available by the glass. Indecisive types can let the staff put together a wine sampler to accompany a full meal or a snack of cheese and dried meat. **Known for:** generous lunchtime specials; snacks available all day; lovely outdoor seating area. *Average main: 34 SF ✉ Klösterlistutz 16, Bärengraben ☎ 031/3501000 🌐 www.kloesterlibern.ch.*

$$ ITALIAN ✕ **Lorenzini.** This two-story complex of bars and a restaurant is a popular gathering place for stylish patrons looking for an Italy fix. Eclectic photos, prints, and paintings adorn the walls, and various sculptures add interest throughout. **Known for:** outdoor seating sheltered by arcades; elegant but not stuffy dining; tempting dessert case. *Average main: 31 SF ✉ Hotelg. 10, Altstadt ☎ 031/3185067 🌐 www.lorenzini.ch.*

$$$ EUROPEAN Fodor's Choice ★ ✕ **Meridiano.** A sweeping view of the Altstadt and the Alps pairs perfectly with the opulent yet refined interior in gold, cream, and black, and at night it's a perfect location for a romantic splurge. Try the four-course "Genuinely Swiss" menu for a culinary tour of Switzerland, or, if you're feeling flush and decadent, go for the six-course tasting menu. **Known for:** creative presentation using items like stones and moss; award-winning wine list, including rare Swiss vintages; its Michelin star. *Average main: 57 SF ✉ Hotel Allegro, Kornhausstr. 3, City Center ☎ 031/3395245 🌐 www.kursaal-bern.ch ⊙ Closed Sun. and Mon. No lunch Sat.*

$ VEGETARIAN FAMILY **Tibits.** Following the success of its train station branch, Tibits opened this larger and more glamorous version nearby. The food is 100% vegetarian and sold by weight from a buffet of hot, cold, and sweet selections with an international flair. **Known for:** large buffet available all day; free tap water and bread rolls; Sunday brunch. *Average main: 22 SF* *Gurteng. 3, City Center* *031/3130222* *www.tibits.ch.*

$$ ITALIAN Fodor's Choice ★ **Verdi.** The menu sees cold-weather ingredients like truffles, cream, and polenta transition to tomatoes, basil, and fennel as the weather warms up. Meat lovers should consider the classic "Bollito misto" dish served with a green sauce. **Known for:** plentiful antipasti buffet; elegant decor with distinct seating areas; being dedicated to the Italian composer. *Average main: 34 SF* *Gerechtigkeitsg. 7, Altstadt* *031/3126368* *www.bindella.ch/de/verdi.*

$$ FRENCH **Zimmermania.** A deceptively simple local favorite and one of the most typically French bistros in Bern, this cultural transplant tucked away on a backstreet near the Rathaus has been serving classics like entrecôte Café de Paris (beef in butter sauce) with French fries, escargots in herb garlic butter, and calf's head since 1848. In a city that celebrates the onion, this is a good place to try onion soup. **Known for:** simple yet elegant atmosphere; business lunches; tarte au citron. *Average main: 42 SF* *Brunng. 19, Altstadt* *031/3111542* *www.zimmermania.ch* *Closed Sun. and Mon. and for a month in summer.*

MARZILI AND MATTE

Along the River Aare and downhill from the Altstadt, the Marzili and Matte neighborhoods are good places for chilling out by the water. Upriver from the waterworks at Schwellenmätteli, the Marzili bathing complex attracts masses of swimmers and sunbathers on hot summer days.

$$ ECLECTIC **Gartenrestaurant Marzilibrücke.** The menu at this casual bohemian spot on the Marzili side of the river reaches to the far corners of the globe. Expect Indian curries, Thai dishes, Italian pasta, German schnitzel, and Greek salads to share the menu. **Known for:** many locally sourced ingredients; in summer, the gourmet pizza garden; Sunday brunch. *Average main: 32 SF* *Gasstr. 8, Marzili* *031/3112780* *www.taberna.ch.*

$$ MEDITERRANEAN **Schwellenmätteli.** A chest-high glass barrier stands between you and white water at the tip of this stylish, sun-soaked restaurant and bar. The dining area, indoors or outside beneath a retractable roof, serves Mediterranean-inspired dishes and a fair amount of seafood as well as a Sunday brunch. **Known for:** one-of-a-kind location; extensive cocktail menu; afternoon cake buffet. *Average main: 33 SF* *Dalmaziquai 11, Matte* *031/3505001* *www.schwellenmaetteli.ch.*

$$$ MEDITERRANEAN Fodor's Choice ★ **Zum Zähringer.** With its typical bistro, covered terrace overlooking the River Aare, and a garden that hosts barbecues in summer, this place is a chameleon with a lot of atmosphere. The kitchen produces excellent, mostly Mediterranean dishes such as lamb carpaccio, veal scaloppine, and sauerbraten (beef marinated in red wine). **Known for:** four-course, mix-and-match gourmet meals; idyllic location for outdoor dining; warm, welcoming service. *Average main: 47 SF* *Badg. 1, Matte* *031/3120888* *www.restaurant-zaehringer.ch* *Closed Sun.*

WHERE TO STAY

Bern has plenty of top-quality hotels, many of them with magnificent 19th-century characteristics: towering ceilings ornately accented with stucco moldings, balconies with curlicue belle époque iron railings, domed corner turrets, and miles of marble floors. A step or two below, price-wise, are some older venues that tend toward the generic. But today's owners and managers are waking up to the fact that flowered prints and dusty blue carpeting are just a little too 1980s, even if they're spotlessly clean. These new entrepreneurs are ripping up old floor coverings to expose and polish up the often centuries-old parquet underneath; they're whitewashing the walls, installing state-of-the-art entertainment systems, upgrading the bathrooms (or just plain adding them), and fixing up the rooms with simple, modular furniture that keeps the prices at a level the average traveler can afford.

One truism here is that most, if not all, of Bern's hotel staffers are professional, cheerful, and accommodating. And most of them speak at least three languages comfortably, one of which is sure to be English. If you can, book in advance, because music festivals, trade conventions, sports events, and parliamentary sessions (March, June, September, and December) can fill rooms fast. Rates drop on weekends, when there is less demand.

Hotel reviews have been shortened. For full information, visit Fodors.com.

WHAT IT COSTS IN SWISS FRANCS

	$	$$	$$$	$$$$
For Two People	Under 201 SF	201 SF–300 SF	301 SF–500 SF	Over 500 SF

Hotel prices are the lowest cost of a standard double room in high season, including taxes.

9

ALTSTADT (OLD TOWN) AND CITY CENTER

$$$$ HOTEL Fodor's Choice ★ **Bellevue Palace Bern.** A pretension-free mix of belle époque elegance and contemporary ease defines this impeccable hotel, built in 1913 to accommodate government visitors. **Pros:** two loungeable lobbies great for decompressing; fabulous Alpine views from south-facing rooms and outdoor terrace; good for people-watching, especially politicians. **Cons:** modern rooms may seem spare; no in-room coffee/tea facilities, but kettle provided on request; no real spa. *Rooms from: 504 SF* ✉ *Kocherg. 3–5, Altstadt* ☎ *031/3204545* 🌐 *www.bellevue-palace.ch* *126 rooms* *Breakfast.*

$$ HOTEL **Hotel Allegro.** In a town renowned for its antiquities, Hotel Allegro stands out as thoroughly modern. **Pros:** heated tile floors in bathrooms; upper south-facing rooms with Alpine views; gym, plus free bikes to borrow. **Cons:** slightly off the beaten path; a/c can seem slow; large numbers of conference guests. *Rooms from: 210 SF* ✉ *Kornhausstr. 3, City Center* ☎ *031/3395500* 🌐 *www.allegro-hotel.ch* *172 rooms* *No meals.*

$$ HOTEL **Hotel Bären am Budesplatz.** Occupying much of a city block between the Hauptbahnhof and the Bundeshaus, this business-class hotel is perfectly placed at the heart of Bern's commercial district. **Pros:** good value; in-room coffee machines; practical desks for working. **Cons:** not all rooms have air-conditioning; more business than leisure vibe; can be loud, depending on neighbors. *Rooms from: 245 SF* ✉ *Schauplatzg. 4, City Center* ☎ *031/3113367, 800/780–7234 in U.S.* 🌐 *www.baeren-bern.ch* *57 rooms* *Breakfast.*

$$ HOTEL **Hotel Belle Epoque.** Pay close attention to the walls in this boutique gem, which are furnished entirely with belle époque originals: Steinlen graces the bathrooms and breakfast area, Ferdinand Hodler and Gustav Klimt spice up suites named for them, and the bar has photos of Henri Toulouse-Lautrec standing next to the Moulin Rouge poster. **Pros:** attractive bar, restaurant, and sidewalk café; on a charming and quiet cobblestone street; fine art on display. **Cons:** evening entertainment can draw a boisterous crowd; unimpressive breakfast costs extra; corridors rather gloomy. *Rooms from: 280 SF* ✉ *Gerechtigkeitsg. 18, Altstadt* ☎ *031/3114336* 🌐 *www.belle-epoque.ch* *17 rooms* *No meals.*

$$ HOTEL FAMILY **Hotel Bern.** Stepping inside this energetic property with an imposing facade, you may be pleasantly surprised to find a wholly modern interior, making for a fantastic juxtaposition of old and new. **Pros:** kids under 12 stay free; lactose- and gluten-free breakfast options; live music on Wednesday. **Cons:** restaurant is a bit staid; business vibe during the week; limited views. *Rooms from: 210 SF* ✉ *Zeughausg. 9, City Center* ☎ *031/3292222* 🌐 *www.hotelbern.ch* *99 rooms* *No meals.*

$$ HOTEL **Hotel Goldener Schlüssel.** This 500-year-old property—the oldest in Bern—is within earshot of the Zytglogge bells. Rooms are small but nicely conceived, with dark parquet floors, modular furniture, white pillows and duvet covers, and flat-screen TVs; all have showers. Its solidly popular restaurant serves a mix of rib-sticking favorites like bratwurst with Rösti and an authentic Wiener schnitzel. **Pros:** great Altstadt location near station; quiet street with little traffic; nice pillow menu. **Cons:** rooms are small; bathrooms generally small; clock tower rings all night. *Rooms from: 220 SF* ✉ *Rathausg. 72, Altstadt* ☎ *031/3110216* 🌐 *www.goldener-schluessel.ch* *34 rooms* *Breakfast.*

$ HOTEL **Hotel Kreuz Bern.** Decorated in soft, mainly neutral colors, this tastefully appointed hotel offers a range of room types and sizes with some fun and unexpected touches, like giant maps of Bern on the walls. **Pros:** excellent central location; modern, well-designed rooms; tea and coffee corner on fourth floor. **Cons:** rooms in the "grandlit" (queen-size bed) category are very small; front rooms noisy, especially on weekends; combination shower gel/shampoo. *Rooms from: 186 SF* ✉ *Zeughausg. 41, City Center* ☎ *031/3299595* 🌐 *www.kreuzbern.ch* *99 rooms* *Breakfast.*

$ HOTEL **Hotel Nydeck.** In this small, tidy corner hotel near the Nydeggbrücke—an excellent location near the main attractions of the Old Town—rooms are small but pleasant, and the medieval city views are hard to beat. **Pros:** cheerful environment; perfect medieval neighborhood setting; four-person suite with kitchen available. **Cons:** the bed barely fits in some of the rooms; street noise can be a problem with open windows; no elevator. *Rooms from: 180 SF* ✉ *Gerechtigkeitsg. 1, Altstadt* ☎ *031/3118686* 🌐 *www.hotelnydeck.ch* *12 rooms* *Breakfast.*

$$$ HOTEL Fodor's Choice ★ **Hotel Schweizerhof Bern.** Luxurious yet practically appointed, this hotel's rooms feature neutral tones that appeal to both business and leisure travelers. **Pros:** luxe rooms and design elements; lovely rooftop terrace; free in-room beverages. **Cons:** location across from train station isn't very glamorous; views from rooms and lobby bar are limited; confusing controls for lights and window shades. *Rooms from: 455 SF* ✉ *Bahnhofpl. 11, City Center* ☎ *031/3268080* 🌐 *www.schweizerhof-bern.ch* *99 rooms* *Some meals.*

$$ HOTEL **Savoy Hotel.** This neatly tailored hotel is just minutes from the main train station, as well as the city's markets and arcaded shopping streets. **Pros:** proximity to train station; rooms have soundproofed windows; bistro serves food all day. **Cons:** a/c could be stronger; vibe more business than leisure; no elevator from fourth to fifth floor. *Rooms from: 220 SF* ✉ *Neueng. 26, City Center* ☎ *031/3114405* 🌐 *www.hotelsavoy-bern.ch* *64 rooms* *Breakfast.*

$$ HOTEL **Sorrell Hotel Ador.** Nicely appointed and located just west of the Hauptbahnhof, this boxy hotel is a good deal if you're price conscious but still want something stylish. **Pros:** well-designed modern interiors; close to everything; breakfast included. **Cons:** uninspiring exterior; located on a block heavy with early-1970s concrete; frosted-glass bathroom walls in some rooms. *Rooms from: 205 SF* ✉ *Laupenstr. 15, City Center* ☎ *031/3880111* 🌐 *www.sorrellhotels.com* *59 rooms* *Breakfast.*

GREATER BERN

$$ HOTEL **Unique Hotel Innere Enge.** Art nouveau accents, pristine Alpine views, exposed beams, and jazz memorabilia from greats like Lionel Hampton, John Lewis, Hazy Osterwald, and Clark Terry punctuate the spacious, sunny rooms in this half-timbered inn that dates to the early 1700s. **Pros:** lush private park with large outdoor terrace; individually themed rooms; restaurants and jazz club on-site. **Cons:** just outside the city center; curtains rather garish; rooms can get hot. *Rooms from: 260 SF* ✉ *Engestr. 54, Greater Bern* ☎ *031/3096111* 🌐 *www.innere-enge.ch* *26 rooms* *Breakfast.*

NIGHTLIFE AND PERFORMING ARTS

Twice a year, Bern Tourismus widely disseminates *Bern Guide,* a free, pocket-sized, bilingual (German/English), and comprehensive guide to what's on in the city (exhibits, nightlife, festivals, shopping, excursions, and useful telephone numbers). The website 🌐 *www.bern.com* fills in any remaining gaps.

DID YOU KNOW?

Albert Einstein wrote and published his *Special Theory of Relativity* in Bern, in 1905.

NIGHTLIFE

The Bernese like to party, and nightlife options accordingly run the gamut from plush-velvet seating and belle époque refinement to jazz lounges, casual sidewalk bars, and plugged-in clubs where DJs spin the latest. Bärenplatz and Kornhausplatz bubble over with revelers on summer evenings; many restaurants transition into bars as the night wears on.

ALTSTADT (OLD TOWN) AND CITY CENTER

BARS

Adriano's. This friendly, glassed-in coffee bar serves fresh croissants from 7 am (10 am on Sunday), sandwiches throughout the day, and wine or beer to a sidewalk crowd come nightfall. ✉ *Theaterpl. 2, Altstadt* ☎ *031/3188831* 🌐 *www.adrianos.ch.*

Bar Toulouse-Lautrec. Exquisite belle époque paintings and live entertainment grace the Bar Toulouse-Lautrec. ✉ *Hotel Belle Epoque, Gerechtigkeitsg. 18, Altstadt* ☎ *031/3114346* 🌐 *www.belle-epoque.ch.*

Bellevue Bar. Well-heeled travelers (and local politicians) come to see and be seen at the wood-paneled Bellevue Bar. In summer, the terrace out back is the place for sipping fancy cocktails and enjoying the view of the Alps and the River Aare. ✉ *Hotel Bellevue Palace, Kocherg. 3–5, Altstadt* 🌐 *www.bellevue-palace.ch.*

Fodor's Choice ★ **Kornhauskeller.** Entering the Kornhauskeller is akin to entering a cathedral, except that the stunning vaulted ceilings and frescoes are underground and the lounge-bar in the gallery stocks an incredible array of whiskeys, rums, and bourbons. The building has focused on food throughout its long life, first as a wine cellar–granary, then as a beer hall. In addition to its vast lounge of leather sofas and chairs, the Kornhauskeller houses a classy restaurant. ✉ *Kornhauspl. 18, Altstadt* ☎ *031/3277272* 🌐 *www.kornhauskeller.ch.*

Martini Terrazza. The Riviera vibe at the outdoor Martini Terrazza and indoor lounge, both part of the Schwellenmätteli restaurant complex in the Matte, lures folks down to the river. It's also a popular morning-after haunt. ✉ *Dalmaziquai 11, Matte* ☎ *031/3505001* 🌐 *www.schwellenmaetteli.ch.*

Matte Brennerei. Hidden in a semi-industrial area along the Aare River, this bar distills its own gin and absinthe, and there are plenty of other drinks on offer, too. The quirky two-floor structure has plush furniture, a pool table, and a smoking lounge. Check online for events like tastings and concerts. ✉ *Mühlenpl. 5, Matte* ☎ *077/4856675* 🌐 *mattebrennerei.ch.*

DANCING

Du Théâtre. On Thursday, smart young professionals stop by after work for a mellow glass of wine at the Düdü Bar. On weekends, the dance floor is on duty until 3:30 am at Du Théâtre. ✉ *Hotelg. 10, Altstadt* ☎ *031/3185067* 🌐 *www.dutheatre.ch.*

GREATER BERN

CASINO

Grand Casino Bern. All 350 slot machines and 14 gaming tables at the Kursaal's Grand Casino Bern function until 4 am on Thursday, 5 am Friday and Saturday, and 2 am the rest of the week. ✉ *Kornhausstr. 3, Kornhausbrücke* ☎ *031/3395555* 🌐 *www.grandcasino-bern.ch* 🎫 *10 SF.*

PERFORMING ARTS

Bern's three-pronged arts scene covers opera and symphonic classics, seasonal festivals, and cubbyhole theaters buried underground.

ALTSTADT (OLD TOWN) AND CITY CENTER

MUSIC AND THE PERFORMING ARTS

Berner Puppentheater. From approximately October to May, marionettes, stick puppets, hand puppets, shadow puppets, and masks come to life on stage at the Berner Puppentheater. ✉ *Gerechtigkeitsg. 31, Altstadt* ☎ *031/3119585* 🌐 *www.berner-puppentheater.ch.*

Berner Symphonie-Orchester. Orchestral work and chamber music are performed by this orchestra in venues all over Bern, as well as in other cities. ✉ *Bern* ☎ *031/3282424* 🌐 *www.bsorchester.ch.*

Gurten Festival. Altstadt streets empty briefly in mid-July as A-list rockers draw crowds up the hill to the four-day open-air Gurten Festival. ✉ *Bern* 🌐 *www.gurtenfestival.ch.*

Fodor's Choice ★ **Mahogany Hall.** Billed as Bern's oldest music club, Mahogany Hall hosts a wide range of Swiss and international artists that play a variety of musical styles. There's also a monthly salsa night featuring a dance workshop. Check online for the calendar or grab a paper copy outside the building. ✉ *Klösterlistutz 18, Bärengraben* ☎ *031/3316000* 🌐 *www.mahogany.ch.*

Stadttheater. Each year, the Stadttheater presents full-scale operas, dramas, and contemporary dance pieces. ✉ *Kornhauspl. 20, Altstadt* ☎ *031/3295111* 🌐 *www.konzerttheaterbern.ch.*

Theater am Käfigturm. Three levels below Spitalgasse, the Theater am Käfigturm presents pantomime, modern dance, avant-garde plays, stand-up comedy, and the occasional film or piece aimed at children. ✉ *Spitalg. 4, City Center* ☎ *031/3116100* 🌐 *www.theater-am-kaefigturm.ch.*

GREATER BERN

Fodor's Choice ★ **Marians Jazzroom.** This popular place hosts top international jazz, blues, and gospel artists between September and May. ✉ *Engestr. 54, Bern* ☎ *031/3096111* 🌐 *www.mariansjazzroom.ch* 🎫 *30 SF.*

SPORTS AND THE OUTDOORS

BIKING

There are about 300 km (186 miles) of marked trails in and around Bern, and the city began a new bike-share program in May 2018.

SWIMMING

Swimmers have headed into the cold, swift Aare just before its U-turn around the Altstadt since Bern was founded. These days a hot Sunday may see scantily clad (or, in certain sections, naked) crowds of more than 10,000 sprawled on beach towels on the grass, swimming laps in the pools, or bobbing happily in the river (a system of handrails projected over the water prevents bathers from traveling too far downstream).

SHOPPING

Bern's official store hours are 9 to 7 weekdays and 8 to 5 on Saturday. Thursday hours are extended to 9; stores in the Hauptbahnhof may open on Sunday. Smaller stores, particularly in the Altstadt, may stay shuttered Monday morning, close for lunch, close before 9 pm on Thursday, and/or open as late as 10 am.

SHOPPING STREETS

No street or side alley in downtown Bern is without interest to shoppers, and you never know what fabulous discovery may await at the end of an intriguing passageway or the bottom of cellar stairs. **Spitalgasse** and **Marktgasse** form the city center's main shopping drag; parallel streets such as **Neuengasse, Aarbergergasse,** and **Amthausgasse** can also be very rewarding. The Altstadt, from **Brunngasse** to **Junkerngasse** by way of **Kramgasse** and **Gerechtigkeitsgasse,** is lined and honeycombed with fine specialty boutiques.

ALTSTADT (OLD TOWN) AND CITY CENTER

BOOKS

Orell Füssli. At this German-language chain store lodged in the basement of the Loeb department store, globes, dictionaries, multilingual travel guides, English-language fiction and biographies, a play area for kids, and a sizable selection of books about Switzerland are highlights. ✉ *Spitalg. 47–51, City Center* ☎ *031/3202020* 🌐 *www.orellfuessli.ch.*

Stauffacher. It is easy to get lost in the sprawling multilingual Stauffacher, emporium of books, maps, and multimedia, but there are far worse fates. The substantial English Bookshop occupies the third floor of the west wing; regular readings (some in English) are held in the Café Littéraire. ✉ *Neueng. 25–37, City Center* ☎ *031/3136363* 🌐 *www.stauffacher.ch.*

CHOCOLATE

Beeler. The specialty at Beeler is the Caramelina, where truffle meets caramel in seven flavors, including mocha-cardamom and cassis. There's also plenty of seating for those who like to linger over tea and cake. ✉ *Spitalg. 36, City Center* ☎ *031/3112808* 🌐 *www.confiserie-beeler.ch.*

SUNDAY TEA

Many chocolatiers' shops have tearoom areas at the back and are, therefore, allowed to open on Sunday. If you go, be sure to try the Bernese specialty *Lebkuchen*, a dense, flat spice cake made with hazelnuts, honey, and almonds.

Eichenberger. Find an assortment of pralines and truffles, as well as hazelnut gingerbread emblazoned with the iconic bear, at Eichenberger. There are five stores in Bern, three of which have cafés. ✉ *Bahnhofpl. 5, City Center* ☎ *031/3113325* 🌐 *www.confiserie-eichenberger.ch.*

Fodor's Choice ★ **Läderach.** Giant slabs of chocolate studded with nuts and fruit are the main attraction here. The samplers sold in cellophane bags are fun for immediate sharing, or choose the sturdy wooden gift box for an indulgent souvenir. ✉ *Spitalg. 2, Altstadt* ☎ *031/3110425* 🌐 *www.laederach.com.*

Tschirren. The self-styled prince of Bernese chocolatiers, Tschirren has been making its divine assortment of artfully rough-hewn truffles since 1919. ✉ *Kramg. 73, Altstadt* ☎ *031/3111717* 🌐 *www.swiss-chocolate.ch.*

DEPARTMENT STORES

Globus. Good-quality, stylish, often vibrantly colorful home accessories and cooking gear fill the upper stories at Globus. On the lower levels, fashionable hats and scarves, cosmetics, and designer labels give way to foodstuffs—from specialty oils to cheese—in the upscale supermarket downstairs. ✉ *Spitalg. 17–21, City Center* ☎ *058/5784040* 🌐 *www.globus.ch.*

Loeb. Clothing for women, men, and children dominates the floor space at Loeb. Also worth a browse: toys, craft supplies, and housewares. At ground level you'll find accessories, hosiery, stationery, and cosmetics. ✉ *Spitalg. 47–51, City Center* ☎ *031/3207111* 🌐 *www.loeb.ch.*

GIFTS AND SOUVENIRS

Boutique Nelli. The warrenlike boutique has a whimsical selection of glassware, jewelry, candles in rainbow colors, and imaginative kitchen gadgets. ✉ *Gerechtigkeitsg. 3, Altstadt* ☎ *031/3111040* 🌐 *www.boutiquenelli.ch.*

Fodor's Choice ★ **Heimatwerk.** A high-quality emporium of Swiss-made handicrafts, textiles, jewelry, cosmetics, and ceramics, Heimatwerk also sells pocketknives and other typically Swiss souvenirs at all price points. The basement is devoted to toys and children's clothing. ✉ *Kramg. 61, Altstadt* ☎ *031/3113000* 🌐 *www.heimatwerk-bern.ch.*

Holz Art. Colorful handmade wooden figures and candelabras, delicate shaved-wood trees, and lacy wooden cutouts adorn Holz Art. ✉ *Münsterg. 36, Altstadt* ☎ *031/3126666* 🌐 *www.holz-art-bern.ch.*

Bern has been a market town since the Middle Ages, and seasonal outdoor markets are still an integral part of daily life.

HOME ACCESSORIES

Cachet. This unusual store stocks items such as iron Japanese teapots, colored grass baskets, camel-hair rugs, Turkish lamps, multicolored bottles, whimsical mobiles, and soulful carved-wood furniture from India, Indonesia, and Pakistan. ✉ *Amthausg. 1, City Center* ☎ *031/3118466* 🌐 *www.cachet.ch.*

Depot. Clean, livable, often joyously colorful and affordable designs channel faraway locales at Depot, where the focus is on decorative items like candles and vases, plus necessities like towels, sheets, and dishes. ✉ *Spitalg. 4, City Center* ☎ *031/3115667* 🌐 *www.depot-online.com.*

MARKETS

Tuesday and Saturday are Bern's formal year-round market days, with most of the action concentrated in the morning along Bundesplatz, Bärenplatz, Waisenhausplatz, Schauplatzgasse, Gurtengasse, and Bundesgasse in the center of town.

Fodor's Choice ★ **Crafts Fair.** Arts-and-crafts stands fill the Münsterplatz on the first Saturday of the month between March and December. ✉ *Münsterpl., Altstadt* 🌐 *handwerkermaerit.ch.*

Fodor's Choice ★ **Meat and Cheese Market.** Münstergasse, between Zytglogge and Münster, offers meats and dairy products every Tuesday and Saturday. ✉ *Münsterg., City Center.*

Trader's Market. This awning-covered warren is the place for handmade soaps, antique copper pots, silver jewelry, handmade hammocks, tie-dyed scarves, and toys, including helium-filled balloons. Open on

Tuesday and Saturday, the market also adds late-night hours on Thursday between April and October. ✉ *Waisenhauspl., Altstadt.*

TOYS

FAMILY **Bilboquet.** The old red cash register still works at Bilboquet, which turned 50 in 2016. Kid-sized umbrellas have animal handles, and the plush toys range from snowy owls to llamas. ✉ *Münsterg. 37, Altstadt* ☎ *031/3113671* 🌐 *bilboquet.ch.*

FAMILY **Chlätterbär.** This shop sells fully stocked wooden kitchens, xylophones, beaded jewelry, drum kits, hand puppets, and wooden dollhouse furniture. ✉ *Amthausg. 3, City Center* ☎ *031/3111196* 🌐 *spielkiste.ch/cb.*

FAMILY **Puppenklinik.** The owner of the Puppenklinik has a passion for restoration. The result is a huge collection of vintage dolls, toys, teddy bears, and puppets from around the world. ✉ *Gerechtigkeitsg. 36, Altstadt* ☎ *031/3120771.*

FAMILY **U-Tiger.** There are few hard edges at U-Tiger, where cloud sofas, green-dragon bean bags, quilted soccer fields, and fuzzy sheep hot-water bottles headline the creative selection of room furnishings and other accoutrements for children. ✉ *Gerechtigkeitsg. 69, Altstadt* ☎ *031/3279091* 🌐 *www.utiger-kindermoebel.ch.*

SPAS

Fodor's Choice ★ **Oktogon Hammam.** Housed in a former gasworks, the three-story building follows the Middle Eastern hammam tradition. You pass through a series of serene rooms where you steam, scrub, shower, and soak. Admission includes an exfoliation mitt and a linen sheet to wear for modesty's sake. At the end of the process, you recline on a bed under the wooden eaves. You can also book extras like a soapsuds massage. The on-site café serves free tea and sells light snacks. On Tuesday, only women can visit the spa. ✉ *Weiherg. 3, Matte* ☎ *031/3113101* 🌐 *www.hammam-bern.ch.*

The Spa at Hotel Schweizerhof. Though fairly compact, this underground refuge features a wealth of amenities. There's a sauna, steam bath, plunge pool, and relaxation pool with bubble jets—not to mention a fitness room for those who want to do more than just relax. The spa offers massages and a variety of cosmetic treatments; a quiet room with waterbeds extends the pampering. The spa is free for hotel guests; for others, the base rate is 39 SF for two hours. Guests are asked to wear a swimsuit or a towel at all times. ✉ *Hotel Schweizerhof Bern, Bahnhofpl. 11, Bern* ☎ *031/3268080* 🌐 *www.schweizerhof-bern.ch.*

BERNER OBERLAND

10

WELCOME TO BERNER OBERLAND

TOP REASONS TO GO

★ **Top of the world:** At 11,333 feet, the Jungfraujoch isn't the highest place on the planet, but it certainly feels like it, with the Alps' longest glacier and scores of snow-slathered peaks so close.

★ **Twin peaks:** The upwardly mobile head to the adjacent mountaintop villages of Wengen and Mürren to find the Switzerland of cheese, chalet, and chic cliché.

★ **Shangri-la found:** Complete with 72 cascading waterfalls (among Europe's highest), the Lauterbrunnen Valley is like a massive version of Yosemite National Park.

★ **Gilded Gstaad:** Money attracts money, and there's certainly a lot of it here. Mere mortals can indulge in exquisite meals, skiing, and overnight stays in paradise.

★ **Old Switzerland, in a nutshell:** Ballenberg is a delightfully reconstructed Swiss village—à la America's Colonial Williamsburg—with traditional crafts on show.

Blessed with nine valleys, the lovely lakes of Thun and Brienz, jet-set Gstaad, and the ageless grandeur of the Jungfrau, this compact region contains a universe of sights. No wonder Switzerland's tourist industry began here in the early 1800s, with English gentry flocking to gape at its gorgeous Alpine scenery.

1 Jungfrau Region. A transportation hub, bustling Interlaken has upward of 130 hotels and makes the perfect base camp (it also has a lively nightlife). A short ride away are the magnificent summits of summits—the Eiger, Mönch, and Jungfrau (with the highest train station in Europe). Nestled below are the villages of Grindelwald, Lauterbrunnen, Wengen, and Mürren, all chalets and geraniums. In winter they have the ambience that every North American "alpine village" resort aims for—and misses.

2 Brienzersee. In the Oberland a wide variety in altitude creates a great diversity of scenery, so you can bathe comfortably in Lake Brienz after skiing on the Jungfrau slopes in July. Waterfront Brienz is home to famed wood-carvers and the storybook museum village of Ballenberg. Nearby, the plot thickens in Meiringen—Sherlock Holmes

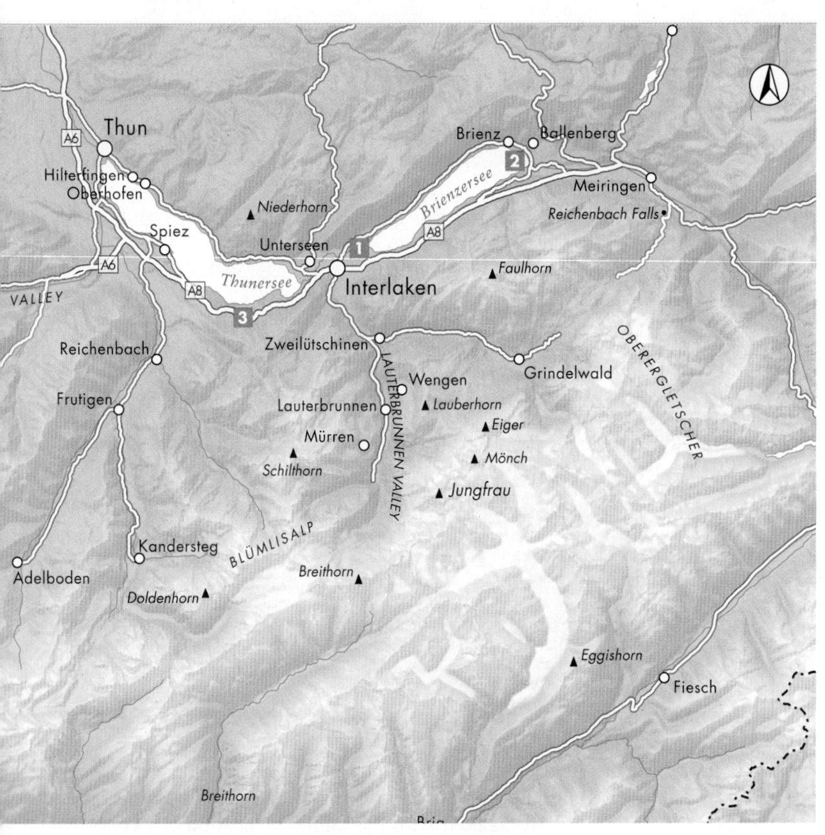

nearly met his match here at Reichenbach Falls.

3 Thunersee. This idyllic lake is named for Thun, a resort town of medieval dignity. Between bouts of waterskiing and wakeboarding, castle-hop to your heart's content: the shoreline villages of Spiez, Hilterfingen, and Oberhofen all have fairy-tale-worthy extravaganzas.

4 Simmental and Gstaad. From Spiez, the highway leads southwest into the Simmental Valley, where forest gorges hide Gstaad, a chic and modish winter resort.

Updated by
Susan Misicka

There are times when the reality of Switzerland puts postcard idealization to shame, surpassing advertising-image peaks and skies. Those times happen most often in the Berner Oberland, for this rugged region concentrates some of the best features of rural Switzerland: awesome mountain panoramas, massive glaciers, crystalline lakes, dramatic gorges and waterfalls, chic ski resorts, dense pine forests, and charming gingerbread chalets. Before the onslaught of visitors inspired many locals to switch from farming to innkeeping, agriculture was the prime industry—and this is still true today, evidenced by the frequent sight of cattle dotting the hillsides, as though conveniently placed for photo ops.

The houses of the Berner Oberland are classics: the definitive Swiss chalet, whose broad, eaved roofs cover fancifully scalloped and carved gables. Facades are painted with the family dedication on wood that has weathered to dark sienna. From early spring through autumn, window boxes spill torrents of well-tended geraniums and petunias, and adjacent woodpiles are stacked with mosaiclike precision in readiness for dropping temperatures.

The region is arranged tidily enough for even a brief visit. Its main resort city, Interlaken, lies in green lowlands between the gleaming twin pools of the Brienzersee and the Thunersee, which are linked by the River Aare. Behind them to the south loom craggy, forested foothills, and behind those foothills stand some of Europe's noblest peaks, most notably the snowy crowns of the Eiger (13,026 feet), the Mönch (13,475 feet), and the fiercely beautiful Jungfrau (13,642 feet).

Because nature has laid the region out so conveniently, it has become the most popular in Switzerland for tourism. Its excursion and transportation systems carry enormous numbers of visitors to its myriad viewpoints, overlooks, and wonders. The railroad to the Jungfraujoch transports masses of tour groups to its high-altitude attractions, and on a peak-season day its crowded station can look like the Sistine Chapel in August or the Chicago Board of Trade. But the tourist industry handles the onslaught with ease, offering such an efficient network of boats, trains, and funiculars, such a variety of activities and attractions, and such a wide range of accommodations, from posh city hotels to rustic mountain lodges, that every visitor can find the most suitable way to take in the marvels of the Bernese Alps.

BERNER OBERLAND PLANNER

WHEN TO GO

The Oberland has four distinct seasons, each more beautiful than the last. Valley springs and summers are perfect for outdoor activities, from hiking and biking to swimming. Fall becomes crisp around October, and winter brings snow. Keep in mind that snow can stay as late as May and come as early as August at over 6,500 feet.

Winter versus summer? Everyone loves the magic of snow, but all that white can easily lend a sameness to all those mountains—something you avoid if you enjoy an Alpine summer. Warm weather can also mean haze, which can taint your photos of spectacular valleys, so be sure to pack your camera's polarizer filter. Gstaad hosts the Yehudi Menuhin Music Festival every summer, which draws crowds. If crowds aren't your thing, try the off-season (early spring or late fall).

No matter the season, sports enthusiasts will be in their element: hiking, biking, waterskiing, sailing, parasailing and gliding, bungee jumping, skiing, snowboarding, and sledding are just a few activities available.

GETTING HERE AND AROUND

AIR TRAVEL

Within 90 minutes, Bern Airport brings you via bus and train to Interlaken, the hub of the Berner Oberland. Near Basel, EuroAirport (across the border in France) is under 2½ hours by train or bus. The Zürich Airport is also less than a 2½-hour train ride away. Geneva's Cointrin is just under 3 hours away.

BOAT AND FERRY TRAVEL

In warmer months, round-trip boat cruises around Lake Thun and Lake Brienz provide an ever-changing view of the craggy foothills and peaks. Boats run in winter, too, though on a reduced schedule. Buy tickets and catch boats for Lake Thun at Interlaken West station. For Lake Brienz, go to Interlaken Ost (East).

The round-trip from Interlaken to Thun takes about four hours; the trip one way takes about two hours and includes stops for visits to the castles of Oberhofen, Spiez, and Hilterfingen. A round-trip from Interlaken to Brienz takes around 2½ hours, to Iseltwald about 1¼ hours. These boats are public transportation as well as pleasure cruisers; just disembark whenever you feel like it and check timetables when you want to catch another.

Contacts BLS Schifffahrt Berner Oberland. ✉ *Lachenweg 19, Thun* ☎ *058/3274811* 🌐 *www.bls.ch.*

BUS TRAVEL

Postbuses (also called postautos or postcars) travel into much of the area not served by trains, including most smaller mountain towns.

CAR TRAVEL

Driving in the Berner Oberland allows you the freedom to find your own views and to park at the very edges of civilization before taking off on foot or by train. The site 🌐 *www.route.search.ch* offers detailed driving directions and maps in English.

TRAIN TRAVEL

The Berner Oberland is crawling with federal and private railways, funiculars, cogwheel trains, and cable lifts designed with the sole purpose of getting you closer to its spectacular views.

DISCOUNTS AND DEALS

Contacts Berner Oberland Regional Pass. ☎ *058/3274750* 🌐 *www.regiopass-berneroberland.ch.*

HOTELS

This is the most visited region in Switzerland, so book as early as possible. High season here means winter, with summer making up a second-place high season.

Decide on which experience you want: the townie feel of a place like Interlaken, which has many bars, nightclubs, restaurants, and movie theaters; the much quieter Grindelwald, with fewer venues; or the cliff-top-secluded Mürren or Wengen, where you'll be getting most of your evening's entertainment from the hotel—usually including meals.

RESTAURANTS

Eating in the Berner Oberland can be a tasty lesson in the local dialect. Take *Gstampfti Chrugli, Suure Mocke,* and *Chalbsläberli mit Röschti.* Fortunately, these traditional meals—that's mashed potatoes, braised beef, and sliced calf's liver with butter hash browns to us—taste much better than they sound.

Although no Swiss citizen would think of eating fondue in summer, the region teems with restaurants full of wood-and-cowbell decorations that serve exactly what tourists want, which includes melted cheese in its many forms. Other restaurants go sleek, with 20 SF cocktails, dim track lighting, and duck à la European fusion. There's no shortage of pizza and pasta joints either, though the better ones will have wood-fired ovens and homemade dough.

Hotel and restaurant reviews have been shortened. For full information, visit Fodors.com.

WHAT IT COSTS IN SWISS FRANCS				
	$	$$	$$$	$$$$
Restaurants	Under 26 SF	26 SF–45 SF	46 SF–65 SF	Over 65 SF
Hotels	Under 201 SF	201 SF–300 SF	301 SF–500 SF	Over 500 SF

Restaurant prices are the average cost of a main course at dinner or, if dinner is not served, at lunch. Hotel prices are the lowest cost of a standard double room in high season, including taxes.

TOURS

Alpinzentrum Gstaad. Adrenaline is the main ingredient of this tour operator, which specializes in activities like river rafting, rock climbing, glacier hiking, and high-rope parks. But they also have a gentle side, whether it's an easy snowshoe outing or a mild ride from Thun to Bern on the River Aare. ✉ *Cheserypl. 1, Gstaad* ☎ *033/7484161* 🌐 *www.alpinzentrum.ch* 🎫 *From 35 SF.*

GrindelwaldBus. The hop-on/hop-off Grösse Scheidegg round-trip is especially popular and covers Interlaken, Brienz, Meiringen, Grosse Scheidegg, and Grindelwald. You can get your ticket at any of the stations for 89 SF–110 SF, depending on whether you want to add a boat ride. It's also possible to charter a van or a bus for custom excursions in the region. ✉ *Grundstr. 32, Grindelwald* ☎ *033/8541616* 🌐 *www.grindelwaldbus.ch.*

VISITOR INFORMATION

The Berner Oberland website is a good place to start; its tourism wing points you to a number of regional tourist boards.

Contacts Berner Oberland Tourismus. 🌐 *www.berneroberland.ch.*

THE JUNGFRAU REGION

10

The thriving resort town of Interlaken lies between two spectacularly positioned lakes, the Brienzersee (Lake Brienz) and the Thunersee (Lake Thun), and is the gateway to two magnificent mountain valleys, one leading up to the popular sports resort of Grindelwald, the other to Lauterbrunnen and the famous car-free resorts of Wengen and Mürren. Looming over both valleys, the Jungfrau and its partner peaks—the Eiger and Mönch—can be admired from various high-altitude overviews.

INTERLAKEN

58 km (36 miles) southeast of Bern.

Often touted as a town without character, Interlaken has patiently borne the brunt of being called "the best place in Switzerland to get away *from*"—but this, it turns out, is a tribute to the town's proximity to many of the wonders of the Bernese Alps. This bustling Victorian resort town is a centrally located home base for travelers planning to

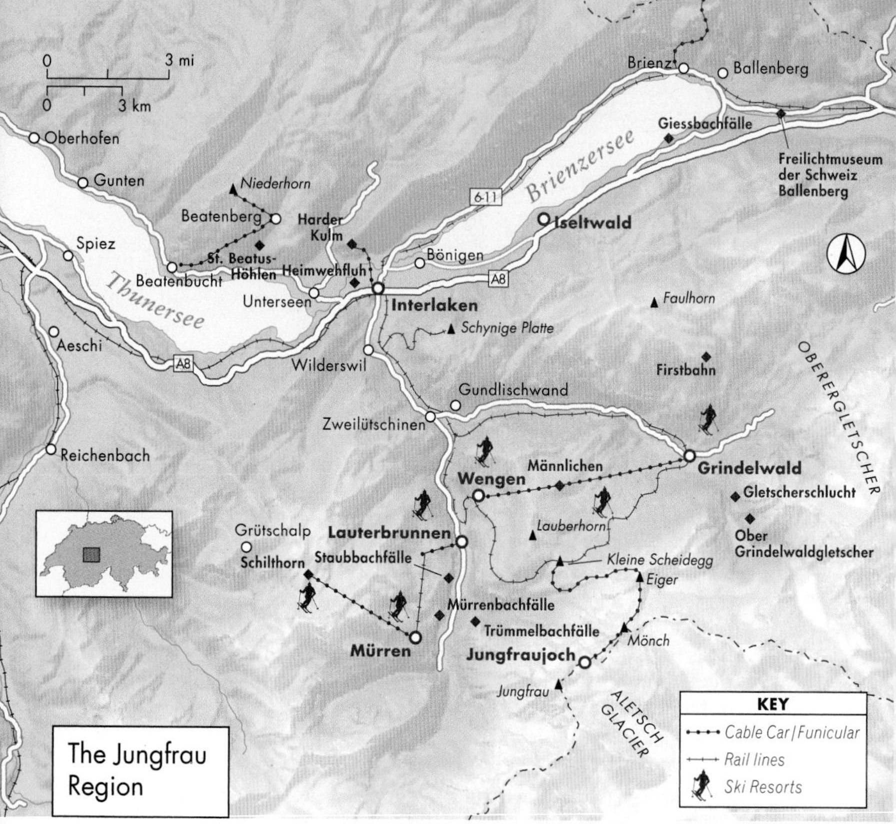

visit the region's two lakes and the mountains towering behind them. Those who want up-close mountain views more than nightlife, however, will want to consider staying in one of the smaller resort towns. The name *Interlaken* has a Latin source: *interlacus* (between lakes). At 1,860 feet, Interlaken dominates the Bödeli, the branch of lowland between the lakes that Interlaken shares with the nearby towns of Unterseen, Wilderswil, Bönigen, Goldswil, and Matten. The town's two train stations, Interlaken Ost (East) and Interlaken West, are good orientation points; most sights are just a few minutes' walk from one of the stations. There are unlimited excursion options, and it is a pleasant, if urban, place to stay.

GETTING HERE AND AROUND

Interlaken has two train stations: Interlaken West, where trains arrive from Bern, Thun, and Spiez; and Interlaken Ost (East), which connects you to Brienz and the Jungfrau region. West is the more central station, but check with your hotel—some of the town's fine hotels are clustered nearer the East station, and all Brienzersee boat excursions leave from the docks nearby. The direct train that comes from Bern stops at both stations. From Zürich, a line leads through Bern to Interlaken and takes about two hours; a more scenic trip over the Golden Pass route via Luzern takes about three hours.

Buses to nearby towns leave from the train stations, both of which have taxis to help you schlep your luggage to your hotel; there are also carriage rides for the romantically inclined.

Swift and scenic roads link both Bern and Zürich to Interlaken. From Bern, take A6 to Spiez, then A8 to Interlaken. From Zürich, travel by Highway A3 south to pick up first A4 and then A14 in the direction of Luzern. South of Luzern, pick up the A8 in the direction of Interlaken.

TOURS **GoldenPass Line.** Interlaken lies at the center of the picturesque rail line from Montreux to Luzern. Depending on the leg, you can enjoy the landscape from a panoramic wagon, or perhaps a retro train-car version resembling the Orient Express. There are also chocolate- and cheese-themed tours. ☎ *021/9898190* ⊕ *www.goldenpassline.ch.*

Interlaken carriage rides. For a nostalgic tour of the streets of greater Interlaken by horse-drawn carriage, line up by the Interlaken West or Ost train station and hitch a ride. Check with Interlaken Tourism for providers. ✉ *Interlaken* ☎ *033/8265300.*

VISITOR INFORMATION

The Interlaken Tourist Office, at the foot of the Hotel Metropole, provides information on Interlaken and the Jungfrau region. Arrange your excursions here.

Contacts Interlaken Tourismus. ✉ *Marktg. 1, Interlaken* ☎ *033/8265300* ⊕ *www.interlaken.ch.*

EXPLORING

TOP ATTRACTIONS

Fodor's Choice ★ **Schynige Platte.** For a most splendid overview of the region, head to this 6,454-foot plateau for a picnic, or wander down any of its numerous footpaths, or visit its Alpine Botanical Garden, where more than 600 varieties of mountain flowers grow. A cogwheel train dating from 1893 takes you on the round-trip journey, though you may opt to walk either up or (more comfortably) down. If you are only going in one direction, make sure to specify your direction of travel when you buy your ticket. Trains run from approximately 7:25 am to 4:45 pm. To get there, take the four-minute ride on the Bernese Oberland Railway from Interlaken East to Wilderswil. ✉ *Wilderswil* ☎ *033/8287233* ⊕ *www.jungfrau.ch* 🎫 *64 SF round-trip* ⏲ *Closed Oct.–May (depending on snow conditions).*

10

FAMILY **St. Beatus-Höhlen.** For a dose of nature blended with history, check out the St. Beatus caves. Their legend goes back to the 6th century, when the missionary St. Beatus arrived on the Thunersee to find the local population terrorized by a dragon that lived in the lake and surrounding grottoes. Exorcised by Beatus, the fleeing dragon fell to his death on the rocks. Today you can see the stalagmites, stalactites, and pools inside, as well as a colorful rendering of Ponzo, the dragon. The on-site cave museum offers scientific and historical information about caves around the world. Take a jacket, because it's cold inside the caves. You can reach them by taking Bus 21 from either train station or by crossing by boat from the Interlaken West station to Sundlaunen, then hiking 20 minutes to the caves. ✉ *Seestr., Sundlauenen* ☎ *033/8411643* ⊕ *www.beatushoehlen.ch* 🎫 *18 SF.*

The Berner Oberland rewards hikers with spectacular vistas, like this one of the Jungfrau.

WORTH NOTING

Harder Kulm. This 4,337-foot peak and its scenic overlook can be reached via an eight-minute funicular ride, making it a good bet when you don't have time for a longer excursion. From the top you'll enjoy views south over the city, the lakes, and the whole panorama of snowy peaks. The chalet-style restaurant offers sumptuous traditional dishes on a sunny terrace. The funicular station is north of River Aare, across Beaurivagebrücke. ✉ *Interlaken* ☎ *033/8287233* 🌐 *www.jungfrau.ch* 🎫 *Funicular 32 SF round-trip* ⏲ *Closed Dec.–Apr.*

FAMILY **Heimwehfluh.** An old-fashioned funicular railway chugs to the top of this 2,194-foot mountain, where you get views of both lakes as well as a peek at the Jungfrau, the Eiger, and the Mönch. There's the usual terrace restaurant at the top, along with a children's playground and a model-train show with music and lights. On the way down you can opt for a ride on the 985-foot-long bobsled run. The funicular station is a five-minute walk from the Interlaken West station down Rugenparkstrasse, with departures every 15 minutes between 10 and 5. The train show costs an extra 7 SF. ✉ *Interlaken* ☎ *033/8223453* 🌐 *www.heimwehfluh.ch* 🎫 *16 SF* ⏲ *Closed Oct.–Easter.*

Touristik-Museum der Jungfrau Region. This museum traces the history of tourism in the area over the last 200 years. Exhibits include souvenir production, models of early transportation, and primitive mountain climbing and skiing equipment. ✉ *Obere Gasse 28, Unterseen* ☎ *079/4769626* 🌐 *www.touristikmuseum.ch* 🎫 *5 SF* ⏲ *Closed Mon.–Wed. from Oct.–Apr.*

Unterseen. On the north side of the River Aare is this tiny town, founded in 1279 on land rented from the Augustinians. Unterseen retains some of the region's oldest buildings, including the 17th-century Stadthaus (city hall) and the 14th-century church, its steeple dating from 1471. The Schloss Unterseen (Unterseen Castle), built in 1656, stands at the opposite end of the square from these structures, near a medieval arched gateway. You can get here via a 10-minute bus ride from the center of Interlaken, or by walking from the Interlaken West train station. ✉ *Interlaken* 🌐 *www.unterseen.ch.*

WHERE TO EAT

$$ SWISS

✕ **Alpenblick.** This carved-wood-and-shingle 17th-century landmark attracts both locals and travelers with its two restaurants. The Bistro serves old-style Swiss cuisine—try the *Felchen* (a kind of whitefish) from nearby Lake Brienz, or an Alpenblick *Rösti* (similar to hash browns). The Gourmetstübli, a showcase for chef Richard Stöckli's renowned international fare, may include fish and mussels in a saffron-pepper sauce or veal ravioli and vegetables. **Known for:** award-winning gourmet cuisine; less expensive bistro fare; local favorite. $ *Average main: 36 SF* ✉ *Oberdorfstr. 8, Wilderswil* ☎ *033/8283550* 🌐 *www.hotel-alpenblick.ch.*

$$ ECLECTIC

✕ **Krebs.** Established in 1875, this old-world spot offers a well-balanced mix of tradition and modern comfort, with starched-collar service. Traditional Swiss cuisine and homey daily plates share menu space with the occasional French or Asian creation—tenderloin of pork with balsamic reduction and panfried shiitake noodles could be a good place to start. **Known for:** cheese fondue and Rösti; large, sunny terrace; proximity to the train station. $ *Average main: 30 SF* ✉ *Bahnhofstr. 4, Interlaken* ☎ *033/8260330* 🌐 *www.krebshotel.ch.*

$$ SWISS Fodor's Choice ★

✕ **Restaurant Bären.** In the late 1600s, postal workers traveling the Oberland needed a place to eat and swap horses. They found what they needed in this lumbering wood chalet, one of the oldest buildings in the area. **Known for:** rustic atmosphere; traditional Swiss fare; mountain views from patio. $ *Average main: 30 SF* ✉ *Seestr. 2, Unterseen* ☎ *033/8227526* 🌐 *www.baeren-unterseen.ch* ⏲ *Closed Mon. No lunch Tues.–Thurs.*

$$ ECLECTIC

✕ **Schuh.** With a luxurious shady terrace spilling into the Höhematte in summer and mellow piano sounds enhancing the classically elegant interior, this café-restaurant serves rich, hot Swiss meals (as well as some Chinese and Thai dishes). The recipes may date all the way back to 1818, but most of the dishes are freshly made in-house on a daily basis. **Known for:** fresh chocolate made on-site; daily chocolate shows at 5 pm for 16 SF; Swiss and Asian meals. $ *Average main: 29 SF* ✉ *Höheweg 56, Interlaken* ☎ *033/8888050* 🌐 *www.schuh-interlaken.ch.*

$$ SWISS

✕ **Stellambiente.** For something nicely out of the ordinary, try this family-run gem that defies its outdated 1960s exterior and residential setting. Along with marvelous, friendly service, you'll enjoy modern, flavorful cuisine: order the "surprise" menu and be treated to six inventive courses served on beautiful, individually selected pieces of china. **Known for:** flambéed beef fillet "Medici" with a red-wine-and-herb sauce; weekday lunch buffet; seasonal fare. $ *Average main: 30 SF* ✉ *Stella Swiss Quality Hotel, General-Guisan-Str. 2, Interlaken* ☎ *033/8228871* 🌐 *www.stella-hotel.ch* ⏲ *Closed Sun.*

WHERE TO STAY

$$ HOTEL **City Hotel Oberland.** The exterior of this hotel's main building is bristling with mansard windows and stucco trim, and the wing across the street is pierced by a life-size statue of a cow. **Pros:** central location for shopping and nightlife; the breakfast fills you up for sightseeing; bar and two restaurants on-site. **Cons:** noisy neighborhood; limited parking given the number of rooms; can get hot, depending on room and season. *Rooms from: 236 SF* *Höheweg 7, Interlaken* *033/8278787* *www.city-oberland.ch* *192 rooms* *Breakfast.*

$ B&B/INN **Hotel Alphorn.** This modern bed-and-breakfast sits on a quiet side street between Interlaken West and the Heimwehfluh. **Pros:** free Wi-Fi in every room; peaceful location; homemade jam at breakfast. **Cons:** some rooms are tiny; extra charge for balcony; limited "reception" hours. *Rooms from: 180 SF* *Rothornstr. 29a, Interlaken* *033/8223051* *www.hotel-alphorn.ch* *Closed early Jan.–late Mar.* *13 rooms* *Breakfast.*

$$ HOTEL Fodor's Choice ★ **Hotel Interlaken.** The oldest hotel in town, the Hotel Interlaken has been hosting overnight guests since 1323—first as a hospital, then as a cloister, and by the early 15th century as a tavern. **Pros:** cozy, attractive rooms with Alpine flair; in-room tea/coffeemakers; in the historic part of town. **Cons:** rooms can get hot in summer; not all rooms have a minibar; bit of a walk from town center. *Rooms from: 293 SF* *Höheweg 74, Interlaken* *033/8266868* *www.hotelinterlaken.ch* *61 rooms* *Breakfast.*

$$$ HOTEL **Hotel Royal–St. Georges.** If you are a fan of Victoriana, this impeccably restored grand hotel is for you, with original moldings, built-in furnishings, and fantastical bath fixtures. **Pros:** enjoyable for architecture lovers; easy access to trains and boats; spa with hot tub and sauna. **Cons:** artwork and color schemes in modern rooms won't appeal to everyone; noisy on street side; no a/c. *Rooms from: 360 SF* *Höheweg 139, Interlaken* *033/8227575* *www.hotelroyal.ch* *92 rooms* *Breakfast.*

$$$ RESORT **Lindner Grand Hotel Beau Rivage.** Set well back from the road and surrounded by gardens, this grande dame maintains an unruffled sense of calm. **Pros:** good location; fabulous views; spa facilities. **Cons:** no a/c; needs some renovation; rooms at the back are very close to train tracks. *Rooms from: 380 SF* *Höheweg 211, Interlaken* *033/8267007* *www.lindnerhotels.ch* *101 rooms* *Breakfast.*

$$$$ RESORT Fodor's Choice ★ **Victoria-Jungfrau Grand Hotel & Spa.** Restoration has taken this 1865 grande dame firmly into the 21st century, with glitzy touches such as the burled-wood entryway and a vast belle époque lobby that spirals off into innumerable bars and tea salons. **Pros:** location with view of Jungfrau; wonderful spa; elegant common areas. **Cons:** so gargantuan that you can feel like a mouse among many; some call this place overpriced; rooms can get hot in summer. *Rooms from: 650 SF* *Höheweg 41, Interlaken* *033/8282828* *www.victoria-jungfrau.ch* *212 rooms* *Breakfast.*

NIGHTLIFE AND PERFORMING ARTS

BARS

Brasserie 17. You'll always find a lively mixed crowd at Brasserie 17. Except in summer, Thursday means free live music. ✉ *Happy Inn Lodge, Rosenstr. 17, Interlaken* ☎ *033/8223225* 🌐 *www.brasserie17.ch.*

Market Fine Wine and Food. This classy wine bar has leather furnishings and lovely architectural flourishes. In warm weather, there's sidewalk seating with a view of the Höhematte. Tapas and pasta are on the menu along with a good variety of wines. ✉ *Jungfraustr. 46, Interlaken* ☎ *033/8237374* 🌐 *www.wineart.ch.*

THEATER

Fodor's Choice ★ **Tellfreilichtspiele.** For a real introduction to the local experience, don't miss the Tellfreilichtspiele, an outdoor pageant presented in Interlaken every summer by a cast of Swiss amateurs. Wrapped in a rented blanket and seated in a 2,200-seat sheltered amphitheater that opens onto illuminated woods and a permanent "medieval" village set, you'll see 180 players in splendid costumes acting out the epic tale of Swiss hero Wilhelm Tell. The text is Friedrich Schiller's famous play, performed in German with the guttural singsong of a Schwyzerdütsch accent—but don't worry; with galloping horses, flower-decked cows, bonfires, parades, and, of course, the famous apple-shooting climax, the operatic story tells itself. ✉ *Interlaken* ☎ *033/8223722* 🌐 *www.tellspiele.ch.*

SPAS

Victoria-Jungfrau Spa. An architecturally splendid indoor swimming pool with columns rising from the water is the anchor of the Victoria-Jungfrau spa, a sprawling wellness playground spanning 59,000 square feet. Whether it's sunny or snowy, the outdoor hot tub with a view of Harder Kulm is a particular treat. Adjacent to the pool, the "heat experience zone"—referring to the saunas and steam baths—features walnut trim, iridescent tiles, and flickering candles. The science of antiaging is the focus at the adjacent Spa Nescens. In addition to treatment rooms, it has its own saunas, steam baths, and relaxation rooms where guests are encouraged to unwind before or after a treatment. There are separate facilities for men and women, but couples can reserve the private spa and enjoy a few romantic hours together. A gym, tennis courts, and fitness studios provide the chance to exercise, and a small bistro serves light meals. ✉ *Victoria-Jungfrau Grand Hotel & Spa, Höheweg 41, Interlaken* ☎ *033/8282730* 🌐 *www.victoria-jungfrau.ch.*

LAUTERBRUNNEN

10 km (6 miles) south of Interlaken.

Fodor's Choice ★ Acclaimed by Alfred, Lord Tennyson, as "the stateliest bit of landstrip," the Lauterbrunnen Valley is often ranked as one of the most beautiful places in Switzerland. A Swiss Shangri-la, it encloses a nearly perfect set piece of earth, sky, and water. The mountains here seem to part like the Red Sea as two awesome, bluff-lined rock faces line the vast valley, where grassy meadows often lie in shadow as 1,508-foot rocky shoulders rise on either side. What really sets this mountainous masterpiece apart are the more than 70 waterfalls (*Lauterbrunnen* means "only

Laced with waterfalls, including the 941-foot Staubbach Falls (pictured) Lauterbrunnen Valley is one of the most beautiful spots in Switzerland.

springs") that line the length of the 3-km-long (2-mile-long) valley. Some plummet from sky-high crags, others cascade out of cliff-face crevasses, and many are hidden within the rocks themselves; the largest, the Staubbach Falls, were immortalized by Johann Wolfgang von Goethe, William Wordsworth, and Lord Byron, who described them as "the tail of a white horse blowing in the breeze." For scenery supreme, Lauterbrunnen can't be topped.

The relentlessly picturesque panorama opens up as you get off the train. This tidy town of weathered chalets also serves as a starting point for the region's two most famous excursions: to the Schilthorn and to the Jungfraujoch. Super-efficient parking and a rail terminal allow long- and short-term parking for visitors heading for Wengen, Mürren, the Jungfraujoch, or the Schilthorn. To save a lot of money on hotels, consider choosing this valley as a home base for day trips by train, funicular, or cable. But don't ignore its own wealth of hiking options through some of the most awe-inspiring scenery in Europe. Several lovely trails line the valley, including the **Panorama Spazierweg,** which connects Lauterbrunnen with Wengen. Get a map of it (and lots of brochures) from the tourist office on the main street.

GETTING HERE AND AROUND

The Bernese Oberland Railway runs trains once or twice an hour from Interlaken Ost station to the village of Lauterbrunnen; the trip takes 20 minutes and stops in such hamlets as Wilderswil and Zweilütschinen.

TOURS

Air-Glaciers. If you have the stomach for it, hop on a breathtaking helicopter tour of the amazing mountain ranges from Air-Glaciers. The heliport is south of town off the main road. ✉ *Lischmaad, Lauterbrunnen* ☎ *033/8560560* 🌐 *www.airglaciers.ch.*

VISITOR INFORMATION

Contacts Lauterbrunnen Tourism. ✉ *Stutzli 460, Lauterbrunnen* ☎ *033/8568568* 🌐 *lauterbrunnen.swiss.*

EXPLORING

Staubbachfälle (*Staubbach Falls*). Magnificent waterfalls adorn the length of the Lauterbrunnen Valley, the most famous being the 974-foot Staubbachfälle, which are illuminated at night and visible from town. These falls draw you like a magnet through the village of Lauterbrunnen itself, past a bevy of roadside cafés and the town center (marked by a church and the small Museum of the Lauterbrunnen Valley). Just opposite the falls is a centuries-old graveyard. ✉ *Lauterbrunnen.*

Fodor's Choice ★ **Trümmelbachfälle** (*Trümmelbach Falls*). A series of 10 glacier waterfalls hidden deep inside rock walls make up the spectacular Trümmelbachfälle, which you can access by a tunnel lift. Approach the departure point via a pretty creek-side walkway and brace yourself for some steep stair climbing. Be sure to bring along a light jacket—the spray can seem less than refreshing in the cool Alpine air. ✉ *Lauterbrunnen* ☎ *033/8553232* 🌐 *www.truemmelbachfaelle.ch* 🎟 *11 SF* ⏲ *Closed Dec.–Mar.*

WHERE TO STAY

$ B&B/INN FAMILY **Chalet-Hotel Rosa.** Housed in a 350-year-old chalet, this B&B is charming yet modern. **Pros:** bright and modern bathrooms; orthopedic beds; some waterfall views. **Cons:** right on main road; late check-in, early checkout; cash only. Ⓢ *Rooms from: 160 SF* ✉ *Hauptstr., Lauterbrunnen* ☎ *033/8551073* 🌐 *www.chaletrosabb.com* ▭ *No credit cards* 🛏 *11 rooms* 🍽 *Breakfast.*

$ HOTEL **Hotel Silberhorn.** Across from the train station and next to the cable car to Mürren, this wonderful family-owned hotel with a lovely garden is a surprisingly quiet option. **Pros:** excellent cuisine; peaceful vibe; amazing views. **Cons:** no elevator; rooms can get hot in summer; no pets allowed. Ⓢ *Rooms from: 189 SF* ✉ *Zuben, Lauterbrunnen* ☎ *033/8562210* 🌐 *www.silberhorn.com* ⏲ *Closed late Oct.–mid-Dec.* 🛏 *30 rooms* 🍽 *Breakfast.*

$ B&B/INN FAMILY **Hotel Staubbach.** Across from the Staubbach Falls, this excellent lodging opens directly onto Lauterbrunnen's main street, which is handily lined with shops and cafés. **Pros:** views of Staubbach Falls; children's play area; free tea and coffee all day. **Cons:** no restaurant; in-room facilities are limited; can be noisy. Ⓢ *Rooms from: 160 SF* ✉ *Hauptstr., Lauterbrunnen* ☎ *033/8555454* 🌐 *www.staubbach.com* ⏲ *Closed Nov.–early Jan.* 🛏 *27 rooms* 🍽 *Breakfast.*

CLOSE UP

When the Cows Come Home

It's difficult to grow more than grass on the steep slopes of the Alps, so much of the area has traditionally been used to graze sheep, goats, and, of course, dairy cattle, who supply fresh milk to the cheese and chocolate industries that make up such an important part of the country's agricultural economy. Brown Swiss, said to be the oldest breed in the world, has been a reliable producer of dairy products for centuries. Browns are highly prized in the region, as they adapt to all kinds of weather, have strong feet and legs, and produce more milk (which also happens to be higher in protein than that from other cows). Their robust nature has made them increasingly popular throughout the world.

The seasonal movement of livestock from lowland pastures to Alpine meadows is a tradition that goes back to ancient times. In spring, herders in regional costume spruce up their animals with flowers and embroidered bell collars and move them up to the grazing areas in a ceremony known as the *Alpaufzug* (Alpine ascent). In fall they come down the same way in the *Alpabfahrt* (Alpine descent). All cows are fitted with bells to help make them easier to find if they wander away from the rest of the herd, and the collective clang can echo through an entire valley. If you're driving along during one of the ceremonies, be prepared to pull over for a half hour or more while the cows lumber past, taking up the entire road.

MÜRREN

7 km (4 miles) southwest of Lauterbrunnen, 16 km (10 miles) south of Interlaken, plus a five-minute cable car ride from Stechelberg.

Fodor's Choice ★

Mürren is perched on a mountaintop shelf—5,361 feet high, to be precise. This village, along with neighboring Wengen, has always lured the rich and famous. The birthplace of downhill and slalom skiing (in the 1920s), Mürren offers extraordinarily peaceful mountain nights and an unrivaled panorama of the Jungfrau, Mönch, and Eiger, all set so close, you feel you can almost reach out and touch them. Skiers may want to settle here for daredevil skiing at the top (the annual Inferno Race in January is the largest amateur downhill in the world). Hikers can combine bluff-top trails with staggering views. This is a car-free resort, so no parking lots spoil the scenery.

GETTING HERE AND AROUND

Mürren is usually accessed via a cable car from the center of Lauterbrunnen and then a cogwheel train from Grütschalp (20.80 SF round-trip for both), but these may be shut down for maintenance (global warming's permafrost melt has increased closings). Alternatively, take the bus to Stechelberg—at the far end of the valley—where two even more dizzying cable cars (31.60 SF round-trip) have you reaching for the sky in no time. Upon arrival, Mürren splays out along a long mountain ridge road lined with hotels, restaurants, shops, a few historic chalets, and a large *Sportzentrum* (sports center).

VISITOR INFORMATION

Contacts Mürren Tourism. ✉ *Höhematte (in the Sportzentrum), Mürren* ☎ *033/8568686* 🌐 *www.mymuerren.ch.*

EXPLORING

Bergbahn Lauterbrunnen-Mürren. To reach Mürren from Lauterbrunnen take the aerial cable car across the street from the Lauterbrunnen train station. You then connect to the cogwheel rail from Grütschalp, which runs along the cliff and affords some magnificent views. The whole trip takes about 30 minutes and drops you at the Mürren rail station, at the opposite end of town from the cable car stop and a nice walk away. There are departures every 15 to 30 minutes. As you ascend, point your binoculars at the gleaming dome on the Jungfraujoch across the valley: you can almost hear the winds howling off the Aletsch Glacier. ✉ *Lauterbrunnen* ☎ *033/8287233* 🌐 *www.jungfrau.ch* 🎫 *22.80 SF round-trip.*

Schilthorn. Mürren boasts some of the longest downhill runs because it is at the foot of the Schilthorn (9,748 feet) mountain, famed for its role in the James Bond movie *On Her Majesty's Secret Service*. The peak of this icy megalith is accessed by a four-stage cable-lift ride past bare-rock cliffs and stunning slopes. At each level you step off the cable car, walk across the station, and wait briefly for the next cable car. At the top is the much-photographed revolving restaurant Piz Gloria, where you can see clips of the film. There's also an interactive, multimedia exhibition that is a must-see for James Bond fans called *Bond World*. Attractions include a flight simulator inside a helicopter and a 40-seat theater showing 007's Alpine adventures. The cable car station is in the town of Stechelberg, near the spectacular Mürrenbachfälle (Mürrenbach Falls). ✉ *Stechelberg* ☎ *033/8260007* 🌐 *www.schilthorn.ch* 🎫 *Cable car 105 SF round-trip.*

WHERE TO STAY

$$ HOTEL **Hotel Alpenruh.** Clad in time-burnished pine, fitted with gables, and sporting some great gingerbread trim, the Alpenruh is as picturesque a hotel as you can get in Mürren. **Pros:** views straight out of a postcard; tasteful interiors at relatively low prices; sauna. **Cons:** nearby cable car girders mar the view from some rooms; only three bathrooms have bathtubs—if you like a long hot soak après-ski, be sure to book one of them; no bar or lounge area. *Rooms from: 240 SF* ✉ *Eggli, Mürren* ☎ *033/8568800* 🌐 *www.alpenruh-muerren.ch* *26 rooms* *Breakfast.*

$$ HOTEL FAMILY Fodor's Choice ★ **Hotel Bellevue.** Distinguished by its lovely yellow-brick-and-shutter facade, this longtime landmark is a traditional ski lodge with full modern comforts. **Pros:** a welcome home-away-from-home abode; sauna; handy coin laundry. **Cons:** one room lacks a balcony—be sure to avoid it; no elevator; no hot food served at breakfast. *Rooms from: 250 SF* ✉ *Lus 1050A, Mürren* ☎ *033/8551401* 🌐 *www.bellevuemuerren.ch* *Closed mid-Apr.–early June and mid-Oct.–mid-Dec.* *19 rooms* *Breakfast.*

$$ RESORT **Hotel Eiger.** With a front-row perch directly across from the Eiger, Mönch, and Jungfrau, this is the most stylish hotel in Mürren. **Pros:** fantastic views; plush and cozy environment; adjacent to the Bergbahn

Mürren is a picturesque village with unbeatable views of the Jungfrau, Mönch, and Eiger peaks.

cliff-top station. **Cons:** the location is all about peace and tranquility, not excitement; spa zone can get crowded; train station across the street can emit some noise. $ *Rooms from: 290 SF* ✉ *Aegerten, Mürren* ☎ *033/8565454* 🌐 *www.hoteleiger.com* *49 rooms* *Breakfast.*

SPORTS AND THE OUTDOORS

SKIING

Schilthorn Ski Resort. Home to the Inferno amateur ski race, the Schilthorn has nearly 30 runs, most of them red (medium difficulty). There are also mogul pistes as well as winter hiking and sledding trails. Snowboarders and freeskiers will appreciate the Skyline Snowpark. ☎ *033/8260007* 🌐 *www.schilthorn.ch* *Skiing from 63 SF, hiking and sledding from 41 SF.*

FAMILY **Swiss Snowsports School.** For ski or snowboard lessons, contact the school office at Chalet Finel, directly behind the Hotel Jungfrau. ✉ *Chalet Finel, Mürren* ☎ *033/8551247* 🌐 *www.swiss-snowsports-muerren.ch.*

WENGEN

10 km (6 miles) north of Mürren.

Fodor's Choice ★ Lord Byron, Consuelo Vanderbilt (the Duchess of Marlborough), and other posh folks put Wengen on the map, spreading the word about its incomparable eagle's-nest perch on a plateau over the Lauterbrunnen Valley. Few places offered such magnificent panoramas and such elegant hotels. And because of its setting, its *Alpenglühen* ("Alpine glow," in which mountains turn pink in the sunset) was said to be the prettiest in all of Switzerland. Alas, success breeds its own problems. Today you can barely drink in the famous view 4,180 feet over the valley, because hundreds of chalets are in the way. Innerwengen, the town center, is crowded with large buildings and shops with plate-glass windows. But once up on your hotel balcony—the higher the better, of course—you may experience the wonder of yore.

What draws most visitors today is some of the Oberland's most challenging skiing (it connects with the trail network at Grindelwald), choicest hotels, and pinkest sunsets. You can aim for centrally located upscale hotels, near shopping and nightlife options, or head downhill to pleasant, more isolated lodging, all artfully skewed toward the view. Half-board is just short of obligatory, since only a few restaurants are not attached to a hotel. It's a car-free town; most hotels have porters that meet the trains.

GETTING HERE AND AROUND

Famously, cars cannot drive to Wengen, and the only transport is provided by the little Wengernalp Mountain Railway, or Wengernalpbahn. This departs and arrives from the lower-valley-floor town of Lauterbrunnen and chugs up the mountainside to Wengen every quarter hour, with departures as early as 4:50 am and as late as 2:40 am, depending on the day and season.

VISITOR INFORMATION

Contacts Wengen Tourism. ✉ *Dorfstr., Wengen* ☎ *033/8568585* 🌐 *www.wengen.ch.*

EXPLORING

In summer Wengen is a wonderful place to hike. You can also be inspired—and thrilled—by taking the famous **Männlichen Cable Car,** complete with a rooftop balcony for those who like to feel the wind in their hair. From Wengen it soars up to the top of the Männlichen ridge, a nearly five-minute ride. In Männlichen, hike up to the viewing station for a spectacular view of the Grindelwald and Lauterbrunnen valleys framed by the Eiger and Jungfrau peaks. You'll also find there the Berggasthaus Männlichen (Mountain Guest House), with several restaurants and guest accommodations. The cable car descends to the town of Grindelwald. Many, however, opt to head down under their own steam to **Kleine Scheidegg,** a tiny hamlet that serves as a hub for the mountain trains. This nearly two-hour descent is one of the most beloved and scenic hikes in the world. Another option is the "Summer Gemel," a three-wheeled mountain sled that you steer with your body weight.

10

But Wengen is a place to get intellectual as well as physical; get out onto those forest trails and you may understand why Byron was inspired to compose *Manfred* when he hiked to nearby Wengernalp in 1816, creating the first Byronic hero and influencing the development of Romanticism in the 19th century.

WHERE TO STAY

$$$ RESORT **Beausite Park Hotel.** On the hill above Wengen (a bit of a hike from the town center, but that may be a virtue), this lodging offers the kind of views that made Wengen world-famous—a vista of mountain majesty

with the nearby buildings nearly hidden by trees. **Pros:** peaceful location with sweeping views; ideal for skiers; family run. **Cons:** 10-minute walk uphill from cable car; back rooms can be dark because of trees; modern facade looks out of place. *Rooms from: 374 SF ⊠ Wengi, Wengen ☎ 033/8565161 ⊕ www.parkwengen.ch 42 rooms Breakfast.*

$$$ HOTEL **Hotel Alpenrose.** One of Wengen's first lodgings, this welcoming inn—downhill and away from the center—has been run by the same family for more than a century. **Pros:** traditional family-run business; relaxing salon for tired skiers or hikers; tables and lounge chairs maximize garden's unique views. **Cons:** an uphill walk to central Wengen; no wellness or spa facilities; carpets might not appeal. *Rooms from: 384 SF ⊠ Roossi 1371C, Wengen ☎ 033/8553216 ⊕ www.alpenrose.ch ⊙ Closed early Apr.–mid-May and early Oct.–Christmas 40 rooms Breakfast.*

$$ HOTEL FAMILY **Hotel Bären.** This family-run chalet just below the center of town has bright interiors and good views. **Pros:** hosts are top-notch; excellent food; free Wi-Fi. **Cons:** uphill walk to town center; limited views from rear rooms; no spa facilities. *Rooms from: 230 SF ⊠ Am Acker, Wengen ☎ 033/8551419 ⊕ www.baeren-wengen.ch ⊙ Closed mid-Oct.–mid-Dec. and for 2 wks after Easter 18 rooms Breakfast.*

$$$ HOTEL **Hotel Falken.** Built in 1895, soon after train tracks reached this mountain retreat, the Hotel Falken maintains its turn-of-the-century feel and its family-run friendliness. **Pros:** sociable atmosphere prevails; generous amenities in bathroom; great balcony views. **Cons:** some textiles could use a face-lift; no spa services; quite close to train tracks. *Rooms from: 380 SF ⊠ Gruebi, Wengen ☎ 033/8565121 ⊕ www.hotelfalken.com ⊙ Closed Nov.–early Dec. 44 rooms Breakfast.*

$$$ HOTEL **Hotel Regina.** At this genteel Victorian hotel with its plush and handsome lobby, you might be greeted by the owners' cocker spaniel, Caramel. **Pros:** stunning views from nearly all rooms; award-winning cuisine; lovely grounds. **Cons:** the hotel's restaurants, wine bar, and shop close in the off-season; some rooms looking quite worn; no minibar, coffee machine, or (free) Wi-Fi in room. *Rooms from: 400 SF ⊠ Schonegg, Wengen ☎ 033/8565858 ⊕ www.hotelregina.ch ⊙ Closed mid-Oct.–mid-Dec. 78 rooms Breakfast.*

SPORTS AND THE OUTDOORS

SKIING

Just over the ridge from Grindelwald, Wengen is nestled on a sheltered plateau high above the Lauterbrunnen Valley. From there a complex transport system connects to Grindelwald, Kleine Scheidegg, and Männlichen. From Wengen you can take a cogwheel train toward Jungfraujoch or Lauterbrunnen. There's also a cable car to Männlichen plus numerous lifts to serve the ski slopes. The Lauberhorn run is tough; it's used for World Cup ski races in January. One-day lift tickets for Grindelwald–Wengen cost 64 SF, and a two-day pass costs 118 SF. Lift passes for the whole Jungfrau region cost 73 SF for one day, and 145 SF for two days.

GRINDELWALD

19 km (12 miles) southeast of Interlaken.

Fodor's Choice ★ Not counting its sheer Alpine beauty (3,393 feet), this town remains among the most popular in the Berner Oberland for the simple reason that it is one of the most accessible of the region's mountaintop resorts. Strung along a mountain roadway with one main train station (and another used mainly for excursions to and from the mountains), it makes an excellent base for skiing, shopping, and dining—if you don't mind a little traffic. Once you get off the main road, there are gorgeous Alpine hikes in all directions.

Grindelwald may be surrounded by the peaks of the Wetterhorn, Schreckhorn, Mönch, and Jungfrau, but it is best known as the "Eiger village"—it faces the terrifying north face of the peak that has claimed so many mountain climbers' lives that some call it the "death wall." In the summer of 2006 the Eiger almost claimed Grindelwald itself as its newest victim: headlines around the world described the large chunk of rock face that broke off (because of unseasonably warm temperatures) and plummeted down the mountainside, covering Grindelwald in dust for several days.

GETTING HERE AND AROUND

Bernese Oberland Railway trains run the 35-minute route between Grindelwald and the Interlaken Ost station twice per hour.

VISITOR INFORMATION

Contacts Grindelwald Tourism. ✉ *Dorfstr. 110, Grindelwald* ☎ *033/8541212* 🌐 *www.grindelwald.ch.*

EXPLORING

Find out how climate change is affecting the region using an app developed by researchers at the University of Bern. The app works like this: hikers can explore seven climate paths and use their smartphones (and GPS technology) to listen to specific information about their surroundings. 🌐 *www.jungfrau-klimaguide.ch*

FAMILY **Firstbahn.** After a lovely 25-minute gondola ride on one of Europe's longest lifts, the peak called First (7,112 feet above sea level) is the launchpad for various adventures. For example, you can soar along a zipline in summer and sled down in winter. First is also the starting point for an easy 3-km (2-mile) walk to Lake Bachalpsee. Ask about combo tickets to save money on the gondola ride and activities. ✉ *Grindelwald* ☎ *033/8287233* 🌐 *www.jungfrau.ch* 🎫 *Gondola 30 SF, zipline 29 SF, sled run 33 SF* ⏲ *Closed Nov.–Mar.*

Gletscherschlucht (*Glacier Gorge*). Travel down into the valley below Grindelwald, and visit the Gletscherschlucht. You can either drive or take the bus to the hotel of the same name. From there you can walk a trail along the river and over bridges about 1 km (½ mile) into the gorge. Although you can't see the glacier itself while walking along the edges of the spectacular gorge it sculpted, you'll get a powerful sense of its slow-motion, inexorable force. ✉ *Grindelwald* 🌐 *www.grindelwald-sports.ch/en/glacier-canyon.html* 🎫 *19 SF* ⏲ *Closed mid-Oct.–late May.*

Continued on page 380

THE BERNESE ALPS

TOURING THE SUMMITS

A veritable chorus line of soaring peaks—the Jungfrau, Mönch, Eiger, Männlichen, and Schilthorn—are among Switzerland's mightiest mountains. To take your sightseeing to new heights, use this mini-guide to the cable-cars, gondolas, and trains that scale these sky-high Alps.

The Jungfrau mountain as seen from the Lauterbrunnen hinterlands

THE SUMMIT OF SUMMITS
CHOOSE YOUR BEST TRIP

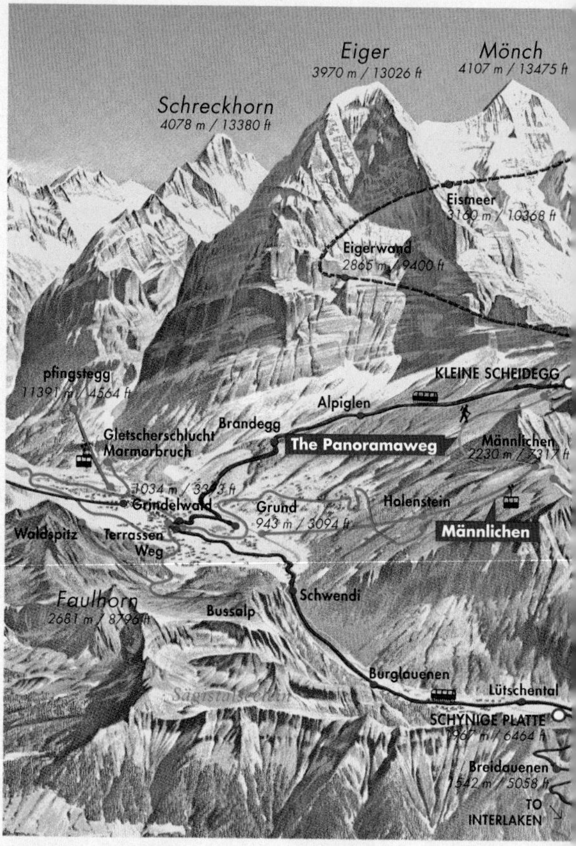

THE JUNGFRAU: A Train Ride to the Top of the World. You can't see the whole continent from the Jungfraujoch, Europe's highest accessible peak, but it sure seems like you can. It took some 16 years of work to dig the tunnel through the Eiger that today makes it possible for passengers aboard the **Jungfraujochbahn** to reach the "Top of Europe" in just 30 minutes from Kleine Scheidegg. During its ascent to the 11,333-foot-high station at the icy saddle, or "joch," that links the Mönch and the Jungfrau peaks, the train stops to afford terrifying views down the treacherous Eiger North Face and across yawning crevasses. At the top, hike over the Alps' longest glacier if the elevation (and scenery) haven't taken your breath.

THE WENGERNALP: One of Europe's Longest Rack-Railways. The Wengernalp train runs from Lauterbrunnen up the Männlichen Ridge and down to Kleine Scheidegg and Grindelwald. In between, this train route offers a fine first-act in acquainting visitors with the Bernese Oberland because it stretches through 12 miles of Switzerland's most beautiful ecozones.

Wengen–Männlichen cable car

THE MÄNNLICHEN: Europe's Longest Aerial Ride. Männlichen, a cluster of buildings perched overlooking a vista so spectacular it inspired Lord Byron's "Manfred," is accessible from both Grindelwald and Lauterbrunnen. From Grindelwald the **Männlichen gondola** stretches an amazing 3¾ miles to an airy station at 7,317 feet. From the Lauterbrunnen side, first take a train to Wengen, then board the cable car to Männlichen.

THE PANORAMAWEG: Switzerland's Most Hiker-Friendly Trail. No matter how travelers get to the top of the Wengernalp or the Männlichen Ridge, many opt to descend by foot along the relatively easy but

spectacular **Panoramaweg** trail. This unforgettable hike heads over to Kleine Scheidegg, where trains will then take you down to Grindelwald or Wengen or sky-high up the Jungfrau.

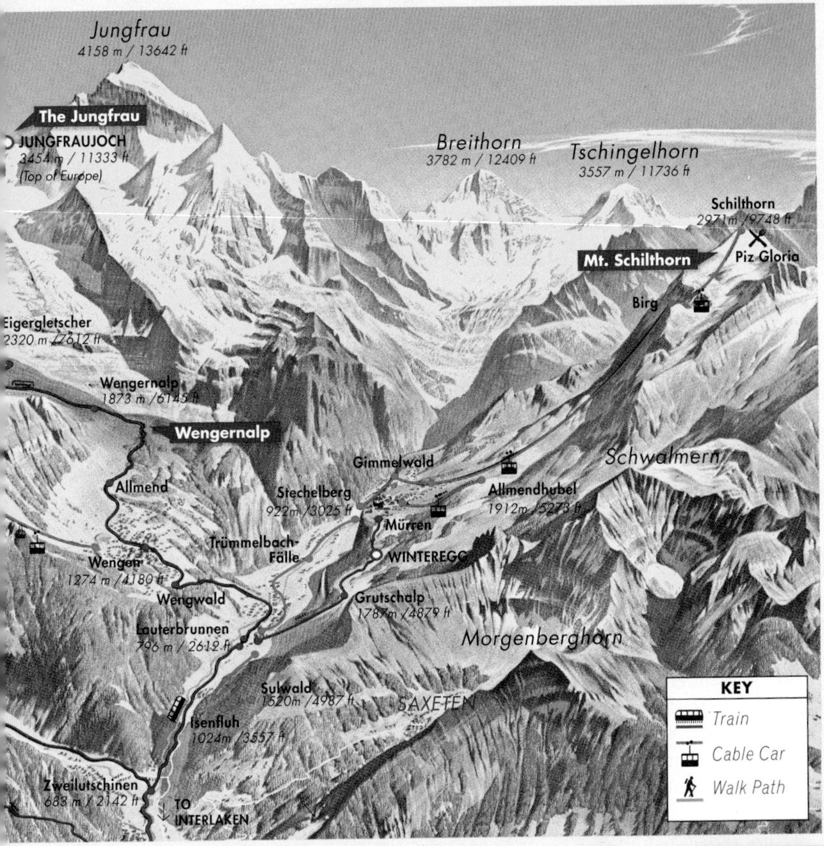

MT. SCHILTHORN: Sky-high Dining at James Bond's Piz Gloria. A dizzying, four-stage cable-car ride up the Schilthorn whisks visitors up to 9,748 feet, where the dominating peaks of the Bernese Oberland offer a far more memorable spectacle than the Bond movie filmed here in 1969, *On Her Majesty's Secret Service*. Head up early for the James Bond breakfast at the revolving Piz Gloria restaurant or linger in the warm afternoon light on the 360-degree deck that affords views so splendid your photos may look fake.

Skiing at Männlichen

THE JUNGFRAU: A TRAIN RIDE TO THE "TOP OF EUROPE"

The otherworldly landscape (or maybe it is just the lack of oxygen?) will make you feel like you're on the moon.

WHERE IT STARTS

Granddaddy of all high-altitude excursions is the famous journey to the **Jungfraujoch**—site of the highest railroad station in Europe—and is one of the most popular adventures in Switzerland. From the station at Lauterbrunnen you take the green cogwheel Wengernalp Railway as it grinds steeply up the wooded mountainside.

Get a seat on the right side of the car and watch the valley and the village shrink down below. On the hilltop, the resort town of Wengen pops into view but the train continues to climb and reaches Kleine Scheidegg, a tiny, isolated settlement above the timberline and surrounded by vertiginous scenery.

Top, Jungfraujoch—or the "Top of Europe"—leads to unforgettable vistas of the Aletsch Glacier from the Sphinx Terrace.

WHAT YOU SEE

At Kleine Scheidegg you change to the Jungfraubahn train, which tunnels straight into the rock of the **Eiger,** notorious as one of the most deadly ascents for mountain-climbers. If possible, for the 30- minute train ride up, snag a seat (again, one on the right-hand side) on one of the modern trains, which feature televisions screening a documentary about how the track was built. The train also stops twice, briefly, for icy views down the Eiger North Face and then again for tumbling glaciers framed by enormous picture windows blasted through the mountain's stony face. These are well worth the sprint out of the train for photos (even if someone grabs your seat). These stops only occur on the upward journey. Finally, you reach the **Jungfraujoch terminus** at 11,333 feet. Follow signs to the Top of Europe restaurant, a gleaming white glass-and-steel pavilion. The expanse of rock and ice you will see from here is simply blinding—bring your sunglasses.

FROM THE SPHINX TERRACE

Want to go even higher? Ride a high-tech, high-speed elevator up another 364 feet to the **Sphinx Terrace**: to the south crawls the vast **Aletsch Glacier**, to the northeast stand the Mönch and the Eiger, and to the southwest—almost close enough to touch—towers the tip of the Jungfrau herself. Hope that the outside Sphinx Terrace is open when you visit, as it is a delight to bathe in the sun and, if you're lucky, only a light mountain breeze (toast the moment with a glass of prosecco from the bar near the elevator). If the weather is good, a one-hour hike across a vast snow field lets you reach the **Mönchsjochhütte**, a hiker's dorm with refreshments and grand views.

SKY-HIGH ACTIVITIES

From June to mid-September sign up for a beginner's ski lesson, a dogsled ride, or tour the chill blue depths of the **Ice Palace,** a novelty attraction reminiscent of a wax museum, full of incongruous, slightly soggy ice sculptures. Admission to the attraction is included in the price of the excursion. ☎ 033/8287233 🌐 *www.jungfrau.ch* ⏲ *April–Oct., daily 6:35 am (first train up)–5:45 pm (last train down); Nov.–March, daily 6 am (first train up)–4:40 pm (last train down). The schedule is weather-dependent in winter: call ahead.*

Top, railway passes below the notorious Eiger North Wall.

TRIP TIP

Return trains, especially toward the end of the day, can be standing room only. You can possibly beat the crowds and get a cheaper price if you go really early in the morning or very late in the afternoon. Even if this isn't an exercise in solitude—the Jungfraujoch restaurants combined can seat 700 people at once—the touch-the-sky experience is worth it.

FROM THE WENGERNALP TO THE PANORAMAWEG

For breathtaking views of Switzerland's mountain heavyweights, nothing beats the gondola or cable-car up the Wengernalp and Männlichen or the famous hike along the Panoramweg.

UP THE WENGERNALP

The Wengernalp train chugs from the relatively balmy flats of the Lauterbrunnen Valley, through the quiet village of Wengen and up to the windswept mountainsides of the Kleine Scheidegg. From there the tracks drop down to bustling Grindelwald and more spectacular views. For many, a trip on this rack railway—one of the planet's longest—is just the first stage of the train journey up to the otherworldly ice fields of the Jungfraujoch. Yet it remains a worthy pursuit in itself because the Wengernalp ridge is sensational: the vista here (toward the 6,464-foot peak of Schynige Platte) inspired Lord Byron to write "Manfred" (the poem which kickstarted the Romanticism movement). The trip from either side up to Kleine Scheidegg takes 30-45 minutes.

☏ *033/8287233* 🌐 *www.jungfrau.ch*
⏲ *Departures about every 25 mins from 7 am–5:40 pm. Schedules are weather-dependent in winter: call ahead.*

ACROSS THE MÄNNLICHEN RIDGE

Ready to stretch your legs? The Männlichen lifts in summer provide access to a bevy of well-marked trails bathed in glorious views and punctuated by

Top, couple hiking the Männlichen Panoramaweg. Above, the car-free resort of Wengen sits on a mountainside below the notorious Eiger.

quaint mountain restaurants. Männlichen, a collection of buildings near the Jungfrau, Mönch, and Eiger peaks, can be accessed from lifts on either side—Lauterbrunnen or Grindelwald—of the ridge it sits on. One of the longest gondola rides in the world departs from the Grindelwald side, traveling 6 kilometers (3¾ miles) in 30 minutes. Or, take the five-minute zip up by cable car from Wengen. A spectacular view of both valleys, as well as the Berggasthaus Männlichen (Mountain Guest House), which offers food and guest accommodations, greets you upon arrival.

ALONG THE PANORAMAWEG TRAIL

From Männlichen, warm the legs up by climbing more than 100 meters in elevation to the Männlichen Gipfel (or Männlichen summit), at the edge of the ridge, for great views. Or, if you're reasonably fit, tackle the famous Panoramaweg trail from Männlichen to Kleine Scheidegg, taking about an hour-and-30-minutes on a mild descent along a well-maintained but uneven path. As this is one of the classic hikes in Europe, you will not be alone but there are enough rugged views to go around. The trail curves around the ridge by the Lauberhorn (where World Cup ski races are held); benches about halfway along the route make for a perfect picnic break. When you reach the hamlet of Kleine Scheidegg, catch a train toward either Grindelwald, or Wengen and Lauterbrunnen. ■ **TIP→ For the ultimate loop, first ride the gondola from Grindelwald to Männlichen, then hike over to Kleine Scheidegg, and hop trains back to Lauterbrunnen or Grindelwald.**

TIMES AND PRICES

Check the Web or the lift stations for full details about times and prices; various offers combine lifts and trains if you plan on hiking between points.

☎ 033/8552933 Wengen-Männlichen, ☎ 033/8548080 Grindelwald-Männlichen ⊕ www.maennlichen.ch

BY TRAIN ✉ *Trains from Lauterbrunnen Train Station to Kleine Scheidegg Train Station ☎ 0900/300300 ⊕ www.sbb.ch ⏲ Departures daily about every 25 mins 7 am–5:40 pm.*

BY GONDOLA AND CABLE CAR: *⏲ Gondola rides between Grindelwald-Männlichen every 30 mins, roughly 8 am–5:15 pm in summer, roughly 8 am–4 pm in winter. Cablecar between Wengen-Männlichen: June–Sept., every 15 minutes, 8 am–5:15 pm; Oct.–May every 15 mins, roughly 8 am–4 pm.*

Top, Wengen–Männlichen cable car.

BREAKFAST WITH BOND: ATOP MT. SCHILTHORN

James Bond had to use all of his wits to scale the Schilthorn but all you need is a ride up a string of the world's highest cable cars.

Second only to the Jungfraujoch for jaw-dropping views, the trip up the **Schilthorn** (9,748 feet) is truly a must for visitors to the Berner Oberland. Cue the Hallelujah chorus as you rise beside Yosemite-esque cliffs, past idyllic alpine farms, and at last rise to a mountain pinnacle that normally only the most hearty would ever set foot upon. From there not only are the Jungfrau, Mönch, and Eiger in full view, but a 360-degree riot of ragged peaks are as well.

"VIEWTIFUL" MÜRREN

The ride up is a four-stage cable-car extravaganza. From Lauterbrunen take the postbus toward Stechelberg and its Schilthornbahn station. Head up to a real cliff-hanger of a village, **Mürren**. Packed with Gemütlichkeit, it has superb hiking trails, beautiful hotels, and the Allmendhubel funicular. After a sky-high lunch on a terrace over the Lauterbrunnen valley, change cars once more at Birg for the final cable-car ascent.

Top, cable car ascending the Schilthorn.

The Piz Gloria revolving restaurant offers great views of the Eiger, Mönch, and Jungfrau.

IN THE PIZ GLORIA

The last lap soars across impossible heights to reach the Schilthorn peak, famed for its role in the 1969 James Bond action-film *On Her Majesty's Secret Service*. Here sits the flying-saucer-like lair of the film's villain, Ernest Blofeld, now known as the revolving restaurant **Piz Gloria.** Die-hard fans head here for the James Bond breakfast (no martinis, however), but visitors anytime can enjoy clips of the film in the Touristorama or the metal deck around the circular building for staggering 360-degree views of the scenery. Hiking down from the Schilthorn is a knee-smashing affair, so it is best to return to earth via cable-car. ☎ *033/8260007* 🌐 *www.schilthorn.ch* ⏲ *Departures yr-round, twice hourly 7:25 am–4:25 pm; last departure from the top 6:03 pm in summer, 5:03 pm in winter.*

TRIP TIPS

Remember these tips and you won't get into a pique over peaks.

- Prices for many cable-car and rack train rides can be as high as the peaks themselves. So wallet-watchers may want to consider a Jungfraubahnen Pass. Valid for 6 consecutive days, it entitles the holder to unlimited trips within the Jungfrau district network. For an extra fee, you can add the trip to Jungfraujoch. Pass prices are cheaper for those who already have a Swiss Travel Pass or Half-Fare Card. Another euro-stretcher are the special "Good Morning" rates that are offered for the first (as early as 6:30 am, and also sometimes second) departures of the day, with returns by 12 noon during the peak summer months, or returns any time of the day during November–April.
- Don't let high altitude sickness get you down. If you might suffer from a mild headache (the usual malady) atop the Jungfrau or Schilthorn peaks, consider taking aspirin before heading skyward. Move slowly. Breathing at the top nets just 67 percent oxygen. Plus: drink plenty of liquids (but not alcohol).
- Cable cars close twice annually for servicing—usually at the end of April and the end of November.
- Get a fix on the weather before heading out. Check with your hotel concierge. Make sure you pick a good-weather day, as the views are the thing when you are up high. Take sunglasses, warm clothes, and sturdy shoes with good tread.

Oberer Grindelwaldgletscher. From Grindelwald you can take a 20-minute drive, hop aboard a postbus, or hike up to the Oberer Grindelwaldgletscher, a craggy, steel-blue glacier—act fast, though, because 30% of it has melted since 1963, and forecasts have it shrinking another 20% by 2030. You can approach its base along wooded trails, where there's an instrument to measure the glacier's daily movement. ✉ *Grindelwald.*

THE DEADLY EIGER

Landmarked by its famous "White Spider" (the conjunction of snowfields and icy chutes), the Eiger's notorious north face was first climbed in the summer of 1938 via a wandering route. It was not until 1961 that the first group of climbers successfully conquered the almost vertical rock face by climbing straight up its middle. As you look up from the Jungfrau Railway train, the surprise is not that more than 45 people have lost their lives on the north face, but that anyone should have succeeded. Rumor has it that townspeople used to make bets on who would make it and who would not.

WHERE TO EAT

$ ECLECTIC **Bistro Memory.** A no-fuss, family-style bistro, this welcoming place is known for its youthful, smiley staff. With a well-stocked bar, varied menu, and street-side tables for watching the world go by, it has the relaxed feel of an English pub. **Known for:** all kinds of Rösti; casual, homey atmosphere; good for families. *Average main: 24 SF* ✉ *Hotel Eiger, Dorfstr. 133, Grindelwald* ☎ *033/8543131* 🌐 *www.eiger-grindelwald.ch.*

$ PIZZA Fodor's Choice ★ **Onkel Tom's Hütte.** Set in a rustic A-frame cabin on the main drag, this tiny pizza parlor is as cozy as they come. Rough-hewn floors accommodate ski boots, and a smattering of wooden tables share space with a huge iron cookstove where the young owner produces fresh pizzas in three sizes (the smallest of which is more than enough for most people). **Known for:** 400 kinds of wine; besides pizza, generous salads; popularity with hikers. *Average main: 24 SF* ✉ *Hauptstr., near the cable car station, Grindelwald* ☎ *033/8535239* 🌐 *onkel-toms.ch* *Closed Wed. and Thurs.*

WHERE TO STAY

$$$ RESORT Fodor's Choice ★ **Hotel Belvedere.** As you wind your way into Grindelwald, you can't help but notice this large pink structure perched precariously above the road. **Pros:** excellent facilities and cuisine; astounding views; peaceful surroundings. **Cons:** expensive rates; decor varies by room and might not suit all tastes; food is so good, it may be hard to go farther afield. *Rooms from: 450 SF* ✉ *Dorfstr. 53, Grindelwald* ☎ *033/8889999* 🌐 *www.belvedere-grindelwald.ch* *56 rooms* *Breakfast.*

$ HOTEL **Hotel Cabana.** Brimming with personal warmth, this family-run hotel has become a favorite among those who value tranquility and convenience. **Pros:** good value; quiet and pretty setting; honor system fridge in lobby. **Cons:** no restaurant; uphill walk into town; extra charge for robes. *Rooms from: 180 SF* ✉ *Dorfstr. 46, Grindelwald* ☎ *033/8545070* 🌐 *www.cabana-grindelwald.ch* *Closed Easter–mid-May, Oct., and Nov.* *15 rooms* *Breakfast.*

The only way to reach the charming village of Wengen is on the Wengernalp Mountain Railway.

$$ HOTEL Fodor's Choice ★ **Hotel Gletschergarten.** An expanded version of the standard chalet-style lodging, the Gletschergarten has been in the same family for four generations. **Pros:** homey feel with friendly hosts; small spa; magnificent views over glacier. **Cons:** some room elements could use a makeover; a bit of a walk to main street attractions; carpets not to everyone's taste. *Rooms from: 230 SF Obere Gletscherstr. 1, Grindelwald 033/8531721 www.hotel-gletschergarten.ch Closed mid-Apr.–mid-May and mid-Oct.–mid-Dec. 26 rooms No meals.*

$ HOTEL **Hotel-Restaurant Wetterhorn.** Overlooking the magnificent ice-blue glacier—as well as a sprawling parking lot—this pretty, wood-trimmed inn offers generous lunches on the terrace and good regional dining inside the comfortable restaurant. **Pros:** perfect base location for skiing and hiking; popular stop for meals; great views. **Cons:** the crowds are also savoring the sights; no coffee- or tea-making facilities in room; parking lot somewhat mars views. *Rooms from: 200 SF Obere Gletscherstr. 159, Grindelwald 033/8531218 www.hotel-wetterhorn.ch Closed late Oct.–late Nov. and 2 wks around Easter 10 rooms Breakfast.*

$$$$ RESORT **Romantik Hotel Schweizerhof.** Behind its dark-wood, red-shuttered chalet facade dating from 1892, this large, welcoming hotel invites you in with cozy wing chairs and bookcases in the lobby lounge and dining rooms—perfect spots to lounge in on rainy days. **Pros:** nothing is rushed, so you can truly relax; small library has books in seven languages; large garden and spa. **Cons:** rooms are well appointed but not lavish; can get hot in rooms in summer; carpets not to everyone's taste. *Rooms from: 670 SF Off Dorfstr., Grindelwald 033/8545858 www.hotel-schweizerhof.com Closed mid-Oct.–mid-Dec. and for 1 month around Easter 40 rooms Breakfast.*

DID YOU KNOW?

A bit of Switzerland crumbled away on July 13, 2006, with the headline-making rockfall from the Eiger's notorious north face due to the melting of the rock permafrost.

NIGHTLIFE

BARS

Avocado. Artfully furnished with thrift-shop treasures, the Avocado serves up whiskey, beer, and the occasional shot of live music. ✉ *Dorfstr. 158, Grindelwald* ☎ *079/9552704.*

SPORTS AND THE OUTDOORS

HIKING

Grindelwald is a hiker's paradise, both in summer and winter. Detailed maps of mountain trails are available at the tourist office.

Eiger Trail. The 6-km (3¾-mile) Eiger Trail extends from Alpiglen (near Grindelwald) to Eigergletscher (above Kleine Scheidegg). It abruptly climbs 2,300 vertical feet through cool copses of firs and spruce. Strategically placed benches offer a welcome breather or the perfect spot for lunch. Using only hand tools, the trail was built in 1997 in just 39 days. *Moderate.* 🌐 *grindelwald.ch/en/summer/product/track/36-eiger-trail-eigerletscher-alpiglen/.*

GrindelwaldSports. Head into the mountains on a guided hike led by GrindelwaldSports. With a day or two's notice, you can set out with a local, trained guide who can talk terrain as you cross beneath those lofty peaks. The Grindelwald tourist office also sometimes organizes outings. The tourist office and GrindelwaldSports are both at Grindelwald's Sportszentrum on Dorfstrasse. ✉ *Dorfstr. 103, Grindelwald* ☎ *033/8541280* 🌐 *www.grindelwaldsports.ch.*

SKIING

An ideal base for the Jungfrau ski area, Grindelwald provides access to the varied trails of Grindelwald First and Kleine Scheidegg–Männlichen. From here you'll have access to a whopping 45 lifts, cable cars, and funiculars that service no less than 206 km (128 miles) of downhill runs. Some slopes go right down to the village; there are special areas for snowboarders and beginning skiers. One-day lift tickets that cover the First-Kleine Scheidegg–Männlichen areas (plus Wengen) cost 64 SF. A two-day pass costs 118 SF. A two-day pass for the entire region, which adds Mürren and the Schilthorn, costs 145 SF.

BRIENZERSEE

One of the cleanest lakes in Switzerland—which surely means one of the cleanest in the world—the magnificent bowl that is the Brienzersee mirrors the mountain-scape and forests, cliffs, and waterfalls that surround it. Along the shore are some top attractions: the wood-carving center of Brienz, the wonderful open-air museum village of Freilichtmuseum Ballenberg—Switzerland's Colonial Williamsburg—and Meiringen, the site of Reichenbach Falls, where Sherlock Holmes fought with Moriarty. You can cruise alongside Lake Brienz at high speed on the A8 freeway or crawl along its edge on secondary waterfront roads. You can also cut a wake across it on a steamer, exploring each stop on foot before cruising to your next destination.

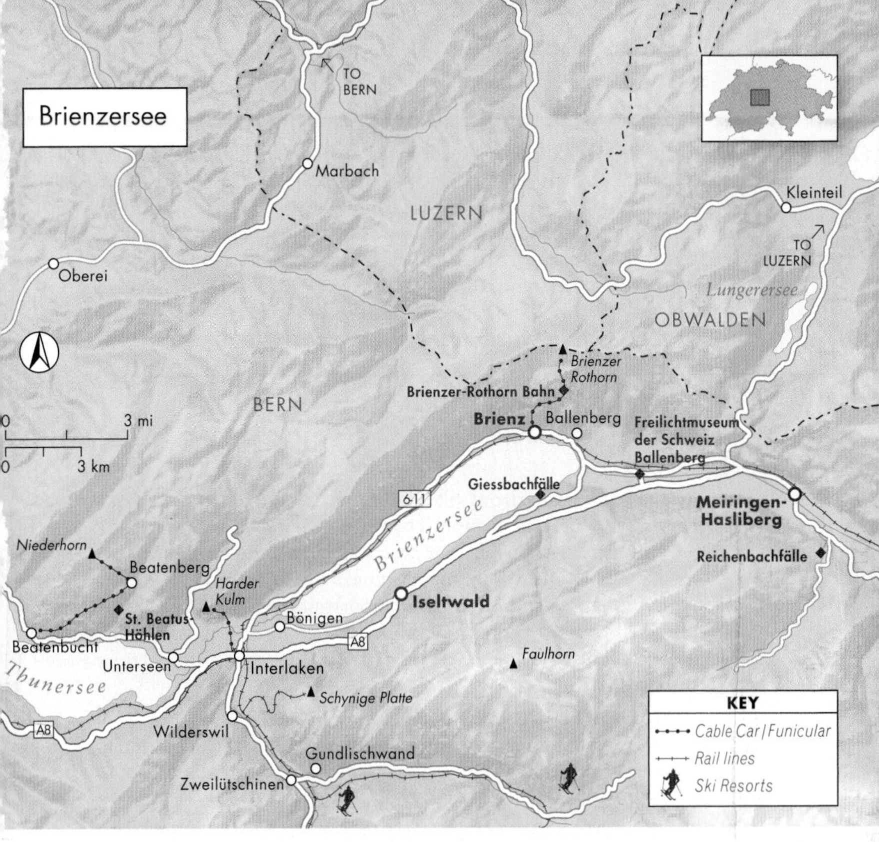

ISELTWALD

9 km (6 miles) northeast of Interlaken.

Set on a lovely and picturesque peninsula jutting out into the quiet waters of the lake, Iseltwald has a bevy of cafés, rental chalets, and hotels clustered at the water's edge. And every restaurant prides itself on its fish dishes.

GETTING HERE AND AROUND

By land, the most scenic route to Iseltwald from Interlaken is via the south-shore road; follow the black-and-white "Iseltwald" signs. You can also take the A8 expressway, following the signs for Meiringen.

EXPLORING

Giessbachfälle. From the edge of Iseltwald, an idyllic forest walk of about 1½ hours brings you to the falls of the Giessbach, which tumble in several stages down rocky cliffs to the lake. They are easy to find, being right next to the 19th-century extravaganza that is the Grandhotel Giessbach. You can also get to the falls via the Brienzersee steamer, which departs from Brienz or Interlaken Ost. ✉ *Brienz.*

WHERE TO STAY

$$ HOTEL Fodor's Choice ★ **Grandhotel Giessbach.** Overlooking the famed Giessbach Falls, this 19th-century belle époque showplace trimmed with fancy woodwork and topped with turrets offers lovely scenic views from almost any vantage point. **Pros:** stunning location; old-world charm; outdoor swimming pool with water lilies. **Cons:** day-trippers come for lunch at the terrace, so it can be crowded; might be hard to sleep in rooms facing the waterfall; takes some effort to get there. *Rooms from: 230 SF ✉ Am Brienzersee, Brienz ☎ 033/9522525 🌐 www.giessbach.ch ⏲ Closed late Oct.–late Apr. 70 rooms Breakfast.*

BRIENZ

12 km (7 miles) northeast of Iseltwald, 21 km (13 miles) northeast of Interlaken.

The romantic waterfront village of Brienz, world renowned for its wood carving, is a favorite stop for people traveling by boat as well as by car. Several artisan shops display the local wares, which range in quality from the ubiquitous, winningly simple figures of cows to finely modeled Nativity figures and Hümmel-like portraits of Wilhelm Tell. Brienz is also a showcase of traditional Oberland architecture, with some of its loveliest houses (at the west end of town, near the church) dating from the 17th century.

GETTING HERE AND AROUND

Brienz is on the direct rail line with Interlaken, with very frequent train connections.

VISITOR INFORMATION

Contacts Brienz Tourismus. *✉ Hauptstr. 143, Brienz ☎ 033/9528080 🌐 www.brienz-tourismus.ch.*

EXPLORING

FAMILY Fodor's Choice ★ **Brienzer-Rothorn Bahn.** Switzerland's last steam-driven cogwheel train runs from the waterfront of Brienz up to the summit of Brienzer-Rothorn, 7,700 feet above the town. The ride takes an hour and rolls under huge craggy peaks and through verdant meadows to afford stunning views of the lake. (The town will be so far below, you'll need pictures to remember the whole excursion wasn't fake.) A restaurant up top serves decent soups and sandwiches on a terrace that makes the most of the views. Trains depart about once an hour, but to avoid long waits at peak times, purchase your timed ticket in advance on the day you will make the trip. *✉ Hauptstr., Brienz ☎ 033/9522222 🌐 www.brienz-rothorn-bahn.ch 88 SF round-trip ⏲ Closed Nov.–May.*

FAMILY Fodor's Choice ★ **Freilichtmuseum der Schweiz Ballenberg** (*Ballenberg Swiss Open-Air Museum*). More than 100 typical houses from virtually every part of Switzerland are on display in this magnificent outdoor exhibit down a small road just east of Brienz. Dotting the meadows are 19th-century barns, pastel-shuttered houses, antique lace-making shops, traditional haberdasheries, and plenty of carefully reconstructed chalets. Even the gardens and farm animals are true to type. Spinning, forging, and lace making are demonstrated using original tools. The settlement, between

The train up to Brienzer-Rothorn is the last steam-driven cogwheel in the country.

the villages of Hofstetten and Brienzwiler, ranges over many acres, and you can easily spend at least a half day here. Via public transport, take the train to Brienz or Brünig and then a short bus ride to Ballenberg. ✉ *Museumsstr. 131* ☎ *033/9521030* 🌐 *www.ballenberg.ch* 🎫 *24 SF* ⏲ *Closed Nov.–mid-Apr.*

Fuchs Holzschnitzkurse. At Brienz you may want to try your hand at wood carving. From May to October, you can learn to carve the typical Brienzer cow during a two-hour lesson at the atelier of Paul Fuchs. Make a reservation through the Haslital tourist office in Meiringen. His workshop is in Hofstetten, between Brienz and Ballenberg. ✉ *Scheidweg 19D, Hofstetten* ☎ *033/9725050* 🌐 *www.fuchs-holzschnitzkurse.ch* 🎫 *30 SF* ⏲ *Closed Nov.–Apr.*

10

Schweizer Holzbildhauerei (*Swiss Woodcarving Museum*). To learn about the history of traditional Swiss woodworking, stop by the Schweizer Holzbildhauerei, where you can also buy locally carved pieces. ✉ *Hauptstr. 111, Brienz* ☎ *033/9521317* 🌐 *www.museum-holzbildhauerei.ch* 🎫 *5 SF* ⏲ *Closed Nov.–Apr.*

WHERE TO EAT

$$ ECLECTIC ✕ **Bären.** Mature trees strung with lights shade a brick terrace perched above the lake, making this establishment a lovely spot for a meal. The lighter choices include poached whitefish in a white-wine sauce. **Known for:** Indian cuisine as well as Swiss specialties; splendid lakeside setting; live entertainment. [$] *Average main: 30 SF* ✉ *Hauptstr. 72, Brienz* ☎ *033/9512412* 🌐 *www.seehotel-baeren-brienz.ch.*

$$ SWISS ✕ **Steinbock.** At this carved-wood chalet dating from 1787, you can sit out on the flower-lined terrace and choose from among no fewer than

10 interpretations of Lake Brienz whitefish and perch. The menu also has a range of veal classics. **Known for:** fresh, seasonal menu; traditional decor with lots of wood; sunny location. *Average main: 32 SF* ✉ *Hauptstr. 123, Brienz* ☎ *033/9514055* 🌐 *www.steinbock-brienz.ch.*

WHERE TO STAY

$ RESORT FAMILY **Hotel Lindenhof.** Families often settle in for a week or two at this hotel high above the lakefront, their evenings spent by the immense stone fireplace, in the panoramic winter garden, or on the spectacular terrace. **Pros:** indoor pool and sauna; manicured gardens; quirky decor. **Cons:** standard rooms are fairly small; a 15-minute uphill walk from the lake; no in-room kettle or coffeemaker. *Rooms from: 180 SF* ✉ *Lindenhofweg 15, Brienz* ☎ *033/9522030* 🌐 *www.hotel-lindenhof.ch* *Closed Jan.–mid-Mar. and Mon. and Tues. in late Mar., Apr., Nov., and Dec.* *40 rooms* *Breakfast.*

MEIRINGEN–HASLIBERG

12 km (7 miles) northeast of Iseltwald, 21 km (13 miles) northeast of Interlaken.

Set apart from the twin lakes and saddled between the roads to the Sustenpass and the Brünigpass, Meiringen is a resort town with more than 300 km (186 miles) of marked hiking trails and 60 km (37 miles) of ski slopes at the Hasliberg ski region. Historically, its claim to fame is as the place where meringue was invented—the (dubious) legend is that the resident chef had too many egg whites left over and decided to do something different for visiting celeb Napoléon. But there is little history left here, and today Meiringen is merely a pleasant town whose main street is lined with shops selling all sorts of kitschy Swiss merchandise (don't laugh—this stuff is hard to find in many parts of the country).

GETTING HERE AND AROUND

Frequent trains run the 35-minute route between Meiringen and Interlaken.

VISITOR INFORMATION

Contacts Tourist Information Meiringen. ✉ *Bahnhofpl. 12, Meiringen* ☎ *033/9725050* 🌐 *www.haslital.ch.*

EXPLORING

Aare Gorge. You can explore the imposing Aare Gorge (Aareschlucht, as it's known in German) via a sturdy walkway. On hot summer days, the rush of river water below you has a welcome cooling effect. ✉ *Meiringen* ☎ *033/9714048* 🌐 *www.aareschlucht.ch* *8.50 SF* *Closed Nov.–Apr.*

FAMILY **Reichenbachfälle** (*Reichenbach Falls*). Meiringen's one showstopper is the Reichenbachfälle, where Sir Arthur Conan Doyle's fictional detective Sherlock Holmes and his archenemy, Professor Moriarty, plunged into the "cauldron of swirling water and seething foam in that bottomless abyss above Meiringen." This was the climax of the "last" Holmes story, "The Final Problem" (the uproar over the detective's untimely end was such that the author was forced to resurrect his hero for further fictional adventures). The falls, 2,730 feet up a mountain a little way outside

Sherlock Holmes is commemorated by this statue in Meiringen. The famous detective "died" after a struggle with Professor James Moriarty on the Reichenbach Falls, just above the city.

of town, can be visited via a funicular. ✉ *Meiringen* ☎ *033/9822626* 🌐 *www.grimselwelt.ch* 🎫 *10 SF* ⏲ *Closed mid-Oct.–early May.*

Sherlock Holmes Museum. Buffs of the famous detective will like the Sherlock Holmes Museum in the center of town. Housed in a small chapel, it contains a replica of the fictional sleuth's front room at 221B Baker Street. ✉ *Bahnhofstr. 26, Meiringen* ☎ *033/9726008* 🌐 *www.sherlock-holmes.ch* 🎫 *4 SF* ⏲ *Closed Mon., Tues., and Thurs.–Sat. Dec.–Apr.*

THUNERSEE

If you like your mountains as a picturesque backdrop and like to relax on the waterfront, take a drive around the Thunersee (Lake Thun) or crisscross it on a leisurely cruise boat. More populous than Lake Brienz, its allures include the marina town of Spiez and the large market town of Thun, spread at the feet of the spectacular Schloss Zähringen (Zähringen Castle). There are other castles along the lake, and yet another high-altitude excursion above the waterfront to take in Alpine panoramas—a trip up the Niederhorn.

SPIEZ

19 km (11¾ miles) west of Interlaken.

With its mild climate and lakeside location, Spiez provides a striking contrast to the snowy Alps. A good reason to visit might be the nearby vineyards, which produce about 75,000 bottles of wine per year.

GETTING HERE AND AROUND

A rail line connects this summer lake resort with Thun and Interlaken.

VISITOR INFORMATION

Contacts Thunersee Tourismus. *Spiez Bahnhof, Seestr. 2, Spiez* *033/6559000* *www.thunersee.ch.*

EXPLORING

FAMILY **Schloss Spiez.** The town's enormous waterfront castle, Schloss Spiez, was home to the family Strättligen and, in the 13th century, its great troubadour, Heinrich. The structure spans four architectural epochs, starting with the 11th-century tower. Its halls contain beautiful period furnishings, some dating back to Gothic times. The early Norman church on the grounds is more than 1,000 years old. *Schlossstr. 16, Spiez* *033/6541506* *www.schloss-spiez.ch* *10 SF* *Closed mid-Oct.–mid-Apr.*

WHERE TO EAT

$ ITALIAN **Hotel Seegarten Marina.** Choose between a marble-columned pizzeria in one wing and two dining rooms that stretch comfortably along the waterfront. The lake fish specialties are excellent, but there is also a huge range of steaks, pastas, and salads, plus a children's menu—you will be spoiled for choice. **Known for:** pretty waterfront location; large sunny terrace; free Wi-Fi. *Average main: 25 SF* *Schachenstr. 3, Spiez* *033/6556767* *www.seegarten-marina.ch.*

WHERE TO STAY

$$$ RESORT **Strandhotel Belvédère.** Amid beautiful lawns and gardens, this graceful old mansion has its own manicured beach for secluded swimming. **Pros:** elegant dining; lakeside location; sparkling spa. **Cons:** seminar groups might remind vacationers of the office; not much to do in town; gap between beds might bother couples. *Rooms from: 360 SF* *Schachenstr. 39, Spiez* *033/6556666* *www.belvedere-spiez.ch* *36 rooms* *Breakfast.*

THUN

10 km (6 miles) north of Spiez, 29 km (18 miles) northwest of Interlaken.

Built on an island in the River Aare as it flows from Lake Thun, this picturesque market town is laced with rushing streams crossed by wooden bridges, and its streets are lined with arcades. On the Old Town's main shopping thoroughfare pedestrians stroll along flowered terrace sidewalks built on the roofs of the stores' first floors and climb down stone stairs to visit the "sunken" street-level shops.

GETTING HERE AND AROUND

A rail line connects Thun, Spiez, and Interlaken. From Bern you can catch A6 south, toward Thun.

VISITOR INFORMATION

Contacts Thunersee Tourismus. *Bahnhof, Seestr., Thun* *033/2259000* *www.thunersee.ch.*

Set against a beautiful mountain backdrop, the Thunersee is studded with castles.

EXPLORING

OFF THE BEATEN PATH

Niederhorn. The trip up the 6,397-foot Niederhorn lets you sit back and soak in the glory of the entire region. From the summit, you can appreciate not only the Jungfrau's splendor but also the rugged terrain surrounding the Gemmi Pass to the west and Grosse Scheidegg to the east. The journey can begin with a funicular from the lakeside stop called Beatenbucht (get here via boat or postbus from Thun). If you'd rather, you can catch a gondola in the hamlet of Beatenberg (accessible by postbus from Interlaken). You'll change to a cable car at Vorsass, where you'll find a lovely restaurant, on your way to the Niederhorn. Keep your eyes peeled for chamois and Alpine ibex along the ridge. In winter, you can go skiing, snowboarding, walking, or sledding. ☎ *033/8410841* 🌐 *www.niederhorn.ch* 🎫 *60 SF–75 SF round-trip from Thun or Interlaken, depending on transportation mode.*

10

Fodor's Choice ★

Schloss Thun (*Thun Castle*). From the charming medieval Rathausplatz, a covered stairway leads up to the great Schloss Thun, its broad donjon (inner tower) surrounded by four stout turrets. Built in 1186 by Berchtold V, Duke of Zähringen, it houses the fine Schlossmuseum Thun (Thun Castle Museum) and provides magnificent views from its towers. The Knights' Hall has a grand fireplace, an intimidating assortment of medieval weapons, and tapestries, one from the tent of Charles the Bold. The hall is often the imposing venue for concerts. Other floors display local Steffisburg and Heimberg ceramics, 19th-century uniforms and arms, and Swiss household objects, including charming Victorian toys. ✉ *Schlossberg 1, Thun* ☎ *033/2232001* 🌐 *www.schlossthun.ch* 🎫 *10 SF* 🕑 *Closed Mon.–Sat. Nov.–Jan.*

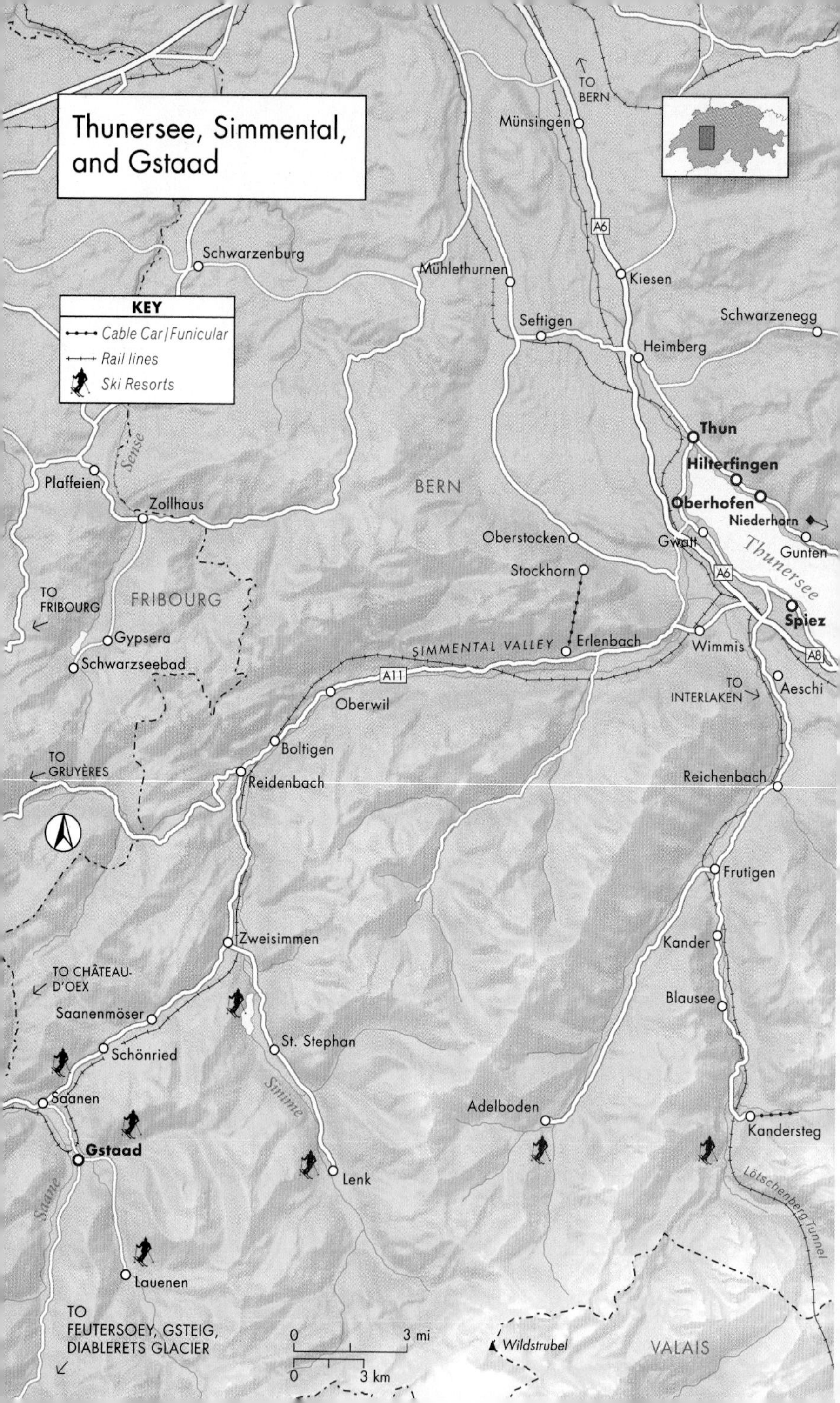
Thunersee, Simmental, and Gstaad
KEY
Cable Car/Funicular
Rail lines
Ski Resorts
TO BERN
Münsingen
A6
Schwarzenburg
Mühlethurnen
Kiesen
Seftigen
Schwarzenegg
Heimberg
Thun
Hilterfingen
Oberhofen
Niederhorn
Gunten
Thunersee
Sense
Plaffeien
Zollhaus
BERN
Oberstocken
Gwatt
Stockhorn
TO FRIBOURG
FRIBOURG
Spiez
Gypsera
Schwarzseebad
SIMMENTAL VALLEY
Erlenbach
Wimmis
A8
A11
Oberwil
TO INTERLAKEN
Aeschi
Boltigen
TO GRUYÈRES
Reidenbach
Reichenbach
Frutigen
Zweisimmen
Kander
TO CHÂTEAU-D'OEX
Saanenmöser
Blausee
Schönried
St. Stephan
Simme
Saanen
Adelboden
Kandersteg
Gstaad
Lenk
Lötschenberg Tunnel
Saane
Lauenen
TO FEUTERSOEY, GSTEIG, DIABLERETS GLACIER
0
3 mi
3 km
Wildstrubel
VALAIS

WHERE TO STAY

$$ HOTEL **Krone.** On the charming town hall square, this landmark hotel has some fine river views. **Pros:** historic character and central location; bountiful breakfast buffet; riverside terrace. **Cons:** paid parking is limited; can be noisy during the busiest times; no a/c. *Rooms from: 220 SF* *Obere Hauptg. 2, Thun* *033/2278888* *www.krone-thun.ch* *31 rooms* *Breakfast.*

$ HOTEL **Zu Metzgern.** At the base of the castle hill, this shuttered and arcaded *Zunfthaus* (guildhall) overlooks the Town Hall Square. **Pros:** great atmosphere; central location in the Old Town; traditional Swiss restaurant on-site. **Cons:** sinks in the room, but bathrooms are down the hall; breakfast not included in rates; revelers outside can be noisy. *Rooms from: 139 SF* *Untere Hauptg. 2, Thun* *033/2222141* *www.zumetzgern.ch* *10 rooms* *No meals.*

SPORTS AND THE OUTDOORS

SAILING

Lake Thun offers the area's best sailing.

Von Allmen Sailing School. From April to August, the Von Allmen Sailing School near Spiez offers courses and boat rentals. *Interlakenstr. 103A* *033/8225693* *www.motor-segelbootschule.ch.*

SHOPPING

Erlebnis-Töpferei. A good spot for traditional pottery, Erlebnis-Töpferei is just north of Thun. *Bernstr. 295, Heimberg* *033/4371472* *www.danielhowald.ch.*

HILTERFINGEN AND OBERHOFEN

5 km (3 miles) southeast of Thun.

Lake Thun is famous for its waterside castles, and Hilterfingen and Oberhofen, a little farther along the shore, have two of the best.

Schloss Hünegg. Hilterfingen's castle, Schloss Hünegg, was built in 1861 and furnished over the years with a bent toward art nouveau. The stunning interiors have remained unchanged since 1900. Outside is idyllic parkland. *Staatsstr. 52, Hilterfingen* *033/2431982* *www.schlosshuenegg.ch* *10 SF* *Closed mid-Oct.–mid-May.*

10

Schloss Oberhofen. Even Walt Disney would have a hard time topping Schloss Oberhofen for sheer fairy-tale splendor. The jewel of the village, this delightful hodgepodge of towers and spires sits on the waterfront. Begun during the 12th century, it was repeatedly altered over a span of 700 years. Inside, a museum has a display of the lifestyles of Bernese nobility, along with salons done up in the plushest 19th-century style, plus a Turkish "smoking room," a display of magical medieval stained glass, and a 13th-century chapel with noted Romanesque frescoes. In the Seetürmchen is a lovely, candlelit chamber where all eyes are drawn to an extraordinary carved-wood mermaid chandelier. Those in the know touch the mermaid's belly for good luck. *Schlossg., Oberhofen* *033/2431235* *www.schlossoberhofen.ch* *10 SF* *Closed late Oct.–mid-May.*

SIMMENTAL AND GSTAAD

Separate in spirit and terrain from the rest of the Berner Oberland, this craggy forest gorge follows the Lower Simme into the Saanenland, a region as closely allied with French-speaking Vaud as it is with its Germanic brothers. Here the world-famous resort of Gstaad has linked up with a handful of neighboring village resorts to create the almost limitless outdoor opportunities of the Gstaad "Mountain Rides" region. From Gstaad it's an easy day trip into the contrasting culture of Lake Geneva and the waterfront towns of Montreux and Lausanne. From Interlaken, take A8 toward Spiez, then cut west on A11, following the signs toward Zweisimmen, which leads to Gstaad. The forest gorges of the Simmental Valley lead you through Zweisimmen to the Saanenland and Gstaad.

GSTAAD

49 km (30 miles) southwest of Spiez, 67 km (42 miles) southwest of Interlaken, 68 km (43 miles) northwest of Montreux.

The four fingerlike valleys of the Saanenland find their palm at Gstaad, the Berner Oberland's most glamorous resort. Linking the Berner Oberland with the French-speaking territory of the Pays-d'Enhaut of Canton Vaud, the holiday region of Gstaad blends the two regions' natural beauty and cultures, upholding Pays-d'Enhaut folk-art traditions such as *papier découpage* (paper silhouette cutouts) as well as decidedly Germanic ones (cowbells, wood carvings, and alpenhorns).

In Gstaad, neither culture wins the upper hand—in fact, both cultures take a backseat to a more cosmopolitan attitude. During high season the folksy Gemütlichkeit of the region gives way to jet-set international style. Although weathered-wood chalets are the norm (even the two tiny supermarkets are encased in chalet-style structures), the main street is lined with designer boutiques. Prince Rainier of Monaco, Roger Moore, and Elizabeth Taylor have all owned chalets in Gstaad, as well as the late musician and conductor Yehudi Menuhin, who founded his annual summer music festival here. (The Menuhin Festival takes place from mid-July through early September, and hotels fill quickly then—as they do for the Swiss Open tennis tournament, held every July.)

Gstaad is a see-and-be-seen spot, with equal attention given to its plentiful skiing and its glamorous gatherings—après-ski, après-concert, après-match. The Christmas–New Year's season brings a stampede of glittering socialites. But you can escape the social scene. There are several unpretentious inns, hotels, and vacation apartments, and dozens of farmhouses that rent rooms, either in Gstaad itself or in one of the nearby Saanenland hamlets (Gsteig, Feutersoey, Lauenen, Turbach, Schönried, Saanenmöser, Saanen). What paradoxically defies and maintains Gstaad's socialite status is its setting: richly forested slopes, scenic year-round trails, working dairy farms, and, for the most part, stubbornly authentic chalet architecture keep it firmly anchored in tradition.

GETTING HERE AND AROUND

There are train connections from Bern; change in Spiez and Zweisimmen. There's also a narrow-gauge train from Montreux every hour that costs 27 SF one way. The center of Gstaad itself is reserved for pedestrians. You can leave your car at the parking facilities at either end of the main street.

VISITOR INFORMATION

Contacts Gstaad Saanenland Tourismus. ✉ *Promenade 41, Gstaad* ☎ *033/7488181* 🌐 *www.gstaad.ch.*

EXPLORING

Museum der Landschaft Saanen (*Saanenland Museum*). On Saanen's main street, upstairs from the Heimatwerk handicrafts shop, the Museum der Landschaft Saanen traces the history of the area through tools, costumes, furniture, and decorative pieces. ✉ *Dorfstr. 62a, Saanen* ☎ *033/7447988* 🌐 *www.museum-saanen.ch* 🎫 *8 SF* ⏲ *Closed Mon.*

Saanen Church. The first recorded mention of the Saanen Church, the oldest building in the region, was in 1228, and it is no doubt older than that. Just off Saanen's main street, the church is open daily for visits unless a service is being held. This Romanesque structure was renovated in the 20th century to reveal portions of medieval frescoes on the interior walls. ✉ *Bortgässli, Gstaad* 🌐 *www.kirchesaanen.ch/saanen.php.*

WHERE TO EAT

$$$$ MODERN FRENCH Fodor's Choice ★

✕ **Die Chesery.** Brie stuffed with truffles, lobster "cappuccino" (a foamy bisque), and le pigeon "royal": with such showstoppers as these, the well-regarded chef, Robert Speth, scales the summits of culinary excellence. He masterfully marries exotic flavors with local ingredients, and his results have foodies and millionaires fighting for reservations; book way ahead in high season. **Known for:** mouthwatering food, eye-watering prices; good-value lunch specials; selling stock and seasoning. 💲 *Average main: 73 SF* ✉ *Alte Lauenenstr. 6, Gstaad* ☎ *033/7442451* 🌐 *www.chesery.ch* ⏲ *Closed Mon., Easter–early June, and early Oct.–early Dec.*

WHERE TO STAY

$$$$ RESORT Fodor's Choice ★

The Alpina Gstaad. In a vast park above the village, this exquisite hotel manages to be posh and homey at the same time. **Pros:** every room has a balcony with a beautiful view; excellent food in three restaurants, including Japanese; large spa with indoor and outdoor pools. **Cons:** uphill walk from town; awfully high prices for drinks and spa treatments; you'll have to check out eventually. 💲 *Rooms from: 850 SF* ✉ *Alpinastr. 23, Gstaad* ☎ *033/8889888* 🌐 *www.thealpinagstaad.ch* ⏲ *Closed mid-Mar.–early June and Oct.–early Dec.* *55 rooms* 🍽 *Breakfast.*

$$$$ RESORT

Gstaad Palace Hotel. Towering above tiny Gstaad, this fantasyland castle is as costly as it looks. **Pros:** sense of history and stardust in this century-old hotel; plethora of amenities; stunning views. **Cons:** coffeemakers are only in suites; 15-minute walk uphill from town; prices to match the lofty location. 💲 *Rooms from: 740 SF* ✉ *Palacestr., Gstaad* ☎ *033/7485000* 🌐 *www.palace.ch* ⏲ *Closed mid-Mar.–mid-June and mid-Sept.–mid-Dec.* *100 rooms* 🍽 *Breakfast.*

DID YOU KNOW?

Gstaad is known for its après-ski scene and high-profile vacationers. If you want to arrive in style, book a room at the Palace, an extravagantly appointed castlelike hotel perched above the resort—you might be chauffeured in a Rolls-Royce to check in.

$$$$ HOTEL **Hotel Le Grand Chalet.** A 15-minute walk from the center of Gstaad, the hilltop Le Grand Chalet commands a spectacular view of the surrounding mountains and village below. **Pros:** fine food in the restaurant; amazing views; spacious rooms. **Cons:** not close to Gstaad nightlife; decor somewhat old-fashioned; fitness and wellness essentially in same room. *Rooms from: 505 SF* *Neueretstr. 43, Gstaad* *033/7487676* *www.grandchalet.ch* *Closed late Mar.–late May and early Oct.–mid-Dec.* *23 rooms* *Breakfast.*

$$$ HOTEL **Hotel Olden.** At the eastern end of the main thoroughfare, this charming Victorian-style inn has an elaborately painted facade and intricately carved woodwork in every interior niche. **Pros:** unique but traditional hotel; fine dining and entertainment on-site; central location. **Cons:** no elevator; no spa; potentially noisy revelers nearby. *Rooms from: 450 SF* *Promenade 35, Gstaad* *033/7484950* *www.hotelolden.com* *Closed mid-Apr.–early June and late Oct.–mid-Dec.* *12 rooms* *Breakfast.*

$$$$ RESORT **Le Grand Bellevue.** Set in a nicely landscaped park at the northern edge of the village, this resort features whimsical decor, several on-site dining options, and a very large spa with numerous relaxation chambers. **Pros:** complimentary minibars and coffeemakers in rooms; vast and gorgeous spa; sushi bar, fondue hut, and renowned restaurant. **Cons:** in-room color schemes a bit drab; luxe spa towels rather heavy for saunas; rumble of trains might disturb some. *Rooms from:* *Hauptstr., Gstaad* *033/7480000, 033/7480001* *www.bellevue-gstaad.ch* *57 rooms* *Breakfast.*

$$$$ RESORT **Park Gstaad.** Pairing wool-and-wooden materials with high-end entertainment systems, this handsome hotel blends old chalet style with contemporary flair in its well-designed rooms and suites. **Pros:** truly top-notch wellness program and facilities; pairing modern luxe with a modern-chalet abode is a winning combination; outdoor pool with lawn. **Cons:** gray wool seems a bit cold next to warm wood tones; everything is expensive; some rooms can get hot in summer. *Rooms from: 680 SF* *Wispilestr. 29, Gstaad* *033/7489800* *www.parkgstaad.ch* *Closed mid-Sept.–late Dec. and mid-Mar.–early June* *94 rooms* *Breakfast.*

$$ HOTEL **Posthotel Rössli.** This comfortable inn, dating back to 1845, combines down-home knotty-pine decor with soigné style. **Pros:** refreshing escape from more overblown places nearby; great low-key, traditional atmosphere; outdoor seating perfect for people-watching. **Cons:** limited parking; no bar area; no elevator. *Rooms from: 260 SF* *Promenade 10, Gstaad* *033/7484242* *www.posthotelroessli.ch* *18 rooms* *Breakfast.*

SPAS

Le Grand Bellevue Spa. With its 17 "heat treatment" features, the Thermal Oasis is the centerpiece of the spa at Le Grand Bellevue resort. Each sauna and steam chamber has its own distinct character, temperature, and humidity. There is also a swimming pool, and there are two hot tubs, one of which is outside. The full-service spa offers various massage and facial treatments. *Le Grand Bellevue, Hauptstr., Gstaad* *033/7480101* *www.bellevue-gstaad.ch/spa.*

10

Palace Spa. Gorgeous wood, stone, and other materials are the hallmark of the spa at the Gstaad Palace, where you might indeed feel like royalty. The facilities include separate steam baths and saunas for men and women, who can reunite for a swim in the indoor or outdoor pools or to enjoy the warmth of the fireplace-in-the-round at the heart of the 19,000-square-foot facility. There's also a private spa suite, plus a seven-room hammam that can be reserved for private use. The varied treatment menu includes massages, body exfoliations, and antiaging oxygen facials. Sports enthusiasts will appreciate the squash court as well as the Pilates and fitness studios. ✉ *Gstaad Palace Hotel, Palacestr., Gstaad* ☎ *033/7485000* 🌐 *www.palace.ch.*

Six Senses Spa. At the Alpina Gstaad, this is the first Swiss branch of Six Senses, an international spa chain. Outdoors, a heated pool beckons in all seasons. Indoors, the pool area features limestone boulders, wooden beams, two hot tubs, and a slide for children, whose access is limited to certain hours. There are separate sauna and steam facilities for men and women, as well as numerous themed treatment rooms. A fresh juice bar and tea lounge provide refreshments and a wealth of reading material. Day passes are available. ✉ *Alpina Gstaad, Alpinastr. 23, Gstaad* ☎ *033/8889898* 🌐 *www.thealpinagstaad.ch.*

SPORTS AND THE OUTDOORS

SKIING

Fodor's Choice ★ **Gstaad Mountain Rides.** With its 53 lifts, this immense resort can transport more than 50,000 skiers per hour to its network of 220 km (136 miles) of marked runs. In fact, these lifts are spread across a large territory: 20 km (12 miles), from Zweisimmen and St-Stefan in the east to Château-d'Oex in the west, and 20 km (12 miles) to the Diablerets Glacier in the south. The Glacier 3000 Snow Park is open from early November until May, and the Gstaad Snow Park is a highlight for freestyle fans. There are also more than 50 km (30 miles) of well-groomed cross-country trails in the area. Gstaad's expansive area means that most of its lifts are not reachable on foot, and since parking is in short supply, public transport, either by the train or the postbus, is the best option. Some hotels provide shuttle service as well. ✉ *Gstaad* 🌐 *www.gstaad.ch* 🎫 *Lift tickets from 63 SF.*

Gstaad Snowsports. Head here if you want lessons in snowboarding, or downhill or cross-country skiing. ✉ *Promenade 63, Gstaad* ☎ *033/7441865* 🌐 *www.gstaadsnowsports.ch.*

VALAIS

WELCOME TO VALAIS

TOP REASONS TO GO

★ **The Matterhorn:** Shutter-snap this glorious enigma from all angles, be it a luxury hotel room at its base or the sky-high Gornegrat–Monte Rosa Bahn.

★ **Great downhill skiing:** In Valais there's a ski resort for everyone, from family-friendly Saas-Fee to tourist-beloved Zermatt to chic Crans-Montana and Verbier.

★ **Cantonal capital:** Presided over by the castle of Tourbillon, Sion is a fortified link in the giant web of precipitous passes.

★ **Mineral baths:** Known for its natural thermal baths, the year-round destination of Leukerbad lets you dip into Switzerland's healing mineral-rich waters.

★ **Wine route:** Bike-friendly Valais offers a verdant landscape with centuries-old vineyards and unique varietals grown nowhere else.

Switzerland's third-largest canton, Valais is a complex network of valleys, rivers, and peaks harboring an A-to-Z of ski resorts. Its bottom half, a wide, fertile riverbed flanked by bluffs, is the region's most characteristic and imposing. It's fed from the north and south by remote, narrow valleys that snake into the mountains and peter out in Alpine wilderness or lead to the region's most famous landmarks—including that Swiss superstar, the Matterhorn. Not all of Valais covers Alpine terrain, however. The western stretch—between Martigny and Sierre—comprises one of the two chief sources of wine in Switzerland (the other is in Vaud, along Lac Léman). Valaisan wines come from ancient vineyards that grace the hillsides flanking the Rhône.

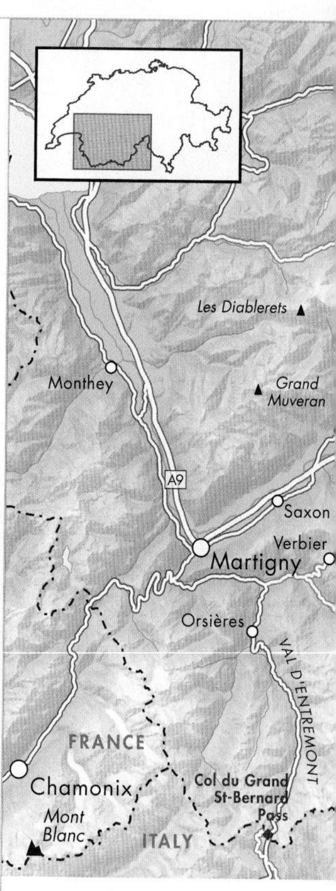

1 Bas Valais and Sion. If you have to pick one Valais wild valley to explore, head to the Val d'Entremont. Martigny is a treasure trove of art and history, Verbier has great facilities, and the famous Col du Grand St-Bernard pass connecting Switzerland to Italy is, weather permitting, unforgettable. Sion, the canton's capital, is marked by two rocky hills that materialize in front of you like a fairy-tale landscape, one crowned by the Tourbillon castle.

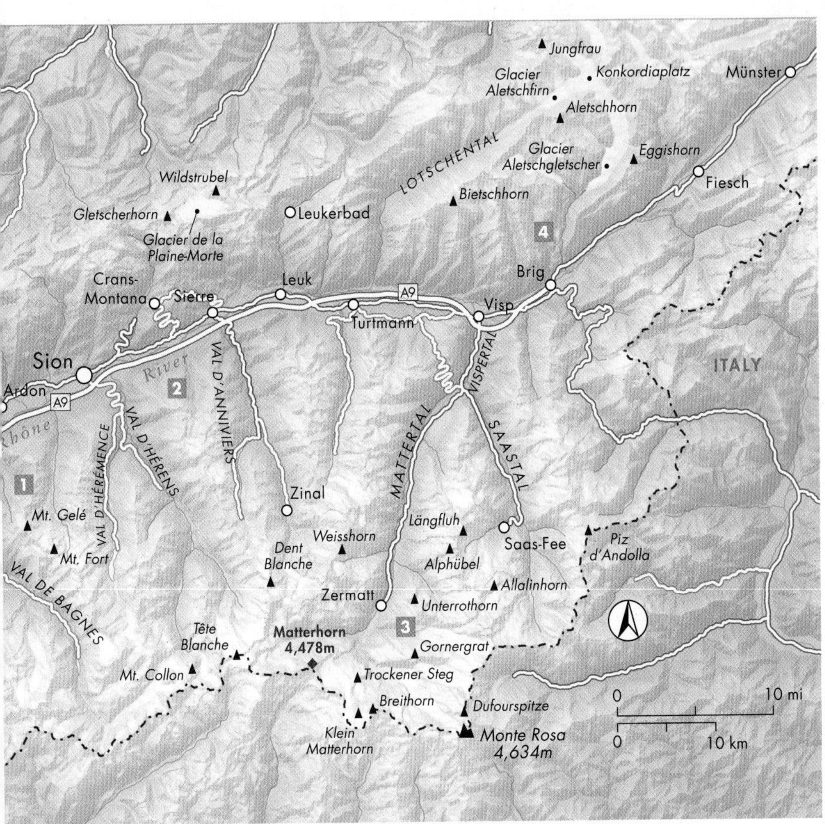

2 Conversion de la Vallèe. The adjoining modern ski resorts of Crans-Montana are attractively perched 5,000 feet up on a sunny plateau among woods, grasslands, and small lakes. In nearby Val d'Anniviers, tiny villages are noted for their folkloric *mazots* (small wooden barns balanced on stone disks and columns).

3 Zermatt and Saas-Fee. Feast your eyes on the Matterhorn in tourist-beloved Zermatt, where you can amble through the bustling village's streets before taking a lift or a train to even higher elevations. Allow half a day to get here and back, enjoying spectacular views from the train en route. Nearby is Saas-Fee, famed for its snowboarding, tamed marmots, glacier skiing, and a lower-key vibe favored by Swiss families and more serious hikers.

4 Brig and the Alpine passes. All mountain passes lead to or through Brig. Traffic and rail lines pour into and out of Italy, Ticino, central Switzerland, and the Berner Oberland via the Simplon, Nufenen, Furka, and Grimsel passes.

Updated by Liz Humphreys

For many visitors, Valais is the only part of Switzerland they ever see—and for good reason. After all, 40 of the 52 13,000-foot peaks in the Alps can be found here—including the famed Matterhorn—making it a skiing, snowboarding, and hiking paradise. With more than 300 sunny days a year, it's also the country's premiere wine region, home to more than 22,000 winegrowers and 700 winemakers. Add to the mix a handful of medieval castles, ancient mountain passes, natural thermal springs, and a network of bike trails, and you've got the best of Switzerland packed into 5,180 square km (2,000 square miles).

More than 500 km (310 miles) of mountains and glaciers span the Bietschhorn, Aletsch, and Jungfrau summits. In 2001, UNESCO named this area a World Heritage Site, joining such other natural wonders as the Galapagos Islands, Yellowstone National Park, and the Serengeti Desert. Today, Valais remains a region where Italian-, French-, and German-speaking cultures converge and the predominant language changes from valley to valley. Nearly everyone speaks English and is exceptionally welcoming to travelers from all over the world.

The Matterhorn is the region's most iconic site, and many newcomers feel unsatisfied if they don't get a glimpse of Switzerland's most photographed peak. Though it's definitely an image to behold, the Matterhorn is just one of many otherworldly gems, along with Monte Rosa, Weisshorn, and Dame Blanche (Mont Blanc). The best viewpoint for the Matterhorn is from the lovely resort town Zermatt.

To best experience Valais, don't try to explore every valley that ribs out from the Rhône; better to choose one region and spend a few days hiking, driving, or skiing. Enter from Lac Léman and visit the Gianadda museum in Martigny. Spend the night and next day exploring the citadel and Old

Town of Sion. Be sure to get up high in the mountains to magnificent resorts like Saas-Fee, Verbier, Zermatt, Leukerbad, and Crans-Montana.

The broad upper valley of the mighty Rhône is a region still wild, remote, and slightly unruly. Its *raccards* (typical Valaisan barns balanced on stone disks) still dot the slopes where meadow-grazing cows live at vertiginous angles. For the prettiest scenery, opt for the slow switchback crawl over the mountain passes rather than the more efficient tunnels. And as always, trains are preferable over cars, offering consistently better views and a more stress-free way to travel.

VALAIS PLANNER

WHEN TO GO

Valais is at its sunny best in high summer and midwinter; foggy dampness overwhelms in late autumn and spring. Mountain weather is impetuous, embracing with its warmth one day and obliterating views and trails the next. Take your cues from local forecasts and mountain operators who have an experienced sense about shifting patterns. Misty clouds move away in short order, opening up the path or vista for those who are patient.

Some of the best skiing and hiking can be had in March and September when crowds are the lightest and the sun is at its perfect arc. May, June, and November to mid-December are renovation, repair, and getaway times for locals. Facilities rotate closing periods, though, so there's always a fluffy bed and good meal.

GETTING HERE AND AROUND

AIR TRAVEL

For international arrivals, choose between two airports when flying to Valais: Geneva International Airport or Zürich Airport. Connecting service through London and Paris makes Geneva preferable for those heading to the west (French) end of Valais. Zürich brings passengers closer to the east (German) side, but the Alps are in the way; you must connect by rail tunnel or drive over one of the passes, which takes two to three hours.

BUS TRAVEL

As in other parts of the country, an efficient network of postbuses covers the region, even to the most remote hamlets. If you're staying in a car-free resort, traveling by bus frees you from finding a place to keep your car. Inquire about special bus passes for the region, including the Valais Central Pass for 48 SF (three days of travel within the same week).

Buses are also a convenient way to return to starting points from long-distance hikes. Resorts like Verbier, Crans-Montana, and Saas-Fee, with its contingent valleys, have free shuttles that loop a circuit for skiers and snowboarders, as well as summer guests.

CAR TRAVEL

Valais is something of a dead end by nature: a fine expressway (A9) carries you in from Lac Léman, but to enter—or exit—from the east end, you must park your car on a train and ride through the Furka Pass tunnel to go north or under the Simplon Pass to go southeast. (The serpentine roads over these passes are open in summer; weather permitting, the Simplon road stays open all year.) You also may cut through from or to Kandersteg in the Berner Oberland by taking a car train to Goppenstein or Brig. A summer-only road twists over the Grimsel Pass as well, heading toward Meiringen and the Berner Oberland or, over the Brünig Pass, to Luzern.

To see the tiny back roads, you need a car. The A9 expressway from Lausanne turns into a well-maintained highway at Sierre,which continues on to Brig. Additional tunnels and expanded lanes are being carved out of existing highways. Distances in the north and south valleys can be deceptive: apparently short jogs are full of painfully slow switchbacks and distractingly beautiful views. Both Zermatt and Saas-Fee are car-free resorts, though you can drive all the way to a parking lot at the edge of Saas-Fee's main street. Zermatt must be approached by rail from Täsch, the end of the line for cars (there's a garage).

TRAIN TRAVEL

There are straightforward rail connections to the region by way of Geneva and Lausanne to the west and Brig to the east. The two are connected by one clean rail sweep that runs the length of the valley. The run to main connections midvalley takes about two hours. Add on another hour to arrive at mountain destinations. Routes into smaller tributary valleys are limited, although most resorts are served by postbuses running directly from train stations. The Mont Blanc–St. Bernard Express, with its signature red-and-white cars, passes through Le Châble for connections to Verbier on its way from Martigny to Chamonix. In Le Châble, take the cableway or bus for the 10- to 20-minute ride.

⇨ *For more information on getting here and around, see Travel Smart Switzerland.*

Contacts Mont Blanc/St. Bernard Express. ☎ *027/7216840* 🌐 *www.tmrsa.ch.*

HOTELS

Valais hotels are in a constant state of flux, and every year at least one old hotel is given a makeover. The most appealing hotels in Valais are historic sites that have maintained their rustic ambience. Most of those built after 1960 popped up in generic, concrete-slab, balconied rows to accommodate the 1960s ski boom. They are solid enough but anonymous, depending on the personality of their owners.

Valais is home to some of Switzerland's most famous resorts, and prices vary widely between top-level lodgings in resorts and simple auberges (inns) in humbler towns, as well as between seasons. In some resorts, especially Zermatt, there is more than one high season, with the highest prices generally seen over Christmas and New Year's and from mid-February to mid-March. Remember that many resorts shut down during the lulls in May and from November to mid-December.

RESTAURANTS

For Valaisans, the midday meal remains the mainstay. Locals gather at a bistro for a hearty *plat chaud* (warm meal) that includes meat, vegetable or pasta, and salad for under 20 SF. The evening meal is lighter, perhaps comprising an *assiette* (platter) of cheese and cold cuts shared by the table, accompanied by bread and fruit.

Keep in mind that most eateries do not offer continuous service; lunch winds down around 2 and dinner does not begin before 6. Unless a host greets you or you have a reservation, it is fine to take a seat at an open table.

Multiple dining options can share the same entrance and kitchen. A brasserie, or *Stübli,* is the homey casual section just inside the doorway, with paper place mats, straightforward dishes, and lively conversation. The quieter *salle à manger* (dining room) has tables dressed in linen and a *carte* (menu) of multicourse meals and more complicated preparations. If cheese specialties are served, a *carnotzet,* a cozy space in the cellar or a corner away from main dining, is designated to confine the aroma and foster conviviality.

Hotel and restaurant reviews have been shortened. For full information, visit Fodors.com.

WHAT IT COSTS IN SWISS FRANCS

	$	$$	$$$	$$$$
Restaurants	Under 26 SF	26 SF–45 SF	46 SF–65 SF	Over 65 SF
Hotels	Under 201 SF	201 SF–300 SF	301 SF–500 SF	Over 500 SF

Restaurant prices are the average cost of a main course at dinner or, if dinner is not served, at lunch. Hotel prices are the lowest cost of a standard double room in high season, including taxes.

TOURS

Alpenwild. This tour agency runs guided 10-day treks on the Haute Route from Chamonix or Verbier to Zermatt. Gentler 10-day hikes from Chamonix to Zermatt are also available, with less arduous ascents and descents, as are hiking trips in Zermatt that include a Jungfrau excursion. ☎ *801/226–9026* 🌐 *www.alpenwild.com* *From 3,450 SF, including guided hikes, accommodations, meals, and ground transportation.*

Alpinehikers. This operator specializes in moderate to strenuous guided hikes in Switzerland for small groups (14 people or fewer), including a seven-day Matterhorn hike in Zermatt and Saas-Fee, the Haute Route from Chamonix to Zermatt (plus a less taxing Haute Route Highlights tour), and the Glacier Express hiking tour in Zermatt and Riederalp. ☎ *928/7780345* 🌐 *www.alpinehikers.com* *From $2,000 including guided hikes, accommodations, most meals, and rail passes.*

Valais Wine Tours. Catherine Antille Emery, who grew up in Crans-Montana, leads half- and full-day walking tours of the Valais wine region. ☎ *079/2254054* 🌐 *www.valaiswinetours.com* *From 140 SF.*

VISITOR INFORMATION

The main tourist office for the entire Valais region is in Sion.

Contacts Valais/Wallis Promotion. ✉ *6 rue Pré-Fleuri, Sion* ☎ *027/3273590* 🌐 *www.valais.ch.*

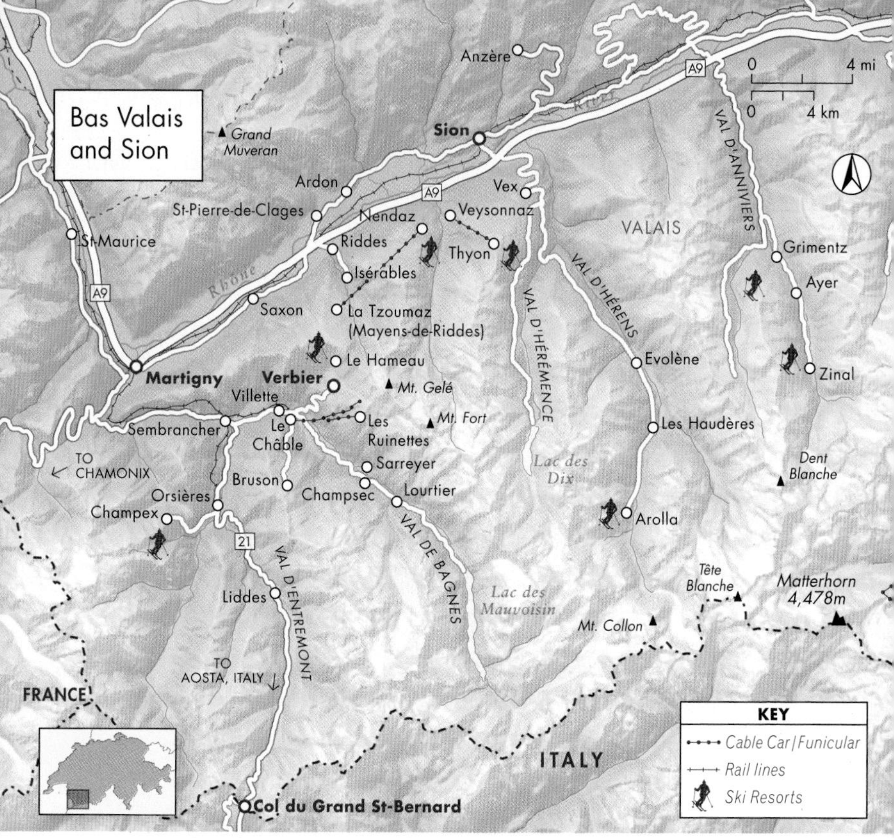

BAS VALAIS AND SION

As you cross from the canton of Vaud into Bas Valais (Lower Valais), the Rhône and its valley start to lose their broad, flat, delta character. The mountains—the Dents du Midi to the west and the Dents de Morcles to the east—begin to crowd in. The river no longer flows placidly but gives a taste of the mountain torrent it will become as you approach its source. At the Martigny elbow, the most ancient of Alpine routes leaves the Rhône and ascends due south to 8,098 feet at the Col du Grand St-Bernard before descending into Italy's Valle d'Aosta.

The Rhône Valley is most fertile east of Martigny, its flatlands thick with orchards and vegetable gardens and its south-facing slopes quilted with vineyards. This patch of Valais demonstrates the region's dramatic contrasts. Over the fertile farmlands looms the great medieval stronghold of Sion, its fortress towers protecting the gateway to the Alps.

MARTIGNY

23 km (14 miles) southwest of Sion.

At the foot of the Col du Grand St-Bernard, Martigny has long been a commercial crossroads. A small, primarily residential town backed by vineyards, it calls itself the "Art City," and indeed, its main attraction is the delightful Fondation Pierre Gianadda museum, which holds an intriguing collection of modern and ancient art. Sculptures by Swiss artists are scattered throughout the town. Martigny is also home to a number of Gallo-Roman ruins, including thermal baths, living quarters, and, most impressively, an amphitheater that once seated up to 5,000 people for gladiator events. If possible, time your visit to catch an amphitheater concert, an open-air movie, or the "Combat des Reines" (cow fights) in the fall.

GETTING HERE AND AROUND

Martigny is the transportation hub for the Lower Valais. Trains often stop at its rail station on the line running between Lausanne (50 minutes away) and Brig (one hour away). Postbuses connect all the towns of the Lower Valais.

VISITOR INFORMATION

Contacts Martigny Tourist Information. ✉ *6 av. de la Gare, Martigny* ☏ *027/7204949* 🌐 *www.martigny.com.*

EXPLORING

FAMILY **Fondation Barry du Grand-St-Bernard.** Storyboards and films at the Fondation Barry du Grand-St-Bernard praise the lifesaving work of a breed of dog that has come to symbolize the Alpine zone straddling Switzerland and Italy. Ten St. Bernard dogs live year-round at the museum, which is in a restored arsenal adjacent to Martigny's Roman amphitheater. Visitors may watch the dogs in their grassy outdoor enclosure from both inside the museum and the park outside. Occasionally a handler brings one of them out for a meet and greet. Cuddly toy St. Bernards are sold in the museum shop. Le Collier d'Or (Gold Collar), the museum's terraced café, opens a half-hour before the museum for an energizing coffee or snack. ✉ *34 rue du Levant, Martigny* ☏ *027/7204920* 🌐 *www.fondation-barry.ch* 🎫 *12 SF* ⏲ *Closed Mon. from Apr. 15–Oct. 15.*

Fodor's Choice ★ **Fondation Pierre Gianadda.** The Fondation Pierre Gianadda rises in bold geometric shapes around the Roman ruins on which it is built. Recent retrospectives have spotlighted works by Renoir and Monet. The **Musée Gallo-Romain** displays Gallo-Roman relics excavated from a 1st-century temple—striking bronzes, statuary, pottery, and coins—though descriptions are only in French and German. A marked path leads through the antique village, baths, drainage systems, and foundations to the fully restored 5,000-seat amphitheater, which dates from the 2nd century. In the gracefully landscaped garden surrounding the foundation, a wonderful **Parc de Sculpture** displays works by Rodin, Brancusi, Miró, Arman, Moore, Dubuffet, and Max Ernst. There's also a sizable **Musée de l'Automobile,** which contains some 50 antique cars, all in working order. They include an 1897 Benz, the Delaunay-Belleville of Czar Nicholas II of Russia, and a handful of Swiss-made models. You may also spot posters for concerts by international classical stars such as Cecilia Bartoli or Itzhak Perlman—the space doubles as a concert hall. ✉ *59 rue du Forum, Martigny* ☎ *027/7223978* 🌐 *www.gianadda.ch* 🎫 *20 SF.*

VERBIER

28 km (18 miles) east of Martigny, 54 km (34 miles) southwest of Sion.

A big part of Verbier's appeal is skiing on sunny slopes and the fact that it has a high-tech, state-of-the-art sports complex that links Quatre Vallées (four valleys) and multiple ski areas, which include Thyon, Veysonnaz, Nendaz, and La Tzoumaz. Verbier has a huge aerial cableway, with a cabin that accommodates 150, plus 89 smaller transportation installations. There is plenty of vertical drop, to which extreme ski and snowboard competitions can attest.

Summer sports here are equally serious: hiking, mountain biking, and hang gliding and its variations compete with golf as the principal activities. Perched on a sunny shelf high above the Val de Bagnes, with wraparound views and the 10,923-foot Mont Fort towering above, Verbier is protective of its picturesque wooden chalet architecture, yet stays current with modern amenities and comforts. Thanks to its compact layout and easygoing locals, the town has a friendlier feel than the traffic-snarled sprawl of Crans-Montana or hotel-packed Zermatt. Don't be surprised to hear a lot of English spoken in Verbier—it's a haven for moneyed Brits who are big into chalet rentals.

WATCH A COW FIGHT

In fall, the annual Foire de Martigny celebration hosts the "Combat des Reines," or cow fights, in Martigny's ancient Roman amphitheater. Massive, bell-wearing, naturally combative Hérens cows lock horns (but do not hurt each other) to establish dominance. Smaller fights like this take place in rural areas of Valais during the summer. With other activities like flag throwing, *lutte suisse* (Swiss wrestling), alpenhorn playing, *Hornussen* (like golf and baseball in one), and *Steinstossen* (stone hurling), it doesn't get any more Swiss. For more information, visit 🌐 *www.foireduvalais.ch.*

GETTING HERE AND AROUND

Verbier is a compact resort town with excellent shuttle service between hotels, chalets, and the lifts. In high season, unless there is parking space at your lodging, a car is an additional expense and nuisance, so public transportation is recommended. From Martigny, the train trip takes about an hour: take the St. Bernard Express bound for Orsières, its bright-red rail cars emblazoned with the region's famous mascot. Disembark in Le Châble, where a connecting bus takes you up the steep, winding road to the post office in the center of Verbier. If you are traveling light, there is a gondola cable car that departs from this base station.

Another option is to drive to Le Châble, leave your car in the large parking lot, and then transfer to the resort using the bus or cableway; this way, you can avoid driving the switchback roads to the resort. Once here, you can easily navigate the village by foot or shuttle bus, and all hotels are clearly signposted.

VISITOR INFORMATION

Contacts Verbier Tourist Information. ✉ *2 pl. Centrale, Verbier* ☎ *027/7753888* 🌐 *www.verbier.ch.*

WHERE TO EAT

$$ FRENCH ✕ **La Grange.** At clubby, rustic-chic La Grange, you'll always find lots of grilled specialties, particularly beef and lamb, on the menu, as well as inspired epicurean choices such as foie gras with plum sauce or Asian-inspired turbot with saffron and vegetable pearls—saffron from Mund being a Valais specialty. Chef Thierry Corthay's cuisine is not only seasonal (read: frequent menu changes) but also of the terroir, which is to say he serves regional products with pride. **Known for:** grilled meats; seasonal fare with a focus on regional products; wine list with good selection of local vintages. [$] *Average main: 38 SF* ✉ *70 rte. de Verbier Station, Verbier* ☎ *027/7716431* 🌐 *www.lagrange.ch* ⏲ *Closed June.*

$ SWISS ✕ **Le Mayentzet.** On the mountain right below the Mayentzet chairlift, this rustic Alpine chalet offers a cozy place for hot chocolate or lunch and a terrace with stunning panoramic views. The friendly staff serves Swiss fare like *assiete Valaisian*, a plate of local dried meats, and fondue. **Known for:** stunning views from the terrace; Swiss fare; lively lunch crowd during the ski season. [$] *Average main: 25 SF* ✉ *Les Hauts de Verbier, Verbier* ☎ *027/7752549.*

$$$ SWISS ✕ **W Kitchen.** Urban chic meets traditional Alpine style at this restaurant on the lower level of the W Verbier, where polished copper lights and leather banquettes meld seamlessly with floor-to-ceiling windows, faux fur pillows, and exposed wood. The menu puts a modern spin on local Swiss fare with a seasonal menu that might highlight pumpkin and deer in the fall and asparagus and fish in the spring. **Known for:** chic, but relaxed crowd and atmosphere; modern Swiss food; lovely views of the valley. [$] *Average main: 54 SF* ✉ *W Hotel Verbier, 70 rue de Medran, Verbier* ☎ *027/4728888* 🌐 *www.wkitchen-verbier.ch/en* ⏲ *No lunch.*

WHERE TO STAY

$$$ B&B/INN **Chalet d'Adrien.** Named for the owner's grandfather, a baron who discovered the village in the early 1900s, this luxury Relais & Châteaux hotel is packed with antiques and collectibles from old farmhouses and châteaux. **Pros:** private ski-mansion feel; friendly, personalized service; great mountain views from rooms. **Cons:** 10-minute walk uphill from village; country decor and teddy-bear collection in lobby may prove too cutesy for some; breakfast buffet is a particularly expensive supplement. [$] *Rooms from: 420 SF* ✉ *Chemin des Creux, Verbier* ☎ *027/7716200* 🌐 *www.chalet-adrien.com* ⏲ *Closed late Apr.–early July and late Sept.–early Dec.* *29 rooms* *No meals.*

$$$ HOTEL **Hotel Farinet.** Located in the heart of Verbier, the freshly rehabbed Hotel Farinet offers ski-lodge style with modern touches. **Pros:** ski chalet vibe with modern upgrades; central location; happening nightlife. **Cons:** rooms above the bars can be noisy; no in-room phones to reach reception; no parking. [$] *Rooms from: 420 SF* ✉ *6 Central Pl., Verbier* ☎ *027/7716626* 🌐 *www.hotelfarinet.com* ⏲ *Closed May, June, Oct., and Nov.* *20 rooms* *Breakfast.*

$$$ HOTEL **La Cordée des Alpes.** This centrally located luxury hotel has a refined contemporary ski-lodge atmosphere, eager-to-please service, and a well-regarded Italian restaurant, La Cordée. **Pros:** friendly staff; relaxing spa area; close to center of town. **Cons:** lacks that "wow" factor; parking is an expensive per-night charge; staffing can be light. *Rooms from: 470 SF ✉ 24 rte. du Centre Sportif, Verbier ☎ 027/7754545 🌐 www.hotelcordee.com ⊙ Closed Sept.–early Dec. and late Apr.–early July ⇨ 36 rooms 🍽 Breakfast.*

$$$$ HOTEL Fodor's Choice ★ **W Hotel Verbier.** The first Alpine branch of the W hotel chain draws a hip, urban crowd that appreciates the mountain-ski-lodge-meets-modern-design aesthetic. **Pros:** cool, contemporary design; location near the Médran gondola is perfect for ski-in ski-out or summer hikes; lovely spa. **Cons:** strange layout of public spaces with long, dark hallways connecting several different buildings; lower-level rooms lack views; rooms above the terrace off the bar can be noisy. *Rooms from: 700 SF ✉ 70 rue de Médran, Verbier ☎ 027/4728888 🌐 www.wverbier.com ⇨ 123 rooms 🍽 Breakfast.*

NIGHTLIFE AND PERFORMING ARTS

BARS AND CLUBS

Crock No Name. The popular club has a sunny terrace for après-ski cocktails and live music or DJs nightly for dancing into the wee hours. *✉ 22 rte. des Creux, Verbier ☎ 027/7716934.*

Farm Club. The Farm Club is the place to be seen in Verbier—it stays open until 4 in the winter season. *✉ Nevai Hotel, 55 rte. de Verbier Station, Verbier ☎ 079/1278754, 079/2577883 🌐 www.hotelnevai.com.*

Ice Cube. The après-ski scene at this slope-side bar below Les Ruinettes kicks into high gear at 3 pm, before skiers have their last runs. *✉ Les Ruinettes, Verbier ☎ 027/7711979 🌐 www.lesruinettes.ch.*

South. Hôtel Farinet features a collection of bars and clubs, some with live music, some with cocktails. For the more hard-core partyers, the basement club South is open until 4 in the winter high season. *✉ Farinet, 4 rte. des Creux, Verbier ☎ 027/7716626 🌐 www.hotelfarinet.com.*

MUSIC FESTIVALS

Fodor's Choice ★ **Verbier Festival.** For more than two weeks overlapping July and August, the Verbier Festival hosts an impressive classical music festival of performances and master classes. Two Verbier Festival orchestras and soloists of the caliber of Elisabeth Leonskaja, Evgeny Kissin, and Joshua Bell put on a stunning 17-day, 60-concert program that plays out in various venues all over Verbier. *✉ Verbier ☎ 084/8771882 🌐 www.verbierfestival.com.*

SPORTS AND THE OUTDOORS

Verbier offers a variety of summer and winter high-altitude sports, ranging from rock and ice climbing to rafting and snow tubing, all led by specialist outfitters.

BIKING

About 250 km (188 miles) of trails range from difficult distance rides across the passes to simpler runs closer to town.

Backside. The pros at Backside can help you plan your entire outing, plus rent standard or high-performance bikes, helmets, and shells. ✉ *Rue de Medran, Verbier* ☎ *027/7715556* 🌐 *backsideverbier.ch.*

Médran Sports. This company sells equipment at competitive rates. ✉ *59 rte. de Verbier Station, Verbier* ☎ *027/7716048* 🌐 *www.medransports.ch.*

GOLF

Golf Club Verbier. High in the mountains at 5,250 feet, with fabulous views, the Esserts golf course challenges the experienced player. Less advanced golfers enjoy the pitch-and-putt Les Moulins course inside the resort. Both courses contain hazards, including mountain streams and changes in elevation, that increase the difficulty. Most of the Esserts course takes you down the mountain, whereas Les Moulins is uphill the entire time. The Verbier Golf Club is open for play only May through November since it is transformed into a ski hill during the winter. ✉ *5 chemin des Esserts, Verbier* ☎ *027/7715314* 🌐 *www.verbiergolfclub.ch* *Esserts Course: July and Aug. 95 SF; May, June, Sept., and Oct. 70 SF weekdays and 80 SF weekends. Moulins Course: May–Nov. 30 SF* *Esserts Course: 18 holes, 5350 yards, par 69; Moulins Course: 18 holes, 1090 yards, par 54* *Closed Dec.–Apr.*

HIKING AND CLIMBING

Trails thread from ridgeline to valley floor in 400 km (300 miles) of pathways that cross nature reserves, highland streams, and historic villages. Sign up at 🌐 *www.guideverbier.com*, **La Fantastique** (☎ *027/7714141*), or **Verbier SportPlus** (☎ *027/7753363*) for everything from hut-to-hut trekking tours to technical rock climbing and rappelling sessions.

For an easy 2½-hour hike with amazing views of the Alps, Rhône Valley, and the town of Verbier, take the gondola up from Médran to Les Ruinettes at 7,190 feet. From there, the Route de la Plaine is wide and relatively flat as it gently winds over to the Croix de Coeur, where you can stop for a hearty fondue lunch before hiking back down to Verbier through Les Planards and Les Esserts. You can also return to Verbier via a short but steep uphill walk to Savoleyres at 7,700 feet to catch the gondola back down to Les Creux.

SKIING

Adrenaline. Sign up for skiing lessons at the Adrenaline counter in the Hardcore Snow and Fashion Shop, which rents ski and snowboarding equipment. It's in the Galerie Alpina, on the main square opposite the post office. ✉ *Galerie Alpina, 11 rue de la Poste, Verbier* ☎ *027/7717459* 🌐 *www.adrenaline-verbier.ch.*

École Suisse de Ski. If you're looking to fine-tune your ski or snowboard technique, book a private instructor at this Verbier skiing school. ✉ *2 rue de Médran, Verbier* ☎ *027/7753363* 🌐 *www.essverbier.ch.*

4 Vallées. Verbier is the center of Switzerland's famous transit network, 4 Vallées, which consists of 12 gondolas, five cable cars, 18 chairlifts, and 33 other ski lifts, giving access to 410 km (253 miles) of marked pistes. From this hub an immense complex of resorts has developed—some modest, others exclusive—covering four valleys in an extended ski area whose extremities are 15 km (9 miles) or so apart as the crow flies and several dozen kilometers apart by way of winding mountain roads. 🌐 *www.4vallees.ch.*

Verbier is connected to multiple ski areas, and has preserved its charming wooden chalets.

Mont Fort. Verbier's ski area culminates at Mont Fort, at 10,923 feet. This is reached by an aerial tram, Le Jumbo, equipped with a cab that accommodates 150. La Chaux Express, a chondola (combination chairlift and gondola on the same cable) sweeps skiers to the upper station. Keep your skis or snowboard on for the chair, or take them off to enter the gondola. This entire sector is crisscrossed by a dense network of astonishingly varied pistes. There are several strategic passes, including Les Attelas, Chassoure, Col des Gentianes, and Tortin. The snow park of La Chaux offers a variety of jumps, big air, rails, and a ski-cross. You can get either one-day or six-day lift tickets to ski Verbier-Mont Fort, Bruson, and Savoleyres–La Tzoumaz. Automated ski passes streamline the lift check-in process; free tickets and discounts for children are available. ✉ *Verbier* 🌐 *www.verbier.ch* 🎫 *1-day lift tickets from 75 SF.*

Sledge Run La Tzoumaz. For a different Alpine experience, rent a sled at any of the village sports outlets and take a run down the 10-km (6-mile) toboggan track from Savoleyres to La Tzoumaz. ✉ *Téléverbier SA, Savoleyres.*

FAMILY **Verbier Ski School European Snowsport.** This ski school offers skiing, snowboarding, telemarking, Nordic skiing, and ski touring lessons in a variety of languages. ✉ *Rue de Medran, Verbier* ☎ *027/7716222* 🌐 *europeansnowsport.com.*

COL DU GRAND ST-BERNARD

40 km (25 miles) south of Martigny, 69 km (43 miles) southwest of Sion.

GETTING HERE AND AROUND

The opening of the Col du Grand St-Bernard, the pass connecting Switzerland and Italy, is weather dependent. This ancient high-mountain crossing is closed to cars during the winter months, when it makes an excellent snowshoeing or skiing course. The roadway also can be shut down in summer because of random snowfalls. On a clear day the narrow twisting roads threading in and out of avalanche breaks make for an unforgettable drive. The traffic on the approach to the pass is dramatically reduced once vehicles driving through to the Italian city of Aosta leave the highway at the tunnel entrance.

During summer, public transport to the Great St. Bernard Hospice is available from Martigny. The journey starts with train service to the village of Orsières, terminus of the rail line, and then switches to bus. It's a one-hour drive by car; add an additional half hour for the rail-bus connection.

EXPLORING

Fodor'sChoice ★ **Col du Grand St-Bernard.** Breasting the formidable barrier of the Alps at 8,101 feet, this pass is the oldest and most famous of the great Alpine crossings, and the first to join Rome and Byzantium to the wilds of the north. Used for centuries before the birth of Christ, it has witnessed an endless stream of emperors, knights, and simple travelers—think of Umberto Eco's *Name of the Rose,* with its two friars crossing on donkey in howling winter winds. Napoléon took an army of 40,000 across it en route to Marengo, where he defeated the Austrians in 1800.

L'Hospice du Grand St-Bernard. In operation since the Middle Ages, L'Hospice du Grand St-Bernard has played host to kings, princes, and writers like Charles Dickens. Within these walls you'll find cozy, inexpensive guest rooms and a stone dining hall where you can revive yourself with bowls of soup, slabs of creamy cheese, honey-sweetened tea, and carafes of red wine produced in the Valais. The facility includes an excellent museum with exhibits about the history of the pass and the devoted monks of the Order of St. Augustine, who live here. Displays of church treasures—chalices, crosses, and altar clothes in gold, silver, and jewels—are on view in another wing. The fresco-bedecked baroque church remains open for daily prayers. Behind the hospice is **Chenil au Col du Grand St-Bernard,** a kennel full of the landmark's enormous, furry namesakes: the famous St. Bernard dogs, who for centuries helped the monks find travelers lost in the snow. They supposedly came to Switzerland with silk caravans from Central Asia and were used by Romans as war dogs; today they're kept more for sentimental than functional reasons. The foundation is named after the most famous St. Bernard of them all: Barry, who saved more than 40 people in the 19th century and today stands stuffed in Bern's Naturhistorisches Museum

(Museum of Natural History). Souvenir stands sell plush versions of St. Bernards, and there are a handful of dining options on either side of the pass. ✉ *Col du Grand St-Bernard, Bourg-Saint-Pierre* ☎ *027/7871153* 🌐 *www.aubergehospice.ch* 🎫 *Museum 10 SF* ⏲ *Closed mid-Oct.–May.*

SION

54 km (34 miles) northeast of Verbier.

Rearing up in the otherwise deltalike flatlands of the western Valais, two otherworldly twin hills flank the ancient city of Sion. The two hills together are a powerful emblem of the city's 1,500-year history as a bishopric and Christian stronghold. If you're up for it, climb to the top of either hill (though not mountains, they're still steep) for dramatic views of the surrounding flatlands and the mountains flanking the valley.

A shortage of high-quality hotels gives the impression that the town is not as hospitable to travelers as the tourist-oriented ski resorts, but don't be deterred; there are ample reasons to spend some time here, including a vibrant Old Town with modern boutiques and restaurants, some interesting museums, and those unbeatable hilltop vistas.

GETTING HERE AND AROUND

Sion is a main stop on the railway running between Lausanne (one hour) and Brig (40 minutes); many postbuses threading the region stop at the train station. The town itself can be comfortably explored on foot in an afternoon, unless you lose yourself in one of its museums or labyrinthine antiques shops. In summer a trolley called Le P'tit Sédunois (4 SF) shuttles between the Place de la Panta and elevated sights.

VISITOR INFORMATION

Contact Sion Tourist Information. ✉ *2 pl. de la Planta, Sion* ☎ *027/3277727* 🌐 *www.siontourism.ch.*

EXPLORING

TOP ATTRACTIONS

Château de Tourbillon. Crowning Tourbillon, the higher of Sion's hills, the ruined château was built as a bishop's residence at the end of the 13th century and destroyed by fire in 1788. If you take the rugged hike up the steep hill, try to visit the tiny chapel with its ancient, layered frescoes. ✉ *14 rue des Châteaux, Sion* 🎫 *Free* ⏲ *Closed mid-Nov.–mid-Mar.*

Fodor's Choice ★ **Église-Forteresse de Valère** (*Church-Fortress of Valère*). On Valère, Sion's lower hill, the Église-Forteresse de Valère is a striking example of sacred and secular power combined—reflective of the church's heyday, when it often subjugated rather than served its parishioners. Built on Roman foundations, the massive stone walls enclose both the château and the 11th-century **Église Notre-Dame de Valère** (Church of Our Lady of Valère). This structure stands in a relatively raw form, rare in Switzerland, where monuments are often restored to perfection. Over the engaging Romanesque carvings, 16th-century fresco fragments, and 17th-century stalls painted with scenes of the Passion, is a rare organ, with a cabinet painted with two fine medieval Christian scenes. Dating from the 15th century, it's the oldest playable organ in the world (though it doesn't appear old, as it was restored in 2005), and an annual organ festival celebrates its musical virtues.

The château complex also houses the **Musée d'Histoire** (History Museum), which displays a wide array of medieval sacristy chests and religious artifacts. Expanded exhibits trace daily life and advances in the canton from these early centuries to the present day. Explanations are in three languages, including English. To reach the museum and church, you have to trek up uneven stone walkways and steep staircases, but you won't regret it. ✉ *24 rue des Châteaux, Sion* ☎ *027/6064715* 🌐 *www.musees-valais.ch* 🎟 *Church free, guided tour 4 SF; museum 12 SF (free first Sun. of the month)* ⏲ *Church and museum closed Mon. Oct.–May. No guided tours Mon.–Sat. Oct.–May.*

OFF THE BEATEN PATH

Isérables. High up in the bluffs and valleys to the south of Sion are scores of isolated eagle's-nest towns, including Isérables. Set on a precarious slope that drops 3,280 feet into the lowlands, the town has narrow streets that weave between crooked old stone-shingle mazots. Since the arrival of the cable car, Isérables has prospered and modernized itself. Yet the inhabitants of this village still carry the curious nickname *Bedjuis*. Some say it's derived from "Bedouins" and that the people are descended from the Saracen hordes who, after the battle of Poitiers in 732, overran some of the high Alpine valleys. Excursions to the sights and villages of this *haute vallée* (high valley) can be accomplished in a day, with a little time to hike and explore before returning to Sion. ✉ *Iserables.*

FAMILY **Lac Souterrain St-Léonard.** For an activity the whole family can enjoy, take a half-hour boat ride across the largest natural subterranean lake in Europe at 984 feet long, where you can see strange rock formations and even fish under the crystal clear water. Bring an extra sweater, even in summer, as it gets chilly when you descend into the cave. Watch for monthly boat concerts on the lake, where the acoustics are exceptional. ✉ *21 rue du Lac* ✣ *6 km (4 miles) east of Sion* ☎ *027/2032266* 🌐 *www.lac-souterrain.com* 🎟 *10 SF* ⏲ *Closed mid-Nov.–mid-Mar.*

Maison Supersaxo (*House of Supersaxo*). This grand old home, tucked into a passageway off Rue Supersaxo, was built in 1505 by Georges Supersaxo, the local governor, to put his rivals to shame. This extravagantly decorated building includes a Gothic staircase and grand hall, whose painted wood ceiling is a dazzling work of decorative art. ✉ *Passage Supersaxo, Sion* ☎ *027/3238550* 🎟 *Free* ⏲ *Closed weekends.*

Notre-Dame du Glarier (*Our Lady of Glarier*). The cathedral is dominated by its Romanesque tower, built in the Lombard style and dating from the 12th century. The rest of the church is late Gothic in style. ✉ *Rue de la Cathédrale, Sion.*

WORTH NOTING

OFF THE BEATEN PATH

Musée d'Art du Valais (*Valais Art Museum*). One of the main reasons to visit the Musée d'Art, housed in the remains of two 12th-century castles, is to discover the work of Swiss artist Ernest Biéler (1863–1948). For three decades from around 1905, he painted life in Savièse, a community in the Sion district. The naive vibe of these scenes and portraits offers a glimpse into the Valais as it once was. The museum also features

In the bike-friendly Valais, the area around Sion is where many of Switzerland's centuries-old vineyards can be found.

a small but intriguing collection of canvases, photography, and other works from the 18th century to today by international and local artists. ✉ *15 pl. de la Majorie, Sion* ☎ *027/6064690* 🌐 *www.musees-valais.ch* 🎫 *8 SF. Free first Sun. of the month* ⏲ *Closed Mon.*

Musée de la Nature du Valais (*Valais Museum of Nature*). Opened in 2013 in the former Archaeological Museum, this space's theme is "Man and Nature in the Valais," which aims to inspire visitors to consider their relationship with the natural environment in the Valais, from the Mesolithic age to today. Installations feature typical flora and life-size representations of fauna that inhabit this diverse land. ✉ *12 rue des Châteaux, Sion* ☎ *027/6064730* 🌐 *www.musees-valais.ch* 🎫 *8 SF. Free first Sun. of the month* ⏲ *Closed Mon.*

Old Town. Up Rue de Lausanne, the Old Town is a blend of attractive 16th-century houses, modern shops, and a host of sights worth seeing. ✉ *Sion.*

OFF THE BEATEN PATH

St-Pierre-de-Clages. Known for its 11th-century church, this village is also known as the only "book town" in Switzerland. Secondhand-book-dealers' shops are clustered around the Place and Rue de l'Eglise, and some of them, like Nico's Books, also sell titles in English. A main attraction is one of Switzerland's quirkiest mom-and-pop stores, **La Potagère** (✉ *3 rue de l'Eglise* ☎ *027/3064344* 🌐 *www.lapotagere.ch)*, crammed to (and including) the rafters with local oils, vinegars, organic teas, syrups, dried fruit, and delicious jams made in-house. ✢ *15 km (9 miles) southwest of Sion* 🌐 *www.village-du-livre.ch.*

WHERE TO EAT

$ **Le Verre à Pied.** It's a tight squeeze to get into Old Town's popular
WINE BAR *caveau-oenothèque* (wine bar–cum-store) Le Verre à Pied, where 180 regional vintages are poured seven days a week. Light snacks like local cheese and meats, tapenade, and foie-gras toasts are available. **Known for:** extensive collection of local wines; tapas; amiable service. *Average main: 20 SF* *29 rue du Grand-Pont, Sion* *027/3211380* *www.sioncapitaledesvins.com.*

NIGHTLIFE AND PERFORMING ARTS

Sion attracts many musicians and scholars to its festivals celebrating the medieval organ in its church-fortress.

Festival International de l'Orgue Ancien Valère (*International Festival of the Ancient Valère Organ*). One of the region's most popular events, the Festival International de l'Orgue Ancien Valère takes place throughout July and August. Tickets are sold at the tourist office and online in advance and at the church after 3 pm the day of the concert. Note that you need to walk up a steep road and stairs to reach the venue. *Basilique de Valere, 24 rue des Châteaux, St-Luc* *027/3235767* *www.orgueancien-valere.ch.*

CONVERSION DE LA VALLÉE

Secured above the plateau north of Sierre and Leuk is the ski town of Crans-Montana and the hot springs resort of Leukerbad, each with a different personality. Crans-Montana offers expansive skiing, name-brand boutiques, and clubby restaurants. Although Leukerbad also has first-class hotels and ski runs (albeit fewer of them), it is the restorative pools and spas and authentic Alpine village that attract visitors. Along this stretch of the Rhône, the switchback of language and culture begins. Valais, as it is referred to by French speakers, is called Wallis by locals with Germanic ties. To the south the remote Val d'Anniviers offers a glimpse of a simpler life before high-speed lifts and Internet cafés.

CRANS-MONTANA

12 km (7 miles) northwest of Sierre, 19 km (11 miles) northeast of Sion.

This French-speaking resort rises above the valley on a steep, sheltered shelf at 4,904 feet. It commands a broad view across the Rhône Valley to the peaks of the Valaisan Alps, and its grassy and wooded plateau gets the benefit of Sierre's sunshine and fresh air. Behind the towns, the **Rohrbachstein** (9,686 feet), the **Gletscherhorn** (9,653 feet), and the **Wildstrubel** (10,637 feet) combine to create a complex of challenging ski slopes.

The resort towns themselves—basically one town, with two areas—have an American-style ambience marked by golf courses, chain fashion boutiques, and 1970s architecture that's likely to disappoint those seeking cozy charm. The crowds are young, wealthy, international, roving in cocoons of the fit, fun-loving, and fashionable.

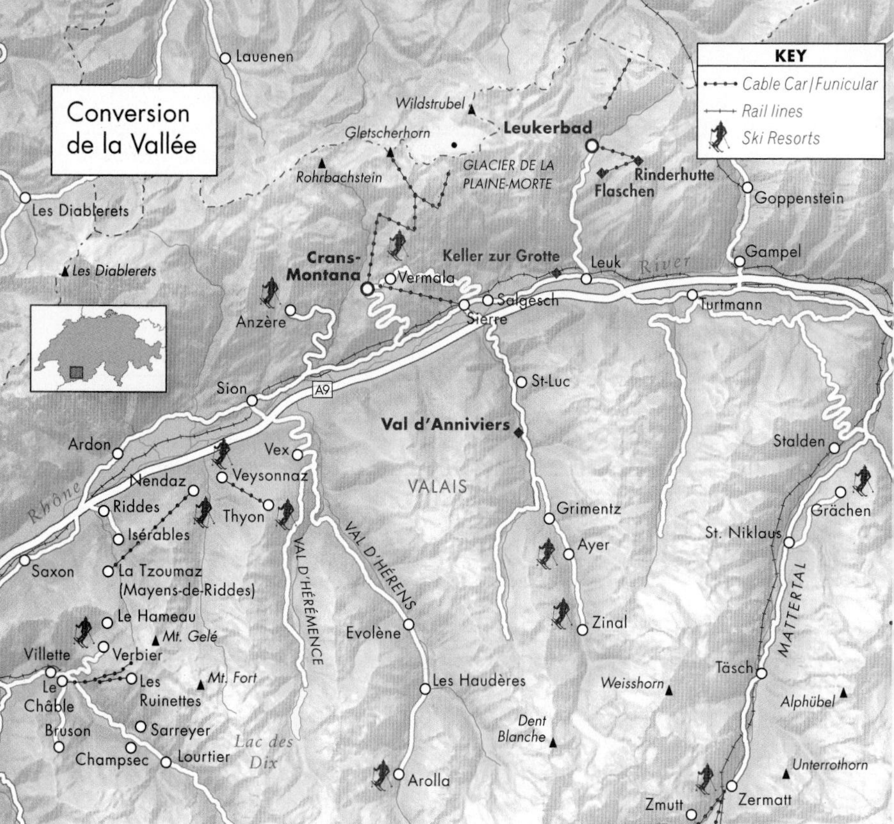

GETTING HERE AND AROUND

From the train station in Sierre, follow the painted red line on the sidewalk to the SMC (Sierre Mollens Crans-Montana) station, where a steep funicular connects the town of Sierre with the resort area of Crans-Montana. The 12-minute ride delivers you to the Montana side of town, where free shuttles head to hotels and chalets. Car traffic is almost always heavy, so it's best to get around on foot or shuttle bus. As in other resorts, signs point the way to the hotels.

Contact SMC. ☎ *027/4813355* 🌐 *www.cie-smc.ch.*

VISITOR INFORMATION

Contact Crans-Montana Tourist Information. ✉ *20 av. de la Gare, Crans-Montana* ☎ *084/8221012* 🌐 *www.crans-montana.ch.*

WHERE TO EAT

$ BURGER ✕ **Burger Lounge.** This cozy basement lounge and pub features minimalist decor—small, wooded high-top tables, bar seating, and a large couch—that lets the burgers shine. Diners get a choice of a single or double burger, made with local meat and toppings—bacon, cheese, lettuce, and tomato—and the whole thing is served on a freshly baked bun from local patisserie Taillens. **Known for:** delicious burgers; inexpensive, casual fare; cozy, intimate atmosphere. *Average main: 18 SF ✉ 6 rue Centrale, Crans-Montana ☎ 079/9368492 🌐 www.burgerlounge.org ⊙ Closed Mon. and Tues.*

$ CAFÉ **Taillens.** This overflowing tearoom with exquisite pastries is a must-stop before or after an activity-packed day. Run today by the third generation of the Taillens family, this landmark is beloved by locals and visitors alike. **Known for:** cakes, pastries, and specialty breads; central location; terrace with great people-watching. *Average main: 12 SF ✉ 8 av. de la Gare, Crans-Montana ☎ 027/4854030 🌐 www.boulangerietaillens.ch.*

WHERE TO STAY

$$$ HOTEL Fodor's Choice ★ **Chetzeron.** A former gondola station high above the village offers an idyllic, away-from-it-all oasis. **Pros:** panoramic views of Rhône valley, Matterhorn, and Mont Blanc; peaceful mountain resort away from it all; friendly, personalized service. **Cons:** getting here can be a challenge; evening arrivals and departures depend on snowcat with limited schedule; small spa. *Rooms from: 380 SF ✉ 9 chemin de Cry d'Er, Crans-Montana ☎ 027/4850800 🌐 www.chetzeron.ch 16 rooms Breakfast.*

$$$ HOTEL **Crans Ambassador.** Built in the shape of mountain peaks, this classic hotel perched high on a hillside above Montana has been refurbished in a contemporary style that's purposefully understated to let the views take center stage. **Pros:** welcome drink in the spacious lounge bar, with open fireplace and panoramic views; only a few minutes' walk to the Grand Signal ski lift; delectable cuisine and top-notch wine selection at the restaurant. **Cons:** rooms on the bland side; a 15-minute hike downhill (or shuttle ride) to Montana; shared balconies limit privacy. *Rooms from: 450 SF ✉ 3 rte. du Petit Signal, Crans-Montana ☎ 027/4854848 🌐 cransambassador.ch ⊙ Closed late Sept.–mid-Dec. and late Apr.–June 56 rooms Breakfast.*

$$$$ RESORT **Guarda Golf Hotel & Residences.** This resort hits the trifecta: comfortable American-style accommodations, impeccable Swiss service, and warm Brazilian hospitality. **Pros:** halcyon views of the Alps; excellent service, including a knowledgeable waitstaff; prompt pick-up and drop-off shuttle. **Cons:** food can be hit or miss; art gallery space could be put to better use; service, luxury, and all the amenities come at a price. *Rooms from: 650 SF ✉ 14 rte. des Zirès, Crans-Montana ☎ 027/4862000 🌐 www.hotelguardagolf.com ⊙ Closed mid-Sept.–mid-Dec. and late Mar.–mid-June 31 rooms Breakfast.*

$$$$ B&B/INN **LeCrans Hotel & Spa.** Located high above Crans-Montana's luxury-shop-lined streets, this Alpine-meets-contemporary hotel remains a chic perch for deep-pocketed travelers. **Pros:** warm, modern design; top-quality restaurant with amazing views; sybaritic spa. **Cons:** theme rooms a bit over-the-top when the Alpine views dominate; location is far away from everything; à la carte breakfast (no buffet) time-consuming. *Rooms from: 550 SF ✉ 1 chemin du Mont Blanc, Crans-Montana ☎ 027/4866060 🌐 www.lecrans.com ⊙ Closed late Apr.–early June and Nov. 15 rooms Breakfast.*

$$$$ B&B/INN Fodor's Choice ★ **L'Hostellerie du Pas de l'Ours.** In a town known for blocklike towers, this petite Relais & Châteaux–listed auberge stands out with its preserved wooden facade, plush lobby, and inviting fireplace. **Pros:** plush rooms rich with amenities; magnificent wellness center with indoor-outdoor pool; highly regarded restaurant. **Cons:** somewhat of a walk into the town center; feels like navigating a maze to reach the spa area; expensive. *Rooms from: 720 SF* ✉ *41 rue du Pas de l'Ours, Crans-Montana* ☎ *027/4859333* 🌐 *www.pasdelours.ch* ⊙ *Closed mid-Apr.–early June and mid-Oct.–late Nov.* *15 rooms* *Breakfast.*

NIGHTLIFE

BARS AND CLUBS

Amadeus. The small but convivial Amadeus, beneath the Olympic Hotel in Montana, is a popular après-ski venue. ✉ *Olympic Hotel, 4 rue Louis Antille, Crans-Montana* ☎ *027/4812495* 🌐 *www.amadays.ch.*

Le Pacha. The dance floor buzzes at Le Pacha, a popular spot in Crans. ✉ *2 rue du Prado, Crans-Montana* ☎ *079/4350635* 🌐 *www.lepacha.ch.*

Fodor's Choice ★ **Le Tirbouchon.** Run by oenophile Patrick Jenny, this no-frills wine shop with a wine bar is a great place to sample regional producers. The chummy local go-to houses more than 250 wines, including many lesser-known varieties of Valais wines like Humagne Rouge and Petite Arvine. You can also order Valaisan-style tapas to accompany your pours. ✉ *15 av. de la Gare, Crans-Montana* ☎ *079/5413445* 🌐 *www.letirbouchon.ch.*

Monk'is. If music, videos, shots, and burgers until 1 am interest you, Monk'is is a hot, primate-themed venue in Crans. ✉ *19 rue Centrale, Crans-Montana* ☎ *079/4093285* 🌐 *www.monkis.ch.*

SPORTS AND THE OUTDOORS

BOATING

Étang Long is directly in Crans. Lac Grenon and Lac Moubra, two crystalline lakes near the connected villages, are filled with pedal boats and windsurfers on long summer days. Rentals are available at shore-side kiosks.

Étang Long. Wakeboarding and waterskiing services are available on Étang Long through a city-run kiosk in the park on the lakeside. Bookings are required. ✉ *Crans-Montana* ☎ *078/6663703.*

GOLF

Fodor's Choice ★ **Golf Club Crans-sur-Sierre.** If playing while enjoying phenomenal Alpine views, including the Matterhorn and Mont Blanc, excites you, the wonderfully situated, beautiful courses at Golf Club Crans-sur-Sierre might be just your ticket. Spanish golf legend Severiano Ballesteros designed the 18-hole course, home to the annual Omega European Masters, and Jack Nicklaus designed the challenging and equally stunning 9-hole. The season generally lasts from the time snow disappears in June through the first snowfall in October; the actual dates can vary from year to year. ✉ *20 rue du Prado, Crans-Montana* ☎ *027/4859797* 🌐 *www.golfcrans.ch* *High-season rates from 60 SF* *Severiano Ballesteros: 18 holes, 6935 yards, par 72; Jack Nicklaus: 9 holes, 2984 yards, par 35* ⊙ *Closed Nov.–Apr.*

HIKING

About 301 km (187 miles) of well-marked trails branch out from both villages, sometimes intersecting but more often leading in opposite directions. Unless you want to scale higher peaks, all that is needed is a good pair of boots and a map to guide you to signed pathways through open terrain, forests, or along the *bisses* (irrigation channels), beloved by butterflies and wildflowers in the summer. Keep an eye out for fast-paced Nordic walkers (power hikers using ski poles).

One of the more popular hikes in Crans-Montana between June and October is an easy 10-km (6-mile) trail that follows the irrigation channel built in the 15th century, leading you upstream from Vermala, just to the west of the Barzettes-Violettes cable car station. Enjoy the panoramic views along the way before stopping at the Colombire Hamlet for some fresh local cheese. Then head along another gentle slope to end up in Aminona, where you can catch a bus back to Montana. The whole hike takes about three hours.

Swiss Mountain Sports. If it's an extreme hiking or climbing challenge you're looking for, contact the pros at Swiss Mountain Sports for guidance. They also offer ski and snowboard school in the winter. ✉ *3 rte. du Parc, Crans-Montana* ☎ *027/4804466* 🌐 *www.sms04.ch.*

SKIING

Crans-Montana is known for its sunny slopes—which can be a great thing during the early part of the season, which runs from late November to late April—but may cause problems as the snow starts to melt. Nevertheless, it's especially good for intermediate skiers, with 140 km (87 miles) of slopes, and cross-country skiers, with 24 km (15 miles) of trails within the resort, including several classic circuits across snow-covered golf courses and around the village lakes, plus a lovely trail atop the glacier. Begin your ascent up the mountain with a cable car leaving from one of four locations: Crans or Montana, which both reach Cry d'Er (via a second lift); Barzettes-Violettes, which reaches Les Violettes and then Plaine Morte; or Aminona, which ascends to Petit Bonvin. Lift tickets cost 69 SF for one day and 349 SF for six days.

Violettes Plaine-Morte. The views during the ascent on the gondola from Les Violettes to Plaine Morte, virtually under assault by crowds during the high season, in themselves justify your stay in Crans-Montana, either in winter or summer. ✉ *Crans-Montana.*

Les Bosses. The incredibly steep-pitched Les Bosses is a challenge for pros. Reach it by chairlift from Les Violettes. ✉ *Crans-Montana.*

Petit Bonvin. The eastern section of the ski area connects to Aminona, where a park for snowboarders and a 6-km (3¾-mile) bobsled run drop from 7,874-foot-tall Petit Bonvin. ✉ *Crans-Montana.*

Piste Nationale. Expert skiers may prefer the Piste Nationale—a 7-km (4½-mile) descent, the longest in the region—site of previous world championships. Get here from the Cry d'Er cable car station. ✉ *Crans-Montana.*

The cross-country ski trails at Plaine Morte, near Crans-Montana, are open seven months a year.

Plaine Morte. The pearl of the region is the Plaine Morte, a flat glacier that's perched like a pancake at an elevation of 9,840 feet. A 6-km (3½-mile) cross-country ski trail is open seven months of the year, although there's snow year-round. ✉ *Crans-Montana.*

SHOPPING

At times the streets of stylish Crans can feel like a fashion runway, with the leather-and-fur-trimmed crowd hidden behind logo sunglasses and cashmere hats. This tiny village has taken a cue from Gstaad and St. Moritz, assembling the most high-end shops and designer boutiques in the entire region. Though the usual suspects of luxury fashion can be found here—Louis Vuitton, Bulgari, Chanel, Hublot, Moncler, and Prada—several family-owned shops and an outdoor market remain affordable spots to sample local wines, meats, and cheeses.

Alex Sports. Don't be deceived by its name: Alex Sports stocks such labels as Bogner, Escada, Ralph Lauren, and Zegna. Yes, you can buy a down jacket or rent a pair of skis. There are four smaller branches in Crans-Montana, including one that specializes in bikes and accessories and one in the Crans-Ambassador hotel. ✉ *31 rue du Prado, Crans-Montana* ☎ *027/4814061* 🌐 *www.alexsports.ch.*

VAL D'ANNIVIERS

25 km (16 miles) south of Sierre.

If you drive east of Sierre and south of the Rhône, following signs for Vissoie, you enter a wild and craggy valley called Val d'Anniviers. The name is said to come from its curious and famous (among anthropologists, at least) nomads, known in Latin as *anni viatores* (year-round travelers). A stopover in any one of these windswept mountain hideouts to walk, climb, ski, or relax by the fire is a reward. In late September, when herds of bell-toting cows are brought down from the mountains, there's a clangy seasonal celebration called Désalpe.

VISITOR INFORMATION

Contact **Val d'Anniviers Tourist Information.** ☎ *027/4761700* 🌐 *www.valdanniviers.ch.*

EXPLORING

Grimentz. In summer you can drive down a narrow forest road to Grimentz. With a population of 490, this ancient 13th-century village has preserved its weathered-wood houses and mazots in its tiny center. It is particularly known for its *vin du glacier,* or glacier wine, which is traditionally drunk directly from the barrel rather than bottled. ✉ *Grimentz* 🌐 *www.grimentz.ch.*

St-Luc. Head up a switchback road to the tiny village of St-Luc for a taste of rural life and celestial viewing at the observatory an easy funicular ride up the mountain. ✉ *St-Luc.*

WHERE TO STAY

$$ B&B/INN **Grand Hôtel Bella Tola.** A mountain retreat since the late 1800s, and a member of Swiss Historic Hotels, the designer setting of this stately mansion perched above St-Luc's main thoroughfare mixes antiques and collectibles with sepia photos, rippled mirrors, orchids, and fur pillows—the handiwork of the woman who owns the hotel with her husband. **Pros:** feels like staying with an old friend; beautiful location with stunning views; charming, typically Swiss vibe. **Cons:** many rooms no bigger than a breadbasket; children allowed into the spa only before 5:30 pm, which can be tricky après-ski; some find the decor cluttered. $ *Rooms from: 290 SF* ✉ *Rue Principale, St-Luc* ☎ *027/4751444* 🌐 *www.bellatola.ch* ⏲ *Closed mid-Apr.–mid-June and mid-Oct.–mid-Dec.* *30 rooms* *Breakfast.*

SPORTS AND THE OUTDOORS

HIKING

Le Chemin des Planètes. Walk through the universe on an astronomically themed 6-km (4-mile) trail called Le Chemin des Planètes. The Tignousa funicular from St-Luc (round-trip 16 SF) delivers you to the starting point at 7,218 feet. Models of the planets are set along a pathway that begins at the base of the **Observatoire François-Xavier Bagnoud** (*027/4755808; www.ofxb.ch*). Allow two hours to make the ascent from there, past the Hotel Weisshorn. For 26 SF (including funicular; free June–Sept. with the "Anniviers Liberté" pass if you stay in the region one night or longer) you can view the night sky through the reflecting and refracting telescopes at the observatory; sign up for a night visit at the St-Luc Tourist Office. ✉ *St-Luc.*

LEUKERBAD

21 km (13 miles) northeast of Sierre.

At 4,628 feet, Leukerbad, called Loèche-les-Bains in French, is Europe's highest spa village; travelers have been ascending to this Alpine retreat for centuries to take the curative waters and fill their lungs with cleansing mountain air. Leukerbad is a pleasant alternative to the larger resorts, and its rejuvenating hot mineral pools are a soothing winter après-ski option.

Summer brings hikers who love the combination of trekking and soaking. High-altitude crossings via the Gemmi Pass go back to 500 BC. The ancient connection between the Valais and the Berner Oberland can be traversed easily in a day.

Calcium sulfite hot springs flow beneath the village, filling stone troughs with warm vapor, keeping thoroughfares free of snow, and circulating to private tubs and public pools daily. In the late 1960s an arthritis and rheumatism treatment facility was established, but it has since been overshadowed by upscale wellness hotels and sports clinics. The two largest bath facilities in Leukerbad are Leukerbad Therme and Walliser Alpentherme & Spa. Both have pools, fountains, whirlpools, jets, and sprays of thermal waters. Towels and robes can be rented at the reception desk. The local tap water, which comes from the same source, is also said to have health benefits, so don't forget to drink a glass of water.

GETTING HERE AND AROUND

To get to the thermal village of Leukerbad by public transportation, you'll need to transfer to an LLB Lines bus from the Leuk-Susten train station. If you arrive by car, the road from Leuk-Susten to Leukerbad is an easy drive all year-round.

Contacts LLB. ☎ *027/4727171* 🌐 *www.llbreisen.ch.*

VISITOR INFORMATION

Contact Leukerbad Tourist Information. ✉ *Rathaus, Rathausstr., Leukerbad* ☎ *027/4727171* 🌐 *www.leukerbad.ch.*

EXPLORING

Keller zur Grotte. Just outside Leukerbad is this cozy winery with a tasting room where you can sample wonderful Humagne Rouges, Fendants, Walliser rosés, and Cornalins, among other unique Valais varietals. The town makes for a great half-day bike ride from Leukerbad, and it is downhill all the way. For those who don't want to climb up again, you can easily throw your bike on the bus as you head back uphill. ✉ *Kegelpl. 7, Varen* ☎ *027/4733647* 🌐 *www.kellerzurgrotte.ch* ⌚ *Closed Sun. and Mon.*

FAMILY **Leukerbad Therme.** With its indoor and outdoor pools, this multilevel facility is more water park than thermal bath. It's usually packed with families, so don't come expecting peace and quiet. But the views of Leukerbad's mountains are terrific, though no better than at Alpentherme, which is better suited to those seeking tranquility. Leukerbad Therme has a sauna, solarium, and snack bar, as well as giant slides that corkscrew their way down into one of the thermal baths. ✉ *Rathausstr. 32,*

Leukerbad ☎ 027/4722020 ⊕ www.leukerbadtherme.ch ☏ 25 SF for 3-hr pass; 30 SF for day pass; 10 SF extra for sauna and Turkish bath.

Fodor's Choice ★ **Walliser Alpentherme & Spa.** Sporting expansive Palladian windows set in marble, the Alpentherme looks like a temple perched on the hill. Annexes contain a beauty center, shopping arcade, and bistro. The unique spa treatments here are the Roman-Irish bath, a two-hour succession of hot and cold soaks, vapor treatments, and a soap-brush massage; and the Valaisan sauna village, a course of steam rooms and saunas. Massage, herbal wraps, scrubs, and medical consultations are also on the menu. Children under eight are welcome with an adult at the pools for free, but they are not permitted in the sauna village or Roman-Irish baths. ✉ *Dorfpl., Leukerbad* ☎ *027/4721010* ⊕ *www.alpentherme.ch* ☏ *25 SF for 3 hrs in thermal baths; 40 SF for 5 hrs in baths and sauna; 55 SF day pass for baths and sauna.*

WHERE TO STAY

$$$ HOTEL **Hotel Waldhaus.** With the friendliness that comes from a family-run establishment, this chalet-style guesthouse is set on a quiet street overlooking the village and houses one of the best restaurants in town. **Pros:** quiet location; excellent service; top-notch food in the restaurant. **Cons:** per-day supplement per person for stays fewer than three nights; not all rooms face mountain; parking can be a challenge. [$] *Rooms from: 308 SF* ✉ *Promenade 17, Leukerbad* ☎ *027/4703232* ⊕ *www.hotel-waldhaus.ch* *16 rooms* *Breakfast.*

$$$ B&B/INN Fodor's Choice ★ **Les Sources des Alpes.** When it first opened in 1834, this Relais & Châteaux hotel received tourists on the "Grand Tour" through Europe; now it plays to those who want *des vacances cocooning* (pampered downtime) in an exclusive setting with its own lovely outdoor thermal pool. **Pros:** sitting in a hot pool on a cold day is a great experience; friendly staff; top-quality food and wine at the hotel restaurant. **Cons:** restaurant atmosphere a bit stuffy; indoor spa area could use an update; minimum booking required Dec. 24–Jan. 10. [$] *Rooms from: 450 SF* ✉ *Tuftstr. 17, Leukerbad* ☎ *027/4722000* ⊕ *www.sourcesdesalpes.ch* ⊙ *Closed last 2 wks of Apr.* *30 rooms* *Breakfast.*

SPORTS AND THE OUTDOORS

HIKING

Hiking trails totalling 200 km (124 miles) range from easy walks alongside lakes to rugged treks in mountainous terrain. Hikes for the whole family include a unique **thermal spring trek,** which takes walkers on a 3-km (2-mile) stroll through town to learn more about Leukerbad's famous waters. More difficult walks include the **Leukerbad to Albinen hike,** which involves scrambling up eight ladders en route. Begin hikes of all levels at the Torrent and Gemmi cable car stops. For instance, from the Gemmipass, a gentle two-hour hike leads to the beautiful scenery of **Daubensee lake.** For exact routes, pick up the hiking guide from the Leukerbad tourist office.

SKIING

Leukerbad has 80 km (49 miles) of downhill and cross-country runs at varying levels of difficulty, including some used for World Cup training and testing. The ski season usually runs mid-December–mid-April.

Skiers can choose between taking the Torrent cable car, which whisks skiers to as high as 8,563 feet and offers 50 km (31 miles) of slopes, from beginner to expert, or the Gemmi cable car, which reaches 7,710 feet and is great for cross-country skiing (30 km [18 miles] of trails), tobogganing, and snowshoeing. A one-day ski pass including a visit to one of the public spas is 66 SF; from June to October the price (without ski pass) is reduced to 43 SF.

Expert skiers are challenged by the 9¾-km (6-mile) run from Schwalbennest mountain station, reached by funicular to the Rinderhütte mountain station followed by chairlift to the highest skiing point in Leukerbad.

The frozen Daubensee lake makes a lovely setting for cross-country skiing. From the Gemmipass cable car station, take an aerial tram to the Daubensee, where you can choose from a 7-km (4-mile) or 8-km (5-mile) trail.

ZERMATT AND SAAS-FEE

Immediately east of Sierre you'll notice a sharp change: *vals* become *tals,* and the sounds you overhear at your next pit stop are no longer the mellifluous tones of the Suisse Romande but the sharper Swiss-German dialect called Wallisertiitsch. Welcome to Wallis (*vahl*-is), the Germanic end of Valais. This sharp demographic frontier can be traced to the 6th century, when Alemannic tribes poured over the Grimsel Pass and penetrated as far as Sierre.

ZERMATT AND THE MATTERHORN

28 km (18 miles) south of Visp, plus a 10-km (6-mile) train ride from Täsch.

Fodor's Choice ★ Despite its fame—which stems from the iconic Matterhorn and its excellent ski facilities—Zermatt is a resort with its feet on the ground. It protects its regional quirks along with the wildlife and tumbledown mazots, which crowd between glass-and-concrete chalets like old tenements between skyscrapers. Streets twist past weathered-wood walls, flower boxes, and haphazard stone roofs until they break into open country that inevitably slopes uphill. Despite the throngs of tourists, you're never far from the wild roar of a silty river or vertiginous mountain path.

In the mid-19th century Zermatt was virtually unheard of; the few visitors who came to town stayed at the vicarage. The vicar and a chaplain named Joseph Seiler persuaded Seiler's younger brother Alexander to start an inn. Opened in 1854 and named the Hotel Monte Rosa, it's still one of five Seiler hotels in Zermatt. In 1891 the cog railway between Visp and Zermatt took its first summer run and began disgorging tourists with profitable regularity—though it didn't plow through in wintertime until 1927. Today the town remains a car-free resort (though electric carts run by the hotels clog the streets). If you're

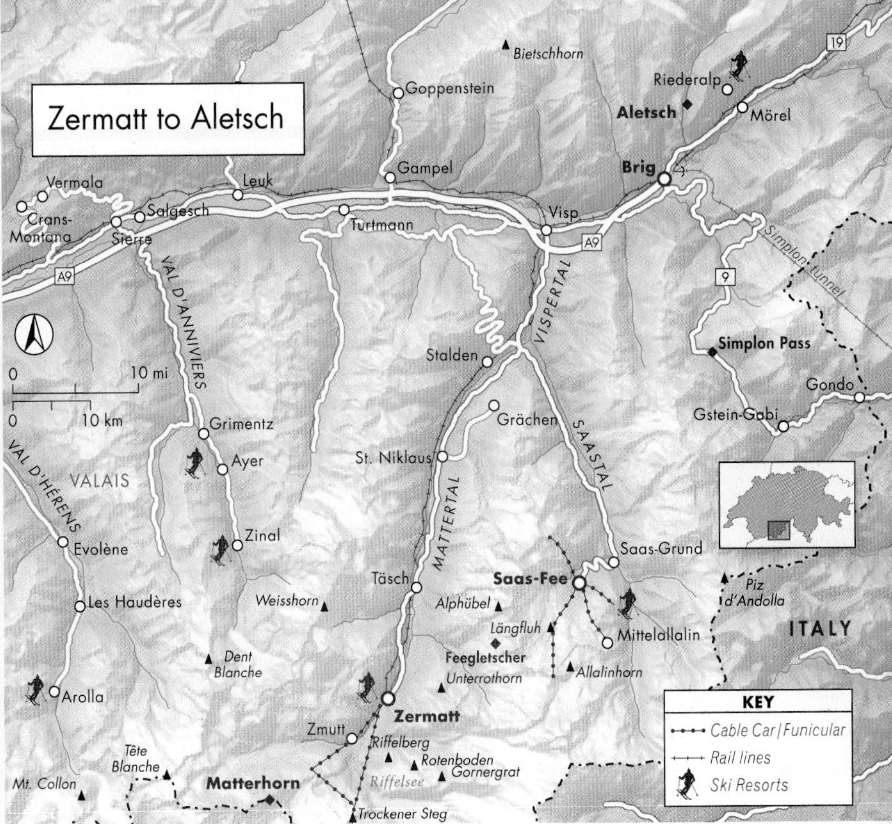

traveling primarily by car, park it in the multistory terminal connected to the station in Täsch, where you catch the train into Zermatt.

GETTING HERE AND AROUND

Zermatt, the world's most famous car-free Alpine village, requires residents and guests to leave their vehicles in the village of Täsch. The Matterhorn Gotthard Bahn ferries passengers from Brig and Visp to Zermatt, and operates frequent shuttle service from Täsch to the village on a private railway system. It also connects with the Glacier Express, a very touristy train that runs between Zermatt and St. Moritz. Once in Zermatt, another arm of the network, the pricey Gornergrat Bahn takes skiers and day hikers to the Gornergrat.

In Täsch, five-star hotels like those in the Seiler group have separate valet terminals plus private transfer that can be booked with your room reservation. In addition, there are open lots where the rates are less expensive, but plan to add at least 15 SF per day for parking to your vacation expenses. If you don't want to make the half-hour drive on mountain roads into the Matter Valley, use rail service that connects through Visp. The scenic ride takes about an hour.

If the weather is clear when you arrive, hustle to the end of the village to see the mountain. Then split your day of exploring between taking

DID YOU KNOW?

Nestled beneath the Matterhorn, Zermatt has been entirely car-free since 1947. Only electric vehicles that don't run on fuel are permitted in this resort, and they are ubiquitous.

a lift or the train to higher elevations and strolling the narrow streets and shops, being sure to stop at one of the local restaurants for raclette.

Contact Gornergrat Bahn. ☎ *084/8642442* 🌐 *www.gornergrat.ch.* **Matterhorn Gottard Bahn.** ☎ *084/8642442* 🌐 *www.mgbahn.ch.* **Matterhorn Terminal Täsch.** ☎ *027/9668100* 🌐 *www.zermatt.ch/anreise/Matterhorn-Terminal-Taesch.*

VISITOR INFORMATION

Contacts Zermatt Tourist Information. ✉ *Bahnhofpl. 5, Zermatt* ☎ *027/9668100* 🌐 *www.zermatt.ch.*

EXPLORING

Gornergrat–Monte Rose Bahn. It's quite simple to gain the broader perspective of high altitudes without risking life or limb. A train trip on the Gornergrat Bahn functions as an excursion as well as a ski transport. Part of its rail system was completed in 1898, and it's the highest open-air rail system in Europe (the tracks to the Jungfraujoch, though higher, bore through the face of the Eiger). It connects out of the main Zermatt train station and heads sharply left, at a right angle to the track that brings you into town. Its stop at the **Riffelberg,** at 8,469 feet, presents wide-open views of the Matterhorn. Farther on, from **Rotenboden,** at 9,246 feet, a short downhill walk leads to the **Riffelsee,** which obligingly provides photographers a postcard-perfect reflection of the famous peak. At the end of the 9-km (5½-mile) line, the train stops at the summit station of **Gornergrat,** at 10,266 feet, and passengers pour onto the observation terraces to take in the majestic views of the Matterhorn, Monte Rosa, Gorner Glacier, and an expanse of peaks and glaciers. Make sure to bring warm clothes, sunglasses, and sturdy shoes, especially if you're planning to ski or hike down. ✉ *Bahnhofpl. 7, Brig* ☎ *084/8642442* 🌐 *www.gornergratbahn.ch* 🎫 *94 SF round-trip, 47 SF one way.*

Fodor's Choice ★ **Matterhorn.** At 14,685 feet, the Matterhorn's peculiar snaggletooth form rears up over the village of Zermatt, larger than life and genuinely awe inspiring. As you weave through crowds along Bahnhofstrasse, the town's main street, you're assaulted on all sides by Matterhorn images—on postcards, sweatshirts, calendars, beer steins, and candy wrappers—though not by the original, which is obscured by resort buildings (except from the windows of pricier hotel rooms). But break past the shops and hotels onto the main road into the hills, and you'll reach a slightly elevated spot where you'll probably stop dead in your tracks. There it is at last, its twist of snowy rock blinding in the sun. Surely more pictures are taken from this spot than from anywhere else in Switzerland. It was Edward Whymper's spectacular—and catastrophic—conquest of the Matterhorn, on July 14, 1865, that made Zermatt a household word. After reaching the mountain's summit, his climbing party began its descent, tying themselves together and moving one man at a time. One of the climbers slipped, dragging the others down with him. Though Whymper and one of his companions braced themselves to stop the fall, the rope between climbers snapped and four mountaineers fell nearly 4,000 feet to their deaths. One body was never recovered, but the others lie in modest graves behind the park near the village church, surrounded by scores of other failed mountaineers. In summer the streets of Zermatt fill with sturdy, weathered climbers. They continue to tackle the peaks, and climbers have mastered the Matterhorn thousands of times since Whymper's disastrous victory. ✉ *Zermatt.*

DID YOU KNOW?

Zermatt lies in a hollow of meadows and trees ringed by mountains—among them the broad **Monte Rosa** and its tallest peak, the **Dufourspitze** (at 15,200 feet, the highest point in Switzerland)—plus 36 others that tower above 13,000 feet—of which visitors hear relatively little, so all-consuming is the cult of the Matterhorn.

FAMILY **Matterhorn Museum – Zermatlantis.** To get a sense of life in this high-altitude region and the risks involved in climbing, visit the Matterhorn Museum – Zermatlantis, a sunken village of chalets, mazots, and dwellings depicted as an archaeological site that visitors walk through, experiencing different periods of time along the way. The personal accounts of local docents liven up the displays of antiquated equipment, clothing, and historical documents about those who lived and climbed here. There is a farmer's cottage, hotel, and church interior, plus stuffed and mounted animals. ✉ *Kirchpl., Zermatt* ☎ *027/9674100* 🌐 *www.zermatt.ch/museum* 🎫 *10 SF.*

St. Peter's Zermatt - The English Church. Climb the winding pathway behind Pizzeria Molino to the white church on the hill, St. Peter's. Anglican services are still held in the tiny sanctuary established by the British, who ignited a climbing fervor to conquer the Matterhorn and other towering peaks in the region. Take time to pause in the cemetery that holds the graves of those not fortunate enough to return safely and others who remained in this beloved community to live out their lives. ✉ *Bodmen 5, Zermatt* ☎ *027/9675566.*

WHERE TO EAT

$$ SWISS Fodor's Choice ★ ✕ **Findlerhof.** Ideal for long lunches between sessions on the slopes or a panoramic break on an all-day hike, this place perched in tiny Findeln, between the Sunnegga and Blauherd ski areas, has astonishing Matterhorn views to accompany decidedly fresh and creative food. Franz and Heidi Schwery tend their own Alpine garden to provide lettuce for their salads and berries for vinaigrettes and hot desserts. **Known for:** astonishing Matterhorn views; cozy atmosphere; local Swiss specialties. $ *Average main: 30 SF* ✉ *Findeln* ☎ *027/9672588* 🌐 *www.findlerhof.ch* ⏲ *Closed May–mid-June and mid-Oct.–Nov.*

$$ SWISS ✕ **Grill-Room Stockhorn.** The moment you step across the threshold into this low-slung, two-story restaurant decked with mountaineering memorabilia, the tantalizing aroma of melting cheese should sharpen your appetite. Downstairs, watch meat roasting on the wood-fired grill while enjoying the chalet-style decor. **Known for:** grilled meats and regional dishes; cozy, chalet-style decor; friendly service. $ *Average main: 42 SF* ✉ *Hotel Stockhorn, Riedstr. 11, Zermatt* ☎ *027/9671747* 🌐 *www.hotelstockhorn.ch* ⏲ *Closed Mon. Closed late Apr.–mid-June and Oct.–mid-Nov.*

$$ SWISS ✕ **Whymper-Stube.** At this little restaurant in the Hotel Monte Rosa, plates of melted raclette and bubbling pots of fondue are delivered to

tightly packed tables by an agile waitstaff. Be sure to try the unusual variations on cheese dishes like the fresh mushroom or pear-laced fondue. **Known for:** Swiss specialties and unique variations on fondue; cozy atmosphere; friendly staff. *Average main: 28 SF* ✉ *Hotel Monte Rosa, Bahnhofstr. 80, Zermatt* ☎ *027/9672296* 🌐 *www.whymper-stube.ch* ⏲ *Closed May and last 2 wks of Oct.*

$$ SWISS — **Zum See.** In the hamlet (little more than a cluster of mazots) of the same name, this restaurant turns out inventive meals that merit acclaim. A half-hour's walk from Zermatt, it overflows until late afternoon with diners sunning on the terrace or packed into the 400-year-old log house. (The quickest way to get here is to walk or ski down from Furi.) Hosts Max and Greti Mennig masterfully prepare such seasonal specials as venison salad with wild mushrooms and handmade tortelloni with spinach-ricotta filling. **Known for:** creative, seasonal fare; Thursday night fondue Chinoise dinner during the winter season; extensive selection of wines and brandies. *Average main: 35 SF* ✉ *Zum See 24, Zermatt* ☎ *027/9672045* 🌐 *www.zumsee.ch* ⏲ *Closed mid-Apr.–late June and mid-Oct.–mid-Dec. No dinner.*

WHERE TO STAY

Many Zermatt hotels, especially larger ones, decide on a year-by-year basis to close during low season, which lasts from "meltdown" (anywhere from late April to mid-June) until "preseason" (November through mid-December). If you plan to travel during the low season, be sure to call ahead. That noted, the summer "low season" can prove more popular than the winter ski season, with rates and availability to match.

$$$ HOTEL — **Hotel Monte Rosa.** Behind the graceful, shuttered facade of this historic hotel, you'll find an ideal balance between modern convenience and history in the original ceiling moldings and Victorian dining hall. **Pros:** old-world charm with modern conveniences; in the heart of Zermatt; friendly, attentive staff. **Cons:** no in-house pool or spa facilities; bar is trendy but narrow and uncomfortably cramped; front-facing rooms can be noisy. *Rooms from: 474 SF* ✉ *Bahnhofstr. 80, Zermatt* ☎ *027/9660333* 🌐 *www.monterosazermatt.ch* ⏲ *Closed mid-Apr.–mid-June and Oct.–mid-Dec.* *41 rooms* *Breakfast.*

$$$$ HOTEL Fodor's Choice ★ — **Mont Cervin Palace.** The central location and luxurious setting help this Zermatt grande dame stand out, with rooms divided between the main building and connecting annexes. **Pros:** station pickup in a red antique horse-drawn carriage; wellness and spa facilities that are tops; attentive staff and luxurious accommodations. **Cons:** big-city luxury removes you somewhat from the village atmosphere; many hotel restaurants open only in the winter; parking and transport cost extra. *Rooms from: 660 SF* ✉ *Bahnhofstr. 31, Zermatt* ☎ *027/9668888* 🌐 *www.montcervinpalace.ch* ⏲ *Closed late Apr.–mid-June, Oct., and Nov.* *165 rooms* *Breakfast.*

$$$ HOTEL Fodor's Choice ★ — **Omnia Mountain Lodge.** This sophisticated glass-and-steel hotel on the hillside above the Kirchplatz not only has great service and superlative town and mountain views, but is an engineering marvel, a sleek standout in a village of traditional hoteliers. **Pros:** sophisticated, sleek

Many hotels and resorts in Zermatt have stunning views of the iconic Matterhorn.

design; lovely wellness area; Bose sound systems and designer toiletries. **Cons:** not so close to cable cars; staggered building layout can be disorienting; books quickly and getting in can be tough. *Rooms from: 500 SF* ✉ *Auf dem Fels, Zermatt* ☎ *027/9667171* 🌐 *www.the-omnia.ch* ⏲ *Closed late Apr.–mid-June* *30 rooms* 🍽 *Breakfast.*

$$$$ HOTEL **Riffelalp Resort 2222m.** Sitting at 7,290 feet amid open fields and dense forests, this mountaintop option has direct views of the Matterhorn—especially breathtaking in the orange glow of early morning. **Pros:** stunning Matterhorn views; peaceful mountain retreat away from the village hubbub; precise service. **Cons:** 7-night minimum in winter season and 10-night minimum over New Year's; overly formal and reserved attitude; already pricey hotel with add-ons like transportation and minibar. *Rooms from: 815 SF* ✉ *Riffelalp, Zermatt* ☎ *027/9660555* 🌐 *www.riffelalp.com* ⏲ *Closed mid-Apr.–late June and Oct.–mid-Dec.* *72 rooms* 🍽 *Breakfast.*

$$ HOTEL **Walliserhof Hotel.** This cozy, family-run charmer, a five-minute walk from the main train station, offers both a convenient location and friendly service that have helped make it a favorite since its opening in 1896. **Pros:** central location; spacious rooms; good, Swiss-centric restaurant. **Cons:** the cramped spa feels like an afterthought; rooms facing the street may be noisy; few in-room amenities. *Rooms from: 290 SF* ✉ *Bahnofstr. 30, Zermatt* ☎ *027/5302020* 🌐 *www.walliserhof-zermatt.ch* ⏲ *Closed May and Nov.* *23 rooms* 🍽 *Breakfast.*

NIGHTLIFE

Gee's Bar. Located in what locals call the "Bermuda Triangle" because of its concentration of nightspots, this is a lively bar where you can enjoy cocktails, including the Matterhorn Mule, made with homemade ginger beer. ✉ *Bahnhofstr. 70, Zermatt* ☎ *027/9677788* 🌐 *zermattgees.com.*

Hexen Bar. A great place for après-ski drinks, this chatty witch-themed bar and pub has a subtle gay vibe. *Gespritzer weissers* (white-wine spritzers) are a local favorite, but the dark-wood paneling and cozy booths might make you want to sample something from the extensive whiskey menu. ✉ *Bahnhofstr. 43, Zermatt* ☎ *027/9675533* 🌐 *www.grampis.ch.*

Josef's Wine Lounge. For excellent wines served with a modern flair, head down the pathway beside the Hotel Mirabeau to Josef's Wine Lounge. Though open all winter season, it's sometimes closed in summer, so check before you go. ✉ *Hotel Mirabeau, Untere Mattenrstr. 12–14, Zermatt* ☎ *027/9662660* 🌐 *www.hotel-mirabeau.ch.*

Schwyzer Stübli. A double dose of regional song and dance can be had at the Schwyzer Stübli, open only in winter. Be prepared for rowdy sing-alongs and accordion music. It's incidentally also a great place to sample traditional Swiss food. ✉ *Hotel Schweizerhof, Bahnhofstr. 5, Zermatt* ☎ *027/9660000* 🌐 *www.schweizerhofzermatt.ch.*

Unique Hotel Post. Across the cobblestones from Gee's Bar is the Unique Hotel Post, which houses a concert hall, lounge where DJs spin tunes for late-night revelers (both open only in winter), disco with a high-energy beat, cocktail and cigar lounge, and mellow pub serving chicken wings and burgers. ✉ *Unique Hotel Post, Bahnhofstr. 41, Zermatt* ☎ *027/9671931* 🌐 *www.hotelpost.ch.*

Vernissage. For one-stop entertainment, eating, and drinking, swing by the cinema, concert hall, lounge bar, café, or innovative restaurant at the Vernissage, the brainchild of local artist-architect Heinz Julen. ✉ *Backstage Hotel Vernissage, Hofmattstr. 4, Zermatt* ☎ *027/9666970.*

SPORTS AND THE OUTDOORS

HIKING

With 400 km (248 miles) of marked trails available, you'll have plenty of options for exploring the mountains on foot. Outfitted with scarred boots, backpacks, and walking sticks, trekkers strike out in all directions for daylong excursions ranging from easy to exhausting. Free route guides are available at the tourist office. Be sure to pack rain gear and a warm jacket along with sunscreen, because the weather changes quickly. Multiday lift passes ease the way up and leave some change in your pocket for an after-hike beer.

Fodor's Choice ★ **Five Lakes Walk.** Although any hike with views of the Matterhorn is worth the effort, particularly special is the 9-km (6-mile) route from Blauherd to Sunnegga, passing lakes like Stelli, Grindji, and Grün along the way. A funicular and cable car ride to Blauherd at 8,200 feet brings you to the start, and a funicular ride takes you back to town. The route is relatively easy but still requires a climb of 800 vertical feet. An alternative is to end your hike at Findeln for a restorative lunch with mountain views, though you need to walk the 40 minutes back downhill to town afterward. ✉ *Zermatt.*

MOUNTAIN BIKING

Mountain bikers may use all the area's paths but must respect hikers on the trail. There are six routes specifically for mountain bikes, covering a total of 100 km (62 miles). Bikes can be transported on the Gornergrat, Rothorn, and Schwarzsee lifts.

Slalom Sport. A wide variety of bikes can be rented at Slalom Sport. ✉ *Kirchstr. 17, Zermatt* ☎ *027/9662366* 🌐 *www.zermattbike.com.*

MOUNTAIN CLIMBING

The climb up the Matterhorn must be taken seriously; you have to be in top physical condition and have climbing experience to attempt the summit. You also need to spend 7 to 10 days acclimatizing once in the area. Less experienced climbers have plenty of alternatives, though, such as a one-day climb of the Riffelhorn (9,774 feet) or a half traverse of the Breithorn (13,661 feet). For those wanting a challenge without such extreme altitudes, try a guided trip across the rugged Gorner gorge.

Zermatt Alpin Center. For detailed information, advice, instruction, and climbing guides for the Matterhorn, contact the Zermatt Alpin Center. ✉ *Bahnhofstr. 58, Zermatt* ☎ *027/9662460* 🌐 *www.alpincenter-zermatt.ch.*

SKIING

Zermatt's skiable terrain lives up to its reputation: the 52 lifts and mountain railways are capable of moving well more than 90,000 skiers per hour up to its approximately 360 km (224 miles) of marked pistes—if you count those of Cervinia in Italy. Among the lifts are the cable car that carries skiers up to an elevation of 12,746 feet on the Matterhorn Glacier Paradise (previously known as Klein Matterhorn), the small Gornergratbahn that creeps up to the Gornergrat, and a subway through an underground tunnel that gives more pleasure to ecologists than sun-loving skiers.

The skiable territory on this royal plateau was once separated into three separate sectors, but the installation of a gondola to Riffelberg has linked the three together. The first sector is **Sunnegga-Blauherd-Rothorn,** which culminates at an elevation of 10,170 feet. **Gornergrat-Stockhorn** (11,155 feet) is the second. The third is the region dominated by the **Matterhorn Glacier Paradise,** which goes to Italy. The best way to prioritize your ski day is still to concentrate on one or two areas, especially during high season. Thanks to snowmaking machines and the eternal snows, Zermatt is said to guarantee skiers 7,216 feet of vertical drop no matter what the snowfall—an impressive claim—as well as year-round skiing. A one-day lift ticket costs 79 SF and a six-day, 380 SF; if you want to ski to Italy, it costs 92 SF and 434 SF, respectively.

Snowpark Zermatt. This snowboarding center on Theodul Glacier has pipes, kickers, and rails to thrill. Take the cable car to Matterhorn Glacier Paradise to reach the snowpark. ✉ *Schluhmattstr. 28, Zermatt* ☎ *027/9660101* 🌐 *www.snowpark-zermatt.ch.*

Swiss Ski and Snowboard School. This outfit runs group classes from mid-December until mid-April, but can provide private instruction all year. ✉ *Bahnhofstr. 58, Zermatt* ☎ *027/9662466* 🌐 *www.skischulezermatt.ch.*

SHOPPING

Zermatt is Switzerland's souvenir capital, offering a broad variety of goods, including scarves, watches, knives, logo clothing, and Matterhorn-in-a-box stones. Popular folk crafts and traditional products include large grotesque masks of carved wood, and lidded *channes* (tankards) in pewter or tin, molded in graduated sizes; they're sold everywhere, even in grocery stores.

You'll see lots of stores offering state-of-the-art sports equipment and apparel, from collapsible grappling hooks for climbers and lightweight hiking boots in brilliant colors to pairs of lightweight, spiked walking sticks for hikers to add a bit of upper-body workout to their climb.

Bayard. Bayard has sporting-goods shops scattered throughout the village, including this one on the Bahnhofstrasse. It's an ideal place to rent ski gear or shop for a new pair of downhill racing goggles. ✉ *Bahnhofstr. 35, Zermatt* ☎ *027/9664960* 🌐 *www.bayardzermatt.ch.*

Glacier Sport. This popular shop specializes in ski and climbing equipment and accessories. ✉ *Bahnhofstr. 19, Zermatt* ☎ *027/9681300* 🌐 *www.glacier-intersport.ch.*

SAAS-FEE

36 km (22 miles) south of Visp.

Quieter and more low-key than Zermatt is the village of Saas-Fee, a car-free mountain resort with a family-friendly vibe. Saas-Fee also has a fantastic network of trails that allows you to get up close and personal with the wild marmots, who live in subterranean dwellings on the mountain. At the end of the switchback road from Saas-Grund lies a parking garage where you must abandon your car for the length of your stay. Even by the garage the view on arriving at this lofty (5,871 feet) plateau is humbling. (In true Swiss-efficient fashion, drop off your bags curbside and call an electric shuttle that arrives to fetch you in the time it takes to park your car.) If you're staying in Saas-Fee overnight, your hotel gives you a Citizens' Pass that includes free bus travel and discounts to area attractions; in the summer, two nights or longer also gets you free travel on most cableways. Also consider buying a Saaspass (5 SF per night per person) for even steeper discounts on entrance fees, mountain guides, parking fees, and more.

GETTING HERE AND AROUND

Car-free Saas-Fee has a bus connection with Brig (about one hour, 20 minutes) and Visp (one hour); take the train here from Brig by transferring at Visp or connecting with Zermatt by rail, with a transfer at Stalden-Saas.

VISITOR INFORMATION

Contact **Saas-Fee Tourist Information.** ✉ *Obere Dorfstr. 2, at the entrance to the village, Saas-Fee* ☎ *027/9581858* 🌐 *www.saas-fee.ch.*

EXPLORING

Dom. Saas-Fee is at the heart of a circle of mountains called the Mischabel, 13 of which tower more than 13,120 feet. Among them is the Dom (14,908 feet), the highest mountain entirely on Swiss soil. ✉ *Saas-Fee.*

FAMILY **Eis Pavillon** (*Ice Pavilion*). The Eis Pavillon combines fascinating construction with a dash of kitsch and lets you look beneath the frozen surface of the earth. More than 25 feet below the ice pack, the cavernous facility provides an impressive view of the surreal, frozen environment inside glacial formations. Bring a coat or sweater—it's literally freezing down there. There are ice sculptures, exhibits on glaciology and crevasse rescue, and even a chapel-like room for meditation, concerts, and art shows. To reach the Eis Pavillon, take the Alpin Express or Felskinn cable car up to Felskinn before switching to the underground funicular—the world's highest (prepare yourself for a drastic change in altitude). ✉ *Mittelallalin, Saas-Fee* ☎ *027/9581100* 🎟 *10 SF.*

Fee Glacier. Saas-Fee lies in a deep valley that leaves no doubt about its source—it seems to pour from the vast, intimidating Fee Glacier. *Fee* can be translated as "fairy," and this primordial landscape could illustrate a fairy tale. See it up close by taking a gondola up to Spielboden and then a cable car to Längfluh, right on the glacier's edge, where there's a restaurant with magnificent glacial views. ✉ *Saas-Fee.*

WHERE TO EAT

Saas-Fee has always been known for good food, but it's really come into its own in terms of culinary excellence in the last few years. Chefs here provide much more than the usual fondue and raclette.

$$ SWISS ✕ **Restaurant Skihütte.** During the winter high season you'll have to be quick in order to snag a table on the sun-filled deck of this traditional restaurant on the main drag. A great location on the way back from the lifts, it's perfect for a cold after-ski brewski or tummy-warming Williamine pear schnapps. **Known for:** lively, sun-filled deck; local favorites; slow service when it's crowded. $ *Average main: 26 SF* ✉ *Dorfstr. 43, Saas-Fee* ☎ *027/9589280* 🌐 *hotel-burgener.ch/skihuette.html.*

$$$$ FRENCH Fodor's Choice ★ ✕ **Restaurant-Vinothek Fletschhorn.** Markus Neff presides over this gourmand's paradise in the Waldhotel Fletschhorn. The vibe is innovative, the flavors are superb, many ingredients are local, and dishes rotate seasonally. **Known for:** innovative, seasonal fare; charming country vibe; extensive wine list. $ *Average main: 70 SF* ✉ *Waldhotel Fletschhorn, Saas-Fee* ☎ *027/9572131* 🌐 *www.fletschhorn.ch* ⊗ *Closed late Apr.–mid-June and late-Oct.–mid-Dec.*

WHERE TO STAY

$$ HOTEL Fodor's Choice ★ 🏨 **The Dom Hotel.** Saas-Fee's oldest hotel has embraced a winning mixture of old and new with a clean but rustic design and big picture windows that fling open to incredible views of the surrounding mountains and glaciers. **Pros:** homey touches blend with discreet high-tech amenities; location in the center of town can't be beat; popular restaurant with extensive wine list. **Cons:** no spa facilities; nearby church bells may wake up light sleepers; transfer to the station can be slow to arrange. $ *Rooms from: 270 SF* ✉ *Dorfpl. 2, Saas-Fee* ☎ *027/9587700* 🌐 *www.domcollection.ch* ⊗ *Closed late Apr.–mid-June* 🛏 *35 rooms* 🍽 *Breakfast.*

$$ RESORT 🏨 **Ferienart Resort & Spa.** In the center of town, this wood-chalet hotel has some of the best views around, an appealing spa area, and a fine choice of on-site restaurants. **Pros:** top-of-the-line wellness facilities;

DID YOU KNOW?

There are many opportunities to climb peaks higher than 13,000 feet in this region. From Saas-Fee, an easy option is Allalinhorn; there climbers can ride a mountain train much of the way up before tackling the remaining route to the summit.

babysitting and day care center a plus for families; gorgeous restaurants. **Cons:** rooms vary drastically; inconsistent service; kitschy megaresort-y vibe. *Rooms from: 280 SF* ✉ *Dorfweg 1, Saas-Fee* ☎ *027/9581900* 🌐 *www.ferienart.ch* *71 rooms* *Breakfast.*

$$$ HOTEL **Hotel Schweizerhof.** This hotel has the town's best spa, not to mention lofty views of the mountains and glaciers, and the rates include a six-course dinner in addition to breakfast. **Pros:** excellent spa; secluded hilltop locale; friendly service. **Cons:** shuttle bus to and from the slopes can get crowded; extremely high charge for drinking water; not all rooms have views. *Rooms from: 360 SF* ✉ *Hallenstr. 10, Saas-Fee* ☎ *027/9587575* 🌐 *www.schweizerhof-saasfee.ch* *Closed mid-Apr.–mid.-June and mid-Nov.–mid-Dec.* *46 rooms* *Breakfast.*

$$$ B&B/INN Fodor's Choice ★ **Waldhotel Fletschhorn.** A member of the Relais & Châteaux collection of hotels, this sophisticated *Landgasthof* (country inn) is set apart from town at the end of a woodsy lane and includes one of the top restaurants in the region. **Pros:** staff picks you up at the station; worth a stay just to eat at the restaurant; posh, elegant mountain experience. **Cons:** 25-minute walk from the village; tiny spa area; pricey. *Rooms from: 350 SF* ✉ *Saas-Fee* ☎ *027/9572131* 🌐 *www.fletschhorn.ch* *Closed late Apr.–mid-June and late-Oct.–mid-Dec.* *12 rooms* *Breakfast.*

NIGHTLIFE

BARS AND CLUBS

Nesti's. Patrons squeeze into Nesti's, a perennial après-ski favorite. ✉ *Dorfstr. 23, Saas-Fee* ☎ *079/8681453.*

Popcorn Bar. A younger crowd congregates for drinks at Popcorn Bar. The all-in-one spot features a shop stuffed with übercool snowboard clothes and gear, reasonably priced hotel rooms, and—of course—DJs and dancing. ✉ *Obere Dorfstr. 6, Saas-Fee* ☎ *027/9585000* 🌐 *www.popcorn.ch.*

SPORTS AND THE OUTDOORS

HIKING

Larch forests, flower- and herb-filled meadows, and glacial zones host 350 km (218 miles) of trails at all levels of difficulty. Historic routes cross passes into Italy and extend outbound along ridgelines toward the river. Bus and lift services make it easy to return to the village in time for dinner. Most hotels happily pack a lunch for the outing, or you can stop at *buvettes* (snack bars) scattered along the trails.

One popular option is to take a cable car over to Hannig mountain station at 7,710 feet for a three-hour hike to a glacial lake and back down to Saas-Fee. To start from Hannig, follow the path toward Schönegg.

Another option is the timeworn pilgrimage route from Saas-Fee to Saas-Grund, which offers stops at 15 shrines with costumed wooden statues strung along the path like beads on a rosary.

MOUNTAIN CLIMBING

Mountaineering Office Saas-Fee Guides. This mountaineering company conducts daily guided forays throughout the year and rents season-appropriate equipment. A popular activity is gorge crossing, which uses safety cables and pulleys to traverse the valley's deep divide. There are also a few *via ferrata* (iron way), preset routes with ladders and cables secured in place to challenge climbers at all stages of competence. ✉ *Obere Dorfstr. 75, Saas-Fee* ☎ *027/9574464* 🌐 *www.saasfeeguides.ch.*

SKIING

The first glacier to be used for skiing here was the **Längfluh** (9,414 feet), accessed by gondola, then cable car. The run is magnificent, sometimes physically demanding, and always varied. From the Längfluh you can take a lift to reach *the* ski area of Saas-Fee, the **Felskinn-Mittelallalin** sector (9,840–11,480 feet).

Lifts don't connect with other resorts in the valley—Saas-Almagell, Saas-Balen, or Saas-Grund. Nevertheless, good days of skiing can be found a bus ride away, and hiking trails open in winter and summer link all four valleys. A one-day lift ticket costs 73 SF; a six-day pass costs 365 SF with the Citizens' Pass.

Felskinn-Mittelallalin. Felskinn harbors its own surprise: to preserve the land and landscape, the Valaisans have constructed a subterranean funicular, the Métro Alpin, which climbs through the heart of the mountain to Mittelallalin, that is, halfway up the Allalinhorn (13,210 feet). Tourists debark in a rotating restaurant noted more for the austere grandeur of its natural surroundings than its food. Felskinn-Mittelallalin's exceptional site, its high elevation, 20 km (12½ miles) of runs, and ample facilities (cable car, funicular, and three ski lifts) have made Saas-Fee the number one summer-skiing resort in Switzerland. ✉ *Saas-Fee.*

SLEDDING

FAMILY **Feeblitz.** Your stay won't be complete without a few runs on the Feeblitz Toboggan Run, the curved and looped track of the *Rodelbobbahn* (bobsled) near the Alpin Express cable car station. ✉ *Alpin Express, Saas-Fee* ☎ *027/9573111* 🌐 *www.feeblitz.ch* 🎫 *6.50 SF.*

SPORTS CENTER

BRIG AND THE ALPINE PASSES

This region is the Grand Central Station of the Alps. All mountain passes lead to or through Brig, as traffic and rail lines pour in from Italy, Ticino, central Switzerland, and the Berner Oberland. It is also a transit link for Paris, Brussels, London, and Rome. The Simplon, Nufenen, Grimsel, and Furka passes provide exit options and stunning vistas dependent on destination. Northeast of this critical junction the spectacular Aletsch Glacier, the largest in Europe and a UNESCO World Heritage Site, straddles the cantons of Valais and Bern. The Rhône River becomes increasingly wild and silty until you arrive at its source in Gletsch, at the end of the valley called Goms.

BRIG

19 km (12 miles) southeast of Leukerbad.

A rail and road junction joining four cantons, this small but vital town for centuries has been a center of trade with Italy. Often overlooked as merely a transit point, the town has a legacy that can be appreciated

The imposing Stockalperschloss is a must-see if you're passing through Brig.

in a couple of hours: a restored core with cobblestone streets, shops, cafés, and the main attraction, a fairy-tale-worthy merchant's castle.

VISITOR INFORMATION

Contact Brig Simplon Tourism Information. ✉ *Bahnhofstr. 2, Brig* ☎ *027/9216030* 🌐 *www.brig-simplon.ch.*

EXPLORING

Stockalperschloss. The fantastical Stockalperschloss, a massive baroque castle, was built between 1658 and 1678 by Prince Kaspar Jodok von Stockalper und Thurm (1609–91), a Swiss tycoon who made his fortune in Italian trade over the Simplon Pass. Soaring spectacularly with three towers topped with gilt onion domes and containing a courtyard lined by elegant Italianate arcades, it was once Switzerland's largest private home and is now restored. Inside are libraries, archives, and some baroque period rooms. Though you can visit the gardens, public tours are offered in German only, but group tours in English, French, and Italian can be booked through Brig Simplon Tourism. ✉ *Alte Simplonstr. 28, Brig* ☎ *027/9216030* 🎫 *Garden free; German-language tours 8 SF* ⏲ *No tours Mon. May–Oct.*

ALETSCH

13 km (8 miles) north of Brig.

Ice-capped peaks with small mountain resorts staggered up their spines rim the Aletsch, a glacier that shares its name with the area surrounding it, paralleling the valley floor. A variety of ecological zones—from deep, frozen expanses in the center to forests emerging

CLOSE UP

Aletsch: Europe's Longest Glacier

Aletsch's famous glacier—23 km (14 miles)—was at its longest 155 years ago, but now recedes 100 to 165 feet per year. Concern about the recession of the earth's ice formations has made preserving the Aletsch Glacier internationally significant, so UNESCO designated a 250-square-km (97-square-mile) area around the glacier, shared between the cantons of Valais (77%) and Bern (23%), as a protected site. Generations ago the Swiss sensed the need to safeguard the area and began placing parts in conservationist hands.

The glacier's starting point, Concordia Platz, is the confluence of three ice masses that move down from the Bernese Alps. Here the ice has been measured as deep as 2,952 feet—over twice the height of the Empire State Building. Another magnificent formation, the Märjelensee is a lake with icebergs floating on top, carved into the glacier field with walls of ice and stone. As the glacier's ice recedes, nature reclaims the land, first with moss and small plants, then forest. Pro Natura, the conservation organization that oversees the region, describes the process as "forest emerging from ice." Though some of the area's pine and larch are 600 to 700 years old, extreme conditions keep them short. Animals thought to be extinct thrive here; chamois, martens, badgers, lizards, and birds have adapted to the elevation and temperature.

Cable cars ferry tourists to ridgetops above Riederalp, Bettmeralp, and Fiescheralp, where 360-degree views of the sweep of ice are framed by extraordinary peaks. You can see the Bernese Alps, including the Sphinx station on the Jungfraujoch called the "Top of Europe"; the Valaisan Alps; and even into Italy and France. Hiking trails lead to the glacier's edge, and guides take trekkers across parts of the ice field. All around are places to admire nature's grandeur and be grateful that it is being protected.

at the fringes—are part of a wilderness region that is now firmly in the hands of conservationists, protected as a UNESCO international nature site. In contrast to these extreme expanses, sunny south-facing slopes are active with skiers and hikers staying in the villages of Riederalp, Bettmeralp, and Fiescheralp.

GETTING HERE AND AROUND

You have three choices to reach the Aletsch villages and the UNESCO viewpoints near the glacier. The cable car from Fiesch takes you to either the village of Fiescheralp (27 SF round-trip) or directly up to Eggishorn, the highest viewpoint on the glacier's edge (9,413 feet; 42.80 SF round-trip). The village of Bettmeralp is reached via cable car from the Betten train station (19.60 SF round-trip); from there, walk about 15 minutes to the gondola up to Bettmerhorn (8,684 feet; 24 SF round-trip). Arrive at Riederalp by a giant gondola that lifts passengers from the village of Mörel; the 16-minute ride covers nearly 6,500 feet and costs 19.60 SF round-trip. Take another gondola to reach the Moosfluh viewpoint (7,654 feet; 20 SF round-trip). The Riederalp Bahnen, where the cable car starts, is across the street from the Mörel train station, a stop on the Matterhorn Gotthard line.

VISITOR INFORMATION

Contact **Aletsch Arena.** 🌐 *www.aletscharena.ch.*

EXPLORING

Fiesch Cable Car. If the day is clear, grab the chance for a spectacular ride to the top of one of the lofty peaks that shadow the roadway by taking the Fiesch cable car up to Eggishorn (9,413 feet). The panoramic views of Alps and glaciers leave most breathless. As the cable car rotates 360 degrees, you can tick off famous Bernese and Valaisan peaks from your to-see list. The Jungfrau, Eiger, Matterhorn, and Dom are clearly visible, as are peaks that lie across the border in Italy and France. ✉ *Fiesch, Furkastr. 61* ☎ *027/9712700.*

SPORTS AND THE OUTDOORS

HIKING

Beautiful hikes of all levels abound throughout the Aletsch region. You can start hikes directly from the villages of Riederalp, Bettmeralp, and Fiescheralp, or take a cable car up to begin amazingly scenic hikes along the glacier's edge. If you're planning a lot of hiking in the area, consider purchasing a Hiking Pass Aletsch, which gives you access to all the cable cars (49 SF for one day, 127 SF for six days).

Fodor's Choice ★ **Aletsch Panorama Trail.** From Brig catch a train to the Betten Talstation cable car, which whisks you up to Bettmeralp for amazing views. A gondola takes you to about 8,700 feet up the Bettmerhorn. From there, expect to climb about 1,300 vertical feet and drop more than 2,700 on this 11-km (7-mile) route, arriving at a cable car in Fiescheralp to take you back to train service in Fiesch. The trail, accessible between June and September, goes along the massive Aletsch Glacier, through a valley dotted with pristine Alpine lakes. Along the way, stop at the Gletscherstube, a rustic hut set near the Märjelensee, at 8,640 feet, where you can eat lunch or get a bed for the night to prolong the adventure. ✉ *Bettmeralp.*

SKIING

The three resorts of **Riederalp, Bettmeralp,** and **Fiescheralp** are connected by trails, lifts, and shuttle buses. There are 35 lifts and 104 km (65 miles) of runs, a quarter of which are expert and peak at 9,415 feet. A one-day lift ticket for access to the whole Aletsch ski area costs 60 SF; a six-day pass costs 335 SF. All the essentials are in place in these picture-book villages, but don't expect lots of amenities, varied dining choices, or glitzy nightlife.

Swiss Ski School Riederalp. Anyone requiring a ski school up here should contact the Swiss Ski School Riederalp. ✉ *Riederalp* ☎ *027/9271001* 🌐 *www.skischule-riederalp.ch.*

12

VAUD

WELCOME TO VAUD

TOP REASONS TO GO

★ **Montreux's Promenade du Lac:** Walk 3 magical miles along Lac Léman (Lake Geneva) to the Château de Chillon, Switzerland's most beautiful castle.

★ **Tramping with Charlie Chaplin:** Vevey commemorates its celebrated citizen in bronze at its lake rose garden and at Chaplin's World, a new museum in his honor in Corsier.

★ **Lausanne's table for two:** Acolyte of superchef Benoit Violier, Franck Giovannini is the new culinary king to watch.

★ **The grape escape:** From La Côte to Chablais, vineyards and wine cellars allow you to sip vintages that seldom make it beyond the border.

★ **Palatial pursuits:** Grandes dames of luxury, the Beau-Rivage Palace and Montreux Palace hotels even synchronize their gilded awnings to the sun's daily tour over the lake.

Lac Léman is a graceful swelling in the Rhône River, which passes through the northern hook of the Valais and channels between the French and Vaudoise Alps before breaking into the open at Bouveret, west of Villeneuve. The lake is shared by three of Switzerland's great French cities, grandes dames of the Suisse Romande: Lausanne, Montreux, and Geneva. Though the lake's southern shore lies in France's Haute-Savoie, the green hillsides of the north portion and the cluster of nearby Alps that looms over its east end are all part of the canton of Vaud.

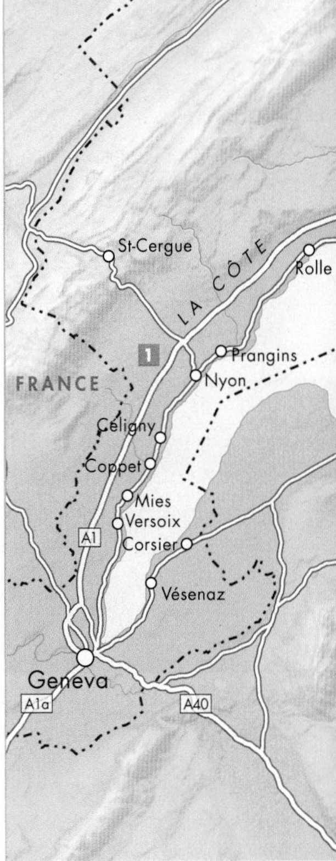

1 La Côte. Studded with wine villages, this region is famed for its châteaux—Prangins displays Swiss history, and Morges has 10,000 miniature lead soldiers in residence. But don't miss waterside Nyon, founded by Julius Caesar.

2 Lausanne. Not quite the city it was when Voltaire, Jean-Jacques Rousseau, and Victor Hugo waxed passionate about its beauty, Lausanne is largely a modern maze, but here and there you'll enjoy a burnt-orange jumble of medieval rooftops, shuttered windows with flower boxes, and misty Lac Léman and the Alps. Happily, the art and nightlife scenes are lively.

3 Lavaux Vignobles and Riviera. Set amid wine villages, the gorgeously picturesque Corniche de Lavaux heads toward Vevey, home to food giant Nestlé.

12

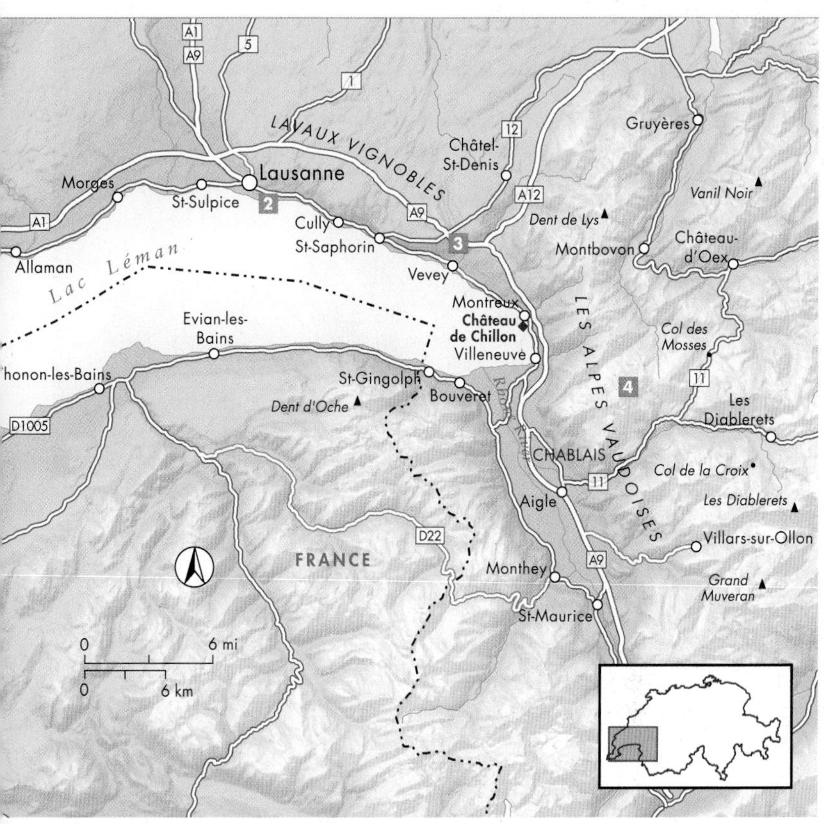

Globe-trotters have always loved this romantic town—Rousseau, Henry James, and Ernest Hemingway are just a few who enjoyed taking walks here. More modern is Montreux: spilling down the hill to a sunny bay, this usually tranquil city goes hot-cool when the Jazz Festival takes over in July.

4 Les Alpes Vaudoises. Framed by a stunning castle, Aigle is the gateway to many of the small, family-friendly resort towns high in the mountains above. Just across the steep summit of the Col des Mosses lies Château-d'Oex, home to hot-air balloons and richly carved wooden chalets unique to the Pays d'Enhaut highlands.

EATING WELL IN VAUD

The marvelous culinary delights of the region range from the elaborate concoctions of star chefs to the simplest fare.

Vaud's French influences are evident in the region's dishes, from fish caught in Lac Léman (above), to wines from the lakeside slopes (above, right). Sausages (below, right) are part of many traditional meals.

What's the common denominator? In any eatery worth its salt, it'll be *cuisine du marché:* cooking based on fresh market produce. Seasonal is the name of the game.

Like the rest of Switzerland, this region was part of France's Helvetic Republic from 1798 through 1803 and—although Vaud did some time under the House of Burgundy, and borders France to the west—French cooking here, as in *la cuisine française,* does not come out of historical tradition, but out of the relatively recent, essentially 20th-century phenomenon that saw French restaurants spring up around the globe.

Which is not to say there aren't cross influences, French and otherwise, in Vaudois cooking, best sampled in cozy *pintes* (wine pubs that serve food) that feature the finest local wines.

MALAKOFFS

The villages of Vinzel and Bursins are the best sources for a very local specialty, the *Malakoff,* which consists of a slice of Gruyère on a piece of toast that is then deep fried. These cheesy delights have always been a favorite of the Vaudois, but after the Crimean Wars they were renamed after a beloved officer who led his army of Vaud-born mercenaries to victory in the siege of Sebastopol.

PAPET VAUDOIS

The highlight of Vaudois cuisine, this dish is the unbeatable combination of slowly stewed leeks and potatoes, white wine, and spices, served with the classic pork-and-cabbage-stuffed sausage, *saucisse aux choux*.

FILETS DE PERCHE

Whether dusted with flour and fried in sweet cream butter *à la meunière*, or sautéed in a simple white-wine sauce, this local fish has a ubiquitous place on every lakeside restaurant menu. There is a reason folks order it year-round—when served with thin, crispy frites and washed down with a chilled Chasselas, your taste buds will find themselves in seventh heaven. Beware that some perch in less trustworthy establishments comes from Eastern Europe, so be sure to ask for the real deal.

SAUSAGES

Legend has it that the occupied Vaudois chopped up the biggest hanks of ham to avoid giving them to their Bernese rulers. With copious small pieces of meat on their hands, it is only natural that charcuterie reigns supreme in the canton of Vaud. From the traditional Easter or Pentecôte *boutefas* (sausage stuffed in a pork bladder), to the famous cabbage-stuffed saucisse aux choux typically enjoyed from September to April, there is a smoked sausage to suit all tastes.

SWEETS

Desserts here are some of the best, and most unusual, in the country. The *salée au sucre* is a popular breakfast item for special occasions. A yeasty, salty doughnut of sorts, it is topped with a deliciously sweet, creamy cheese—a Vaudois "cheese Danish," if you will. Real sweet tooths will prefer the *carac*, a miniature pie filled with dense chocolate ganache and glazed with neon-green icing. And if you're tempted by historic desserts of yore, the *gâteau à la raisinée* or *gâteau au vin cuit*—sweetened with a thick syrup of reduced pear or apple juice—is a must-try.

WINE

Chasselas is to Vaud what Fendant is to Valais—a light, often slightly sparkling white wine whose popularity is unparalleled in the region. Although some say it lacks complex aromatic notes, crisp, clean Chasselas is a perfect match for buttery regional specialties like filets de perche. Be sure to try Chasselas in all its incarnations—the prestigious Dézaley, Mont-sur-Rolle, or Yvorne all make fine additions to any wine cellar.

Updated by
Alexis Munier

In just one region, you can experience a complete cultural, gastronomic, and scenic sweep of Switzerland. Vaud (pronounced Voh) has a stunning Gothic cathedral (Lausanne) and one of Europe's most evocative châteaux (Chillon), palatial hotels and weathered-wood chalets, sophisticated culture and ancient folk traditions, snowy Alpine slopes and balmy lake resorts, simple fondue and the finesse of some of the world's great chefs. Everywhere there are roadside vineyards with luxurious rows of vines and rich, black loam.

This is the region of Lac Léman, a grand body of water graced by Lausanne and Montreux. The lake's romance—Savoy Alps looming across the horizon, steamers fanning across its surface, palm trees rustling along its shores—made it a focal point of the budding 19th-century tourist industry and an inspiration to the arts. In a Henry James novella the imprudent Daisy Miller made waves when she crossed its waters unchaperoned to visit Chillon; Byron's Bonivard languished in chains in the fortress's dungeons. In their homes outside Montreux, Igor Stravinsky wrote *The Rite of Spring* and Richard Strauss, his transcendent *Four Last Songs*. And perhaps going from the sublime to the ridiculous, film fans of James Bond will remember Sean Connery's car chase through the hillsides around Lac Léman in hot pursuit of Auric Goldfinger's Rolls as it swept its way to the villain's Swiss factory, neatly tucked in the mountains north of the lake.

Throughout the canton French is spoken, and the temperament the Vaudois inherited from the Romans and Burgundians sets them apart from their Swiss-German fellow citizens. It's evident in their humor, their style, and—above all—their love of their own good wine.

VAUD PLANNER

WHEN TO GO

The lake sparkles and clouds lift from Mont Blanc from spring to fall; November tends to be drizzly gray, and then winter brightens things up above the plain (as they call the flatter terrain surrounding the lake).

Crowds monopolize Montreux and Chillon year-round, but overwhelm them in July (jazz festival time) and August (Europe-wide vacations). However, it's worth aiming for the concert and dance season in Lausanne: from September through May.

Remember that at these latitudes, summer daylight extends until 9 pm, allowing you to pack a lot into one day; the reverse is true in winter.

PLANNING YOUR TIME

To experience the highlights of lake and mountain, reserve five days. Spend two savoring Lausanne and its Old Town, museums, and hyperactive waterfront. The Corniche route winds its way through the vineyards and hamlets of the Lavaux. Pull-offs are strategically interspersed for photo ops and to steady the nerves of drivers not used to narrow, cantilevered roadways. Get out and walk a section of the wine trail and definitely taste a glass of white wine. A few hours in the harbor-front town of Vevey, especially its older section, and the glitzy, Riviera-like city of Montreux will suffice. A visit to the region would be incomplete without a tour of Chillon—the fabled fortress that inspired Lord Byron to pen his famous poem "Prisoner of Chillon."

GETTING HERE AND AROUND

AIR TRAVEL

Geneva International Airport is the most convenient hub for Vaud. Trains connect the airport to Nyon, Lausanne, Morges, Vevey, and Montreux—if you're heading to one of the smaller lakeside villages, you will likely have to make a connection in one of these towns. Taxis abound, but fares are steep—the one-way fare to Lausanne runs approximately 220 SF for the 45-minute ride. A *navette,* or shuttle bus, runs twice hourly to major cities in Vaud; most fares are under 50 SF.

Contacts Navette Leman. ☎ *0800/107107* 🌐 *www.navetteleman.ch.*

BOAT AND FERRY TRAVEL

Like all fair-size Swiss lakes, Lac Léman is crisscrossed with comfortable and reasonably swift steamers, here run by the Compagnie Générale de Navigation. In summer they sometimes run more often than the trains that parallel their routes. You can embark and disembark freely at ports along the way. The trip from one end of the lake to the other will take the better part of a day, as routes are designed to serve a third of the lake per circuit, connecting towns on both the French and Swiss sides. Shorter trips like the one from Lausanne to Vevey will take an hour.

Contacts Compagnie Générale de Navigation *(CGN).* ☎ *0848/811848* 🌐 *www.cgn.ch.*

BUS TRAVEL

A useful network of postbus routes covers the region if you want connections to outlying villages and hamlets. Throughout the Riviera, bus service is provided by VMCV (Vevey-Montreux-Chillon-Villeneuve). The Line 1 trolley bus parallels the lakefront and is the most heavily used. ■ **TIP→ Hotel guests receive a Riviera Card that allows gratis rides on buses and reduced fares on other modes of transportation.**

Contacts VMCV. ☎ *021/9891811* 🌐 *www.vmcv.ch.*

CAR TRAVEL

There are two major arteries leading to Lac Léman, one entering from the north via Bern and Fribourg (A12), the other arcing over the north shore of Lac Léman from Geneva to Lausanne (A1), then to Montreux and on south through the Alpes Vaudoises toward the Col du Grand St-Bernard (A9) in Canton Valais. They are swift and often scenic expressways, and the north-shore artery (A1 and A9) traces a route that has been followed since before Roman times.

Secondary highways parallel the expressways, but this is one case where, as the larger road sits higher on the lakeside slopes, the views from the expressway are often better than those from the highway. Be sure, however, to detour for the Corniche road views between Lausanne and Vevey.

Rent the smallest car you and your luggage will allow, because narrow lanes in wine villages and parking in cities are headaches. Although expensive, opt for public garages that are clearly signed whenever possible. Take the ticket with you after entry, as payment is made via automated machines at the pedestrian entrance; many locations accept credit cards. The ticket returned after payment is your access card to exit.

TRAIN TRAVEL

Lausanne lies on a major train route between Bern and Geneva, with express trains connecting from Basel and Zürich. Regional trains along the waterfront, connecting major lake towns, are frequent and swift unless you board one of the S-trains that stop at every village. Travel time between centers like Geneva and Nyon, or Lausanne and Vevey, is about 15 minutes; count on doubling that on an S-train.

There are also several private rail systems leading into small villages and rural regions, including the Montreux–Oberland–Bernois (MOB) Railroad's Golden Pass, which climbs sharply behind Montreux and cuts straight over the pre-Alps toward Château-d'Oex and the Berner Oberland. Reserve space in one of its glass-dome, panoramic cars and take in the countryside, with food and beverage service brought to your seat. The historic Blonay–Chamby Railroad has steam-powered seasonal excursions, as does the Rochers-de-Naye line.

Contacts Blonay–Chamby Railroad. ☎ *021/9432121* 🌐 *www.blonay-chamby.ch.* **Montreux–Oberland–Bernois Railroad** (*MOB*). ☎ *0840/245245* 🌐 *www.goldenpass.ch.*

HOTELS

It's a pleasure unique to Vaud to wake up, part floor-length sheers, and look out over Lac Léman to Mont Blanc. A series of 19th-century grand hotels with banks of balconied lake-view rooms were created to offer this luxury, yet there's no shortage of charming inns offering similar views on an intimate scale. The hotels of Lausanne and Montreux are long on luxury and grace, and low prices are not easy to find. Especially at peak periods—Christmas to New Year's and June to August—it's important to book ahead. Small auberges in the villages along the lake and in the vineyards offer traditional dishes and simple comforts.

RESTAURANTS

As in all great wine regions, *dégustation* (wine tasting) and *haute gastronomie* (refined cuisine) go hand in hand here. In inns and auberges throughout La Côte and Lavaux (the two stretches of vineyard-lined shore), you'll dine beside nattily attired oenophiles who lower their half lenses to study a label, then go on to order a multicourse feast to complement their extensive tastings.

To experience Vaud's best cuisine, look for *déjeuners d'affaires* (business lunches), plats du jour, and prix-fixe menus, which can offer considerable savings over à la carte dining.

Of course, you will be spoiled for choice by the quality of Lausanne's restaurants. Prices can be high, but if you wander through the backstreets, you will see that the less affluent in Lausanne eat well, too.

Hotel and restaurant reviews have been shortened. For full information, visit Fodors.com.

WHAT IT COSTS IN SWISS FRANCS

	$	$$	$$$	$$$$
Restaurants	Under 26 SF	26 SF–45 SF	46 SF–65 SF	Over 65 SF
Hotels	Under 201 SF	201 SF–300 SF	301 SF–500 SF	Over 500 SF

Restaurant prices are the average cost of a main course at dinner or, if dinner is not served, at lunch. Hotel prices are the lowest cost of a standard double room in high season, including taxes.

TOURS

A wealth of tours are organized by the local tourism offices, which can also arrange for customized packages through an association of independent travel guides. Walking tours led by historians in Lausanne, Vevey, and Montreux are increasingly popular and given year-round. The Lausanne tourist office also runs a daily two-hour coach trip into the Old Town, including a visit to the cathedral and an extended city coach tour that takes in the Lavaux vineyards.

Most local tourist offices offer daily general tours in summer to Gruyères, to Chamonix and Mont Blanc, and to Les Avants and Château-d'Oex by the Montreux–Oberland–Bernois railroad line's panoramic train. There is also a chocolate excursion to the Cailler factory in Broc. To ensure a tour with English commentary, reserve in advance.

Lausanne à Pied. This group offers nearly a dozen different tours dedicated to everything from the city's important trees to its bridges. Tours may be booked through the Lausanne tourist office or online. ☎ *021/3201262* 🌐 *www.lausanne-a-pied.ch* 🎟 *From 30 SF.*

FAMILY **mobileo.** Adventurous travelers might consider booking a Segway tour with Mobileo, which offers several different routes. You can ride from "Lake to Sky," starting at the old fishing village of Ouchy and making your way uphill to Lausanne's loveliest neighborhoods. ☎ *840/424242* 🌐 *www.mobileo.ch* 🎟 *From 120 SF.*

Swiss Riviera Wine Tours. For a luxurious private tour in the Lavaux, contact specialist Swiss Riviera Wine Tours. You'll meet the friendliest winemakers in the area, sample their best wines, dine on a gourmet picnic lunch overlooking the lake, and even receive a surprise gift. The company also runs combination tours to Chateau de Chillon and Chateau d'Aigle. ☎ *21/9653237* 🌐 *www.swissrivierawinetours.com* 🎟 *From 22 SF.*

VISITOR INFORMATION

The main regional tourist office is in Lausanne.

Contacts Office du Tourisme du Canton de Vaud. ✉ *60 av. d'Ouchy, Lausanne* ☎ *021/6132626* 🌐 *www.lake-geneva-region.ch.*

LA CÔTE

Just northeast of Geneva, La Côte (the shore) of Lac Léman has been settled since Roman times, with its south-facing slopes cultivated for wine. It is thus peppered with ancient waterfront and hillside towns, castles, and Roman remnants. Train and bus service connects most towns and villages, but a car is a must if you want to wind through tiny wine villages. Do get out and walk—if only to hear the trickling of any number of Romanesque trough fountains and to saunter along a lakefront promenade. Be willing to travel back and forth from the slopes to the waterfront a few times if you're determined to cover all the region's charms; sticking exclusively to either the diminutive Route du Vignoble or the shore road deprives you of some wonderful sights.

NYON

27 km (17 miles) southwest of Lausanne.

Lovely Nyon, with its waterfront drive, shops, museums, and a castle dominating its cliff-top Old Town, was founded by Julius Caesar around 45 BC as a camp for war veterans. Lovely views can be had from the château-museum's terrace and the town's waterfront promenade, where boats and swans bob in the waves.

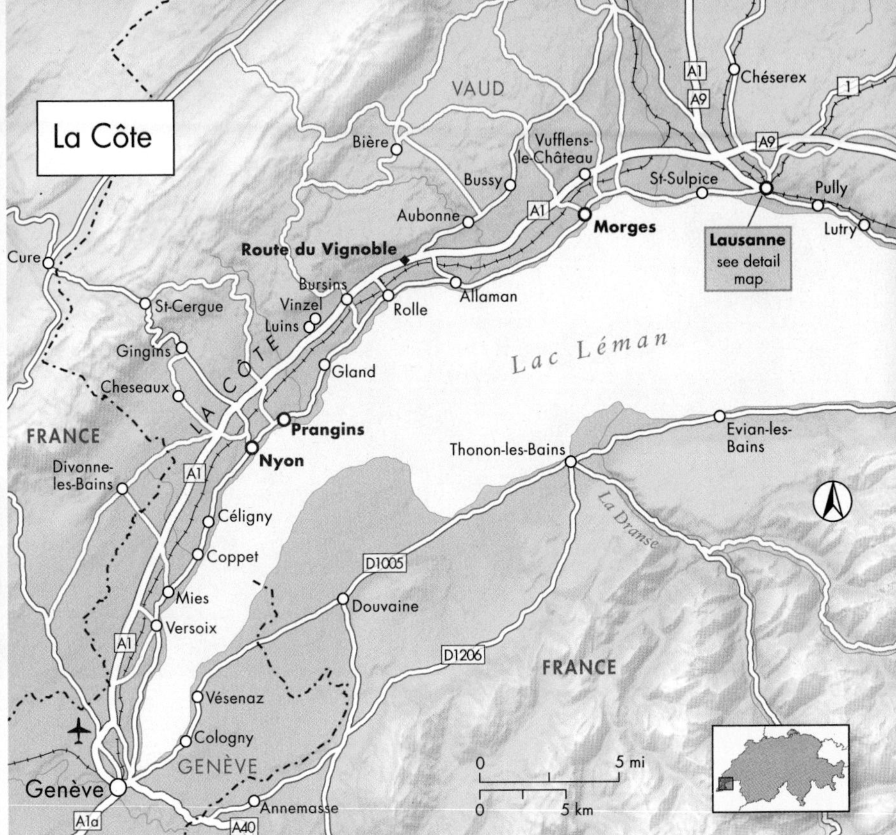

GETTING HERE AND AROUND

Nyon is one of the primary stations of the main rail line that goes along the shore of Lac Léman, served by all trains (regional and interregional). There are multiple arrivals and departures every hour. Most sights can be easily reached by foot, as the station is centrally located and just a five-minute walk from the historic Old Town.

VISITOR INFORMATION

Contacts Nyon Région Tourisme. ✉ *8 av. Viollier, Nyon* ☎ *022/3656600* 🌐 *www.nyon-tourisme.ch.*

EXPLORING

Château de Nyon. Dominating Nyon's hilltop over the waterfront is the Château de Nyon, a magnificent 12th-century multispire fortress with a terrace that takes in sweeping views of the lake and Mont Blanc. Its spacious rooms hold the collection of the Musée Historique, which traces the history of the castle inhabitants from residence by the dukes of Savoy (1293–1536) through occupation by the Bernese (1536–1798) to reclamation by the canton after the Vaud revolution. The upper floors held prisoners until 1979, and the city council and courts met in chambers here until 1999. Exhibits throughout highlight the city's position as a renowned porcelain center. Modern-day conversions include a marriage salon and a *caveau des vignerons*

La Château de Nyon sits prominently above the lakeside town's waterfront.

(wine cellar) featuring wines of local growers. ✉ *Pl. du Château, Nyon* ☎ *022/3164273* 🌐 *www.chateaudenyon.ch* 🎫 *8 SF, includes Musée du Léman and Musée Romain* ⏲ *Closed Mon.*

FAMILY **Musée du Léman.** Nestled in a charming floral park that parallels the water, the Musée du Léman has interactive exhibits about the fragile ecosystems of the lake, recreational boating activities, and coast-guard rescue techniques. There's a sizable aquarium, housed in a shuttered 18th-century hospital. ✉ *8 quai Louis-Bonnard, Nyon* ☎ *022/3164250* 🌐 *www.museeduleman.ch* 🎫 *8 SF, includes Musée Romain and Le Château de Nyon* ⏲ *Closed Mon.*

Musée Romain (*Roman Museum*). Graced by a statue of Caesar, the Musée Romain contains an attractively mounted collection of sumptuously detailed architectural stonework, fresco fragments, statuary, mosaics, and earthenware. The museum was built atop the foundation of a 1st-century AD basilica; a pristine miniature model inside and an excellent trompe l'oeil palace on an outside wall evoke the remarkable original structure. A listing of the exhibits is available in English, as are guided tours. ✉ *Rue Maupertuis, Nyon* ☎ *022/3164280* 🌐 *www.mrn.ch* 🎫 *8 SF, includes Musée du Léman and Château de Nyon* ⏲ *Closed Mon.*

WHERE TO EAT

$$ ITALIAN ✕ **Auberge du Château.** This Italian eatery, just steps from Nyon's château, serves straightforward fare, well-priced plats du jour, and specialty items like shrimp and vegetables on a pillow of saffron cream. An expansive terrace lets diners study the château; in winter, broad windows reveal the comings and goings on the municipal plaza. **Known**

for: fall game menu; locally picked mushrooms in season; lively Italian atmosphere. *Average main: 27 SF ✉ 8 pl. du Château, Nyon ☎ 022/3610032 🌐 www.aubergeduchateau.ch.*

WHERE TO STAY

$ HOTEL **Hôtel de l'Ange.** This unusually chic property in a convenient location proves that good things come in small packages. **Pros:** swanky design; immaculate housekeeping; Parisian-style bar specializes in gin. **Cons:** rooms are quite small; not bookable on some travel aggregate websites; no a/c means that rooms are warm in summer. *Rooms from: 175 SF ✉ 22 rue St-Jean, Nyon ☎ 022/3615509 🌐 www.hoteldelange.ch 14 rooms Breakfast.*

PRANGINS

3 km (2 miles) northeast of Nyon.

You'll see the elegant hillside château that's home to the national museum before you reach this little commune, where the pace of life moves gently between the boulangerie, post office, and café.

GETTING HERE AND AROUND

Take a train to the Nyon station, then switch to local bus service that picks up passengers outside the main entrance. The ride takes seven minutes to the village stop; from there it is a three-minute walk to the château.

EXPLORING

Musée National Suisse (*Swiss National Museum*). The 18th-century Château de Prangins is home to the Suisse Romande branch of the Musée National Suisse. The castle once had land holdings that stretched all the way to Rolle. Its four floors detail (in four languages, including English) Swiss life in the 18th and 19th centuries. Surrounded by parks and gardens (take note of the extensive culinary plantings set according to ancient documents), the museum is also a major venue for cultural events and regional celebrations. A café with terrace is open for lunch and refreshments. *✉ Av. Général Guiguer, Prangins ☎ 022/9948890 🌐 www.nationalmuseum.ch/e/prangins/ 10 SF Closed Mon.*

QUICK BITES

Rapp Chocolatier. After strolling the galleries and gardens of the National Museum, head to Rapp Chocolatier, a petite chocolate shop in the heart of town. Here handmade confections are stacked in perfect pyramids, and a school and demonstration kitchen are adjacent, so if your timing is right, you'll see artisans shaping molten cocoa and plying their forms with heavenly fillings. Known for: handmade chocolate in all shapes and sizes; chocolate-making classes for beginners; flaky, mouthwatering pastries. *✉ 6 rue des Alpes, Prangins ☎ 022/3617914 🌐 www.chocolaterie-rapp.com Closed Sun.*

WHERE TO STAY

$$$ HOTEL **La Barcarolle.** Hidden in a parklike setting off the lake road, this mustard-colored *relais* (inn) sits amid historic châteaux and country homes. **Pros:** secluded idyllic retreat; grand rooms with lots of amenities; spacious, luxurious bathrooms. **Cons:** must have a car to cover the distance to other villages; Swiss-style furnishings lack pizzazz; bus stop 15-min walk away. *Rooms from: 330 SF* *Rte. de Promenthoux, Prangins* *022/3657878* *www.labarcarolle.ch* *39 rooms* *Breakfast.*

EN ROUTE **Rolle.** About 12 km (7 miles) northeast of Nyon, the lakefront village of Rolle merits a detour for a look at its dramatic 13th-century château, built at the water's edge by a Savoyard prince. While in town you can visit the Moinat Antiques and Decoration shop for a sample of what it takes to furnish a grand country home. *Rolle* *www.tourisme-rolle.ch.*

ROUTE DU VIGNOBLE

36 km (22 miles) between Nyon and Lausanne.

Parallel to the waterfront highway, threading through the steep-sloping vineyards between Nyon and Lausanne, the Route du Vignoble (Vineyard Road) unfolds a rolling green landscape high above the lake, punctuated by noble manors and vineyards.

Luins, home of the flinty, fruity white wine of the same name, is a typical pretty village. Just up the road, the village of **Vinzel** develops its own white wines on sunny slopes and sells them from the *vin-celliers* (wine cellars) that inspired its name. The route continues through **Bursins,** home of an 11th-century Romanesque church, and goes all the way to **Morges.** The road is clearly signposted throughout.

MORGES

23 km (14 miles) northeast of Prangins, 8 km (5 miles) west of Lausanne.

On the waterfront just west of the urban sprawl of Lausanne, Morges is a pleasant lake town favored by sailors and devotees of its **Fête de la Tulipe** (Tulip Festival), held annually in April and May.

VISITOR INFORMATION

Contacts Morges Région Tourisme. *2 rue du Château, Morges* *021/8013233* *www.morges-tourisme.ch.*

EXPLORING

FAMILY **La Liberté.** The oar-powered warships of the Greeks, Romans, and Phoenicians once crossed the waters of Lac Léman. Now you can follow in their wake on *La Liberté*, a reconstruction of a 17th-century galley. This brainchild of historian Jean-Pierre Hirt is part public works project, part historical re-creation. The 183-foot ship sails the lake Wednesday and Saturday evenings and twice Sunday afternoon from mid-May to mid-October for two-hour tours. Reservations are required. *45 rue de Lausanne, Morges* *021/8035031* *www.lagalere.ch* *38 SF.*

Musée Alexis Forel. In the heart of town, a 16th-century courtyard-centered mansion, once home to renowned engraver Alexis Forel, displays the holdings of the Musée Alexis Forel. Although most of Forel's exceptional engravings are in the Musée Jenisch, in Vevey, here you can experience his home surroundings. Thick-beamed salons filled with high-back chairs, stern portraits, and delicate china remain as they were in the 1920s, when musicians and writers such as Stravinsky, Ignacy Paderewski, and Romain Rolland gathered for lively discussions and private concerts. An attic room has a selection of 18th-century puppets and porcelain dolls. ✉ *54 Grand-Rue, Morges* ☎ *021/8012647* 🌐 *www.museeforel.ch* 🎫 *10 SF* ⏲ *Closed Mon. and Tues.*

Musée du Château. The town's castle, built by the Duke of Savoy around 1286 as a defense against the bishop-princes of Lausanne, now houses the Musée du Château. The eclectic collection includes weapons, military uniforms, and 10,000 miniature lead soldiers. In the Salle Général Henri Guisan, you'll find memorabilia of this World War II general, much honored for keeping both sides happy enough to leave Switzerland safely alone. ✉ *1 rue de Château, Morges* ☎ *021/3160990* 🌐 *www.chateau-morges.ch* 🎫 *10 SF* ⏲ *Closed Mon. and mid-Dec.–Feb.*

OFF THE BEATEN PATH

Vufflens-le-Château. This village, 2 km (1 mile) northwest of Morges, is known for its namesake château, a 15th-century Savoyard palace with a massive donjon and four lesser towers, all trimmed in fine Piedmont-style brickwork. It's privately owned, but the grounds are open to the public. ✉ *Av. du Château, Vufflens-le-Château.*

WHERE TO EAT

$$$ FRENCH

L'Ermitage des Ravet. A multicourse gastronomic treat awaits at the restaurant in this 17th-century farmhouse set beneath old, draping trees where chef Bernard Ravet and his family serve the classics with a modern twist. Son Guy, who trained at top addresses in France and the United States, leads the kitchen in tandem with his father, while daughter and sommelier Nathalie pours carefully paired vintages. **Known for:** dazzling dessert creations; various types of foie gras; family business with a warm atmosphere. 💲 *Average main: 65 SF* ✉ *26 rte. du Village, Vufflens-le-Château* ☎ *021/8046868* ⏲ *Closed Sun.–Tues.*

WHERE TO STAY

$$ HOTEL

Hotel Fleur du Lac. This lakefront retreat, just outside town on the main route to Lausanne, is surrounded by abundant gardens and stately old trees. **Pros:** resort feel, with private dock and lake access; connected to town by lakefront pathway; renovated rooms. **Cons:** not close to the train station; bland decor; some guests report less than enthusiastic staff. 💲 *Rooms from: 275 SF* ✉ *70 rue de Lausanne, Morges* ☎ *021/8115811* 🌐 *www.fleur-du-lac.ch* 🛏 *38 rooms* 🍽 *No meals.*

Visit Palace de la Palud in Lausanne on Wednesday or Saturday to browse the market.

LAUSANNE

66 km (41 miles) northeast of Geneva, 108 km (67 miles) southwest of Bern.

"Lausanne is a block of picturesque houses, spilling over two or three gorges, which spread from the same central knot, and are crowned by a cathedral like a tiara. On the esplanade of the church … I saw the lake over the roofs, the mountains over the lake, clouds over the mountains, and stars over the clouds." Such was Victor Hugo's impression of this grand and graceful tiered city. Voltaire, Rousseau, Byron, and Jean Cocteau all waxed equally passionate about Lausanne—and not only for its visual beauty. It has been a cultural center for centuries, the world drawn first to its magnificent Gothic cathedral and the powers it represented, then to its university, and during the 18th and 19th centuries to its vibrant intellectual and social life. Today the Swiss consider Lausanne a most desirable city in which to live.

Rising in tiers from the lakeside at Ouchy, Lausanne covers three hills that are separated by gorges that once channeled rivers. The rivers have been built over, and huge bridges span the gaps across the hilltops. On one hill in particular, modern skyscrapers contrast brutally with the beautiful proportions of the cathedral rising majestically from its crest. Atmospheric alleys and narrow streets have mostly been demolished, yet the Old Town clustered around the cathedral has been painstakingly restored.

Below the Old Town spreads the commercial city center, and in the bottom of the hollow between Avenue Jules Gonin and Rue de Genève is the Flon, a neighborhood with plenty of nightspots. Still farther south, along the lake, is the separate township of Ouchy, an animated resort area dominated by the Château d'Ouchy, with a tower dating from the Middle Ages.

GETTING HERE AND AROUND

Lausanne serves as gateway to the region and connector for the east–west routes across the Alps to Milan (three hours) and the TGV to Paris or Avignon (four hours). From Geneva, trains take about 30 minutes and arrive in Lausanne up to four times an hour; from Bern they take a little more than an hour and arrive twice an hour.

While you're here, you will exhaust yourself if you attempt to walk the hillsides of Lausanne from lakefront Ouchy to hilltop Old Town. So do what the locals do and use the Transports Publics de la Région Lausannoise, a subway, rail, and bus network. The Métro subway is the quickest vertical ride from lake to suburbs with stops at the main train station, trendy Flon, and Bessières (cathedral) before terminating in Epalinges. The automated ticket machines can be confusing, as they list all routes.

There are two handy branches of Lausanne Tourisme, one at the main train station and the other at the subway station in Ouchy. The former is open daily 9–7, and the latter has the same hours April–September and closes an hour earlier October–March. The main office is open weekdays 9–5. Mobilis, a pass that combines all rail and bus services, starts at 8.60 SF for a daily pass. ■ **TIP→ The Lausanne Transport Card provided to all hotel guests is free, and so are your rides on local buses, trains, and the Métro.**

VISITOR INFORMATION

Contacts Lausanne Tourisme. ✉ *2 av. de Rhodanie, Lausanne* ☎ *021/6137373* 🌐 *www.lausanne-tourisme.ch.*

EXPLORING

TOP ATTRACTIONS

Fodor's Choice ★ **Cathédrale de Notre-Dame** (*Cathedral of Our Lady*). A Burgundian Gothic architectural treasure, this cathedral is Switzerland's largest church—and probably its finest. Begun in the 12th century by Italian, Flemish, and French architects, it was completed in 1275. Pope Gregory X came expressly to perform the historic consecration ceremony—of double importance, because it also served as a coronation service for Rudolf of Habsburg as the new Holy Roman emperor. Eugene Viollet-le-Duc, a renowned restorer who worked on the cathedrals of Chartres and Notre-Dame-de-Paris, brought portions of the building to Victorian Gothic perfection in the 19th century. His repairs are visible as paler stone contrasting with the weathered local sandstone.

Streamlined to the extreme, without radiating chapels or the excesses of later Gothic trim, the cathedral wasn't always so spare; in fact, there was brilliant painting. Zealous Reformers plastered over the florid colors, but in so doing they unwittingly preserved them, and now you can see portions of these splendid shades restored in the right transept.

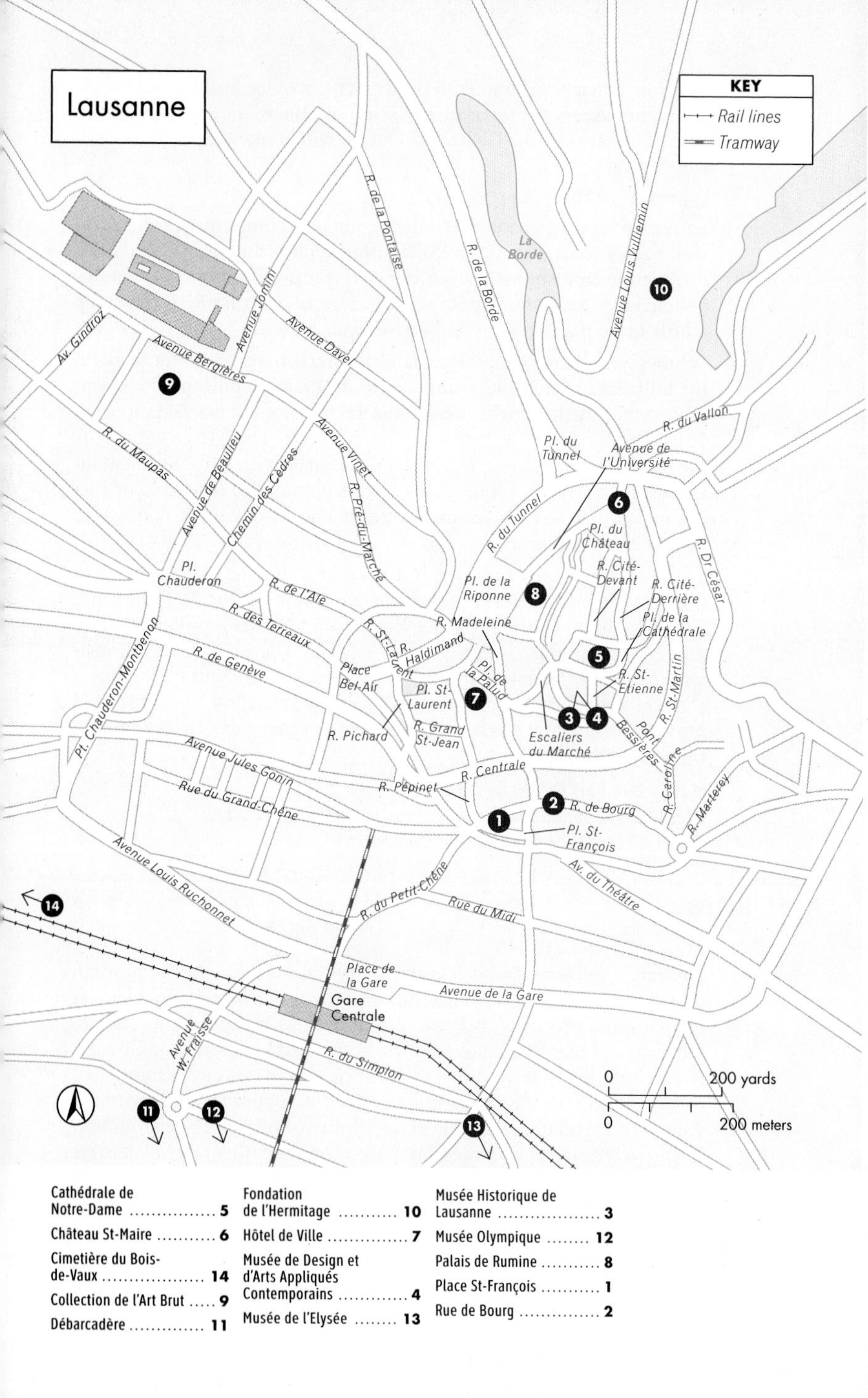

Cathédrale de Notre-Dame 5
Château St-Maire 6
Cimetière du Bois-de-Vaux 14
Collection de l'Art Brut 9
Débarcadère 11
Fondation de l'Hermitage 10
Hôtel de Ville 7
Musée de Design et d'Arts Appliqués Contemporains 4
Musée de l'Elysée 13
Musée Historique de Lausanne 3
Musée Olympique 12
Palais de Rumine 8
Place St-François 1
Rue de Bourg 2

The Cathédrale de Notre-Dame is Switzerland's largest church.

The dark and delicate choir contains the 14th-century tomb of the crusader Otto I of Grandson and exceptionally fine 13th-century choir stalls, unusual for their age alone, not to mention their beauty. The church's masterpiece, the 13th-century painted portal, is considered one of Europe's most magnificent. A tribute to 21st-century technology, the 7,000-pipe organ fills the sanctuary with swells of sacred music.

Holding fast to tradition, the cathedral has maintained a *guet,* or "lookout," since 1405. The guet sleeps in the belfry and is charged with crying out every hour on the hour between 10 pm and 2 am.

Protestant services (the cathedral was reformed in the 16th century) exclude nonworshipping visitors on Sunday at 10 am and 8 pm. You may want to come instead for the evening concerts given on an almost weekly basis in spring and autumn. Guided tours are given July to mid-September. ✉ *Pl. de la Cathédrale, Old Town* ☎ *021/3167161.*

Château St-Maire. The fortresslike elements of this 15th-century stone cylinder certainly came into play. The castle was built for the bishops of Lausanne; during the 16th century the citizens wearied of ecclesiastical power and allied themselves with Bern and Fribourg against the bishops protected within. Before long, however, Bern itself marched on Lausanne, put a bailiff in this bishops' castle, and stripped the city fathers of their power. Today the Château St-Maire is the seat of the cantonal government. ✉ *Pl. du Château, Old Town.*

OFF THE BEATEN PATH

Cimetière du Bois-de-Vaux. Always adorned with white flowers, as was her signature style, the grave of Coco Chanel lies within a large wooded cemetery park on the western edge of the city. Urban legend has it that Madame Chanel's beloved companion, her dog, is buried not far away

A GOOD WALK: LAUSANNE

Begin in the commercial hub of the city, the **Place St-François** (nicknamed "Sainfe" by the Lausannois), where you'll see the former Franciscan Église St-François. Behind the church, take a near hairpin turn right onto the fashionable main shopping street, the ancient **Rue de Bourg.** At the top of Rue de Bourg, Rue Caroline leads you left and left again over the Pont Bessières, where you can see the city's peculiar design spanning gorges and covered rivers.

Crossing the bridge and bearing right brings you up into the Old Town. On your left, the imposing palace of the Old Bishopric now houses the **Musée Historique de Lausanne.**

Adjacent is the **Musée de Design et d'Arts Appliqués Contemporains,** known as the "Mudac" to locals. Straight ahead, at the top of Rue St-Étienne, towers the tremendous **Cathédrale de Notre-Dame,** which is on par with some of Europe's finest churches.

With the cathedral on your left, walk up the narrow passage of Rue Cité-Derrière to the Place du Château and its eponymous monument, the **Château St-Maire.** As you face the château, turn left and walk down the Rue Cité-Devant.

As you pass the cathedral again, veer right toward a flight of wooden steps that leads down to the dramatic Escaliers du Marché, a wood-roof medieval staircase, and the Place de la Palud and the **Hôtel de Ville,** the seat of the municipal and communal councils. Turning right, just up Rue Madeleine, you will come upon the Place de la Riponne and the imposing **Palais de Rumine.**

A long hike up Avenue Vinet, northwest of the Old Town, will take you to the **Collection de l'Art Brut,** an unusual museum of fringe art.

South of the Old Town, Ouchy's **Débarcadère** has typical quayside attractions—vendors and people strolling on a promenade. It can be easily reached by the steep subway Métro; there are stations across from the Gare Centrale and under the Rue du Grand-Chêne in the Flon. (There's also a large underground parking garage, a boon in this space-pressed city.)

Just east of Ouchy, on a hillside overlooking the lake, the dramatic **Musée Olympique** tells about the history and sports of the Olympic Games. It's less than half a mile from the Débarcadère along the Quai de Belgique, which turns into the Quai d'Ouchy.

Uphill and connected by garden pathways, the **Musée de l'Elysée** is a photography museum housed in a restored 18th-century *campagne* (country manor home).

The Collection de l'Art Brut features "psychopathological" art from a variety of nontraditional artists.

in the pet cemetery on the grounds of the stately Beau-Rivage Palace. The cemetery is accessible by the No. 25 bus toward Bourdonnette, or the Nos. 1 and 6 toward Maladière. ✉ *2 rte. de Chavannes, Lausanne.*

Collection de l'Art Brut. This singular museum focuses on the genre of fringe or "psychopathological" art, dubbed *l'art brut* (raw art) in the 1940s by French artist Jean Dubuffet. His own collection forms the base of this ensemble of raw material from untrained minds—prisoners, schizophrenics, or the merely obsessed. Strangely enough, the collection is housed in the Château de Beaulieu, a former mansion of Madame de Staël, she of the sophisticated salons. The exhibits range from intricate yarn and textile pieces to a wall full of whimsical seashell masks. One of the most affecting works is a panel of rough carvings made by an asylum patient in solitary confinement; it was shaped with a broken spoon and a chamber-pot handle. You can get here by walking up Avenue Vinet or by taking Bus No. 2 from Place St-François in the direction of Désert. ✉ *11 av. des Bergières, Beaulieu* ☎ *021/3152570* 🌐 *www.artbrut.ch* 🎫 *10 SF, free the first Sat. of month* ⏲ *Closed Mon. Sept.–June.*

FAMILY **Débarcadère** (*Wharf*). In fine weather the waterfront buzzes day and night—strollers, diners, concertgoers, in-line skaters, artisans selling their wares—while the white steamers that land here add to the traffic. ✉ *Pl. du Port, Ouchy.*

Fodor's Choice ★ **Fondation de l'Hermitage.** A 15-minute bus ride from Old Town takes you to this beautifully set 19th-century country home. The estate is now an impressive art gallery with a fine permanent collection of Vaudois artists and headline-grabbing, yet seriously presented, blockbuster shows. Exhibits have included the works of Pablo Picasso, Alberto Giacometti, and the American impressionists. Details of the elegant villa have been preserved, including intricate moldings, carved fireplaces, and multipatterned parquet floors. Allow time for a walk on the grounds and coffee at L'esquisse, the café surrounded by the outlying orangery. To get here, take Bus No. 3 from Gare Centrale to the Motte stop or Bus No. 16 from Place St-François to Hermitage. ✉ *2 rte. du Signal, Sauvabelin* ☎ *021/3125013* 🌐 *www.fondation-hermitage.ch* 🎫 *19 SF* ⏲ *Closed Mon.*

Hôtel de Ville (*Town Hall*). Constructed between the 15th and 17th century, this is the seat of municipal and communal councils. A painted, medieval **Fontaine de la Justice** (*Justice Fountain*) draws strollers to lounge on its heavy rim. Across the street you can watch the modern **animated clock,** donated to the city by local merchants; moving figures appear every hour on the hour. A street market is held in the square every Wednesday and Saturday morning. ✉ *2 pl. de la Palud, City Center* ☎ *021/3152556* 🎫 *Free.*

Musée Historique de Lausanne. The Ancien-Évêché (Old Bishopric) holds a wealth of both temporary and permanent historical exhibits about the city. Don't miss the 250-square-foot scale model of 17th-century Lausanne, with its commentary illuminating the neighborhoods' histories. Also look for the re-created 19th-century shop windows. ⚠ **The museum is closed for renovation until fall 2018.** ✉ *4 pl. de la Cathédrale, Old Town* ☎ *021/3154101* 🎫 *8 SF* ⏲ *Closed Mon. Sept.–June.*

Place St-François (*St. Francis Square*). The stone-paved square is dominated by the massive post office and the former Franciscan **Église St-François** (*Church of St. Francis*), built during the 13th and 14th centuries. From 1783 to 1793, Edward Gibbon lived in a house on the site of the post office and there finished his work *The Decline and Fall of the Roman Empire.* ✉ *St-François.*

Rue de Bourg. Once a separate village isolated on a natural ridge, this is now Lausanne's fashionable main shopping street. Narrow and cobblestoned, it's lined with platinum-card stores such as Hermès and Louis Vuitton. Boutiques have been built into the centuries-old buildings, though some have added fittingly modern facades. ✉ *St-François.*

WORTH NOTING

Musée de Design et d'Arts Appliqués Contemporains (*Museum of Contemporary Design and Applied Arts*). A museum of contemporary design seems amiss in this ancient quarter of the city, but it demonstrates the passion for art in everyday life. Temporary and permanent installations in the restored Maison Gaudard feature glassworks, textiles, and graphics. Creative and performing arts merge in multimedia shows. ✉ *6 pl. de la Cathédrale, Old Town* ☎ *021/3152530* 🌐 *www.mudac.ch* 🎫 *10 SF* ⏲ *Closed Mon.*

FAMILY **Musée de l'Elysée.** Stark white walls and parquet floors form an inviting backdrop for the changing array of contemporary photography assembled by this museum in an 18th-century country manor. Wander the rooms, cellar, and attic spaces to view multiple exhibitions—some interactive and designed especially for children. The park surrounding the estate is a quiet place to find a shaded bench and critique the current show. ✉ *18 av. de l'Elysée, Ouchy* ☎ *021/3169911* 🌐 *www.elysee.ch* 🎫 *8 SF* ⏲ *Closed Mon.*

FAMILY **Musée Olympique** (*Olympic Museum*). With high-tech presentations and touching mementos, this complex pays tribute to the athletic tradition in ancient Greece, the development of the modern Games, the evolution of the individual sports, Paralympic competitions, and the athletes themselves. There are art objects—an Etruscan torch from the 6th century BC, Auguste Rodin's *American Athlete*—as well as archival films and videos, interactive displays, photographs, coins and stamps, and medals from various eras throughout Olympic history. A sculpture park, museum shop, and lovely café overlooking the lake complete this ambitious, world-class endeavor. Brochures and guided tours are available in English. ✉ *1 quai d'Ouchy, Ouchy* ☎ *021/6216511* 🌐 *www.olympic.org* 🎫 *18 SF* ⏲ *Closed Mon. Nov.–Apr.*

FAMILY **Palais de Rumine.** Built at the turn of the last century, this enormous neo-Renaissance structure houses several museums, all with a local spin. The top exhibit at the **Musée Cantonal d'Archéologie et d'Histoire** (Cantonal Archaeology and History Museum) is the gold bust of Marcus Aurelius discovered at nearby Avenches in 1939. The **Musée Cantonal de Géologie** (Cantonal Geology Museum) has an excellent fossil collection, including a mammoth skeleton. Besides its collection of regional fauna, the **Musée Cantonal de Zoologie** (Cantonal Zoology Museum) has a rare collection of comparative anatomy. The **Musée Cantonal des Beaux-Arts** (Cantonal Museum of Fine Arts) has an enlightening collection of Swiss art, not only by the Germanic Hodler and Anker but also by Vaud artists—especially Francois Bocion, whose local landscapes are well worth study during a visit to this region. Each museum has some descriptions or an abbreviated guide in English. All of these museums are free. ✉ *6 pl. de la Riponne, City Center* 🌐 *www.musees.vd.ch* 🎫 *Free* ⏲ *Closed Mon.*

WHERE TO EAT

$$$ SWISS Fodor's Choice ★ **Café Beau-Rivage.** As if turning its back on star sibling Anne-Sophie Pic and the aristocratic Beau-Rivage Palace, which shelters both, this young, lively brasserie-café faces the lake and the Ouchy waterfront scene. Its flashy brass-and-Biedermeier dining area and bar fill with smart Lausannois and internationals enjoying trendy cuisine du marché. **Known for:** Asian-inspired dishes like tandoori prawns with lemongrass; the best club sandwich in Lausanne; gracious summer terrace overlooking rose gardens. *$ Average main: 50 SF* ✉ *17–19 pl. du Port, Ouchy* ☎ *021/6133330* 🌐 *www.brp.ch.*

$ SWISS **Café Romand.** All the customers seem to know each other at this traditional dining institution, where shared wooden tables and clattering china create the perfect ambience for fondue, mussels, sausage, or *choucroûte* (sauerkraut). Prominent members of Lausanne's arts community swarm here after rehearsals and concerts, as service continues until 11 pm—late by Swiss standards. **Known for:** charmingly indifferent waitstaff; excellent regional and old-fashioned specialties; good fondue. *$ Average main: 25 SF* ✉ *2 pl. St-François, St-François* ☎ *021/3126375* 🌐 *www.cafe-romand.ch* ⏲ *Closed Sun.*

$$ ECLECTIC **Etoile Blanche.** This hip café, bar, and restaurant is beloved by students, business executives, and artists alike. The simple yet eclectic

decor features vintage advertisements and polished-wood seating, and several tables are available outside during the summer months. **Known for:** good selection of beers on tap; tasty, American-style cheeseburgers; packed bar a popular place for singles. *Average main: 30 SF Pl. Benjamin-Constant, City Center 021/3512460 www.etoileblanche.ch.*

$ FAST FOOD **Holy Cow!** At this self-proclaimed gourmet burger bar, Lausannois can feast on freshly grilled, juicy burgers while avoiding the town's McDonald's and Burger King. The chain has a refreshing "go-local" philosophy, and most ingredients are produced within a 25-mile radius. **Known for:** Elvis burger featuring blue cheese and bacon; thick, crispy British-style fries; selection of herbal sodas and microbrews. *Average main: 17 SF 10 rue des Terreaux, City Center 079/8197050 www.holycow.ch.*

$$ ECLECTIC **La Pomme de Pin.** Behind the cathedral, this winsome pinte—one of Lausanne's oldest—produces an eclectic menu ranging from French to Italian to Swiss (rabbit and Rösti, anyone?), along with reasonably priced plats du jour, served in the casual café and the adjoining linen-decked restaurant. The glass-panel door is often left ajar by neighbors dropping in for a glass of wine or espresso and a quick round of gossip. **Known for:** historic location in Old Town; inventive autumn game menu; exceptionally juicy roasted coquelet (baby chicken). *Average main: 45 SF 11–13 rue Cité-Derrière, Old Town 021/3234656 www.lapommedepin.ch Closed Sun.*

$$ MODERN FRENCH **Nomade.** This trendy restaurant–wine bar is one of Lausanne's rendezvous spots for the 30-and-over crowd. Chic yet comfy decor prevails in the cocktail area, and tall communal tables in the wine bar allow for easy mixing and mingling. **Known for:** over 30 wines available by the glass; panfried scallops in seafood sauce; older yet trendy clientele. *Average main: 38 SF 9 pl. de l'Europe, Flon 021/3201313 www.restaurantnomade.ch No credit cards No lunch Sun.*

$$$$ FRENCH Fodor's Choice ★ **Restaurant de l'Hôtel de Ville.** Since the tragic loss of world-renowned chef Benoit Violier, his determined widow, Brigitte, has continued to oversee the three-Michelin-star restaurant, propelling it to even higher accolades. Chef Franck Giovannini is already winning hearts—and stomachs—with his fresh twist on haute cuisine. **Known for:** finely orchestrated prix-fixe menus; consistently ranked one of the best restaurants in the world; exceptional service with a smile that is rare for such establishments. *Average main: 95 SF 1 rue d'Yverdon, Crissier 7 km (4 miles) west of Lausanne 021/6340505 www.restaurantcrissier.com Closed Sun. and Mon.*

$$ MODERN ITALIAN **Restaurant du Théâtre.** Locals come to this upscale spot for oven-fired pizzas—without a doubt the best in town. The elegant dining room is a year-round hit with locals; in summer there is nothing more delightful than sitting under the garden's sprawling trees and umbrellas. **Known for:** veal filet mignon in morel sauce; hot spot for pre- and post-performance operagoers; gorgeous summer terrace framed by tall trees. *Average main: 38 SF 12 av. du Théâtre, City Center 021/3515115 www.restaurant-du-theatre.ch Closed Sun. No dinner Mon.*

12

WHERE TO STAY

$$ HOTEL Fodor'sChoice ★ **Angleterre & Résidence Hôtel.** Within four graceful 18th- and 19th-century villas and a historic hotel near the waterfront, this small complex has been modernized without ruffling its gentility or disturbing its graceful stone arches, marble floors, or discreet gardens. **Pros:** urban feel steeped in history; part of energetic lakefront scene; especially pretty grounds surround the outdoor pool. **Cons:** alley entrance to garage and reception difficult to find; hard to snag a table on the patio for lunch or a sunset cocktail; lots of stairs make it less than ideal for physically challenged guests. *Rooms from: 280 SF* *11 pl. du Port, Ouchy* *021/6133434* *www.angleterre-residence.ch* *75 rooms* *No meals.*

$$$$ HOTEL **Beau-Rivage Palace.** Of the scores of luxury hotels in Switzerland, this gleaming grande dame stands apart—its neoclassical flourishes seamlessly restored to period opulence, its vast waterfront grounds manicured like a country estate. **Pros:** old-world elegance with modern flair; park setting with lake views is incomparable; extraordinary breakfast buffet. **Cons:** grand interiors missing a personal touch; staff formality adds to upper-crust ambience; rooms above event spaces can be noisy. *Rooms from: 540 SF* *17–19 pl. du Port, Ouchy* *021/6133333* *www.brp.ch* *168 rooms* *No meals.*

$ HOTEL **Carlton Lausanne Boutique Hotel.** A quiet tree-lined street in one of Lausanne's nicest neighborhoods masks this lodging's proximity to the train station. **Pros:** residential setting is a respite; well-priced neighborhood eateries nearby; just a short walk from the lakeside. **Cons:** no porter to help with luggage; bathrooms are on the small side; not wheelchair accessible. *Rooms from: 185 SF* *4 av. de Cour, Sous-Gare* *021/6130707* *www.carltonlausanne.ch* *47 rooms* *No meals.*

$$ HOTEL **Hotel Alpha-Palmiers by Fassbind.** Behind this historical facade you'll find a courtyard hotel of modern proportions. **Pros:** family-run operation eschews chain feel; garage parking a godsend in this hilly city; train station just five minutes away. **Cons:** access via a one-way street is tricky to navigate by car; popular for group meetings; up a steep cobblestone hill. *Rooms from: 225 SF* *34 rue du Petit-Chêne, City Center* *021/5555599* *byfassbind.com* *210 rooms* *Breakfast.*

$ HOTEL **Hôtel Regina Garni.** The owners of this friendly lodging spent more than a decade in the United States, so the language barrier is nonexistent. **Pros:** sights and shopping just outside the front door; well priced in an expensive lodging city; well-mannered staff. **Cons:** although driving up to the entrance is hypothetically possible, it's hard to find the way; no restaurant, although many options are nearby; dated, unattractive linens in some rooms. *Rooms from: 180 SF* *18 rue Grand-St-Jean, City Center* *021/3202441* *www.hotel-regina.ch* *36 rooms* *Breakfast.*

$ HOTEL **Lausanne Guest House.** This tidy 19th-century town house not far from the train station tends to attract a young crowd who are willing to give up some comforts like shared baths and breakfast on-site for budget rates. **Pros:** helpful staff; homey atmosphere; short walk from train station. **Cons:** front desk not staffed around the clock; simple furnishings without decoration; most rooms have shared baths. *Rooms from:*

125 SF ✉ 4 Epinettes, City Center ☎ 021/6018000 🌐 www.lausanne-guesthouse.ch ⇨ 25 rooms 🍽 No meals.

$$$$ HOTEL **Lausanne Palace & Spa.** This Edwardian landmark, distinctly urbane in setting and style, stands on a hill high over the lake, with layers of city scenery draped behind. **Pros:** top-drawer address sure to impress; easy access to nightlife of the Flon; popular bars on-site. **Cons:** staid linens in some rooms; doorman and concierge are quick to size you up; room service is limited at night. $ *Rooms from: 540 SF ✉ 7–9 rue du Grand-Chêne, City Center ☎ 021/3313131 🌐 www.lausanne-palace.ch ⇨ 154 rooms 🍽 No meals.*

$$$ HOTEL Fodor's Choice ★ **Royal Savoy.** After a six-year, top-to-bottom renovation, the historic Royal Savoy has been unveiled as the latest—and perhaps the finest—five-star hotel in all of Suisse Romande. **Pros:** excellent quality-price rapport for a five-star property; rooftop lounge provides a panoramic view over the lake; large spa area for a pampered soak in various marbled pools. **Cons:** gray interiors are not for those who dislike a neutral palette; moneyed guests (and some staff) give off a haughty vibe; outdoor pool is quite small. $ *Rooms from: 370 SF ✉ 40 av. d'Ouchy, Ouchy ☎ 021/6148888 🌐 www.royalsavoy.ch ⇨ 186 rooms 🍽 No meals.*

NIGHTLIFE AND PERFORMING ARTS

NIGHTLIFE

BARS

Bar du Palace. An after-hours crowd heads to the stately Bar du Palace. If it's not your thing, the stylish, pared-down LP Bar is just a corridor away. ✉ *Lausanne Palace & Spa, 7–9 rue du Grand-Chêne, City Center ☎ 021/3313131 🌐 www.lausanne-palace.ch.*

Le Bar. One of the city's choicest and liveliest gathering spots is the sophisticated Le Bar. There's an armchair-filled lounge and a tiny wine bar where you can sip your favorite cocktail or wine. Upstairs, Bar Anglais offers spectacular lake views from its clubby setting and terrace chaises. ✉ *Beau-Rivage Palace, 17–19 pl. du Port, Ouchy ☎ 021/6133333 🌐 www.brp.ch.*

Le Chorus. Look for a range of styles at Le Chorus, a renowned jazz cellar that serves food and drinks. ✉ *3 av. du Mon-Repos, City Center ☎ 021/3232233 🌐 www.chorus.ch.*

Yatus. To explore the vintages of the country, and the world, drop in at this wine bar where they pour dozens of different wines at the minimalist bar or on the hidden terrace. ✉ *11 rue Petit-Chêne, St-François ☎ 021/3124501 🌐 www.yatus.ch.*

DANCE CLUBS

Since most nighttime activity is centered on the Flon and Place St-François areas, it's easy to sample several hot spots. Things don't get going until midnight and rock on until 5 am. If you pass a crowded club where the music is to your taste, duck inside.

D! Club Inside a converted cinema, this nightspot is a mix of film, fashion, and music. ✉ *Pl. Centrale, City Center ☎ 021/3515140 🌐 www.dclub.ch.*

MAD. Clubbers come from as far away as Zürich and Basel to hear their favorite DJs and live bands at MAD. On Sunday night the club hosts a gay crowd. ✉ *23 rue de Genève, Flon* ☎ *021/3406969* 🌐 *www.madclub.ch.*

PERFORMING ARTS

Lausanne is one of Switzerland's arts capitals. Event seasons generally run from September to May, though summer brings outdoor concerts and more-casual events. A listing of free and ticketed offerings can be found in *Allons-y,* and monthly updates appear in *Reg'art* (in French). Check out the daily newspaper *24 Heures* for listings as well.

MUSIC

Salle Métropole. The Orchestre de Chambre de Lausanne shares the stage at Salle Métropole with the riveting experiments of the Maurice Béjart ballet company as well as a varied selection of concert performances. ✉ *1 pl. Bel-Air, City Center* ☎ *021/3450025* 🌐 *www.sallemetropole.ch.*

Théâtre de Beaulieu. Across from the Collection de l'Art Brut, the Théâtre de Beaulieu hosts full-scale musical performances. Keep an eye out for appearances by the Orchestre de la Suisse Romande, which Lausanne shares with Geneva. ✉ *10 av. des Bergières, Beaulieu* ☎ *021/6432110* 🌐 *www.theatredebeaulieu.ch.*

SPORTS AND THE OUTDOORS

BIKING

Gare CFF de Lausanne. The train station, **Gare CFF de Lausanne,** rents bikes. It's best to make a reservation at least one day in advance; in summer three days is recommended. ✉ *5a pl. de la Gare, City Center* ☎ *051/2242162.*

Guy Delessert. For an afternoon of paddleboating or a lakefront bicycle ride, check out Guy Delessert. Bikes (and boats) are available March through November. ✉ *2 pl. du Vieux Port, Ouchy* ☎ *079/6223918.*

Maison du Vélo. This shop provides free bike rentals year-round—all you need is a 20 SF deposit. It's first-come, first-serve. ✉ *1b pl. de l'Europe, Flon* ☎ *021/5330115.*

SWIMMING

Bellerive. You have access to the lake and three pools at Bellerive, which has generous lawns that are perfect for lounging, and a self-service restaurant. ✉ *23 av. de Rhodanie, Ouchy* ☎ *021/3154860.*

Mon-Repos. The indoor pool at Mon-Repos is open from September through June. ✉ *4 av. du Tribunal-Fédéral, City Center* ☎ *021/3154888.*

Piscine de Montchoisi. The pool at Piscine de Montchoisi makes artificial waves, so it's popular with kids. It's open from mid-May through August. ✉ *30 av. du Servan, Montchoisi* ☎ *021/3154962.*

SHOPPING

High-end designer names and funky boutiques are found on **Place St-François, Rue St-François, Rue de Bourg,** and **Rue du Grand-Pont.** Less expensive shopping is along **Rue St-Laurent** and **Rue de l'Ale.** Generally, store hours are weekdays 9:30–7, 9:30–6 on Saturday, closed Sunday.

BOOKS

FNAC. For magazines, travel guides, and other reading material, FNAC is *the* superstore. It even has a hyperactive coffee bar and a ticket kiosk. ✉ *6 rue de Genève, Flon* ☎ *021/2138585* 🌐 *www.fnac.ch.*

DEPARTMENT STORES

Bongénie. This department store has clusters of designer areas on several levels. ✉ *10 pl. St-François, St-François* ☎ *021/3452727* 🌐 *www.bongenie-grieder.ch.*

Globus. This upscale department store has a splendid food hall on the lower level. ✉ *Rue Centrale at Rue du Pont, City Center* ☎ *021/3429090* 🌐 *www.globus.ch.*

Manor. Value-priced Manor stocks a full range of merchandise, including souvenirs. It has bountiful food offerings, too. ✉ *7 rue St-Laurent, City Center* ☎ *021/3213699* 🌐 *www.manor.ch.*

MARKETS

There are fruit and vegetable markets in Lausanne along **Rue de l'Ale, Rue de Bourg,** and **Place de la Riponne** every Wednesday and Saturday (8–2:30). **Place de la Palud** adds a flea market to its Wednesday and Saturday produce markets and is the site of a handicrafts market the first Friday of the month from March through December. A weekly flea market sets up on Thursday on **Place Chauderon.** Seasonal additions include summer produce found Sunday along the **Allée Bacounis** in Ouchy, and the Marché Noël (Christmas Market) in December on the transformed **Place St-François** and **Place de la Riponne.**

WATCHES

Most watch shops specialize in brands and are clustered in the St-François neighborhood. Large Swatch boutiques are in the Globus and Manor department stores.

Boutique Tourbillon. When you're in the market for a watch, keep in mind that this shop sells high-end brands like Blancpain and Omega. ✉ *8 pl. St-François, City Center* ☎ *021/3235145* 🌐 *www.tourbillon.com.*

Bucherer. Rolex, Tag Heuer, and Baume & Mercier are on offer at Bucherer. ✉ *1 rue de Bourg, City Center* ☎ *021/3123612* 🌐 *www.bucherer.com.*

Guillard. If you are searching for brands like Ebel, go to Guillard. ✉ *1 pl. du Palud, City Center* ☎ *021/3126886* 🌐 *www.guillard.ch.*

LAVAUX VIGNOBLES AND RIVIERA

To the east of Lausanne stretches the Lavaux Vignoble (the Lavaux wine region), a UNESCO-designated World Heritage Site with remarkably beautiful vineyards that rise up the hillsides all the way from Pully, on the outskirts of Lausanne, to Montreux—a distance of 24 km (15

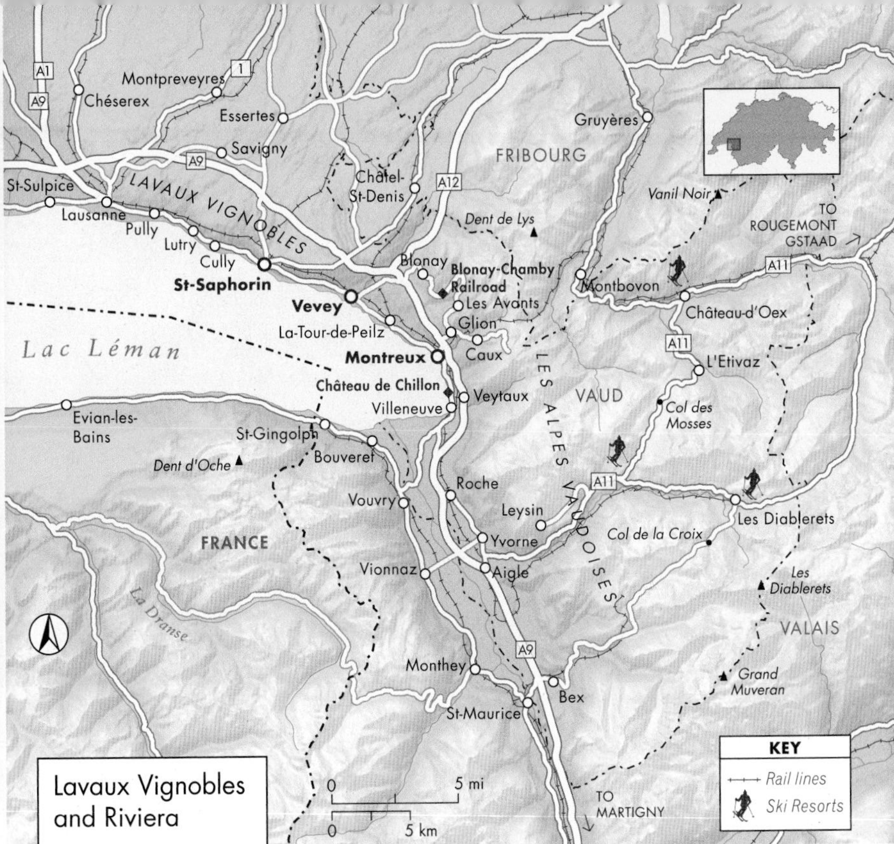

miles)—and then beyond to the fortress-crowned town of Aigle. Brown-roof stone villages in the Savoy style, old defense towers, and small baronial castles stud the green-and-black landscape. The vineyards, enclosed within low stone walls, slope so steeply that all the work has to be done by hand. Fertilizer is carried in containers strapped to workers' backs. In early October pickers harvest the fruit, carrying the loads to the nearest road and driving them by tractor to the nearest press. Some Lavaux vintages are excellent and in great demand, but unfortunately, as with so much of Switzerland's wine, the yield is small, and the product is rarely exported. Throughout the year, especially on weekends, winegrowers' cellars and some of the private châteaux-vignobles open for tastings (and, of course, sales). A listing of cave open hours, festivals, and eateries can be found at *www.lavaux.ch*.

ST-SAPHORIN

5½ km (3 miles) southeast of Lausanne.

At the end of the Corniche Road, just west of Vevey, St-Saphorin is perched above the water. With its impossibly narrow, steep cobbled streets and ancient winemakers' houses crowded around fountains and crooked alleys, this is a village that merits a stop. It lies along the ancient Roman highway, and its small church sits atop Roman foundations.

Many of Lavaux's famous wines are not available outside Switzerland.

There's a tiny **museum** of Roman artifacts (including a sizable millstone) in the church. Go through the low door near the altar; you can see the museum whenever the church is unlocked and services are not being held. The explanations are all in French, but it's easy to chart the church's expansion through its ruins.

For additional vineyard explorations accompanied by jaw-dropping vistas, take the vertical grade uphill—on foot or by car—to Chexbres. ■ **TIP→ Be attentive, as the close-walled street relies on tight pull-offs to pass oncoming vehicles.** The reward is a different orientation on the working wine village, complete with rail connections to whisk you back down to the active waterfront via Vevey.

The scenic **Corniche de Lavaux** stretches some 17 km (10 miles) through Lavaux, threading above the waterfront from Lausanne to Vevey, between the autoroute and the lakeside Route 9. This is Switzerland at its most Franco-European, reminiscent in its small-scale way of the Riviera or the hill towns of Alsace. You'll career around hairpin turns on narrow cobbled streets, with the Savoy Alps glowing across the sparkling lake and the Dents du Midi looming ahead. Stop to gaze at the scenery from roadside overlooks or wander down a side lane into the vineyards of Riex, Épesses, Rivaz, Cully, or Dézaley, the sources of some of Switzerland's loveliest white wines and all part of the Lavaux UNESCO heritage site.

WHERE TO EAT

$$$ SWISS ✕ **L'Auberge de l'Onde.** Once the main relais (stagecoach stop) between the Simplon Pass and Geneva, this vineyard stop is out of central casting, groaning with history and heady with atmosphere: Igor Stravinsky

and Charlie Chaplin were among the artists loyal to its charms. The tiny wood-paneled pinte, where winemakers come to read the daily papers with a pitcher of St-Saph, as they call it, and devour the upscale plat du jour, is enticing, as are the adjacent, white-tablecloth salons and upstairs-attic-beamed grillroom. **Known for:** wine selection curated by lauded sommelier Jérôme Aké Béda; perfect spot for a gourmet lunch after a vineyard hike; local dessert specialties like tarte au vin cuit. *Average main: 47 SF* ✉ *Centre Ville, St. Saphorin* ☎ *021/9254900* 🌐 *www.aubergedelonde.ch* ⏲ *Closed Mon. and Tues.*

CELEBRITY SIGHTINGS IN THE LAVAUX

Among the notables who have been drawn to Vevey are Graham Greene, Victor Hugo, Jean-Jacques Rousseau (who set much of his *Julie, ou la Nouvelle Héloïse* here), Fyodor Dostoyevsky, Gustave Courbet, Oskar Kokoschka, Charlie and Oona Chaplin (buried in the cemetery at Corsier), and Swiss native Édouard Jeanneret, known as Le Corbusier. By following an excellent brochure-map published by the tourist office, you can travel to the homes and haunts of some 40 luminaries.

WHERE TO STAY

$$ B&B/INN **L'Hôtel Baron Tavernier.** Lodging high up on the Corniche Road yields superlative views with elegant comfort. **Pros:** jaw-dropping views of lake, vineyards, and mountains; solitude adjacent to wine trails and cellar doors; small spa area with many treatment options. **Cons:** overflow crowds drawn to outdoor restaurant on weekends; complicated to access without a car; although friendly, service can be slow. *Rooms from: 300 SF* ✉ *Rte. de la Corniche, Chexbres* ☎ *021/9266000* 🌐 *www.barontavernier.com* *11 rooms, 7 suites* *Breakfast.*

SPORTS AND THE OUTDOORS

HIKING

Lavaux Vineyard Terraces Trail. This 11-km (6¾-mile) route connects Lutry and St-Saphorin, offering stunning views of Lac Léman, the steep walled terraces of the Lavaux wineries, and a glimpse of snowy peaks in the distance. Portions of the trail can be steep, but a lot of it is paved, too. No roughing it here: stop to sample Chasselas, Gamays, and other *vins*, as tasting rooms and bistros flourish in achingly picturesque villages along the route. ✉ *St. Saphorin.*

VEVEY

4 km (2½ miles) east of St-Saphorin, 7 km (4½ miles) west of Montreux, 19 km (12 miles) east of Lausanne.

In the 1870s Henry James captured this waterfront town's mood of prim grace while writing (and setting) *Daisy Miller* in the Hôtel des Trois Couronnes. Indeed, despite its virtual twinning with glamorous Montreux, Vevey retains its air of isolation and old-world gentility. Loyal visitors have been returning for generations to gaze at the Dent d'Oche (7,288 feet), across the water in France, and make sedate steamer excursions into Montreux and Lausanne. Today there are some

Continued on page 480

The Vineyards of Lavaux

Switzerland's most stunning wine-producing region is the Lavaux, where vineyards and villages perch on steep terraces that zigzag down to the shoreline of Lac Léman. The UNESCO World Heritage site comprises 10,000 terraces of Chasselas, Gamay, and Pinot Noir vines spread over 40 levels. The area is also full of cellars and wineries worth visiting. Here's how to get the most out of a day trip to wine country from Lausanne.

WINE-TASTING DAY TRIP FROM LAUSANNE

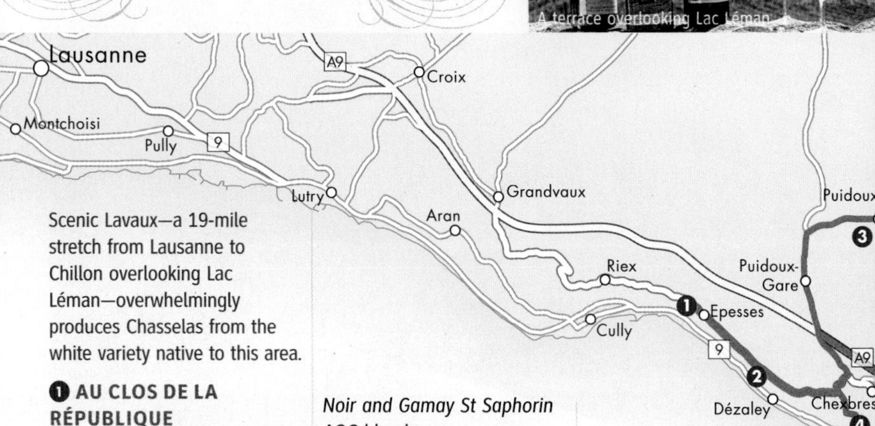

A terrace overlooking Lac Léman

Scenic Lavaux—a 19-mile stretch from Lausanne to Chillon overlooking Lac Léman—overwhelmingly produces Chasselas from the white variety native to this area.

❶ AU CLOS DE LA RÉPUBLIQUE

A 13th-generation winemaker whose stunning cellars hold wines from across Lavaux. The wines bear witness to its different soil types. *Try: Passerillé de Lavaux, a Chasselas dessert wine.*

✉ Ruelle du Petit-Crêt, Epesses
☎ 021/7991444
🌐 www.patrick-fonjallaz.ch

❷ LE TREYTORRENS EN DÉZALEY

The Testuz winery's tasting room offers wines from all of Vaud's wine regions: Pinot Noir, Gamay, and Chasselas predominate. *Try: a full-bodied Pinot Noir and Gamay St Saphorin AOC blend.*

✉ Route du Lac, Dézaley
☎ 021/7999911
🌐 www.testuz.ch

Vineyards abut the tracks in Dézaley

❸ ARC EN VINS

Featuring a range of wines from Lavaux and other Swiss regions, this winery also makes blends combining less prevalent varieties. *Try: an unusual white, Charmont de Lavaux, which is a cross of Chasselas and Chardonnay.*

✉ 19 rte. du Verney
☎ 021/9463344
🌐 www.arc-en-vins.ch

❹ LAVAUX VINORAMA

Most Lavaux wineries have meager opening hours or are open by appointment, so this center featuring a savvy selection of some 200 Lavaux wines is a boon. *Try: a red with a hint of black cherry and spice made from an ancient local variety, Plant Robert.*

✉ 2 route du Lac, Rivaz
☎ 021/9463131
🌐 www.lavaux-vinorama.ch

Grapes ready to harvest in Dézaley

❺ ASSOCIATION VITICOLE DE CORSEAUX

Worth a visit for the lake-and-mountain views alone—and while this group of winemakers presents fewer than 20 selections, there are pleasant surprises. *Try: Pinot Noir Le Corsalin, powerfully structured yet silky.*

✉ 20 rue du Village, Corseaux
☎ 021/9213185
🌐 www.avc-vins.ch

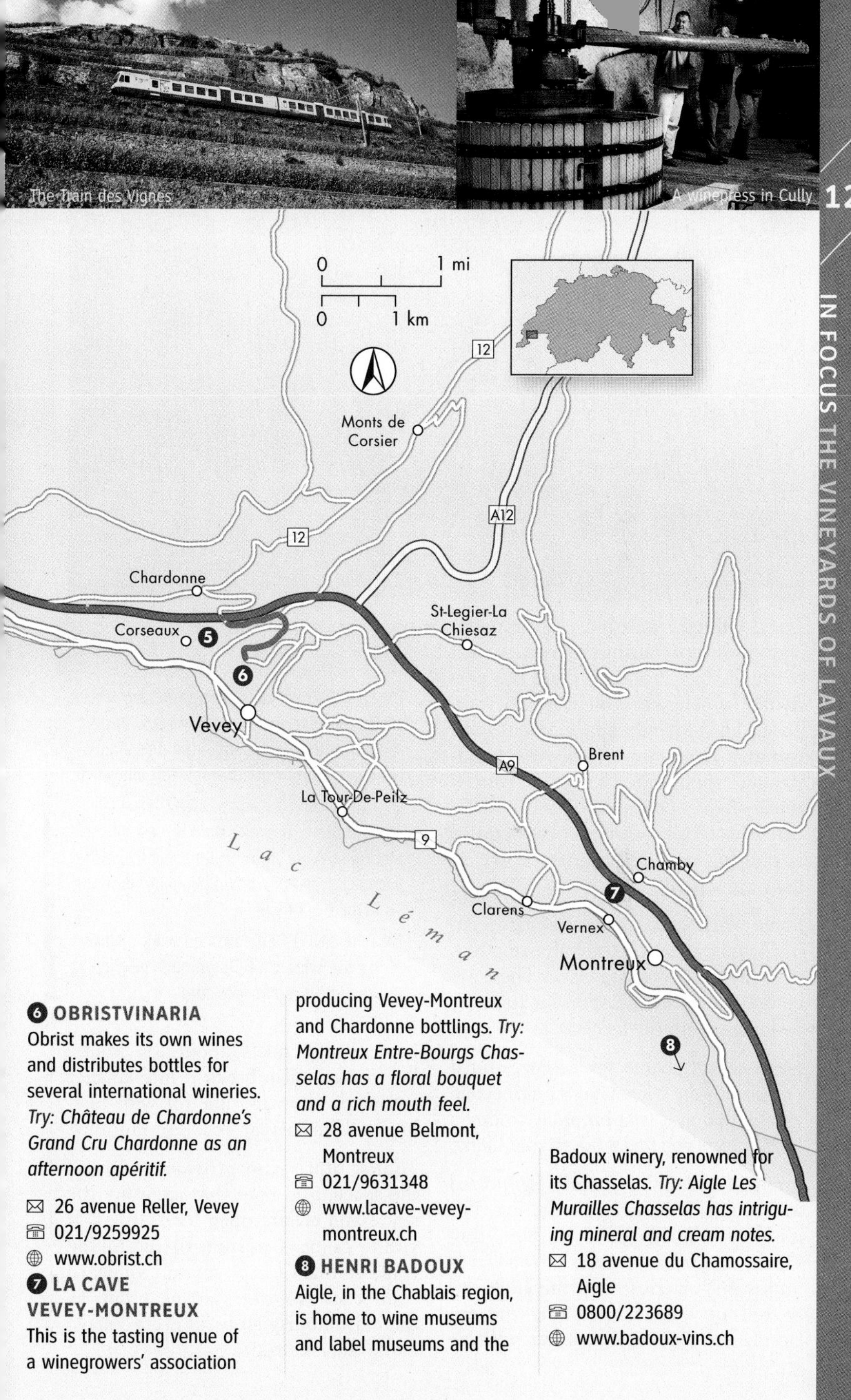

The Train des Vignes

A winepress in Cully

6 OBRISTVINARIA

Obrist makes its own wines and distributes bottles for several international wineries. *Try: Château de Chardonne's Grand Cru Chardonne as an afternoon apéritif.*

✉ 26 avenue Reller, Vevey
☎ 021/9259925
🌐 www.obrist.ch

7 LA CAVE VEVEY-MONTREUX

This is the tasting venue of a winegrowers' association producing Vevey-Montreux and Chardonne bottlings. *Try: Montreux Entre-Bourgs Chasselas has a floral bouquet and a rich mouth feel.*

✉ 28 avenue Belmont, Montreux
☎ 021/9631348
🌐 www.lacave-vevey-montreux.ch

8 HENRI BADOUX

Aigle, in the Chablais region, is home to wine museums and label museums and the Badoux winery, renowned for its Chasselas. *Try: Aigle Les Murailles Chasselas has intriguing mineral and cream notes.*

✉ 18 avenue du Chamossaire, Aigle
☎ 0800/223689
🌐 www.badoux-vins.ch

LAVAUX TOURING TIPS

Local vintners welcome visitors year-round, except during harvest, which is usually in October. If there is a particular winemaker you want to visit, phone ahead for an appointment. You can also keep an eye peeled for hand-painted signs announcing "*caveau ouvert*" or "*dégustation*"; this indicates that a cellar owner or cooperative is pouring wine. (Designate a driver; laws are strict.)

Some wineries have sophisticated tasting rooms; others feature a tasting barrel within the working cellar. These are communal gathering spots so you may be tasting with the locals.

Most cellars charge for tasting, and if you occupy the winemaker's time beyond a casual pour, it is appropriate to buy a bottle unless you find it not to your liking.

Interconnected hiking trails (signposted in several languages, including English) span the length of the shore from Ouchy to Chillon, traversing vineyards and traffic arteries from the lakefront to hillside villages. Walking the entire 32-km (19-mile) *parcours viticole* (wine route) takes about 8½ hours, but you can also break it into smaller segments, allowing time for wine tastings and meals at local restaurants.

Tourist offices can provide a copy of the specialized map that identifies the route and cellars open for tastings. If you're doing a portion of the hiking trail, you can easily catch a vineyard train back to your starting point, as there are hourly stops in every village along the lakefront.

GETTING THERE

BY TRAIN: From Lausanne, there are tracks along the lake to Vevey, Montreux, and Aigle. Another track, the Train des Vignes (vineyard train) rolls through the vineyards.

BY CAR: From Lausanne-Ouchy, head straight along the lake road to Vevey/Montreux/Aigle. Turn off (and up) into wine villages, then back down. Signage abounds; you won't get lost.

BY BIKE AND FOOT: You can walk or bike along the wine trail. Download the map at *www.montreuxriviera.com*

Conne wine cellar in Chexbres

WINE-TASTING PRIMER

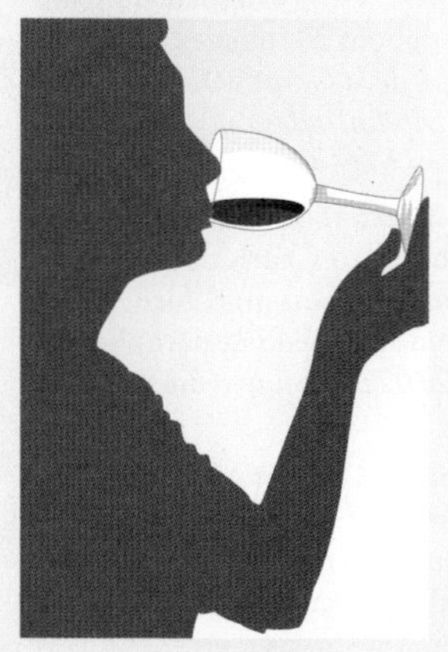

Ordering and tasting wine—whether at a winery, bar, or restaurant—is easy once you master a few simple steps.

LOOK AND NOTE

Hold your glass by the stem and look at the wine in the glass. Note its color, depth, and clarity.

For whites, is it greenish, yellow, or gold? For reds, is it purplish, ruby, or garnet? Is the wine's color pale or deep? Is the liquid clear or cloudy?

SWIRL AND SNIFF

Swirl the wine gently in the glass to intensify the scents, then sniff over the rim of the glass. What do you smell? Try to identify aromas like:

- **Fruits**—citrus, peaches, berries, figs, melon
- **Flowers**—orange blossoms, honey, perfume
- **Spices**—baking spices, pungent, herbal notes
- **Vegetables**—fresh or cooked, herbal notes
- **Minerals**—earth, steely notes, wet stones
- **Dairy**—butter, cream, cheese, yogurt
- **Oak**—toast, vanilla, coconut, tobacco
- **Animal**—leathery, meaty notes

Are there any unpleasant notes, like mildew or wet dog, that might indicate that the wine is "off?"

SIP AND SAVOR

Prime your palate with a sip, swishing the wine in your mouth. Then spit in a bucket or swallow.

Take another sip and think about the wine's attributes. Sweetness is detected on the tip of the tongue, acidity on the sides of the tongue, and tannins (a mouth-drying sensation) on the gums. Consider the body—does the wine feel light in the mouth, or is there a rich sensation? Are the flavors consistent with the aromas? If you like the wine, try to pinpoint what you like about it, and vice versa if you don't like it.

Take time to savor the wine as you're sipping it—the tasting experience may seem a bit scientific, but the end goal is your enjoyment.

who come just to see the bronze statue of Charlie Chaplin in a rose garden on the lakefront quay, and to take the funicular or mountain train up to Mont Pèlerin. Vevey is also a great walking town, with more character in its shuttered Old Town; better museums, landmarks, and shops; and more native activity in its wine market than cosmopolitan Montreux can muster.

GETTING HERE AND AROUND

The regional and local S-trains linking the adjacent cities Vevey and Montreux have departures every 10 to 15 minutes, but the trolleybus that snakes along the lake road is more scenic—its route extends from Villenuve to the Vevey Funicular and is the best way (other than by car) to reach Château de Chillon.

Contacts Transports VMCV Publics. ⊕ *www.vmcv.ch.*

VISITOR INFORMATION

Contacts Montreux-Vevey Tourisme. ✉ *29 Grand-Pl., Vevey* ⊕ *www.montreux-vevey.com.*

EXPLORING

FAMILY **Alimentarium.** The Nestlé Foundation, a dynamic force in the region, sponsors this unconventional museum devoted to the celebration and study of food. In a stainless-steel kitchen, chefs demonstrate their skills, and displays on food preparation cover everything from the campfire to futuristic equipment. Other sections focus on merchants, supermarkets, food presentation, and marketing; you can also stroll through herb and vegetable gardens. The exhibits have material in English; some are interactive. The museum underwent a major renovation in 2015. ✉ *Quai Perdonnet, Vevey* ☎ *021/9244111* ⊕ *www.alimentarium.ch* 🎟 *13 SF* ⏲ *Closed Mon.*

OFF THE BEATEN PATH

Blonay–Chamby Railroad. From Vevey and Montreux, a number of railways climb into the heights, which in late spring are carpeted with an extravagance of wild narcissus blooms. If you like model railroads, you will especially enjoy a trip on the Blonay–Chamby Railroad, whose real steam-driven trains alternate with electric trains. You can depart from either end (parking is more plentiful in Blonay); trains make a stop at a small museum of railroad history in between. The trip takes about 20 minutes each way, not including a browse in the museum. ✉ *3 pl. de la Gare* ☎ *021/9432121* ⊕ *www.blonay-chamby.ch* 🎟 *20 SF round-trip (includes museum admission)* ⏲ *Closed Nov.–Apr. and weekdays from May–Oct.*

Musée Historique du Vieux Vevey (*Historical Museum of Old Vevey*). This grand 16th-century manor house, briefly home to Charlotte de Lengefeld, wife of Friedrich von Schiller, retains some original furnishings as well as collections of arms, art, keys, and winemaking paraphernalia. ✉ *2 rue du Château, Vevey* ☎ *021/9210722* ⊕ *www.museehistoriquevevey.ch* 🎟 *5 SF* ⏲ *Closed Mon.*

Musée Suisse de l'Appareil Photographique (*Swiss Camera Museum*). The Musée Suisse de l'Appareil Photographique displays an impressive collection of cameras, photographic equipment, and mounted work. ✉ *99 Grande-Pl., Vevey* ☎ *021/9253480* ⊕ *www.cameramuseum.ch* 🎟 *9 SF* ⏲ *Closed Mon.*

QUICK BITES **Läderach. If sweets are on your mind, pick up a handcrafted chocolate in the shape of Charlie Chaplin's shoes from Läderach, on a pedestrian walkway near the tourist office. The chocolate showroom features live demonstrations and course offerings for budding chocolatiers. Known for: chocolate-making courses in first-class workshop; delicately rolled pralines; master chocolatier Blaise Poyet.** ✉ ***8 rue du Théâtre, Vevey*** ☎ ***021/9213737*** 🌐 ***www.laederach.com*** ⏲ ***Closed Sun.***

FAMILY **Musée Suisse du Jeu** (*Game and Toy Museum*). Just east of town, the Musée Suisse du Jeu fills a 13th-century castle. Games of strategy and chance, ranging from dice to video games, are represented in displays spanning centuries. Tours are available in English. Its excellent gift shop is stocked with puzzles and board games. The courtyard eatery, in a former gardener's cottage, serves snacks and light meals. ✉ *11 rue du Château, La Tour-de-Peilz* ☎ *021/9772300* 🌐 *www.museedujeu.ch* 🎟 *9 SF* ⏲ *Closed Mon.*

WHERE TO EAT

$$$ FRENCH ✕ **La Haut.** This elegant, intimate restaurant is in a restored home in the wine village of Chardonne. Perched high on a hill, it offers a view of the lake (from part of the dining room) that is worthy of a Champagne toast. **Known for:** incredible views from high-up Chardonne; main courses are smartly garnished with fresh herbs and vegetables; exceptionally fresh goat cheese from Rossinière. $ *Average main: 54 SF* ✉ *21 rue du Village, Chardonne* ☎ *021/9212930* 🌐 *www.restaurant-la-haut.ch* ⏲ *Closed Sun. and Mon.*

$$ SWISS ✕ **Le Mazot.** After years of overseeing bubbling pots of fondue—the popular draw at this tiny eatery—the hand-painted murals and mirrors set in dark frames have a smoky patina. It's a casual neighborhood place where local wines are poured from pewter pitchers and the people at the next table eavesdrop. **Known for:** tender entrecôte of beef or cheval (horse); consistently packed to the rafters at only 10 feet wide; lake-caught perch fillets and crispy fries. $ *Average main: 28 SF* ✉ *7 rue du Conseil, Vevey* ☎ *021/9217822* ⏲ *Closed Wed. and Thurs. No lunch Sun.*

$$ ECLECTIC ✕ **National.** A thriving bar with extended service hours and proximity to the cinema attracts late diners of all ages. The trendy vibe overflows onto the patio, with seating under twinkling lights—a respite from the serious smoking crowd. **Known for:** porc massalé wrapped in banana leaf; funky, international crowd; desserts with a twist that include spicy mango crème brûlée. $ *Average main: 34 SF* ✉ *9 rue du Torrent, Vevey* ☎ *021/9237625* 🌐 *www.natio.ch.*

WHERE TO STAY

$$$ HOTEL 🏨 **Grand Hôtel du Lac.** Anita Brookner set her novel *Hotel du Lac* in this lakefront doyenne, where readers find an abundance of refinement and global sophistication proffered beneath the Relais & Châteaux banner. **Pros:** historically elegant; pool and garden plus harbor access are sensational in summer; exceptional service staff add a personal touch to your requests. **Cons:** at the outer edge of town; lakefront festivals and neighborhood block parties can engulf; some standard rooms are in

need of refurbishment. $ *Rooms from: 500 SF* ✉ *1 rue d'Italie, Vevey* ☎ *021/9250606* 🌐 *www.grandhoteldulac.ch* *50 rooms* 🍽 *Breakfast.*

$$ HOTEL **Hostellerie Bon Rivage.** This hotel blends right in with the estates facing the lake on the main road between Vevey and Montreux. **Pros:** price-value relationship is tops; hotel often features art exhibitions and musical evenings; picturesque marina setting with superb views. **Cons:** no a/c necessitates closed shutters against the afternoon sun; most guest rooms have only a shower; isolated location. $ *Rooms from: 250 SF* ✉ *18 rue de St-Maurice, La Tour-de-Peilz* ☎ *021/9770707* 🌐 *www.bon-rivage.ch* *50 rooms* 🍽 *Breakfast.*

$$$ HOTEL Fodor's Choice ★ **Hôtel des Trois Couronnes.** Honeycombed by dramatic atrium stairwells that look down on marble columns and gleaming floors inlaid with golden coronets, this regal landmark was Henry James's home base when he wrote (and set here) the novella *Daisy Miller.* Burgundy brocade with floral swags and coverlets contrast boldly with striped wallpaper in generously sized guest rooms. **Pros:** from valet to spa attendant, the staff is superb; perfect balance of modern refinement and history; long indoor pool makes swimming laps a pleasure. **Cons:** noise wafts up into rooms from terrace parties; Sunday brunch doesn't live up to its former reputation; some rooms could benefit from a freshening up. $ *Rooms from: 420 SF* ✉ *49 rue d'Italie, Vevey* ☎ *021/9233200* 🌐 *www.hoteltroiscouronnes.com* *71 rooms* 🍽 *No meals.*

NIGHTLIFE

Despite its quiet, small-town appearance, Vevey has gathering spots where the music is loud and revelers dance until dawn.

Diva Club. Patrons warble karaoke nightly at Diva Club, which offers full-throttle clubbing on the weekend. ✉ *30 av. General Guisan, Vevey* ☎ *021/9212196.*

Rex Good Vibes. Gays and straights gather for music and cocktails plus imaginative theme parties hosted by Il Baretto at Rex Good Vibes, in the Rex cinema complex. ✉ *22 rue de la Madeleine, Vevey* ☎ *021/9258890* 🌐 *www.cinerive.com/resto.*

SPORTS AND THE OUTDOORS

As you drive along the highway, you will see sunbathers lounging on rocks jutting out into the lake and swimmers playing on the stony beaches. It's difficult to tell if they are on private property or have public access. There *are* swimming areas open to everyone that include a mix of facilities—toilets, showers, changing cabins, and snack bars—but lifeguards are only at the pools, so be careful. Slippery rocks, drop-offs, and water traffic on the lake require special attention.

Jardin Doret. Access to the lake, a generous lawn with a children's play area, and a snack bar are among the pluses at Jardin Doret. ✉ *Av. Louis-Ruchonnet, Vevey* ☎ *0848/868484.*

Vevey/Corseaux Plage. West of Nestlé headquarters, the Vevey/Corseaux Plage has both lake swimming and two large pools, one indoors, the other out. ✉ *19 av. de Lavaux, Corseaux* ☎ *021/9212368.*

SHOPPING

Boutiques and galleries in the Old Town east of Place du Marché deserve your attention.

Tuesday and Saturday bring neighbors, politicians, and foodies to the center of Old Town for the **Vevey Open-Air Bazaar** where wagons circle and stalls fill tidy rows, each piled high with produce from nearby farms, meats cut to order, or seafood netted at dawn. Because Vevey is a marketing center for regional wines, the local white is sold in summer at the Saturday market, adding to the spirit of a folkloric festival; you buy your own glass and taste *à volonté* (at will). Most shops are closed on Sunday.

La Laiterie de la Grenette. The town's best cheese shop sells coveted double-crème from a dairy in Gruyéres that locals line up to purchase before the limited daily supply runs out. ✉ *27 rue des Deux-Marchés, Vevey* ☎ *021/9212345.*

Saint-Antoine. A modern, multilevel complex diagonally across from the train station, Saint-Antoine clusters large and small retailers within its glass panels. The underground parking is a smart alternative to the cramped, restricted parking in Old Town. ✉ *1 av. Général-Guisan, Vevey.*

MONTREUX

4 km (2 miles) southeast of Vevey, 21 km (13 miles) southeast of Lausanne.

Montreux might be called the Cannes of Lac Léman—though it might raise an eyebrow at the slur. Spilling down steep hillsides into a sunny south-facing bay, its waterfront thick with magnolias, cypresses, and palm trees, the historic resort earns its reputation as the capital—if not the pearl—of the Swiss Riviera. Unlike the French Riviera, it has managed, despite overwhelming crowds of conventioneers, to keep up appearances. Its Edwardian-French deportment has survived considerable development, and though there are plenty of harsh modern high-rises with parking-garage aesthetics, its mansarded landmarks still unfurl yellow awnings to shield millionaires from the sun.

Famed for the nearby lakeside Château de Chillon, Montreux is where Stravinsky composed *Petrouchka* and *Le Sacre du Printemps,* and where Vladimir Nabokov resided in splendor. Indeed, Montreux and its suburbs have attracted artists and literati for 200 years: Byron, Percy Bysshe Shelley, Leo Tolstoy, Hans Christian Andersen, and Gustave Flaubert were drawn to its lush shoreline. The resort is best known for its annual jazz festival, which lately has strayed from its original focus to include rock, R&B, Latin, and hip-hop. Each July, Montreux's usually composed promenade explodes in a street festival of food tents, vendor kiosks, and open band shells, which complement standing-room-only concert hall venues.

The iconic Château de Chillon is one of the most photographed sights in Switzerland.

GETTING HERE AND AROUND

Montreux is accessible via regional and local trains on the rail line that runs from Lausanne to the Valais. It is a 20- to 30-minute ride from Lausanne. By car it takes approximately 30 minutes on the A9 motorway; Exit 19 from the elevated roadway winds down to the lakefront road and into the center of town.

VISITOR INFORMATION

Contacts Montreux-Vevey Tourisme. ✉ *5 rue du Théâtre, Montreux* ☎ *084/8868484* 🌐 *www.montreuxriviera.com.*

EXPLORING

Fodor's Choice ★ **Château de Chillon.** One of Switzerland's must-sees is the Château de Chillon, the awe-inspiringly picturesque 12th-century castle that rears out of the water at Veytaux, down the road from and within sight of Montreux. Chillon was built on Roman foundations under the direction of Duke Peter of Savoy with the help of military architects from Plantagenet England. For a long period it served as a state prison, and one of its shackled guests was François Bonivard, who supported the Reformation and enraged the Savoyards. He spent six years in this prison, chained most of the time to a pillar in the dungeon before being released by the Bernese in 1536.

While living near Montreux, Lord Byron visited Chillon and was so transported by its atmosphere and by Bonivard's grim sojourn that he was inspired to write his famous poem "The Prisoner of Chillon." Like a true tourist, Byron carved his name on a pillar in Bonivard's still-damp and chilly dungeon; his graffito is now protected under a plaque.

In high season visitors to Chillon must now file placidly from restored chamber to restored turret, often waiting at doorways for entire busloads of fellow tourists to pass. Yet the 19th-century Romantic-era restoration is so evocative and so convincing, with its tapestries, carved fireplaces, period ceramics and pewter, and elaborate wooden ceilings, that even the jaded castle hound may become as carried away as Byron was. While you're waiting your turn, you can gaze out the narrow windows over the sparkling, lapping water and remember Mark Twain, who thought Bonivard didn't have it half bad. Proceeds from the purchase of a bottle of Clos de Chillon, the white wine from estate vineyards, goes to restoration activities. ✉ *Veytaux* ☎ *021/9668910* 🌐 *www.chillon.ch* 🎫 *12.50 SF.*

Maison Visinand. Montreux's cultural center, the Maison Visinand is housed in a restored mansion in the Old Town. Its calendar of events mixes exhibitions and performances with classes and studios for painting, photography, and dance. ✉ *32 rue du Pont, Montreux* ☎ *021/9630726* 🌐 *www.maisonvisinand.ch* 🎫 *Free* ⏲ *Closed Mon. and Tues.*

QUICK BITES

Zurcher. The lunch-and-tearoom set (ladies with poodles, Brits in tweeds, fashionistas in Gucci) regularly descends on Zurcher, the irresistible confiserie on Montreux's main drag. A green salad, the *potage du jour* (soup of the day), and a chocolate torte make a great quick meal. Known for: buttery pastries and rich chocolate desserts; scrambled free-range eggs with black truffles; historic establishment more than 100 years old. ✉ *45 av. du Casino, Montreux* ☎ *021/9635963* 🌐 *www.confiserie-zurcher.ch* ⏲ *Closed Mon.*

Musée de Montreux (*Museum of Montreux*). Above the train station, a cluster of 17th-century homes once belonging to the town's successful winemakers is now the Musée de Montreux. This historical museum traces regional development from the time when Roman coins were used as tender, focusing on agricultural life and the shift to tourism. Profiles of famous residents and visitors who lived and worked in the area are highlighted. The museum's cellar restaurant, open from 6 pm, is a good place to sample typical local cuisine. ✉ *40 rue de la Gare, Montreux* ☎ *021/9631353* 🌐 *www.museemontreux.ch* 🎫 *6 SF* ⏲ *Closed Nov.–Mar.*

WHERE TO EAT

$$ ITALIAN

✕ **La Rouvenaz.** If it's an oven-fired pizza or plate of pasta you crave, there's no place more convivial or convenient than this trattoria on the main drag. The atmosphere is warmed by terra-cotta walls with bold blue accents and endless pitchers of wine. **Known for:** large crowds on weekends, when reservations are recommended; fresh seafood specialties; authentic tiramisu and other Italian desserts. [$] *Average main: 34 SF* ✉ *1 rue du Marché, Montreux* ☎ *021/9632736* 🌐 *www.rouvenaz.ch.*

$$$$ FRENCH

✕ **Le Pont de Brent.** Fresh twists on modern French and Swiss cuisine are the specialty at this Michelin-starred restaurant. You can sample unique dishes at a price that won't break the bank by trying the "Menu de Midi," which includes amuse-bouche, entrée, main course, and dessert. **Known for:** creative frogs'-legs dishes; lovely hillside location in the winding roads above Montreux; copious use of fresh herbs. $ *Average main: 195 SF* ✉ *4 rte. de Blonay, Brent* ✣ *7 km (4½ miles) northwest of Montreux* ☎ *021/9645230* 🌐 *www.lepontdebrent.ch* ⏲ *Closed Sun. and Mon.*

$$ THAI **Mai Thai.** If you're weary of regional cuisine, freshly made spring rolls, satays, and spicy dishes from this storefront eatery on the edge of Clarens will lighten up the program. This longtime resident of the neighborhood draws locals to its Asian-accented dining room, but at the first hint of warmth they scurry to tables on the terrace built directly on the water. **Known for:** traditional pad Thai and colorful curries; gorgeous lakeside terrace for dining alfresco; easily the best Thai food in the canton. $ *Average main: 36 SF* ✉ *40 rue du Lac, Clarens* ☎ *021/9642536* ⏲ *Closed Mon.*

WHERE TO STAY

$$$ HOTEL Fodor's Choice ★ **Fairmont Le Montreux Palace.** Silver mansards and yellow awnings flag this vast institution as a landmark, though its aristocratic interiors are now filled with cell-phone-chatting travelers. **Pros:** halls and salons are replete with history and decorative architecture; discreet staff can handle any request; exceptional bathrooms feature whirlpool tubs. **Cons:** easy to feel lost in the shuffle of high-end conferences; prices are steep for basics like breakfast and parking; some mattresses are extra-firm, proving too hard for guests. $ *Rooms from: 400 SF* ✉ *2 av. Claude-Nobs, Montreux* ☎ *021/9621212* 🌐 *www.fairmont.com* *236 rooms* *No meals.*

$ B&B/INN **Hotel Masson.** If you enjoy being away from the downtown resort scene, look up this demure little inn on a hillside in Veytaux, between Chillon and Montreux. **Pros:** serene old family-estate feel; genial hostess is an accomplished innkeeper; buffet breakfast with homemade breads and jams. **Cons:** need a car unless you want to trek uphill from the bus stop; no other restaurants nearby; could use a bit of sprucing up. $ *Rooms from: 200 SF* ✉ *5 rue Bonivard, Veytaux* ☎ *021/9660044* 🌐 *www.hotelmasson.ch* ⏲ *Closed Oct.–Apr.* *31 rooms* *Breakfast.*

$$ HOTEL **Tralala Hotel.** In a town of world-renowned musical heritage, the rooms of this small modern inn tucked in the sharp curve of an Old Town thoroughfare are themed for jazz, rock, and blues stars. **Pros:** refreshing contrast to the town's stately hotel scene; attracts a well-heeled thirtysomething crowd; the only hotel in Montreux's Les Planches (Old Town). **Cons:** limited kitchen requires that you dine elsewhere; public street or pay garage parking can be a headache and costly; up a steep hill from the train station and lakeside. $ *Rooms from: 220 SF* ✉ *2 rue du Temple, Montreux* ☎ *021/9634973* 🌐 *www.tralalahotel.ch* *32 rooms, 3 suites* *Breakfast.*

NIGHTLIFE AND PERFORMING ARTS

Montreux's famous festivals and arts events are listed in a seasonal booklet published by the tourist office; tickets are sold from its booth at the waterfront. In summer Montreux offers a variety of free outdoor concerts from its bandstand on the waterfront near the landing stage.

DID YOU KNOW?

The first hot-air balloon to circumnavigate the world was launched from Château-d'Oex in 1999. Every year the resort hosts "Balloon Week," a festival in January dedicated to the sport.

TICKETS

Ticket Corner. Ticket Corner sells tickets to concerts, sports, and other events. ✉ *Montreux* ☎ *0900/800800* 🌐 *www.ticketcorner.ch.*

BARS

Funky Claude's Bar. This happening jazz bar at the Fairmont Le Montreux Palace is named for local legend Claude Nobs, the founder of the Montreux Jazz Festival. With spacious, wood-paneled interiors and burgundy leather chairs, enthusiastic bartenders shake up inspired house cocktails to the beat of live musicians. A full menu features traditional Caesar salads and club sandwiches, alongside more exotic fare like crab tempura with ponzu sauce. All this fun, however, comes at the standard high prices of a hotel bar. ✉ *Fairmont Le Montreaux Palace, 2 av. Claude-Nobs, Montreux* ☎ *021/9621212* 🌐 *www.fairmont.com/montreux/.*

La Vinoteca. Adjacent to a popular Italian restaurant, the eclectic La Vinoteca is the smallest bar in town. Look for an excellent selection of Italian wines. ✉ *1 rue du Marché, Montreux* ☎ *021/9632736* 🌐 *www.rouvenaz.ch.*

Mayfair House. An urbane, designer-clad crowd flocks to the Mayfair House to take in the afternoon sun and make plans for the evening. ✉ *52 Grand-Rue, Montreux* ☎ *021/9667978* 🌐 *www.mayfair.ch.*

DANCE CLUBS

Black Pearl. Techno and Latin sounds accompanied by colorful lighting pulse at Black Pearl, where weekend partying goes until 5 am. ✉ *92 Grand-Rue, Montreux* ☎ *021/9635288* 🌐 *www.leblackpearl.ch.*

Millésime Club. Rotating DJs attract a young crowd to Millésime Club, which has all-white designer couches for a swank, Miami Beach feel. ✉ *2 av. Claude-Nobs, Montreux* ☎ *079/5091067* 🌐 *www.millesime-club.ch.*

MUSIC FESTIVALS

Fodor's Choice ★ **Montreux Jazz Festival.** The renowned Montreux Jazz Festival takes place every July in the ultramodern Auditorium Stravinski and other lakeside venues. Popular events sell out in hours. ✉ *5 av. Claude-Nobs, Montreux* 🌐 *www.montreuxjazzfestival.com.*

SPORTS AND THE OUTDOORS

BOATING

Water sports are popular along Montreux-Vevey's waterfront. Lessons and rentals are available at locations in marinas and from docks that rim the lake.

Nautic Loisirs. All types of equipment, from paddle- to motorboats, kayaks to windsurfers, can be rented at Nautic Loisirs. ✉ *Quai des Fleurs, Montreux* ☎ *078/6061588* 🌐 *www.nauticloisirs.ch.*

SHOPPING

Souvenir shops, tony boutiques, and jewelry stores are interspersed randomly along the Grand-Rue.

Forum. This modern complex is topped with shops and restaurants. Underground parking is connected to the Place du Marché, a large covered pavilion where the weekly open-air food market is held every Friday morning. ✉ *6 pl. du Marché, Montreux* 🌐 *www.forum-montreux.ch.*

13

GENEVA

WELCOME TO GENEVA

TOP REASONS TO GO

★ **Falling water:** The feathery Jet d'Eau, Geneva's iconic harbor fountain, is visible for miles in every direction.

★ **Blue zone:** At the foot of the Alps, Lac Léman offers the opportunity to sail, picnic, and relax with jaw-dropping views.

★ **Historical crossroads:** Geneva's past as an independent crossroads of people and trade and home to the Calvinist Reformation movement has left the city with a rich history.

★ **Block party:** The Fêtes de Genève gives everyone a midsummer break by turning La Rade into a 10-day smorgasbord of international foods.

★ **Exclusive baubles:** To wander the Rue du Rhône is to take a roll call of the world's finest jewelers—only here, many are homegrown.

★ **Clink glasses:** Swiss wines aren't widely available outside the country, so explore Gamays from Geneva and Merlots from Montreux at a wine bar here.

1 Rive Droite (Right Bank). Clustered around a central downtown area (Centre Ville) that includes Cornavin, the main train station, are the business, shopping, and mixed-market residential areas of St. Gervais and Les Pâquis. To the north, about 10 minutes from the train station by tram, is the International Area, home to the UN's European headquarters and other international organizations.

2 Rive Gauche (Left Bank). Crossing over from the Right Bank on any of several bridges, you'll link up with the Centre Ville Rive Gauche, which includes the shopping streets known as Rues Basses. If you take the Ponts de l'Ile, the Rues Basses are to your left; the Vieille Ville (Old Town) is straight ahead; and to your right is the Plainpalais banking, university, and art-and-theater district. Crossing over on Pont du Mont-Blanc gives you access to the Eaux-Vives waterfront area, behind which a residential, business, and shopping neighborhood opens up.

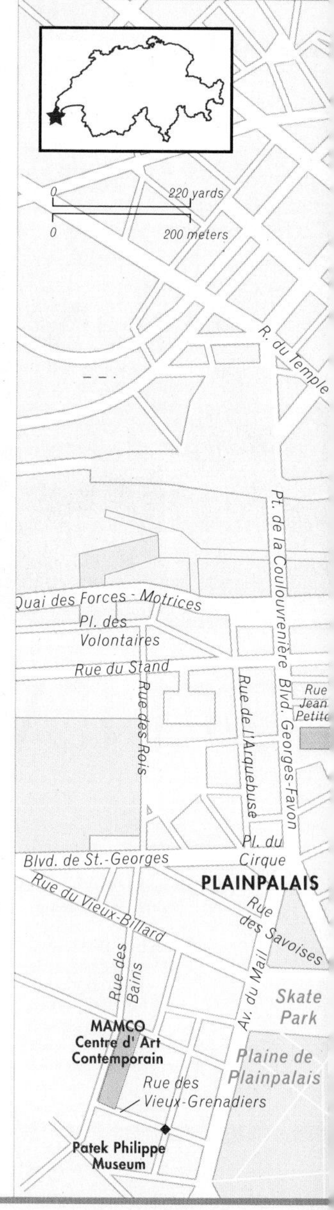

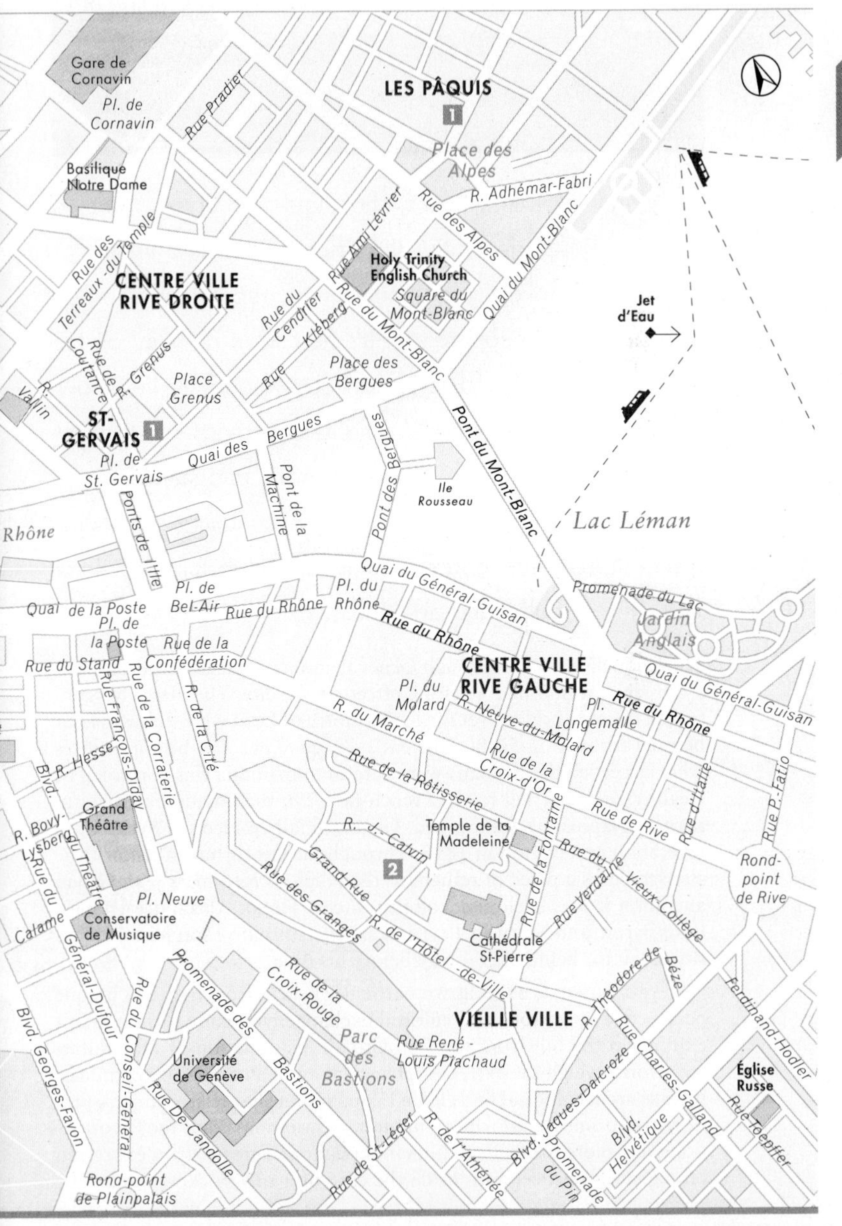

Gare de Cornavin
Pl. de Cornavin
Rue Pradier
LES PÂQUIS
1
Place des Alpes
R. Adhémar-Fabri
Basilique Notre Dame
Rue des Terreaux-du-Temple
Rue Ami-Lévrier
Rue des Alpes
Quai du Mont-Blanc
Holy Trinity English Church
Square du Mont-Blanc
CENTRE VILLE RIVE DROITE
Rue du Cendrier
Rue Kléberg
Rue du Mont-Blanc
Jet d'Eau
Rue de Coutance
R. Grenus
Place Grenus
Place des Bergues
R. Vallin
ST-GERVAIS
1
Quai des Bergues
Pont du Mont-Blanc
Pl. de St. Gervais
Pont de la Machine
Pont des Bergues
Ile Rousseau
Rhône
Ponts de l'Ile
Lac Léman
Quai du Général-Guisan
Pl. de Bel-Air
Pl. du Rhône
Promenade du Lac
Jardin Anglais
Quai de la Poste
Rue du Rhône
Pl. de la Poste
Rue de la Confédération
Rue du Rhône
Rue du Stand
CENTRE VILLE RIVE GAUCHE
Quai du Général-Guisan
Rue François-Diday
Rue de la Corraterie
R. de la Cité
Pl. du Molard
R. Neuve-du-Molard
Pl. Longemalle
Rue du Rhône
R. du Marché
Blvd.
R. Hesse
Rue de la Croix-d'Or
Rue de la Rôtisserie
Rue d'Italie
Rue P.-Fatio
Grand Théâtre
Rue de Rive
R. Bovy-Lysberg
R. J.-Calvin
Temple de la Madeleine
Rue de la Fontaine
Rue du Théâtre
Rue du Vieux-Collège
Rond-point de Rive
Rue du Calame
Grand Rue
2
Pl. Neuve
Rue des Granges
Rue Verdaine
Conservatoire de Musique
R. de l'Hôtel-de-Ville
Cathédrale St-Pierre
Général-Dufour
Promenade des Bastions
Rue de la Croix-Rouge
R. Théodore-de-Bèze
Rue du Conseil-Général
VIEILLE VILLE
Ferdinand-Hodler
Blvd. Georges-Favon
Parc des Bastions
Rue René-Louis Piachaud
Rue Charles-Galland
Université de Genève
Blvd. Jaques-Dalcroze
Église Russe
Rue De-Candolle
R. de l'Athénée
Blvd. Helvétique
Rue Toepffer
Rue de St-Léger
Promenade du Pin
Rond-point de Plainpalais

Updated by Kelly DiNardo

Long known for its watches, chocolate, and banks, Geneva is a postcard-perfect city with a rich history as a haven for cultural freethinkers and a modern-day reputation as a hub of international cooperation. It's nestled in a valley on the southwestern end of Lac Léman and ringed by the snow-capped Alps, and the dazzling surroundings are a playground for skiers, snowboarders, hikers, and sailors. In the city, cobblestone streets lined with cafés, luxury boutiques, grand monuments, and museums beckon to foodies, shoppers, history buffs, and art fiends.

The Rhône River cuts through Geneva, and its strategic importance as a crossing ground had a lasting effect on the city. The Genevois controlled the only bridge over the Rhône north of Lyon when Julius Caesar breezed through in 58 BC; the early Burgundians and bishop-princes who succeeded the Romans were careful to maintain this control. The wealthy city-state fell to the French in 1798, then made overtures to Bern as Napoléon's star waned. Geneva finally joined the Swiss Confederation as a canton in 1815. Throughout this turbulent history, the city served as a place of refuge for the religious reformers Jean Calvin and John Knox; sheltered Voltaire, Victor Hugo, Alexandre Dumas, Lord Byron, and Mary Shelley; and expelled its native son Jean-Jacques Rousseau for being liberal way before his time.

Geneva's museums have drawn particular benefit from the city's unique perspective on history and cultural exchange: you can visit a military exhibit up the hill from the Red Cross's examination of humanitarian efforts; weigh the extremes of ancient and contemporary ceramics; browse archaeological finds from Egypt and the Far East; compare pre-Christian primitive art with its modern incarnation; relive the Reformation; or explore the fruits of human thought and creativity as expressed on paper, in science, and inside the case of a tiny pocket watch. The

Palais des Nations forms the ultimate living (and working) museum of 20th-century history.

Today, Switzerland's famous neutrality has made it a hotbed of international activity with a thriving community of expatriates from around the world. The result is a bustling city filled with busy shops and lively cafés during the week and a more serene lakeside retreat on the weekends as many use this gateway city to explore the natural beauty of the region.

Hiking or skiing the nearby Alps and Jura are popular weekend activities, and there are options for newbies, extreme adventurists, day-trippers, and those lucky enough to extend their holiday. From meandering through the wine trails to hiking and skiing, Geneva provides a great home base for exploring the surrounding countryside.

GENEVA PLANNER

WHEN TO GO

Hot and sunny with a slight breeze in summer, crisp and clear in spring and autumn, rainbow-prone in June—Geneva's weather, when it's good, is spectacular. The Alps glow pink and the Jura fades to silhouette at the end of the day; restaurants set tables outside from March through October.

There are other days—whole weeks of them in winter—when stratus clouds coagulate between the mountains and gray out everything in sight. But relief comes from La Bise, the often bitingly cold north wind that blows in off the lake, clears away *la grisaille* (the grayness), and reveals sparkling snow-covered peaks.

PLANNING YOUR TIME

A curious tension exists in Geneva between dour intellectual concepts and breathtaking physical beauty, and you will probably find yourself torn between the urge to wander the quays and the sense that you ought to hit the museum trail. Don't choose: try to divide whatever time you have in the city equally between an extended stroll along the waterfront and a thorough exploration of the Vieille Ville.

Make time for the International Area if it interests you—never mind if it doesn't. Do not, however, skip Carouge, the creative, convivial warren of craftspeople and artists to the south of the city. Try to see some specialist collections (the Fondation Bodmer and the Patek Philippe Museum are stars), check out the Rues Basses shopping scene, and make sure that you go somewhere—Port Noir, the tip of the Jet d'Eau jetty, the cathedral towers, La Perle du Lac, Cologny—where you can see distance: Geneva genuinely does look equally good from up close and far away.

GETTING HERE AND AROUND

AIR TRAVEL

Geneva International Airport, Switzerland's second largest, lies 5 km (3 miles) northwest of downtown Geneva, in Cointrin. ■ **TIP→ When you arrive, pick up a free ticket from the dispensers in the baggage hall**

just before customs. The ticket is valid for 80 minutes from the time it's dispensed and gives you free transportation on trains, buses, trams, and *mouettes* (water shuttles).

GROUND TRANSPORTATION

There's no easier way to get from the airport to the city than the trains that depart every few minutes for the Gare Cornavin, Geneva's main train station. Amazingly, the trip takes just six minutes. The Nos. 5 and 10 buses connect the airport and downtown in about 20 minutes. Taxis are plentiful but expensive: expect to pay 35 SF or more to reach the city center.

Canton-wide public transport is clean, punctual, ubiquitous, and cheap. In fact, it's free if you're staying at a hotel or hostel, or if you're camping. Ask for your **Geneva Transport Card** at your lodging's front desk; it will give you free use of trains, buses, trams, and shuttle boats for the length of your stay.

BIKE TRAVEL

Bike lanes, indicated by a yellow line and a yellow bicycle symbol on the pavement, are ubiquitous downtown. Yellow signs indicate routes elsewhere in the canton. Genèv'Roule "lends" bicycles from May to October in all their locations, which include Place du Rhône in Centre Ville Rive Gauche, Ruelle des Templiers in Eaux-Vives, Bains des Pâquis in Pâquis, Plaine de Plainpalais in Plainpalais, and Place de l'Octroi in Carouge. Show valid identification, pay a deposit of 20 SF, and the bike is yours for four hours and must be returned the same day.

Contacts Genèv'Roule. ✉ *17 pl. Montbrillant, Centre Ville Rive Droite* ☎ *022/7401343* 🌐 *www.geneveroule.ch.*

BOAT AND FERRY TRAVEL

The Compagnie Générale de Navigation operates steamship connections between Geneva and lake towns in Vaud and France. Swiss Pass holders travel free; those with a Swiss Boat Pass pay half price. Smaller-scale lake travel, including a shuttle service across Geneva's harbor, is entrusted to the Mouettes Genevoises.

Contacts Compagnie Générale de Navigation (*CGN*). ☎ *0900/929929* 🌐 *www.cgn.ch.* **Mouettes Genevoises.** ✉ *8 quai du Mont-Blanc, Les Pâquis* ☎ *022/7322944* 🌐 *www.mouettesgenevoises.ch.*

BUS AND TRAM TRAVEL

Local buses and trams operate every few minutes on all city routes from 5 or 6 am to around midnight (depending on the day of the week and the route). On Friday and Saturday, the Noctambus night-bus service kicks in between 2 and 4 am.

The standard one-ride fare is 3.50 SF. Day passes, known as *cartes journalières,* are available from vending machines, Unireso sales points, and the Transports Publics Genevois (TPG) booths at the train station and Rond-point de Rive. Unlimited city-center travel between 9 am and the last bus costs 7 SF; 10.60 SF will buy you a ticket that allows two people to travel for the price of one on weekends.

Contacts Transports Publics Genevois (*TPG*). ☎ *0800/02202120* 🌐 *www.tpg.ch.*

13

CAR TRAVEL

Geneva's long border with France makes for easy access from all points French. The Swiss A1 expressway, along the north shore, connects Geneva to the rest of Switzerland by way of Lausanne. Traffic along the quays clogs easily, and parking in town is both restricted and expensive; look for electric signs on major incoming roads that note the whereabouts of (immaculate) municipal parking garages and their current number of empty spaces.

TAXI TRAVEL

Taxis are clean and drivers are polite, but rates are very expensive. Be prepared to pay a 6.30 SF minimum charge plus 3.20 SF per kilometer (about half a mile) traveled. In the evening and on Sunday, the rate climbs to 3.80 SF per kilometer. Cabs won't stop if you hail them; go to a designated taxi stand (marked on the pavement in yellow) or call.

Contacts Taxi-Phone. ☎ *022/3314133* 🌐 *www.taxi-phone.ch.*

TRAIN TRAVEL

Express trains from most Swiss cities arrive at and depart from the Right Bank Gare Cornavin every hour. Regional trains leave every 15 minutes en route to Nyon and Lausanne.

TOURS

BUS AND TRAIN TOURS

FAMILY **Key Tours.** These two-hour bus tours of the city leave from Place Dorcière daily at 2 pm as well as at 10 am from May through September, and recorded commentary is in English. It's a good idea to arrive at least 15 minutes early, as the Swiss are known for their punctuality. ✉ *7 rue des Alpes, Les Pâquis* ☎ *022/7314140* 🌐 *www.keytours.ch* 🎫 *From 45 SF.*

FAMILY **STT.** Between March and December pick up the minitrain at Place du Rhône for a trip around the Vieille Ville. A second minitrain leaves from there and the Quai du Mont-Blanc for a tour of the International Area with its scenic lake and mountain views. From March to October, a third minitrain departs from the Quai du Mont-Blanc for a "parks and residences" ride to the Botanical Gardens and back. Each loop lasts between 35 and 75 minutes. ✉ *36 bd. St-Georges, Plainpalais* ☎ *022/7810404* 🌐 *www.sttt.ch* 🎫 *From 8.90 SF.*

WALKING TOURS

FAMILY **Service des Guides.** An English-speaking guide at Genève Tourisme leads a two-hour walk through the Vieille Ville every Saturday at 10 am. Additional weekday circuits at 10 am take place between June and late September. English-language audio guides to the Vieille Ville last 2½ hours. You can arrange tailor-made thematic tours that trace the history of watchmaking, Jean Calvin's legacy, or any one of 14 other subjects. ✉ *Genève Tourisme, 18 rue du Mont-Blanc, Centre Ville Rive Droite* ☎ *022/9097030* 🎫 *From 15 SF.*

VISITOR INFORMATION

Genève Tourisme is headquartered inside the large post office building halfway between the Pont du Mont-Blanc and the Gare Cornavin. Additional information booths serve the airport and, from June through September, the train station. The Arcade d'Information de la Ville de

Genève, run by the city on the Pont de la Machine, is another excellent, multilingual source of information about all things Geneva.

Contacts Genève Tourisme. ✉ *18 rue du Mont-Blanc, Centre Ville Rive Droite* ☎ *022/9097070* 🌐 *www.geneve-tourisme.ch.*

EXPLORING

The *République et Canton de Genève* (Republic and Canton of Geneva) commands sweeping views of the French Alps and the French Jura from its fortuitous position at the southwestern tip of Lac Léman. The water flows straight through the city center and into the River Rhône en route to Lyon and the Mediterranean, leaving museums, shops, restaurants, and parks to jostle for space on its history-laden south shore, known as Rive Gauche. Busy shopping streets underline the hilltop Vieille Ville, the Plaine de Plainpalais lies to its west, and Eaux-Vives stretches along the quays to the east.

The *quartier international* (International Area), the Gare Cornavin, and sumptuous waterfront hotels dominate the north shore, or Rive Droite. St-Gervais, just north of the Ponts de l'Ile, was once a watchmaking quarter. Les Pâquis, a mix of artists, ethnic communities, and scrappy pleasure seekers, extends north from the Pont du Mont-Blanc. The International Area, on the outer edge of the city, is a short tram ride from Gare Cornavin; all other neighborhoods are easily toured on foot.

RIVE DROITE (RIGHT BANK)

INTERNATIONAL AREA

The Palais des Nations, 10 minutes north of the Gare Cornavin by tram, is the focal point of Geneva's humanitarian and diplomatic zone. Modern structures housing UN agencies dominate streets leading to it; embassies, 19th-century villas full of nongovernmental organizations, and museums surround them.

To get to this sector, take Tram No. 13 or No. 15 from the Gare Cornavin to the end of the line (Nations), and disembark onto the pedestrian Promenade des Nations. Towering over the 84 computer-managed water fountains is Swiss artist Daniel Berset's *Broken Chair,* a memorial to land-mine victims.

TOP ATTRACTIONS

FAMILY Fodor's Choice ★ **Jardin Botanique** (*Botanical Garden*). These 69 peaceful acres of winding paths and streams bear witness to Geneva's early-19th-century fascination with botany. They also include tropical greenhouses, beds of irises and roses, rock gardens, an aviary, a deer park, a garden of scent and touch, a living catalog of economically useful and medicinal plants, a seed bank, and a formidable research institute. Several of the trees predate 1700. The main entrance is opposite the World Trade Organization. ✉ *154 rue de Lausanne, International Area* ☎ *022/4185100* 🌐 *www.ville-ge.ch/cjb* 🎟 *Free.*

Musée d'Histoire des Sciences (*Museum of the History of Science*). Walk-around glass cases display age-old sundials and astrolabes, microscopes

Geneva's tranquil botanical garden is on the Right Bank in the city's busy humanitarian and diplomatic zone.

and telescopes, barometers and ornate globes that collectively document the evolution of modern science. Descriptions are in English. The neoclassical Italianate jewel that houses the collection, the Villa Bartholoni, dates from 1830. ✉ *128 rue de Lausanne, International Area* ☎ *022/4185060* 🌐 *www.ville-ge.ch/mhs* 🎫 *Free* ⏲ *Closed Mon.*

Fodor's Choice ★ **Musée International de la Croix-Rouge et du Croissant-Rouge** (*International Red Cross and Red Crescent Museum*). The museum focuses on three major challenges in today's "Humanitarian Adventure": defending human dignity, restoring family links, and reducing natural risks. The artifacts and artwork in each section are complemented by the life-size videos of 12 witnesses sharing their heart-wrenching personal stories that include surviving a land mine in Kabul and identifying tsunami victims in Japan. An audio guide, available in English, is included in the price. ✉ *17 av. de la Paix, International Area* ☎ *022/7489525* 🌐 *www.redcrossmuseum.ch/en/* 🎫 *15 SF* ⏲ *Closed Mon.*

Palais des Nations (*Palace of Nations*). Built between 1929 and 1936 for the League of Nations, this monumental compound became the European office of the United Nations in 1946 and quickly evolved into the largest center for multilateral diplomacy in the world. Today it hosts some 9,000 conferences and 25,000 delegates each year; it is also the largest nexus for United Nations operational activities after New York.

Security is tight: be prepared to show your passport. Points of particular interest include the **Assembly Hall,** the largest of 34 conference rooms, where the UN General Assembly and scores of world leaders have met, and the ornate **Council Chamber,** home to the Conference on Disarmament, which glows with allegorical murals. Tours last about one hour and are conducted in 15 languages, including English. ✉ *14 av. de la Paix, International Area* ☎ *022/9174896* 🌐 *www.unog.ch* 🎫 *12 SF* ⏲ *Closed weekends.*

WORTH NOTING

Musée Ariana. An architectural anachronism when it was completed in 1887, this serene Italianate structure now houses the Musée Suisse de la Céramique et du Verre (Swiss Museum of Ceramics and Glass). Stoneware, earthenware, porcelain, and glass covering 700 years of East–West exchange populate the upper floors; contemporary work rotates through the basement. ✉ *10 av. de la Paix, International Area* ☎ *022/4185450* 🌐 *www.ville-ge.ch/ariana* 🎫 *Free* ⏲ *Closed Mon.*

Musée Militaire Genevois (*Geneva Military Museum*). The humble setting adds authenticity to this detailed look at a neutral but thoroughly competent military force. Uniformed models, weapons, prints, and documents proceed in chronological order through the eventful history of la Garde Genevoise from 1814 to the present, including a Napoleonic officer's outfit, Guillaume-Henri Dufour's personal effects, and a full-scale re-creation of a Genevois border post during World War II. ✉ *18 chemin de l'Impératrice, Chambésy, International Area* ☎ *022/7342406* 🎫 *Free* ⏲ *Closed Mon.*

LES PÂQUIS

The Rive Droite neighborhood known as Les Pâquis is lively and diverse, with luxury hotels and expensive apartments lining the waterfront. The crisscrosses of narrow streets opening up behind the five-star glamour have a multiethnic character and house everything from quirky boutiques, bars, and restaurants to the Red Light District.

TOP ATTRACTIONS

Mont Blanc. At 15,767 feet, Mont Blanc is the highest mountain in Europe and the crown jewel of the French Alps. Geneva's Right Bank—particularly its waterfront parkland—has a front-row view framed by three less lofty acolytes: Les Voirons, to the left; Le Môle, in the center; and Le Salève, to the right. ✉ *Geneva.*

WORTH NOTING

Beau-Rivage. Jean-Jacques Mayer's descendants still own and operate the hotel he built in 1865. It has discreetly witnessed the birth of a nation (Czechoslovakia, in 1918), the death of an empress (Empress Elisabeth of Austria, in 1898), the sale of royal treasure (the Duchess of Windsor's jewels, in 1987), and the passage of crowned heads from around the world. ✉ *13 quai du Mont-Blanc, Les Pâquis* ☎ *022/7166666* 🌐 *www.beau-rivage.ch.*

Monument Brunswick. Charles d'Este-Guelph, the famously eccentric (and deposed) duke of Brunswick, died in Geneva in 1873 and left his vast fortune to the city on condition that his mausoleum, the Gothic design of which is based on the 14th-century Scaligeri tombs in Verona, be given prominence. No one is sure why his sarcophagus faces inland. ✉ *Bounded by Rue des Alpes, Quai du Mont-Blanc, and Rue Adhémar-Fabri, Les Pâquis.*

Palais Wilson. The largest of Geneva's grandes dames, this former hotel leaped to international prominence on April 28, 1919, when the peace negotiators in Paris chose Geneva to host the newborn League of Nations. International civil servants began work here in November 1920, and the building was renamed in honor of U.S. President Woodrow Wilson in 1924. By 1936 the faltering League had run out of space and moved to the custom-built Palais des Nations. Ten years later it was dismantled. The Palais Wilson was gutted by fire in 1987, meticulously restored in 1998, and now houses the headquarters of the United Nations High Commissioner for Human Rights. It is not open to the public. ✉ *51 rue des Pâquis, Les Pâquis.*

LOCAL CELEBRATIONS

Nothing is too insignificant, it would seem, to be feted in Geneva: it enthusiastically supports a stream of celebrations, including wine harvest, jazz, and cinema-arts festivals. The three-day Fête de la Musique marks the summer solstice with more than 500 open-air concerts; the Fête de l'Escalade rolls back the clock to 1602 each December. The flamboyantly raunchy Lake Parade grinds its way along the quays in July. The 10-day Fêtes de Genève fill the waterfront each August with Ferris wheels, open-air discos, international foods, and a massive display of fireworks set to music.

RIVE GAUCHE (LEFT BANK)

CENTRE VILLE RIVE GAUCHE

Unlike its Right Bank counterpart, which extends vertically down toward the lake and river from the main train station, Cornavin, the Centre Ville Rive Gauche is aligned horizontally with the Rhône and comprises Quai du Général Guisan and the Rues Basses shopping area. Both parts of downtown Geneva—Rive Droite and Rive Gauche—are business, shopping, and to some extent residential areas. Geneva's equivalent of 5th Avenue, or Rodeo Drive, is the Left Bank's Rue du Rhône.

TOP ATTRACTIONS

Horloge Fleurie (*Flower Clock*). The city first planted this gigantic, and accurate, floral timepiece in 1955 to highlight Geneva's seminal role in the Swiss watchmaking industry. Some 6,500 plants are required four times a year to cover its 16-foot-wide surface. ✉ *Quai du Général-Guisan and Pont du Mont-Blanc, Centre Ville Rive Gauche.*

WORTH NOTING

Ile Rousseau. Jean-Jacques Rousseau, born in Geneva and the son of a Genevois watchmaker, is known to history as a liberal philosopher in part because the conservative governments in Geneva and Paris so thoroughly rejected his views. His statue on this former city bastion, erected reluctantly in 1835 (57 years after his death), was surrounded by trees and his face deliberately hidden from view until the 1862 construction of the Pont du Mont-Blanc gave Rousseau the last laugh. In 2012, for Rousseau's 300th birthday, the statue was turned so visitors can once again see his face. ✉ *Off Pont des Bergues, Centre Ville Rive Gauche.*

Temple de la Fusterie. Designed by Huguenot refugee Jean Vennes and completed in 1715, Geneva's first specifically Calvinist church was built to accommodate the flood of French Protestants that followed the 1685 revocation of the Edict of Nantes. The baroque facade blended into the secular landscape around it; the well-lighted and whitewashed galleries within allowed 750 people to hear every word the minister said. ✉ *Pl. de la Fusterie, Centre Ville Rive Gauche.*

Tour de l'Ile. On the border of the Rive Gauche's Plainpalais and Centre Ville neighborhoods is the lone surviving fragment of a 13th-century castle built by Bishop Aymon de Grandson to protect Geneva from attack via the bridge. The castle was demolished in 1677; this carefully preserved lookout tower now houses the Banque Safdié. It is not open to the public. ✉ *Rue de la Tour-de-l'Ile, Centre Ville Rive Gauche.*

EAUX-VIVES

Overall a tad more sedate in feel than the heart of Pâquis, which lies across the water, Eaux-Vives is nevertheless a bustling mix of residential, commercial, and business life. Quai Gustave-Ador echoes some of the grandeur of the opposite shore with fine old apartment buildings and prestigious office space.

TOP ATTRACTIONS

FAMILY
Fodor's Choice ★

Jet d'Eau (*Water Jet*). The city's landmark fountain, which shoots 132 gallons of water—the equivalent of four standard bathtubs—459 feet into the air every second at 125 mph, can be seen throughout downtown. The parks and promenades around the lake offer the opportunity to see it from almost 360 degrees, and a new wooden walkway on the pier at dock Gustave-Ador makes it easier to view up close. ✉ *Off Quai Gustave-Ador, Eaux-Vives.*

WORTH NOTING

Fodor's Choice ★

Fondation Martin Bodmer (*Martin Bodmer Foundation*). The museum that sources this humbling exhibition of original texts—from cuneiform tablets, papyrus scrolls, and parchment to a dizzying array of first editions—maps the history of human thought. Dramatic displays of bas-reliefs and dimly lighted Egyptian books of the dead give way to Homer's *Iliad*; handwritten Gospels according to Matthew and John; exquisite copies of the Koran; a perfectly preserved Gutenberg Bible; Shakespeare (the complete works, published in 1623); an autographed score by Mozart; *Oliver Twist*; the *Communist Manifesto*; and *Alice in Wonderland*. A comprehensive printed guide is available in English. Energetic sightseers can get here on foot; otherwise, take the A bus from Rond-point de Rive and get off at Cologny-Temple. The ride takes 12 minutes. ✉ *19–21 Martin Bodmer, Cologny* ☎ *022/7074436* 🌐 *fondationbodmer.ch/en/museum/* 🎫 *15 SF* ⏲ *Closed Mon.*

La Neptune. Old photos of Geneva show scores of black masts and graceful, cream-colored sails crowding the lake. Now *La Neptune* is one of only four authentic traditional barges still in existence. Built in 1904 and restored twice, in 1976 and 2005, she hauled stone and sand between far-flung construction sites until 1968. Today, it can be hired out for day sails. ✉ *Off Quai Gustave-Ador, Eaux-Vives* ☎ *022/7322944.*

QUICK BITES

Gelateria Arlecchino. The ice-cream maestros at Gelateria Arlecchino, across the street from the Jet d'Eau, crank out some 50 homemade flavors, including ginger-lime, tiramisu, pineapple mint, green tea, licorice, and several sugar-free options. Known for: wide selection of flavors; creative flavors like basil and ginger-lime; location near waterfront park and Jet d'Eau. ✉ ***1 rue du 31-Décembre, Eaux-Vives*** ☎ ***022/7367060*** 🌐 ***www.larlecchino.ch.***

FAMILY **Parc La Grange.** The remnants of a 1st-century Roman villa crown the hillside in this gracious, sun-dappled park, once the private grounds of an 18th-century villa overlooking the lake. William Favre's bequest of his family's domain to the city in 1917 stipulated that the park be made available to the public during the day and closed at night. It is still the only green space in Geneva to be locked when the sun goes down. The Orangerie and the Théâtre de Verdure stage performances and open-air concerts through the summer months. ✉ *Quai Gustave-Ador, Eaux-Vives.*

VIEILLE VILLE

Geneva's Old Town (Vieille Ville), a tight cluster of museums, boutiques, historical sites, and sidewalk cafés capped by the cathedral, represents the city's core. The cantonal government's executive, legislative, and judicial branches operate within its walls; the Left Bank radiates out from its slopes.

The **Passeport Musées** is a little booklet that, when stamped at the door like a passport, allows one free entrance each to the Fondation Baur, Fondation Martin Bodmer, Musée des Suisses dans le Monde, Musée Barbier-Mueller, Musée International de la Croix-Rouge et du Croissant-Rouge, Musée International de la Réforme, and Patek Philippe Museum. Many hotels (and the museums themselves) sell the booklets. They are valid for three months, cost 40 SF, and can be handed off to a friend.

TOP ATTRACTIONS

Auditoire Calvin (*Calvin's Lecture Hall*). Reformed services in English, Italian, and Dutch made this simple Gothic structure, built in the 15th century on the site of two prior churches, a potent international gathering place for 16th-century Protestant refugees. The Scots reformer John Knox preached here from 1556 to 1559 while he translated the Bible into English, initiating the Presbyterian Church; Calvin and his successors used the space to teach theology. Today the auditoire hosts the Church of Scotland, the Dutch Reformed Community, and the Waldensian Church of Italy. ✉ *1 pl. de la Taconnerie, Vieille Ville* 🎫 *Free.*

Cathédrale St-Pierre (*St. Peter's Cathedral*). A stylistic hybrid scarred by centuries of religious upheaval and political turmoil, this imposing cathedral somehow survived the ages with its dignity intact. The massive neoclassical facade was an 18th-century addition meant to shore up 12th-century Romanesque-Gothic walls; stained-glass windows, the Duke of Rohan's tomb, a few choir stalls, and the 15th-century **Chapel of the Maccabees** hint at lavish alternatives to Calvin's plain chair. Fifteenth-century bells and bird's-eye city views reward those who

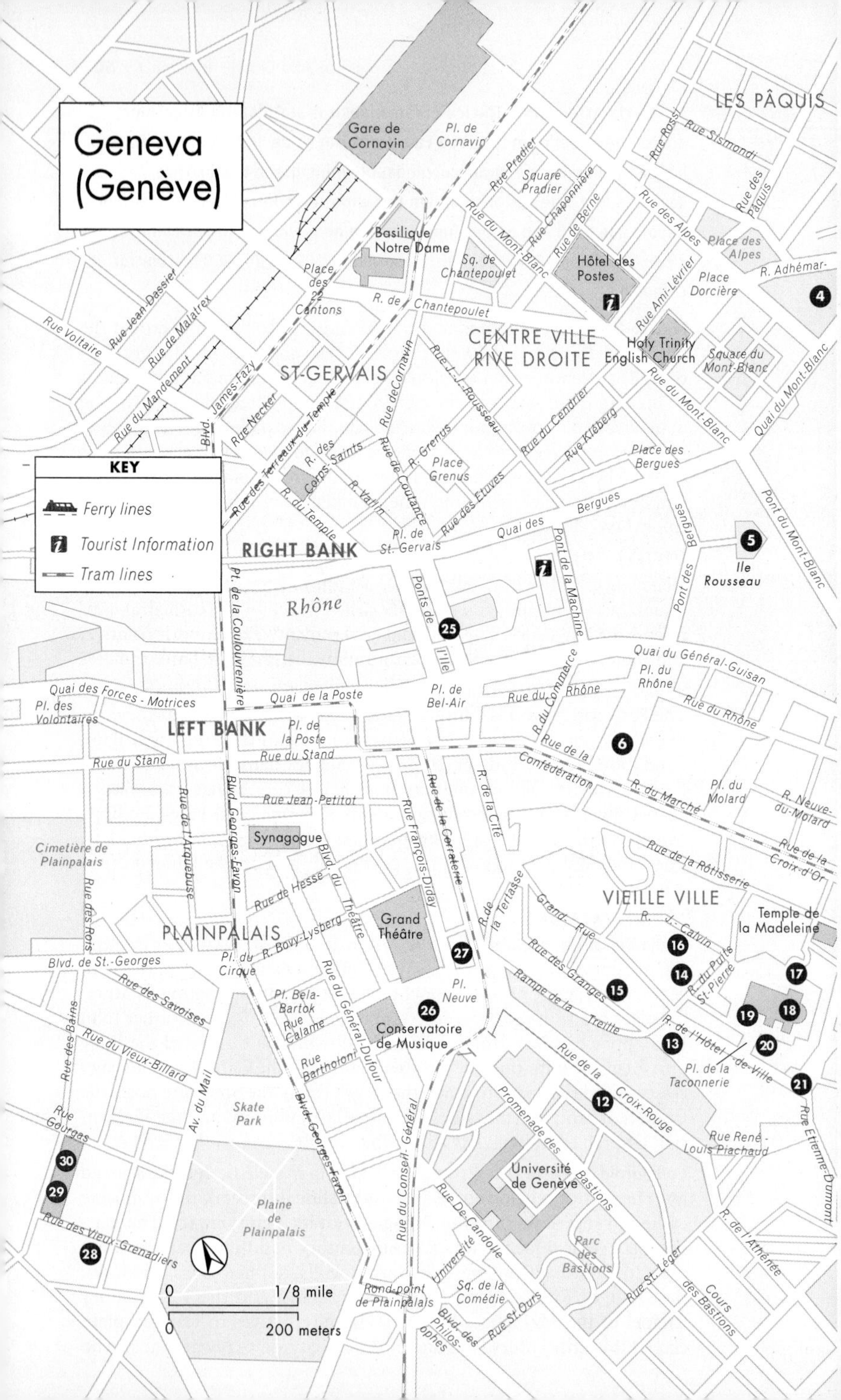

Geneva (Genève)
KEY
Ferry lines
Tourist Information
Tram lines
LES PÂQUIS
Gare de Cornavin
Pl. de Cornavin
Basilique Notre Dame
Place des 22 Cantons
Square Pradier
Sq. de Chantepoulet
Hôtel des Postes
Place des Alpes
Place Dorcière
Holy Trinity English Church
Square du Mont-Blanc
CENTRE VILLE RIVE DROITE
ST-GERVAIS
Place Grenus
Place des Bergues
Pl. de St.-Gervais
RIGHT BANK
Rhône
Ile Rousseau
LEFT BANK
Pl. des Volontaires
Pl. de la Poste
Pl. de Bel-Air
Pl. du Rhône
Pl. du Molard
Synagogue
Cimetière de Plainpalais
VIEILLE VILLE
Temple de la Madeleine
PLAINPALAIS
Grand Théâtre
Pl. du Cirque
Pl. Neuve
Pl. Bela-Bartok
Conservatoire de Musique
Pl. de la Taconnerie
Skate Park
Université de Genève
Plaine de Plainpalais
Parc des Bastions
Rond-point de Plainpalais
Sq. de la Comédie
Rue Voltaire
Rue Jean-Dassier
Rue de Malatrex
Rue du Mandement
Blvd. James-Fazy
Rue Necker
Rue des Terreaux-du-Temple
R. des Corps-Saints
R. du Temple
R. Vallin
Rue deCornavin
Rue de Coutance
R. Grenus
Rue J.-J.-Rousseau
Rue des Etuves
Rue du Cendrier
Rue Kléberg
R. de Chantepoulet
Rue Pradier
Rue du Mont-Blanc
Rue Chaponnière
Rue de Berne
Rue Rossi
Rue Sismondi
Rue des Pâquis
Rue des Alpes
Rue Ami-Lévrier
R. Adhémar-
Quai du Mont-Blanc
Pont du Mont-Blanc
Quai des Bergues
Pont des Bergues
Pont de la Machine
Ponts de l'Ile
Pl. de la Coulouvrenière
Quai des Forces - Motrices
Quai de la Poste
Quai du Général-Guisan
Rue du Rhône
R. du Commerce
Rue de la Confédération
R. du Marché
R. Neuve-du-Molard
Rue de la Croix-d'Or
Rue de la Rôtisserie
Rue du Stand
Rue Jean-Petitot
Rue de l'Arquebuse
Blvd. Georges-Favon
Rue François-Diday
Rue de la Corraterie
R. de la Cité
R. de la Tertasse
Grand-Rue
R. J.-Calvin
R. du Puits-St-Pierre
Rue des Granges
Rampe de la Treille
R. de l'Hôtel-de-Ville
Rue de Hesse
Blvd. du Théâtre
R. Bovy-Lysberg
Rue des Rois
Blvd. de St.-Georges
Rue des Savoises
Rue Calame
Rue Bartholoni
Rue du Général-Dufour
Rue du Vieux-Billard
Rue des Bains
Rue Gourgas
Av. du Mail
Rue des Vieux-Grenadiers
Rue du Conseil-Général
Rue de la Croix-Rouge
Promenade des Bastions
Rue René-Louis Piachaud
Rue Etienne-Dumont
R. de l'Athénée
Rue De-Candolle
Université
Rue St. Léger
Cours des Bastions
Rue St.-Ours
Blvd. des Philosophes
0 1/8 mile
0 200 meters
4
5
6
12
13
14
15
16
17
18
19
20
21
25
26
27
28
29
30

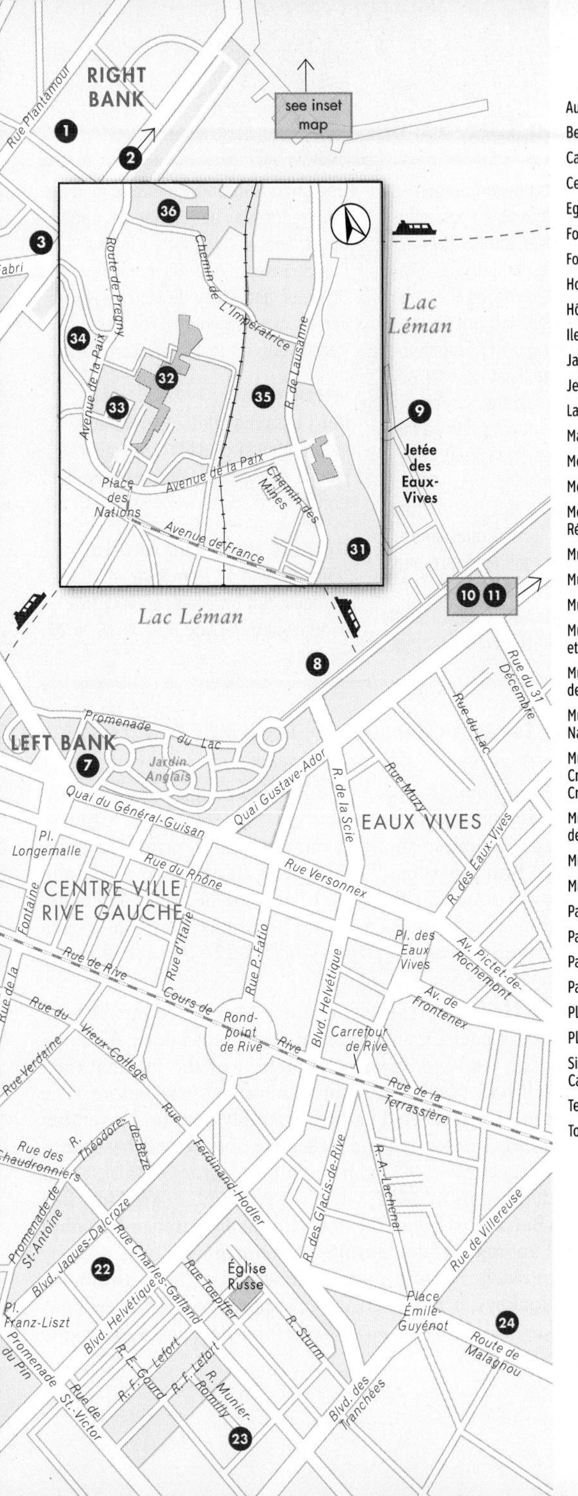

Auditoire Calvin **20**
Beau-Rivage **3**
Cathédrale St-Pierre **18**
Centre d'Art Contemporain **29**
Eglise Saint-Germain **15**
Fondation Baur **23**
Fondation Martin Bodmer **11**
Horloge Fleurie **7**
Hôtel de Ville **13**
Ile Rousseau **5**
Jardin Botanique **35**
Jet d'Eau **9**
La Neptune **8**
Maison Tavel **14**
Mont Blanc **1**
Monument Brunswick **4**
Monument de la Réformation **12**
Musée Ariana **33**
Musée Barbier-Mueller **16**
Musée d'Art et d'Histoire **22**
Musée d'Art Moderne et Contemporain **30**
Musée d'Histoire des Sciences **31**
Musée d'Histoire Naturelle **24**
Musée International de la Croix-Rouge et du Croissant-Rouge **34**
Musée International de la Réforme **17**
Musée Militaire Genevois **36**
Musée Rath **27**
Palais des Nations **32**
Palais Wilson **2**
Parc La Grange **10**
Patek Philippe Museum **28**
Place du Bourg-de-Four **21**
Place de Neuve **26**
Site Archéologique Cathédrale St-Pierre **19**
Temple de la Fusterie **6**
Tour de l'Ile **25**

CLOSE UP

Carouge: La Citè Sarde

Carouge (from *quadruvium*) began life in the Roman era as a crossroads next to a bridge over the River Arve. It remained a mere hamlet until 1754, when the Duke of Savoy, by then also king of Sardinia, annexed it with the intention of creating a rival commercial hub for Geneva. That never happened, courtesy of the French Revolution, but the town grew so fast that the royal planners in Turin drew up five separate development plans between 1772 and 1783; their harmonious architecture, plazas, and courtyard gardens still recall Mediterranean ways unheard of in Geneva. Colorful shop windows, sidewalk cafés, friendly restaurants, hole-in-the-wall galleries, tree-lined fruit-and-vegetable markets (on Wednesday and Saturday), open doors, and working artists infuse Rue St-Joseph, Rue Ancienne, Rue St-Victor, and Place du Marché with vibrant creative energy. For more information go to 🌐 *www.carouge.ch.*

WHEN TO GO

Don't miss the outdoor street fairs in late August or early September (Vogue de Carouge) or the December Christmas Market.

GETTING HERE AND AROUND

Trams 12 and 13 from Rive and Gare Cornavin run on average every five minutes and get you here in 15 to 20 minutes.

climb the **North Tower.** ✉ *Cour St-Pierre, Vieille Ville* ☎ *022/3117575* 🌐 *www.saintpierre-geneve.ch* 🎫 *North tower 5 SF.*

Fondation Baur (*Baur Foundation*). Alfred Baur's lovingly preserved collection of Far Eastern art packs more than 10 centuries of Chinese ceramics and jade, Japanese smoking paraphernalia, prints, lacquerware, and sword fittings—some 9,000 objects in all—into a tranquil 19th-century town house on the edge of the Vieille Ville. Thematic temporary exhibits occupy the basement. English texts introduce each room. ✉ *8 rue Munier-Romilly, Vieille Ville* ☎ *022/7043282* 🌐 *www.fondation-baur.ch* 🎫 *10 SF.*

Hôtel de Ville (*City Hall*). Representatives from 14 of 16 countries present signed the first Geneva Convention in the ground-floor Alabama Hall on August 22, 1864, enforcing the action of the International Red Cross, which had been created in Geneva the year before. The League of Nations also convened its first assembly here on November 15, 1920. The canton's executive and legislative bodies meet here; until 1958 government functionaries lived here. But the history of this elegant vaulted compound begins in 1455, when the city built a large fortified tower, the Tour Baudet, to house the State Council Chamber. Its ramp, an architectural anomaly added during the Reformation, was used by the councilors to reach the third-floor meeting hall without dismounting from their donkeys, a practice that gave name to the tower: *baudet* means donkey in French. ✉ *2 rue de l'Hôtel-de-Ville, Vieille Ville* ☎ *022/3272118* 🎫 *Free.*

The landmark Jet d'Eau shoots water 459 feet into the air.

Fodor's Choice ★ **Monument de la Réformation** (*Reformation Wall*). Conceived on a grand scale and erected between 1909 and 1917, this solemn 325-by-30-foot swath of granite pays homage to the 16th-century religious movement spearheaded by Guillaume Farel, Jean Calvin, Théodore de Bèze, and John Knox. Smaller statues of major Protestant figures, bas-reliefs, and inscriptions connected with the Reformation flank the lifelike giants as they hover over Bern, Geneva, and Edinburgh's coats of arms. Roger Williams is surrounded by Pilgrims praying on the deck of the *Mayflower,* and near Oliver Cromwell is the 1689 presentation of the Bill of Rights to King William and Queen Mary by the English Houses of Parliament. The Reformation's—and Geneva's—motto, *Post Tenebras Lux* (After Darkness, Light), spreads over the whole. The location lies just below the Vieille Ville. ✉ *Parc des Bastions, Vieille Ville.*

Musée Barbier-Mueller. Josef Mueller began acquiring fine primitive art from Africa, Southeast Asia, and the Americas in 1907. Today his family's vast, inspired collection of sculpture, masks, shields, textiles, and ornaments spans six continents and seven millennia. A small selection is on view at any given time, displayed like jewels in warm, spotlighted vaults of scrubbed stone. ✉ *10 rue Jean-Calvin, Vieille Ville* ☎ *022/3120270* 🌐 *www.barbier-mueller.ch* 🎫 *8 SF.*

Fodor's Choice ★ **Musée International de la Réforme** (*International Museum of the Reformation*). Period artifacts, carefully preserved documents, and engaging audiovisuals explain the logic behind the Protestant Reformation. This sophisticated, modern, and remarkably friendly museum explores its influence as a religious, cultural, and philosophical phenomenon and traces its roots from the early 16th century through today. The sparkling

The Wall of the Reformers commemorates major figures in the 16th-century Protestant Reformation.

18th-century premises, on the site where Geneva voted to adopt the Reform, connect by underground passage to the Site Archéologique. The free audio guide is in English, as is all the signage. ✉ *4 rue du Cloître, Vieille Ville* ☎ *022/3102431* 🌐 *www.musee-reforme.ch* 🎫 *13 SF, 18 SF with Site Archéologique, Cathedral, and towers* ⏲ *Closed Mon.*

Place du Bourg-de-Four. Ancient roads met in this layered Vieille Ville square before heading south to Annecy and Lyon, east to Italy and the Chablais, north to the Rues Basses, and west through the center of town to the bridge. Once a Celtic cattle market, later flooded with refugees, it's still the quintessential Genevois crossroads where shoppers, lawyers, workers, and students all meet for drinks around an 18th-century fountain. ✉ *Meeting point of Rue Etienne-Dumont, Rue Saint-Léger, and Rue de l'Hôtel-de-Ville, Vieille Ville.*

FAMILY
Fodor's Choice ★

Site Archéologique Cathédrale St-Pierre. Archaeologists found multiple layers of history underneath the Cathédrale St-Pierre when its foundations began to falter in 1976. Excavations have so far yielded remnants of two 4th-century Christian sanctuaries, mosaic floors from the late Roman Empire, three early churches, and an 11th-century crypt. The first Romanesque cathedral on the site was built in 1000. Audio guides in English and careful lighting help navigate the (reinforced) underground maze that remains. ✉ *6 cour St-Pierre, Vieille Ville* ☎ *022/3117574* 🌐 *www.site-archeologique.ch* 🎫 *8 SF.*

WORTH NOTING

Eglise Saint-Germain (*Saint-Germain Church*). This pristine 15th-century sanctuary served as a Protestant temple, a butcher's warehouse, a foundry, and a government meeting hall before Napoléon's troops

A GOOD WALK: VIEILLE VILLE

Stroll through Parc des Bastions from its Place Neuve entrance. Geneva's university (on your right) is descended from Calvin's groundbreaking academy; the **Monument de la Réformation** spreads along the park wall to your left. Access Rue de la Croix-Rouge, then Promenade de la Treille, from steps to the monument's right.

Past the *Marronnier Officiel* (Official Chestnut Tree) is the **Hôtel de Ville,** seat of Geneva's cantonal government. By the statue of statesman Charles Pictet de Rochemont, head right through the 18th-century portico, then right again at No. 2 rue de l'Hôtel-de-Ville into the government complex courtyard.

Across the street, **Maison Tavel** is worth a stop. Turn right after leaving Maison Tavel, then right again into Grand-Rue. Espace Jean-Jacques Rousseau (No. 40), the philosopher's birthplace, features an audiovisual overview of his life. By No. 28, turn left into Ruelle du Sautier, which empties out by the **Eglise Saint-Germain.** Follow Rue des Granges; the 18th-century rooms of Fondation Zoubov (No. 2) can be visited on weekday afternoons.

Continue through Place du Grand-Mézel, Geneva's 15th-century Jewish ghetto. To the left, Rue de la Cité connects the Old Town with its ancient river crossing. Head back up Grand-Rue and turn left down Rue de la Pélisserie, which becomes Rue Jean-Calvin; the **Musée Barbier-Mueller** is here. Calvin and his family lived across from No. 11 from 1543 until his death in 1564.

Proceed via Rue Otto-Barblan to Cour Saint-Pierre, home to the **Musée International de la Réforme, Cathédrale St-Pierre,** and the **Site Archéologique.** This has been Geneva's spiritual center since the time of Celtic goddesses. Take Rue du Cloître to the Reformation museum. Upon leaving the museum, turn left then right into Rue de l'Evêché behind the cathedral. The chapel straight ahead is the **Auditoire de Calvin.** Back at Cour Saint-Pierre, you'll see the entrance to the Site Archéologique to your right. Finish with the view from the cathedral towers.

Via Rue de l'Evêché, go to Rue des Barrières; ascend the stairs leading to Terrasse Agrippa-d'Aubigné for a terrific view of the cathedral and 15th-century Madeleine church below.

Then head down the ramp to the right into Rue de la Fontaine. Walk up past the Lutheran Church to **Place du Bourg-de-Four** and into Rue Etienne-Dumont.

Continue straight to Place Franz-Liszt—after the composer, who lived here—and turn left onto Promenade de Saint-Antoine. Descend the steps marked **Site Archéologique** to stroll through the massive remains of Geneva's defense walls, then ride the elevator up and cross the bridge to the **Musée d'Art et d'Histoire.**

You can't miss the cupolas crowning the 19th-century Eglise Russe, which may be visited. Follow Rue François Le Fort to Rue Munier-Romilly, where the **Fondation Baur** museum is the last building on the right.

returned it to Catholicism in 1803. The second chapel on the left maps a structural lineage that began in AD 400, and the steeple dates from the 14th century. Today's whitewashed walls, strategic lighting, and stained glass frame weekly classical music concerts in summer. Attending a concert or a service (the latter occurs at 10 on Sunday) is usually your only chance to see the inside. ✉ *9 rue des Granges, Vieille Ville* 🌐 *www.concertstgermain.ch.*

Maison Tavel (*Tavel House*). Vaulted cellars and ground-floor kitchens display medieval graffiti, 15th-century tiles, and a guillotine in Geneva's oldest house, now a museum focused on life in the city from 1334 to the 1800s. Seventeenth-century ironwork, doors, and other fragments of long-demolished houses fill the first floor; a bourgeois home complete with 18th-century wallpaper is re-created on the second. The enormous Magnin Model (which depicts Geneva as it looked before its elaborate defense walls came down in 1850) is housed in the attic. Audio guides are available in English, French, German, and Russian. ✉ *6 rue du Puits-St-Pierre, Vieille Ville* ☎ *022/4183700* 🌐 *www.ville-ge.ch/mah* 🎫 *Free* ⏲ *Closed Mon.*

Musée d'Art et d'Histoire (*Museum of Art and History*). The 15th-century *Miracle of the Fishes,* in which Jesus paces the waters of Lac Léman, keeps things focused locally at this museum built in 1910. The collection includes Switzerland's largest concentration of Egyptian art, Escalade-era weapons, Alpine landscapes from both ends of the 19th century, and substantial modern art. There is often a fee for temporary exhibits. ✉ *2 rue Charles-Galland, Vieille Ville* ☎ *022/4182600* 🌐 *www.ville-ge.ch/mah* 🎫 *Free* ⏲ *Closed Mon.*

FAMILY **Muséu d'Histoire Naturelle** (*Museum of Natural History*). Large, evocative wildlife dioramas complete with sound effects cover most major animal types at this spacious museum. Large quantities of fossils, gigantic crystals, precious stones, and a case full of polyhedrons ensure that the place is always swarming with local school groups. Swiss geology, the history of the solar system, and thematic temporary exhibits round out the collection; most labels are in French. The museum is a short walk away on the outskirts of the Vieille Ville. ✉ *1 rte. de Malagnou, Florissant-Malagnou* ☎ *022/4186300* 🌐 *www.ville-ge.ch/mhng* 🎫 *Free* ⏲ *Closed Mon.*

PLAINPALAIS

Reclaimed from the swamps that formed the confluence of the Rhône and Arve rivers as recently as 1850, the area centered on the diamond-shaped Plaine de Plainpalais is now home to contemporary art galleries, traveling circuses, weekly markets, local and regional media, the sprawling Université de Genève, and remnants of a late-19th-century industrial past.

TOP ATTRACTIONS

Centre d'Art Contemporain (*Center for Contemporary Art*). Andy Warhol, Cindy Sherman, Nan Goldin, Pipilotti Rist, Thomas Scheibitz, and Shirana Shahbazi are some of the pioneering Swiss and international artists who have presented work here since 1974. The center's four annual exhibits tend to be transdisciplinary displays highlighting

The Patek Philippe Museum underscores Geneva's watchmaking reputation with a beautiful collection of timekeeping pieces and other artifacts.

emerging artists who examine the practice of art in a cultural context. Guided visits in English are available upon request. ✉ *10 rue des Vieux-Grenadiers, Plainpalais* ☎ *022/3291842* 🌐 *www.centre.ch* 🎫 *5 SF* ⏲ *Closed Mon.*

Place de Neuve. Aristocratic town houses now overlook Geneva's opera house, the Musée Rath, the Conservatoire de Musique, and the gilded wrought-iron entrance to the Parc des Bastions, but until 1850 this wide-open space was the city's heavily fortified main southern gate. The equestrian statue at the center of the square honors Guillaume-Henri Dufour, the first general of Switzerland's federal army and the first person to map the country. The large bust of Henry Dunant, founder of the International Red Cross, marks the spot where public executions once took place. ✉ *Intersection of Bd. du Théâtre, Rue de la Corraterie, Rue de la Croix-Rouge, and Rue Bartholoni, Plainpalais.*

WORTH NOTING

Musée d'Art Moderne et Contemporain (*Museum of Modern and Contemporary Art*). Concrete floors and fluorescent lighting set the tone for this gritty collection of stark, mind-stretching, post-1960 art. Better known as MAMCO, the museum shares its former factory compound with separate centers for contemporary art and photography. The industrial surroundings help juxtapose aesthetic approaches; temporary exhibits add current artists to the mix. ✉ *10 rue des Vieux-Grenadiers, Plainpalais* ☎ *022/3206122* 🌐 *www.mamco.ch* 🎫 *8 SF* ⏲ *Closed Mon.*

Musée Rath. Switzerland's original fine arts museum, inaugurated in 1826 and named for its late benefactor, Simon Rath, housed Geneva's growing collections of art and archaeology until they overflowed to the Musée d'Art et d'Histoire in 1910. Now the Rath hosts two major temporary exhibitions each year; they range in focus from archaeology to contemporary art. ✉ *Pl. Neuve, Plainpalais* ☎ *022/4183340* 🌐 *institutions.ville-geneve.ch/fr/mah* 🎫 *15 SF* ⏲ *Closed Mon.*

Patek Philippe Museum. In this breathtaking private collection you'll discover delicate gold watch cases, complicated watch innards, lifelike portrait miniatures, and softly lighted enameled fans, pens, pocketknives, snuffboxes, telescopes, and vanity pistols that shoot singing birds. Most of the objects displayed in this former watchmaking workshop are hundreds of years old; many were created in Geneva by Patek Philippe, one of the city's most venerable watchmaking companies. Meticulously restored workbenches, audiovisual displays, classical music, and a horological library complete the picture; the two-hour guided tour (in English at 2:30 on Saturday) puts it all in context. All signage is in English. ✉ *7 rue des Vieux-Grenadiers, Plainpalais* ☎ *022/8070910* 🌐 *www.patekmuseum.com* 🎫 *10 SF* ⏲ *Closed Sun. and Mon.*

WHERE TO EAT

For years Geneva's restaurants dished up menus heavily reliant on French, German, and northern Italian fare. Increasingly, there's a more international spin to the city's dining scene with Japanese, Peruvian, Indian, and Nordic cuisine popping up with fanfare. Tapas-style grazing menus have become as common as those offering five-course meals, and signature restaurants run by well-known chefs as prevalent as casual burger joints.

Although dress-code days are gone, casual elegance is the rule of thumb. Hours for meals generally remain noon to 2 pm and 7 to 9:30 or 10 pm; pubs, bars, and clubs satisfy hungry night owls. And yes, after the stores close on Saturday afternoon, Geneva's city center is virtually dormant—and most, but by no means all, restaurants close. That's because the Genevois spend their weekends eating at country inns and village cafés.

Geneva restaurants (and bars and clubs) are all nonsmoking. Some are now charging for the *carafe d'eau* (tap water). Since it is not local custom to take small children to better restaurants, amenities (and welcome) may be poor if you arrive with babies in tow. Tipping? Local diners may leave the change as a gesture when they leave, but tipping for exceptional service is up to the customer and is still the exception, not the rule.

Use the coordinate (⊕ B2) at the end of each listing to locate a site on the Where to Eat and Stay in Geneva map.

WHAT IT COSTS IN SWISS FRANCS

	$	$$	$$$	$$$$
At Dinner	Under 26 SF	26 SF–45 SF	46 SF–65 SF	Over 65 SF

Restaurant prices are the average cost of a main course at dinner or, if dinner is not served, at lunch.

RIVE DROITE (RIGHT BANK)

LES PÂQUIS

$$$$ SCANDINAVIAN Fodor's Choice ★ **Fiskebar.** Overlooking the lake, this Nordic-inspired restaurant has a minimalist look reliant on natural materials like wood, leather, and glass. Four connected spaces include a stunning emerald-green banquette and a fresh-fish counter with communal seating in front of a shimmering glass wall. **Known for:** creative Nordic cuisine; seafood-centric menu; relaxed atmosphere. *Average main: 75 SF* *11 quai du Mont-Blanc, Les Pâquis* *022/9096071* *Closed Sun. and Mon.* *E2.*

$ AMERICAN FAMILY Fodor's Choice ★ **The Hamburger Foundation.** Launched as a food truck, the Hamburger Foundation expanded to a classic, American-style burger joint decorated with simple black-and-white tile and red-umbrella-shaded picnic tables on the patio. The menu features three items—a burger, cheeseburger, and bacon cheeseburger, all made from locally sourced Swiss ingredients, including beef that is ground each morning by the in-house butcher. **Known for:** local meat, buns, produce, and beer; American-style burgers; fun, laid-back environment and staff. *Average main: 25 SF* *37 rue Philippe-Plantamour, Les Pâquis* *022/3100044* *www.thehamburgerfoundation.ch* *F1.*

$$ FRENCH **La Perle du Lac.** Built in 1827, this sprawling lakeside chalet set amid magnificently manicured public parks comes dramatically into its own in summer. Although the wine list is good and the French-accented seasonal cuisine competent, if it's haute gastronomy you're after, don't come here; this place is about location, location, location. **Known for:** idyllic location and excellent views; adequate food and service, but great ambience; classic French fare. *Average main: 45 SF* *126 rue de Lausanne, International Area* *022/9091020* *www.laperledulac.ch* *Closed Mon.* *G1.*

$$$$ FRENCH Fodor's Choice ★ **Le Chat Botté.** The elegant dining room of the Beau-Rivage is dressed in rich creams and browns with the occasional pop of apple green, but with majestic views of the Jet d'Eau and Mont Blanc the terrace steals the show. The menu evolves with the seasons: Michelin-starred chef Dominique Gauthier tweaks the details of his lineup every few months, and dishes may include such delights as zucchini blossom stuffed with mushrooms and topped with Parmesan foam, duckling lacquered with spices and a caramelized peach with ginger, or the local lake perch. **Known for:** stunning terrace views; elegant, seasonal French fare; vast wine list. *Average main: 170 SF* *Beau-Rivage Hotel, 13 quai du Mont-Blanc, Les Pâquis* *022/7166920* *www.beau-rivage.ch* *Closed Sat. and Sun.* *F1.*

$$$ MEDITERRANEAN **Le Jardin.** The dining room of Le Richemond is adorned in crimson and crystal, but it's the terrace with views of the lake that steals the show at this see-and-be-seen destination. The menu features seasonal dishes and Mediterranean classics like sea bass ceviche, spaghetti with clams, and a baked, salt-crusted fish. **Known for:** beautiful terrace setting and views of the lake; seasonal and local fare; excellent food and service. *Average main: 62 SF* *Le Richemond, Jardin Brunswick, Les Pâquis* *022/7157100* *www.lerichemond.com* *E1.*

13

CENTRE VILLE RIVE DROITE

$$$ FRENCH ✕ **Café Calla.** With a casual bistro vibe and health-conscious cuisine, the Mandarin Oriental's restaurant draws both business travelers and pleasure-seekers. The café, which offers gluten-free and vegetarian options, serves modern Swiss and French fare with a focus on local and seasonal ingredients. **Known for:** healthful, local fare; Parisian-style shaded terrace; vegetarian and gluten-free options. *Average main: 50 SF ✉ Mandarin Oriental Geneva, 1 quai Turrettini, Centre Ville Rive Droite ☎ 022/9090000 🌐 www.mandarinoriental.com ✣ B3.*

$$$$ ITALIAN ✕ **Il Lago.** Decorated with rich brocades, glittering chandeliers, and bright frescoes, this robin's-egg-blue dining room has plenty of light streaming through a wall of windows. Diners enjoy classic dishes from northern Italy and a menu of Italian, French, and Swiss wines. **Known for:** elegant decor and service; classic Italian dishes; expense account prices. *Average main: 75 SF ✉ Four Seasons Hotel des Bergues, 33 quai des Bergues, Centre Ville Rive Droite ☎ 022/9087110 🌐 www.fourseasons.com/geneva ✣ E2.*

$$$ JAPANESE ✕ **Izumi.** This rooftop restaurant serves up panoramic views of the city and Japanese-fusion fare, which is a rarity in Geneva. Nestled on top of the Four Seasons, the simple, modern decor lets the natural beauty of the nearby Alps take center stage while dishes like lobster and spinach salad with yuzu-truffle dressing tempt the taste buds. **Known for:** stunning panoramic views; well-prepared Japanese-fusion food; relaxed, lounge atmosphere. *Average main: 50 SF ✉ Four Seasons Hotel des Bergues, 33 quai des Bergues, Centre Ville Rive Droite ☎ 022/9087522 🌐 www.fourseasons.com/geneva ✣ E2.*

RIVE GAUCHE (LEFT BANK)

CENTRE VILLE RIVE GAUCHE

$$$ FRENCH ✕ **Brasserie Lipp.** The "Années Folles" decor—green-and-white tiles, mustard-yellow ceilings, warm wood—and busy waiters in ankle-length aprons channel Paris. Local diners of all stripes come to tuck into hearty portions of choucroute (sauerkraut) with pork and potatoes, vegetable couscous, tartares of beef or fish, and heaping platters of seafood. **Known for:** lively atmosphere; French bistro fare; charming outdoor terrace and gardens. *Average main: 50 SF ✉ Confédération-Centre, 8 rue de la Confédération, Centre Ville Rive Gauche ☎ 022/3188030 🌐 www.brasserie-lipp.com ✣ D4.*

$$$ STEAKHOUSE ✕ **Chez Philippe.** Inspired by New York steak houses, local powerhouse Philippe Chevrier created this modern restaurant with exposed brick and sleek black leather banquettes in the heart of downtown. The meat-centric menu features top-quality beef from Switzerland, Ireland, and Japan as well as an extensive wine list. **Known for:** modern, lively vibe; terrace seating; steak-house fare. *Average main: 50 SF ✉ 8 rue du Rhône, Centre Ville Rive Gauche ☎ 022/3161616 🌐 www.chezphilippe.ch ✣ D4.*

VIEILLE VILLE

$$ FRENCH

Au Pied-de-Cochon. Low ceilings, whitewashed beams, and a worn zinc bar give context to simple regional dishes like cassoulet, *émincé de veau* (veal strips in a cream sauce), *filets de perches,* and the namesake pigs' feet (served grilled or stuffed)—the selection varies. The crowd can be noisy, and table service can occasionally be a tad gruff, but locals and tourists keep streaming in, not least because it's one of the few places in town that serves meals straight through from noon to 10 pm. **Known for:** regional dishes; people-watching on the terrace; ongoing service from noon to 10 pm. *Average main: 35 SF 4 pl. du Bourg-de-Four, Vieille Ville 022/3104797 www.pied-de-cochon.ch E5.*

$ FRENCH

Chez Ma Cousine. There are three of these appealingly decorated restaurants around town: this one in Vieille Ville, as well as one on Rue Lissignol in Centre Ville Rive Droite, and one in the International Area. The idea is basic: lunch and dinner, you get half a roast chicken, Provençal-style potatoes, and green salad for 15.90 SF. **Known for:** inexpensive, good, quick fare; rotisserie chicken and simple sides; people-watching on the terrace of two of the locations. *Average main: 15 SF 6 pl. du Bourg-de-Four, Vieille Ville 022/3109696 www.chezmacousine.ch E5.*

$$ SWISS

Les Armures. A robust Swiss menu has made this Vieille Ville institution a magnet for local street sweepers, foreign heads of state, and everyone in between. Before tucking into a fondue or *raclette* (melted cheese served with small potatoes in their skins, pickled pearl onions, and gherkins), order a starter of air-dried meat cut paper thin—a specialty of the canton of Grisons. **Known for:** Swiss specialties like fondue and raclette; cozy, convivial atmosphere; celebrity diners like former President Clinton. *Average main: 40 SF 1 rue du Puits-St-Pierre, Vieille Ville 022/3103442 www.hotel-les-armures.ch E5.*

$$ FRENCH

L'Hôtel-de-Ville. It's hard to get more Genevois than this: diners reflect the city's mix of locals, tourists, expats, and politicians. The menu specializes in local favorites like filets de perches, *longeole* sausage, and game in season. **Known for:** local specialties and wines; a late-for-Geneva kitchen; people-watching on the terrace. *Average main: 40 SF 39 Grand-Rue, Vieille Ville 022/3117030 www.hdvglozu.ch E5.*

PLAINPALAIS

$$ ECLECTIC

Fodor's Choice ★

Café des Bains. Right across from MAMCO (Geneva's museum of contemporary art), in an arty neighborhood that has come to be known as QuARTier des Bains, this trendy-chic eatery-cum-bar that spills out onto a sidewalk terrace during the summer months mixes a classic-French-café look with contemporary touches and regularly changing artwork. World flavors are injected into a basically French seasonal repertoire, although one thing that's always on the dessert menu is American-style cheesecake. **Known for:** traditional French bistro with a creative, worldly twist; beautiful garden and sidewalk terrace; American-style cheesecake for dessert. *Average main: 40 SF 26 rue des Bains, Plainpalais 022/3215798 www.cafedesbains.com Closed Sun. A6.*

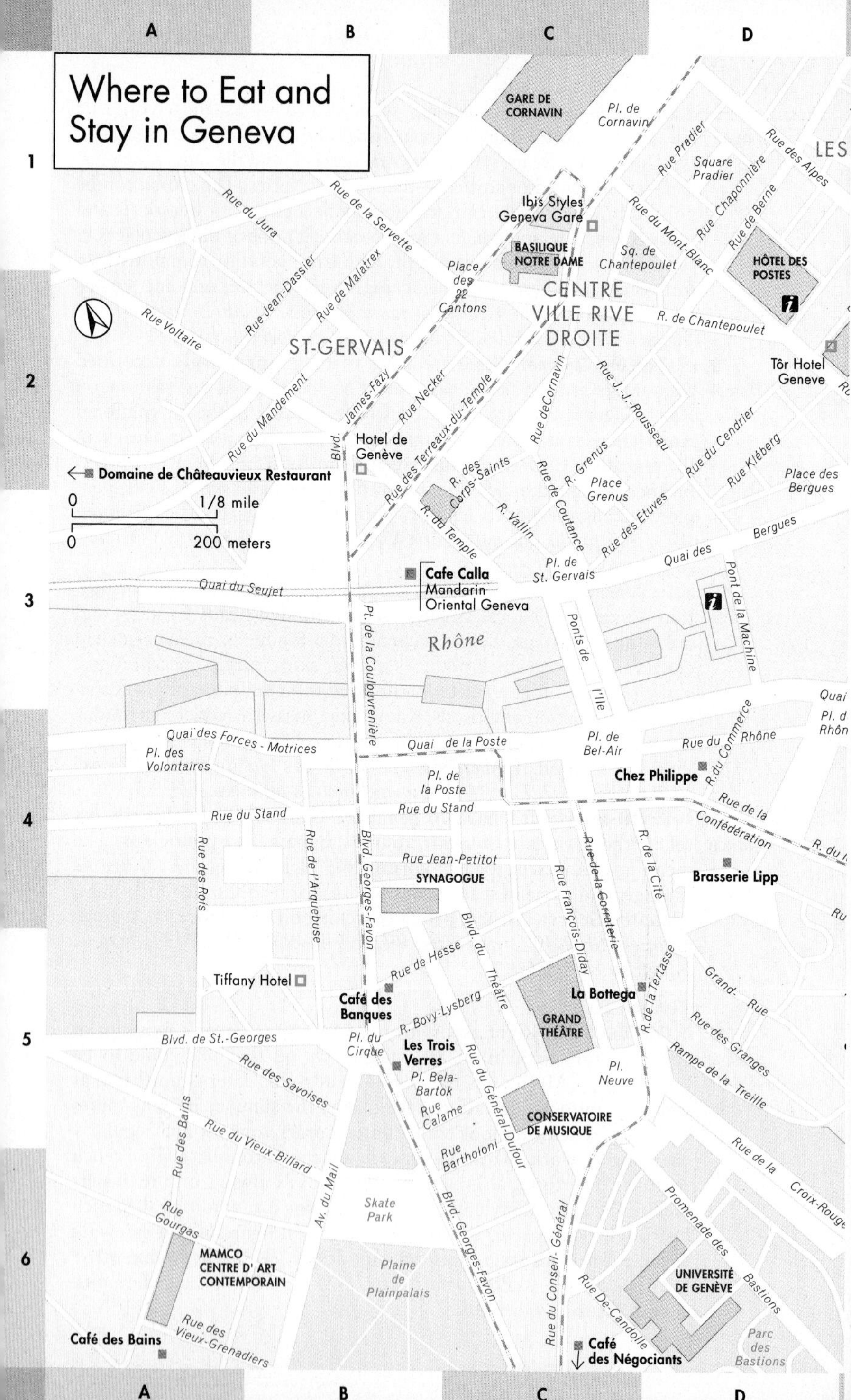

Where to Eat and Stay in Geneva
A
B
C
D
1
2
3
4
5
6
GARE DE CORNAVIN
Pl. de Cornavin
Ibis Styles Geneva Gare
BASILIQUE NOTRE DAME
Sq. de Chantepoulet
HÔTEL DES POSTES
CENTRE VILLE RIVE DROITE
ST-GERVAIS
Tôr Hotel Geneve
Hotel de Genève
Domaine de Châteauvieux Restaurant
0
1/8 mile
0
200 meters
Cafe Calla
Mandarin Oriental Geneva
Rhône
Chez Philippe
Brasserie Lipp
SYNAGOGUE
Tiffany Hotel
Café des Banques
Les Trois Verres
La Bottega
GRAND THÉÂTRE
CONSERVATOIRE DE MUSIQUE
MAMCO CENTRE D' ART CONTEMPORAIN
Café des Bains
UNIVERSITÉ DE GENÈVE
Café des Négociants
Skate Park
Plaine de Plainpalais
Parc des Bastions
Rue du Jura
Rue de la Servette
Rue Voltaire
Rue Jean-Dassier
Rue de Malatrex
Place des 22 Cantons
Rue du Mandement
Blvd. James-Fazy
Rue Necker
Rue des Terreaux-du-Temple
R. des Corps-Saints
R. du Temple
R. Vallin
Rue deCornavin
Rue de Coutance
R. Grenus
Place Grenus
Rue des Etuves
Rue J.-J.-Rousseau
Rue du Cendrier
Rue Kléberg
Place des Bergues
Quai des Bergues
Rue Pradier
Square Pradier
Rue Chaponnière
Rue de Berne
Rue des Alpes
Rue du Mont-Blanc
R. de Chantepoulet
Pl. de St. Gervais
Pont de la Machine
Quai du Seujet
Pt. de la Coulouvrenière
Ponts de l'Ile
Quai des Forces - Motrices
Pl. des Volontaires
Quai de la Poste
Pl. de Bel-Air
Rue du Rhône
R. du Commerce
Pl. de la Poste
Rue du Stand
Rue de la Confédération
Rue des Rois
Rue de l'Arquebuse
Blvd. Georges-Favon
Rue Jean-Petitot
Rue François-Diday
Rue de la Corraterie
R. de la Cité
Rue de Hesse
Blvd. du Théâtre
R. Bovy-Lysberg
R. de la Tertasse
Grand-Rue
Rue des Granges
Rampe de la Treille
Blvd. de St.-Georges
Pl. du Cirque
Pl. Bela-Bartok
Rue Calame
Rue Bartholoni
Rue du Général-Dufour
Pl. Neuve
Rue des Savoises
Rue du Vieux-Billard
Rue des Bains
Rue Gourgas
Av. du Mail
Rue des Vieux-Grenadiers
Rue du Conseil- Général
Rue De-Candolle
Promenade des Bastions
Rue de la Croix-Rouge

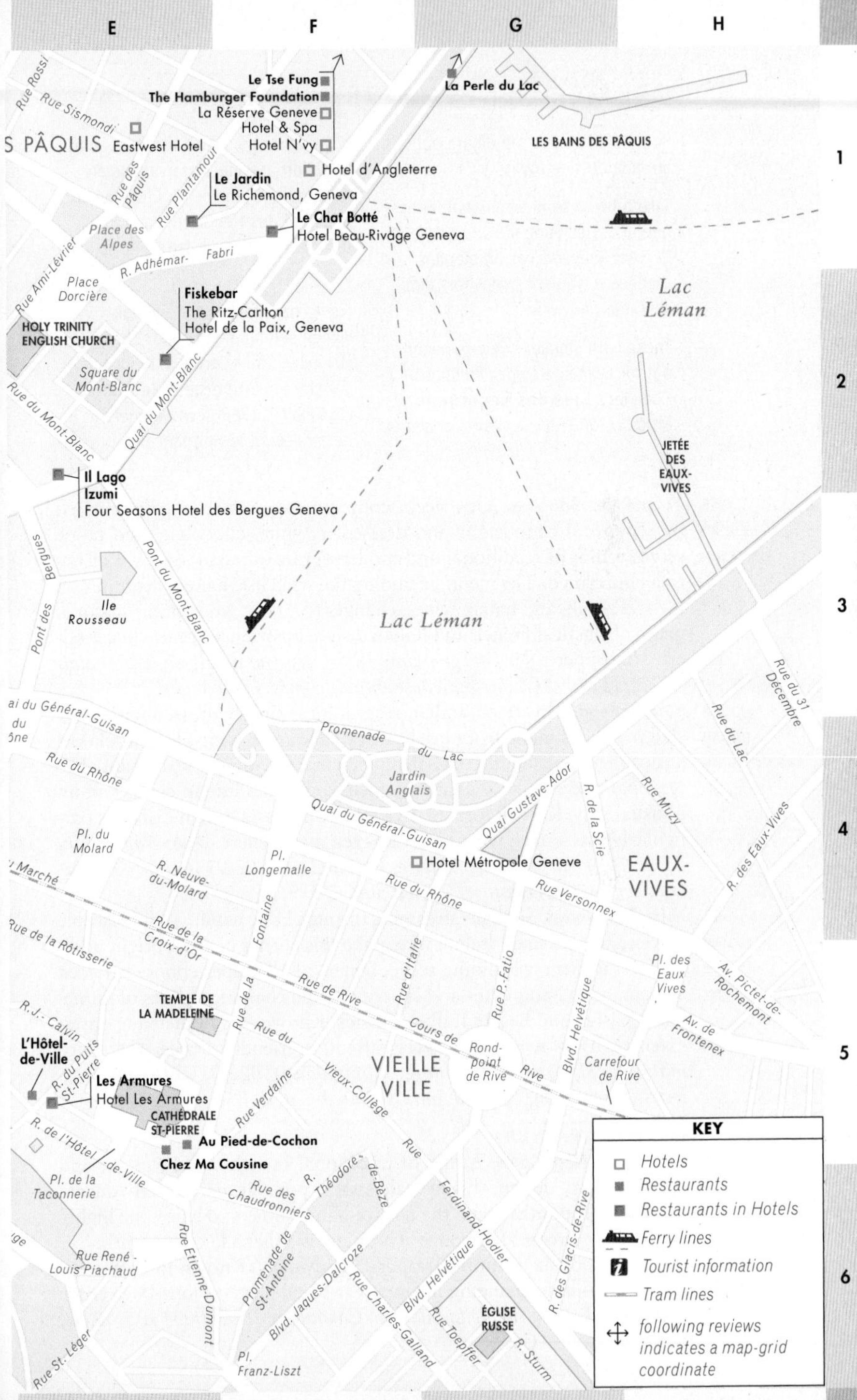

E
F
G
H
1
2
3
4
5
6
Le Tse Fung
The Hamburger Foundation
La Réserve Geneve
Hotel & Spa
Hotel N'vy
Eastwest Hotel
La Perle du Lac
LES BAINS DES PÂQUIS
Hotel d'Angleterre
Le Jardin
Le Richemond, Geneva
Le Chat Botté
Hotel Beau-Rivage Geneva
Fiskebar
The Ritz-Carlton
Hotel de la Paix, Geneva
HOLY TRINITY ENGLISH CHURCH
Il Lago
Izumi
Four Seasons Hotel des Bergues Geneva
Lac Léman
JETÉE DES EAUX-VIVES
Ile Rousseau
Jardin Anglais
Hotel Métropole Geneve
EAUX-VIVES
TEMPLE DE LA MADELEINE
L'Hôtel-de-Ville
Les Armures
Hotel Les Armures
CATHÉDRALE ST-PIERRE
Au Pied-de-Cochon
Chez Ma Cousine
VIEILLE VILLE
ÉGLISE RUSSE
KEY
Hotels
Restaurants
Restaurants in Hotels
Ferry lines
Tourist information
Tram lines
following reviews indicates a map-grid coordinate

GREATER GENEVA EATS

Some of Geneva's top dining options are just outside town.

Take a break from traditional Swiss fare at Le Tse Fung (☎ *022/9595959* 🌐 *www.lareserve.ch*), an elegant Chinese restaurant that offers dim sum and fine wines.

Those with smaller budgets might opt for Domaine owner Philippe Chevrier's **Café des Négociants** (☎ *022/3003130* 🌐 *www.negociants.ch*) in Carouge, which boasts a good selection of wine. Reservations are required at Domaine de Châteuvieux and Café des Négociants and highly recommended at Le Tse Fung, so plan ahead.

For a cozy meal in a storybook-village setting, head about 16 km (10 miles) from Centre Ville Rive Gauche to **L'Auberge d'Hermance** (☎ *022/7511368* 🌐 *www.hotel-hermance.ch*) in Hermance.

$$ MODERN EUROPEAN

Café des Banques. This sleek, contemporary restaurant illuminated by sculptural chandeliers and dressed in white, chocolate, and taupe serves a mix of traditional and modern Franco-Italian seasonal dishes to a chic crowd. The menu, including the wine list that concentrates on Swiss, French, and Italian wines, changes regularly. **Known for:** seasonal menu of classical French and Italian dishes; busy lunch scene; chic, modern atmosphere. *Average main: 38 SF* ✉ *6 rue de Hesse, Plainpalais* ☎ *022/3114498* 🌐 *www.cafedesbanques.com* *Closed weekends* ✣ *B5.*

$$$ ITALIAN Fodor's Choice ★

La Bottega. This rustic Italian restaurant is simply dressed with recycled materials made from brick, wood, and iron, which lend a relaxed atmosphere unusual for a Michelin-starred, fine-dining restaurant. The seasonal and regularly changing menu reinvents Italian classics in an unusual way. **Known for:** creative takes on classic Italian dishes; a particularly interesting wine list; a relaxed atmosphere. *Average main: 55 SF* ✉ *21 rue de la Corraterie, Plainpalais* ☎ *022/7361000* 🌐 *www.labottegatrattoria.com* *Closed Sun.* ✣ *D5.*

$$ ITALIAN Fodor's Choice ★

Les Trois Verres. Sunlight streaming through large windows, impeccable service, and seasonal Italian fare make this corner bistro a bright addition to the Genevois dining scene. Diners of all stripes choose between dark maroon banquettes and cherry-colored chairs for plates of homemade pastas and hearty Italian classics. **Known for:** homemade pasta; extensive list of wines by the glass; attentive, friendly service. *Average main: 40 SF* ✉ *8 rue Hornung, Plainpalais* ☎ *022/3208462* 🌐 *www.lestroisverres.ch* *Closed Sun. No lunch Sat.* ✣ *B5.*

GREATER GENEVA

$$ FRENCH

Café des Négociants. A mix of traditional French café furniture and contemporary design, this upscale spot is popular, particularly during the summer months when the terrace allows diners to enjoy the highly picturesque streets of Carouge. The menu is either à la carte or prix fixe (for groups of six or more, arranged in advance). **Known for:** attentive service; regularly changing menu; great-value plats du jour. *Average main: 45 SF* ✉ *29 rue de la Filature, Carouge* ☎ *022/3003130* 🌐 *www.negociants.ch* ✣ *C6.*

Geneva's Vieille Ville has many delightful outdoor cafés.

$$$$ FRENCH **Domaine de Châteauvieux Restaurant.** Philippe Chevrier's expansive kitchen, out in the heart of Geneva's wine country, draws inspiration and the culinary equivalent of spun gold from local and regional foods (some of which are sold on-site in a little *épicerie* [grocery]). The country estate offers sweeping hilltop views of the Rhône and Jura and Salève mountains. **Known for:** bucolic setting and commanding views; award-winning gastronomic experience; the chef's table inside the kitchen that offers an immersive and personal experience. *Average main: 290 SF* *16 chemin de Châteauvieux, Satigny* *022/7531511* *www.chateauvieux.ch* *Closed Sun. and Mon.* *A2.*

$$$$ CHINESE **Le Tse Fung.** Plush red velvet chairs and golden accents encourage guests to linger at Le Tse Fung, an elegant Chinese restaurant tucked into the lower level of this resort overlooking the lake. The menu offers several prix-fixe meals with traditional dishes like Peking duck with pancakes, and an à la carte, dim sum approach that includes 15 types of steamed or grilled dumplings and two styles of Peking duck served over two courses. **Known for:** elegant Asian decor; upscale Chinese food; extensive wine list. *Average main: 75 SF* *La Reserve, 301 rte. de Lausanne, Bellevue* *022/9595959* *www.tsefung.ch* *F1.*

WHERE TO STAY

The palace-style hotel continues to be the defining image of the city's hospitality. There is something quintessentially Geneva about the wealth these places ooze, and the waterfront ones on the Right Bank give you sweeping views of the city's other iconic features: the Jet d'Eau, Old Town, La Rade (the waterfront), river, lake, and mountains. They're also near parks—another of the city's points of pride—for that early-morning jog as the sun rises across the water.

Overall, the hospitality sector has seen an overhaul in Geneva these past years, as owners recognize that decor matters and that updates (and upkeep) are essential. Genuinely gracious, go-the-extra-mile-with-a-smile service remains vexingly confined to the professionally trained top and family-run bottom of the rate structure, but the good news is that the concept of gracious service is making across-the-board inroads.

Geneva hotels do err on the expensive side, and the practice of massively hiking up rates during events like the annual car show in March persists. Speaking of which, large events can suddenly fill entire hotels, so book as early as you can. And, because this is a conference-and-convention-driven town, leisure visitors will find lower prices on weekend stays.

As for breakfast (if not included), you won't readily find places outside the big hotels that do bacon and eggs, but if you're happy with croissants and coffee, head for the nearest café. As for practicalities, many places accept children up to a certain age for free, or another bed can be put in your room for a low extra. Wi-Fi is now common (often at an added cost). Depending on the category of hotel, there is a *taxe de séjour* between 1.50 SF and 6 SF per person and per night. Check when you are booking if they are including this in the quoted rate or not.

Hotel reviews have been shortened. For full information, visit Fodors.com. Use the coordinate (⊕ B2) at the end of each listing to locate a site on the Where to Eat and Stay in Geneva map.

WHAT IT COSTS IN SWISS FRANCS				
	$	$$	$$$	$$$$
For Two People	Under 201 SF	201 SF–300 SF	301 SF–500 SF	Over 500 SF

Hotel prices are the lowest cost of a standard double room in high season, including taxes.

RIVE DROITE (RIGHT BANK)

LES PÂQUIS

$$$ HOTEL **Eastwest Hotel.** This small hotel has sleek interiors with both Asian and European design elements. **Pros:** welcoming staff; sophisticated aesthetic; central location. **Cons:** space (closets, etc.) can be a little tight for some; the sensibilities may be a tad too refined; reservation required for parking. *Rooms from: 480 SF ✉ 6 rue des Pâquis, Les Pâquis ☎ 022/7081717 🌐 www.eastwesthotel.ch 41 rooms No meals ⊕ E1.*

$$$$ HOTEL Fodor's Choice ★ **Hotel Beau-Rivage Geneva.** This grande dame along Geneva's waterfront shook off its fusty image with a multimillion-dollar renovation that added a floor, several suites, luxe furnishings, and modern-day technology. **Pros:** elegant, comfortable, luxurious rooms; display of artifacts from Austrian Empress Sissi, who was killed outside the hotel; to-die-for location and views. **Cons:** decor on the lower floors is still a

little outdated; no wellness or spa area; pricey. $ *Rooms from: 600 SF* ✉ *13 quai du Mont-Blanc, Les Pâquis* ☎ *022/7166666* 🌐 *www.beau-rivage.ch* *95 rooms* *No meals* ✥ *F1.*

$$$$ HOTEL Fodor's Choice ★ **Hotel d'Angleterre.** Impeccable taste, total discretion, and a passion for detail mark this stylish boutique hotel, where thematic decorations stretch from African to baroque. **Pros:** one of the best examples of a luxurious boutique hotel you'll find anywhere; beautifully maintained; smiling, friendly service. **Cons:** cramped elevator; some will find it stuffy; lower lakeside rooms can be noisy. $ *Rooms from: 720 SF* ✉ *17 quai du Mont-Blanc, Les Pâquis* ☎ *022/9065555* 🌐 *www.dangleterrehotel.com* *45 rooms* *No meals* ✥ *F1.*

13

$$ HOTEL **Hôtel N'vy.** Tucked into a quiet neighborhood just a stone's throw from the lake, this trendy hotel marries a rock-and-roll, high-tech sensibility with four-star service. **Pros:** guests receive 15% off Manotel restaurants; energetic and creative vibe and aesthetics; rooms feature travel-friendly technology, like built-in adapters. **Cons:** breakfast not included; some find it noisy at night from the nearby bars and clubs; parking is pricey. $ *Rooms from: 250 SF* ✉ *18 rue Richemont, Les Pâquis* ☎ *022/5446666* 🌐 *www.hotelnvygeneva.com* *159 rooms* *No meals* ✥ *F1.*

$$$$ HOTEL **Le Richemond, Geneva.** Dressed up in crimson and crystal grandeur, this stately hotel wins over guests with its pied-à-terre vibe and impeccable service. **Pros:** opulent, luxe atmosphere; chill-out zone; his-and-hers massage therapy room. **Cons:** corporate-style decor in many rooms; floral arrangements in the public spaces can seem incongruous; opulence has a price. $ *Rooms from: 600 SF* ✉ *Jardin Brunswick, Les Pâquis* ☎ *022/7157000* 🌐 *www.roccofortecollection.com* *109 rooms* *No meals* ✥ *E1.*

$$$$ HOTEL Fodor's Choice ★ **The Ritz-Carlton Hotel de la Paix, Geneva.** After an extensive top-to-bottom renovation, the historic Hotel de la Paix reopened as a Ritz-Carlton property, marking the luxury hotel brand's debut in Switzerland. **Pros:** first-class service; large and luxurious rooms; premier location. **Cons:** some will find the lake-view rooms noisy; no spa; luxury comes at a price. $ *Rooms from: 550 SF* ✉ *11 quai du Mont-Blanc, Les Pâquis* ☎ *022/9096000* 🌐 *www.ritzcarlton.com* *75 rooms* *No meals* ✥ *E2.*

CENTRE VILLE RIVE DROITE

$$$$ HOTEL Fodor's Choice ★ **Four Seasons Hotel des Bergues Geneva.** Unpretentious service, lavish decor, luxurious details, and a first-rate location gives this palace an inner glow. **Pros:** excellent location within walking distance of the train, Old Town, and Jet d'Eau; spacious and luxurious spa; first-rate, personal service. **Cons:** perfection has its price; Wi-Fi for more than two devices costs extra; breakfast not included and pricey. $ *Rooms from: 795 SF* ✉ *33 quai des Bergues, Centre Ville Rive Droite* ☎ *022/9087000* 🌐 *www.fourseasons.com/geneva* *115 rooms* *No meals* ✥ *E2.*

$$ HOTEL **Ibis Styles Geneva Gare.** Across the street from the train station, this modern hotel provides a comfortable and convenient base. **Pros:** great location, great value; Wi-Fi and breakfast included; friendly, accommodating staff. **Cons:** rooms are on the small side; street-side rooms can be noisy; no frills and low on character. $ *Rooms from: 250 SF* ✉ *8 pl. de Cornavin, Centre Ville Rive Droite* ☎ *022/9064700* *52 rooms* *Breakfast* ✥ *C1.*

$ HOTEL **Tor Hôtel Geneve.** Within easy walking distance of both the main train station and the lake, this simply done hotel occupies three floors of a building across from the English Church. **Pros:** super-central location; staff gets kudos for friendliness; simple, clean, good-value rooms. **Cons:** space can be tight; noise may be a problem; during hot weather the lack of air-conditioning is felt. *Rooms from: 140 SF 3 rue Ami-Lévrier, Centre Ville Rive Droite 022/9098820 www.torhotel.com 26 rooms Breakfast D2.*

ST-GERVAIS

$ HOTEL **Hotel de Genève.** This family-run place has its own brand of charm and an exceptionally caring staff. **Pros:** personal, original decor; they take pride in good service; inexpensive. **Cons:** chalet lobby-cum-breakfast area can get very crowded; noisy; no air-conditioning. *Rooms from: 150 SF 1 pl. Isaac-Mercier, St-Gervais 022/7323264 www.hotel-de-geneve.ch 39 rooms Breakfast B2.*

$$$$ HOTEL **Mandarin Oriental, Geneva.** Elegant interiors, attentive service, and fabulous Rhône views add to the appeal of this Asian-influenced hotel. **Pros:** central location; a natural, easy vibe; the luxury of spaciousness. **Cons:** at these prices, there shouldn't be a charge for Wi-Fi; breakfast and parking are extra and pricey; no spa. *Rooms from: 655 SF 1 quai Turrettini, St-Gervais 022/9090000 www.mandarinoriental.com/geneva 182 rooms No meals C3.*

RIVE GAUCHE (LEFT BANK)

CENTRE VILLE RIVE GAUCHE

$$$ HOTEL **Hotel Metropole Geneve.** Massive scrubbed-stone arches, swirled wrought-iron sconces, lush carpeting, and the immediate proximity of high-voltage Rue du Rhône shopping give this 1854 Left Bank palace an air of urban gentility and center-city bustle. **Pros:** central location; bar has a cozy feel; integrated and accessible technology. **Cons:** no on-site parking; some find it too loud; small gym and no pool or spa. *Rooms from: 380 SF 34 quai du Général-Guisan, Centre Ville Rive Gauche 022/3183200 www.metropole.ch 127 rooms Breakfast G4.*

VIEILLE VILLE

$$$$ HOTEL **Hotel Les Armures.** Original 17th-century stonework, colorful frescoes, painted beams, and tapestries adorn the lobby and some rooms in this low-key luxury hotel near the cathedral; others have clean modern lines and restful deep-brown accents. **Pros:** in the heart of Geneva's Old Town; cozy, well-decorated traditional Swiss style; friendly, accommodating staff. **Cons:** not a lot of amenities; too quiet for some; breakfast and parking are extra. *Rooms from: 600 SF 1 rue du Puits-St-Pierre, Vieille Ville 022/3109172 www.hotel-les-armures.ch 32 rooms No meals E5.*

PLAINPALAIS

$$ HOTEL **Tiffany Hotel.** This pretty art nouveau–style hotel blends its 19th-century originality with a contemporary edge. **Pros:** friendly and accommodating staff; breakfast gets rave reviews, even though it's

extra; cozy common areas to read or have a glass of wine. **Cons:** some bathrooms could use updating; rooms in the front of the building can be noisy; tiny elevator. *Rooms from: 300 SF* ✉ *20 rue de l'Arquebuse, Plainpalais* ☎ *022/7081616* 🌐 *www.hotel-tiffany.ch* *65 rooms* *No meals* ✣ *B5.*

GREATER GENEVA

$$$ RESORT FAMILY **La Réserve Geneve Hotel & Spa.** Nestled on the shores of Lac Léman, this contemporary resort in a residential suburb resembles a grand African lodge. **Pros:** idyllic atmosphere; abundant amenities; complete and utter pampering. **Cons:** outside the center of the city; meals are extra and pricey, and the remote location leaves few other options; front-facing rooms overlook parking lot and can be loud. *Rooms from: 450 SF* ✉ *301 rte. de Lausanne, Bellevue* ☎ *022/9595959* 🌐 *www.lareserve.ch* *102 rooms* *No meals* ✣ *F1.*

NIGHTLIFE

A successful night out in Geneva—whether exclusive, trendy, or pub based—can hinge on understanding that you are not in a major metropolis. Though bars and clubs have lots of life, much of it English speaking, it may not always be possible to party 'til dawn.

The *Genève Agenda* publishes monthly English and French listings of concerts, performances, temporary exhibits, restaurants, and clubs. A popular guide, it is also called the *Monthly Guide of Geneva* (🌐 *www.le-guide.ch*)—free copies are available from tourist information booths and hotels, and the publication can also be downloaded from the website.

RIVE DROITE (RIGHT BANK)

LES PÂQUIS

BARS

Mr. Pickwick Pub. Popular with English speakers is Mr. Pickwick Pub. ✉ *80 rue de Lausanne, Les Pâquis* ☎ *022/7316797* 🌐 *www.mrpickwick.ch.*

ST-GERVAIS

BARS

Mulligan's. Guinness is on tap and soccer matches are on the telly at Mulligan's, which is proudly Irish owned and operated. ✉ *14 rue Grenus, St-Gervais* ☎ *022/7328576* 🌐 *www.ireland.ch.*

13

RIVE GAUCHE (LEFT BANK)

CENTRE VILLE RIVE GAUCHE

BARS

5. This rooftop lounge atop the Hotel Metropole offers breathtaking views of the Jet d'Eau, tapas, and craft cocktails for a chic, after-work crowd from May to September. ✉ *34 quai du Général-Guisan, Centre Ville Rive Gauche* ☎ *022/3183355* 🌐 *www.metropole.ch.*

La Clémence. In the warmer months you can sit outside at quintessentially Genevese La Clémence. ✉ *20 pl. du Bourg-de-Four, Vieille Ville* ☎ *022/3122498* 🌐 *www.laclemence.ch.*

Fodor's Choice ★ **L'Atelier Cocktail Club.** This dark, cozy bar with a speakeasy vibe pours craft cocktails that include classics and inventive, new concoctions. ✉ *11 rue Henri-Blanvalet, Centre Ville Rive Gauche* ☎ *022/7352247* 🌐 *www.ateliercocktailclub.ch.*

Fodor's Choice ★ **Le Verre à Monique.** This elegant cocktail club features shabby-chic, retro decor, and exquisite craft cocktails. ✉ *19 rue des Savoises, Centre Ville Rive Gauche* ☎ *022/3202307* 🌐 *verreamonique.ch.*

PLAINPALAIS

BARS

Boulevard du Vin. When it comes to wine bars, Boulevard du Vin tops a lot of lists. ✉ *3 bd. Georges-Favon, Plainpalais* ☎ *022/3109190* 🌐 *www.boulevard-du-vin.ch.*

PERFORMING ARTS

Geneva's legacy as a cultural crossroads has produced an unusually rich arts scene for a city of its size: most performance spaces in town are roadhouses, through which flow a steady stream of foreign as well as Swiss artists. Tickets remain on sale from theater box offices up to the day of performance, but it's wise to book ahead.

FNAC Rive. The ticket service at FNAC Rive manages sales for an ever-changing list of events. ✉ *16 rue de Rive, Centre Ville Rive Gauche* ☎ *022/8161256* 🌐 *www.ch.fnacspectacles.com.*

MUSIC AND DANCE

Bâtiment des Forces Motrices. Classical music, opera, contemporary dance, and the occasional film festival cycle through the Bâtiment des Forces Motrices. ✉ *2 pl. des Volontaires, Plainpalais* ☎ *022/3221220* 🌐 *www.bfm.ch.*

Grand Théâtre. The Grand Théâtre stages more than a dozen operas, ballets, and recitals in a newly renovated theater. ✉ *Pl. Neuve, Plainpalais* ☎ *022/4183130* 🌐 *www.geneveopera.ch.*

Sud des Alpes. Nervy improvisation and contemporary jazz is on the bill at Sud des Alpes. ✉ *10 rue des Alpes, Les Pâquis* ☎ *022/7165630* 🌐 *www.amr-geneve.ch.*

Victoria Hall. Geneva's classical concert venue is the 19th-century Victoria Hall, with an imposing stone facade and an interior that uses liberal

There are many antiques shops to browse in Vieille Ville.

amounts of gold leaf. Victoria Hall is home to the venerable Orchestre de la Suisse Romande. ✉ *14 rue du Général-Dufour, Plainpalais* ☎ *022/4183500* 🌐 *www.ville-ge.ch/vh*.

THEATER

FAMILY **Am Stram Gram.** The creative, colorful French children's theater Am Stram Gram draws inspiration from myths, traditional tales, lyric poetry, and contemporary writing. ✉ *56 rte. de Frontenex, Eaux-Vives* ☎ *022/7357924* 🌐 *www.amstramgram.ch*.

Comédie de Genève. Comédie de Genève stages modern dramas and international classics in French. ✉ *6 bd. des Philosophes, Plainpalais* ☎ *022/3205001* 🌐 *www.comedie.ch*.

Théâtre du Grütli. The experimental Théâtre du Grütli fills its spare, flexible space with contemporary Swiss and foreign plays in French. ✉ *16 rue du Général-Dufour, Plainpalais* ☎ *022/8884488* 🌐 *www.grutli.ch*.

SHOPPING AND SPAS

Most shops are open Monday through Wednesday from 9 to 7, Thursday and Friday until 7:30, and Saturday until 6. Many stores close on Sunday. A word to the wise: myriad variations on this basic picture will continue, including closing over lunch, so if you want to be sure, call ahead.

RIVE DROITE (RIGHT BANK)

CENTRE VILLE RIVE GAUCHE

BOOKS

Payot. The popular chain Payot has an English-language section and English-speaking staff, who help you keep abreast of current trends. ✉ *7 rue de la Confédération, Centre Ville Rive Droite* ☎ *022/3161900* 🌐 *www.payot.ch.*

LES PÂQUIS

SPAS

Le Spa at Le Richemond. Tucked away on the lower level of this grande dame, this cozy spa radiates calm with soft lighting, soothing music, and golden-hued mosaics. In a relatively small space, the spa includes a sauna, fitness center, five treatment rooms, and a Turkish-style hammam. The individually tailored treatments—which include massages, facials, and beauty treatments—include Eastern rituals. ✉ *Le Richemond, Jardin Brunswick, Les Pâquis* ☎ *022/7157000* 🌐 *www.lerichemond.ch.*

RIVE GAUCHE (LEFT BANK)

CENTRE VILLE RIVE DROITE

CHOCOLATE

Auer. Local cobblestones inspired Henri Auer's *pavés glacés,* creamy bite-size delicacies that have become Genevois classics. His descendants at Auer maintain the tradition. ✉ *4 rue de Rive, Centre Ville Rive Droite* ☎ *022/3114286* 🌐 *www.chocolat-auer.ch.*

Du Rhône. This shop has sold chocolate since 1875 when (it's said) even passing coach horses stopped and wouldn't budge until someone gave them a praline. ✉ *3 rue de la Confédération, Centre Ville Rive Droite* ☎ *022/3115614* 🌐 *www.du-rhone.ch.*

Rohr. Even though this kitchen models its smooth, rich signature truffles after old Geneva garbage cans, don't be fooled: Rohr stocks the best chocolate in town. Another location is at 4 rue de l'Enfer in Centre Ville Rive Gauche. ✉ *3 pl. du Molard, Centre Ville Rive Droite* ☎ *022/3116303* 🌐 *www.rohr.ch.*

DEPARTMENT STORES

Bongénie. This boutique has floor after floor filled with designer clothing and high-end cosmetics. ✉ *34 rue du Marché, Centre Ville Rive Droite* ☎ *022/8181111* 🌐 *www.bongenie-grieder.ch.*

Globus. This department store excels at home accessories, kitchen utensils, and men's and women's clothing. The ground floor Food Hall offers meals, light snacks, and gourmet groceries throughout the day. ✉ *48 rue du Rhône, Centre Ville Rive Droite* ☎ *022/3195050* 🌐 *www.globus.ch.*

JEWELRY

Bucherer. Bucherer sells luminous pearls and diamonds of all sizes. It's also the place for prestigious, indestructible Rolex models. Look for another branch at 1 quai du Mont-Blanc in Centre Ville Rive Droite. ✉ *45 rue du Rhône, Centre Ville Rive Droite* ☎ *022/3196266* 🌐 *www.bucherer.com.*

Cartier. This luxury brand famously renders feline grace in diamonds, rubies, and emeralds. ✉ *35 rue du Rhône, Centre Ville Rive Droite* ☎ *022/8185454* 🌐 *www.cartier.com.*

Chopard. This Swiss-based luxury company creates elegant watches, jewelry, cuff links, and more. Another location can be found at 27 rue du Rhône, Centre Ville Rive Gauche. ✉ *8 rue de la Confédération, Centre Ville Rive Droite* ☎ *022/3113728* 🌐 *www.chopard.com.*

Gilbert Albert. After working for Patek Philippe, Geneva-born Gilbert Albert made a name for himself creating jewelry with unusual-for-the-time materials like fossils, feathers, and minerals. Today, nature still inspires the line with stones wrapped in curvaceous, coral-like gold. ✉ *23 quai des Bergues, Centre Ville Rive Droite* ☎ *022/3114833* 🌐 *www.gilbertalbert.com.*

MARKETS

Halle de Rive. Flavorful cheeses, fresh flowers, local wines, and fine Swiss chocolate are among the items on offer all day Monday through Saturday at Halle de Rive. A vibrant seasonal fruit-and-vegetable market fills Boulevard Helvétique on Wednesday and Saturday mornings. ✉ *17 rue Pierre-Fatio/29 bd. Helvétique, Centre Ville Rive Droite* 🌐 *www.halle-de-rive.com.*

Place de la Fusterie. Arts-and-crafts vendors crowd Place de la Fusterie every Thursday. ✉ *Off Rue du Marché, Centre Ville Rive Droite.*

PAPER GOODS

Brachard. This shop has wonderful papers, cards, pens, exquisite notebooks—and don't miss Brachard Contemporary across the street to the right, up the stairs at No. 7, then upstairs again in the passageway. ✉ *10 rue de la Corraterie, Centre Ville Rive Droite* ☎ *022/8170555* 🌐 *www.brachard.ch.*

WATCHES

Franck Muller. This shop, one of many outlets in Geneva, creates complicated modern timepieces. ✉ *1 rue de la Tour-de-l'Ile, Centre Ville Rive Droite* ☎ *022/8180030* 🌐 *www.franckmuller.com.*

Patek Philippe. A bit of history: Patek Philippe occupies the 1839 building where Antoine Norbert de Patek invented the winding mechanism inside all watches. ✉ *41 rue du Rhône, Centre Ville Rive Droite* ☎ *022/8095050* 🌐 *www.patek.com.*

Piaget. This retailer wraps its ultraflat tourbillion watches in sleek white gold. ✉ *40 rue du Rhône, Centre Ville Rive Droite* ☎ *022/8170200* 🌐 *www.piaget.com.*

Vacheron Constantin. The oldest watch company in Geneva, Vacheron Constantin sold its first design in 1755. ✉ *1 pl. Longemalle, Centre Ville Rive Droite* ☎ *022/3161740* 🌐 *www.vacheron-constantin.com.*

VIEILLE VILLE

ANTIQUES

Galerie Grand-Rue. Galerie Grand-Rue deals in largely 19th-century oils and works on paper, including original prints of Geneva and elsewhere. ✉ *25 Grand-Rue, Vieille Ville* ☎ *022/3117685* 🌐 *www.galerie-grand-rue.ch.*

Il Librairie. Head to Il Librairie for leather-bound and gilt first editions. Most are not in English. ✉ *20 Grand-Rue, Vieille Ville* ☎ *022/3102050* 🌐 *http://illibrairie.ch/.*

Regency House. Well-polished English furniture fills the Regency House. ✉ *3 rue de l'Hôtel-de-Ville, Vieille Ville* ☎ *022/3103540* 🌐 *www.regencyhouse.ch.*

BOOKS

Librairie Bernard Letu. An inspired range of multilingual art and photography titles fills Librairie Bernard Letu. ✉ *2 rue Jean-Calvin, Vieille Ville* ☎ *022/3104757* 🌐 *www.letubooks.com.*

CHOCOLATE

Arn. Silky, handmade white-chocolate truffles top the selection at Arn. ✉ *12 pl. du Bourg-de-Four, Vieille Ville* ☎ *022/3104094* 🌐 *www.swiss-chocolates.ch.*

GIFTS AND SOUVENIRS

Mercerie Catherine B. This boutique sells Swiss-themed samplers—hearts, flowers, chalets, cows—already framed or ready for you to embroider yourself. ✉ *17 rue de la Cité, Vieille Ville* ☎ *022/3107779* 🌐 *www.merceriecatherineb.com.*

PLAINPALAIS

MARKETS

Plaine de Plainpalais. Flea market stalls move into position around the Plaine de Plainpalais on Wednesday and Saturday, replacing the Tuesday, Friday, and Sunday morning fruit-and-vegetable stands. ✉ *Plainpalais.*

GREATER GENEVA

GIFTS AND SOUVENIRS

Epsetera. Crafts, including carved wooden toys, make Epsetera fun for all ages. There's also a downtown location at 64–66 rue du Grande-Pre (☎ *022/92900299*). ✉ *29 rue St-Joseph, Carouge* ☎ *022/9490263* 🌐 *www.epsetera.ch.*

SPAS

La Réserve Spa. On the shores of Lac Léman, this spa includes more than 21,000 square feet of creamy white fabrics and dark, rich wood. Inside are 17 treatment rooms, sauna and steam rooms, a health-conscious café, and a large fitness center with tennis courts and an indoor pool. Guests are pampered by therapists who offer a mix of traditional offerings, like body wraps, and innovative options that include lymph-draining techniques. The spa also offers a full menu of fitness classes. ✉ *La Réserve, 301 rte. de Lausanne, Bellevue* 🌐 *www.lareserve.ch.*

TRAVEL SMART SWITZERLAND

GETTING HERE AND AROUND

Switzerland offers perhaps the best transit network in Europe: impeccable expressways studded with emergency phones; trams and buses winding through city streets; steamers crisscrossing crystal clear lakes; and the famous trains, whose wheels roll to a stop under the station clock just as the second hand sweeps to 12.

Once you're at the station, a web of transportation options gets you even closer to those spectacular views: cogwheel trains grind up 45-degree slopes, lifts and gondolas sail silently to majestic vantage points, tiny Alpine "metros" (called funiculars) bore through granite up to green tundra above 8,000 feet.

Traveling by car is the surest way to penetrate every nook and cranny of the Swiss landscape, but if you invest in a rail pass, you will not feel cut off. Most Swiss trains intersect with private excursion networks and allow for comfortable sightseeing itineraries without huge layovers. And there's always a sturdy yellow postbus, following its appointed rounds at minimal cost; connections to obscure villages and trails are free to holders of the Swiss Travel Pass, and accessible by public transport.

AIR TRAVEL

The entire country of Switzerland is smaller in area than the state of West Virginia, so flying from one region to another is a luxury that, considering how efficient the trains are, few travelers require—unless there's a convenient connection from your intercontinental arrival point (Geneva, Zürich) to a smaller airport (Basel, Bern, Lugano, and Sion).

In Switzerland you will not usually need to check in more than an hour before boarding. Be sure to check your airline's limit on checked and carry-on luggage; most airlines accept one carry-on item, although Swiss and other national carriers will turn a blind eye to two.

For 22 SF per bag, passengers on Swiss and partner airlines who fly into Zürich or Geneva airports with tickets on Swiss Federal Railways can forward their luggage to their final destination, allowing them to travel unencumbered. For the return trip, baggage check-in and airline boarding passes can be arranged at more than 30 train stations around Switzerland, but this can only be done less than 36 hours in advance; Swiss passengers can collect their luggage at their final destination airport, and passengers on other airlines can pick it up from the SBB (Swiss Federal Railways) counter at the Zürich or Geneva airports.

Flying time to Geneva or Zürich is about 1 hour from London, 8 hours from New York, 9 hours from Chicago, 11 hours from Los Angeles, 11 hours from San Francisco, and 23 to 25 hours from Sydney.

AIRPORTS

The major gateways into the country are the Zürich Airport (ZRH) and Geneva's Cointrin Airport (GVA). Most Swiss flights will fly via Zürich Airport, the airline's hub. Be sure to allow yourself at least an hour to transfer to your connecting flight. The EuroAirport on the outskirts of Basel is used by many airlines as a stopover and has low-cost flights to numerous destinations across Europe. Its proximity to Zürich makes it very convenient.

Contacts EuroAirport Basel Mulhouse Freiburg (*BSL/MLH/EAP*). ☎ *03/89903111* 🌐 *www.euroairport.com*. **Genève Aéroport** (*GVA*). ☎ *022/7177105* 🌐 *www.gva.ch*. **Zürich Airport** (*ZRH*). ☎ *043/8162211* 🌐 *www.zurich-airport.com*.

FLIGHTS

Swiss flies from Boston, Chicago, Los Angeles, San Francisco, Miami, Montréal, and New York–JFK to Zürich, as well as from New York and Montréal to Geneva. United flies from New York–JFK, Newark, and Washington–Dulles to Geneva and from Washington–Dulles, Miami, Chicago, Houston, Newark, Boston, San Francisco, and Los Angeles to Zürich. American Airlines connects Philadelphia with Zürich, and Delta flies from New York–JFK to Zürich.

British Airways flies from London to Geneva and Zürich, and KLM flies from Amsterdam to the two Swiss cities. Other options to Geneva include easyJet (from London and many European cities), Adria Airways Switzerland (from Lugano, Rome, Dusseldorf, and other European cities), flybe (from locations throughout the United Kingdom), and Vueling (from Barcelona, Rome, and Gran Canaria). If you're headed to Zürich, then easyJet (from London Gatwick and Luton, Amsterdam, Berlin, Lisbon, Nice, Venice, and others) and Vueling (from Rome, Barcelona Alicante, Lisbon, Prague, and more) are the main low-cost carriers. Finally, easyJet also flies from Basel's EuroAirport to nearly 60 European destinations.

Contacts **American Airlines.** ☎ *800/4337300 in U.S., 0848/289–289 in Switzerland* 🌐 *www.aa.com.* **British Airways.** ☎ *0844/493–0787 in U.K., 044/8009222 in Switzerland* 🌐 *www.britishairways.com.* **Delta Airlines.** ☎ *800/221–1212 for U.S. reservations, 800/241–4141 for international reservations, 0848/000872 in Switzerland* 🌐 *www.delta.com.* **easyJet.** ☎ *0848/282828 in Switzerland, 0330/3655000 in U.K.* 🌐 *www.easyjet.com.* **flybe.** ☎ *0371/7002000 in U.K., 0207/3080812 international* 🌐 *www.flybe.com.* **KLM.** ☎ *020/4747747 in the Netherlands, 0848/874444 in Switzerland* 🌐 *www.klm.com.* **Swiss.** ☎ *877/359–7947 in U.S., 0848/700700 in Switzerland* 🌐 *www.swiss.com.* **United Airlines.** ☎ *800/864–8331 for U.S. reservations, 022/4177280 in Switzerland (English)* 🌐 *www.united.com.* **Vueling.** ☎ *0900/000370 in Switzerland (1.50 SF per min), 093/1221291 international ticket sales, 093/1518158 international customer service* 🌐 *www.vueling.com.*

BOAT TRAVEL

All of Switzerland's larger lakes are crisscrossed by elegant steamers, some of them restored paddle steamers. Their café-restaurants serve drinks, snacks, and hot food at standard mealtimes; toilet facilities are provided. Service continues year-round but is greatly reduced in winter. Unlimited travel is free to holders of the Swiss Travel Pass. The Swiss Travel Pass Flex may also be used for boat travel. For some travel such as night or themed cruises, you may have to pay a fee even with the Swiss Travel Pass.

Tickets can be purchased at ticket booths near the docks before departure; tickets for some shorter boat rides are also sold at a counter on board before departure. Tourism offices usually have the latest schedules, though it may be better to check with the boat companies. Credit cards are generally accepted, as are Swiss francs and euros.

The Compagnie Générale de Navigation offers excursion boat rides on Lac Léman (Lake Geneva), which range in price depending on the distance covered and the type of excursion. Numerous options are available on Lake Luzern, including with Schifffahrtsgesellschaft des Vierwaldstättersees. In Ticino, the Navigazione Lago di Lugano and Navigazione Lago Maggiore-Bacino Svizzero run frequent daily boat trips. In Zürich, boat rides of 1½ to 7 hours are available in summer with Zürichsee Schifffahrtsgesellschaft. In winter, the number of boat rides dwindles.

Contacts **Compagnie Générale de Navigation.** ✉ *17 av. de Rhodanie, Lausanne* ☎ *0900/929929* 🌐 *www.cgn.ch.* **Navigazione Del Lago di Lugano.** ✉ *Viale Castagnola 12, Lugano* ☎ *091/2221111* 🌐 *www.lakelugano.ch.* **Navigazione Lago Maggiore.** ✉ *P. le Baracca 1, Arona* ☎ *0322/233200, 0848/091091*

Lago Maggiore Tourist Office 🌐 *www.navigazionelaghi.it.* **Schifffahrtsgesellschaft des Vierwaldstättersees.** ✉ *Werftestr. 5, Luzern* ☎ *041/3676767* 🌐 *www.lakelucerne.ch.* **Zürichsee Schifffahrtsgesellschaft.** ✉ *Mythenquai 333, Zürich* ☎ *044/4871333, 0848/988988 Zürich transport information (SF.80 per minute)* 🌐 *www.zsg.ch.*

BUS TRAVEL

Switzerland's famous yellow postbuses (called *Postautos, cars postaux, autopostali*), with their loud tritone horns, link main cities with villages off the beaten track and even crawl over the highest mountain passes. Both postbuses and city buses follow posted schedules to the minute: you can set your watch by them. For schedules, check the Swiss PostBus website or the Swiss train web site (🌐 *www.sbb.ch*). Watch for the yellow sign with a picture of the distinctive curly horn. Postbuses are handy for hikers: walking itineraries are available at some postbus stops. The Swiss Travel Pass includes unlimited travel on postbuses. However, be sure to ask whether reservations are required, as is the case for some Alpine pass routes.

There's also a special scenic postbus route, the Palm Express. This route goes from St. Moritz to Lugano via the Maloja Pass with a stop in Italy. The buses run daily from mid-June through mid-October and from late December through the first week of January. From the second week of January to the first week of June and from late October to mid-December, the Palm Express schedule is curtailed and the buses run only from Friday to Sunday. Reservations are obligatory and must be made by 8:30 am on the day of departure. They can be made online, as well as at any train station or tourist office.

Contacts PostBus. ☎ *0848/888888* 🌐 *postauto.ch.*

CAR TRAVEL

GASOLINE

If there's one thing that's generally cheaper in Switzerland than elsewhere in western Europe, it's gasoline. If you are crossing borders, try to fill the tank in Switzerland, because both regular and diesel gasoline are cheaper than in neighboring countries. Prices are slightly higher in mountain areas. Be sure to have some 10 SF and 20 SF notes available, because many gas stations (especially in the mountains) have vending-machine pumps that operate even when the station is closed. Simply slide in a bill and fill your tank. Many of these machines also accept major credit cards. You can request a receipt (*Quittung* in German, *quittance* in French, *ricevuta* in Italian) from the machine.

PARKING

Parking areas are clearly marked. In blue or red zones a *Parkenscheibe, disque de stationnement*, or *disco orario* (provided in rental cars or available free from banks, tourist offices, or police stations) must be placed clearly in the front window noting the time of arrival. These zones are slowly being replaced by metered-parking white zones. Each city sets its own time allotments for parking; the limits are posted. Metered parking is often paid for at communal machines that vary from city to city. Some machines simply accept coins and dispense tickets. At others you'll need to punch in your parking space or license plate number, then add coins. The ticket for parking may or may not have to be placed in your car window; this information is noted on the machine or ticket. The price of parking in public lots varies by location, with cities charging more than small towns.

ROAD CONDITIONS

Road signs throughout the country use a color-coded system, with the official route numbers in white against a colored background. Expressway signs are green, and other major roads have signs in blue (unlike in the rest of Europe, where the colors are reversed). Signs for smaller roads are white with black lettering. All signage indicates the names of upcoming towns as well, and it is generally easiest to use these names for navigating.

Swiss roads are well surfaced, but when you are dealing with mountains, they do wind a lot, so don't plan on achieving high average speeds. When estimating likely travel times, look carefully at the map: there may be only 32 km (20 miles) between one point and another—but the road may cross an Alpine pass. There is a well-developed expressway network, though some notable gaps still exist in the south along an east–west line, roughly between Lugano and Sion. In addition, tunnels—notably the St. Gotthard—are closed at times for repairs or weather conditions, or they become bottlenecks in heavy traffic, especially over holiday weekends. A combination of steep or winding routes and hazardous weather means some roads will be closed in winter. Signs are posted at the beginning of the climb.

To find out about road conditions, traffic jams, itineraries, and so forth, and for breakdown services, dues-paying members can turn to two places: the Swiss Automobile Club or the Touring Club of Switzerland. For frequent and precise information in Swiss languages, you can dial 163, or tune in to local radio stations.

Contacts Swiss Automobile Club. ☎ *031/3283111* 🌐 *www.acs.ch.* **Touring Club of Switzerland.** ☎ *0844/888111* 🌐 *www.tcs.ch.*

ROADSIDE EMERGENCIES

All road breakdowns should be called in to the countrywide emergency numbers, 117 (for the police and roadside assistance), or 144 (for accidents and ambulance assistance). If you are on an expressway, pull over to the shoulder and look for arrows pointing you to the nearest orange radiotelephone, called *bornes SOS*; use these phones instead of a mobile phone because they allow police to find you instantly and send help. There are SOS phones every kilometer (roughly every ½ mile), on alternating sides of the expressway.

RULES OF THE ROAD

As in most of Europe, driving is on the right. Vehicles on main roads have priority over those on smaller roads. At intersections, priority is given to the driver on the right except when driving on a road with right-of-way and when merging into traffic circles, where priority is given to the drivers coming from the left (i.e., those already in the traffic circle). In some residential areas—notably Geneva—traffic coming from the right has the right-of-way.

In urban areas the speed limit is 50 kph (30 mph); on major roads it's 80 kph (50 mph), and on expressways, the limit ranges from 100 kph (60 mph) to 120 kph (75 mph). On expressways the left lane is only for passing other cars; you must merge right as soon as possible, and passing on the right is a no-go. It is illegal to make a right-hand turn on a red light. The blood-alcohol limit is 0.05.

Despite its laid-back image, Switzerland suffers from aggressive driving. Tailgating, though illegal, is a common problem, as is speeding. If you are being tailgated on the expressway, just move into the right lane and ignore any high-beam flashing and visible signs of road rage behind you. If you are driving extra slowly, let the people behind you pass.

Headlights are compulsory and should be switched on at all times. Always carry your valid license and car-registration papers; there are occasional roadblocks to check them. Wear seat belts in the front and back seats—they are mandatory.

To use the expressways, you must display a sticker, or *vignette,* on the top center or lower corner of the windshield. You can buy one at the border or in post offices, gas stations, and garages. A vignette costs 40 SF, or €34, and is valid for a year. Driving without a vignette puts you at risk for getting a 200 SF fine. Cars rented within Switzerland already have these stickers; if you rent a car elsewhere in Europe, ask if the rental company will provide the vignette for you.

Traffic going up a mountain has priority, except for postbuses coming down, in which case the ascending traffic must make way for the buses. A sign with a yellow post horn on a blue background means that postbuses have priority. On winding mountain roads, a brief honk as you approach a curve is a good way of warning any oncoming traffic. In winter it's mandatory in Switzerland to have snow chains in the trunk; snow tires are recommended but not required. Snow-chain service stations have signs marked *service de chaînes à neige* or *schneekettendienst,* meaning that snow chains are available for rent.

TIP→ Switzerland is exceedingly pedestrian-friendly, so whether you are walking or behind the wheel, be on the lookout for crosswalks. Cars must stop for people waiting to cross, and it is common for someone to walk right out in front of you. Caution should be your modus operandi when driving through towns.

CAR RENTAL

Car rental rates in Zürich and Geneva begin around $65 to $100 a day for an economy car with air-conditioning, a manual transmission, and unlimited mileage. Some, but not all, prices include the 8% tax on car rentals. Although you can usually rent a car upon arrival, significant savings can be made by booking in advance through a third-party wholesale website. European companies like Europcar and Sixt often have better deals.

Your driver's license is acceptable in Switzerland, but an International Driving Permit (IDP)—available from the American and Canadian automobile associations and, in the United Kingdom, from the Automobile Association and Royal Automobile Club—is a good idea. An official translation of your license done in 10 languages, it can help local law enforcement understand the terms of your license (IDPs are valid only in conjunction with a valid license). The minimum age to rent a car is generally 18. Note that some agencies do not allow you to drive cars into Italy. In Switzerland some rental agencies charge daily fees of about 25 SF for drivers under 25. If you wish to pay cash, agencies will request a deposit.

TIP→ All children under the age of 12 who are less than 59 inches tall must be fastened in an infant car seat, child seat, or booster seat while riding in a motor vehicle. If you are traveling with children and renting a car, be sure to ask the rental car company for the appropriate seats in advance, or plan on taking trains and buses instead. (There are no exemptions to this rule for taxis, and finding a taxi willing to provide the seats is nearly impossible.)

CAR RENTAL RESOURCES

Major Agencies Alamo. ☎ *0800/000675* 🌐 *www.alamo.ch.* **Avis.** ☎ *0848/811818* 🌐 *www.avis.ch.* **Budget.** ☎ *800/472–3325 outside U.S., 800/218–7992 U.S. reservations* 🌐 *www.budget.com.* **Enterprise.** ☎ *0848/445522* 🌐 *www.enterprise.ch.* **Europcar.** ☎ *044/8044646, 0848/808099 international reservations* 🌐 *www.europcar.ch.* **Hertz.** ☎ *0848/822020* 🌐 *www.hertz.ch.* **National Car Rental.** ☎ *844/382–6875 U.S. reservations, 844/393–9989 customer service* 🌐 *www.nationalcar.com.* **Sixt.** ☎ *0848/884444* 🌐 *www.sixt.ch.*

Wholesalers Auto Europe. ☎ *888/223–5555* 🌐 *www.autoeurope.com.* **Kemwel.** ☎ *877/820–0668* 🌐 *www.kemwel.com.*

TRAIN TRAVEL

The Swiss Federal Railways, or SBB/CFF/FFS, boasts one of the world's densest transportation networks. Trains and stations are clean and, as you'd expect, service is extremely prompt. Trains described as Inter-City or Express are the fastest, stopping only in main towns. *Regionalzug, train régional,* and *treno regionale* mean "local train" and make frequent stops.

In addition to the federal rail lines there are some private rail lines, such as the GoldenPass and the Rhätische Bahn.

Most private lines are integrated into the main network and generally accept discount rail passes or offer other reductions on the price.

If you're planning to use trains extensively, you can download the official timetable (*Kursbuch*, *horaire*, or *orario*) at 🌐 *www.fahrplanfelder.ch*. The comprehensive Swiss Federal Railways website and mobile app allow you to work out itineraries, including suburban trains, trams, and buses, and buy tickets online.

■ TIP→ Tickets aren't available on board any trains, so make sure to buy them in advance. Fines for riding without a valid ticket are a painful 90 SF.

TRAIN TIPS

If you are eager to read or get some work done on the train, look for the quiet zone compartments, available on a number of routes in Switzerland. Travelers are asked not to use cell phones, listen to music, or engage in loud conversation. Most InterCity and Express trains feature power outlets in both first- and second-class cars. If you need Internet access, you will need a hot spot, as Swiss trains generally do not have Wi-Fi on board. Swisscom does offer Wi-Fi hot spots at 80 stations.

If you happen to suffer from motion sickness, note that the Swiss ICN trains—and the German ICE, the French TGV, and the Italian Trenitalia—all use "tilt technology" for a less jerky ride. One side effect, however, is that some passengers might get "seasick," especially if the track is curvy (as it is between Biel/Bienne and Geneva). An over-the-counter drug for motion sickness should help. Also, close the shades and avoid looking out the window.

Consider a first-class ticket only if the extra comfort is worth the price. The principal difference between first and second class, the only two options, is space: first-class cars are less crowded. Seat size is also larger, upholstery fancier, and you usually will be delivered to the track position closest to the station.

RAIL PASSES

If Switzerland is your only destination in Europe, there are numerous passes available for visitors. The **Swiss Travel Pass** is the best value, offering unlimited travel on Swiss Federal Railways, postbuses, Swiss lake steamers, and the local bus and tram services of 75 cities. It also gives reductions on many privately owned railways, cable cars, and funiculars. And it gives you access to 500 museums in the country.

The card is available from Switzerland Tourism and from travel agents outside Switzerland, including Rail Europe. You can get a card valid for 3 days (216 SF second-class; 344 SF first-class); 4 days (259 SF second-class; 412 SF first-class); 8 days (376 SF second-class; 596 SF first-class); or 15 days (458 SF second-class; 722 SF first-class). There's also the **Swiss Travel Pass Flex,** offering the same for 3, 4, 8, or 15 days in a 30-day period at the user's convenience (248 SF–502 SF second-class; 396 SF–793 SF first-class). With both passes, reservation fees may be applicable on certain routes.

The **Swiss Family Card** is available at no cost to all Swiss Travel Pass and Swiss Travel Pass Flex travelers. With this card, children ages 6 to 15 accompanied by a parent travel for free.

Within some tourist areas, regional holiday passes are available. Their discount offers vary; prices vary widely, too, depending on the region and period of validity. Passes are available from Switzerland Tourism and local tourist boards, as well as the train stations, but to be on the safe side, inquire well in advance.

Switzerland is one of 28 countries in which you can use a **Eurail Global Pass,** which provides unlimited first- or second-class rail travel in all the participating countries. If you plan to rack up the miles, get a standard pass. These are available for 5 days within one month ($391 second-class, $479 first-class), 7 days within one month ($475 second-class, $584 first-class), 10 days within two months ($585 second-class, $719 first-class), 15 days within two months ($766 second-class, $941 first-class), 15 continuous days ($498 second-class, $611 first-class), 22 continuous days ($640 second-class, $786 first-class), one continuous month ($785 second-class, $964 first-class), two continuous months ($1,006 second-class, $1,359 first-class), and three continuous months ($1,362 second-class, $1,675 first-class).

If your plans call for limited train travel, look into a less-expensive **Eurail Select Pass.** You get a set number of travel days during a specified time period. For example, a two-month pass allows between 5 and 10 days of rail travel; costs range between $544 and $790. Keep in mind that the Eurail Select Pass is good only for two, three, or four countries that border each other, depending on which pass you choose.

In addition to standard Eurail Passes, ask about special rail-pass plans. Among these are the Eurail Youth Pass (for those aged 12–27) and the Eurail Saver Passes (which give a 15% discount for two or more people traveling together).

Many travelers assume that rail passes guarantee them a seat. Not so. You should book seats ahead even if you are using a rail pass. Seat reservations are required on some European trains, particularly high-speed trains, and are a good idea during busy seasons and on popular routes. You also will need a reservation if you purchase sleeping accommodations. Whichever pass you choose, remember that you must make your purchase before you leave for Europe. The Swiss Federal Railways has a user-friendly site that lets you check fares and schedules. You can also call its hotline, which has information in English.

Contacts Eurail. 🌐 *www.eurail.com.* **GoldenPass.** ☎ *021/9898190* 🌐 *www.goldenpass.ch.* **Jungfraubahnen.** ☎ *033/8287233* 🌐 *www.jungfrau.ch.* **Matterhorn Gotthard Bahn.** ☎ *0848/642442* 🌐 *www.matterhorngotthardbahn.ch.* **Rail Europe.** ☎ *800/622–8600 in U.S., 800/361–7245 in Canada, 847/916–1028 international* 🌐 *www.raileurope.com.* **Railtour Suisse.** ✉ *Bernstr. 164, Zollikofen* ☎ *031/3780101* 🌐 *www.railtour.ch.* **Rhätische Bahn.** ☎ *081/2886565* 🌐 *www.rhb.ch.* **Swiss Federal Railways.** ☎ *0900/300300 1.19 SF per min* 🌐 *www.sbb.ch.*

CHANNEL TUNNEL

With the Channel Tunnel completing a seamless route, you can leave London around noon on the Eurostar and (thanks to connections via Paris–Lyon on the French *train à grande vitesse,* or TGV) have a late supper in Geneva. Note that the TGV tracks connecting Geneva and Paris are a bit bumpy, which can be unsettling for sensitive passengers.

SCENIC ROUTES

Switzerland makes the most of its Alpine rail engineering, which cuts through the icy granite landscape above 6,560 feet, by offering special trains that cross over spectacular passes with panoramic cars. The most popular sightseeing itineraries take 4 to 11 hours of travel time. For information on these and other scenic routes, contact Swiss Federal Railways or Railtour Suisse, Switzerland's largest train-tour company.

For more information on scenic routes, see the Scenic Journeys feature in Chapter 1.

ESSENTIALS

ACCOMMODATIONS

Switzerland is almost as famous for its hotels as it is for its mountains, watches, and chocolates; its standards in hospitality are extremely high. Rooms are impeccably clean and well maintained, but prices are accordingly steep. Americans accustomed to spacious hotels with two double beds, a big TV, and a bath-shower combination may be disappointed in their first venture into the legendary Swiss hotel's small spaces and limited facilities.

TIP→ Where no address is provided in the hotel listings, none is necessary: in smaller towns and villages, a postal code is all you need. To find the hotel on arrival, watch for the official street signs pointing the way to every hotel that belongs to the local tourist association.

Air-conditioning is not as prevalent as in the United States; evenings are generally cool, so Alpine air often stands in for air-conditioning, but even those hotels that offer it may shut it off after the summer).

Most hotels in Switzerland allow children under a certain age to stay in their parents' room at no extra charge, but others charge for them as extra adults. The Swiss Hotel Association has listings of family-friendly hotels throughout the country.

Particularly in ski resorts or in hotels where you'll be staying for three days or more, you may be quoted a room price per person including demipension (half-board). This means you've opted to have breakfast included and to eat either lunch or (more often) dinner in the hotel, selecting from a limited, fixed menu. Unless you're holding out for a gastronomic adventure, your best (and most economical) bet is to take half-board. Most hotels will be flexible if you come in from the slopes craving a steaming pot of fondue, and they will then subtract the day's pension supplement from your room price, charging you à la carte instead.

BED-AND-BREAKFASTS

You can order brochures and get information about bed-and-breakfasts from the user-friendly website of Bed and Breakfast Switzerland, 🌐 *www.bnb.ch*. You can also make reservations through the site.

HOTELS

When selecting a place to stay, an important resource can be the *hotelleriesuisse*, the Swiss Hotel Association (SHA), a rigorous and demanding organization that maintains a specific rating system for lodging standards. Four out of five Swiss hotels belong to this group and take their stars seriously.

Many hotels close for a short period during their region's off-season (usually during May and November). Closing dates often vary from year to year, so be sure to call ahead and check.

Contact hotelleriesuisse (Swiss Hotel Association). ✉ *Monbijoustr. 130, Bern* ☎ *031/3704111* 🌐 *www.hotelleriesuisse.ch.*

SAVING MONEY

Travelers on a budget can get a helping hand from the Swiss Budget Hotels group; its 90 participating hotels are in the one- to three-star bracket and generally comply with the SHA's quality standards. These comfortable little hotels have banded together to dispel Switzerland's intimidating image as an elite, overpriced vacation spot and offer down-to-earth standards in memorable packages.

Another resource both at home and abroad is 🌐 *Airbnb.com*, which allows locals to open up their private or shared rooms, apartments, and chalets to travelers worldwide. Prices are competitive, and it's a nice way to get a local perspective.

Contacts Swiss Budget Hotels. ☎ *031/3781835* 🌐 *www.rooms.ch.*

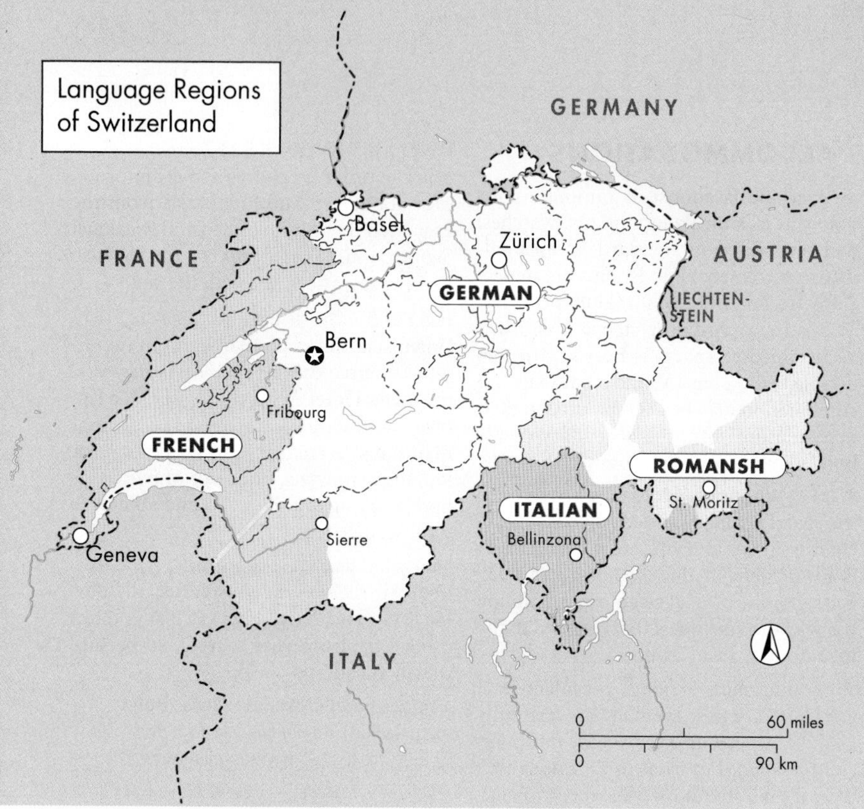

COMMUNICATIONS

INTERNET

Nearly all hotels and some public places have Wi-Fi hot spots. Most hotels and many bars, cafés, and restaurants provide the service for free. A few cities (such as Geneva) provide Wi-Fi service at nearly 650 access points throughout the city at no charge.

The cheapest and easiest way to talk to people internationally is over the Internet, using a service like Skype, FaceTime, Google Hangouts, or WhatsApp.

CELLULAR PHONES

Mobile roaming charges can be steep ($1/minute, $20/MB, and tolls for incoming calls are the norm), so it's a good idea to ask your service provider about any international plans it offers before setting out. Once abroad, it's almost always cheaper to send a text message than to make a call, since texts have a low set fee (often less than 5¢).

If you want to make local calls and your smartphone is already unlocked (or your provider will unlock it), consider buying a Swiss prepaid SIM card, which can be cheaper and easier than using your U.S. card abroad. SIM cards are available in phone stores (Lycamobile, Salt, Swisscom, Sunrise) and supermarkets (Coop, Migros, etc.) in Switzerland, or online (Cellular Abroad, Mobal) before you travel. Purchase requires a passport, and costs start at approximately 20 SF, which usually includes 15 SF of credit/data.

LANDLINES

Calling from a hotel is almost always the most expensive way to keep in touch; hotels usually add huge surcharges to all calls, particularly international ones. In

Switzerland pay phones (increasingly difficult to find, but often available at post offices, train stations, and airports) and calling cards keep costs to a minimum, but only if you purchase the cards locally.

The country code for Switzerland is 41. When dialing a Swiss number from abroad, drop the initial 0 from the local area code.

CALLING WITHIN SWITZERLAND

Dial 1811 for information within Switzerland (1.90 SF for the initial connection and the first minute, and around 0.22 SF thereafter) 24 hours a day. All telephone operators speak English, and instructions are printed in English in all telephone booths. You can also send an SMS to 1811 (1 SF) with last name and place of residence to receive information on phone numbers and addresses.

Dial the local area code (including the 0) when calling any local number.

There's direct dialing to everywhere in Switzerland. Include the area code preceded by 0 when dialing anywhere within Switzerland.

To make a local call on a pay phone, pick up the receiver, insert a phone card, and dial the number. A local call costs 0.60 SF plus 0.10 SF for each additional unit. Toll-free numbers begin with 0800. Swisscom phone cards are available in 5 SF, 10 SF, 20 SF, or 50 SF units; they're sold at post offices, train stations, airports, and kiosks. Slip a card into an adapted public phone, and a continual readout will tell you how much money is left on the card. The cost of the call will be counted against the card, with any remaining value still good for the next time you use it. If you drain the card and still need to talk, the readout will warn you: you can either pop in a new card or make up the difference with coins. Many phone booths now also accept Visa, MasterCard, and American Express cards.

CALLING OUTSIDE SWITZERLAND

The country code is 1 for the United States and Canada, 61 for Australia, 64 for New Zealand, and 44 for the United Kingdom.

You can dial most international numbers direct from Switzerland, adding 00 before the country code. If you want a number that cannot be reached directly, or if you need an international phone number, dial 1811 for a connection. It's cheapest to use the booths in train stations and post offices: calls made from your hotel cost a great deal more.

CALLING CARDS

A variety of international phone cards in denominations of 5 to 50 SF are available in kiosks located in every train station. They often offer the cheapest rates. You can use the code on the card until you run out of units.

■ TIP→ If you travel internationally frequently, save one of your old mobile phones or buy a cheap, unlocked one on the Internet; you can then get various pay-as-you-go SIM cards in each destination.

Contacts Cellular Abroad. ☎ *800/287–5072* 🌐 *www.cellularabroad.com.* **CoopMobile.** ☎ *078/7807820 international, 0800/780782 in Switzerland* 🌐 *www.coopmobile.ch/en.* **Lycamobile.** ☎ *077/9000122* 🌐 *www.lycamobile.ch/en/.* **Migros.** ☎ *062/8394727 international, 0800/151728 in Switzerland* 🌐 *shop.m-budget.migros.ch.* **Mobal.** ☎ *888/888–9162* 🌐 *www.mobal.com.* **Salt.** ☎ *078/7007000 international, 0800/078078 in Switzerland* 🌐 *www.salt.ch/en.* **Sunrise.** ☎ *058/7770101 international, 0800/707505 in Switzerland* 🌐 *www.sunrise.ch.* **Swisscom.** ☎ *062/2861212 international, 0800/800800 in Switzerland* 🌐 *www.swisscom.ch/en/residential.html.*

CUSTOMS AND DUTIES

When entering Switzerland, a visitor who is 17 years or older may bring in a total of 250 units/grams of tobacco products (250 cigarettes or 50 cigars or 250 grams of tobacco); 5 liters of alcohol up to 36 proof (beer, wine, and liqueurs); and 1 liter over 36 proof. Visitors over 17 may bring gifts valued at up to 300 SF duty-free. Medicine, such as insulin, is allowed for personal use only.

Contacts Federal Customs Administration. 🌐 *www.ezv.admin.ch/index.html.*

EATING OUT

Breakfast spreads in Switzerland tend to include coffee and a selection of bread, marmalade, lunch meat, and local cheese. If you prefer a lot of milk in your coffee, ask for a *renversé* in French (literally, *upside-down*) or a *Milchkaffee* in German. The signature *Bircher muesli*—invented by Dr. Maximilian Oskar Bircher-Benner at his diet clinic at the end of the 19th century—is available in most supermarkets (such as Migros and Coop) and can make a hearty breakfast or lunch, especially when served with plain or fruit yogurt instead of milk.

Many restaurants close after lunch (as of 3 pm) and reopen for dinner (about 6 pm). In remote regions it may prove difficult to find kitchens open past 9 or 10 pm, so plan ahead. It's not unusual for restaurants to close on Sunday; those in Ticino may close for the entire month of August, and resort restaurants may close for a month in the late spring and fall. Bars generally close at 1 or 2 am, although clubs continue serving into the wee hours.

Children's menus are available in many restaurants around Switzerland; otherwise, you can usually request a child-size portion and the prices will be adjusted accordingly.

Unless otherwise noted, the restaurants listed in this guide are open daily for lunch and dinner. Restaurant prices in the reviews are the average cost of a main course at dinner or, if dinner is not served, at lunch.

PAYING

Credit cards are widely accepted. Euros are sometimes accepted, though change will come in Swiss francs. Note that service is included unless indicated on the menu. It is customary to leave a small tip in cash (up to 10%, depending on how pleased you are with the service).

WORD OF MOUTH

Before your trip, be sure to check out what other travelers are saying in Talk on 🌐 *www.fodors.com*

RESERVATIONS AND DRESS

Regardless of where you are, it's a good idea to make a reservation if you can. For famed restaurants, book as far ahead as you can (often 30 days), and reconfirm as soon as you arrive. (Large parties should always call ahead to check the reservations policy.)

ELECTRICITY

The electrical current in Switzerland is 220 volts, 50 cycles alternating current (AC); wall outlets take plugs that have two or three round prongs. The two-pronged Continental-type plugs can be used throughout the country.

Consider making a small investment in a universal adapter, which has several types of plugs in one lightweight, compact unit. Most laptops and mobile-phone chargers are dual voltage (i.e., they operate equally well on 110 and 220 volts) so require only an adapter. These days the same is true of small appliances such as hair dryers. Always check labels and manufacturer instructions to be sure. Don't use 110-volt outlets marked "for shavers only" for high-wattage appliances such as hair dryers.

EMERGENCIES

U.S. Embassies and Consulates American Embassy. ✉ *Sulgeneckstr. 19, Bern* ☎ *031/3577011, 031/3577777 24-hour emergency hotline* 🌐 *ch.usembassy.gov.* **U.S. Consular Agency Geneva.** ✉ *7 rue Versonnex, Geneva* ☎ *022/8405160.* **U.S. Consular Agency Zürich.** ✉ *Dufourstr. 101, Zürich* ☎ *043/4992960.*

HEALTH

When hiking or skiing in the mountains, be aware of the dangers of altitude sickness: numbness, tingling, nausea, drowsiness, headaches, and vision problems. If you experience discomfort, return to a lower altitude as soon as possible. It's a good idea to limit strenuous activity on the first day at extra-high-altitude resorts and to drink plenty of water. Adults with heart problems may want to avoid all excursions above 6,500 feet. If you're traveling with a child under two years old, you may be advised by locals not to carry him or her on excursions above 6,500 feet; check with your pediatrician before leaving home.

Travelers should also be mindful of other afflictions such as heatstroke, dehydration, sunstroke, frostbite, and snow blindness. To avoid snow blindness, wear sunglasses with side shields or goggles, especially if you have light-colored eyes. You should wear sunscreen all through the year; many different brands are available at ski shops near the slopes. In rural areas, take precautions against ticks, especially in spring and summer.

OVER-THE-COUNTER REMEDIES

Basic over-the-counter medicines are available from pharmacies (*pharmacie, Apotheke, farmacia*), which are recognizable thanks to signs with green crosses.

HOURS OF OPERATION

Most businesses still close for lunch in Switzerland, generally from noon or 12:30 to 1:30 or 2, but this is changing, especially in larger cities and in the German-speaking part of the country. All remain closed on Sunday. Banks are open weekdays from 8:30 to 4:30 or 5, and always close during lunch. Post offices generally are open limited hours on Saturday.

Gas station kiosks are usually open daily from 6:30 am until 9 pm. Automatic pumps, which accept major credit cards and Swiss bank notes, are in service 24 hours a day.

Museums generally close on Monday. There is, however, an increasing trend toward staying open late one night a week, usually on Thursday or Friday evening.

Pharmacies generally are open weekdays from 9 to 1 and 2 to 6, and Saturday 9 to 1. In cities, they tend to stay open through the lunch hour. To find out which pharmacy is covering the late-night shift, check listings posted near or on the front window.

Shops are generally open every day except Sunday. They usually close early (4 or 5 pm) on Saturday, except in larger cities, where they stay open until 6 on Saturday and often stay open until 8 or 9 at least one day a week. Smaller stores close for an hour or two for lunch. Stores in train stations in larger cities often open daily until 9 pm, even on Sunday; in the Geneva and Zürich airports, shops are open on Sunday.

HOLIDAYS

National holidays include New Year's Day, Good Friday (March or April), Easter Sunday and Monday (March or April), Ascension Day (May), Whitsunday and Whitmonday (May), Swiss National Holiday (August 1), and Christmas and Boxing Day (December 25–26). Labor Day (May 1) is also celebrated in some regions.

MAIL

Mail rates are divided into first-class "A" (airmail) and second-class "B" (surface). Letters and postcards to North America weighing up to 20 grams (about.70 ounce) cost 2 SF and 1.70 SF. It generally takes 3 to 7 business days to reach the United States when mailed first class and 7 to 15 in second class.

Postal codes precede the names of cities and towns in Swiss addresses.

SHIPPING PACKAGES

FedEx and UPS operate out of Basel, Bern, Geneva, Lugano, and Zürich, although overnight service is guaranteed only to selected European destinations. An envelope weighing up to 1.1 pounds will cost about 193 SF to the United States and Canada. Packages can also be sent through the Swiss Post; however, due to the high cost of any mailing, it could be more economical simply to check a second bag on your trip home.

MONEY

Switzerland remains one of the most expensive countries on the Continent for travelers, and you may find yourself shocked by the price of a light lunch or a generic hotel room. A cup of coffee or a small beer costs about 5 SF in a simple restaurant; ordinary wines, sold by the deciliter ("déci"), a small pour of roughly 3.5 ounces, start at about 8 SF. These prices almost double in resorts, city hotels, and fine restaurants. A plain, one-plate daily lunch special averages 18 SF to 25 SF. A city bus ride costs between 3 SF and 4 SF, a short cab ride 18 SF.

Prices here are given for adults. Substantially reduced fees are almost always available for children, students, and senior citizens.

ATMS AND BANKS

ATMs are common and are always the best way to get local currency, even if your bank charges you a fee.

CREDIT CARDS

Credit cards are best for large purchases, but check with your bank for any foreign transaction fees. We strongly advise against using a debit card to make purchases abroad. If your card is compromised, the money in your bank account may disappear, at least temporarily, unlike with a credit card, where you can dispute a specious charge before having to pay your bill.

TIP→ Before you charge something, ask the merchant whether or not he or she plans to do a dynamic currency conversion (DCC). In such a transaction the credit-card processor (shop, restaurant, or hotel, not Visa or MasterCard) converts the currency and charges you in dollars. In most cases you'll pay the merchant a 3% fee for this service in addition to any credit-card company and issuing-bank foreign-transaction surcharges.

Dynamic currency conversion (DCC) programs are becoming increasingly widespread. You should always have the option to be charged in local currency.

Reporting Lost Cards American Express. *800/528–4800 in U.S., 336/3931111 collect from abroad www.americanexpress.com.* **Diners Club.** *800/234–6377 in U.S., 514/8771577 collect from abroad www.dinersclub.com.* **MasterCard.** *800/627–8372 in U.S., 636/7227111 collect from abroad www.mastercard.com.* **Visa.** *800/847–2911 in U.S., 303/9671096 collect from abroad www.visa.com.*

CURRENCY AND EXCHANGE

The unit of currency in Switzerland is the Swiss franc (SF), available in notes of 10, 20, 50, 100, 200, and 1,000 (the currency symbol for the franc is CHF). Francs are divided into *centimes* (in Suisse Romande) or *Rappen* (in German Switzerland). There are coins for 5, 10, 20, and 50 centimes. Larger coins are the 1-, 2-, and 5-franc pieces.

At this writing, 1 Swiss franc equals 0.99 U.S. dollars, 1.28 Canadian dollars, and 0.77 pounds sterling. Keep in mind that more than 300 train stations have currency exchange offices that are open daily, including lunch hours, when most banks are closed. These booths swap currency and buy and sell traveler's checks in various currencies.

TIP→ Even if a currency-exchange booth has a sign promising no commission, rest assured that there's some kind of huge, hidden fee. (Oh, that's right. The sign didn't say no fee.) And as for rates, you're almost always better off getting foreign currency at an ATM or exchanging money at a bank.

Contact XE.com. *www.xe.com.*

PACKING

In most of Switzerland, dress is casual. City dress is more formal. Men would be wise to pack a jacket and tie if dining in any of the expensive restaurants reviewed in this book, even in mountain resorts; otherwise, a button-up shirt or elegant sweater are standard at night. Also keep in mind that sneakers or jeans won't cut it for most upscale restaurants or clubs, even when paired with a good shirt. Women wear skirts more frequently in Switzerland than in the United States, though anything fashionable is fine. Except at the chicest hotels in international resorts, you won't need formal evening dress.

PASSPORTS

Australian, British, Canadian, New Zealand, and U.S. citizens need only a valid passport to enter Switzerland for stays of up to 90 days.

TAXES

What you see is what you pay in Switzerland: restaurant checks and hotel bills include all taxes.

If your purchases in a single shop total 300 SF and the goods are exported within 30 days of the purchase date, you may reclaim the V.A.T. (8% in Switzerland). This tax is included in the sales price of most items.

When making a purchase, ask for a V.A.T. refund form and find out whether the merchant gives refunds—not all stores do. Have the form stamped like any customs form by customs officials when you leave the country or, if you're visiting several European Union countries, when you leave the EU. After you're through passport control, take the form to a refund-service counter for an on-the-spot refund (which is usually the quickest and easiest option), or mail it to the address on the form after you arrive home. You receive the total refund stated on the form, but the processing time can be long, especially if you request a credit card adjustment.

Global Blue is a worldwide service with more than 300,000 affiliated stores and more than 250 refund counters at major airports and border crossings. Its refund form, called a Tax Free Form, is the most common across the European continent. The service issues refunds in the form of cash, credit card adjustment, money transfer, or bank check.

V.A.T. Refunds Global Blue. ☎ *866/706–6090 in U.S., 0800/3211111 in Switzerland* 🌐 *www.globalblue.com.*

TIME

Situated in the same time zone as Paris (GMT+1), Switzerland is one hour ahead of London, six hours ahead of New York, nine hours ahead of Los Angeles, and nine hours behind Sydney. Daylight saving time starts one to three weeks earlier in the United States, so during that period the time difference is one hour less.

Time Zones Timeanddate.com. 🌐 *www.timeanddate.com/worldclock.*

TIPPING

Despite all protests to the contrary and menus marked *service compris,* the Swiss *do* tip at restaurants, but it's not done as a percentage. Instead, they give quantities anywhere from the change from the nearest franc to 10 SF or more for a world-class meal that has been exquisitely served.

If, in a café, the server settles the bill at the table, fishing the change from her leather purse, give her the change on the spot—or calculate the total, including tip, and tell her the full sum before she counts it onto the tabletop. If you need to take more time to calculate, leave it on the table, though this isn't common practice in outdoor cafés. If you're paying for a meal with a credit card, try to tip with cash instead of filling in the tip slot on the slip:

not all managers are good about doling out the servers' tips in cash. Bartenders are also tipped along these lines.

Tipping porters and doormen is easier: 2 SF per bag is adequate in good hotels, 1 SF per trip in humbler lodgings (unless you travel heavy). To tip other hotel personnel, you can leave an appropriate amount with the concierge or, for cleaning staff, with a note of thanks in your room. Porter service fees at Geneva and Zürich airports depend on the distance covered and number of bags, but average out at around 5 SF per bag. Tip taxi drivers the change or an extra couple of francs, depending on the length of the drive and whether they've helped with your bags.

TRIP INSURANCE

Comprehensive trip insurance is valuable if you're booking a very expensive or complicated trip (particularly to an isolated region), or if you're booking far in advance. Comprehensive policies typically cover trip cancellation and interruption, letting you cancel or cut your trip short because of illness, or, in some cases, acts of terrorism in your destination. Such policies might also cover evacuation and medical care. (For trips abroad you should have medical coverage at the very least.) Some policies also cover you for trip delays because of bad weather or mechanical problems, as well as for lost or delayed luggage.

Another type of coverage to consider is financial default—that is, when your trip is disrupted because a tour operator, airline, or cruise line goes out of business. Generally you must buy this when you book your trip or shortly thereafter, and it's available to you only if your operator isn't on a list of excluded companies.

Always read the fine print of your policy to make sure that you're covered for the risks that most concern you. Compare several policies to be sure you're getting the best price and range of coverage available.

Insurance Comparison Info Insure My Trip. ☎ *800/487–4722* 🌐 *www.insuremytrip.com.* **Square Mouth.** ☎ *800/240–0369* 🌐 *www.squaremouth.com.*

Comprehensive Insurers Allianz. ☎ *866/884–3556* 🌐 *www.allianztravelinsurance.com.* **Generali Global Assistance.** ☎ *800/874–2442* 🌐 *www.generalitravelinsurance.com.* **Travelex Insurance.** ☎ *800/228–9792* 🌐 *www.travelexinsurance.com.* **Travel Insured International.** ☎ *800/243–3174* 🌐 *www.travelinsured.com.* **World Nomads.** ☎ *844/207–1930* 🌐 *www.worldnomads.com.*

VISITOR INFORMATION

The Switzerland Tourism website (🌐 *www.myswitzerland.com*) allows you to research destinations and activities and book accommodations. When you're in Switzerland, AngloPhone is an English-language information service giving details on hotels, restaurants, museums, nightlife, skiing, what to do in an emergency, and more. Lines are open weekdays 9–noon and 2–7. Calls cost 2.15 SF per minute.

All About Switzerland AngloPhone. ☎ *0900/576444* 🌐 *www.swissstyle.com/anglophone-information-services.* **Federal Department of Foreign Affairs.** 🌐 *www.eda.admin.ch.* **Pro Helvetia.** 🌐 *prohelvetia.ch/en.* **Swissart Network.** 🌐 *www.swissart.ch.* **Swiss Broadcasting Corporation.** 🌐 *www.swissinfo.ch.* **Switzerland Tourism.** ☎ *0800/10020029* 🌐 *www.myswitzerland.com.*

UNDERSTANDING SWITZERLAND

VOCABULARY

VOCABULARY

	ENGLISH	FRENCH	FRENCH PRONUNCIATION
BASICS			
	Yes/no	Oui/non	wee/no
	Please	S'il vous plaît	seel voo **play**
	Thank you	Merci	mare-**see**
	De rien	You're welcome	deh ree-**enh**
	Excuse me	Pardon	pahr-**doan**
	Hello	Bonjour	bohn-**zhoor**
	Goodbye	Au revoir	o ruh-**vwahr**
NUMBERS			
	One	Un	un
	Two	Deux	deuh
	Three	Trois	twa
	Four	Quatre	**cat**-ruh
	Five	Cinq	sank
	Six	Six	seess
	Seven	Sept	set
	Eight	Huit	weat
	Nine	Neuf	nuf
	Ten	Dix	deess
DAYS			
	Today	Aujourd'hui	o-zhoor-**dwee**
	Tomorrow	Demain	deh-**menh**
	Yesterday	Hier	yair
	Morning	Matin	ma-**tenh**
	Afternoon	Après-midi	ah-pray-mee-**dee**
	Night	Nuit	nwee
	Monday	Lundi	**lahn**-dee
	Tuesday	Mardi	**mahr**-dee
	Wednesday	Mercredi	**mare**-kruh-dee
	Thursday	Jeudi	**juh**-dee
	Friday	Vendredi	**vawn**-dra-dee
	Saturday	Samedi	**sam**-dee
	Sunday	Dimanche	**dee**-mawnsh

* *Prevalent Swiss-German dialect*

GERMAN	GERMAN PRONUNCIATION	ITALIAN	ITALIAN PRONUNCIATION
Ja/nein	yah/nine	Sí/No	see/no
Bitte	**bit**-uh	Per favore	pear fa-**voh**-reh
Danke	**dahn**-kuh	Grazie	**grah**-tsee-ay
Bitte schön	**bit**-uh **shern**	Prego	**pray**-go
Entschuldigen Sie *Äxgüsi	ent-**shool**-de-gen-zee	Scusi	**skoo**-zee **ax**-scu-see
Guten Tag *Grüezi *Grüss Gott	**goot**-en **tahk** **grit**-zee groos got	Buon giorno	bwohn **jyohr**-noh
Auf Widersehen *Ufwiederluege *Tschüss (*familiar*)	Auf **vee-der**-zane oof-**vee-der**-lawgah choohs	Arrivederci	a-ree-vah-**dare**-chee
Eins	eints	Uno	**oo**-no
Zwei	tsvai	Due	**doo**-ay
Drei	dry	Tre	tray
Vier	fear	Quattro	**kwah**-troh
Fünf	fumph	Cinque	**cheen**-kway
Sechs	zex	Sei	say
Sieben	**zee**-ben	Sette	**set**-ay
Acht	ahkt	Otto	**oh**-to
Neun	noyn	Nove	**no**-vay
Zehn	tsane	Dieci	dee-**eh**-chee
Huete	**hoi**-tah	Oggi	**oh**-jee
Morgen	**more**-gehn	Domani	do-**mah**-nee
Gestern	geh-**shtairn**	Ieri	ee-veh-ree
Morgen	**more**-gehn	Mattina	ma-**tee**-na
Nachmittag	nahkt-**mit**-ahk	Pomeriggio	po-mer-**ee**-jo
Nacht	nahkt	Notte	Noh-teh
Montag	**mohn**-tahk	Lunedì	**loo**-neh-dee
Dienstag	**deens**-tahk	Martedì	**mahr**-teh-dee
Mittwoch	**mit**-vohk	Mercoledì	**mare**-co-leh-dee
Donnerstag	**doe**-ners-tahk	Giovedì	**jo**-veh-dee
Freitag	**fry**-tahk	Venerdì	**ven**-air-dee
Samstag	**zahm**-stahk	Sabato	**sah**-ba-toe
Sonntag	**zon**-tahk	La Domenica	lah doe-**men**-ee-ca

ENGLISH	FRENCH	FRENCH PRONUNCIATION
USEFUL PHRASES		
Do you speak English?	Parlez-vous anglais?	par-lay-vooz awng-**gleh**
I don't speak French/ German/ Italian.	Je ne parle pas français.	juh nuh parl pah fraun-**seh**
I don't understand.	Je ne comprends pas.	juh nuh kohm-prawhn **pah**
I don't know.	Je ne sais pas.	juh nuh say **pah**
I am American/ British.	Je suis américain/	jhu anglais sweez a-may-ree-**can**/awn-**glay**
I am sick.	Je suis malade.	juh swee ma-**lahd**
Please call a doctor.	Appelez un docteur s'il vous plâit.	a-pe-lay uhn dohk-**tore** seel voo **play**
Have you any rooms?	Est-ce que vous avez une chambre?	Ehskuh vooz- ah-vay-oon **shahm**-br
How much does it cost?	C'est combien?	say comb-bee-**enh**
Do you accept . . . (credit card)	Est-ce que vous acceptez . . .	Ehskuh voo zahksehptay . . .
Too expensive	Trop cher	troh **shehr**
It's beautiful.	C'est très beau.	say tray boh
Help!	Au secours!	o say-**koor**
Stop!	Arrêtez!	a-ruh-**tay**
GETTING AROUND		
Where is . . .	C'est où . . .	say oo
The train station?	la gare?	la gahr
The post office?	la poste?	la pohst
The hospital?	l'hôpital?	lo-pee-**tahl**
Where are the rest rooms?	Où sont les toilettes?	oo sohn lay **twah**-let
Left	A gauche	a **gohsh**
Right	À droite	a **drwat**
Straight ahead	Tout droit	**too drwat**

**Prevalent Swiss-German dialect*

GERMAN	GERMAN PRONUNCIATION	ITALIAN	ITALIAN PRONUNCIATION
Sprechen Sie Englisch?	Shprek-hun zee **eng**-glish	Parla inglese?	**par**-la een **glay**-zay
Ich sprech kein Deutsch.	ihkh **shprek**-uh kine doych	Non parlo italiano.	non **par**-lo ee-tal-**yah**-no
Ich verstehe nicht.	ihkh fehr-**stay**-eh nikht	Non capisco.	non ka-**peess**-ko
Ich habe keine Ahnung.	ihkh hah-beh kine-eh **ah**-nung	Non lo so.	non lo **so**
Ich bin Amerikaner(in). Engländer(in).	ihkh bin a-mer-i **kah**-ner(in)/ **eng**- glan-der(in)	Sono americano(a)/ Sono inglese.	**so**-no a-may-ree-**kah**-no(a)/**so**-no een-**glay**-zay
Ich bin krank.	ihkh bin **krahnk**	Sto male.	sto **ma**-lay
Bitte rufen einen Arzt.	**bit**-uh **roof**-en ine-en **ahrtst**	Chiami un dottore per favore.	kee-**ah**-mee oon doe-**toe**-ray pear fah-**voh**-reh
Haben sie ein Zimmer?	**Ha**-ben zee ine **tsimmer**	C'e una camera libera?	chay **oo**-nah **cam**-er-ah **lee**-ber-eh
Wieviel kostet das?	**vee**-feel **cost**-et dahs	Quanto costa?	**kwahn**-toe-**coast**-a
Nehmen Sie . . .	**nay**-men zee . . .	Posso pagare . . .	**pohs**-soh pah-**gah**-reh . . .
Es kostet zu viel.	es **cost**-et tsu feel	Troppo caro	**troh**-poh **cah**-roh
Das ist schön.	dahs is **shern**	É bello(a).	eh **bell**-oh
Hilfe!	**hilf**-uh	Aiuto!	a-**yoo**-toe
Halt!	hahlt	Alt!	ahlt

Wo ist . . .	**vo** ist	Dov'è . . .	doe-**veh**
Der Bahnhof?	dare **bahn**-hof	la stazione?	la sta-tsee-**oh**-nay
Die Post?	dee **post**	l'ufficio postale?	loo-**fee**-cho po-**sta**-lay
Das Krankenhaus? *Das Spital?	dahs **krahnk**-en-house dahs shpee-**tahl**	l'ospedale?	lo-spay-**dah**-lay
Wo ist die Toilette?	vo ist dee twah-**let**-uh	Dov'è il bagno?	doe-**vay** eel**bahn**-yo
Links	links	a sinistra	a see-**neess**-tra
Rechts	rechts	a destra	a-**des**-tra
geradeaus	geh-**rod**-uh ouse	Avanti dritto	a-**vahn**-tee **dree**-to

ENGLISH	FRENCH	FRENCH PRONUNCIATION

DINING OUT

ENGLISH	FRENCH	FRENCH PRONUNCIATION
Waiter/Waitress	Monsieur/ Mademoiselle	muh-**syuh**/ mad-mwa-**zel**
Please give me . . .	S'il vous plait, donnez-moi . . .	see voo **play** doh nay **mwah**
The menu	La carte	la cart
The bill/check	L'addition	la-dee-see-**ohn**
A fork	Une fourchette	ewn four-**shet**
A knife	Un couteau	uhn koo-**toe**
A spoon	Une cuillère	ewn kwee-**air**
A napkin	Une serviette	ewn sair-vee-**et**
Bread	Du pain	due penh
Butter	Du beurre	due bur
Milk	Du lait	due lay
Pepper	Du poivre	due **pwah**-vruh
Salt	Du sel	due sell
Sugar	Du sucre	due **sook**-ruh
Coffee	Un café	uhn kahfay
Tea	Un thé	uhn tay
Mineral water *carbonated/still*	De l'eau minéral *gazeuse/non gazeuse*	duh loh meenehrahl gahzuhz/noh(n) gahzuhz
Wine	Vin	venh
Cheers!	A votre santé!	ah vo-truh sahn-**tay**

GERMAN	GERMAN PRONUNCIATION	ITALIAN	ITALIAN PRONUNCIATION
Herr Ober/ Fraülein	hehr **oh**-ber **froy**-line	Cameriere(a)	kah-meh-**ryeh**-reh(rah)
Bitte geben sie mir . . .	**bit**-uh gay behn zee-**meer**	Mi dia por favore	mee **dee**-a pear-fah-**voh**-reh . . .
Die speisekarte	dee **shpie**-zeh-car-tuh	Il menù	eel may-**noo**
Die Rechnung	dee **rekh**-nung	Il conto	eel **cone**-toe
Eine Gabel	**ine**-eh-**gah**-buhl	Una forchetta	oona for-**ket**-a
Ein messer	I-nuh-**mess**-ehr	Un coltello	oon kol-**tel**-o
Einen Löffel	I-nen **ler**-fuhl	Un cucchiaio	oon koo-kee-**ah-yo**
Die Serviette	dee zair-vee-**eh**-tuh	Il tovagliolo	eel toe-va-lee-**oh-lo**
Brot	broht	Il pane	eel **pa**-nay
Butter	**boo**-tehr	Il burro	eel **boo**-roh
Milch	meelch	Il latte	eel **lot**-ay
Pfeffer	**fef**-fehr	Il pepe	eel **pay**-pay
Salz	zahlts	Il sale	eel **sah**-lay
Zucker	**tsoo**-kher	Lo zucchero	loh **tsoo**-ker-o
eine Kaffee	**ine**-eh **kah**-feh	un caffè	oon kahf-**feh**
einen Tee	**ine**-en tay	un tè	oon teh
Mineral wasser *mit gas/ohne gas*	mi-neh-**raal**-**vahs**-sehr mit gahz/**oh**-nuh gahz	L'acqua minerale *gassata/naturale*	l'ah kwa mee-neh-**rah**-leh gahs-**sah**-tah/ nah-too-**rah**-leh
Wein	vine	Il vino	eel **vee**-noh
Zum Wohl! *Proscht	zoom vole prosht	Salute!	sah-**loo**-teh

INDEX

A

Aare Gorge, *388*
Air travel. ⇨ *See* **Plane travel**
Al Portone ✕, *206*
Alfred Escher statue, 53
Aletsch, *440–442*
Aletsch Glacier, *441*
Aletsch Panorama Trail, *442*
Alimentarium, *480*
Alpina Gstaad, The 🏨, *395*
Alpine Passes, *439–442*
Alpineum, *229*
Altdorf, *249–250*
Altes Rathaus (Luzern), *225*
Altstadt (Basel), *260, 264–267*
Altstadt (Bern), *325–331*
Altstadt (St. Gallen), *108*
Altstadt (Zürich), *52–61*
Angleterre & Résidence Hôtel 🏨, *467*
Animated clock (Lausanne), *464*
Appenzell, *114–118*
Appenzell embroidery, *116*
Appenzeller Volkskunde Museum, *116*
Arcades (Bern), *328*
Arenenberg, *105*
Arosa, *140–145*
Arosa Kulm Hotel & Alpin Spa 🏨, *141–142*
Art galleries and museums. ⇨ *See* **Museums**
Arts. ⇨ *See* **Nightlife and the arts**
Ascona, *198–201*
Atlantis by Giardino 🏨, *77*
Auberge aux *4 Vents* 🏨, *299*
Auberge des Clefs ✕, *309*
Auditoire de Calvin, *501*
Augusta Raurica, *270–271*
Automates Jaquet-Droz, *312*
Aventicum, *309*

B

Bach & Buck ✕, *313–314*
Badrutt's Palace Hotel 🏨, *172*
Bahnhofstrasse (Zürich), *52*
Bas Valais, *406–417*
Basel, *21, 254–284*
Altstadt, 260, 264–267
discounts and deals, 264
festivals and seasonal events, 267
Greater Basel, 270–272
itineraries, 265
Kleinbasel, 269
lodging, 276–278
nightlife and the arts, 278–280
restaurants, 264, 272–276
St. Alban, 269–270
shopping, 280–282
sightseeing, 259–272
spas, 283–284
timing the visit, 257
tours, 259
transportation, 257–258
visitor information, 259
Zoo, 270
Basler Münster, *260*
Basler Papiermühle, *269*
Basse-Ville (Fribourg), *294*
Baur au Lac 🏨, *71*
BearPark, *328*
Beau-Rivage (Geneva), *498*
Beckenried, *245–246*
Bel Étage ✕, *273–274*
Bellevue Palace Bern 🏨, *339*
Bellinzona, *189–194*
Bergbahn Lauterbrunnen-Mürren, *365*
Berggasthaus Aescher-Wildkirchli ✕, *117*
Bern, *22, 320–348*
Altstadt *(Old Town)* **and City Center,** *325–331*
festivals and seasonal events, 344, 347–348
greater Bern, 333–335
itineraries, 326
lodging, 339–341
museum district: Kirchenfeld, 331, 333
nightlife and the arts, 341–344
restaurants, 330, 331, 335–338
shopping, 345–348
spas, 348
sports and outdoor activities, 345
timing the visit, 323
transportation, 324
visitor information, 324
Berner Oberland, *12, 350–398*
Brienzersee, 384–398
discounts and deals, 354
festivals and seasonal events, 361
Jungfrau region, 355–369, 372, 374–375, 380–384
lodging, 354, 360, 363, 365–366, 367–368, 380–381, 388, 390, 393, 395, 397
nightlife and the arts, 361, 384
restaurants, 354, 359, 379, 380, 387–388, 390, 395
shopping, 393
Simmental and Gstaad, 394–398
skiing, 366, 368, 384, 398
spas, 361, 397–398
sports and outdoor activities, 366, 368, 384, 393, 398
Thunersee, 389–393
timing the visit, 353
tours, 355, 357, 363
transportation, 353–354
visitor information, 355
Bernisches Historisches Museum, *331, 333*
Bethlehemhaus, *252*
Bicycling
Bern, 345
Eastern Switzerland and Liechtenstein, 102, 106, 108, 123–124
Fribourg and Neuchâtel, 291–292
Geneva, 494
Graubünden, 144, 147, 154, 160, 168, 176
Luzern and Central Switzerland, 219, 236
Ticino, 183
Valais, 410–411, 434
Vaud, 469, 478
Zürich, 51
Bistro Gentiana ✕, *152*
Blaues und Weisses Haus, *264, 266*
Blonay-Chamby Railroad, *480*
Boat and ferry travel, *529–530*
Berner Oberland, 353–354
Eastern Switzerland and Liechtenstein, 94
Fribourg and Neuchâtel, 292
Geneva, 494
Luzern and Central Switzerland, 219, 221–222
Ticino, 183, 186
Vaud, 449, 456
Zürich, 50
Boating and sailing
Berner Oberland, 393
Fribourg and Neuchâtel, 310, 316
Graubünden, 154
Luzern and Central Switzerland, 236
Valais, 420
Vaud, 488
Bobsledding, *176*
Bodensee, *105–108*
Bogn Engiadina Scuol (spa), *159*
Bourbaki-Panorama, *225*
Brauquöll Appenzell, *115*
Brienz, *386–388*
Brienzer-Rothorn Bahn, *386*
Brienzersee, *384–398*
Brig, *439–442*
Bulle, *303, 306*
Bundesbriefmuseum, *252*
Bundeshaus (Bern), *328*
Bündner Kunstmuseum Chur, *137*
Bürgenstock, 247
Bürgenstock Resort Lake Lucerne 🏨, **247**
Bürglen, *252*

Bursins, *456*
Bus travel and tours, *24, 530*
Bern, 324
Berner Oberland, 354, 355
Eastern Switzerland and Liechtenstein, 94
Fribourg and Neuchâtel, 292
Geneva, 494–495
Graubünden, 129
Luzern and Central Switzerland, 222
Ticino, 186
Valais, 403
Vaud, 450
Zürich, 51

C

Cable cars
Berner Oberland, 365, 367, 377, 379
Eastern Switzerland and Liechtenstein, 110
Luzern and Central Switzerland, 243, 245–246
Valais, 442
Caduff's Wine Loft ✕, *69*
Café Beau-Rivage ✕, *465*
Café des Bains ✕, *513*
Campione, *212–213*
Car travel and rentals, *24, 39, 44, 530–532*
Basel, 258
Bern, 324
Berner Oberland, 354
Eastern Switzerland and Liechtenstein, 94
Fribourg and Neuchâtel, 292
Geneva, 495
Graubünden, 129–130
Luzern and Central Switzerland, 222
Ticino, 186–187
Valais, 403–404
Vaud, 450, 478
Zürich, 50
Carnival, *235*
Carouge, *504*
Carriage rides, *168–169, 357*
Casa dei Canonici, *196*
Casinos
Bern, 344
Fribourg and Neuchâtel, 316
Graubünden, 153, 175
Luzern, 234
Ticino, 197, 211, 213
Castelgrande, *192*
Castelgrande ✕, *193*
Castello di Montebello, *191*
Castello di Sasso Corbaro, *191*
Castles and mansions
Basel, 264, 266
Berner Oberland, 390, 391, 393
Fribourg and Neuchâtel, 301–302, 313, 317, 318
Geneva, 498, 499, 500, 508
Graubünden, 134, 158
Ticino, 191, 192
Valais, 414, 440
Vaud, 453–454, 461, 484–485
Cathédrale de Notre-Dame, *459, 461*
Cathédrale St-Nicholas, *294*
Cathédrale St-Pierre, *501, 504*
Cattedrale di San Lorenzo, *206*
Caves, *357*
Central Switzerland. ⇨ See **Luzern and Central Switzerland**
Centre d'Art Contemporain, *508–509*
Centre Dürrenmatt, *312–313*
Centro Storico (Bellinzona), *191*
Channel Tunnel, *534*
Chapelle du St-Sépulcre, *294*
Château de Chenaux, *307*
Château de Chillon, *484–485*
Château de Grandson, *317*
Château de Gruyères, *301–302*
Château de Neuchâtel, *313*
Château de Nyon, *453–454*
Château de Tourbillon, *414*
Château de Yverdon-les-Bains, *318*
Château St-Maire, *461*
Cheese-making
Eastern Switzerland and Liechtenstein, 116
Fribourg and Neuchâtel, 288–289, 302
Chenil au Col du Grand St-Bernard, *413–414*
Chetzeron 🏨, *419*
Cheval Blanc by Peter Knogl ✕, *274*
Chiesa Collegiata di San Pietro e San Stefano, *192*
Chiesa di San Francesco, *195*
Chiesa di Santa Maria degli Angioli, *203*
Chiesa di Sant'Antonio, *196*
Chiesa Nuova, *195*
Chiesa San Biagio, *192–193*
Chiesa Santa Maria del Sasso, *213*
Chiesa Santa Maria delle Grazie, *191–192*
Chocolate, *298, 455*
Christmas market, *84*
Christoffelturm, *331*
Chur, *136–140*
Churches and cathedrals
Basel, 260, 266–267
Bern, 329, 330, 331
Berner Oberland, 395
Eastern Switzerland and Liechtenstein, 98, 109
Fribourg and Neuchâtel, 294, 296, 307, 311
Geneva, 500, 501, 504, 506, 508
Graubünden, 137–138, 139, 145, 151
Luzern and Central Switzerland, 228, 229, 230, 243, 251
Ticino, 191–193, 195–196, 203, 206, 213
Valais, 414–415, 416, 430
Vaud, 459, 461, 464
Zürich, 53, 57, 61
Cimetère du Bois-de-Vaux, *461, 463*
City Center (Bern), *325–331*
Clock tower (Bern), *330*
Col du Grand St-Bernard, *413–414*
Collection de l'Art Brut, *463*
Communications, 536–537
Confiserie Schiesser (shop), *282–283*
Conversion de la Vallée, *417–426*
Corniche de Lavaux, *472*
Cows, *364, 408*
Crafts Fair (Bern), *347*
Crans-Montana, *417–422*
Crypt (Basel), *260*
Curling, *144*
Currency and exchange, *540*
Customs and duties, *537–538*

D

Dairy Trail, *289*
Davos, *145, 150–155*
Débarcadère, *463*
Dellago 🏨, *214*
Der Teufelhof Basel 🏨, *277*
Des Trois Tours ✕, *299*
Die Chesery ✕, *395*
Dining. ⇨ See **Restaurants; under specific areas**
Discounts and deals
Basel, 264
Berner Oberland, 354
Eastern Switzerland and Liechtenstein, 115
Luzern and Central Switzerland, 223
Dolder Grand, The 🏨, *79*
Dolder Grand Spa, The, *85*
Dom, *435*
Dom Hotel, The 🏨, *436*
Drei Weieren, *110*
Duties, *537–538*

E

Eastern Switzerland and Liechtenstein, *20, 88–124*
Bodensee to Walensee, 105–120
discounts and deals, 115
Liechtenstein, 120–124
lodging, 95, 101–102, 104, 105, 112, 117–118, 119, 123
restaurants, 95, 101, 103–104, 109, 110–112, 116–117, 122
Schaffhausen and the Rhine, 96–105
shopping, 106, 114, 116, 118, 123–124
skiing, 119–120
spas, 112, 114

sports and outdoor activities, 102, 106, 108, 112, 114, 119–120, 123
timing the visit, 93
tours, 98
transportation, 94–95
visitor information, 96
Ebenalp, *115*
Église Abbatiale, *307*
Église Collégiale, *311*
Église des Cordeliers, *294, 296*
Église-Forteresse de Valère, *414–415*
Église Notre Dame de Valère, *414–415*
Église St-François, *464*
Eglise Saint-Germain, *506, 508*
Eiger, *374, 380*
Einstein St. Gallen Hotel Congress Spa ⌂, *112*
Einsteinhaus, *328–329*
Eis Pavillon, *436*
Electricity, *538*
Embroidery, *116*
Emergencies, *531, 538*
Escher, Alfred, *53*
Esel, *239, 242*
Espace Jean Tinguely-Niki de Saint Phalle, *296*
Estavayer-le-Lac, *307*

F

Fairmont Le Montreux Palace ⌂, *486*
Fasnacht, *267*
Fasnacht-Brunnen, *260*
Fee Glacier, *436*
Festivals and seasonal events, *25.* ⇨ *See also under specific cities and areas*
Fiesch cable car, *442*
Film festivals
Locarno, 197
Zürich, 82
Findlerhof ✕, *430*
Firstbahn, *369*
Fiskebar ✕, *511*
Five Lakes Walk, *433*
Flea markets, *106*
Flower Clock, *499*
Fondation Barry du Grand St-Bernard, *407*
Fondation Baur, *504*
Fondation Beyeler, *271*
Fondation de l'Hermitage, *463–464*
Fondation Martin Bodmer, *500*
Fondation Pierre Gianadda, *407*
Fontaine de la Justice (Lausanne), *464*
Fondue, *289*
Fossils, *192*
Fountains
Basel, 260
Bern, 328
Geneva, 500
Lausanne, 464
Four Seasons des Bergues, Geneva ⌂, *519*
Franziskanerkirche, *229*
Fraumünster, *53*
Freilichtmuseum der Schweiz Ballenberg, *386–387*
Fribourg and Neuchâtel, *22, 286–318*
festivals and seasonal events, 301
Fribourg, 293–307
Lac de Neuchâtel, 310–318
lodging, 292, 299–300, 303, 309–310, 315
Murten, 307–310
nightlife and the arts, 300, 316
restaurants, 292–293, 297, 298–299, 302–303, 309, 313–315
skiing, 303
spas, 318
sports and outdoor activities, 303, 310
timing the visit, 291
transportation, 291–292
Fronwagplatz (Schaffhausen), *96*
Fuchs Holzschnitzkurse, *387*
Funiculars
Bern, 335
Berner Oberland, 358
Eastern Switzerland and Liechtenstein, 110
Graubünden, 166
Luzern and Central Switzerland, 243
Ticino, 204

G

Galeries de l'Histoire, *313*
Gandria, *212*
Gardens and parks
Bern, 328, 330
Eastern Switzerland and Liechtenstein, 110
Geneva, 496, 501
Graubünden, 161–164
Ticino, 199, 203, 206, 208, 213
Vaud, 482
George Bar & Grill ✕, *66*
Geneva, *23, 490–526*
Carouge, 504
festivals and seasonal events, 499, 522
International area, 496–498
itineraries, 507
Les Pâquis, 498–499
lodging, 517–521
nightlife and the arts, 521–523
Plainpalais, 508–510
restaurants, 501, 510–517
Rive Droite, 496–499
Rive Gauche, 499–501
shopping, 523–526
sightseeing, 496–510
spas, 524, 526
timing the visit, 493
tours, 495
transportation, 493–495
visitor information, 495–496
Vieille Ville, 501, 504–508
Geneva Transport Card, *494*
Gerberstube, *99*
Giardino Ascona ⌂, *201*
Giardino Belvedere, *203*
Giardino Mountain ⌂, *172*
Gissebachfälle, *385*
Giger Museum, *302*
Gletschergarten, *229*
Gletscherhorn, *417*
Gletscherschlucht, *369*
GLOW by Armin Amrein ✕, *152*
Golf
Graubünden, 144, 147, 176
Valais, 411, 420
Golf Club de Crans-sur-Sierre, *420*
Gondola rides, *369, 377*
Gornergrat, *429*
Gornergrat Monte Rose Bahn, *429*
Gottlieben, *105*
Grand Hotel Kronenhof ⌂, *167*
Grand Hotel Les Trois Rois ⌂, *266, 277*
Grandhotel Giessbach ⌂, *386*
Grandson, *317*
Graphische Sammlung, *57*
Graubünden, *20, 126–178*
festivals and seasonal events, 153, 175
Heidiland, 132–145
lodging, 130–131, 135, 139, 141–143, 146, 152–153, 155, 158–159, 164, 167–168, 172–174
Lower Engadine, 155–164
nightlife and the arts, 140, 143–144, 153, 168, 174–175
Prättigau and Davos, 145–155
restaurants, 131, 134, 139, 141, 146, 151–152, 166, 171–172
skiing, 144–145, 147, 148, 154–155, 160 –161, 169, 178
spas, 136, 140, 159, 168, 175
sports and outdoor activities, 134, 144–145, 147–148, 150, 154–155, 160 –161, 168–169, 175–178
timing the visit, 129
tours, 131–132
transportation, 129–130, 159
Upper Engadine, 164–178
visitor information, 132
Greater Basel, *270–272*
Greater Bern, *333–335*
Grimentz, *423*
Grindelwald, *369, 380–381, 384*
Grossmünster, *57*
Grotto du Rii ✕, *199*
Gruyères, *300–303*

Gstaad, *394–398*
Gstaad Mountain Rides, *398*
Guarda, *155*
Gurten, *335*

H

Hamburger Foundation, The, *511*
Harder Kulm, *358*
Hauptbahnhof, *53*
Haus Konstruktiv, *53, 56*
Haus zum Ritter, *99*
Haus zum Rüden, *68*
Health concerns, *539*
Heidi-Weg, *134*
Heididorf, *132, 134*
Heidiland, *132–145*
Heiliggeistkirche, *329*
Heimatwerk (shop), *346*
Heimwehfluh, *358*
Helicopter tours, *363*
Helmhaus, *57*
Helvetia statue, *269*
Herman Hesse Museum, *203*
Hiking. *See* **Walking and hiking**
Hilterfingen, *393*
Hinz und Kunz Bar, *279*
Historisches Museum (Basel), *261*
Historisches Museum (Luzern), *225, 228*
Hofkirche, *230*
Hof-Torturm, *137*
Hohenklingen, *102*
Horloge Fleurie, *499*
Horse-drawn carriage rides, *168–169, 357*
Hotel Appenzell, *118*
Hotel Beau-Rivage Geneva, *518–519*
Hotel Bellevue, *365*
Hotel Belvedere, *380*
Hotel de l'Ours, *309*
Hôtel de Ville (Fribourg), *296*
Hôtel de Ville (Geneva), *504*
Hôtel de Ville (Lausanne), *464*
Hôtel de Ville (Yverdon-les-Bains), *318*
Hôtel des Trois Couronnes, *482*
Hotel Drachenburg und Waaghaus, *105*
Hotel Gletschergarten, *381*
Hotel Interlaken, *360*
Hotel Krafft Basel, *278*
Hotel Palafitte, *315*
Hotel Schatzalp, *152*
Hotel Schweizerhof Bern, *341*
Hotel Silvapina, *146*
Hotel Splendide Royal, *210*
Hotels, *17, 535*
Basel, 276–278
Bern, 339–341
Berner Oberland, 354, 360, 363, 365–366, 367–368, 380–381, 388, 390, 393, 395, 397
Eastern Switzerland and Liechtenstein, 95, 101–102, 104, 105, 112, 117–118, 119, 123
Fribourg and Neuchâtel, 292, 299–300, 303, 309–310, 315
Geneva, 517–521
Graubünden, 130–131, 135, 139, 141–143, 146, 152–153, 155, 158–159, 164, 167–168, 172–174
Luzern and Central Switzerland, 222, 232–233, 244, 245, 257
price categories, 17, 71, 131, 188, 223, 276, 293, 339, 354, 405, 450, 518
Ticino, 187, 193–194, 197, 200–201, 210–211, 214
Valais, 404, 409–410, 419–420, 423, 425, 431–432, 436, 438
Vaud, 451, 455, 456, 457, 467–468, 473, 481–482, 486
Zürich, 71–79

I

Ice Palace, *375*
Ice sports, *160, 169, 176, 178*
Il Lungolago, *203*
Ile Rousseau, *499*
InterContinental Davos, *152–153*
Interlaken, *355–361*
Isérables, *415*
Isole di Brissago, *199*
Ital-Redinghaus, *252*
Itineraries, *34–44.* *See also under specific cities and areas*

J

Jägerhof, *111*
James Joyce's grave, *63*
Jardin Botanique, *496*
Jesuitenkirche, *228*
Jet d'Eau, *500*
Joyce, James, *63*
Jungfrau region, *355–369, 372, 374–375, 380–384*
Jungfraujoch, *374*

K

Käfigturm, *331*
Kaiser's Reblaube, *66*
Kapellbrücke, *228*
Kaserene (bar), *279*
Kathedrale (St. Gallen), *109*
Kathedrale St. Maria Himmelfahrt, *137–138*
Kaufleuten (club), *81*
Keller zur Grotte, *424*
Kirche St. Johann, *151*
Kirche St. Martin, *138*
Kirche St. Peter, *53*
Kirchenfeld, *331, 333*
Kirchgasse, *61*
Kirchner Museum, *151*
Klee, Paul, *334*
Kleinbasel, *269*
Kleine Scheidegg, *367*
Kloster St. Georgen, *102–103*
Kloster St. Johann Müstair, *161*
Klösterli Weincafé, *337*
Klosters, *145–150*
Kornhaus, *331*
Kornhausforum, *331*
Kornhauskeller, *343*
Kreis 8 (Zürich), *64*
Kreis 5 (Zürich), *62–63*
Kreis 1 (Zürich), *52–61*
Kreis 7 (Zürich), *63–64*
Kreis 2 (Zürich), *61–62*
KrippenWelt Stein-am-Rhein, *103*
Kronenhalle, *68, 80*
Kulm Hotel St. Moritz, *173*
Kultur-und Kongresszentrum, *229*
Kunsthalle (Basel), *261*
Kunsthalle (Zürich), *63*
Kunsthalle Bern, *333*
Kunsthaus (Zürich), *57*
Kunstmuseum (Bern), *329*
Kunstmuseum Basel, *261*
Kunstmuseum Basel | Gegenwart, *270*
Kunstmuseum Liechtenstein, *122*

L

La Côte, *452–457*
La Liberté, *456*
La Neptune, *500*
La Vetta, *141*
Lac de Neuchâtel, *310–318*
Lac Souterrain St-Léonard, *415*
Läderach (shop), *346*
Lake Luzern, *218–219*
Lake Zürich, *65*
Language, *136, 544–549*
Laténium, *311–312*
L'Atelier Cocktail Club, *522*
Lausanne, *458–470*
Lauterbrunnen, *361–363*
Lavaux Vignobles, *470–488*
Le Bateau, *103–104*
Le Bocca, *314*
La Bottega, *516*
Le Chat Botté, *511*
La Désalpe, *301*
Le Tirbouchon (wine café), *420*
Le Verre à Monique (bar), *522*
Leonhardskirche, *266*
Les Sources des Alpes, *425*
Les Trois Verres, *516*
Leukerbad, *424–426*
Leukerbad Therme, *424–425*
L'Hospice du Grand St. Bernard, *413–414*
L'Hostellerie du Pas de l'Ours, *420*
Libraries, *109–110*

Liechtenstein. ⇨ *See* **Eastern Switzerland and Liechtenstein**
Liechtensteinisches Landesmuseum, *122*
Lindenhof, *56*
Locarno, *194–198*
Lodging, *17, 535.* ⇨ *See also Hotels; under specific cities and areas*
Löwendenkmal, *229*
Lower Engadine, *155–164*
Lugano, *202–212*
Luzern and Central Switzerland, *21, 216–252*
discounts and deals, 223
festivals and seasonal events, 235
Lake Luzern, 218–219
lodging, 222, 232–233, 244, 245, 257
Luzern environs, 238–246
nightlife and the arts, 233–235
restaurants, 223, 230–232
shopping, 237–238
spas, 238, 245
sports and outdoor activities, 236–237
timing the visit, 218, 221
transportation, 218, 221–222
Urnersee, 246–252
visitor information, 223

M

Mahogany Hall, *344*
Maienfeld, *132, 134–136*
Marians Jazzroom, *344*
Maison Cailler, *298*
Maison d'Ailleurs, *318*
Maison du Gruyère, *302*
Maison Supersaxo, *415*
Maison Tavel, *508*
Maison Visinand, *485*
Männlichen , *372, 376–377*
Männlichen Cable Car, *367*
Marktgasse Hotel 🏨**,** *77*
Marktplatz (Basel), *261*
Martigny, *407–408*
Matterhorn, *426–435*
Matterhorn Museum – Zermatlantis, *430*
Meat and Cheese Market (Bern), *347*
Meierei ✕**,** *172*
Meiringen-Hasliberg, *388–389*
Meridiano ✕**,** *337*
Migros Museum für Gegenwartskunst, *63*
Mittlere Rheinbrücke, *264*
Monasteries and convents
Gottlieben, 105
Parc Naziunal Svizzer, 161
Stein am Rhein, 102–103
Mönchsjochhütte, *375*
Money matters, *17, 540*
Money-saving tips, *24, 33, 535*
Mont Blanc, *498*
Mont Cervin Palace 🏨**,** *431*
Monte Brè, *204*
Monte Generoso, *204*
Monte San Salvatore, *204*
Monte Verità, *199*
Montreux, *483–488*
Monument Brunswick, *498*
Monument de la Réformation, *505*
Monument to Arnold von Winkelried, *242*
Morat. ⇨ *See* **Murten**
Morcote, *213–214*
Morges, *456–457*
Mt. Pilatus, *239–242*
Mt. Rigi, *244*
Mt. Säntis, *119*
Mt. Schilthorn, *365, 373, 378–379*
Mt. Titlis, *243*
Mountain climbing
Graubünden, 169
Valais, 411, 434, 438–439
Mühleggbahn, *110*
Mülenenschlucht, *110*
Munot, *98*
Münster (Bern), *330*
Münster zu Allerheiligen, *98*
Muottas Muragl, *166*
Mürren, *364–366, 378*
Murten, *307–310*
Musée Alexis Forel, *457*
Musée Ariana, *498*
Musée Barbier-Mueller, *505*
Musée Cantonal d'Archéologie et d'Histoire, *465*
Musée Cantonal de Géologie, *465*
Musée Cantonal de la Vigne et du Vin, *313*
Musée Cantonal de Zoologie, *465*
Musée Cantonal des Beaux-Arts, *465*
Musée d'Art du Valais, 415–416
Musée d'Art et d'Histoire (Geneva), *508*
Musée d'Art et d'Histoire (Neuchâtel), *312*
Musée d'Art et d'Histoire de Fribourg, *296–297*
Musée d'Art Moderne et Contemporain, *509*
Musée de Design et d'Arts Appliqués Comtemporains, *464*
Musée de la Nature du Valais, *416*
Musée de l'Automobile, *407–408*
Musée de l'Elysée, *464*
Musée de Montreux, *485*
Musée de Morat, *309*
Musée des Grenouilles, *307*
Musée d'Histoire (Sion), *415*
Musée d'Histoire des Sciences, *496–497*
Musée du Château, *457*
Musée du Léman, *454*
Musée Gallo-Romain, *407*
Musée Gruérien, *306*
Musée Historique de Lausanne, *464*
Musée Historique du Vieux Vevey, *480*
Musée International de la Croix-Rouge et du Croissant-Rouge, *497*
Musée International de la Réforme, *505–506*
Musée Militaire Genevois, *498*
Musée National Suisse, *455*
Musée Olympique, *465*
Musée Rath, *509–510*
Musée Romain (Nyon), *454*
Musée Suisse de la Machine à et Objets Insolites, *297*
Musée Suisse de l'Appareil Photographique, *480*
Musée Suisse du Jeu, *481*
Museo Cantonale di Storia Naturale, *206*
Museo Civico e Archeologico, *196*
Museo d'Arte della Svizzera italiana, Lugano (MASI) – LAC, *204, 206*
Museo d'Arte della Svizzera italiana, Lugano (MASI) – Palazzo Reali, *206*
Museo Doganale, *212*
Museo Villa dei Cedri, *193*
Museum Alpin, *165–166*
Museum Appenzell, *116*
Museum der Landschaft Saanen, *395*
Muséum d'Histoire Naturelle, *508*
Museum Engiadinais, *171*
Museum für Appenzeller Brauchtum, *116*
Museum für Gestaltung, *63*
Museum für Kommunikation, *333*
Museum Rietberg, *61–62*
Museum Tinguely, *269*
Museum zu Allerheiligen, *98*
Museums
Basel, 262, 264, 267, 269, 270, 271–272
Bern, 328–329, 331, 333, 334
Berner Oberland, 358, 386–387, 395
Eastern Switzerland and Liechtenstein, 98, 103, 105, 110, 116, 122
Fribourg and Neuchâtel, 296–297, 302, 306, 307, 309, 311–313, 318
Geneva, 496–497, 498, 500, 501, 504, 505–506, 508–510
Graubünden, 137, 141, 145, 151, 165–166, 171

Luzern and Central Switzerland, 225, 228, 229, 230, 252
Ticino, 193, 196, 203, 204, 206, 212
Valais, 407–408, 413–414, 415–416, 430
Vaud, 454, 455, 457, 463–465, 472, 480–481, 485
Zürich, 53, 56, 57, 61–63
Music, classical
Basel, 279
Bern, 344
festivals, 82, 153, 201, 235, 410, 417
Geneva, 522–523
Graubünden, 144, 153, 175
Luzern, 235
Ticino, 201
Valais, 410, 417
Vaud, 469
Zürich, 82
Music, popular
Basel, 279–280
Bern, 344
festivals, 175, 197, 201, 211–212, 235, 344, 488
Graubünden, 175
Luzern, 235
Ticino, 197, 201, 211–212
Valais, 420
Vaud, 488
Zürich, 81

N

Napoleon Museum Thurgau, *105*
Naturhistorisches Museum (Basel), *267*
Naturhistorisches Museum (Bern), *333*
Natur-Museum, *230*
Neuchâtel. ⇨ *See* **Fribourg and Neuchâtel**
Neuveville, *298*
Niederdorf, *52, 56–61*
Niederhorn, *391*
Nightlife and the arts
Basel, 278–280
Bern, 341–344
Berner Oberland, 361, 384
Fribourg and Neuchâtel, 300, 316
Geneva, 521–523
Graubünden, 140, 143–144, 153, 168, 174–175
Luzern and Central Switzerland, 233–235
Ticino, 197–198, 201, 211–212, 213
Valais, 410, 420, 433, 438
Vaud, 468–469, 482, 486–488
Zürich, 79–82
Nira Alpina 🏨, *173*
Nomad Design & Lifestyle Hotel 🏨, *277*
Notre-Dame du Glarier, *415*
Nutli-Hüschi, *145*
Nydeggkirche, *331*
Nyon, *452–455*

O

Oberdorf, *52, 56–61*
Obere Gasse, *137*
Oberer Grindelwaldgletscher, *380*
Oberhofen, *393*
Oktogon Hammam, *348*
Old Swiss House ✕, *231*
Old Town (Bern), *325–331*
Old Town (Neuchâtel), *313*
Old Town (Sion), *416*
Omnia Mountain Lounge 🏨, *431–432*
Onkel Tom's Hütte ✕, *380*
Opera
Bern, 344
Geneva, 522
Zürich, 82
Osteria del Centenario ✕, *196*

P

Palais de Rumine, *465*
Palais des Nations, *497–498*
Palais Wilson, *499*
Palazzo Civico (Bellinzona), *192*
Palazzo Civico (Lugano), *208*
Panorama Restaurant Muottas Muragl ✕, *166*
Panorama Spazierweg, *362*
Panoramaweg, *372–373, 376–377*
Paradeplatz (Zürich), *53*
Parc de Sculpture, *407*
Parc La Grange, *501*
Parc Naziunal Svizzer, *161–164*
Parco Civico-Ciani, *208*
Parco del Tassino, *208*
Parco Scherrer, *213*
Park Hotel Vitznan 🏨, *245*
Parks, national, *161–164*
Passage, The 🏨, *277*
Passeport Musées, *501*
Payerne, *306–307*
Pinacoteca Comunale Casa Rusca, *196*
Pfarrkirche St. Peter und St. Paul, *243*
Pharmazie-Historisches Museum, *267*
Piazza della Riforma (Lugano), *206*
Piazza Grande (Locarno), *195*
Piazza Motta (Ascona), *199*
Piz Gloria ✕, *379*
Place de Neuve (Geneva), *509*
Place du Bourg-de-Four (Geneva), *506*
Place St-François (Lausanne), *464*
Planche-Supérieure, *297*
Plane travel, *24, 528–529*
Basel, 257–258
Bern, 324
Berner Oberland, 353
Eastern Switzerland and Liechtenstein, 94
Fribourg and Neuchâtel, 291
Geneva, 493–494
Graubünden, 129
Luzern and Central Switzerland, 221
Ticino, 186
Valais, 403
Vaud, 449
Zürich, 50
Pont de Berne, *298*
Pont de Zähringen, *297*
Pontresina, *164–169*
Postmuseum, *122*
Prangins, *455–456*
Prättigau and Davos, *145–155*

R

Rathaus (Basel), *264*
Rathaus (Chur), *138*
Rathaus (Schwyz), *252*
Rathaus (Stein am Rhein), *103*
Rätisches Museum, *137*
Reichenbachfälle, *388–389*
Restaurant Bären ✕, *359*
Restaurant de l'Hôtel de Ville ✕, *466*
Restaurant Stucki ✕, *276*
Restaurant-Vinothek Fletschorn ✕, *436*
Restaurants, *17, 538*
Basel, 264, 272–276
Bern, 330, 331, 335–338
Berner Oberland, 354, 359, 379, 380, 387–388, 390, 395
cuisine, 28–29, 90–91, 288–289, 298, 446–447
Eastern Switzerland and Liechtenstein, 95, 101, 103–104, 109, 110–112, 116–117, 122
Fribourg and Neuchâtel, 292–293, 297, 298–299, 302–303, 309, 313–315
Geneva, 501, 510–517
Graubünden, 131, 134, 139, 141, 146, 151–152, 166, 171–172
Luzern and Central Switzerland, 223, 230–232
price categories, 17, 65, 95, 131, 188, 223, 273, 293, 336, 354, 405, 450, 510
Ticino, 187–188, 193, 196, 199–200, 208–210
Valais, 404–405, 409, 417, 418–419, 430–431, 436
Vaud, 451, 455, 457, 465–466, 472–473, 481, 485–486
Zürich, 52, 64–70
Rhätibahn, *159*
Rheinfall, *98*
Riffelberg, *429*
Riffelsee, *429*
Rimini Bar, *80*
Rindermarkt, *61*

Ritz-Carlton Hotel de la Paix, Geneva 🏨, *519*
Riviera, *470–488*
Rohrbachstein, *417*
Roman artifacts
Basel, 270–271
Fribourg and Neuchâtel, 309, 311–312
Geneva, 501, 506
Graubünden, 137, 139
Valais, 407–408
Vaud, 454, 472
Zürich, 56
Romansh, *136*
Romantik Hotel Chesa Grischuna 🏨, *146*
Romantik Hotel Stern 🏨, *139*
Römermuseum, *271*
Romont, *306*
Rosengarten, *330*
Rotenboden, *429*
Route du Vignoble, *456*
Royal Savoy 🏨, *468*
Rue de Bourg (Lausanne), *464*
Rütli Meadow, *247–248*

S

Saanen Church, *395*
Saas-Fee, *426, 435–439*
Sailing. ⇨ *See* **Boating and sailing**
St. Alban, *269–270*
St. Alban-Tor, *270*
St. Beatus-Höhlen, *357*
St. Bernard dogs, *407, 413–414*
St. Gallen, *108–114*
St. Galler Bauernmarkt, *114*
St. Jacob, *145*
St. Martin Zillis, *139*
St. Moritz, *169–178*
St. Peter's Zermatt - The English Church, 430
St-Luc, *423*
St-Pierre-de-Clages, *416*
St-Saphorin, *471–473*
Sammlung Rosengart, *229*
Santuario della Madonna del Sasso, *195–196*
Schaffhausen and the Rhine, *96–105*
Schanfigger Heimatmuseum, *141*
Schaukäserei, *116*
Schauspielhaus Pfauenbühne, *61*
Schillerstein, *248*
Schilthorn, *365, 373, 378–379*
Schlaf-Fass Riesling-Silvaner Maienfeld 🏨, *135*
Schloss Brandis 🏨, *134*
Schloss Hünegg, *393*
Schloss Oberhofen, *393*
Schloss Salenegg, *134*
Schloss Spiez, *390*
Schloss Tarasp, *158*
Schloss Thun, *391*
Schlosshotel Chastè 🏨, *159*
Schlössli ✕, *111*
Schmiedstube, *99*
Schwabentortum, *99*
Schweizer Holzbildhauerei, *387*
Schweizerisches Alpines Museum, *333*
Schweizerisches Landesmuseum, *62*
Schwyz, *252*
Schynige Platte, *357*
Scuol, *157–161*
Segantini Museum, *171*
Sherlock Holmes Museum, *389*
Shopping. ⇨ *See* **under specific cities and areas**
Simmental, *394–398*
Sion, *406, 414–417*
Site Archéologique Cathédrale St-Pierre, *506*
Skating
Arosa, 144
Davos, 154
Klosters, 148
Skiing
Berner Oberland, 366, 368, 384, 398
Eastern Switzerland and Liechtenstein, 119–120
Fribourg and Neuchâtel, 303
Graubünden, 144–145, 147, 148, 154–155, 160 –161, 169, 178
Valais, 411–412, 421–422, 425–426, 434, 439, 442
Sledding
Graubünden, 148, 150, 161, 176
Valais, 439
Sole Uno (spa), *284*
Sopraceneri, *188–201*
Sottoceneri, *202–214*
Spalentor, *267*
Spas
Basel, 283–284
Bern, 348
Berner Oberland, 361, 397–398
Eastern Switzerland and Liechtenstein, 112, 114
Fribourg and Neuchâtel, 318
Geneva, 524, 526
Graubünden, 136, 140, 159, 168, 175
Luzern and Central Switzerland, 238, 245
Valais, 424–425
Zürich, 85–86
Sphinx Terrace, *375*
Spielzeug Welten Museum Basel, *267*
Spiez, *389–390*
Sports and outdoor activities, *31–32.* ⇨ *See also specific sports; under specific cities and areas*
Spreuerbrücke, *230*
Stadt Lounge, *110*
Stans, *242–243*
Stanserhorn, *243*
Staubbachfälle, *363*
Stein am Rhein, *102–104*
Stiftsbibliothek, *109–110*
Stockalperschloss, *440*
Storchen Zurich 🏨, *75*
Suvretta House 🏨, *174*
Swimming
Bern, 345
Luzern and Central Switzerland, 237
Vaud, 469, 482
Swiss Path, *249*
Swiss Travel Pass, *40*
Swissminiatur, *213*

T

Tarasp-Vulpera, *157–161*
Taxis
Basel, 258
Bern, 324
Geneva, 495
Zürich, 50
Tell, Wilhelm, *250, 251, 252*
Tell monument, *250*
Tell-Museum, *252*
Tell Pass, *223*
Tellfreilichtspiele, *361*
Tellskapelle, *251*
Tellsplatte, *251*
Temple de la Fusterie, *500*
Textilmuseum, *110*
Theater
Basel, 280
Bern, 344
Berner Oberland, 361
Geneva, 523
Luzern, 235
Ticino, 198
Zürich, 61, 82
Thermal Center, *318*
Thermal spas. ⇨ *See* **Spas**
Thun, *390–393*
Thunersee, *389–393*
Tibet Museum, *302*
Ticino, *20–21, 180–214*
festivals and seasonal events, 197, 198, 201, 211–212
itineraries, 205
lakes, 182–183
lodging, 187, 193–194, 197, 200–201, 210–211, 214
nightlife and the arts, 197–198, 201, 211–212, 213
restaurants, 187–188, 193, 196, 199–200, 208–210
shopping, 198, 212
Sopraceneri, 188–201
Sottoceneri, 202–214
sports and outdoor activities, 198, 212
timing the visit, 182, 185–186
tours, 186
transportation, 183, 186–187
visitor information, 188
Tomb of Erasmus, *260*

Tomb of Queen Anna of Habsburg, *260*
Tour de l'Ile, *500*
Touristik-Museum der Jungfrau Region, *358*
Train travel and tours, *24, 39–43, 532–534*
Basel, 258
Bern, 324
Berner Oberland, 354, 357, 365, 374, 375, 377, 379, 386
Eastern Switzerland and Liechtenstein, 94–95
Fribourg and Neuchâtel, 292
Geneva, 495
Graubünden, 130, 159
Luzern and Central Switzerland, 222
Ticino, 187
Valais, 404, 429
Vaud, 450, 478, 480
Zürich, 51
Trams
Basel, 258
Bern, 324
Geneva, 494–495
Zürich, 51
Transportation, 24, 34, 35, 36, 528–534. ⇨ See also under specific cities and areas
Trümmelbachfälle, *363*
Tschuggen Grand Hotel 🏨, *142*
T3e Terre 🏨, *197*

U

Unterseen, *359*
Upper Engadine, *164–178*
Urnersee, *246–252*

V

Vaduz (Liechtenstein), *121–124*
Vaduz Castle, *122*
Val d'Anniviers, *422–423*
Valais, *12–13, 400–442*
Bas Valais and Sion, 406–417
Brig and the Alpine Passes, 439–442
Conversion de la Vallée, 417–426
festivals and seasonal events, 410, 417
lodging, 404, 409–410, 419–420, 423, 425, 431–432, 436, 438
nightlife and the arts, 410, 420, 433, 438
restaurants, 404–405, 409, 417, 418–419, 430–431, 436
shopping, 422, 435
skiing, 411–412, 421–422, 425–426, 434, 439, 442
spas, 424–425
sports and outdoor activities, 410–412, 420–422, 423, 425–426, 433–434, 438–439, 442
timing the visit, 403
tours, 405
transportation, 403–404
visitor information, 405
Zermatt and Saas-Fee, 426–439
Valle Verzasca, *198*
Vaud, *23, 444–488*
festivals and seasonal events, 488
itineraries, 462
La Côte, 452–457
Lausanne, 458–470
Lavaux Vignobles and Riviera, 470–488
lodging, 451, 455, 456, 457, 467–468, 473, 481–482, 486
nightlife and the arts, 468–469, 482, 486–488
restaurants, 451, 455, 457, 465–466, 472–473, 481, 485–486
shopping, 470, 483, 488
sports and outdoor activities, 469, 473, 488
timing the visit, 449
tours, 451–452, 456, 478
transportation, 449–450
visitor information, 452
Verbier, *408–412*
Verbier Festival, *410*
Verkehrshaus, *230*
Vevey, *473, 482–483*
Via Borgo, *199*
Via Mala, *139*
Victoria-Jungfrau Grand Hotel & Spa 🏨, *360*
Vinzel, *456*
Visitor information, *24, 542. ⇨ See also under specific cities and areas*
Vitra Design Museum, *271–272*
Vitromusée, *306*
Vitznau, *244–246*
Vocabulary, *544–549*
Vufflens-le-Château, *457*

W

W Hotel Verbier 🏨, *410*
Waldhotel Fletschhorn 🏨, *438*
Walensee, *105, 119–120*
Walking and hiking, *32*
Basel, 265
Bern, 326
Berner Oberland, 375, 384
Eastern Switzerland and Liechtenstein, 98, 108
Geneva, 495, 507
Graubünden, 134, 144, 147, 154, 169, 176
Luzern and Central Switzerland, 219, 227
Ticino, 183, 198, 205, 212
Valais, 405, 411, 421, 423, 425, 433, 438, 442
Vaud, 462, 473, 478
Zürich, 51, 60
Walliser Alpentherme & Spa, *425*
Wasserkirche, *61*
Water sports, *316*
Waterfalls
Brienzersee, 385
Lauterbrunnen, 363
Meiringen-Hasliberg, 388–389
Schaffhausen, 98
Weesen, *119*
Weggis, *243–244*
Weinmarkt (Luzern), *229*
Wengen, *366–368*
Wengernalp, *372, 376–377*
White-water rafting, *161*
Widder Hotel 🏨, *76*
Wildstrubel, *417*
Wilhelm Tell Monument, *250*
Windsurfing, *154*
Wines, *131, 405, 424, 433, 456, 475–479*
Winkelried, Arnold von, *242*
Wintersportmuseum Davos, *151*
Wirtschaft zum Frieden ✕, *101*
Wirtschaft zum Löwen ✕, *122*
Wood-carving, *387*

Y

Yverdon-les-Bains, *317–318*

Z

Zentrum Paul Klee, *334*
Zermatt, *426–435*
Zoologischer Garten, *270*
Zoologisches Museum, *61*
Zoos
Basel, 270
Bern, 328
Zürich, 63–64
Zum Goldenen Ochsen, *99, 101*
Zum Zähringer ✕, *338*
Zunfthaus zur Saffran, *61*
Zur Wasserquelle, *101*
Zur Zieglerburg, *101*
Zürich, *20, 46–86*
festivals and seasonal events, 49–50, 82
itineraries, 60
lodging, 71–79
nightlife and the arts, 79–82
restaurants, 52, 64–70
shopping, 61, 83–84
sightseeing, 52–64
spas, 85–86
timing the visit, 49–50
tours, 51
transportation, 50–51
visitor information, 51
Zürich West, *62–63*
Zürich Zoo, *63–64*
Zürichsee, *65*
Zwingli, Ulrich, *56*
Zytglogge/Zeitglockenturm, *330*

PHOTO CREDITS

Front cover: Andrey/age fotostock [Description: Zermatt and the Matterhorn, Switzerland]. 1, Janoka82 | Dreamstime.com.2, photogear.ch/iStockphoto. 4, Gevisions | Dreamstime.com. 5 (top), Eder/Shutterstock. 5 (bottom), Labutin.Art/Shutterstock. 6 (top), Morseicinque | Dreamstime.com. 6 (bottom), Marcus Gyger/Switzerland Tourism. 7, Sam74100 | Dreamstime.com. 8 (top left), Algrosskrueg | Dreamstime.com. 8 (top right), Mtkitchn | Dreamstime.com. 8 (bottom right), Christof Sonderegger/Switzerland Tourism. 8 (bottom left), Kitleong | Dreamstime.com. 9 (top left), Huytonthat | Dreamstime.com. 9 (top right), minnystock | Dreamstime.com. 9 (bottom right), Anna Nahabed/Shutterstock. 9 (bottom left), Agnieszka Skalska/Shutterstock. 10 (top left), Dennis Savini/ Switzerland Tourism. 10 (top right), RnDmS / Alamy. 10 (bottom right), Morseicinque | Dreamstime. com. 10 (bottom left), Pathara Buranadilok/Shutterstock. 11, Eddie Gerald / Alamy. 12 (top left), Somatuscani | Dreamstime.com. 12 (top right), ELEPHOTOS/Shutterstock. 12 (bottom right), Neilneil | Dreamstime.com. 12 (bottom left), Gevisions | Dreamstime.com. 13 (top), Alessandro Colle/ Shutterstock. 13 (bottom), Fotoember | Dreamstime.com. 15, Switzerland Tourism/swiss-image.ch/ Max Schmid. **Chapter 1: Experience Switzerland:** 18-19, B van Dierendonck / age fotostock. 38-39 (top), Jungfrau Railways/swiss-image.ch. 38 (bottom left), Switzerland Tourism/swiss-image.ch/ Robert Boesch. 38 (bottom right), Switzerland Tourism/swiss-image.ch/Christof Sonderegger. 40, Switzerland Tourism/swiss-image.ch/Max Schmid. 41 (left), Valais Tourism/swiss-image/Thomas Andenmatten. 41 (right), Switzerland Tourism/swiss-image.ch/Christof Schuerpf. 42, Rhaetische Bahn/swiss-image.ch/Andrea Badrutt. 43, Rhaetische Bahn/swiss-image.ch/Peter Donatsch. 44, Sonderegger Christof / age fotostock. **Chapter 2: Zürich:** 45, Switzerland Tourism / swiss-image.ch/ Christof Schuerpf. 48, Switzerland Tourism / swiss-image.ch/Christof Schuerpf. 54-55, Jürgen Held / age fotostock. 62, Switzerland Tourism / swiss-image.ch/Christof Schuerpf. 64, Switzerland Tourism / swiss-image.ch/Christoph Schuerpf. 67, Switzerland Tourism / swiss-image.ch/Samuel Mizrachi. 75, WIDDER HOTEL. 76, Summit Hotels & Resorts. 78, Switzerland Tourism / swiss-image.ch/Christof Sonderegger. 80, Stefan Schmidlin/The Dolder Grand. **Chapter 3: Eastern Switzerland and Liechtenstein:** 87, Schweiz Tourismus / swiss-image.ch/Lucia Degonda. 90, Stephen French/clubfoto/ iStockphoto. 91 (top), Stefan-Xp/Wikimedia Commons. 91 (bottom), Encoded 9/Wikimedia Commons. 92, Switzerland Tourism / swiss-image.ch/Christof Sonderegger. 99, Switzerland Tourism / swiss-image.ch/Christof Sonderegger. 103, Switzerland Tourism / swiss-image.ch/Christof Sonderegger. 109, Switzerland Tourism / swiss-image.ch/Stephan Engler. 113, Switzerland Tourism / swiss-image. ch//Max Schmid. 117, Switzerland Tourism / swiss-image.ch/Roland Gerth. 121, McPHOTO / age fotostock. **Chapter 4: Graubünden:** 125, Destination Davos Klosters / swiss-image.ch. 128, Switzerland Tourism / swiss-image.ch/Christof Sonderegger. 135, Switzerland Tourism / swiss-image. ch/Christof Sonderegger. 138, Ferienregion Heidiland / swiss-image.ch/Daniel Kalberer. 143, Tschuggen Hotel Group. 149, Destination Davos Klosters / swiss-image.ch/Cedric Kienscherff. 151, Destination Davos Klosters / swiss-image.ch. 157, Sonderegger Christof / age fotostock. 160, Switzerland Tourism / swiss-image.ch/Stephan Engler. 162-63, Switzerland Tourism / ST/swiss-image. ch/Robert Boesch. 165, Pontresina Tourismus / swiss-image.ch/Torsten Krueger. 167, Grand Hotel Kronenhof. 170, ENGADIN St. Moritz / swiss-image.ch/Christian Perret. 177, ENGADIN St. Moritz / swiss-image.ch/Daniel Martinek. **Chapter 5: Ticino:** 179, Ticino Turismo / swiss-image.ch. 182, Ticino Turismo / swiss-image.ch/Remy Steinegger. 183 (top), Ticino Turismo / swiss-image.ch/Remy Steinegger. 183 (bottom) and 184, Ticino Turismo / swiss-image.ch/Christoph Sonderegger. 190, Bellinzona Turismo / swiss-image.ch. 195 and 200, Ticino Turismo / swiss-image.ch/Remy Steinegger. 204, Switzerland Tourism / swiss-image.ch/Roland Gerth. 208, Ticino Turismo / swissimage.ch/Remy Steinegger. **Chapter 6: Luzern and Central Switzerland:** 215, Switzerland Tourism / swiss-image.ch/ Christof Sonderegger. 218, Luzern Tourismus / swiss-image.ch. 219 (top), Chin tin tin/Wikimedia Commons. 219 (bottom), SGV Luzern / swiss-image.ch. 220, Switzerland Tourism / ST/swiss-image. ch. 225, wcpmedia/Shutterstock. 228, Lazar Mihai-Bogdan/Shutterstock. 231, Luzern Tourismus AG / swiss-image.ch. 234, Switzerland Tourism / swiss-image.ch/Christof Sonderegger. 239, Switzerland Tourism / swiss-image.ch/Franziska Pfenniger. 240-41, Switzerland Tourism / swiss-image.ch/Christof Sonderegger. 246, Schweiz Tourismus / swiss-image.ch/Christof Sonderegger. 248, MatthiasKabel/ Wikimedia Commons. 251, Switzerland Tourism / swiss-image.ch/Max Schmid. **Chapter 7: Basel:** 253, Boris Stroujko/Shutterstock. 256 and 259, Basel Tourismus / swiss-image.ch. 266, Ingolf Pompe / age fotostock. 268, Switzerland Tourism / swiss-image.ch/Stephan Engler. 272, Basel Tourismus / swiss-image.ch. 281, Schweiz Tourismus / swiss-image.ch/Christof Sonderegger. **Chapter 8: Fribourg and Neuchâtel:** 285, UFT / swiss-image.ch/OT Moleson. 288, Olivier Savoy/La Maison du Gruyère. 289 (top), swiss-image.ch/Photo by Andy Mettler. 289 (bottom), edseloh/Wikimedia Commons. 290, Switzerland Tourism / swiss-image.ch/Stephan Engler. 296, ventdusud/ Shutterstock. 304-305, José

Fuste Raga / age fotostock. 308, UFT / Swiss-image.ch/Franck Auberson. 314, Switzerland Tourism / swiss-image.ch/Stephan Engler. 316, Switzerland Tourism / swiss-image.ch/Christof Sonderegger. **Chapter 9: Bern:** 319 and 322, Bern Tourism / ST/swiss-image.ch. 325, WYSOCKI Pawel / age fotostock. 329, Alan Smithers/iStockphoto. 332, URF / age fotostock. 336, Etienne / age fotostock. 342, Ingolf Pompe/age fotostock. 347, Switzerland Tourism / swiss-image.ch/Stephan Engler. **Chapter 10: Berner Oberland:** 349, Switzerland Tourism / swiss-image.ch/Christof Sonderegger. 352, Switzerland Tourism / swiss-image.ch/Christof Sonderegger. 358, David Tomlinson / age fotostock. 362, Switzerland Tourism / swiss-image.ch/Roland Gerth. 366, BrendanDias/Shutterstock. 370-71, Switzerland Tourism / swiss-image.ch/Roland Gerth. 372 (bottom left), Wengen-Muerren-Lauterbrunnental Tourismus AG / swiss-image.ch. 372-73 (map), berann.com. 373 (top), Switzerland Tourism / swiss-image.ch/Christof Sonderegger. 373 (bottom), Schweiz Tourismus / swiss-image.ch/Christof Sonderegger. 374 and 375, Jungfrau Railways / swiss-image.ch. 376 (top), Ingolf Pompe / age fotostock. 376 (bottom), Wengen-Muerren-Lauterbrunnental Tourismus AG / swiss-image.ch. 377, Glenn van der Knijff / age fotostock. 378, Doug Pearson/age fotostock. 379, Schilthornbahn AG / swiss-image.ch/Jost von Allmen. 381, Schweiz Tourismus / swiss-image.ch/Christof Sonderegger. 382-83, Ingolf Pompe / age fotostock. 387, Alberto Paredes / age fotostock. 389, Apn68140 | Dreamstime.com. 391, Switzerland Tourism / swiss-image.ch/Max Schmid. 396, Ingolf Pompe / age fotostock. 399, Thomas Andenmatten/Bettmeralp Tourismus. **Chapter 11: Valais:** 402, Switzerland Tourism / swiss-image.ch/Robert Schoenbaechler. 412, Switzerland Tourism / swiss-image.ch/Christof Sonderegger. 416, Milosz Maslanka/Shutterstock. 422, Chachas | Dreamstime.com. 428, Switzerland Tourism / swiss-image.ch/Christof Sonderegger. 432, The Leading Hotels of The World. 437, Saas-Fee Tourism / swiss-image.ch. 440, Roland Zihlmann/Shutterstock. **Chapter 12: Vaud:** 443, Switzerland Tourism / swiss-image.ch/Christof Sonderegger. 446, Aschermann / age fotostock. 447 (top), Switzerland Tourism / swiss-image.ch/Hans-Peter Siffert. 447 (bottom), Joel Bez/Flickr. 448, Switzerland Tourism / swiss-image.ch/Christof Sonderegger. 454, Hubertus Blume / age fotostock. 458, Switzerland Tourism / swiss-image.ch/Christof Schuerpf. 461, Lausanne Tourisme / swiss-image.ch/B.H. Bissat. 463, Switzerland Tourism / swiss-image.ch/Christof Schuerpf. 472, Switzerland Tourism / swiss-image.ch/Peter Maurer. 474-75, Lausanne Tourisme / swiss-image.ch/Urs Achermann. 476 (top), swiss-image.ch/Photo by Andy Mettler. 476 (center), Switzerland Tourism / swiss-image.ch/Stephan Engler. 476 (bottom), Switzerland Tourism / swiss-image.ch/Peter Maurer. 477 (left), Switzerland Tourism / swiss-image.ch/Stephan Engler. 477 (right), Switzerland Tourism / swiss-image.ch/Peter Maurer. 478, Switzerland Tourism / swiss-image.ch/Hans-Peter Siffert. 484, Vladimir Mucibabic/Shutterstock. 487, marco albonico / age fotostock. **Chapter 13: Geneva:** 489, Switzerland Tourism / swiss-image.ch/Samuel Mizrachi. 492, Four Seasons Geneva. 497, Sergio85simoes | Dreamstime.com. 505, Benkrut | Dreamstime.com. 506, Mark Henley / age fotostock. 509, massimo pacifico / age fotostock. 517, Switzerland Tourism / swiss-image.ch/Stephan Engler. 523, Ingolf Pompe / age fotostock. **Back cover, from left to right:** Blende64 | Dreamstime.com; Xantana | Dreamstime.com; Asdf_1 | Dreamstime.com. **Spine:** WEKWEK/iStockphoto. **About Our Writers:** All photos are courtesy of the writers except for the following: Chantal Panozzo, courtesy of Brian Opyd; Kelly DiNardo, courtesy of Stacey Vaeth; Liz Humphreys, courtesy of JF Grossen; Richard Harvell, courtesy of Domenico Sposato; Susan Misicka, courtesy of Thomas Stephens; Vicki Gabathuler, courtesy of Markus Lippuner.

ABOUT OUR WRITERS

Kelly DiNardo keeps waiting to be told to get a real job. Until then, she'll drink cocktails, drive race cars, sweat through Bikram yoga classes, learn the secrets of a burlesque dancer, and travel the world all in the name of work. After graduating from Cornell University, she spent 14 years in Washington, D.C., before moving to Lausanne, Switzerland, where she is learning to appreciate raclette, yodeling, and the Alpine horn. She is the author of *Gilded Lili: Lili St. Cyr and the Striptease Mystique* and the forthcoming *Yoga for the Genius*. Her writing has appeared in the *New York Times,* the *Washington Post, National Geographic Traveler,* AOL Travel, *Glamour, O: The Oprah Magazine, Oz: The Good Life,* and others. For this edition, she updated Zürich, Valais, and Geneva.

Liz Humphreys first fell in love with Switzerland when she sang in the Verbier Festival Chorus in 2006 and tasted some of the Valais's fabulous, hard-to-find wines. Liz is a recent transplant to Europe from New York City, where she spent a decade in editorial positions for media companies, including Condé Nast, Time Inc., and *USA Today*. She has worked on several guidebooks for Fodor's Travel, including Amsterdam, Portugal, Germany, and Italy. Liz has an advanced certificate in wine studies from the WSET (Wine & Spirit Education Trust) and chronicles her travels on her blog, www.winederlust.com. Liz updated Basel, Graunbünden, and Travel Smart.

Susan Misicka was born in Boston but has a few drops of Helvetian blood. She has lived in Switzerland since 2001, mainly in canton Luzern and more recently in the city of Bern. During that time, the journalist/editor has contributed to a variety of media, including *Zürich Dining Out Guide, Living and Working in Switzerland, Swiss News* magazine, World Radio Switzerland, and swissinfo.ch, a division of the Swiss Broadcasting Corporation. Like her Swiss cat Sam, Susan agrees that taking the train is more relaxing than driving. For this edition, she updated Luzern & Central Switzerland, Bern, and Berner Oberland.

Alexis Munier sold everything she owned and relocated to Europe a decade ago. In addition to her position as editorial manager for a large NGO, Munier is the author of nine books, including the infamous Talk Dirty Series and *The Big Black Book of Very Dirty Words*. This opera singer-turned-wordsmith lived and worked in Russia, Slovenia, and Italy before settling down in Lausanne with her two small children and badly behaved poodle. For this edition she updated Experience, Vaud, Ticino, and Fribourg & Neuchâtel.

Chantal Panozzo moved to Switzerland in 2006, pleased to discover a country where people can actually pronounce her name. She is the author of *Swiss Life: 30 Things I Wish I'd Known,* and has also written for CNN Travel, *Brain, Child* magazine, and *The Christian Science Monitor,* among others. In 2010, she co-founded the Zürich Writers Workshop and has planned one international writing conference every year since. A copywriter by trade, Chantal has created advertising campaigns on two continents for brands like Swiss International Airlines, Swissôtel, and Credit Suisse. For this edition, Chantal updated Eastern Switzerland & Liechtenstein.